# PLANNING
# FOR INFORMATION
# SYSTEMS

# PLANNING FOR INFORMATION SYSTEMS

WILLIAM R. KING
EDITOR

ADVANCES IN MANAGEMENT
INFORMATION SYSTEMS
VLADIMIR ZWASS SERIES EDITOR

*M.E.Sharpe*
Armonk, New York
London, England

References to the AMIS papers should be as follows:

Benaroch, Michel. Option-based management of risk in information systems planning. William R. King, ed.,
*Planning for Information Systems. Advances in Management Information Systems,* Volume 14 (Armonk, NY:
M.E. Sharpe, 2009), 318–340.

ISBN 978-0-7656-1950-1
ISSN 1554-6152

Printed in the United States of America

The paper used in this publication meets the minimum requirements of
American National Standard for Information Sciences
Permanence of Paper for Printed Library Materials,
ANSI Z 39.48-1984.

IBT (c)   10   9   8   7   6   5   4   3   2   1

## ADVANCES IN MANAGEMENT INFORMATION SYSTEMS

Forthcoming volumes of this series can be found on the series homepage.
www.mesharpe.com/amis.htm

Editor in Chief, Vladimir Zwass (zwass@fdu.edu)

# *Advances in Management Information Systems*

## Advisory Board

# CONTENTS

## PART III. INFORMATION SYSTEMS INVESTMENT PLANNING

## PART IV. GOALS AND OUTCOMES OF INFORMATION SYSTEMS PLANNING

# SERIES EDITOR'S INTRODUCTION

## VLADIMIR ZWASS, EDITOR-IN-CHIEF

Planning is an organizational and cognitive process of setting objectives for the future, specifying the actions and resources necessary to achieve these objectives, and establishing how the outcomes will be assessed during the planning period and how the plans will be revised. In the turbulent environment of today's business, longer-term plans need to be considered inherently subject to continuous adjustment. It is indeed necessary to plan for flexibility in the hierarchy of plans, ranging from long-term strategic ones that open the perspective for years to project plans.

With the pervasiveness of information technologies (IT) and their strategic importance to many organizations, information systems (IS) planning has been consistently identified as one of the key issues facing senior executives. Several other generally top-ranked issues, such as the pursuit of competitive positioning with IS, or business–IS alignment, are, at their core, planning issues. This *AMIS* volume is, therefore, of value to both general managers and IS managers, while also setting a benchmark for IS researchers who, as we shall see, need to further develop this field. The volume has been written by a most comprehensive group of authorities on its subject and edited by the founder of the study area of strategic planning for IS. The authors show the evolution of IS planning from the early, technology-centered approaches to the present concerns with competitive positioning, organizational learning, and the development of organizational capabilities. The appearance of this volume is timely, as the new approaches to IS planning are necessary both in view of the strategic and operational importance of IT and of the highly dynamic business environment that cannot suffer inflexible plans.

The word "planning" does not appear very commonly these days, either in business books (other than those promoting business plans for start-ups) or in the research literature. One is far more likely to see studies addressing business positioning and reaching for competitive advantage, the development of dynamic capabilities of a firm, or strategic fit of business and IS—that is, planning, by many other names. One may infer several reasons for the—temporary, in my opinion—fading of the term, while the necessary action of planning itself is common enough. How can we plan in an environment of turbulent change? This should not be a rhetorical question—and some of the articles in the volume address it. Does planning not imply an ossifying routine and carry organizational rigidities in its wake? It does not, if done right. Finally, did the planned economies not collapse, leaving a bad odor with the word? The sort of planning they were engaging in—on a national level, and without meaningful prices—earned them the more apt name of command economies, which we are not talking about here.

Planning for IS in the context of a specific enterprise is of vital importance—and of significant difficulty that calls for further, practice-grounded, intensive research. Recent empirical studies of corporate performance persuasively link the deployment of information technologies (IT) to the growing spread between the leaders and the other players in industries with high levels of IT use

(McAfee and Brynjolfsson, 2008). This divergence is attributed to the skillful use of enterprise systems and the Internet–Web compound since the mid-1990s. Beyond that, with the growth of e-commerce and with the progressing digitalization of processes and products in many industries, a great variety of firms have become dependent on IT exploitation and innovation (Zwass, 2003). The outcomes of planning need to combine innovative deployment of IT in the context of the resources and capabilities of a given organization (which are themselves IS-dependent) with the efficient, reliable, and secure operation of the firm. From the technological point of view, which translates into business results, system fragmentation—particularly at the lower levels of the stack—is undesirable and costly. A coherent infrastructure is necessary to rapidly launch new initiatives—say, for a bank to roll out new financial instruments or for an insurance company to offer a new class of underwriting. Integrated Internet-based telecommunications, databases, and data warehouses are needed for flexible support. Well-planned IS architectures, more recently taking advantage of service-oriented approaches, have to be planned to support business operations with flexibility built in at the planning stages.

Planning has always been a difficult activity, not engaged in very willingly by managers (Davis and Olson, 1985, p. 304). The more recent developments have lent further complexity and a far greater degree of uncertainty to longer-term IT-grounded plans in particular. We can point here to several interrelated major factors:

- globalization of competition, including the contestation of firms' competitive positions by new entrants and firms in diverse industries relying on different cost structures;
- partly as a result of the above, heightened market turbulence, in particular in the industries with high IT use (McAfee and Brynjolfsson, 2008);
- competition based on diverse forms of access to resources and capabilities (including outsourcing, offshoring, partnerships, and supply webs) rather than just their ownership;
- dizzying pace of business and technological innovation, some of it disruptive to the existing business models;
- pervasiveness of IT in the business model of many firms, making them vulnerable to the emergence of major new technologies (think of a long-term plan for an IT company drawn up in, say, 1992); and
- availability of massive real-time data from event-driven systems that can be exploited via business analytics to build anticipatory capabilities and adjust plans at various levels almost on the fly—an opportunity to some, and a threat to others. Luxury clothing labels, for example, find the need to respond to consumer demand (rather than rely on the diktat of the creative directors)—because their mass-market competitors, such as Zara, closely track the demand with IT and respond rapidly with IT-based logistics (Passariello, 2008).

This competitive environment requires that planning be done in new ways. To support innovation, planning should be holistic (rather than limited to financial targets), based on continuing environmental scanning and determination of trends, flexible, and involving many people with different perspectives (Barringer and Bluedorn, 1999). For example, at Dolby Laboratories, strategic planning for IS is being designed to mirror the process of the general strategic planning in the company, where the ideas generated by more than 1,000 employees are funneled through a governance process into a manageable number of initiatives for the planning period (Overby, 2008). The critical success factors (CSF) IS planning methodology, elaborated in the present volume by its creator, has been extended to a broadly participative planning process (Peffers, Gengler, and Tuunanen, 2003). The technologies of social computing, such as opinion markets, wiki-based content creation, and idea agoras may not only enrich and facilitate the planning process but also influence the organizational culture to become more planning-oriented. New conceptualizations of the process and product of organizational IS planning in turbulent environments are necessary. Various methods of embedding real options in IT investments (Benaroch et al., 2007), options-oriented thinking in IT project management (Fichman, Keil, and Tiwana, 2005), the fostering of competitive agility by consistently creating digital options with IT (Samabmurthy, Bharadwaj, and Grover, 2003), chunkification of investment projects, and other forms of staged commitment are fruitful and promising research directions in planning for IS. More extensive formulation of IS strategy has been found to lead to greater success in planning for uncertain environments (Newkirk and Lederer, 2006).

It is vital in strategic IS planning to achieve the alignment of IS plans with the corporate business strategy. General and functional managers should be involved in decision making on long-term IS plans and play a key role in several principal decisions that set the overall contour of long-term plans (Ross and Weill, 2002). A variety of actions to achieve the coordination of IS plans with business plans has been established (Lederer and Mendelow, 1989). Shared domain knowledge between line-of-business and IS managers has been found instrumental in the social dimension of long-term alignment (Reich and Benbasat, 2000). The nature of alignment depends on the competitive posture of the firm (Sabherwal and Chan, 2001). As a part of this planning process, IT sourcing decisions should be made within a framework that surfaces and assesses the broad array of potential long-term consequences (King, 2008). All of this having been said, full harmonization of business planning with IS planning eludes most firms (Teo and King, 1997). Some firms, such as Volkswagen of America, have developed a coherent process for prioritizing IT investments in the light of business initiatives (Austin, Ritchie, and Garrett, 2004). Several articles in the present volume shed considerable light on the meaning of this alignment and on the means of obtaining it. Specific IT capabilities have been traced empirically to the competitive advantage of the firms that develop and foster them (Bhatt and Grover, 2005). An interesting recent effort pushes the alignment down to the process level, where the actual business value can be generated—or not (Tallon, 2007–8). Further research is necessary in the area, linking the outcomes to specific planning actions.

It is my hope that this authoritative and comprehensive volume will be a milestone in setting forth our present knowledge of organizational IS planning, a reinforcement of the importance of the planning process, and an encouragement to further research necessary in this domain.

## REFERENCES

Austin, R.D.; Ritchie, W.; and Garrett, G. 2004. Volkswagen of America: managing IT priorities. Harvard Business School Case 9–606–003.

Barringer, B.R., and Bluedorn, A.C. 1999. The relationship between corporate entrepreneurship and strategic management. *Strategic Management Journal*, 20, 421–444.

Benaroch, M.; Jeffery, M.; Kauffman, R.J.; and Shah, S. 2007. Option-based risk management: a field study of sequential information technology investment decisions. *Journal of Management Information Systems*, 24, 2 (Fall), 103–140.

Bhatt, G., and Grover, V. 2005. Types of information technology capabilities and their role in competitive advantage. *Journal of Management Information Systems*, 22, 2 (Fall), 253–277.

Davis, G.B., and Olson, M.H. 1985. *Management Information Systems: Conceptual Foundations, Structure, and Development*, 2d ed. New York: McGraw-Hill.

Fichman, R.G.; Keil, M.; and Tiwana, A. 2005. Beyond valuation: "options thinking" in IT project management. *California Management Review*, 27, 2 (Winter), 74–96.

King, W.R. 2008. A methodology for IT sourcing decisions. In S. Rivard and B.A. Aubert (eds.), *Information Technology Outsourcing*. Vol. 8, *Advances in Management Information Systems*. Armonk, NY: M.E. Sharpe, pp. 67–82.

Lederer, A.L., and Mendelow, A.L. 1989. Coordination of information systems plans with business plans. *Journal of Management Information Systems,* 6, 2 (Fall), 5–19.

McAfee, A., and Brynjolfsson, E. 2008. Investing in the IT that makes a competitive difference. *Harvard Business Review* (July–August), 98–107.

Newkirk, H.E., and Lederer, A.L. 2006. The effectiveness of strategic information systems planning under environmental uncertainty. *Information and Management,* 43, 4 (January), 481–501.

Overby, S. 2008 Strategic planning in the real world. *CIO,* February 1, 28–36.

Passariello, C. 2008. Logistics are in vogue with designers. *Wall Street Journal,* June 27, B1.

Peffers, K.; Gengler, C.E.; and Tuunanen, T. 2003. Extending critical success factors methodology to facilitate broadly participative information systems planning. *Journal of Management Information Systems,* 20, 1 (Summer), 51–85.

Reich, B.H., and Benbasat, I. 2000. Factors that influence the social dimension of alignment between business and information technology objectives. *MIS Quarterly,* 24, 1 (March), 81–113.

Ross, J.W., and Weill, P. 2002. Six IT decisions your IT people shouldn't make. *Harvard Business Review* (November), 84–92.

Sabherwal, R., and Chan, Y.E. 2001. Alignment between business and IS strategies: a study of prospectors, analyzers and defenders. *Information Systems Research,* 12, 1 (March), 11–33.

Sambamurthy, V.; Bharadwaj, A.; and Grover, V. 2003. Shaping agility through digital options: reconceptualizing the role of IT in contemporary organizations. *MIS Quarterly,* 27, 2 (June), 237–263.

Tallon, P.P. 2007–8. A process-oriented perspective on the alignment of information technology and corporate strategy. *Journal of Management Information Systems,* 24, 3 (Winter), 227–268.

Teo, T.S.H., and King, W.R. 1997. Integration between business planning and information systems planning. *Journal of Management Information Systems,* 14, 1 (Summer), 185–214.

Zwass, V. 2003. Electronic commerce and organizational innovation: aspects and opportunities. *International Journal of Electronic Commerce,* 7, 3 (Spring), 7–37.

# PLANNING FOR INFORMATION SYSTEMS

# CHAPTER 1

# PLANNING FOR INFORMATION SYSTEMS

## An Introduction

### WILLIAM R. KING

*Abstract: Strategic planning for information systems was "invented" in the early 1970s. Its application spread rapidly when IBM incorporated the basic ideas into the Business Systems Planning (BSP) methodology that it recommended to many of its clients. In this introduction to the volume, William R. King reviews the various modes of information systems (IS) strategic planning and provides a comprehensive model for performing the activity. The objectives and contents of the volume are also briefly summarized.*

*Keywords: Strategic IS Planning, Modes, IS Strategic Planning Process, IS Strategic Planning*

In the early 1970s, I was one of very few people simultaneously conducting research, consulting, and teaching in both the areas of strategic planning and information systems (IS).

I was, in fact, interested in creating and defining the relationships between the two. I initially lectured, consulted, and wrote on the topic of "strategic decision and information systems," which would later be referred to as "strategic decision support systems."

I also focused on "strategic planning for information systems." In 1975, I wrote a paper with David Cleland, "A New Method for Strategic Systems Planning" (King and Cleland, 1975), which I followed up in 1978 with the better-known paper "Strategic Planning for Management Information Systems" (King, 1978), which was framed around the transformation of "organizational strategy sets," consisting of organizational mission, objectives, strategies, and so forth, into "IS strategy sets." Others subsequently referred to this approach as "strategy set transformation" and later as "alignment."

In 1980, Robert Zmud and I conceptualized a process not only for having the organization's strategy set impact the IS strategy set, but also—the reverse aspect of alignment—having the IS strategy set impact the organization's strategy set (King and Zmud, 1980). This would later spawn the full notion of "alignment" and of "strategic systems"—those systems that could impact an organization's strategic competitive position.

When IBM adopted the essence of my 1978 paper as a basis for its Business Systems Planning (BSP) process (IBM, 1980), which it offered as a systems planning approach to its many customers around the world, the process was widely applied. Indeed, I have seen nothing in my career that was so quickly adopted by so many organizations. In the early 1970s, when I developed these basic ideas in a number of consulting assignments, I could find no company that was linking its strategic business planning with its IS planning in significant ways. By 1983, almost every one of the dozens of firms that I contacted in a survey study claimed to be doing so.

Of course, rudimentary forms of IS planning existed or were prescribed as early as the 1960s. Budget planning, in which next year's IS budgets were derived from last year's budgets by adding planned hardware and software acquisitions, was commonly used. Project planning and scheduling based on critical path notions were also in use, and the notion of a "master plan" that showed how various computer systems and applications were "tied together" into a single overall design were prescriptively discussed, but not well implemented, because most applications systems were "free standing" and developed with little regard to their interactions with other application systems.

For example, working as a consultant for a large bank in the early 1970s, I was asked to propose a strategy for enhancing the bank's revenues that were derived from small businesses. I naively drew up a plan—based on the premise that existing small business customers for some of the bank's products were the best prospects for expanding revenues—that involved interesting these customers in other bank products. When I presented this plan, I was told that it would be prohibitively expensive to determine which products a given small business customer currently utilized because the loan, mortgage, checking, savings, and other application systems were not integrated. When I suggested that this might even be done manually if there were some common identifier—the equivalent of a social security number—for each business in each system, I was told that there was no such common identifier. So, the identification of data across systems would have to be done in terms of the company name. A small-scale test for doing so led me to conclude that the names of companies took many different forms in various systems, which in turn led me to completely give up on the approach.

So, in the early 1970s, the "state of the art" in IS planning was rudimentary at best. Even well accepted ideas such as a "master plan" were not much implemented. Since then, IS strategic planning has developed amazingly rapidly—starting first as a free-standing process and then becoming an integral element of overall organizational strategic business planning.

## ALTERNATIVE MODES OF SPIS

The evolution of strategic planning for information systems (SPIS) may be used as a basis for portraying four significantly different modes of performing SPIS. These modes are important in that they reflect the transformations between the two "strategy sets" and the relationship between strategic business planning and SPIS in terms of the nature and level of integration between the two processes. The modes, shown in Figure 1.1, are:

- Administrative Integration
- Sequential Integration
- Reciprocal Integration
- Full Integration

### Administrative Integration

As shown in Figure 1.1, the least integrated mode, termed "Administrative Integration," is one in which there is two-way flow between the business planning and the IS planning processes, but this concerns only planning administrative matters such as the scheduling of various events in the planning process, the providing of planning information, the formatting of plan submissions, and so on. This administrative flow is depicted by the dashed arrow that shows flows in both directions in Figure 1.1.

Figure 1.1    **Alternate Modes of SPIS**

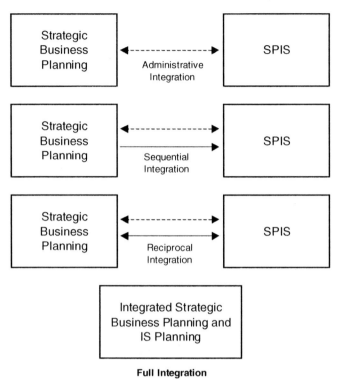

**Full Integration**

## Sequential Integration

The second mode in Figure 1.1 is termed "Sequential Integration." In addition to the two-way flow of administrative information, the primary flow of substantive information is from left to right. This describes the situation in which decisions are made during the strategic business planning process concerning such matters as business strategies and objectives. These choices become inputs to the SPIS process. In this mode, the IS function is envisioned primarily as the implementer of business strategy, and as such, the business strategy and other business information must first be provided so that the SPIS process can focus on the development of the IS infrastructure and programs that are best suited to the business strategy.

## Reciprocal Integration

The mode labeled "Reciprocal Integration" in Figure 1.1 shows a two-way flow of both substantive and administrative information. This reflects a view of IS that recognizes that the organization's information technology (IT) resources may be drivers of business strategy. For instance, if an organization has an IT capability that is complex, sophisticated, and difficult for others to imitate, the business might wish to develop a business strategy in which this IT capability plays an important role. If a firm can provide access to customer data in a unique manner, the business strategy may be adapted to take advantage of this information capability.

**Full Integration**

The last mode in Figure 1.1 is "Full Integration." This suggests that the processes for business strategic planning and SPIS are not separate, but rather are conducted in an integrated and concurrent manner. This represents the recognition that IS is of such critical importance to the enterprise that IS issues must be considered concurrently with other functional issues in the formulation of business strategy.

## EVOLUTION OF THE MODES OF INFORMATION SYSTEMS STRATEGIC PLANNING

There is ample evidence that each of the four modes of SPIS depicted in Figure 1.1 is in current use in a variety of organizations. Thus, the historical evolution of SPIS, which may be loosely thought of as going from a total lack of integration and passing though the four modes from top to bottom in Figure 1.1, does not imply that all organizations will follow an evolutionary path or find it useful to move to the level of full integration. Some firms may determine that the mode best suited to their needs is one that has less-than-full integration.

However, there is evidence that the more "proactive" planning modes—full integration and reciprocal integration—result in better planning performance and outcomes than do the other, more "reactive" modes. This suggests that while all firms may not find it desirable to move to full integration, there is reason to expect better planning performance from the more advanced SPIS modes.

## A MODEL OF ORGANIZATIONAL-LEVEL INFORMATION SYSTEMS PLANNING

Figure 1.2 shows a model of strategic planning for IS in terms of the various elements that must be considered and integrated in a strategic planning process for IS in the organization. In effect, the elements on the left side of Figure 1.2 represent multiple starting points for an SPIS process that is concluded, as shown on the right side of the figure, when choices have been made concerning IS's desired organizational role, mission, capabilities, architectures, and strategic programs, and when implementation plans have been developed.

The SPIS model of Figure 1.2 consists of six key elements:

1. Assessment of external environments
2. Assessment of internal environments
3. Assessment of IS/IT environments
4. Generation and assessments of options for IS/IT change
5. Specification (choice) of IS strategic elements
6. Development and implementation of plans

**Assessment of External Environments**

One of the major inputs to the SPIS process is a set of assessments of external environments. Of particular interest, as shown in Figure 1.2, are assessments of:

- General business and economic trends
- Industry and competitive trends

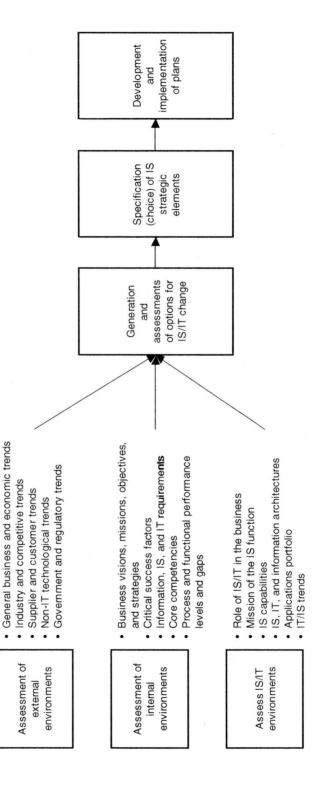

Figure 1.2   A General Model of the SPIS Process

- Supplier and customer trends
- Non–IT technological trends
- Government and regulatory trends

Each of these assessments may have initially been made in the strategic business planning process. However, even so, these assessments need to be analyzed to discern their IS-relevant content. It is almost never adequate for SPIS process managers merely to circulate the external environmental assessments that have been performed by business planners because they will generally not focus either on the aspects of these environments to which IS is most sensitive or on the aspects that are most sensitive to IS.

Each of these external contexts must be assessed as a potential source of opportunities or threats. Evolving trends may indicate new opportunities for IS or suggest new constraints on the evolution of IS.

### General Business and Economic Trends

Forecasts of the future business and economic climate will give some indication of whether the economy is in an expansion or a contraction mode and how long the current situation is expected to continue. This will enable IS planners to "scope" potential opportunities for greater or lesser degrees of change for IS in the organization in the future. For instance, if the economy is expected to go into recession, IS planners may be less aggressive in proposing major investments in new systems and IS capabilities.

Specific forecasts of economic factors that are gathered in this phase, such as productivity improvements, may specify what can be expected of IT, since most productivity improvements are enabled by IT.

### Industry and Competitive Trends

The assessment of industry and competitive trends permits the IS planner to focus on what is happening with regard to technological adoption by firms in the same industry or firms in other industries that might become future competitors.

In making such assessments, it is necessary to recognize that the traditional boundaries of industries are changing. For instance, banks, brokerage firms, investment managers, and other financial firms have been merging and developing new products that blur the traditional definitions of the banking and financial services industries. Firms such as General Electric and General Motors are now heavily involved in financial services. Firms like IBM, which have traditionally provided hardware and software, now derive major portions of their total revenues from consulting services and services provided as an outsourcing vendor. So, the questions of "What is, or will be, our industry?" and "Who will be our competitors?" are of fundamental importance to effective SPIS.

### Supplier and Customer Trends

Supplier and customer trends permit a focus on the changes taking place in the value chain on both the input and output sides. What will our customers and suppliers expect of us in the future? What is the most appropriate and profitable role that our organization can play in the overall value chain? What are the trends in using IT for supply-chain management and for promoting and selling products?

For instance, for some time many firms have been implementing enterprise resource planning (ERP) systems that integrate data reflecting the various functions and processes of the organization. With the rapid development of the Internet, most such firms were forced to address the question of how their ERP systems could be integrated with supply-side systems that would provide them with the opportunity to buy through electronic auctions and to take advantage of other Internet-based purchasing options as well as to implement the promotion or sale of their products and services via the Internet. The Internet so rapidly became a major factor in doing business that many firms were unprepared for the opportunities that it offered and the potential threats from competitors that it posed. Those firms that had conducted good external environmental assessments were certainly better prepared than those that had not.

*Non–IT Technological Trends*

As new technologies such as neural networks or nanotechnologies in materials science become practical or as new production technologies are developed, the demands placed on the IS function within an organization and the opportunities afforded to IS are likely to change. An assessment of such potentially important non-IT technological areas can help IS managers to foresee these changing demands and opportunities.

In some firms, the business strategic planning process involves an assessment of the major technologies that may be relevant to the firm's future success. Because IT enables other technologies, such assessments can be very useful in forecasting future IT issues and requirements.

*Government and Regulatory Trends*

Only a short while ago, IS managers may have thought this environmental area to be of only modest relevance to IS. However, recent government attempts to utilize or limit IT, such as through the establishment of data encryption standards and the implementation of electronic telecommunications surveillance software, have made it clear that the IS function in an organization must be conversant with changes in governmental actions and regulations. In the IT domain, the IS function must be the "eyes and ears" of the firm. In addition, IS must use such assessments as a basis for determining how future systems will be developed, how the firm's intellectual property rights and trade secrets can best be protected, and whether the value of IT investments may be affected by government-imposed constraints on their use. For instance, firms that invest in communications infrastructure may be concerned with the possibility that government will require them to provide open access, thus constraining their opportunity to gain a competitive advantage through such investments. The assessments of such trends can be very useful in establishing a sound basis for such investment choices.

**Assessment of Internal Environments**

Because IS cannot "do everything" that might be possible for it to do, part of the SPIS process is to select those areas within the organization on which IS can most usefully focus. Just as is the case with external environmental assessments, these areas may be thought of either as opportunities to be addressed or as problems to be solved using IS. The starting points for making such determinations in the internal environment are assessments of the following:

- Business visions, missions, objectives, and strategies
- Critical success factors
- Information, IS, and IT requirements
- Core competencies
- Functional and process performance levels and gaps

*Business Visions, Missions, Objectives, and Strategies*

Although SPIS must be conducted in a manner that takes into account IS-enabled opportunities to influence business strategies, it is still an important starting point to have a clear understanding of the vision that top management has for the future of the enterprise, the business missions that have been established, and the business strategies and objectives that have been enunciated.

Sometimes, these are the products of a strategic business planning process; in other instances, they will be best reflected by assessing the past strategic programs that have been prescribed; in still other instances, they may need to be inferred from past strategic actions taken by top management.

*Critical Success Factors*

In order for SPIS to be cost effective, concern must be given to identifying the critical success factors (CSFs) for each business and for the overall enterprise. CSFs are those activities that the organization must do well and the capabilities that it must possess in order to have a chance to be successful. They are the necessary, but not sufficient, conditions for success.

For instance, for an original equipment supplier to the auto industry, one CSF is typically the ability to produce and deliver parts on a "just-in-time" basis. Without this ability, the parts firm has little chance of success, but with it, the firm has the chance to take actions that may lead to success.

Typically, fewer than ten CSFs can be identified for a business. A primary role of IS is to enable and support the development and refinement of capabilities related to these CSFs. Thus, their identification is an important starting point for the SPIS process.

*Information, IS, and IT Requirements*

Although the idea of identifying information resource requirements—whether these requirements are for information, knowledge, systems, services, hardware, or software—is not nearly as practical a notion as it might appear at first, a survey of perceived information resource needs can be a useful input to the SPIS process.

However, at first glance, the notion of requirements is not as practical as it might appear because managers and users of IS resources are not always capable of identifying their requirements, sometimes because they lack an understanding of the latest technologies and sometimes because they cannot conceive of what might be provided to them and therefore cannot "require" what they cannot conceptualize.

At some point in the SPIS process, managers and other system users may be provided with suggestions or information concerning what might be available or what can be feasibly provided by IS. This may be done at an early stage of IS planning or later, in SPIS, when various options are being seriously considered.

*Core Competencies*

The SPIS process must consider the organization's past and potential core competencies. Core competencies are complex and sophisticated "bundles" of capabilities, processes, systems, and procedures that the organization has developed over time and that give it a unique ability to achieve a competitive advantage in the marketplace. For instance, a firm's core competency might be its capacity to rapidly develop and market new versions of existing products and new products. Such a competency would be likely to encompass good market research, concurrent design processes, effective competitive intelligence, and a variety of other organizational activities and systems.

Just as the CSF notion separates out a relatively small number of activities for special attention, the core competency notion identifies a core of activities that are absolutely critical to the future success of the organization. These assessments have become important inputs to making strategic choices for IS for the same reasons that CSFs are important to SPIS.

*Process and Functional Performance Levels and Gaps*

The performance levels of various business processes and functions must be assessed in order to determine which are operating at peak performance and which may be performing inadequately. The term *gap* is widely applied to differences between desired and actual performance levels.

Most enterprises have clearly defined business functions—marketing, operations, human resources, finance, and so on—and most routinely collect performance data for these functions such as the market share achieved by various products or business units and the operating efficiency of the production function. These performance data may be compared with those of competitors that are available through trade associations or vendors of such data. In this fashion, functional performance may be assessed relative to the levels achieved by others and assessments may be made of any gaps that might exist.

Similarly, in business processes such as new product development and order fulfillment, metrics may be available to permit the assessment of process performance. Illustrative of such metrics are cycle times for order fulfillment, levels of customer satisfaction, and quality indicators. Process performance data may not be as readily available for competitors and other firms as are functional performance data. Thus, comparisons across time may have to be relied on to indicate whether progress is being made in each process. It may sometimes be valuable to conduct benchmarking assessments of companies that are acknowledged to be "world class" in some key business processes in order to establish standards of performance that are high, but achievable.

These functional and process performance assessments and identification of gaps can provide insight into areas of opportunity for the application of innovative information systems and technology.

**Assessment of IS/IT Environments**

The third major category of inputs to the SPIS process involves assessing the enterprise's existing IS/IT in terms of:

- Role of IS/IT in the business
- Mission of the IS function
- IS capabilities
- IS, IT, and information architectures
- Applications portfolio
- IS/IT trends

With the exception of IS/IT trends, these are strategic decision elements of SPIS in the areas where choices must subsequently be made in the SPIS process. As such, their current status may have been specified as the result of prior periodic SPIS processes. However, it is not adequate for IS planners to assume that choices made in SPIS in prior years have actually been implemented, because it is not uncommon to discover failures in implementing the results of planning. Alternatively, the current status of these elements may simply reflect the aggregate of many minor choices made throughout the organization over many years rather than a state that is the result of a comprehensive prior choice. In either case, it is important that the IS planner adequately assess the actual current situation with regard to each of these factors.

## Role of IS/IT in the Business

The present role played by IS and IT in the business must be assessed. The role may vary from a service role, in which IS is viewed merely as a service provided to other areas of the organization, to a strategic role in which IS is viewed as something that is crucial to future success.

## Mission of the IS Function

The mission of an organizational entity describes what is expected of it in practical terms that enable its managers to make choices that are sensible, focused toward clear objectives, and internally consistent.

A clearly defined mission enables managers to develop tactics that are consistent with strategies and goals and to choose what they will and will not do. In the area of IS, this is of particular significance because there are so many opportunities for adopting new technologies, developing new systems, and taking initiatives that it is important for the enterprise's top managers to specify an IS mission that will guide IS managers in making the myriad tactical choices that they face routinely.

## IS Capabilities

An organization's IS capability consists of its hardware and software and the shared services, such as e-mail or group support systems, that it provides to organizational participants and the organizational skills and processes that the IS function possesses. These may be skills processed by individuals, such as programming skills or project management skills, or they may be elements of IS's "social capital"—skills that reside in groups rather than in individuals—such as the ability of IS-based teams to rapidly design and implement new applications systems. The IS processes are those that amplify these people skills, such as the availability of systems development techniques and software, the existence of standard templates for successful project management, and SPIS itself.

These capabilities identify the base on which the future of the IS function must be constructed. As such, having a clear understanding of existing capabilities is critical to effective SPIS.

## IS, IT, and Information Architectures

The existing architectures related to information and to IS in the organization will either enable or inhibit change. If the organization has made expensive commitments to particular architectures, it may be reluctant to suffer the costs—both financial and psychological—of change. Thus, existing architectures may impede progress, or if they are scalable and adaptable, they may facilitate change. As a result, a delineation of existing architecture for data, systems, and networks is a fundamental input to the SPIS process.

## Applications Portfolio

The existing portfolio of applications is another baseline that may enhance or inhibit the opportunities for change. For instance, an organization that had implemented ERP in order to integrate data from its business functions may not be willing to consider IS projects that do not conform to its ERP. Even though such a constraint may not be rational in a theoretical sense, some organizations have found that the commitment of time and energy to implement major systems such as ERP is so great that they are not psychologically prepared to consider large-scale additional changes. If this is the case, such factors must be considered in the SPIS process or it will deteriorate into an impractical exercise.

*IS/IT Trends*

Trends in new technologies and applications of IT must be assessed so that the opportunities for future IS developments in the organization can be fully appreciated. This may vary from the application of neural networks applications in creating new products for the business to the development of new methodologies for systems development.

**Generation and Assessment of Options for IS/IT Change**

The next level of the SPIS model, shown in Figure 1.2, involves the generation and assessment of options that may be required, or desired, in order to change the IS function in ways that will best serve the organization.

*Generation of Options*

Some options will naturally evolve from the previously described assessments. For instance, a critical success factor that is not being effectively supported or developed or an information requirement that is not being met will specify options to be considered promptly.

Similarly, a performance gap in a function or process may readily identify an opportunity for the application of IT in improving performance. An important approach to such improvements has been business process reengineering (BPR), which involves the radical redesign of business processes to achieve significant improvements in process performance. IT typically plays a major role in such process redesigns.

Even at the broadest level of IS's role in the organization, it is necessary to periodically consider change. For instance, if IS has operated in a service role, a turnaround may be indicated as appropriate by evolving trends in IS as well as in the assessments that have been made of other internal and external environmental factors.

Other options may need to be creatively generated based on the assessments. For instance, a functional performance deficiency coupled with a newly recognized technology may identify an option for remedying the deficiency using a technology that was not previously available. Such options may make it feasible to address a problem for the first time or present a particularly cost-effective way of doing so.

Other options can be generated through the use of brainstorming and other creativity-enhancing techniques or through logical approaches such as identifying the most significant areas of performance gaps.

*Option Assessment Criteria*

Once options have been generated, they must be assessed. This may be done judgmentally, using some formal scoring technique, or using a combination of subjective judgment and formality. Some criteria that are commonly used in assessing options are:

1. Is this change *required* (e.g., because the new government reporting requirements)?
2. Is it *urgent* (e.g., it might be if the implementation of an IS/IT change is extremely sensitive to a deadline that is not subject to change)?
3. Is it *critical* to business success (e.g., it might be if it were an element of a business critical success factor or if it would significantly enhance a core competence)?
4. Does it have the potential for *high business impact?* (Will it make a real difference? Does it have the potential to improve some aspect of business performance by a significant increment?)
5. Is it *innovative?* (Does it represent a truly new way of doing something?)

**Specification (Choice) of IS Strategic Elements**

Once options for changes in IS/IT have been generated and evaluated, the SPIS process, like any planning process, becomes an exercise in decision making. Decisions must be made and general specifications must be delineated for IS/IT strategic elements:

- Role of IS in the enterprise
- Mission(s) of IS
- IS capabilities to be developed or enhanced
- IS strategic programs
- IS/IT architectures
- Applications portfolio

Any annual or periodic SPIS process may not result in significant changes in all these elements. For instance, the role and missions of IS might be expected to change only infrequently. Other elements may require changes even more frequently than the SPIS process is formally conducted.

Ultimately, the choice of these IS strategic elements is a matter of judgment of the top IS and business managers. However, the conduct of the environmental assessments and the option generation and evaluation phases of SPIS ensures that these judgments can be made on the basis of comprehensive information concerning the options and the likely ramifications of choosing each. As such, the core of SPIS is a process of choice that is based on informed judgment.

**Development and Implementation of Plans**

While the making of strategic choices is often portrayed as the end of a planning process, it is well recognized that in modern organizations, the choices made in any planning process may not be enacted. There are many reasons for such strategy implementation failures, ranging from a lack of understanding as to who is responsible for implementation to reluctance on the part of lower level managers to truly accept the choices made in the SPIS process, perhaps because they disagree with or do not fully understand them.

To avoid these strategic implementation failures, clear implementation plans must be developed. These plans should indicate who is responsible for the implementation of each element of the plan; they should identify specific "milestones" and schedules for the reporting of results to those who are responsible and to top management, and they should specify clear performance goals for each milestone.

Such implementation plans cannot be prepared until the desired changes in the major strategic IS/IT elements have been approved by top management, but they should be developed immediately thereafter and their development should be considered an integral part of the SPIS process.

## OBJECTIVE AND CONTENTS OF THE VOLUME

This volume represents an attempt to pull together the myriad ideas and processes that have come to be identified with IS planning. The focus is not entirely on the strategic planning level, although many of the chapters do deal primarily with that highest level of organizational planning. In addition, I have invited chapters on budget planning, operational planning, project planning, and planning for a variety of desired outcomes that are not necessarily strategic in nature.

I have been fortunate in having been able to induce a variety of knowledgeable and highly visible people to prepare chapters on a wide range of topics.

Part I—Key Concepts of Information Systems Planning—focuses on a description of how IS planning has evolved over the years since its inception (Chapter 2, Lee and Hsu, "The Evolution of Planning for Information Systems"), business–IS strategic alignment (Chapter 3, Tarafdar and Ragu-Nathan, "Business–Information Systems Alignment: Taking Stock and Looking Ahead," and Chapter 4, Teo, "Aligning Business and Information Systems: Review and Future Research Directions"), and the role of dynamic organizational capabilities in leveraging IS competencies (Chapter 5, Bhatt, "The Role of Dynamic Organizational Capabilities in Creating, Renewing, and Leveraging Information Systems Competencies").

Part II—The Organizational Information Systems Planning Process—describes IS planning in terms of critical success factors (Chapter 6, Rockart and Bullen, "Using Critical Success Factors in Setting Information Technology and General Management Resource Priorities"), a knowledge-based view of IS planning (Chapter 7, Sabherwal, Hirschheim, and Jeyaraj, "A Knowledge-Based View of Information Systems Planning and Its Consequences: Review and Propositions"), a practical assessment of strategic alignment (Chapter 8, Bullen and Luftman, "Strategic Alignment: Highly Valued, but Elusive in Practice"), the IT budgeting process (Chapter 9, Smith and McKeen, "Information Technology Budgeting: Planning's Evil Twin"), the search for an optimal level of IS strategic planning (Chapter 10, Philip, "Some Dos and Dont's of Strategic Information Systems Planning," and Chapter 11, Newkirk, Lederer, and Srinivasan, "Strategic Information Systems Planning: The Search for an Optimal Level"), and the role of organizational learning in IS planning (Chapter 12, Otim, Grover, and Segars, "The Role of Organizational Learning in Strategic Information Systems Planning in Uncertain Environments").

Part III—Information Systems Investment Planning—deals with predicting the value that an IS investment project may have (Chapter 13, Davern, "Information Systems Planning: The Search for Potential Value"), a "rational expectations" approach to assessing project payoffs (Chapter 14, Au, Goh, Kauffman, and Riggins, "Planning Technology Investment for High Payoffs: A Rational Expectations Approach to Gauging Potential and Realized Value in a Changing Environment"), assessing the social costs and benefits of projects (Chapter 15, Ryan, "Information Technology Investment Planning: Anticipating Social Subsystem Costs and Benefits"), an options-based approach to managing project risk (Chapter 16, Benaroch, "Option-Based Management of Risk in Information Systems Planning"), planning for project teams (Chapter 17, He, "Creating Better Environments for Information Systems Projects"), and the moderating effects of coordinated planning on project teams (Chapter 18, Mitchell and Zmud, "The Moderating Effects of Coordinated Planning on Project Performance").

Part IV—Goals and Outcomes of Information Systems Planning—considers information strategy as a goal and/or an outcome of IS planning (Chapter 19, Teubner, Mocker, and Pellengahr, "Information Strategy: Confronting Research with Practice"), IT infrastructure as a goal or outcome (Chapter 20, Tallon, "How Information Technology Infrastructure Shapes Strategic Alignment: A Case Study Investigation with Implications for Strategic IS Planning"), and competitive advantage as a goal/outcome (Chapter 21, Barney and Ray, "How IT Resources Can Provide a

Competitive Advantage in Customer Service"). The final two chapters focus on specific IS planning contexts: e-process supply-chain partnerships (Chapter 22, Sawy, Malhotra, and Gosain, "Planning for Successful E-Process Supply-Chain Partnerships"), and Internet-based projects (Chapter 23, Srinivasan, Gallupe, and Wolf, "Planning Successful Internet-Based Projects: A Risk–Performance Framework").

## REFERENCES

IBM Corporation. 1980. Business Systems Planning: Information Systems Planning Guide, GE20-0527-2.
King, W. 1978. Strategic planning for management information systems. *MIS Quarterly,* 2, 1, 27–37.
King, W.R., and Cleland, D.I. 1975. A new method for strategic systems planning. *Business Horizons,* 18, 4, 55–64.

# PART I

## KEY CONCEPTS OF INFORMATION SYSTEMS PLANNING

CHAPTER 2

# THE EVOLUTION OF PLANNING FOR INFORMATION SYSTEMS

## GWO-GUANG LEE AND WEI-LIN HSU

*Abstract: Information systems (IS) planning has consistently been identified as one of the most important issues faced by IS executives and academic researchers, and recently information systems strategic planning (ISSP) in most organizations has shifted toward e-business and e-commerce planning. Numerous researchers argue that ISSP should be seen as one area of business planning and that strategic planning guides a firm's activities in order to achieve organizational goals. The aim of this research is to explore the evolution of information systems strategic planning based on the business planning perspectives. The review suggests that the evolution of ISSP has shifted from the formal rational planning perspectives toward the social cultural learning and political perspectives. The review suggests ISSP may follow the track of the revolution of planning perspectives in strategic planning and take multiple planning perspectives that not only understand the cognitions of strategists but also address their interactions, cultures, and political issues in the situated context.*

*Keywords: Information Systems Strategic Planning*

## INTRODUCTION

### Importance of ISSP

Information systems strategic planning (ISSP) has been identified as one of the most important issues facing IS executives and academic researchers (Basu et al., 2002; Earl, 1993; Kearns, 2006; King, 1978; Lederer and Salmela, 1996; Segars and Grover, 1999; Teo and Ang, 2000). According to surveys of information systems management issues in the past decade, improving ISSP remains one of the key issues facing IS/IT executives and business/corporate managers (Gottschalk, 2001; Pimchangthong, Plaisant, and Bernard, 2003). Moreover, as globalization and electronic commerce/business receive growing attention from organizations, ISSP is progressively becoming a critical medium for developing successful electronic business strategy (Bai and Lee, 2003).

ISSP has been described as a managerial and interactive learning process for integrating IS considerations into the corporate planning process, integrating the application of information systems to business goals, developing detailed information systems plans, and determining information requirements to achieve business objectives (Galliers, 1991; Newkirk and Lederer, 2006; Teo and King, 1997). The ISSP process involves the long-range planning horizon for funds, human services, technical expertise, and the hardware and software capabilities needed to take advantage of any opportunities that may arise (Baker, 1995). Organizations may fail to realize the anticipated benefits of their IS investments if they do not engage in appropriate information systems strategic planning (Salmela, Lederer, and Reponen, 2000). Besides effectively managing information systems/information technology (IS/IT) investments, ISSP can also optimize resource allocation and generate the required IS capability. Incentives for businesses to engage in ISSP have been summarized as follows (Bai and Lee, 2003; Jang, 1989; Scott Morton, 1991; Ward and Peppard, 2002).

- *Turbulent business environment:* It has been argued that the business environment has always been turbulent. The extent of frequent and unpredictable environmental change can dramatically affect organizations in the running of their business. Typical examples include the growth of competition, change in economic systems, globalization and e-business. The use of IS has been seen as a strategic necessity for survival in the increasingly turbulent business environment.
- *Rapid evolution of information technology:* Organizations must reassess available information systems to maintain their competitive position in the light of the rapid evolution in IT, including web-based technology, multimedia technology, client-server architecture, gigabit networking, wireless communication, object-oriented programming and databases, information management security, groupware, and so on.
- *Increasing strategic role of information systems:* IS/IT applications have been widely developed and used in organizations to improve their performance and competitiveness or gain sustainability, including electronic commerce, knowledge management, virtual organizations, customer relationship management, supply chain management, and enterprise resources planning.
- *Resource constraints:* Organizations must efficiently allocate information resources given resource constraints, including software and hardware investments, human resources, time, cost, and other resources spending.
- *Integration of existing and new information systems applications:* The increasing use of IS/IT results in growing IS developments so that incompatible systems must be upgraded or phased out. Accordingly, businesses must develop new IS applications and integrate them with existing systems.

With the rapid evolution in Internet technology and turbulent e-business environments, the focuses of ISSP have shifted toward e-business information systems, including: customer relationship management; enterprise resources planning; supply chain management; and knowledge management systems. Gottschalk (2000, p. 176) predicts several key issues of future studies in IS management around the world in the twenty-first century including: improving links between information systems strategy and business strategy; developing and implementing an information architecture; implementing knowledge management systems; and reducing information technology projects completion time and budget deviations.

## Definition of ISSP

While the importance of ISSP is increasingly recognized in business organizations, a variety of terms are used to describe identical or similar activities related to ISSP in earlier literature. These terms include: information systems strategic planning (ISSP) (Bai and Lee, 2003; Baker, 1995;

Cerpa and Verner, 1998; King, 2000); strategic planning for information systems (SPIS) (Ward and Peppard, 2002); strategic information systems planning (SISP) (Basu et al., 2002; Earl, 1993; Gottschalk, 2001; Segars and Grover, 1998) and information systems strategy formation (ISSF) (Auer and Reponen, 1997; Walsham and Han, 1993).

Lederer and Sethi (1996) provide a popular ISSP definition, which considers the potential impact of IS/IT on business goals and aligns IS/IT plans with business plans to achieve business goals. According to Lee and Gough (1993), ISSP is defined as one area of business strategic planning that aims to achieve business goals through the effective integration of organization management and various information systems in an adaptive and ongoing process. Baker (1995) argues that ISSP involves the identification of prioritized information systems that are efficient, effective, and/or strategic in nature together with the necessary resources (e.g., human, technical, and financial), management of change considerations, control procedures, and organizational structure needed to implement these information systems. Teo and King (1997) define ISSP as the process of formulating IS objectives, defining strategies and policies to achieve them, and developing detailed plans to achieve these objectives. It has been argued that ISSP refers to the process of creating a portfolio for the implementation and use of IS to maximize the effectiveness and efficiency of a corporation, so that it can achieve its objective (Min, Suh, and Kim, 1999).

The ISSP process is an interactive learning process that creates a strategy for business process redesign and incorporates information technology (Auer and Reponen, 1997; Reponen, 1993). This strategy provides viable options for information systems design, implementation, and operation (Reponen, 1993). Typical ISSP activities include the tasks of meeting, interview, and the analysis of documents. The main purpose of information systems strategic planning is to identify the required information systems rather than planning in detail for any specific system. The outputs of ISSP should show which information systems are required and the priority in which they should be implemented.

## EVOLUTION OF PERSPECTIVES ON ISSP

Numerous researchers argue that ISSP should be seen as one area of business planning: for example, Galliers (1987), Lederer and Sethi (1996), Ward and Peppard (2002). Within organizations, strategic business planning guides all activities in order to achieve organizational goals. There are various perspectives, or schools, of ISSP thought, each of which takes a slightly different view of the process and may consequently lead to differences in the formation of information systems strategy.

Strategic business management is necessarily a multiple-paradigmatic discipline that requires varied theoretical perspectives and methodologies (Hoskisson et al., 1999). Many researchers have recognized these and incorporate not only the rational viewpoints but also the power or political, social culture, and strategists' approaches: for example, Idenburg (1993), McCarthy and Leavy (2000), Mintzberg, Ahlstrand, and Lampel (1998), Rajagopalan and Spreitzer (1997), Wit and Meyer (2004), and Whittington (1993). As Mintzberg, Ahlstrand, and Lampel (1998) integrate various schools into a single process and provide more adequate and explicit perspectives, their framework becomes a suitable vehicle to understand the planning perspectives taken during the ISSP. According to Hsu (2006), due to the rapidly changing business environment, the perspectives of information systems strategic planning have shifted from the *design, planning, and positioning* schools to the *learning, cultural,* and *political* schools (Figure 2.1).

Figure 2.1   **Perspectives of Information Systems Strategic Planning (ISSP)**

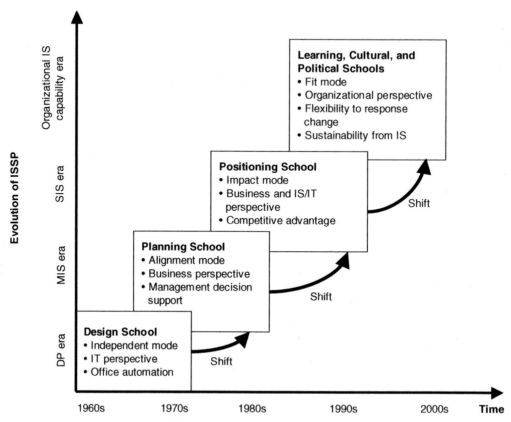

## The Shift from the Design School to the Planning School

From the 1960s onward, the data processing (DP) era, ISSP took the *design* school perspective where top management takes a technology viewpoint and considers using information technology to reduce data processing costs. Researchers that have taken this perspective include, for example, Earl (1993), Sabherwal and Chan (2001), and Salmela, Lederer, and Reponen (2000). ISSP was primarily concerned with gaining computer processing efficiency by handling the most data in the least amount of time (Gallo, 1988). However, most application systems were developed in a piecemeal way and information systems were seen as a matter isolated from the continuing business of the organization (Galliers, 1991). There is no direct link between the business strategy and the IS strategy. The strategy formulation of ISSP in this era has been labeled as "pre-planning" (Jang, 1989) or "independent" (Teo, 1994; Venkatraman and Henderson, 1990). ISSP in this era may be seen as the "independent" mode. The role of the IS function is technically oriented and the purpose of integration between business planning and information systems strategic planning is to support the administration work process (King and Teo, 1997).

From the 1970s onward, the management information systems (MIS) era, the perspective of ISSP shifted to the *planning* school perspective to generate detailed IS/IT plans. Computer applications moved from a transaction-based, batch-processing environment to an interactive environment in which emphasis was placed on day-to-day business operations and short-term tactical needs (Gallo, 1988). There was a growing concern of management to have business-driven information systems, capable of dealing with business problems and the issues they faced (Galliers, 1991). The use of computer applications was considered from an IS, instead of an IT, viewpoint. Business-driven approaches are labeled as the "alignment" mode of information systems strategic planning (Lederer and Sethi, 1988). Popular alignment methodologies include Business Systems Planning (BSP) (IBM, 1975), information engineering (IE) (Martin, 1982) and strategic systems planning (SSP) (Holland Systems Corporation, 1986). BSP combined top-down planning with bottom-up implementation and focused on organizations' business processes to derive data needs. IE provided techniques for building enterprise, data, and process models. Meanwhile, SSP defines a data architecture derived from the business function model by combining information requirements into generic data entities and subject databases. Other researchers who have taken this planning school perspective include, for example, Earl (1993) and Bone and Saxon (2000). The "alignment" mode focuses on using the information systems to assist in achieving business goals (Min, Suh, and Kim, 1999). IS strategies are reactive to business strategies and derived from them (Reich, 1992; Teo, 1994; Venkatraman and Henderson, 1990) and the relationship is unidirectional (Jang 1989; Reich, 1992; Teo and King, 1997).

Several additional terms other than alignment have been used by researchers, for example, coordination (Lederer and Mendelow, 1989), fit (Henderson and Thomas, 1992), linkage (Reich and Benbasat, 1996), and integration (Teo and King, 1997). The major importance of ISSP is to fit information technology, corporate strategies, and organizational factors together: for example, Galliers (1987), Ruohonen (1991), Singh (1993), and Ward and Peppard (2002). The role of the IS function moved toward becoming critical to the long-term success of the organization (King and Teo, 1997).

### The Shift from the Planning School to the Positioning School

The "alignment" mode of ISSP approaches usually includes neither a mechanism for determining whether current systems are either technically or functionally unsatisfactory nor a way of assessing the criticality of various projects or a method for prioritizing IS activities (Dantzig, 1990). These approaches may also be too detailed, time consuming, and costly, and may have problems in securing top management support (Pant and Hsu, 1999). From the 1980s onward, the strategic information systems (SIS) era, the perspective of ISSP began to shift toward the *positioning* school. Researchers who have taken this positioning school perspective include, for example, Al-Qirim (2003), Kearns and Lederer (2004), and Pant and Hsu (1999). The use of IS began to influence organizations' competitive positions and became a strategic weapon for competitive advantage (King, 1988; King and Zmud, 1981; Ward and Peppard, 2002; Wiseman, 1985).

Researchers have suggested exploiting competitive advantage from IS/IT investments by using IT to impact or shape organizational goals (Boynton and Zmud, 1987; Ives and Learmonth, 1984; McFarlan, 1984; Parsons, 1983; Porter, 1985; Porter and Millar, 1985) and/or aligning organizational goals and strategies with IT capabilities rather than the other way around, as was the approach in the "alignment" mode.

There has thus been a continuous growing concern to take both IS/IT and business viewpoints together. ISSP approaches in this era are labeled the "impact" mode (Bergeron, Buteau, and Raymond, 1991), which aims to identify strategic opportunities for organizations by applying IT to optimize business performance (Pant and Ravichandran, 2001). Popular information planning methodologies were proposed, such as value chain analysis (VCA) (Porter and Millar, 1985) and the strategic thrust model (STM) (Rackoff, Wiseman, and Ullrich, 1985). VCA aims to discover how IS can have an impact on the overall performance of a firm by reconstructing the firm's primary and support activities of product or service creation. STM uses a grid, known as a generator of strategic options, which allows a manager to analyze three strategic targets: suppliers, clients, and competitors and also makes the managers aware of the main directions that the firm can take in its quest for competitive advantage. The linkage of business planning and information systems is bidirectional (Premkumar and King, 1991; Reich, 1992; Teo, 1994) and the purpose of IS strategic planning is also to influence business strategy (King and Teo, 1997).

## The Shift from the Positioning School to the Political, Cultural, and Learning Schools

Despite the use of the "alignment" and "impact" modes of ISSP methodologies, organizations have still been unable to effectively deal with IS-related problems (Pant and Hsu, 1999). From the 1990s to now, from the strategy viewpoint, there have been continuous calls for ISSP to take a broader perspective (Hsu, 2006; Lee and Gough, 1993). As globalization and electronic business receives growing attention from organizations, the focus of ISSP shifts from gaining advantages over external competitors to strengthening internal capabilities. The implementation of information systems causes organizational changes, including changes in tasks and skills, organizational structure, organization members, managerial styles, and shared values. The mode of ISSP approaches is described as the "fit" mode (Ruohonen, 1991). Reponen (1993) argues that ISSP is an interactive learning process, where the participants process the knowledge and share the vision of how best to utilize IS/IT. There is significant research taking the learning school perspective, including, for example, Auer and Reponen (1997), Baker (1995), Ciborra (1997), Earl (1993), Grover and Segars (2004), Reponen (1993), Salmela, Lederer, and Reponen (2000), and Simonsen (1999). As ISSP includes negotiations for allocation of organizations' resources and requires top management's commitment and support, ISSP approaches have to consider different stakeholders' perceptions (Earl, 1993). This political concern has been taken by some researchers: for example, Allen, Kern, and Mattison (2002), Basu and others (2002), and Hackney and Little (1999).

Regarding cultural concern, it has been argued that ISSP approaches have to suit the environment, culture, experience, and skills of the organization (Doherty, Marples, and Suhaimi, 1999; Duhan, Levy, and Powell, 2001). King (2000) argues that the best information systems strategic planning uses a methodology to "fit" the organization's culture, style, sophistication, and information systems capabilities. Several researchers have taken the cultural school perspective, including, for example, Allen and Wilson (2003), Allen, Kern, and Mattison (2002), Burn and Szeto (2000), Lewis (2004), Waema and Walsham (1990), Walsham and Han (1993), and Walsham and Sahay (1999). As the focus of organizations shifts from external to internal, the issue of organizational capabilities is an increasing concern in the IS literature (Galliers and Sutherland, 1991; Willcocks, Feeny, and Islei, 1997). To assist organizations in reviewing the level of their capabilities to develop IS projects, based on Nolan's evolutionary model (Gibson and Nolan, 1974; Nolan, 1979), Galliers and Sutherland (1991) proposed a revised "stages of growth" model that addresses the weakness of Nolan's model by improving the organizational and management focus (Galliers, 1991). The revised model consists of six stages, each addressing seven major elements: (1) strategy; (2) structure; (3) systems; (4) staff; (5) style; (6) skills; and (7) superordinate goals, which are called the "seven s's." Lederer and Sethi (1996) indicate that a "fit" between IT capabilities and environmental and competitive conditions is necessary to realize ISSP goals. The globalization and boom of electronic business in the 1990s led IS to the emergence of the fourth era, the organizational IS capability, in which organizations take an internal view and aim to gain sustainability from IS (Ward and Peppard, 2002). The characteristics of the "fit" mode have become the mainstream for developing information systems strategic planning approaches. Earl (1993) defined five types of strategic IS strategic planning approaches, as business-led, method-driven, administrative, technological, and organizational, and claims that the organizational approach is considered the most effective one. There is a need to consider ISSP from an organizational viewpoint. A typical ISSP methodology is the strategic alignment model that fits business strategy, IS strategy, and different organizational factors together (Henderson and Venkatraman, 1994). The relationship between business planning and ISSP can be seen as integrated planning with full integration (King and Teo, 2000).

The evolution of the ISSP perspective has shifted from the *design* school, the *planning* school, and the *positioning* school, toward the *learning, cultural,* and *political* schools. There is little research regarding the environmental, entrepreneurial, cognitive, and configuration schools: for example, Earl (1993), King and Teo (2000), and Knoll and Jarvenpaa (1994). From the *design* perspective, ISSP frameworks can be labeled as the *independent* mode, which focuses on automation and efficiency. Taking the *planning* school perspective, ISSP frameworks can be labeled as the *alignment* mode, which aims to identify the information systems aligned with the business plans and goals with detailed IS related plans. Taking the *positioning* school perspective, ISSP frameworks can be labeled as the *impact* mode, which focuses on identifying information systems that can enhance an organization's competitiveness over their competitors. From the *learning, cultural,* and *political* school perspectives, the fit mode of ISSP emphasizes an internal focus and that the use of IS/IT must be suited to the organization in order to enhance organizations' capabilities.

## EMPIRICAL STUDIES ON ISSP

Similar to strategic planning, by the 1980s, empirical research on ISSP focused on two areas: content and process. The content area emphasizes the exploration of important factors and the impact of information systems strategic planning on firm performance, while the process area emphasizes exploration of how a strategy is actually formed.

### Empirical Studies via the Functionalist Approach

Regarding the content areas, numerous researchers have conducted empirical studies on ISSP (see Table 2.1). Most of them are based on King's (1988) input–process–output–outcomes model (see, e.g., Basu et al., 2002; Kearns, 2006; Kearns and Lederer, 2004; Premkumar and King, 1994; and Teo and King, 1997). These studies are often cited, and were conducted via the dominant functionalist approach, which takes the rational perspective, focusing on content and trying to identify and solve managerial problems.

All of the above studies are dominated by the functionalist approach that focuses on cause–effect relationships and quantitative, rather than qualitative, factors. They provide much information on issues of alignment of IS strategy with business strategy, and the relationships between various factors relating to ISSP and its effectiveness. It is assumed that reality is "concrete," and that manageable problems can be identified and reduced. From a strategy perspective, these theoretical frameworks of ISSP provide a formal, rational, and top-down approach to information systems strategic planning. However, it can be argued that this rational planning perspective underestimates the complexity of reality and therefore involves risks because little attention is paid to the sociocultural context and human issues.

Table 2.1

**Empirical Studies on ISSP in Recent Years via Functionalist Approaches**

| Authors | Research objective |
| --- | --- |
| Kearns, 2006 | Identifying the effect of top management support of SISP on strategic IS management in the U.S. electric power industry |
| Newkirk and Lederer, 2006 | Measuring SISP success as a composite of alignment, analysis, cooperation, and capabilities under environmental uncertainty by a postal survey of 161 IS executives |
| Lee, Lin, and Pai, 2005 | Identifying environmental and organizational factors and the influence on the success of Internet-based interorganizational systems planning |
| Kearns and Lederer, 2004 | Identifying the impact of industry contextual factors on IT focus and the use of IT for competitive advantage |
| Mirchandani and Lederer, 2004 | Identifying IS strategic planning autonomy in U.S. subsidiaries of multinational firms |
| Bai and Lee, 2003 | Identifying organizational factors influencing the quality of the ISSP process |
| Wang and Tai, 2003 | Identifying the impact of organizational context and planning system dimensions on information systems strategic planning effectiveness |
| Hartono et al., 2003 | Examining key predictors of the implementation of strategic information systems plans |
| Basu et al., 2002 | Investigating the impact of organizational commitment, senior management involvement, and team involvement on the success of information systems strategic planning |
| Hussin, King, and Cragg, 2002 | Examining the impact of IT sophistication, CEO commitment, and external IT expertise on IT alignment |
| Kunnathur and Shi, 2001 | Investigating the success of information systems strategic planning in China |
| Sabherwal and Chan, 2001 | A survey examining the impact of alignment on perceived business performance using Miles and Snow's classification of defender, analyzer, and prospector business strategies |
| Teo and Ang, 2001 | Identifying the major planning problems associated with three phases of IS strategic planning (input, process, and outcome) |
| Burn and Szeto, 2000 | A survey examining the differences in perspectives of IT and business managers on which factors contribute to successful strategic alignment |
| Kearns and Lederer, 2000 | Examining the effect of strategic alignment on the use of IS-based resources |
| King and Teo, 2000 | A survey of 600 firms assessing the impact of proactive and reactive modes of strategic information systems strategic planning |
| Reich and Benbasat, 2000 | Finding factors that influence the social dimension of alignment between business and information technology objectives |
| Tai and Phelps, 2000 | Examining the perceptions existing among CEOs and IT executives in Hong Kong |
| Teo and Ang, 2000 | Examining the usefulness of IS plans using a field survey of 136 IS executives |
| Ang et al., 1999 | Investigating the factors that affect the benefits of information systems strategic planning |
| Carayannis, 1999 | Proposing a model of synergy IT and managerial and organizational cognition |

| Authors | Research objective |
|---|---|
| Gottschalk, 1999a | Identifying the implementation predictors of strategic information systems plans |
| Gottschalk, 1999b | A survey examining potential implementation predictors on information technology strategy |
| Luftman, Papp, and Brier, 1999 | Identifying enablers and inhibitors of business–IT alignment |
| Sabherwal, 1999 | Examining relationships between planning sophistication and information systems success |
| Segars and Grover, 1999 | Identifying the profiles of information systems strategic planning |
| Teo and Ang, 1999 | A survey of IS executives on the relative importance of various CSFs for aligning IS plans with business plans |
| Teo and King, 1999 | A survey examining the impacts of BP–ISSP integration on ISSP process, output problems, and organizational performance |
| Choe, Lee, and Park, 1998 | A survey examining the influence of internal, external, and related factors on information systems strategic planning |
| Segars and Grover, 1998 | Measuring the constructs of the success of information systems strategic planning |
| Segars, Grover, and Teng, 1998 | A survey examining the dimensions of information systems strategic planning |
| King and Teo, 1997 | Validating a staged growth model of information systems strategic planning |
| Teo and King, 1997 | Determining factors of alignment between business planning and information systems strategic planning |

## Empirical Studies via the Interpretive Approach

It has been argued that the use of IS/IT has been recognized not as a simple mechanical input–output relationship between a machine and a person (Nardi, 1996). Ciborra (1997) claims that the theories and conceptual models from such rational planning perspectives are not useful in real-world organizations. Additionally, from the cultural perspective, the past experience of managers and social processes in the organization and the impact of culture on IS strategic planning should not be ignored. Existing formal-rational models and frameworks for IS/IT planning are not powerful enough to explain strategic gains as they do not take the sociopolitical perspectives into account for long-term effectiveness (Hackney and Little, 1999). Avison and others (2004) echo McKay and Marshall's (1999) suggestion that the rigorous modular concepts scarcely depict people's thinking and actions in real life. This suggests the limitations of the current dominant functionalist approach in the IS research community. In the process area, other groups of researchers have conducted several empirical studies on ISSP via the interpretive approach (see Table 2.2). These researchers assume that reality is only in the individuals' perceptions and can only be understood from the perspective of the individuals participating.

The above studies and others based on interpretive approaches are often cited and have provided considerable additional information on ISSP, in that they produce "an understanding of the context of the information system, and the process whereby the information system influences and is influenced by the context" (Walsham, 1993, pp. 4–5). This research focuses strongly on the sociocultural and political perspectives, in which the participants involved in the planning process may be expected to more fully reflect real-world situations than is the case using a strictly rational model of ISSP. Similar approaches to IS strategy formulation can produce different levels

Table 2.2

**Empirical Studies on ISSP in Recent Years via Interpretive Approaches**

| Authors | Research objective |
|---|---|
| Peffers and Tuunanen, 2005 | Developing an IS strategic planning method in a project to develop ideas for mobile financial services applications |
| Hasan, 2004 | Using grounded theory to collect data from case and activity theory to analyze the attempt of management to implement organizational change through the introduction of information systems |
| Lewis, 2004 | Using a published case study to illustrate how Ulrich's (1983) purposeful systems paradigm and cultural historical activity theory can be combined and applied to IS alignment issues in practice |
| Allen and Wilson, 2003 | Based on the findings of a longitudinal study and "organization stories," exploring trust or mistrust between superiors and subordinates during the information strategy formation process |
| Allen, Kern, and Mattison, 2002 | Using case studies to explore culture, power, and politics in information and communication tools outsourcing in higher education institutions in the UK to support the required IS |
| Chan, 2002 | Examining alignment of IS and business strategies in eight firms using Henderson and Venkatraman's strategic alignment model |
| Peters, Heng, and Vet, 2002 | Based on evolution theory, analyzing a case study of the evolution of the IS strategy and found no ISSP used; but found that concepts of organizational evolution are useful in analyzing the development of the IS strategy |
| Salmela, Lederer, and Reponen, 2000 | Using action research to examine IS strategic planning in turbulent environments—one practiced, formal, and comprehensive, and the other informal and incremental |
| Hackney and Little, 1999 | Demonstrating the differences between two longitudinal case studies based on the design school and a power behavioral approach and suggesting a trend toward considering sociopolitical perspectives for longer-term effectiveness |
| Simonsen, 1999 | Presenting a bottom-up design approach to contribute to the planning process that suggests how designers can ensure that the design of IT is appropriately aligned with the organization's overall business strategy |
| Walsham and Sahay, 1999 | An in-depth case study, using actor–network theory for analytical purposes to develop and use geographical IS to aid district-level administration in India |
| Auer and Reponen, 1997 | A case study via an action research approach, presenting how the IS strategy process can be embedded into a continuous-experience learning process through user organizational ability analysis |
| Ciborra, 1997 | Presenting a bottom-up approach to alignment where designers and users of the systems also contribute to the planning process |

of effectiveness in different organizations (McLean, 1983). IS strategy formulation must take the specific cultural context into account, as people are key participants in the ISSP process and there are differences between their cognitions and actions. There is little research on understanding the ISSP context through a cultural and historical lens. Hence, broader holistic (e.g., cultural, historical, political, and dynamic) perspectives must be considered and more empirical studies must be conducted in different organizational contexts to explore and understand more information that will be useful in both research and practice.

## THE FUTURE OF ISSP

Although IS/IT strategic planning has been studied extensively, numerous problems remain unresolved. To solve these problems, organizations can improve ISSP by adopting multiple planning perspectives. This chapter addresses the planning perspectives underlying the ISSP process. The ISSP process does not include merely the concerns of formal rational planning such as utilizing a limited budget to support overall information systems technology requirements. It is also concerned with the social, cultural, and political issues derived from community interactions during the planning process. From the strategic planning perspective, the information systems strategic planning has shifted from the design, planning, and positioning schools to the learning, cultural, and political schools. Theoretical frameworks of ISSP always provide a formal, rational, and top-down approach to information systems strategic planning. However, it can be argued that this rational planning perspective underestimates the complexity of reality and therefore involves risks because little attention is paid to sociocultural, context, and human issues. A more interpretive approach is needed to explore the ISSP process within the surrounding organizational context. This chapter provides a valuable reference for business managers, strategic planners, and IS executives in conducting strategic planning for information systems and information technology in the e-business era and IS capability era, as well as for researchers interested in the field of IS/IT, e-commerce, and e-business planning.

## ACKNOWLEDGMENTS

We thank the following people for comments on this chapter: Bill King of the University of Pittsburgh, David Allen of Leeds University Business School, Peter Jimack of Leeds University, and the reviewers.

## REFERENCES

Allen, D., and Wilson, T. 2003. Vertical trust/mistrust during information strategy formation. *International Journal of Information Management*, 23, 3, 223–237.

Allen, D.; Kern, T.; and Mattison, D. 2002. Culture, power and politics in ICT outsourcing in higher education institutions. *European Journal of Information Systems*, 11, 2, 159–173.

Al-Qirim, N.A.Y. 2003. The strategic outsourcing decision of IT and ecommerce: the case of small businesses in New Zealand. *Journal of Information Technology Cases and Applications*, 5, 3, 32–56.

Ang, J.S.K.; Quek, S.A.; Teo, T.S.H.; and Lui, S.H.B. 1999. Modeling IS planning benefits using ACE. *Decision Sciences*, 30, 2, 533–562.

Auer, T., and Reponen, T. 1997. Information systems strategy formation embedded into a continuous organizational learning process. *Information Resources Management Journal*, 10, 2, 32–43.

Avison, D.; Jones, J.; Powell, P.; and Wilson, D. 2004. Using and validating the strategic alignment model. *Journal of Strategic Information Systems*, 13, 3, 223–246.

Bai, R.-J., and Lee, G.-G. 2003. Organizational factors influencing the quality of the IS/IT strategic planning process. *Industrial Management + Data Systems*, 103, 8/9, 622–632.

Baker, B. 1995. The role of feedback in assessing information systems planning effectiveness. *Journal of Strategic Information Systems*, 4, 1, 61–80.

Basu, V.; Hartono, E.; Lederer, A.L.; and Sethi, V. 2002. The impact of organizational commitment, senior management involvement, and team involvement on strategic information systems planning. *Information & Management*, 39, 6, 513–524.

Bergeron, F.; Buteau, C.; and Raymond, L. 1991. Identification of strategic IS opportunities: applying and comparing two methodologies. *MIS Quarterly*, 15, 1, 89–103.

Bone, S., and Saxon, T. 2000. Developing effective technology strategies. *Research Technology Management*, 43, 4, 50–58.

Boynton, A.C., and Zmud, R.W. 1987. Information technology planning in the 1990's: directions for practice and research. *MIS Quarterly,* 11, 1, 58–71.

Burn, J.M., and Szeto, C. 2000. A comparison of the views of business and IT management on success factors for strategic alignment. *Information & Management,* 37, 4, 197–216.

Carayannis, E.G. 1999. Fostering synergies between information technology and managerial and organizational cognition: the role of knowledge management. *Technovation,* 19, 4, 219–231.

Cerpa, N., and Verner, J.M. 1998. Case study: the effect of IS maturity on information systems strategic planning. *Information and Management,* 34, 199–208.

Chan, Y.E. 2002. Why haven't we mastered alignment? the importance of the information organization structure. *MIS Quarterly Executive,* 1, 2, 97–112.

Choe, J.-M.; Lee, Y.-H.; and Park, K.-C. 1998. The relationship model between the influence factors and the strategic applications of information systems. *European Journal of Information Systems,* 7, 137–149.

Ciborra, C.U. 1997. De Profundis? Deconstructing the concept of strategic alignment. *Scandinavian Journal of Information Systems,* 9, 1, 67–82.

Dantzig, D.F. 1990. Understanding information systems. *Journal of Systems Management,* 41, 2, 32–37.

Doherty, N.F.; Marples, C.G.; and Suhaimi, A. 1999. The relative success of alternative approaches to strategic information systems planning: an empirical analysis. *Journal of Strategic Information Systems,* 8, 3, 263–283.

Duhan, S.; Levy, M.; and Powell, P. 2001. Information systems strategy in knowledge-based SMEs: the role of core competencies. *European Journal of Information Systems,* 10, 25–40.

Earl, M.J. 1993. Experiences in strategic information systems planning. *MIS Quarterly,* 17, 1, 1–23.

Galliers, R.D. 1987. Information systems planning in the United Kingdom and Australia: a comparison of current practice. *Oxford Surveys of Information Technology,* 223–255.

———. 1991. Strategic information systems planning: myths, reality and guidelines for successful implementation. *European Journal of Information Systems,* 1, 1, 55–64.

Galliers, R.D., and Sutherland, A.R. 1991. Information systems management and strategy management and strategy formulation: the "stages of growth" model revisited. *Journal of Information Systems Education,* 1, 89–114.

Gallo, T.E. 1988. *Strategic Information Management Planning.* Englewood Cliffs, NJ: Prentice Hall.

Gibson, C.F., and Nolan, R.L. 1974. Managing the four stages of EDP growth. *Harvard Business Review,* 52 (January–February), 76–88.

Gottschalk, P. 1999a. Implementation predictors of strategic information systems plans. *Information & Management,* 36, 2, 77–91.

———. 1999b. Strategic information systems planning: the IT strategy implementation matrix. *European Journal of Information Systems,* 8, 2, 107–118.

———. 2000. Studies of key issues in IS management around the world. *International Journal of Information Management,* 20, 3, 169–180.

———. 2001. Key issues in IS management in Norway: an empirical study based on Q methodology. *Information Resources Management Journal,* 14, 2, 37–45.

Grover, V., and Segars, A.H. 2004. An empirical evaluation of stages of strategic information systems planning: patterns of process design and effectiveness. *Information & Management,* 42, 5, 761–779.

Hackney, R., and Little, S. 1999. Opportunistic strategy formulation for IS/IT planning. *European Journal of Information Systems,* 8, 2, 119–126.

Hartono, E.; Lederer, A.L.; Sethi, V.; and Zhuang, Y. 2003. Key predictors of the implementation of strategic information systems plans. *Database for Advances in Information Systems,* 34, 3, 41–53.

Henderson, J.C., and Thomas, J.B. 1992. Aligning business and information technology domains: strategic planning in hospitals. *Hospital & Health Services Administration,* 37, 1, 71–89.

Henderson, J.C., and Venkatraman, N. 1994. Strategic alignment: a model for organizational transformation via information. In T.J. Allen and M.S. Scott Morton (eds.), *Information Technology and the Corporation of the 1990s: Research Studies.* Oxford: Oxford University Press.

Holland Systems Corporation. 1986. *Strategic Systems Planning,* Document M0154–04861986, Ann Arbor, MI.

Hoskisson, R.E.; Hitt, M.A.; Wan, W.P.; and Yiu, D. 1999. Theory and research in strategic management: swings of a pendulum. *Journal of Management,* 25, 3, 417–456.

Hsu, W.-L. 2006. The process of information systems strategic planning in higher education institutions in Taiwan. Ph.D. diss., School of Computing, University of Leeds.

Hussin, H.; King, M.; and Cragg, P. 2002. IT alignment in small firms. *European Journal of Information Systems*, 11, 2, 108–127.

IBM. 1975. *Business Systems Planning: Information Systems Planning Guide*. Publication No: GE20 0527–4.

Idenburg, P.J. 1993. Four styles of strategy development. *Long Range Planning*, 26, 6, 132–138.

Ives, B., and Learmonth, G. 1984. The information system as a competitive weapon. *Communications of the ACM*, 27, 12, 1193–1201.

Jang, S.Y. 1989. Influence of organizational factors on IS strategic planning. Ph.D. diss., University of Pittsburgh.

Kearns, G.S. 2006. The effect of top management support of SISP on strategic IS management: insights from the US electric power industry. *Omega*, 34, 3, 236–253.

Kearns, G.S., and Lederer, A.L. 2000. The effect of strategic alignment on the use of IS-based resources for competitive advantage. *Journal of Strategic Information Systems*, 9, 4, 265–293.

———. 2004. The impact of industry contextual factors on IT focus and the use of IT for competitive advantage. *Information & Management*, 41, 7, 899–919.

King, W.R. 1978. Assessing the efficacy of IS strategic planning. *Information Systems Management*, 17, 1, 81–83.

———. 1988. How effective is your information systems planning? *Long Range Planning*, 21, 5, 103–112.

———. 2000. Strategic planning for management information systems. *MIS Quarterly*, 2, 1, 27–37.

King, W.R., and Teo, T.S.H. 1997. Integration between business planning and information systems planning: validating a stage hypothesis. *Decision Sciences*, 28, 2, 279–307.

———. 2000. Assessing the impact of proactive versus reactive modes of strategic information systems planning. *Omega*, 28, 6, 667–679.

King, W.R., and Zmud, R.W. 1981. Managing information systems: policy planning, strategic planning and operational planning. In *Proceedings of the Second International Conference on Information Systems*, Cambridge, MA. 299–308.

Knoll, K., and Jarvenpaa, S.L. 1994. Information technology alignment or 'Fit' in highly turbulent environments: the concept of flexibility. In *Proceedings of the 1994 Computer Personnel Research Conference on Reinventing IS: Managing Information Technology in Changing Organizations*, Alexandria, Virginia, 24–26 March, 1–14.

Kunnathur, A.S., and Shi, Z. 2001. An investigation of the strategic information systems planning success in Chinese publicly traded firms. *International Journal of Information Management*, 21, 6, 423–439.

Lederer, A.L., and Mendelow, A.L. 1989. Coordination of information systems plans with business plans. *Journal of Management Information Systems*, 6, 2, 5–19.

Lederer, A.L., and Salmela, H. 1996. Toward a theory of strategic information systems planning. *Journal of Strategic Information Systems*, 5, 3, 237–253.

Lederer, A.L., and Sethi, V. 1988. The implementation of strategic information systems planning methodologies. *MIS Quarterly*, 12, 3, 445–461.

———. 1996. Key prescriptions for strategic information systems planning. *Journal of Management Information Systems*, 13, 1, 35–62.

Lee, G.-G. and Gough, T. 1993. An integrated framework for information systems planning and its initial application. *Journal of Information Technology*, 8, 227–240.

Lee, G.-G.; Lin, H.-F.; and Pai, J.-C. 2005. Influence of environmental and organizational factors on the success of Internet-based interorganizational systems planning. *Internet Research*, 15, 5, 527–543.

Lewis, G. 2004. Strategic alignment: a purposeful perspective. In *Proceedings of "9e Colloque de l'AIM."* INT Evry, France. May.

Luftman, J.N.; Papp, R.; and Brier, T. 1999. Enablers and inhibitors of business-IT alignment. *Communications of the Association for Information Systems*, 1 (March), Article 11.

Martin, J.A. 1982. *Strategic Data-Planning Methodologies*. Englewood Cliffs, NJ: Prentice Hall.

McCarthy, B., and Leavy, B. 2000. Phases in the strategy formation process: an exploratory study of Irish SMEs. *IBAR*, 21, 2, 55–80.

McFarlan, F.W. 1984. Information technology changes the way you compete. *Harvard Business Review*, 62, 3, 98–103.

McKay, J., and Marshall, P. 1999. 2 x 6 = 12, or does it equal action research? In *Proceedings of the Tenth Australasian Conference on Information Systems*, Victoria University of Wellington, 1–3 December, 597–608.

McLean, C. 1983. *Strategic Planning for MIS: An Update.* Information System Working Paper 4–83, Graduate School of Management, University of California, Los Angeles.

Min, S.K.; Suh, E.H.; and Kim, S.Y. 1999. An integrated approach toward strategic information systems planning. *Journal of Strategic Information Systems,* 8, 4, 373–394.

Mintzberg, H.; Ahlstrand, B.; and Lampel, J. 1998. *Strategy Safari: The Complete Guide through the Wilds of Strategic Management.* Englewood Cliffs, NJ: Prentice Hall, 1998.

Mirchandani, D.A., and Lederer, A.L. 2004. IS planning autonomy in US subsidiaries of multinational firms. *Information & Management,* 41, 1021–1036.

Nardi, B.A. (ed.). 1996. *Context and Consciousness: Activity Theory and Human-Computer Interaction,* Cambridge, MA: MIT Press.

Newkirk, H.E., and Lederer, A.L. 2006. The effectiveness of strategic information systems planning under environmental uncertainty. *Information & Management,* 43, 4, 481–501.

Nolan, R.L. 1979. Managing the crises in data processing. *Harvard Business Review,* 52, 2, 115–126.

Pant, S., and Hsu, C. 1999. An integrated framework for strategic information systems planning and development. *Information Resources Management Journal,* 12, 1, 15–25.

Pant, S., and Ravichandran, T. 2001. A framework for information systems planning for e-business. *Logistics Information Management,* 14, 1/2, 85–98.

Parsons, G.L. 1983. Information technology: a new competitive weapon. *Sloan Management Review,* 25, 1, 3–14.

Peffers, K., and Tuunanen, T. 2005. Planning for IS applications: a practical, information theoretical method and case study in mobile financial services. *Information & Management,* 42, 3, 483–501.

Peters, S.C.A.; Heng, M.S.H.; and Vet, R. 2002. Formation of the information systems strategy in a global financial services company. *Information and Organization,* 12, 1, 19–38.

Pimchangthong, D.; Plaisent, M.; and Bernard, P. 2003. Key issues in information systems management: a comparative study of academics and practitioners in Thailand. *Journal of Global Information Technology Management,* 6, 4, 27–44.

Porter, M.E. 1985. Technology and competitive advantage. *Journal of Business Strategy,* 5, 3, 60–77.

Porter, M.E., and Millar, V.E. 1985. How information gives you competitive advantage. *Harvard Business Review,* 63, 4, 149–161.

Premkumar, G., and King, W.R. 1991. Assessing strategic information systems planning. *Long Range Planning,* 24, 5, 41–58.

———. 1994. Organizational characteristics and information systems planning: an empirical study. *Information Systems Research,* 5, 2, 75–109.

Rackoff, N.; Wiseman, C.; and Ullrich, W.A. 1985. Information systems for competitive advantage: implementation of a planning process. *MIS Quarterly,* 9, 4, 285–294.

Rajagopalan, N., and Spreitzer, G.M. 1997. Toward a theory of strategic change: a multi-lens perspective and integrative framework. *Academy of Management Review,* 22, 1, 48–79.

Reich, B.H. 1992. Investigating the linkage between business objectives and information technology objectives: a multiple case study in the insurance industry. Ph.D. diss., University of British Columbia, 1992.

Reich, B.H., and Benbasat, I. 1996. Measuring the linkage between business and information technology objectives. *MIS Quarterly,* 20, 1, 55–81.

———. 2000. Factors that influence the social dimension of alignment between business and information technology objectives. *MIS Quarterly,* 24, 1, 81–113.

Reponen, T. 1993. Information management strategy—an evolutionary process. *Scandinavian Journal of Management,* 9, 3, 189–209.

Ruohonen, M. 1991. Stakeholders of strategic information systems planning: theoretical concepts and empirical examples. *Journal of Strategic Information Systems,* 1, 1, 15–28.

Sabherwal, R. 1999. The relationship between information system planning sophistication and information system success: an empirical assessment. *Decision Sciences,* 30, 1, 137–167.

Sabherwal, R., and Chan, Y.E. 2001. Alignment between business and IS strategies: a study of prospectors, analyzers, and defenders. *Information Systems Research,* 12, 1, 11–33.

Salmela, H.; Lederer, A.L.; and Reponen, T. 2000. Information systems planning in a turbulent environment. *European Journal of Information Systems,* 9, 1, 3–15.

Scott Morton, M.S. (ed.). 1991. *The Corporation of the 1990s: Information Technology and Organizational Transformation.* New York: Oxford University Press.

Segars, A.H., and Grover, V. 1998. Strategic information systems planning success: an investigation of the construct and its measurement. *MIS Quarterly,* 22, 2, 139–163.

———. 1999. Profiles of strategic information systems planning. *Information Systems Research,* 10, 3, 199–232.

Segars, A.H.; Grover, V.; and Teng, J.T.C. 1998. Strategic information systems planning: planning system dimensions, internal coalignment, and implications for planning effectiveness. *Decision Sciences,* 29, 2, 303–345.

Simonsen, J. 1999. How do we take care of strategic alignment? Constructing a design approach. *Scandinavian Journal of Information Systems,* 11, 2, 51–72.

Singh, S.K. 1993. Using information technology effectively: organizational preparedness models. *Information & Management,* 24, 3,133–146.

Tai, L.A., and Phelps, R. 2000. CEO and CIO perceptions of information systems strategy: evidence from Hong Kong. *European Journal of Information Systems,* 9, 3, 163–172.

Teo, T.S.H. 1994. Integration between business planning and IS planning: evolutionary-contingency perspectives. Ph.D. diss., University of Pittsburgh.

Teo, T.S.H., and Ang, J.S.K. 1999. Critical success factors in the alignment of IS plans with business plans. *International Journal of Information Management,* 19, 2, 173–185.

———. 2000. How useful are strategic plans for information systems? *Behaviour & Information Technology,* 19, 4, 275–282.

———. 2001. An examination of major IS planning problems. *International Journal of Information Management,* 21, 6, 457–470.

Teo, T.S.H., and King, W.R. 1997. Integration between business planning and information systems planning: an evolutionary-contingency perspective. *Journal of Management Information Systems,* 14, 1, 185–224.

———. 1999. An empirical study of the impacts of integrating business planning and information systems planning. *European Journal of Information Systems,* 8, 3, 200–210.

Venkatraman, N., and Henderson, J.S. 1990. IT alignment with business strategy. In *An ICL Briefing for Management on the Findings of the Management in the 1990's Research Program,* International Computers Limited, London.

Waema, T.M., and Walsham, G. 1990. Information Systems strategy formulation. *Information & Management,* 18, 1, 29–39.

Walsham, G. 1993. *Interpreting Information Systems in Organizations.* Chichester, UK: Wiley.

Walsham, G., and Han, C.K. 1993. Information systems strategy formation and implementation: the case of a central government agency. *Accounting, Management and Information Technologies,* 3, 3, 191–209.

Walsham, G., and Sahay, S. 1999. GIS for district-level administration in India: problems and opportunities. *MIS Quarterly,* 23, 1, 39–65.

Wang, E.T.G., and Tai, J.C.F. 2003. Factors affecting information systems planning effectiveness: organizational contexts and planning systems dimensions. *Information & Management,* 40, 4, 287–303.

Ward, J., and Peppard, J. 2002. *Strategic Planning for Information Systems.* Chichester, UK: Wiley.

Whittington, R. 1993. *What Is Strategy—and Does it Matter?* London: Routledge.

Willcocks, L.; Feeny, D.; and Islei, G. 1997. *Managing Information Technology As A Strategic Resource.* London: McGraw-Hill.

Wiseman, C. 1985. *Strategy and Computers.* Homewood, IL: Dow Jones-Irwin.

Wit, B.D., and Meyer, R. 2004. *Strategy: Process, Content, Context: An International Perspective.* London: Thomson Learning.

# CHAPTER 3

# BUSINESS–INFORMATION SYSTEMS ALIGNMENT

## Taking Stock and Looking Ahead

MONIDEEPA TARAFDAR AND T.S. RAGU-NATHAN

*Abstract: Information systems research and managerial practice have long emphasized the importance of alignment or fit between IS and business. It is widely acknowledged that organizations that align the strategies, priorities, processes, and structures of the IS function with those of the business can garner superior business value from their information systems/information technology (IS/IT). However, firms continue to find it difficult to achieve alignment, primarily because of insufficient top management awareness of IT, uncoordinated and isolated strategic and IS planning processes, ineffective or powerless IT departments, and barriers to implementation and use arising from political, financial, or technical constraints. What are the key themes and ideas in extant business–IS alignment research? Given developments in the current and emerging business and IT environments, what are the emerging, understudied, and less understood areas? This chapter synthesizes existing knowledge about business–IS alignment by reviewing the IS alignment literature. It further extends it to identify understudied alignment-related issues. In doing so, it suggests for researchers, important areas for future investigation, and for practitioners, a framework for driving, prioritizing, and shaping business–IS alignment efforts.*

*Keywords: Information Systems, Alignment, Fit, IS Strategic Planning*

## INTRODUCTION

Researchers and practitioners have long stressed the importance of alignment or fit or linkage[1] between information systems (IS)[2] and business. The earliest academic discussion of this linkage was in King and Cleland (1975). Subsequently, management practice (IBM, 1981) emphatically highlighted its importance in IS planning. Academic discourse (e.g., Chan et al., 1997; Henderson and Venkatraman, 1993; King, 1978; Pyburn, 1983; Reich and Benbasat, 1996) and professional conversation (Jahnke, 2004) have since investigated various issues in the context of business–IS alignment. It is well understood and widely acknowledged that organizations that align the strategies, priorities, processes, and structures of the IS function with those of the business, can increase the effectiveness of and garner superior business value from their IS/IT. Even so, the subject of business–IS alignment continues to vex organizations, as suggested by the following scenarios.

The authors quote from their conversation (in 2007) with the chief information officer (CIO) of one of the world's leading manufacturers of glass and plastic packaging, with 150 locations globally: "IT planning and organizing were never centralized because our company grew through acquisitions and always retained the IT structures of the companies we bought. That proved to be a disaster [very expensive] because everyone went off doing their own things. We had multiple IT projects of exactly the same things [across the company]. This was encouraged by the reward system because if your division is going to be rewarded purely on divisional performance, you want all the [technology] resources under your control—you don't want someone else controlling those resources."

The authors spoke (in 2006) with the CIO of a large glass manufacturer, who noted that, "The CFO [chief financial officer] and COO [chief operating officer] are part of our Executive Committee. I report to the CFO, and sometimes I sit in on the Committee meetings, to get a sense of [the] strategic issues. However most of the time I come to know of major business decisions only after they are made."

The issue in both of these cases is a lack of business–IS alignment. In the first, there is mismatch between the way that the IT function is organized (decentralized, with divisional control over projects) and the way it is governed at the corporate level (with a cost-centered emphasis). In the second, since the CIO is unaware of likely future strategic decisions, existing IT infrastructure and applications may not be aligned with the requirements of new business initiatives.

The current (and expected future) business and IT environments have four key characteristics. First, the business role of IS/IT continues to expand in terms of functional pervasiveness and technological sophistication. Whereas the last two decades of the twentieth century were about identifying and acquiring IS that could support the business, rapid advancements in IT capabilities have made it possible for organizations to extend and formulate business strategies based on such capabilities (Wheeler, 2002). Second, given continual commercialization of new applications, firms are spending ever-increasing amounts of financial and managerial resources on IT planning, acquisition, deployment, use, and upgrades. Third, recent advances in the use of B2B systems and in outsourcing/offshoring of IT applications and infrastructure have increased the complexity of IT management; crucial IT-related decisions require collaboration and cooperation with vendors and business partners. Fourth, whether or not firms can successfully appropriate benefits from "user-driven" applications such as corporate portals, knowledge management systems, collaborative software, and data-warehousing systems depends on how effectively individual users are able to use them; end-user computing issues are therefore critical in current business-computing environments.

These developments and characteristics lead us to two important implications. First, the cost of misalignment is high. For instance, organizations that adopt applications that do not support their processes and products would find themselves running a costly and ineffective, and ultimately a powerless, IS function; or an end-user IT environment that mandates standardization may stifle innovative and novel use of applications; or firms that fail to match capabilities of emerging information technologies with potential business opportunities could lose their competitive positions. Second, it is more important than ever for organizations not only to acquire and deploy information systems that are aligned to current and future strategic objectives, but also to manage and organize IS/IT resources in line with organizational processes and structures. Toward this end, there is a need to revisit and synthesize existing knowledge about business–IS alignment and conceptually extend them to understand and identify alignment-related issues in these new business and IT environments.

Figure 3.1    **Aspects of Alignment Between Information Systems and Business**

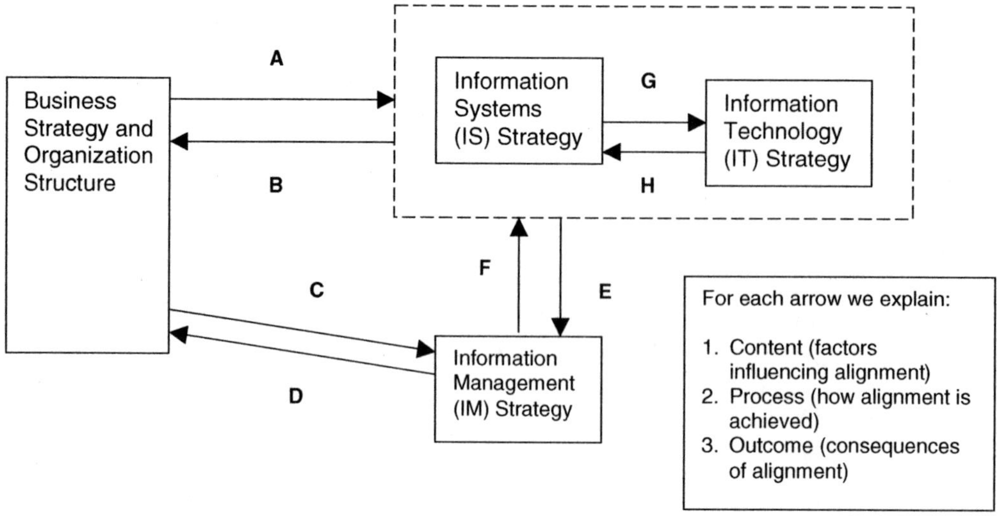

In this chapter, we suggest answers to two questions. One, what are the key themes and ideas in extant business–IS alignment research? Two, what are the emerging, understudied, and less understood areas in business–IS alignment? We do this by reviewing the literature on IS alignment, identifying gaps, and suggesting future research directions. In the next section we describe a model and review framework for studying the alignment between business and IS. In the following section we review the literature and organize its key arguments. Then we identify the gaps in research and establish future areas of study. The final section presents concluding comments.

## MODEL OF ALIGNMENT AND FRAMEWORK FOR REVIEW

There are two broad aspects to alignment between IS and the business. The first involves strategically matching the business and its IT/IS in order to take advantage of IT opportunities and capabilities (Brancheau, Janz, and Wetherbe, 1996; Galliers, Merali, and Spearing 1994; Niederman, Brancheau, and Wetherbe, 1991; Rodgers, 1997), and has been quite widely studied as alignment *between* business strategy and structure, and IS, IT, and IM strategies (Henderson and Venkatraman, 1993; King, 1978). The second aspect involves effectively planning the acquisition, implementation, management, and use of IS and IT for accrual of planned outcomes of IS and IT on the business. This aspect has been conceptualized as alignment *among* IS, IT, and IM strategies (Earl, 1989); it has not been as well studied and has become extremely important in recent years, given the emergence of new IT sourcing options and the dramatic increase in end-user computing. Based on these two aspects, therefore, our review of the literature reveals four distinct components that may be aligned with one another to increase IS effectiveness—*business strategy and organization structure, IS strategy, IT strategy,* and *IM strategy.* We frame our review of the IS-business alignment literature in the model described in Figure 3.1. In this section, we first describe in detail, each component of the model as indicated by the boxes. We then briefly explain alignment implications between the components as represented by the arrows.

*Business strategy and organization structure*[3] describes the *strategy-* and *structure*-related domains of the firm's operations at a business unit level. The *strategy*-related domain consists of the firm's competitive position and its choice of products and markets. It can be understood in a number of ways:

1. By analyzing the firm's emphasis on specific activities; an organization might be a pioneer in product-market development and product innovation and emphasize entrepreneurial activities, or it may offer products and services in a narrow segment and underline cost efficiency, or combine the two approaches (Hambrick, 1983; Miles and Snow, 1978).
2. By considering the relative dominance of different "stances" that the firm might have— aggressiveness toward improving market positions, proactiveness in seeking emerging opportunities, future-based emphasis on long-term considerations such as basic R&D, riskiness in resource allocation and choice of products and markets, defensiveness regarding costs and domain or analysis-driven and systematic decision making (Venkatraman, 1989b).
3. By analyzing the competitive position the firm stakes out, and by understanding the nature of entry barriers, substitutes, the relative influences of the powers of buyers and suppliers (Porter, 1985).

The *structure*-related domain is concerned with choices pertaining to the structure of the firm. These choices include administrative structure (functional or divisional or matrix) (Chandler, 1969), information-processing structure (rules and procedures, hierarchy, creation of slack resources/self-contained tasks/lateral relations) (Galbraith, 1973), interdependencies and coordination among tasks (Thompson, 1967), relative sizes and importance of different organizational parts (line management, operating core, support and technology staff, and strategic apex) (Mintzberg, 1979), and capabilities and specific routines for performing various functions (Grant, 1991; Prahalad and Hamel, 1990; Snow and Hrebeniak, 1980; Stalk, Evans, and Shulman, 1992).

IS, IT and IM strategies are the three aspects of how an organization plans for, delivers, organizes, and controls its information systems-related technologies and resources (Earl, 1989).

*IS strategy* pertains to what a firm should do with information technology. It is typically formulated at the business unit level. It is concerned with determining the firm's information-processing needs and identifying the applications required. Attributes of IS strategy (Sabherwal and Chan, 2001) include IS for efficiency (use of IS primarily for operational support and interorganizational communication), flexibility (use of IS primarily for marketing support and surveillance), and comprehensiveness (use of IS for operational support and marketing surveillance). The orientation of a firm's IS strategy can be assessed by the extent to which it uses applications for enabling particular objectives—increasing efficiency, detailed analysis, forecasting, facilitating creativity and innovation, making risk assessments, or expediting the introduction of new products and services (Chan et al., 1997).

*IT strategy* is concerned primarily with the firm's technological choices—planning, development, and delivery of its computing, communication, applications, and data environment (Earl, 1989). It specifies the technologies and infrastructure that are used for developing applications, as well as the technological architecture used to support them (Weill and Broadbent, 1998). It also pertains to security, vendor selection and policies, and technical standards.

*IM strategy* is the management framework that guides the organization of IS/IT activities. It is management-focused and consists of policies and procedures for managing the roles and responsibilities of the IS function. It focuses on governance structures of the IS function and its relationships with users (Boynton, Zmud, and Jacobs, 1994; Sambamurthy and Zmud, 1999). It also includes activities pertaining to funding, charging for, and evaluating IT applications. The orientation of IM strategy can be assessed by the extent to which development and management of IS and IT are analysis-based, proactive, conservative, defensive, or efficiency based, whether they take into account future technology developments, and whether or not the deployment and use of IS are aggressively promoted within the organization (Ragu-Nathan, et al., 2001).

Arrows *A* and *B* denote the alignment between *business strategy and organization structure, and IS strategy* and *IT strategy*. They describe the fit and integration among business strategy, IS strategy, IT infrastructure, and business infrastructure (Chan, 2002). Reich and Benbasat (1996) (p. 56) conceptualized alignment as "linkage" and defined it as "the degree to which the IT mission, objectives and plans support and are supported by, the business mission, objectives and plans." In particular, *A* signifies that the firm's IS applications and the technologies used for developing and designing them are closely derived from, and support, its business mission, product/market strategies, and structure (Chan, 2002). Examples include using IS to support cost-based or differentiation strategies (Porter, 1985) and applying IS and IT to critical success factors and important activities in the value chain (Goldsmith, 1991; Rockart, 1979). *B* signifies the shaping of the firm's business strategy by its IS applications and technologies. This is possible because existing IS and IT capabilities can create new business opportunities for firms (Porter and Millar, 1985). A firm can also choose to acquire and deploy new IT for entering new or related product market domains (Wheeler, 2002). A good example is that of Baxter Healthcare (Henderson and Venkatraman, 1993). The company launched a new business initiative to take over the materials management function of its customers (hospitals), based on the information-processing capabilities made possible through the use of their automated-purchasing applications. Other examples include credit-processing services that Sears offered to Phillips Petroleum, based on its technologies and capabilities for credit-information processing (Porter, 1985), and Google's entry into online advertising (based on its algorithms for Web-based search).

Arrows *C* and *D* denote the alignment between *business strategy and organization structure*, and *IM strategy*. *C* signifies that the IM strategy must fit the organization's business strategy. That is, the management framework by which the organization guides its IS/IT activities should be aligned with its strategic business goals and structures (Earl, 1989). For instance, a heavily decentralized organization may not support a centralized IM strategy and governance structure. Similarly, a flexible IM structure is required if the organization is to quickly reorient itself to changing contingencies in terms of business structure. *D* denotes the possibility that the IM strategy influences the way that the business is organized. This can happen if, for instance, the IM strategy allows for close relationships between the user and IS communities. In such a case, there could be informal and situational bonding between senior IS managers, and top management and line management (Chan, 2002) or the CIO might participate in strategic business planning (Kearns and Lederer, 2003). Hence IM strategy may influence business strategy or change organizational processes.

Arrows *E* and *F* signify alignment between *IS strategy* and *IT strategy,* and *IM strategy*. In particular, *E* shows that *IS strategy* and *IT strategy* would determine the IM strategy. For example, the nature of applications and particular technologies and platforms selected for their delivery determine the skills and resources needed in the IS function. Similarly, delivery strategies (outsourcing or insourcing, for instance) determine vendor selection and structure of the IS function. Recent studies in IT outsourcing (McFarlan and Delacey, 2004) point to trends where vendors, given their global delivery models, can possibly influence decisions regarding IS applications, IT infrastructure, and platforms, which is illustrated by *F.*

Arrows *G* and *H* denote alignment between *IS strategy* and *IT strategy*. Once the organization determines which applications are required (IS strategy), the technology and infrastructure for delivering those applications are decided (IT strategy). To give an example of *G,* if the IS applications portfolio (part of IS strategy) includes a CRM system, the derived IT strategy would consist of evaluation of available CRM products and choice of an appropriate one. As an example of *H*, in organizations where IT is the means of product and service delivery (Earl, 1989), IT strategy can shape IS strategy because requirements of integration, interfaces, and dependencies in the value chain may determine which applications are selected.

## LITERATURE REVIEW

In this section we review the literature on the aspects of business–IS alignment, as given by the arrows or paths A through G in Figure 3.1. As evident from the descriptions in the previous section, each arrow or aspect has distinct characteristics, which we analyze along three dimensions. First, we describe the *context* of the particular alignment path, that is, the conditions that drive or influence alignment. Second, we explain the *process* of alignment, that is, how alignment takes place for that path. Third, we describe the *outcomes* or consequences of alignment for the path. Such a conceptual structure, used in alignment studies (see, e.g., Kearns and Sabherwal, 2006/2007) takes into account the causes and effects of alignment, and clarifies how alignment takes place.

### Alignment of IS Strategy and IT Strategy with Business Strategy and Structure: Arrow A

Arrow *A* shows the effect of business strategy and structure on IS and IT strategies. Henderson and Venkatraman (1993) conceptualized this as the "strategic fit" between the business strategy (business scope, competencies, and governance) and IS and IT strategies (applications, technology scope, systems competencies, infrastructure, and architecture).

*Context for Arrow A*

There are three kinds of contextual factors that influence how IS strategy and IT strategy are aligned with business strategy and organization structure. First, external factors in the competitive environment include pressure from competition, importance of IT in the industry (King, Thompson, and Teo, 1994, 1996), the form of the firm's competitive advantage (whether it is cost or differentiation based), how key competitive forces such as buyer and supplier power can be neutralized (Goldsmith, 1991; Hatten and Hatten, 1997; Sabherwal and King, 1991), the firm's strategic orientation (Miles and Snow, 1978), and the volatility and complexity of the technical and business environments (Pyburn, 1983). The extent of globalization of the firm's operations and its growth strategies are also important (Weill and Broadbent, 1998)

Second, factors internal to the organization include top management vision, guidance, and support for strategic use of IT, economies of scale for using IT (King, Thompson, and Teo, 1994; Luftman and Brier, 1999; Premkumar and King, 1992), and the capabilities and power of IT leadership (King, Thompson, and Teo, 1996; Luftman and Brier, 1999; Pyburn, 1983). Also important are the quality of IS planning (Premkumar and King, 1992), existing technical resources, experience, and competencies (King, Thompson, and Teo, 1996; Luftman and Brier, 1999), and business IT partnership (Luftman and Brier, 1999). The extent of organizational innovativeness (King, Thompson, and Teo, 1996; Sabherwal and King, 1991) and organizational emphasis on knowledge management (Kearns and Sabherwal, 2006/2007) also influence the propensity for alignment.

Third, factors that indicate the scope or importance of IT in the firm's operations and the perceived need for improvements in various areas determine the extent to which alignment is useful to the firm. The former include the information intensity of the firm's products and value chain (Hatten and Hatten, 1997; Luftman and Brier, 1999; Porter and Millar, 1985; Sabherwal and King, 1991). The latter consist of the need for improved productivity, better information processing and storage, enhancement and maintainenance of firm reputation, more effective decision making, more efficient operations, and greater product and service differentiation (King, Thompson, and Teo, 1994).

*Process for Arrow A*

Broadly speaking, the process for Arrow *A* takes place when an organization's information-processing capabilities are matched with its information-processing requirements (Galbraith, 1973). At a more specific level, it takes place when (a) the content of IS and IT plans are derived from and aligned with the content of business plans, and (b) business executives and IS executives understand one another and have a common mutual understanding of, and commitment to, the role of IT in the firm. The former is referred to as *intellectual* (Reich and Benbasat, 1996) or *strategic* (Chan, 2002) alignment and the latter as *social* (Reich and Benbasat, 1996) or *structural* (Chan, 2002) alignment.

*Intellectual* alignment is accomplished by ensuring that business strategy and planning provide the framework for IS planning (Sambamurthy, Venkatraman, and DeSanctis, 1993). This has been studied from four perspectives. First, through the use of IS planning methodologies that, based on the business or strategic plan, identify activities, processes, and functions where IT can be used. The methodologies include business systems planning (IBM, 1981; Lederer and Sethi, 1988) and the critical success factors approach (Goldsmith, 1991; Rockart, 1979).

The second perspective deals with identifying the broad role of IS and IT in the organization, based on particular aspects of business strategy. That is, the nature of IS and IT support should depend on the overall strategic stance of the firm. In this connection, Das, Zahra, and Warkentin (1991) proposed that the role of IS and IT should be linked to the three types of organizations as described by Miles and Snow (1978), an idea that was empirically studied by Sabherwal and Chan (2001). They suggested that "prospectors" should use IS for flexibility and strategic decision support, "defenders" for efficiency and operational support, and "analyzers" for both flexibility and efficiency. Their results found that alignment between prospectors and use of IS for flexibility, and between analyzers and use of IS for both flexibility and efficiency was positively associated with business performance. In a similar vein Chan and others (1997) suggested an empirically validated alignment between the strategic business orientation of the firm, as given by the STROBE framework (Venkatraman, 1989b) and IS strategy. They found that appropriately using IS in support of particular business orientations of the STROBE framework, such as aggressiveness, analysis, defensiveness, futurity, proactiveness, and riskiness, positively influences IS effectiveness and business performance.

The third perspective matches the characteristics of IS planning process with the organizational role of IS. Studies have suggested that organizations that have a high reliance on IT should design IS planning systems that summarize and route planning information to appropriate members of the planning group and facilitate critical enquiry (Sambamurthy, Venkatraman, and DeSanctis, 1993). They also suggest (Sullivan, 1985) that firms with low (high) IT diffusion and infusion should follow simple (complex) planning methodologies.

The fourth perspective relates to the influence of business strategy and organization structure on technical platforms and architecture. For example, if the organization structure is expected to change as the business grows, then IT systems must not impair flexibility. Or if the organization has global operations, infrastructure technologies must be developed and managed according to global standards. Similarly, if the firm needs to respond rapidly to changes in the marketplace, greater sophistication of IT infrastructure is required. According to Weill and Broadbent (1998), firms that focus on operation excellence emphasize large-scale transaction-processing facilities and technologies, those that concentrate primarily on customer intimacy have shared customer databases, and those that emphasize product leadership have firm-wide messaging services and groupware applications.

*Social* alignment is accomplished in three ways, first, by fostering cross-domain knowledge such that IS professionals understand more about the organization and its business and functional managers become familiar with existing and possible uses of IT in the context of the firm and its industry. When IS (business) professionals are competent in their understanding of the business (IT), there is a greater likelihood of IS—business partnerships and social alignment at various levels in the organization (Bassellier and Benbasat, 2004; Reich and Benbasat, 2000). The second way is through participation of the CIO (chief executive officer; CEO) in the business-planning process (IS-planning process). Such participation promotes discussion between IS and the business; it also ensures that the IS plan reflects the business plan (Kearns and Lederer, 2003; Kearns and Sabherwal, 2006/2007). Third, informal networks and relationships between business and IS executives in the form of proactive, positive, and ongoing interactions between them result in increased social alignment (Chan, 2002).

*Outcome for Arrow A*

There are five kinds of outcomes for Arrow *A*. The first is that IS applications and technologies support particular kinds of business strategies (which can be based on cost, differentiation, innovation, growth, or alliances), by supporting activities that are important to them (Parsons, 1983; Porter and Millar, 1985; Rackoff, Wiseman, and Ullrich, 1985). A second outcome is that IS and IT support various activities associated with the customer interface, such as product search, ordering, using, and upgrading (Ives and Learmonth, 1984). A third outcome is that the use of IS and IT influences parameters that reflect business performance, such as competitive advantage (Bhatt and Grover, 2005; Kearns and Lederer, 2003; King, Thompson, and Teo, 1994). A fourth outcome is that various measures relating to IS performance such as IS planning effectiveness and success, IS contribution to organizational performance (Premkumar and King, 1992), quality of IT project planning, number of implementation problems in IT projects (Kearns and Sabherwal, 2006/2007), and the number or quality of the recommendations from the IS plan that are also included in the business plan (King, 1978) are favorably influenced. In addition, applications most important to the business are developed (Sabherwal and Chan, 2001), and they can be changed with changes in the firm's strategic priorities (Lederer and Mendelow, 1993). Finally, a fifth outcome is that the organization identifies the role of IT that is appropriate for its industry and business strategy (Weill and Broadbent, 1998). For instance, financial services companies or banks that have correctly aligned their IS/IT strategies with their product/market characteristics would likely find themselves in the "strategic" quadrant of the "strategic grid" (Porter and Millar, 1985) or in the "delivery sector" (Earl, 1989). Similarly, defenders, prospectors, and analyzers who have correctly aligned their business strategies with IS strategies would likely use IS for efficiency, flexibility, or comprehensiveness, respectively (Sabherwal and Chan, 2001).

To summarize, what then is the implication of the alignment of *IS strategy* and *IT strategy* with *business strategy and organization structure?* As Table 3.1 shows, the factors influencing this align-

Table 3.1

## Alignment Between Business Strategy and Organization Structure, and IS Strategy and IT Strategy

| Context (factors influencing alignment) | Process (how alignment is achieved) | Outcome (consequences of alignment) |
|---|---|---|
| | *Arrow A: Alignment of IS Strategy and IT Strategy with Business Strategy and Organization Structure* | |
| *External factors*<br>• Competitive pressure, importance of IT in the industry, firm strategy, nature of competitive forces, strategic orientation, and volatility and complexity of business environment (e.g., King and Teo, 1994, 1996; Miles and Snow, 1978; Sabherwal and King, 1991; Weill and Broadbent, 1998)<br>*Internal factors*<br>• Top management vision and guidance for strategic use of IT, power of IS leadership, quality of IS planning, existing technical resources, business–IT partnership, organizational innovativeness, organizational emphasis on knowledge management (e.g., Kearns and Sabherwal, 2006/2007; Luftman and Brier, 1999; Premkumar and King, 1992)<br>*Scope for and perceived importance of IT and need for improvements*<br>• Information intensity of products and value chain (Porter and Millar, 1985; Sabherwal and King, 1991)<br>• Improved productivity and efficiency, more effective decision making, better information storage, product/service differentiation, enhancing firm reputation (Hatten and Hatten, 1997; King and Teo, 1994; Luftman and Brier, 1999) | *Intellectual alignment* (Chan, 2002; Reich and Benbasat, 1996)<br>• Content of IS plans is derived from business plans (Goldsmith 1991; IBM, 1981; Lederer and Sethi, 1988; Rockart, 1979)<br>• Identifying appropriate role of IT in the firm (Chan et al., 1997; Das, Zahra, and Warkentin, 1991; Sabherwal and Chan, 2001)<br>• IS and IT strategy are derived from business strategy (Chan et al., 1997; Das, Zahra, and Warkentin, 1991; Sabherwal and Chan, 2001)<br>• IS planning process matched to the role of IT (Sambamurthy, Venkatraman, and Desanctis, 1993; Sullivan, 1985)<br>• Match between business strategy and IT infrastructure (Weill and Broadbent, 1998)<br>*Social alignment*<br>• Business and IS executives have a common understanding of the role of IT (Bassellier and Benbasat, 2004; Reich and Benbasat, 2000)<br>• Cross-domain knowledge<br>• CEO (CIO) participation in IS (business) planning process (Kearns and Lederer, 2003; Kearns and Sabherwal, 2006/2007)<br>• Informal networks and relationships between business and IS executives (Chan, 2002) | • IS/IT support for business strategies (Parsons, 1983; Porter and Millar, 1985; Rackoff , Wiseman, and Ullrich, 1985<br>• IS/IT support for customer interface activities (Ives and Learmonth, 1984<br>• IS/IT influence on business performance (Bhatt and Grover, 2005; Kearns and Lederer, 2003; King and Teo, 1994)<br>• Favorable influence on IS performance (Kearns and Sabherwal, 2006/2007; King, 1978; Premkumar and King, 1992)<br>• Development of applications most important to the business (Lederer and Mendelow, 1993; Sabherwal and Chan, 2001)<br>• Identification of the appropriate organizational role of IT—Strategic Grid, Sector Model, Infusion/Diffusion Model (Porter and Millar, 1985; Sabherwal and Chan, 2001; Weill and Broadbent, 1998) |

*Arrow B: Alignment of Business Strategy and Organization with Structure IS Strategy and IT Strategy*

- Organizational willingness to analyze the technology environment (Min, Suh, and Kim, 1999; Wheeler, 2002)
- IS (business) literacy of senior functional (IS) management, CIO's understanding of the organizational impacts of IS (Basellier, Reich, and Benbasat, 2001), proactiveness for considering and exploiting IT-based strategic opportunities (Rockart, Earl, and Ross, 1996)
- IT intellectual capital (prior IT knowledge and experience) (Winston and Dologite, 1999)
- IT absorptive capacity (for understanding capabilities of emerging IT and formulating business strategies around them) (Wheeler, 2002; Zahra and George, 2002)
- Governance and communication mechanisms for IT knowledge acquisition and dissemination: steering committees for acquiring and distributing knowledge of emerging IT, exchange of technology-related information with vendors, customerism and competitors (Rockart, Earl, and Ross, 1996; Winston and Dologite, 1999)

- Technology scanning and identification, opportunity matching (Earl, 1989; Wheeler, 2002)
- Think tanks and Delphi techniques (Earl, 1989)
- CEO (CIO) participation in IS (business) planning (Kearns and Lederer, 2003)

- IT-driven product innovation and entry into new markets (Porter and Millar, 1985; Wheeler, 2002)
- Use of IT to alter the basis of industry competition (Porter and Millar, 1985)
- Development of interorganizational configurations and supply-chain partnerships (Malone, Yates, and Benjamin, 1987)
- Sustainable, IT-based competitive advantage (Piccoli and Ives, 2005)

ment may be external (e.g., competitive forces and environmental turbulence) or internal (e.g., top management vision for IT, power of IT leadership), or may relate to the scope and importance of IT and needs for improvements in productivity and efficiency. The process of alignment can be intellectual (where the content of IS and IT plans match that of business plans) or social (where the business and the IS function have a common shared vision of the use of IT in the firm). The outcome of this alignment is a set of IS and IT plans that reflect the appropriate organizational role of IT, support the business strategy, and can positively influence business performance.

### Alignment of Business Strategy and Structure, with IS Strategy and IT Strategy: Arrow B

Arrow *B* shows the effect of IS and IT strategies on business strategy, structure, and processes. Increasing information content in firm products and value chains, combined with capabilities of emerging networking technologies, collaborative and content management tools, and data mining and analysis techniques have made it possible for firms to frame product/market strategies around their IS and IT strategies.

*Context for Arrow B*

Three factors form the context for Arrow *B;* they relate primarily to the propensity and ability of the organization to understand the capabilities of emerging IT and possible implications for new product/market strategies.

The first factor relates to the organization's willingness to analyze the technology environment, and its proactiveness for considering and exploiting IT driven strategic opportunities. Given that technologies continue to evolve, businesses that rely heavily on IT should identify and choose relevant technologies prior to strategy formulation (Wheeler, 2002). Insufficient analysis of the IT environment prevents organizations from being able to identify IT-led disruptive changes in their industry on time (Min, Suh, and Kim, 1999). Firms in which senior management has complementing knowledge—that is, senior functional management is IT literate and senior IS management is strategy and business literate—have a greater ability to understand opportunities available through IT and can more effectively identify technologies that can shape business strategy. This is because CEOs (CIOs) can participate in IS (business) planning (Kearns and Lederer, 2003). Such firms are therefore more likely to proactively consider strategic approaches that use emerging technologies (Rockart, Earl, and Ross, 1996).

The second factor relates to the firm's prior levels of knowledge and experience regarding IT (IT intellectual capital) and its IT absorptive capacity. The knowledge-based view of the firm posits that firms create and maximize knowledge through exchange and combination of new and old knowledge (Grant, 1996a, 1996b). Applied to the context of alignment, this implies that a firm's IT intellectual capital and base of IT experience, reflected in managerial IT knowledge (Winston and Dologite, 1999), help it to understand the business capabilities of new IT. Another factor that helps organizations to understand the value of new (external) information and apply it to commercial ends is their absorptive capacity (Cohen and Levinthal, 1990). In the context of information technology, the firm's IT absorptive capacity[4] helps it to understand and identify technologies that would yield above-normal strategic returns and to formulate competitive strategies around the capabilities provided by such technologies (Wheeler, 2002; Zahra and George, 2002). A higher IT absorptive capacity leads to greater firm propensity for exploiting business opportunities afforded by emerging IT.

The third factor is based on the notion that appropriate organizational configurations that facilitate the exchange of knowledge (referred to as "social capital"), lead to the creation of more knowledge (Nahapiet and Ghoshal, 1998). Applied to the context of Arrow B, such organizational configurations would include governance and communication mechanisms for acquiring and disseminating organizational knowledge about IT and raising the IT awareness of the organization. Governance mechanisms include steering committees for formally acquiring and distributing information about emerging IT (Rockart, Earl, and Ross, 1996). Communication mechanisms facilitate the exchange of technology-related knowledge with buyers, suppliers, IT vendors, and competitors (Cohen and Levinthal, 1990; Winston and Dologite, 1999). Such communication is essential for understanding continuing changes in technologies, their business applications, and their possible consequences on industry competition.

*Process for Arrow B*

The process of alignment for Arrow *B* takes place through three broad activities—technology identification (where emerging IT considered appropriate for influencing and determining future business strategies is identified), opportunity matching (where capabilities and opportunities provided by these technologies are matched to business opportunities as evident in possible new business models, products, or services), and implementation (including organizational routines that facilitate IT adoption and implementation). Some managerial processes that have been mentioned in this context include brainstorming and Delphi techniques, think tanks, and IT environment scanning through interactions with trade associations (Earl, 1989) as well as through CIO participation in business planning and CEO participation in IS planning (Kearns and Lederer, 2003). Much of the literature here is conceptual and draws from the innovation diffusion literature (Earl, 1989; Wheeler, 2002).

*Outcomes for Arrow B*

There are four outcomes for Arrow *B*. The first outcome is that the organization uses capabilities of emerging IT for product innovation and to enter new industries (Porter and Millar, 1985; Wheeler, 2002). This is illustrated by iTunes, where Apple used the digital music and video formats to enter the entertainment content distribution/retailing business. Similar developments have occurred in the telecommunications/cable TV/entertainment industries, where companies have complemented their existing IT with capabilities of emerging technologies to move into related domains. Examples include cell phone service providers such as Verizon offering music downloads and Web-based advertising, and cable TV providers offering broadband Internet services. A second outcome is that firms use the capabilities of emerging IT to alter the rules of competition and change the competitive marketplace. For example, Google has applied its expertise on search algorithms to online advertising. It provides clients with targeted segments of consumers, depending on the key words typed into its search engine. It has also extended its text-search capabilities to video-search capabilities and has acquired video Web sites such as YouTube, a move that has further widened its client base. Moreover, it plans to use the information acquired from its search Web sites for targeted advertising on other media such as television (Delaney and Grant, 2007). These developments have changed the basis of competition in the advertising industry, and the portion of money spent on print and TV advertising has declined steadily in favor of online advertising (Steel, 2007). A third outcome is the development of new interorganizational configurations and decreased coordination and transaction costs in interorganizational information flows, leading to an increase in the formation of "markets," rather than "hierarchies" (Malone, Yates, and Benjamin, 1987). A good example is Dell, which has stitched together a "virtual organization" with the help of tightly integrated electronic interfaces with its supply partners (Magretta, 1998). A fourth outcome is sustainable competitive advantage. Recent ideas on strategic IS (Piccoli and Ives, 2005) show that firms that can constantly launch new competitive actions using capabilities of emerging IT, can build "dynamic" capabilities to stay ahead of competition and build barriers to copying, especially in hypercompetitive and information-intensive industries.

What is the implication of the alignment of *business strategy and organization structure* with *IS strategy* and *IT strategy?* As shown in Table 3.1, factors influencing this alignment are existing organizational IT knowledge, ability to absorb and assimilate new IT knowledge, communication processes for acquiring such knowledge from partners and competitors, and organizational inclination toward using it to identify and exploit new business opportunities. The outcomes of alignment include IT-driven product innovation and entry into new markets, use of IT to alter the basis of industry competition, and sustained, IT-based competitive advantage.

## Alignment of IM Strategy with Business Strategy and Structure: Arrow C

Arrow *C* describes the alignment of IM strategy with business strategy and organization structure, and has been referred to as the functional integration between the business side (administrative infrastructure, processes, and skills) and the IS side (IT management processes and IT skills). The management of IT, which includes IT governance structures, relationships between end users, and IT charge-out strategies, must be aligned with organizational governance structures and strategic orientations, in order to appropriate strategic benefits from IT (Henderson and Venkatraman, 1993). IM strategy must fit the organization's strategy and IM strategies that demand practices unfamiliar to the organization are likely to encounter vigorous resistance from informal and official behaviors, and will not work (Earl, 1989).

### Context for Arrow C

There are four aspects to the context for Arrow *C*. The first consists of factors relating to corporate decision-making structures (centralized/decentralized), diversification and size of the organization, and interaction mechanisms between IS and other functional areas. Corporate centralization (characterized by strong central direction and monitoring) tends to strive for enterprise-wide economies and efficiencies, whereas corporate decentralization (greater autonomy at the business-unit level) tries to address localized business needs and opportunities. Such decision-making structures have a bearing on IM strategy (Ahituv, Neumann, and Aviran, 1989; Brown and Magill, 1994; Earl, 1989; Sambamurthy and Zmud, 2000). The relatedness of diversification also determines the extent of centralization and decentralization of the IS function (Brown and Magill, 1994; Sambamurthy and Zmud, 1999). Firms growing through internal resources typically have related diversification, whereas firms growing through acquisition have, in general, unrelated diversification. As far as size is concerned, larger organizations have a greater scope for architectural synergies across business units (Brown and Magill, 1998), raising the possibility of IS centralization. At the same time, they may have business units with differing IT needs (depending on the extent of diversification), which could lead to a propensity to decentralize IS operations in order to be responsive to individual units (Sambamurthy and Zmud, 1999). Interaction mechanisms and partnerships between the IS department and other functions at the executive level as well as at the middle and junior management levels are also important (Boynton, Zmud, and Jacobs, 1994; Brown and Magill, 1994).

The second factor is the perceived importance of its role in the organization. For example, the organization could perceive the role of IT primarily as a means for reducing costs or generating business value (Ward and Peppard, 1996). For the former, the IT function would likely be managed as an expense center with the objective of minimizing costs. For the latter, the IT function would be looked upon as a resource center or value center integral to the business and would have higher investments in new technologies that might provide a competitive edge (Parsons, 1983; Peppard and Ward, 1999).

The third factor is the strategic orientation of the organization. The nature of the strategic orientation—whether, for example, the firm follows a cost/differentiation strategy or is a defender/analyzer/prospector—determines its IM strategy (Das, Zahra, and Warkentin, 1991).

The fourth aspect includes the performance of the IT function and the economic benefits delivered by IT. When the perceived economic performance of the IT function decreases, management is pressured to look at more efficient means of IT governance. Such evaluation therefore results in attempts to identify more efficient governance and sourcing structures (Loh and Venkatraman, 1992).

*Process for Arrow C*

There are three aspects of the process for Arrow C. The first deals with how the focus of the IS function and decision parameters related to IS and IT management fit with the business strategy. Ward (1987) has proposed that organizations having cost-based business strategies (Porter, 1985) should manage IT as a scarce resource and should focus on a centralized, efficient, and low-cost orientation for the IT department. For firms having differentiation strategies, the management of IT should be driven by requirements of product enhancement. Das, Zahra, and Warkentin (1991) suggest that in "defenders" (given their orientation toward efficiency), the IS infrastructure and applications decisions should be centralized and the IS function should have a low cost orientation, focusing on efficiency and economies of scale. In "prospectors" (given their orientation toward exploration, flexibility, and versatility), IS infrastructure and applications decisions should be under the control of individual business units and the IS department should emphasize flexibility and innovation. In "analyzers," a combination of the two should be followed. Tavakolian (1989) suggests that defender strategies lead to centralization of IT infrastructure and applications decision.

The second aspect addresses the structural fit between IS and business and involves how the IS structure aligns with the organization structure. Earl (1989) suggests that the structure of the IT function should fit that of the host organization. Brown and Magill (1994) suggest that unrelated diversification and high business-unit autonomy should be aligned with primarily decentralized IS structures whereas related diversification, related core businesses, organizational centralization, and strong central direction and monitoring should be aligned with centralized IS structures that emphasize efficiency, standardized controls, and integrative architectures. Similarly, high centralization (decentralization) and strong (weak) corporate direction is associated with centralized (decentralized) IS structures (Ahituv, Neumann, and Aviran, 1989). A more centralized or hybrid IS form is associated with matrix structures and multidivisional companies (Earl, 1989), or with firms that have related diversification, but are in unstable business environments and need to be flexible in their choice and use of applications. In the latter case, related diversification entails infrastructure centralization, and the need to respond to unstable business environments implies applications decentralization. IS structure choices are also influenced by the strategic importance of IT for a particular business unit and opportunities for IT-related cross-unit synergies. For instance, where there are high opportunities for IT-related cross-unit synergies, business units where IT is not perceived to play a strategic role will implement centralized IT decision-making systems. Similarly, where there are few opportunities for IT-related cross-unit synergies, business units where the strategic importance of IT is high will have a decentralized IT decision-making environment (Brown and Magill, 1998).

The third aspect concerns the functioning of the IS–business managerial interface. Characteristics of the IS–business interface such as top management participation in IS planning, CIO participation in business planning (Kearns and Lederer, 2003), and IT councils and steering committees (Sambamurthy and Zmud, 2000) lead to greater interaction and transfer of domain knowledge between IS and the functional areas. This leads to greater mutual understanding about which IS structures and IM strategies will work best and hence results in alignment (Reich and Benbasat, 2000).

*Outcomes for Arrow C*

There are three kinds of outcomes for Arrow C. First, there are sourcing, governance, and decision-making structures with respect to IT architecture development, IT application development, and IT use decisions. Governance can be centralized (all decisions are made at the level of the corporate IT unit), decentralized (all decisions are made at the level of the corporate IT unit), or federal (infrastructure decisions are made at the corporate level, and application and use decisions are made at the business-unit level), depending on where the different decision-making responsibilities are located (Brown and Magill, 1994, 1998; Sambamurthy and Zmud, 2000). Other governance aspects include authority for IS resource allocation, responsibility for IS–business conflict resolution, and IS project prioritization. Sourcing of IT can be done internally or externally (Loh and Venkatraman, 1992) and may be driven by needs for greater economic efficiency in the context of the performance of the IS function.

Second, there are outcomes related to the relationship between the IT function and the broader organization. When the IM strategy is aligned with business strategy and organization structure, the relationship between the IT function and other functional units is integrated and harmonious (Galliers and Sutherland, 1991). Peppard and Ward (1999) similarly mention the "high achieving" IT function where IT is a partner in business, has a good reputation, and feels that the business appreciates them, in contrast with the "low achieving" IT function where the opposite conditions exist.

Third, there are outcomes relating to the effectiveness of the IS function. These include better systems integration and more effective resource allocation (Raghunathan and Raghunathan, 1991). They also include greater end-user satisfaction with the IS function (Brown and Magill, 1994) and the latter's ability to meet corporate needs (Sambamurthy and Zmud, 1999).

To summarize the implication of alignment of IM strategy with business strategy and organization structure, the context of this alignment includes parameters such as centralization/decentralization, diversification, organization size, perceived importance of the role of IT, and perceived economic benefits derived from IT. The process of alignment consists of matching the focus of the IT function and IT decision structures with the organization's business strategy, and matching the IS organization structure with overall organization structure. Outcomes of the alignment include the choice of appropriate IS sourcing and governance decisions, more effective allocation of IS resources, and greater end-user satisfaction with IS.

## Alignment of Business Strategy and Structure with IM Strategy: Arrow D

Arrow D shows the possibility that IM strategy, which includes the way in which the IS department is structured, can influence business strategy and structure.

*Context for Arrow D*

IM strategy can affect business strategy and structure mainly through the influence of IS professionals at the top and middle management levels. The context of Arrow *D* includes the extent to which IS professionals are competent about the business. Business competence of IS professionals (Bassellier and Benbasat, 2004) includes their knowledge of the organization, the reach of their responsibility, their understanding of the organizational impacts of IS, and their interpersonal and leadership skills.

*Process for Arrow D*

If IS governance is such that there is high interaction between the CEO and CIO (Kearns and Lederer, 2003; Kearns and Sabherwal, 2006/2007), and between IS professionals and functional managers, it leads to the intention to form IS–business partnerships (Bassellier and Benbasat, 2004), which results in transfer and exchange of domain knowledge. CIOs can give inputs on organization structure decisions based on their understanding of the impacts of such decisions on the firm's IT architecture and infrastructure. If the CIO is influential enough, such inputs can eventually influence corporate decisions and induce alignment. Likewise, if functional managers have a good understanding of IT management, they can understand the implications of specific IT organization structures on firm organization structure. Interaction born of alliances between the IS and other functional areas can also lead to the development of integration mechanisms such as team-based coordination structures (Sambamurthy and Zmud, 2000), which further facilitate exchange of domain knowledge between the IT function and other departments.

*Outcomes for Arrow D*

Some conceptual studies suggest that the outcome includes an organization structure that is aligned with the IT architecture and infrastructure (Earl, 1989; Sambamurthy and Zmud, 2000). For instance, if IT architecture and infrastructure are standardized across divisions, then the organization structure is such that decisions relating to architecture and infrastructure are made at the corporate level. Little empirical research exists in this area.

What, then, is the implication of the alignment of business strategy and organization structure with IM strategy? As shown in Table 3.2, the contextual factors influencing such alignment include primarily the business competence of IS professionals and functional managers' understanding of IT management. The process consists of interaction between the IS department and other functional areas, at the CIO-CEO level, and at the middle and lower management levels. The outcome of alignment is an organization structure that is matched with the IT architecture and infrastructure.

**Alignment of IM Strategy, with IS Strategy and IT Strategy: Arrow E**

Arrow *E* describes the alignment of *IM Strategy,* with *IS Strategy* and *IT Strategy.* Keen (1993) refers to this as the "fusion" between the deployment of IT (vision and strategic intent) and the management of IT (sourcing strategies and delivery mechanisms), and suggests that such fusion is necessary for organizations to appropriate competitive benefits from IT. Earl (1989) suggests that the way in which IT and IS are managed should be contingent on the nature and criticality of the applications and technologies that are used. For instance, suppose an organization is implementing

Table 3.2

**Alignment Between Business Strategy and Organization Structure, and IM Strategy**

| Context (factors influencing alignment) | Process (how alignment is achieved) | Outcome (consequences of alignment) |
|---|---|---|
| *Arrow C: Alignment of IM Strategy with Business Strategy and Organization Structure* | | |
| • Corporate decision-making structures—centralization/decentralization (Ahituv, Neumann, and Aviran, 1989; Brown and Magill, 1994; Earl, 1989 Sambamurthy and Zmud, 2000)<br>• Related/unrelated diversification (Brown and Magill, 1994; Sambamurthy and Zmud 1999)<br>• Size (Brown and Magill, 1998; Sambamurthy and Zmud, 1999)<br>• Perceived importance of the organizational role of IT (Parsons, 1983; Peppard and Ward, 1999; Ward and Peppard, 1996)<br>• Strategic orientation and business strategy (Das, Zahra, and Warkentin, 1991)<br>• Perceived economic benefits delivered by IT (Loh and Venkatraman, 1992) | • Matching of the focus of the IT function and IT decision-making structures with business strategy (Das, Zahra, and Warkentin, 1991; Tavakolian, 1989; Ward, 1987)<br>• Alignment of IS organization structure with overall organization structure (Ahituv, Neumann, and Aviran, 1989; Brown and Magill, 1994, 1998; Earl, 1989)<br>• IS-functional interface (Kearns and Lederer, 2003; Reich and Benbsasat, 2000; Sambamurthy and Zmud, 2000) | • Sourcing, governance, and decision-making structures with respect to IS application and IT architecture development (Brown and Magill, 1994, 1998; Loh and Venkatraman, 1992; Sambamurthy and Zmud, 2000)<br>• Improved relationships between IS and the broader organization (Galliers and Sutherland, 1991; Peppard and Ward, 1999)<br>• Effectiveness of the IT function: better systems integration, more effective allocation of IS resources, greater end-user satisfaction with the IS function, ability of corporate IS to meet organizational needs (Brown and Magill, 1994; Raghunathan and Raghunathan, 1991; Sambamurthy and Zmud, 1999) |
| *Arrow D: Alignment of Business Strategy and Organization with Structure IM Strategy* | | |
| Business competence of IS professionals:<br>• Knowledge of the organization, responsibility, interpersonal and leadership skills (Bassellier and Benbasat, 2004; Bassellier, Reich, and Benbasat, 2001)<br>• IT competence of business managers—understanding of IT management and resource allocation (Bassellier, Reich, and Benbasat, 2001) | • Interaction between CEO and CIO (Kearns and Lederer, 2003; Kearns and Sabherwal, 2006/2007; Bassellier and Benbasat, 2004)<br>• Interaction between IS professionals and functional managers at other levels (Sambamurthy and Zmud, 2000) | • Organization structure that is matched with IT architecture and infrastructure (Earl, 1989; Sambamurthy and Zmud, 2000) |

an enterprise resource planning application and it is its first big IT application/investment. The IM strategy implications are that the importance and profile of the CIO should be increased. Or, if the organization is planning to implement complex enterprise applications, it would likely need outside implementation consultants, whereas implementation of simple systems can be done in-house.

## Context for Arrow E

The context of Arrow *E* includes the extent of criticality of IS applications and their strategic importance to the business. The planning, organization, and control of the IS function (encompassed in the organization's IM strategy) depends on how critical IS and IT are to the business and what kinds of processes they are used in (Earl, 1989, p. 35). Benefits from IT deployment are fully captured only when there are corresponding changes in the management of IT and IS (Barua, Lee, and Whinston, 1996; Venkatraman, 1994,). A second aspect of the context is the nature of the IS department. The IS department may be technology-focused or service-focused, centralized or decentralized, within or outside the department. A third aspect is the role of the CIO; whether the CIO is more hands on and has technical skills or is a top management member with a business orientation (Edwards, Ward, and Bytheway, 1996).

## Process for Arrow E

The process for Arrow *E* consists of three aspects. The first one involves matching the criticality of IS and IT to appropriate IT management mechanisms. This can be done by matching specific IM strategies with corresponding IS/IT typologies such as the strategic grid (McFarlan, 1984) or the sector model (Earl, 1989). Parsons (1983) suggests that the centrally planned IM strategy (where a central decision-making unit integrates business needs and IT applications, funding is strategic, accounting is profit centered, and evaluation is based on strategic impact) is appropriate for firms in the strategic or turnaround quadrants of the strategic grid. A leading edge IM strategy (where state-of-the-art IT is used to fulfill business objectives, funding is discretional, appraisal and evaluation are based on the extent of strategic change, and IT is a service center) should be used for firms in the strategic or turnaround quadrants. Free-market IM strategies (where users determine their own IT needs and the means to satisfy them, IT specialists compete against outside vendors for users, and IT is a profit center) should be matched to strategic or turnaround quadrants. Monopoly management of IT (which uses an internal IT function to meet IS/IT demand within reasonable costs, where funding is by committee, cost benefit analysis is formal, IT is a cost center, and user satisfaction is the criterion for evaluation) is appropriate for the factory and support quadrants. Scarce-resource management (IT resources and expenditure are constrained, funding is budget driven, cost–benefit analysis is formal, and return-on-investment driven, IT is a cost center, and evaluation is based on resource productivity) is matched with the factory or support quadrants. The "necessary evil" strategy (IT is not used unless there is no alternative, accounting is cost centered, and evaluation is, for all practical purposes, nonexistent) is matched with the support quadrant (Earl, 1989, p. 190). Similarly, Raghunathan and Raghunathan (1990) suggest that resources provided to the IS planning process should vary depending on a firm's position in the strategic grid.

The second aspect is that the role of the CIO should be contingent on the IS and IT strategy and the criticality and strategic importance of applications. For firms in the support quadrant, the CIO should be an IT career person with strong technical skills, and have a "hands-on" approach. For firms in the turnaround quadrant, the hierarchical position of the CIO should be such that it is easy to communicate with top management. The CIO should have a management as well as an IT career, and knowledge of the business. For firms in the factory quadrant, the CIO should be skilled at managing IT operations, have good line-management skills, and should have a management/IT career. For firms in the strategic quadrant, the CIO should be a member of top management and a business leader, with a business or IT career (Earl, 1989, p. 149).

The third aspect is that the focus of the IT department should align with the strategic importance of IS. In terms of the sector model (Earl, 1989), for firms in the delivery sector, the organizational focus of the IS department should be at the corporate level and control should be partly tight (for standardized applications and infrastructure) and partly loose for the function-specific applications. In the dependent sector, IT should be managed at the divisional level and control is similarly partly tight and partly loose. In the drive sector, IT should be managed by line functions and controlled loosely. In the delayed sector, the IS department should manage IT and control should be tight.

*Outcomes for Arrow E*

One of the outcomes of alignment of *IM strategy,* with *IS strategy* and *IT strategy* is improved performance of the IS department. Other outcomes are more effective end-user support, improved relationships between the IS function and functional departments, and appropriateness of the CIO's role.

To summarize the implications of the alignment of IM strategy with IS strategy and IT strategy, as shown in Table 3.3, the context of alignment includes the criticality and strategic importance of IS and IT, the characteristics of the IS department, and the role and skills of the CIO. The process of alignment consists of framing IT management mechanisms appropriate to the criticality of IS and IT, and matching the CIO's role and the focus of the IS department with the strategic importance of IS and IT. The outcome of alignment includes improved performance of the IS department, better end-user support, improved relationships between the IS and other departments, and appropriateness of the CIO's role.

## Alignment of IS Strategy and IT Strategy, with IM Strategy: Arrow F

Arrow *F* shows the possibility that *IM strategy* influences aspects of *IS strategy* and *IT strategy,* and hence the applications and technologies deployed.

*Context for Arrow F*

The context for Arrow *F* includes the business competence and technology understanding of IS professionals (Bassellier and Benbasat, 2004), their knowledge of industry use of current technologies, their interaction with the business side at the top, middle, and line-management levels (Kearns and Lederer, 2003; Kearns and Sabherwal, 2006/2007), and if the IS function is outsourced, the characteristics of vendors (Levina and Ross, 2003).

*Process for Arrow F*

IS professionals who are knowledgeable about the business and have a good understanding of relevant technologies can identify particular applications and platforms that would be appropriate for the firm. In addition, if they build effective networks with functional managers and interact with them at the top management levels, they can influence the choice of applications and technology,

Table 3.3

## Alignment Between IS Strategy and IT Strategy, and IM Strategy

| Context (factors influencing alignment) | Process (how alignment is achieved) | Outcome (consequences of alignment) |
| --- | --- | --- |
| *Arrow E: Alignment of IM Strategy with IS Strategy and IT Strategy* | | |
| • Criticality and strategic importance of IS and IT (Barua, Lee, and Whinston, 1996; Earl, 1989; Venkatraman, 1994)<br>• Characteristics of the IS department: technology focused or service focused, within or outside the organization (Edwards, Ward, and Bytheway, 1996)<br>• Role and skills of the CIO (Edwards, Ward, and Bytheway, 1996) | • Matching appropriate IT management mechanisms with the criticality and strategic importance of IS and IT (Earl, 1989; Parsons, 1983; Raghunathan and Raghunathan, 1990)<br>• Matching the CIO's role with the strategic importance of IS and IT (Earl, 1989)<br>• Matching the focus of the IS department with the strategic importance of IS and IT (Earl, 1989) | • Improved performance of the IS department<br>• More effective end-user support<br>• Improved relationships between the IS department and other functional departments<br>• Appropriateness of the CIO's role (Earl, 1989; Edwards, Ward, and Bytheway, 1996) |
| *Arrow F: Alignment of IS Strategy and IT Strategy with IM Strategy* | | |
| • Business competence and technology understanding of IS professionals (Bassellier and Benbasat 2004)<br>• Interaction between IS professionals and functional managers at top, middle, and line-management levels (Kearns and Lederer, 2003; Kearns and Sabherwal, 2006/2007)<br>• Characteristics of IT vendors and outsourcing arrangements (Levina and Ross, 2003) | • Influence of IS professionals on applications and technology decisions, through networking with functional managers and with top management (Bassellier and Benbasat, 2004)<br>• Influence of outsourcing vendors on applications and technology decisions (Beulen, van Femena, and Currie, 2005) | • Greater user satisfaction with IT<br>• Greater user involvement with IT<br>• Deployment of standardized technologies and solutions, especially for IT infrastructure (Earl, 1989; Edwards, Ward, and Bytheway, 1996) |

and hence determine IS/IT strategy. Moreover, outsourcing arrangements with respect to the IS function can influence the choice of IT platforms and infrastructure. Studies (e.g., Beulen, van Fenema, and Currie, 2005) have shown that outsourcing vendors, because of their wide-ranging experience in developing applications and managing infrastructure, have a technology understanding and knowledge that can be leveraged by their clients. They can bring to the table efficient and standardized solutions, deployed over many different industries, in different companies, and across different locations. Their choice of a particular technology or platform, therefore, often becomes the choice of IT for their clients, and influences IT and IS strategy.

*Outcome for Arrow F*

One outcome for Arrow *F* is increased user satisfaction and possibly greater user involvement with IT. Another outcome is the deployment of standardized technologies and solutions, especially for IT infrastructure.

What are the implications of alignment of *IT strategy* and *IS strategy* with *IM strategy?* As described in Table 3.3, contextual factors that influence alignment include the business competence and technology understanding of IS professionals, their interactions with functional managers and top management, and characteristics of IT vendors and outsourcing arrangements. The process of alignment takes place through the influence of IS professionals and outsourcing vendors on technology and applications decisions. Greater user satisfaction and involvement with IT and the possible deployment of standardized technology and solutions are the outcomes of alignment.

## Alignment of IT Strategy with IS Strategy: Arrow G

The IS strategy specifies applications that a firm plans to acquire. Alignment of IT strategy with IS strategy relates to the choice of appropriate technologies, platforms, hardware, and software regarding the acquisition, development, and implementation of the applications.

*Context for Arrow G*

The context of Arrow *G* consists of four aspects. First, the overall role of IS in the organization (e.g., whether the organization is in the support or strategic quadrants, or in the dependent or drive sectors) determines the nature and criticality of applications. Second, the external IT environment (including available technologies, hardware, software, and vendors) determines what technologies are available, how they can be acquired, and how they are being used by competitors and other firms in the industry. It also affects possible learning-curve implications of new technologies and the extent to which others have been successful in using them. Third, understanding the internal IS and IT environment is important for auditing current technologies, platforms, hardware, and software, as well as for reviewing expected future requirements regarding IS human resources, skills, and development methodologies (Earl, 1989). Fourth, the extent of synergies and common applications across divisions determines opportunities for shared IT platforms and infrastructure.

*Process for Arrow G*

The process of alignment takes place when the policies that govern the choice of particular technologies are based on, and appropriate to, the criticality of IS applications (Earl, 1989; Edwards, Ward, and Bytheway, 1996). For instance, IT planning and the characteristics of the technology should be architectural for firms in the delivery sector or strategic quadrant. It should take into account cross-divisional synergies and opportunities for building standardized and common platforms. For firms in the dependent sector or factory quadrant, IT strategies should result in the use of proven and tested technologies. For firms in the drive sector or turnaround quadrant, IT strategy should result in the deployment of new technologies in areas of greater strategic importance to the firm. For firms in the delayed sector or support quadrant, IT strategies should result in the use of cost-effective and standardized technologies. In all cases, the IT strategy should take into account the business importance and technical sophistication of existing applications and determine appropriate changes required for developing future applications. Alignment can also take place when IT strategy is based on specific information-processing activities that are critical to the firm (Weill and Broadbent, 1998). To give some examples, the need for integrated low cost transaction processing leads to large-scale transaction processing facilities. The need for large databases linking external and internal data and applications for analyzing customer data would lead to shared customer databases. The need for collaborative applications (used in new product development for instance) or knowledge management applications would lead to firm-wide messaging services and groupware applications.

*Outcome for Arrow G*

The primary outcome of Arrow *G* is a portfolio of technologies, platforms, hardware, and software that implements the applications the organization requires and addresses its technological requirements. Another outcome is the development of IT maxims—statements that indicate practical courses of action that the organization wishes to follow with regard to IT. Examples of IT maxims include, "we will migrate toward hardware and software resources that can process complex transactions across a global reach," or "we will electronically process repetitive transactions," or "we will have common order-entry systems across business units that can cross-sell." Such maxims provide the basis for the choice of appropriate hardware, software, vendors, and platforms.

To summarize the implications of the alignment of IT strategy with IS strategy, as shown in Table 3.4, the context for alignment includes the organizational role of IS, the external and internal IT environments, and the extent of application synergies across divisions. The process of alignment includes the development of IT acquisition policies that are consistent with the criticality of IS applications and choice of technologies that are based on information-processing activities that are critical to the firm. The outcomes of alignment include a portfolio of applications that satisfies the technology requirements of the firm and IT maxims that guide the choice and acquisition of hardware and software.

## Alignment of IS Strategy with IT Strategy: Arrow H

Alignment of *IS strategy* with *IT strategy* implies that the choice of applications takes into account the firm's existing technologies and platforms and its architectural requirements.

*Context for Arrow H*

The context for Arrow *H* includes three aspects. First, IT architectural requirements influence application decisions. Second, vendors' technological capabilities and preferences can sometimes influence the firm's choice of applications. Third, the internal IT environment and existing technologies and platforms may form the basis of future applications (Earl, 1989).

Table 3.4

## Alignment Between IS Strategy and IT Strategy

| Context (factors influencing alignment) | Process (how alignment is achieved) | Outcome (consequences of alignment) |
| --- | --- | --- |
| *Arrow G: Alignment of IT Strategy with IS Strategy* | | |
| • Role of IS (e.g., strategic grid, sector model) (Earl, 1989; McFarlan, 1984)<br>• External IT environment: available hardware and software, IT vendors (Earl, 1989)<br>• Internal IT environment: existing technologies and applications (Earl, 1989)<br>• Extent of synergies and common applications across divisions (Weill and Broadbent, 1998) | • Policies governing the choice of particular technologies are appropriate to the criticality of IS applications (Earl, 1989; Edwards, Ward, and Byethway, 1996)<br>• Choice of technologies is based on information-processing activities that are critical to the firm (Weill and Broadbent, 1998) | • Portfolio of technologies and platforms satisfying the firm's IT requirements (Earl, 1989; Edwards, Ward, and Byethway, 1996)<br>• IT "maxims" that provide the basis for the choice of appropriate hardware, software, vendors, and platforms (Weill and Broadbent, 1998) |
| *Arrow H: Alignment of IS Strategy with IT Strategy* | | |
| • Architectural requirements (Earl, 1989)<br>• Technological preferences and capabilities of IT outsourcing vendors and consultants (Beulen, van Femena, and Currie, 2005)<br>• Internal IT environment: existing technologies and platforms (Earl, 1989; Weill and Broadbent, 1998) | • Matching of applications with architectural requirements, vendor's technology capabilities, and existing technologies and platforms (Earl, 1989) | • Portfolio of applications aligned with the firm's architectural requirements and capabilities of existing technologies (Earl, 1989; Edwards, Ward, and Byethway, 1996) |

*Process for Arrow H*

The process for Arrow *H* takes place when applications are aligned with IT architectural requirements. Existing IT platforms, hardware, and software, especially if deployed firmwide and encompassing many divisions, define the context within which future IS strategies and applications are planned. Unless there are changes in products/markets and business strategies, the firm will not usually change its IT architecture frequently. Consequently, the IT architecture defines the constraints within which IS applications can be chosen (Weill and Broadbent, 1998). Also, vendors' choice of specific technologies could potentially restrict the applications choices of the firm. In addition, existing technologies can sometimes suggest the use of new IS applications. For instance, an existing enterprise-resource system might form the basis for data-warehousing applications drawing on its transaction data.

*Outcome for Arrow H*

The outcome for Arrow *H* is a portfolio of IS applications that is aligned with the firm's IT architectural requirements and capabilities of existing technologies.

In summary therefore, when IS strategy is aligned with IT strategy, IT architectural requirements, and vendors' choice of technologies and existing technologies influence the IS applications portfolio. When IS applications are matched with these aspects, the outcome is a portfolio of applications that fits the firm's architectural requirements and builds on existing technology capabilities.

## DIRECTIONS FOR FUTURE STUDY

Three key points emerge from the discussions in the third section on literature review. First, business–IS alignment is a complex and multilayered concept that involves (a) matching business strategy and the IS/IT deployed by the firm and (b) aligning IT managerial practices, technology requirements, and end-user needs. It exists at both strategic and operational levels and involves different management ranks from the IS and functional departments. As such, it is important for an organization to understand which levels of alignment are most important in the particular context of its business and what is required for accomplishing them. For instance, firms in technologically turbulent industries such as software development, computer R&D, and Internet-based search are heavily dependent on capabilities of emerging IT, and usually employ skilled technical people who are comfortable working with IT applications. For such organizations, it may be more important to understand the strategic opportunities from emerging technologies than to provide detailed and involved end-user support. Hence, addressing alignment requirements for Arrows *A* and *B* might be of greater importance than for the other arrows. Similarly, for multinational firms serving global markets, it is important to design appropriate IT architectural platforms and decide what technologies should be centrally acquired and managed. Hence, alignment with respect to Arrows *C, D, E,* and *F* may be more important. To give another example, established and older firms in relatively more stable industries such as low technology manufacturing tend to employ a semiskilled workforce that is not comfortable working with constantly changing IT. Such organizations must use stable technologies and manage and meet end-user expectations in order to receive appropriate operational benefits from IT. Hence, alignment with respect to arrows *E, F, G,* and *H* may be more important.

Second, the concept of alignment is dynamic. As new technologies surface, existing technologies mature, and sourcing for IS and IT becomes part of overall strategic organizational sourcing, new aspects of alignment between IS and business become important, and must be considered. Moreover, the relative importance of different alignment paths can change over time. For instance, undertaking an IT outsourcing initiative might underscore the relative importance of arrows *C, E,* and *H* for the first few years, until the initiative stabilizes. Or large-scale implementation of enterprise systems might mean that arrows *E, F, G,* and *H* need to be especially addressed in order to increase system use by end users. Or, under conditions of a business merger or a restructuring of the IS organization from a decentralized to a centralized one, a firm might be required to choose between comparable technologies and platforms supporting similar applications. In such a situation, the importance of arrows *G* and *H* might be of overriding importance.

Third, it is clear that there are several understudied areas for the alignment paths, which future conceptual and empirical research must address. We describe below, key areas of future research.

In the context of Arrow *A,* recent studies have used the resource-based lens (e.g., Bharadwaj, 2000; Peppard and Ward, 2004) to study IS–business alignment. Powell and Dent-Micallef (1997) state that some firms have gained advantages by using IT to leverage complementary organizational resources such as a flexible culture and supplier relationships. Luftman and Brier (1999) suggest that certain systemic capabilities such as the ability to access information that is important to the achievement of strategic business objectives enhance the effectiveness of the IS function. Kearns and Lederer (2003) found that knowledge-sharing capabilities between IS and business departments can contribute to strategic IT alignment, and that strategic IT alignment is by itself a capability that could lead to competitive advantage. Bhatt and Grover (2005) suggest that the capabilities of IT business experience (the extent to which IT groups are knowledgeable about business strategies, competitive priorities, business policies, and opportunities) and relationship infrastructure (the extent to which IT groups and line management trust, respect, appreciate, and consult with one another in setting IT and business strategy) positively affect competitive advantage. Drawing from this emerging discourse, future research in this domain should address the question of what specific IS resources and capabilities are required for specific kinds of business strategy. What IS capabilities, for instance, are important for business strategies that rely primarily on product innovation? Are there different IS capabilities required for different business strategies? Moreover, recent empirical evidence (Karahanna, Agarwal, and Angst, 2006) suggests that the compatibility of an application or technology with existing work practices, values, and experiences increases its perceived ease of use and usefulness. In this context it is important to continue investigating which technology features are valued by specific end users.

A number of important perspectives are important in the context of research gaps for Arrow *B.* First, recent IS research (Bharadwaj, 2000; Peppard and Ward, 2004) has converged on the notion that sustainable competitive advantages cannot be obtained from just the "technology" part of IS. It is the application of IS resources and capabilities (which are combinations of the technical and human aspects of IS) to organizational functions and processes that results in inimitable, nonapparent, and valuable benefits from IT. Second, the agility view (Sambamurthy, Bharadwaj, and Grover, 2003) suggests that firms can enhance their strategic/business agility by developing appropriate capabilities in IT, process knowledge, and communication technologies. Such agility enables firms to launch many and varied competitive actions and acquire continuing competitive advantage, aided by IT. Third, firms can use IT for creating "barriers to erosion," that is, building resource barriers and preemptive barriers that prevent other firms from copying their IT-dependent competitive advantages. Examples of such IT-facilitated barriers include specialized co-investments in IS with partners and customer-switching costs (Piccoli and Ives, 2005). An example of the latter is investments in terms of time, learning, and music format that customers have made in the case of Apple's iPod. Such barriers create sustained competitive advantage. Fourth, the concept of dynamic capabilities (Eisenhardt and Sull, 2001) suggests that the ability to continually reconfigure IT resources and competencies is important for achieving IT-based strategic advantage in hypercompetitive environments (D'Aveni, 1994). Some of these dynamic capabilities relate to abilities for choosing appropriate emerging technologies, matching them to relevant economic business opportunities (Wheeler, 2002), and implementing them. Finally, it is increasingly being recognized that absorptive capacity (Zahra and George, 2002) and organizational learning (Piccoli and Ives, 2005) as they relate to IT and IS are critical to how and why organizations are able to understand the strategic implications and appropriate sustained benefits of persistently evolving information technologies. Many of the above ideas are conceptual (although some empirical research exists, e.g., Bhatt and Grover, 2005). Future theoretical and empirical research must address the question of why some organizations are more successful than others at identifying business opportunities based on emerging IT and consistently appropriating such opportunities for business value. How, for instance, do firms identify emerging IT that can form the basis of future competitive strategies? What capabilities are required for rapidly acquiring and implementing the identified technologies? What IS capabilities are required for strategic initiatives such as supply chain integration and interorganizational partnerships? How can IS capabilities be combined with specific organizational capabilities to generate firm benefits? How can absorptive capacity and organizational learning be analyzed in the context of IT and how does it enhance other IS capabilities?

Future research in the context of Arrow $C$ could address the issue of alignment of IM strategies (e.g., as given by the STROIM instrument) with various business orientations, as given by the STROBE framework or the Miles and Snow typology.

Many contemporary organizations perceive the primary role of the IS function to be that of an "information services" provider—that is, to appropriately acquire, store, manage, and disseminate information from organizational transactions, activities, and processes. With increasing systems integration across functions, modern IS departments are often in a position to observe and analyze end-to-end processes and acquire valuable process-related knowledge. Arrow $D$ has therefore become critical in recent years and underscores the increasing importance of communication between the CEO and CIO as well as between the IS function and the rest of the business (as given by a number of recent studies—Bassellier and Benbasat, 2004; Bassellier, Reich, and Benbasat, 2001; Kearns and Lederer, 2003; Kearns and Sabherwal, 2006/2007). Future research should investigate questions such as: How can business and process knowledge of CIOs and other IS professionals be appropriated for changing strategy and structure? What structural mechanisms can best facilitate transfer of business knowledge between the CIO and CEO? What are the ways in which such transfer can lead to modifications in products and processes? Given the increasing prevalence of outsourcing, can (external and internal) providers of IT products and services provide inputs to such modifications?

Existing research addressing Arrow $E$ consists primarily of contingency-based managerial frameworks that match various mechanisms for managing IT with appropriate IS and IT strategies (Earl, 1989; Edwards, Ward, and Bytheway, 1996). Future empirical research could address the issue of alignment of IM strategies (e.g., as given by the STROIM instrument) with various IS/IT typologies such as the strategic grid or the sector model. Another unexplored area relates to end-user acceptance and use of applications. Research centered on the technology acceptance model (Taylor, Todd, and Shirley, 1995; Venkatesh et al., 2003) has found that facilitating conditions such as technology support and supporting organizational norms lead to greater system usage. Current ideas on post-adoptive behaviors (Jasperson, Carter, and Zmud, 2005) suggest that most applications are "underused," that is, most of their features are not used. Social structures such as system-use feedback and system-use incentives positively influence an individual's propensity to go beyond the use of basic or mandated features of applications, and engage in "feature extension behaviors," that is, use features not originally mandated or discover ways to apply specific features that go beyond what is defined by the designers. Important questions in this regard relate to understating how IT management practices can facilitate sustained and evolving system use and how these practices should be aligned with the particular role and nature of IS/IT in the firm.

As is the case for Arrow *D*, areas important for future research for Arrow *F* center around mechanisms and contexts for the transfer of knowledge from the IS function to the business. Such knowledge transfer can take place within the firm, between the CIO and CEO (Kearns and Lederer, 2003; Kearns and Sabherwal, 2006/2007), and perhaps even from outsourcing vendor firms to client firms. What are the ways in which such interaction can change IT and IS strategies of the firm? What are the organizational learning processes that take place from such interaction, which lead firms to a better understanding of the possible use of new applications? Is it possible that knowledge can be transferred between IT outsourcing vendors and clients? How?

As in the case of Arrow *E*, existing studies (Earl, 1989; Edwards, Ward, and Bytheway, 1996) addressing Arrow *G* propose a number of practice-based frameworks for matching various orientations toward technology planning and acquisition with particular IS strategies (e.g., as given by the strategic grid). As such, processes and frameworks for deriving appropriate technologies from the IS plan are reasonably well studied, particularly in the areas of systems analysis and design. However, current business and IT environments are characterized, respectively, by fluid organizational forms and availability of many technology choices, primarily as a result of mergers and continually evolving IT. When strategic decisions with respect to mergers fail to take into account characteristics of technology platforms and architectures of the individual organizations, aligning the IT strategy of the combined organization with its IS strategy poses a number of challenges. Important questions in this regard are: What factors influence IT decisions when similar applications exist on different hardware and software platforms? How do end users influence such decisions?

Recent studies (e.g., Hart and Saunders, 1998; Markus et al., 2006) indicate that the choice of B2B applications may be influenced by the technology- and standards-related choices of business partners, supply chain members, and other firms in the industry. Important areas of investigation for Arrow *H* relate to the increasing role of external entities in influencing the choice of applications. How and why do business partners affect a firm's choice of applications? Similarly, a better understanding is required of how outsourcing vendors' technology choices affect a firm's choice of applications.

## CONCLUSION

Alignment has been an important, multifaceted, and complex theme in IS research and practice. A firm that has achieved a high degree of business–IS alignment invests the "right" amount on IS and IT, has a mix of investments appropriate for the firm's strategy, has IS applications that support current business strategies, and IT management practices that facilitate the use of existing applications; IT investments are therefore successfully converted into business value. However, firms continue to find it difficult to achieve alignment (Chan, 2002). The reasons can be attributed to lack of direction in business strategy, insufficient top management awareness of IT, uncoordinated and isolated strategic and IS planning processes, ineffective or powerless IT departments, and barriers to implementation and use arising from political, financial, or technical constraints

(Weill and Broadbent, 1998). As a result, IT decisions are driven by business executives who do not understand the technology, and IT organizations continue to be technology driven rather than business driven. Indeed, according to current practitioner thinking (Jahnke, 2004), business–IS alignment is the "Holy Grail of the IT executive"—essential for appropriating business value from IT, but very difficult to actually achieve. We illustrate using the following scenarios.

> Our conversation with the CIO of the glass and plastics container manufacturer further revealed, "Till very recently, there was no formal business planning, so there was no question of IS planning. IT was acquired in an ad-hoc and piecemeal manner with no thought to architecture or rationalization."

> The chief technical officer of one of the world's largest manufacturers of automotive glass, operating in about forty countries observed (in 2007) that, "Our IT function is empowered and integrated enough at the top [with the business] to suggest specific applications and technologies that the company might need. However most companies are not like that."

There has been a reemergence of academic interest in business–IS alignment (Kearns and Sabherwal, 2006/2007; Umanath, 2003), for example, with particular emphasis on (a) methodological approaches for studying alignment, and (b) specific ways in which alignment can be achieved. As the role of and possibilities from IS expand and diffuse into almost every functional area, it is clear that there is no one best way to alignment; rather, effective alignment depends on addressing particular alignment requirements and contingencies facing the organization at a particular time. The review model developed in this chapter identifies and analyzes key alignment paths that must be considered in order to develop a fit between the business of a firm and its acquisition and use of IT. It contributes to the literature by (a) positioning extant alignment research in the context of current and expected future directions and developments in the use of IT by organizations, and (b) suggesting important areas for future investigation (see Table 3.5). It contributes to practice by delineating and explaining specific alignment paths on which organizations could focus to drive, prioritize, and shape their business–IS alignment efforts.

## NOTES

1. Studies have used interchangeably, the terms "alignment" (Henderson and Venkatraman, 1993; Reich and Benbasat, 1996), "fit" (Das, Zahra, and Warkentin, 1991; Venkatraman, 1989a), "linkage" (Pyburn 1983; Reich and Benbasat 1996, 2000), and "co-ordination" (Lederer and Mendelow, 1989) of different aspects of IS strategy and IS planning with business strategies and plans. In this chapter, we use the term alignment.

2. In this chapter, "IS" stands for information systems-specific applications, "IT" stands for information technology-specific technologies and platforms, and "IM" stands for information management—management and governance of IS and IT activities (Earl, 1989).

3. The fit or alignment between business strategy and organization structure has been extensively discussed (e.g., Chandler, 1969; Thompson 1967), and is not addressed in this chapter. Our interest here is to study the alignment of business strategy and organization structure with strategies relating to planning, acquisition, and management of IS and IT.

4. "Absorptive capacity" of a firm is its ability to "recognize the value of new, external information, assimilate it, and apply it to commercial ends" (Cohen and Levinthal, 1990).

Table 3.5

## Directions for Future Research

| Research questions | Reference domains and models |
|---|---|
| *Arrow A: Alignment of IS Strategy and IT Strategy with Business Strategy and Organization Structure* | |
| • What IS capabilities are important and necessary for different business strategies?<br>• What characteristics of end users—work practices, values, and experience with IT and other characteristics—influence applications and technologies? | • Resource-based view of IS<br>• IS capabilities and competencies (Bharadwaj, 2000; Kearns and Lederer, 2003; Peppard and Ward, 2004)<br>• End-user characteristics and technology adoption (research centered on extensions of technology acceptance model—e.g., Karahanna, Agarwal, and Angst, 2006) |
| *Arrow B: Alignment of Business Strategy and Organization with Structure IS Strategy and IT Strategy* | |
| • How do firms identify emerging IT that can form the basis of future competitive strategies?<br>• What capabilities are required for rapidly acquiring and implementing the identified technologies?<br>• What IS capabilities are required for strategic initiatives such as supply chain integration and interorganizational partnerships?<br>• How can IS capabilities be combined with specific organizational capabilities to generate firm benefits?<br>• How can absorptive capacity and organizational learning be analyzed in the context of IT and how do they enhance other IS capabilities? | • Dynamic capabilities view of IS (Teece, Eisenhardt, and Sull, 2001; Wheeler 2002)<br>• Sustained competitive advantages from IS (Piccoli and Ives, 2005)<br>• Agility and hypercompetitive environments (D'Aveni, 1994; Sambamurthy, Bharadwaj, and Grover, 2003)<br>• Absorptive capacity with respect to IS (Zahra and George, 2002) |
| *Arrow C: Alignment of IM Strategy with Business Strategy and Organization Structure* | |
| • How can different kinds of IM strategy (STROIM—e.g., Ragu-Nathan et al., 2001) be matched to different business orientations (STROBE—Venkatraman, 1985; or Miles and Snow, 1978)? | • IM Strategy orientation (Ragu-Nathan et al., 2001)<br>• Strategic orientation of business enterprises (Venkatraman, 1989b)<br>• Alignment approaches (Drazin and van de Ven, 1992; Venkatraman, 1989a) |

*Arrow D: Alignment of Business Strategy and Organization with Structure IM Strategy*

- What structural mechanisms can best facilitate transfer of business knowledge between the CIO and CEO and between IS professionals and functional managers?
- How can such transfer lead to modifications in products and processes and in strategy and structure?
- Can outsourcing vendors provide inputs to such modifications?

• Interorganizational knowledge transfer
• Interface between IS and business and domain knowledge transfer (Bassellier and Benbasat, 2004; Kearns and Lederer, 2003; Kearns and Sabherwal, 2006/2007)

*Arrow E: Alignment of IM Strategy with IS Strategy and IT Strategy*

- How can different kinds of IM strategy (STROIM—e.g., Ragu-Nathan et al.) be matched to the business role of IT (strategic grid—McFarlan, 1984; or sector model—Earl, 1989)?
- How can IT management practices facilitate post-adoption behaviors such as sustained and evolving system use?
- How should these aspects be aligned with the particular role and nature of IS/IT in the firm?

• IM strategy orientation (Ragu-Nathan et al., 2001)
• IS application typologies such as the strategic grid (McFarlan, 1984) and sector model (Earl, 1989)
• Technology acceptance model (Davis, 1985; Taylor, Todd, and Shirley, 1995; Venkatesh et al., 2003) and post-adoptive behaviors (Jasperson, Carter, and Zmud, 2005)

*Arrow F: Alignment of IS Strategy and IT Strategy with IM Strategy*

- What are the ways in which CIO–CEO interactions can change the firm's IT and IS strategies?
- What organizational learning processes take place from such interaction, thus leading firms to a better understanding of new IS applications that can be used?
- Is it possible that knowledge can be transferred between IT outsourcing vendors and clients? How?

• Interorganizational knowledge transfer (Grant 1996a; Mowery, Oxley, and Silverman, 1996)
• Interface between IS and business and domain knowledge transfer (Bassellier and Benbasat, 2004; Kearns and Lederer, 2003; Kearns and Sabherwal, 2005)

*Arrow G: Alignment of IT Strategy with IS Strategy*

- What factors influence IT decisions when similar applications exist on different hardware and software platforms?
- How do end users influence such decisions?

• Research on technology standards adoption (Markus et al. 2006)
• Technology acceptance model (Taylor, Todd, and Shirley, 1995; Venkatesh et al., 2003)

*Arrow H: Alignment of IS Strategy with IT Strategy*

- How and why do business partners affect a firm's choice of applications?
- How and why do outsourcing vendors' technology choices affect a firm's choice of applications?

• Technology choice of partners (Hart and Saunders, 1998)
• Research on technology standards adoption (Markus et al., 2006)

## REFERENCES

Ahituv, N.; Neumann, S.; and Aviran, M. 1989. Factors affecting the policy for distributing computing resources. *MIS Quarterly,* 13, 4, 389–401.

Barua, A.; Lee, S.C.H.; and Whinston, A.B. 1996. The calculus of reengineering. *Information Systems Research,* 7, 4, 409–428.

Bassellier, G., and Benbasat, I. 2004. Business competence of information technology professionals: conceptual development and influence on IT-business partnerships. *MIS Quarterly,* 28, 4, 673–694.

Bassellier, G.; Reich, B.; and Benbasat, I. 2001. Information technology of competence of business managers: a definition and research model. *Journal of Management Information Systems,* 17, 4, 159–182.

Beulen, E.; van Fenema, P.; and Currie, W. 2005. From application outsourcing to infrastructure management: extending the offshore outsourcing service portfolio. *European Management Journal,* 23, 2, 133–144.

Bharadwaj, A. 2000. A resource-based perspective on information technology and firm performance: an empirical investigation. *MIS Quarterly,* 24, 1, 169–196.

Bhatt, G., and Grover, V. 2005. Types of IT capabilities and their role in competitive advantage: an empirical study. *Journal of Management Information Systems,* 22, 2, 253–277.

Boynton, A.; Zmud, R.; and Jacobs, G. 1994. The influence of IT management practice on IT use in large organizations, *MIS Quarterly,* 18, 3, 299–318.

Brancheau J.C.; Janz, B.D.; and Wetherbe, J.C. 1996. Key issues in information systems management: 1994–95 SIM Delphi results. *MIS Quarterly* 20, 2, 225–242.

Brown, C., and Magill, S. 1994. Alignment of IS functions with the enterprise: Toward a model of antecedents. *MIS Quarterly,* 18, 4, 371–403.

———. 1998. Reconceptualizing the context-design issue for the information system function. *Organization Science,* 9, 2, 176–194.

Chan, Y. 2002. Why haven't we mastered alignment? The importance of the informal organizational structure. *MIS Quarterly Executive,* 1, 2, 97–112.

Chan, Y.; Huff, S.; Barclay, D.; and Copeland, D. 1997. Business strategic orientation, information systems strategic orientation, and strategic alignment. *Information Systems Research,* 8, 2, 125–150.

Chandler, A.D. Jr. 1969. *Strategy and Structure: Chapters in the History of the American Industrial Enterprise.* Boston, MA: MIT Press.

Cohen, W., and Levinthal, D. 1990. Absorptive capacity: a new perspective on learning and innovation. *Administrative Science Quarterly,* 35, 1, 128–152.

Das, S.; Zahra, S.; and Warkentin, M. 1991. Integrating the content and process of strategic MIS planning with competitive strategy. *Decision Sciences,* 22, 5, 953–985.

D'Aveni, R. 1994. *Hypercompetition: Managing the Dynamics Of Strategic Maneuvering.* New York: Free Press.

Delaney, K., and Grant, P. 2007. Google gains on goal of controlling and targeting TV commercials. *Wall Street Journal,* March 10.

Drazin, R., and Van de Ven, A.H. 1985. Alternative forms of fit in contingency theory. *Administrative Science Quarterly,* 30, 4, 514–539.

Earl, M. 1989. *Management Strategy for Information Technology.* New York: Prentice Hall.

Edwards, C.; Ward, J.; and Bytheway, A. 1996. *The Essence of Information Systems.* New Delhi: Prentice Hall.

Eisenhardt, K., and Sull, D. 2001. Strategy as simple rules. *Harvard Business Review,* 79, 1, 107–116.

Galbraith, J. 1973. *Designing Complex Organizations.* Reading, MA: Addison-Wesley.

Galliers, R., and Sutherland, A. 1991. Information systems management and strategy formulation—the stages of growth model revisited. *Journal of Information Systems,* 1, 2, 89–114.

Galliers, R.D.; Merali, Y; and Spearing, L. 1994. Coping with information technology? How British executives perceive the key issues in the mid-1990's. *Journal of Information Technology* 9, 4, 223–238.

Goldsmith, N. 1991. Linking IT planning to business strategy. *Long Range Planning,* 24, 6, 67–77.

Grant, R.M. 1991. The resource-based theory of competitive advantage: implications for strategy formulation. *California Management Review,* 33, 3, 114–135.

———. 1996a. Prospering in dynamically-competitive environments: organizational capability as knowledge integration. *Organization Science,* 7, 4 (July–August), 375–387.

———. 1996b. Toward a knowledge-based theory of the firm. *Strategic Management Journal,* 17 (Winter), 109–122.

Hambrick, D. 1983. High profit strategies in mature capital goods industries: a contingency approach. *Academy of Management Journal*, 26, 4, 687–707.

Hart, P., and Saunders, C. 1998. Emerging electronic partnerships: antecedents and dimensions of EDI use from the supplier's perspective. *Journal of Management Information Systems*, 14, 4, 87–111.

Hatten, M., and Hatten, K. 1997. Information systems strategy: long overdue and still not here. *Long Range Planning*, 30, 2, 254–266.

Henderson, J., and Venkatraman, N. 1993. Strategic alignment: leveraging information technology for transforming organizations. *IBM Systems Journal*, 32, 1, 4–16.

IBM. 1981. *Business Systems Planning: Information Systems Planning Guide*. GE20–0527–3.

Ives, B., and Learmonth, G. 1984. The information systems as a competition weapon. *Communications of the ACM*, 27, 12, 1193–1201.

Jahnke, A. 2004. Why is business–IT alignment so difficult? *CIO Magazine*, June.

Jasperson, J.; Carter, P.; and Zmud, R. 2005. A comprehensive conceptualization of post-adoptive behaviors associated with information technology enabled work systems. *MIS Quarterly*, 29, 3, 525–557.

Karahanna, E.; Agarwal, R.; and Angst, C. 2006. Reconceptualizing compatibility beliefs in technology acceptance research. *MIS Quarterly*, 30, 4, 781–304.

Kearns, G., and Lederer, A. 2003. A resource-based view of strategic IT alignment: how knowledge sharing creates competitive advantage. *Decision Sciences*, 34, 1, 1–29.

Kearns, G., and Sabherwal, R. 2006/2007. Strategic alignment between business and information technology: a knowledge-based view of behaviors, outcome, and consequences. *Journal of Management Information Systems*, 23, 3, 129–162.

Keen, P. 1993. Information technology and the management difference: a fusion map. *IBM Systems Journal*, 32, 1, 17–39.

King, W. 1978. Strategic planning for management information systems. *MIS Quarterly*, 2, 1, 27–37.

King, W.R., and Cleland, D.I. 1975. A new method for strategic systems planning. *Business Horizons*, 18, 4, 55–64.

King, W., and Teo, T.S.H. 1994. Facilitators and inhibitors for the strategic use of information technology. *Information and Management*, 27, 2, 71–87.

———. 1996. Key dimensions of facilitators and inhibitors for the strategic use of information technology. *Journal of Management Information Systems*, 12, 4, 35–53.

Lederer, A., and Mendelow, A. 1989. Co-ordination of information systems plans with business plans. *Journal of Management Information Systems*, 6, 2, 5–19.

———. 1993. Information systems planning and the challenge of shifting priorities. *Information & Management*, 24, 6, 319–328.

Lederer, A., and Sethi, V. 1988. The implementation of strategic information systems planning methodologies. *MIS Quarterly*, 12, 3, 444–461.

Levina, N., and Ross, J. 2003. From the vendor's perspective: Exploring the value proposition in IT outsourcing. *MIS Quarterly*, 27, 3, 331–364.

Loh, L., and Venkatraman, N. 1992. Determinants of information technology outsourcing: a cross-sectional analysis. *Journal of Management Information Systems*, 9, 1, 7–24.

Luftman, J., and Brier, T. 1999. Achieving and sustaining business-IT alignment. *California Management Review*, 42, 1, 109–122.

Magretta, J. 1998. The power of virtual integration: an interview with Dell Computer's Michael Dell. *Harvard Business Review*, March–April, 73–84.

Malone, T.W.; Yates, J.; and Benjamin, R.I. 1987. Electronic markets and electronic hierarchies. *Communications of the ACM*, 30, 6 (June), 484–497.

Markus, M.L.; Steinfield, C.W.; Wigand, R.T.; and Minton, G. 2006. Industry-wide information systems standardization as collective action: the case of the U.S. residential mortgage industry. *MIS Quarterly*, 30, 2, 439–465.

McFarlan, E. 1984. Information technology changes the way you compete. *Harvard Business Review*, 62, 3, 98–103.

McFarlan, F.W., and Delacy, B.J. 2004. *Outsourcing IT: The Global Landscape in 2004*. Boston, MA: Harvard Business School Press.

Miles, R.E., and Snow, C.C. 1978. *Organizational Strategy, Structure, and Process*. New York: McGraw-Hill.

Min, S.; Suh, E.; and Kim, S. 1999. An integrated approach toward strategic information systems planning. *Strategic Information Systems*, 8, 4, 373–394.

Mintzberg, H. 1979. *The Structuring of Organizations.* Englewood Cliffs, NJ: Prentice Hall.

Nahapiet, J., and Ghoshal, S. 1998. Social capital, intellectual capital, and the organizational advantage. *Academy of Management Review,* 23, 1, 242–266.

Niederman, F.; Brancheau, J.; and Wetherbe, J. 1991. Information systems management issues for 1990s. *MIS Quarterly,* 15, 4, 475–500.

Parsons, G.L. 1983. Information technology: a new competitive weapon. *Sloan Management Review,* 25, 1, 3–14.

Peppard, J., and Ward, J. 1999. "Mind the gap": diagnosing the relationship between the IT organization and the rest of the business. *Strategic Information Systems,* 8, 1, 29–60.

———. 2004. Beyond strategic information systems: toward an IS capability. *Strategic Information Systems,* 13, 2, 167–194.

Piccoli, G., and Ives, B. 2005. IT-dependent strategic initiatives and sustained competitive advantage: a review and synthesis of the literature. *MIS Quarterly,* 29, 4, 747–776.

Porter, M. 1985. *Competitive Advantage.* New York: Free Press.

Porter, M., and Millar, V. 1985. How information gives you competitive advantage. *Harvard Business Review,* 63, 4, 49–160.

Powell, T., and Dent-Micallef, A. 1997. Information technology as competitive advantage: the role of human, business, and technology resources. *Strategic Management Journal,* 18, 5, 375–405.

Prahalad, C., and Hamel, G. 1990. The core competence of the organization. *Harvard Business Review,* May, 79–83.

Prekumar, G., and King, W. 1992. An empirical assessment of informational systems planning and the role of information systems in organizations. *Journal of Management Information Systems,* 9, 2, 99–125.

Pyburn, P. 1983. Linking the MIS plan with corporate strategy: an exploratory study. *MIS Quarterly* 7, 2, 1–14.

Rackoff, N.; Wiseman, C.; and Ullrich, W. 1985. Information systems for competitive advantage: implementation of a planning process. *MIS Quarterly,* 9, 4, 285–294.

Raghunathan, B., and Raghunathan, T.S. 1990. Planning implications of the information systems strategic grid: an empirical investigation. *Decision Sciences,* 21, 2, 287–300.

———. 1991. Information systems planning and effectiveness: an empirical analysis. *OMEGA International Journal of Management Science* 19, 2/3, 125–135.

Raghunathan, B; Raghunathan, T.S.; Tu, Q.; and Shi, Z. 2001. Information management strategy: the construct and its measurement. *Journal of Strategic Information Systems,* 10, 4, 265–289.

Reich, B., and Benbasat, I. 1996. Measuring the linkage between business and information technology objectives. *MIS Quarterly,* 20, 1, 55–81.

———. 2000. Factors that influence the social dimension of alignment between business and information technology objectives. *MIS Quarterly,* 24, 1, 81–113.

Rockart, J. 1979. Chief executives define their own data needs. *Harvard Business Review,* 57, 2 (March–April), 81–93.

Rockart, J.; Earl, M.; and Ross, J. 1996. Eight imperatives for the new IT organization. *Sloan Management Review,* 38, 1, 43–55.

Rodgers, L. 1997. Alignment revisited. *CIO Magazine,* May 15, 44–45.

Sabherwal, R., and Chan, Y. 2001. Alignment between business and IS strategies: a study of prospectors, analyzers, and defenders. *Information Systems Research,* 12, 1, 11–33.

Sabherwal, R., and King, W. 1991. Towards a theory of strategic use of information resources. *Information and Management,* 20, 4, 191–212.

Sambamurthy, V., and Zmud, R. 1999. Arrangements for information technology governance: a theory of multiple contingencies. *MIS Quarterly,* 23, 2, 261–290.

———. 2000. Research commentary: the organizing logic for an enterprise's IT activities in the digital era—a prognosis of practice and a call for research. *Information Systems Research,* 11, 2, 105–114.

Sambamurthy, V.; Bharadwaj, A.; and Grover, V. 2003. Shaping agility through digital options: reconceptualizing the role of information technology in contemporary firms. *MIS Quarterly,* 27, 2, 237–263.

Sambamurthy, V.; Venkatraman, S.; and DeSanctis, G. 1993. The design of information technology planning systems for varying organizational contexts. *European Journal of Information Systems,* 2, 2, 23–35.

Snow, C., and Hrebiniak, L. 1980. Strategy, distinctive competence, and organizational performance. *Administrative Science Quarterly* 25, 2, 317–336.

Stalk, G; Evans, P.; and Shulman, L. 1992. Competing on capabilities: the new rules of corporate strategy. *Harvard Business Review,* March/April, 57–69.

Steel, E. 2007. "Measured" Media, Lose in Spending Cuts. *Wall Street Journal,* March 14.

Sullivan, C., Jr. 1985. Systems planning in the information age. *Sloan Management Review,* 27, 2, 3–11.

Tavakolian, H. 1989. Linking the information technology structure with organizational competitive strategy: a survey. *MIS Quarterly,* 13, 3, 309–317.

Taylor, S.; Todd, P.; and Shirley, I. 1995. Understanding information technology usage: a test of competing models. *Information Systems Research,* 6, 2, 144–176.

Thompson, J.D. 1967. *Organizations in Action.* New York: McGraw-Hill.

Umanath, N. 2003. The concept of contingency beyond "it depends": illustration from IS research stream. *Information and Management,* 40, 6, 551–562.

Venkatesh, V.; Morris, M.G.; Davis, G.B.; and Davis, F.D. 2003. User acceptance of information technology: toward a unified view. *MIS Quarterly,* 27, 3, 425–478.

Venkatraman, N. 1989a. The concept of fit in strategy research: toward verbal and statistical correspondence. *Academy of Management Review,* 14, 3, 423–444.

———. 1989b. Strategic orientation of business enterprises: the construct, dimensionality, and measurement. *Management Science,* 35, 8, 942–962.

———. 1994. IT-enabled business transformation: from automation to business scope redefinition. *Sloan Management Review,* 35, 2, 73–87.

Ward, J., and Peppard, J. 1996. Reconciling the IT/business relationship: a troubled marriage in need of guidance. *Strategic Information Systems,* 5, 1, 37–65.

Ward, J.M. 1987. Integrating information systems into business strategies. *Long Range Planning,* 20, 3 (June), 19–29.

Weill, P., and Broadbent, M. 1998. *Leveraging the New Infrastructure: How Market Leaders Capitalize on Information Technology.* Boston, MA: Harvard Business School Press.

Wheeler, B. 2002. NeBIC: a dynamic capabilities theory for assessing net-enablement. *Information Systems Research,* 13, 2, 125–146.

Winston, E., and Dologite, D. 1999. Achieving IT infusion: a conceptual model for small businesses. *Information Resources Management Journal,* 12, 1, 26–38.

Zahra, S., and George, G. 2002. The net-enabled business innovation cycle and the evolution of dynamic capabilities. *Information Systems Research,* 13, 2, 147–150.

# CHAPTER 4

# ALIGNING BUSINESS AND INFORMATION SYSTEMS

## Review and Future Research Directions

### THOMPSON S.H. TEO

*Abstract: Aligning business and information systems (IS) has remained among the top ten key issues facing IS professionals for more than two decades. The aim of this chapter is to review and synthesize the literature on alignment. Specifically, we examine the various terms and definitions of alignment, why alignment is important, how alignment is assessed, factors affecting alignment, changes in alignment over time, and the impact of alignment. We conclude by synthesizing the literature and proposing some directions for future research.*

***Keywords:*** *Alignment, Planning, Strategy, Information Systems*

Over the past twenty years, information systems (IS) planning has consistently remained among the top ten issues facing senior executives (Table 4.1). A key aspect of strategic IS planning is the need for alignment between business planning (BP) and information systems planning (ISP).

In the context of BP and ISP, alignment means that business and IS plans (the outputs of the planning process) should be in harmony and consistent with one another. In other words, similar to aligning things to make them congruent, business and IS strategic alignment can be defined as the alignment of IS goals, strategies and processes with the goals, strategies and the processes of the business enterprise.

From Table 4.1, based on the 2006 SIM survey of IS professionals, it appears that IS planning has decreased in ranking (though it still remains among the top five issues) while business–information technology (IT) alignment has remained the top key issue since 2004. Although this issue has received significant attention in recent years, empirical research focusing specifically on BP–ISP alignment appears to have somewhat slowed down. Note that this chapter focuses on the alignment between IS strategy/plan and business strategy/plan, and between IS planning and business planning.

When the concept of deriving IS strategy from business strategy was first introduced (King, 1978; King and Cleland, 1975), it dealt primarily with the content of plans—that is, deriving the IS mission, strategy and objectives from the mission, strategy and constraints of the strategic business plan. Even when the "reverse" transformation of having IS influence business strategy was first discussed (King and Zmud, 1981), the focus was on content.

Little attention was given to the alignment of the IS strategic planning process with the busi-

Table 4.1

**Ranking of Importance of IS Planning and IT–Business Alignment**

| Study | IS planning | Business–IT alignment |
|---|---|---|
| Ball and Harris (1982) | 1 | — |
| Dickson et al. (1984) | 1 | 7 |
| Hartdog and Herbert (1986) | 1 | 2 |
| Brancheau and Wetherbe (1987) | 1 | 5 |
| Niederman, Brancheau, and Wetherbe (1991) | 3 | 7 |
| Brancheau, Janz, and Wetherbe (1996) | 10 | 9 |
| Watson et al. (1997) | 1 | 2 |
| Luftman and McLean (2004) | 2 | 1 |
| Luftman (2005) | 4 | 1 |
| Luftman, Kempaiah, and Nash (2006) | 4 | 1 |

ness planning process until IBM (1981) used the King (1978) approach as the basis for their business systems planning (BSP) process. IBM's use of these ideas with their customers around the globe was significant in popularizing and extending their application to the consideration of both content and process.

Subsequently, various researchers have emphasized the importance of enterprise architecture (Sowa and Zachman, 1992; Zachman, 1987) and strategic planning methodologies/ frameworks for creating alignment. Examples of IS planning methodologies/frameworks that suggest how IS can support or be aligned with business include: BSP and Business Information Control Study (BICS) (Zachman, 1982), and critical success factors (CSFs) (Rockart, 1979), value chain (Porter and Millar, 1985), customer resource life cycle (Ives and Learmonth, 1984), and strategic thrusts (Rackoff, Wiseman, and Ullrich, 1985). In addition, authors have also examined the creation of business-aligned IS strategy in practice (Earl, 1993; Luftman, 1996). However, a review of such literature, which would include details of different strategic IS planning processes and frameworks, is beyond the scope of this chapter.

Various terms are often used synonymously to describe alignment, namely, "bridge" (Ciborra, 1997), "congruence" (Karimi, Gupta, and Somers, 1996; Scott, 2005), "consistency" (Henderson and Sifonis, 1988), "coordination" (Lederer and Mendelow, 1989), "fit" (Henderson and Venkatraman, 1993), "fusion" (Keen, 1993; Papp, 1998; Smaczny, 2001), "harmony" (Luftman, 2000; Luftman, Papp, and Brier, 1999), "integration" (Teo and King, 1997a, 1997b), "linkage" (Goldsmith, 1991; Reich and Benbasat, 1996), and "match" (Leifer, 1988).

Further, various conceptualizations and definitions of alignment found in the literature include foci on either content or on both content and process:

*Focus on content*

- The degree to which the information technology mission, objectives, and plans support and are supported by the business mission, objectives, and plans (King, 1978; Reich and Benbasat, 1996, 2000).
- Fit between IT and business structures (Jarvenpaa and Ives, 1993).

*Focus on content and process*

- IS strategic alignment: the fit between business strategic orientation and IS strategic orientation (Chan et al., 1997).
- Business–IT alignment: applying information technology in an appropriate and timely way, in harmony with business strategies, goals and needs (Luftman, 2000; Luftman and Brier, 1999; Luftman, Papp, and Brier, 1999).
- Strategic alignment: fit among four domains—business strategy, IT strategy, organizational infrastructure and processes, and IS infrastructure and processes (Henderson and Venkatraman, 1993; Luftman, Lewis, and Oldach, 1993).
- Strategic IS management profile: specifies four types of alignment, namely, strategic alignment (alignment between business strategy and IS strategy), structural alignment (alignment between business structure and IS structure), business alignment (alignment between business strategy and business structure), IS alignment (alignment between IS strategy and IS structure), plus two types of cross-dimensional alignment (alignment between IS strategy and business structure, and alignment between business strategy and IS structure) (Bergeron, Raymond and Rivard, 2004).
- IS alignment has two components: strategic alignment (fit between the priorities and activities of the IS function and those of the business unit) and structural alignment (degree of structural fit between IS and the business, specifically in the areas of IS decision-making rights, reporting relationships, (de)centralization of IS services and infrastructure, and the deployment of IS personnel (Chan, 2002).
- Fit between an organization and its strategy, structure, processes, technology, and environment (Kanellis, Lycett, and Paul, 1999).

In the following sections, we review the literature on the importance of alignment, how alignment is assessed, factors affecting alignment, changes in alignment over time, and the impact of alignment. Then, we propose some suggestions for future research.

## WHY IS ALIGNMENT IMPORTANT?

The need for BP–ISP alignment or more generally, business–IT alignment, has been emphasized in both prescriptive (e.g., King, 1978) and empirical studies (e.g., Chan and Huff, 1993; King and Teo, 1997). The basic premise of the importance of alignment is that greater alignment between IS and business will lead to better performance. Alignment has been examined in various contexts, such as mergers and acquisitions (Brown and Renwick, 1996; Wijnhoven et al., 2006), enterprise systems implementation (Hong and Kim, 2002; Soh and Sia, 2004, 2005), critical success factors of business and IS executives (Khandelwal, 2001), software development processes (Slaughter et al., 2006), Internet usage (Simmers, 2002), and interorganizational relationships (Premkumar, Ramamurthy, and Saunders, 2005). However, the focus of this chapter is mainly on the alignment of business planning/strategies with IS planning/strategies.

Alignment is important because it helps to:

- Ensure that information systems are targeted on areas that are critical to successful business performance (Das, Zahra, and Warkentin, 1991).
- Ensure that the IS function supports organizational goals and activities at every level (Lederer and Mendelow, 1989).

- Enhance top management's understanding of the significance of IS, and increases IS management's understanding of business objectives (Newkirk and Lederer, 2006a).
- Ensure that ISP activities are coordinated with BP activities so that the IS function can better support business strategies and contribute to the achievement of business value (Teo and King, 1996).
- Facilitate acquisition and deployment of information technology that is congruent with the organization's competitive needs rather than existing patterns of usage within the organization (Bowman, Davis, and Wetherbe, 1983).
- Heighten the stature of IS within the organization, thus facilitating the financial and managerial support necessary to effectively implement innovative systems (Das, Zahra, and Warkentin, 1991; Henderson, Rockart, and Sifonis, 1987).
- Maximize returns on IT investment (Avison et al., 2004).
- Help achieve competitive advantage through IS (Avison et al., 2004).
- Provide direction and flexibility to react to new opportunities (Avison et al., 2004).

Given its importance and the varied and complex contexts in which it can be analyzed, IS researchers have operationalized and assessed alignment in different ways. We discuss these in the next section.

## HOW ALIGNMENT IS ASSESSED

Various researchers have proposed methods to assess alignment. A summary of research on various methods used to assess alignment is shown in Table 4.2. For a detailed description and assumptions underlying each method, please refer to the "fit" literature (e.g., Drazin and van de Ven, 1985; Venkatraman, 1989).

### Alignment as Matching

Some of these methods are normative and emphasize bivariate matching between business and IS objectives and strategies. This approach tends to consider alignment as a strategic, top-down process (e.g., King, 1978; King and Cleland, 1975). In terms of normative approaches, researchers have suggested an IT alignment planning process where critical success factors (Rockart, 1979) and goals produced from corporate planning are used to align IT with the business (e.g., Peak, Guynes, and Kroon, 2005).

Alignment can also be assessed through three linkage mechanisms—content, timing, and personnel. Timing and personnel linkages are less often emphasized than content linkages in ISP methodologies (Lederer and Mendelow, 1989).

In terms of *content linkages*, there should be consistency and matching between business plans and IS plans. In other words, the relevant portions of IS plans should be included in business plans and vice versa. For example, IS objectives should be consistent with business objectives. This notion has been tested in an empirical study that found that IS objectives are generally associated with business objectives. Further, there is a correspondence between each organizational objective and specific IS objectives (Zviran, 1990). These results provide support for normative approaches to IS planning (e.g., King, 1978) that advocate linking IS objectives to business objectives.

*Timing linkages* refer to whether IS plans are developed before, after, or at the same time as business plans. Alignment is made easier when both IS plans and business plans are developed simultaneously. Further, for consistency, the planning horizons for both business plans and IS plans should be similar.

Table 4.2

**Assessment of Alignment**

| Authors | Alignment domains |
| --- | --- |
| **Alignment as matching** | |
| King and Cleland (1975) | Business planning (BP) and IS planning (ISP) |
| King (1978) | BP and ISP |
| IBM (1981) | BP and ISP |
| King and Zmud (1981) | BP and ISP |
| Ein-Dor and Segev (1982) | Organizational structure and IS structure |
| Lederer and Mendelow (1989) | Content, timing, and personnel dimensions of BP and ISP |
| Leifer (1988) | IS architecture and organizational structure |
| Tavakolian (1989) | IT structure (degree of centralization) and competitive strategy (prospectors, analyzers, and defenders) |
| Zviran (1990) | Organizational objectives and IS objectives |
| Goldsmith (1991) | BP and ISP |
| Jarvenpaa and Ives (1993) | Business structure and IT strategies |
| Brown and Magill (1994) | IS structure with business strategy and structure |
| Jordan and Tricker (1995) | IS strategy and organizational structures |
| Fiedler, Grover, and Teng (1996) | IT structures and organizational structures |
| Reich and Benbasat (1996) | Intellectual and social dimensions of business and IS plans |
| Brown (1997) | IS structure with business strategy and structure |
| Kearns and Lederer (2000) | Business plans and IS plans |
| Palmer and Markus (2000) | Business strategy and IT strategy |
| Kearns and Lederer (2003) | Process (business planning and IT planning participation) and content (business plans and IS plans) |
| Peak, Guynes, and Kroon (2005) | BP and ISP |
| Tan and Gallupe (2006) | Cognitive commonality between business and IS executives |
| **Alignment as gestalts** | |
| Henderson and Venkatraman (1993) | Strategic alignment model (SAM) encompassing fit among business strategy, IT strategy, organizational infrastructure and processes, and IS infrastructure and processes |
| Burn (1996) | SAM encompassing fit among business strategy, IT strategy, organizational infrastructure and processes, and IS infrastructure and processes |
| Pollalis (2003) | Technological integration, functional integration, and strategic integration |
| Avison et al. (2004) | Validates SAM using data from financial firm |
| Bergeron, Raymond, and Rivard (2004) | Business strategy, IT strategy, business structure, IT structure |
| **Alignment as profile deviation** | |
| Sabherwal and Kirs (1994) | Critical success factors and IT capability (profile deviation) |
| Chan, Sabherwal, and Thrasher (2006) | Business strategy and IS strategy |
| **Alignment as matching/moderator** | |
| Chan et al. (1997) | Business strategic orientation and IS strategic orientation |
| Cragg, King, and Hussin (2002) | Business strategy and IT strategy |

| Authors | Alignment domains |
| --- | --- |
| Hussin, King, and Cragg (2002) | Business strategy and IT strategy |
| Byrd, Lewis, and Byran (2006) | Business strategy and IT strategy. Combines four perspectives of alignment. Process view (coordination and integration) and outcome view (matching and moderator) |
| **Alignment as typology/matching** | |
| Synnott (1987) | BP and ISP |
| Teo and King (1996) | BP and ISP (also examine alignment as mediator) |
| Teo and King (1997a) | BP and ISP (also examine alignment as mediator) |
| King and Teo (1997) | BP and ISP |
| King and Teo (2000) | BP and ISP |
| Luftman (2000) | Business-IT |
| Hoque et al. (2005) | Technology and business strategy |
| Weiss, thorogood, and Clark (2006) | IT–business |
| **Alignment as a success measure** | |
| Segars and Grover (1998) | Alignment as outcome/success of ISP |
| Newkirk and Lederer (2006a, 2006b) | Alignment as outcome/success of ISP |

In contrast, *personnel linkages* are concerned with whether participants involved in BP are also involved in ISP and vice versa. Such mutual involvement is important for ensuring that a common frame of reference exists between business planners and IS planners.

Analogous to above conceptualizations, linkages can also be defined in terms of intellectual and social dimensions (Reich and Benbasat, 1996). The intellectual dimension is a refinement of content linkage since it emphasizes that the content of IT plans and business plans should be internally consistent (i.e., the IT mission, objectives, and plans are consistent with business mission and objectives) and externally valid (i.e., the plans are comprehensive and balanced with respect to external business and IT environments).

In a similar vein, the social dimension is much broader than personnel linkage, as it emphasizes that both business executives and IS executives should understand each other's objectives and plans. Specifically, the social dimension of linkage is defined as "the level of mutual understanding of and commitment to the business and IT mission, objectives, and plans" (Reich and Benbasat, 1996, p. 58) by organizational members. Previous research tended to focus more on the intellectual dimension than the social dimension of alignment.

In addition, there is empirical evidence that the social dimension of linkage can be conceptualized into two timeframes: short term (i.e., understanding of current plans) and long term (i.e., shared vision for the future of IT within the business unit) (Reich and Benbasat, 1996). Further, the cognitive basis of shared understanding between business and IS executives can be examined using personal construct theory (Tan and Gallupe, 2006).

Instead of examining the alignment of IS strategies with business strategies, some researchers focused on alignment of IS structure/strategies with organization structure/strategies. The rationale for this approach is that alignment of strategies may be insufficient since strategy may influence structure and vice versa (Chandler, 1962; Wolf and Egelholf, 2002); hence, there is a need to align structures as well. Research has found that management information system (MIS) structure is significantly associated with organizational structure (Ein-Dor and Segev, 1982), IT structure is strongly related to competitive strategy (Tavakolian, 1989), various IS architectures can be matched with different organizational structures (Leifer, 1988), IT strategy is related to business structure (Jarvenpaa and Ives, 1993), and IS is aligned with some types of organizational structures (Jordan and Tricker, 1995).

In a similar vein, research has also examined how different IS structures (e.g., centralized, decentralized, hybrid) are aligned with organizational context (e.g., structure, strategy) (Brown, 1997; Brown and Magill, 1994) and has derived a taxonomy for matching IT structures to organizational structures (Fiedler, Grover, and Teng, 1996).

## Alignment as Gestalts

Other researchers have assessed alignment in terms of holistic (gestalts) rather than bivariate matching. In other words, instead of bivariate matching (which focus on matching specific dimension(s) of business and IS individually), gestalts examine the alignment of different components of business and IS plans and activities as a group, rather than individually. For example, there are two types of integration between business and IT domains, namely, strategic integration (link between business strategy and IT strategy) and operational integration (link between organizational infrastructure and processes, and IS infrastructure and processes)—called the strategic alignment model (SAM) (Henderson and Venkatraman, 1993). This approach is holistic as it stresses that effective management of IT requires a balance among the choices made across the four domains of business strategy, IT strategy, organizational infrastructure and processes, and IS infrastructure and processes. Researchers have found that the SAM has conceptual and practical value (Avison et al., 2004; Burn, 1996).

Similarly, patterns of coalignment (gestalts) have also been examined in terms of three types of integration that impact the planning process and the overall performance of information-intensive organizations: *technological integration, functional integration, and strategic integration* (Pollalis, 2003). In a similar vein, alignment has been assessed based on a gestalt perspective of fit and theory-based ideal coalignment patterns (Bergeron, Raymond, and Rivard, 2004).

## Alignment as Profile Deviation

Alignment has also been assessed as profile deviation between organizational critical success factors and IT capability (Sabherwal and Kirs, 1994), and by measuring the deviation of an organization's IS strategy from the IS strategy that is theoretically ideal for its business strategy (Chan, Sabherwal, and Thrasher, 2006). The basic premise is that an ideal profile exists and deviations from this profile would result in lower performance (Venkatraman, 1989).

## Combination of Matching and Moderator Alignment Approaches

Some researchers have assessed alignment as moderation (Hussin, King, and Cragg, 2002) while others have assessed it from both matching and moderation perspectives (Chan et al., 1997). The moderation perspective entails modeling alignment as the interaction between business and IT constructs (e.g., between business strategy and IT strategy). In general, research has found that IS strategic alignment is best modeled using holistic "systems" approaches instead of dimension-specific "bivariate" approaches (Bergeron, Raymond, and Rivard, 2001). Further, modeling alignment or fit as moderation using higher level constructs provides more consistent findings than modeling fit as matching using individual dimensions of the business and IS-related constructs (Chan et al. 1997; Cragg, King, and Hussin, 2002). These studies suggest that examining isolated components of strategy and performance can be misleading (Venkatraman, 1989) since performance tends to be affected by multiple components of strategy as a whole (i.e., favoring a holistic approach) rather than individual components (i.e., favoring a bivariate matching approach). Researchers have also examined four perspectives of strategic alignment: two on alignment in the planning process between business and IT (coordination and integration) and two on realized/outcome alignment of business strategy and IT strategy (matching and moderation), and found empirical support for three out of four alignment perspectives as well as general support for alignment as a moderator (Byrd, Lewis, and Bryan, 2006).

**Typologies of Alignment**

In addition, some researchers propose various typologies for alignment. For example, Synnott (1987) conceptualized ISP in terms of varieties of BP–ISP alignment:

1. No planning: No formal BP or ISP.
2. Stand-alone planning: Presence of either business plan or IS plan, but not both.
3. Reactive planning: IS function reacts to business plans and has no input in the planning process.
4. Linked planning: BP is "interfaced" with ISP. Systems resources are matched against business needs.
5. Integrated planning: BP is indistinguishable from ISP. They occur simultaneously and interactively.

Note that alignment is virtually absent for the first and second types in Synnott's typology. Further, Synnott's typology bears some similarities to previous conceptualizations by other researchers. For example, reactive planning is similar to conceptualizations by King (1978) while linked planning is similar to conceptualizations by King and Zmud (1981). Integrated planning is similar to conceptualizations by Goldsmith (1991), who emphasized that rather than separating BP and ISP activities, ISP activities should be integrated within BP activities. Goldsmith further suggested that in order to leverage IT for competitive advantage, it is essential that information strategy and business strategy be developed together in the same process and at the same time.

King and Teo (1997) synthesized the literature on BP–ISP alignment and suggested a four-stage typology of BP–ISP alignment.

- Stage 1: Administrative integration. There is a weak relationship between BP and ISP. In general, there is *little* significant effort to use IT to support business plans.
- Stage 2: Sequential integration. BP *provides directions* for ISP. In other words, ISP focuses primarily on providing support for business plans.
- Stage 3: Reciprocal integration. There is a reciprocal and *interdependent* relationship between BP and ISP. ISP plays a role in both supporting and influencing BP.
- Stage 4: Full integration. There is *little* distinction between the BP process and the ISP process. Business strategy and information strategy are developed *concurrently* in the *same* integrated planning process.

The above typology has been empirically validated and there is general support for a stage model for BP–ISP alignment (King and Teo, 1997). (Note that the extent of alignment was assessed using paragraph descriptions of the four stages.) The stage model suggests not only that there are different types of BP–ISP alignment but also that firms generally evolve from one level to another (generally from lesser levels of alignment to greater levels) as planning matures, becomes more established, and becomes more important to the organization. This evolutionary view suggests that each successive alignment level raises the strategic potential of IT and enables more effective alignment between business strategy and IS strategy.

Analogous to King and Teo (1997) classification, Hoque and colleagues (2005) suggested a three-state typology of the relationships between business and technology:

- Alignment: Technology supports, enables, and does not constrain the firm's current and evolving business strategies.
- Synchronization: Technology not only enables execution of current business strategies but also anticipates and helps shape future business models and strategy.
- Convergence: Business and technology activities intertwine and the leadership teams operate almost interchangeably.

Note that alignment is similar to King and Teo's sequential integration, synchronization is similar to their reciprocal integration, and convergence is similar to their full integration.

Luftman (2000) suggested five levels of alignment maturity:

- Level 1: Initial/ad hoc process
- Level 2: Committed process
- Level 3: Established focused process
- Level 4: Improved/managed process
- Level 5: Optimized process

Each level can be assessed in terms of six criteria: communications maturity, competency/value maturity, governance maturity, partnership maturity, scope and architecture maturity, and skills maturity. The assessment enables an organization to assess where it is and where it needs to go to attain and sustain business–IT alignment.

Weiss (2006) proposed three business–IT alignment profiles based on two dimensions: internal IT–business integration and external market engagement:

- Technical resource: low levels of IT–business integration and IT–market engagement
- Business enabler: IT deployed in some business processes and some engagement with customers and suppliers
- Strategic weapon: IT used to mobilize and extend the enterprise. There is extensive IT deployment internally and externally.

### Alignment as a Success Measure of Strategic ISP

Another stream of research focuses on alignment as an outcome or success measure of strategic ISP. Researchers have empirically derived the dimensions of strategic ISP success as comprising alignment, analysis, cooperation, and capabilities (Segars and Grover, 1998). These dimensions have been used in subsequent studies to measure strategic ISP success (Newkirk and Lederer, 2006a, 2006b).

## Summary

It is evident that there are different methods of assessment of alignment, which can possibly lead to different results. Hence, it is important for researchers to clearly specify and theoretically justify their assessment method of business–IT alignment. The choice of method depends significantly on the objectives and design of the study.

## FACTORS AFFECTING ALIGNMENT

Researchers have examined a wide range of factors affecting alignment. A summary of research on factors affecting alignment is shown in Table 4.3.

### Positive Contributors to Alignment

Factors that have been found to affect alignment include: style of senior management decision making, volatility of business (and applications development portfolio), complexity of IS organization and management task, status and physical location of the IS manager (Pyburn, 1983), communication between business and IT (Coughlan, Lycett, and Macredie, 2005), firmwide strategy formation processes, extent and nature of the interaction between business and IS management (Broadbent and Weill, 1993), business competence of IS executive (Bassellier and Benbasat, 2004; Teo and King, 1997a), senior executive support for IT, IT involved in strategy development, IT understands the business, business–IT partnership, well-prioritized IT projects, IT demonstrates leadership (Luftman, Papp, and Brier, 1999), informal organization structure (rather than formal organizational structure), communication and understanding between business and IS executives, linked business and IS missions, priorities, strategies, planning processes, and plans, line executive commitment to IS issues and initiatives (Chan, 2002), IT maturity, CEO software knowledge (Hussin, King, and Cragg, 2002), IT infrastructure flexibility (in terms of connectivity, modularity, and IT personnel) (Chung, Rainer, and Lewis, 2003), trading partner's influences, CEO/CIO relationship, Internet-based interorganizational system (IIOS) maturity (Lee, Lin, and Pai, 2005), understanding IT and corporate planning, whether the CIO is a member of senior management, shared culture and good communications, deep commitment to IT planning by senior management, shared plan goals, deep end-user involvement, joint architecture/portfolio selection, identity (compatibility) of plan factors (Scott, 2005), shared understanding (cognitive commonality) between business and IS executives (Tan and Gallupe, 2006), planning sophistication, organizational types (business versus academic), business strategy (defender, prospector, analyzer) (Chan, Sabherwal, and Thrasher, 2006), and organizational emphasis on knowledge management and centralization of IT decisions (Kearns and Sabherwal, 2006/2007).

Other researchers have examined critical success factors associated with alignment. These include the following: top management is committed to the strategic use of IT, IS management is knowledgeable about business, top management has confidence in IS department, the IS department provides efficient and reliable services, there is frequent communication between the user and IS, IS is able to keep up with advances in IT, business and IS work together to prioritize IS development, business goals and objectives are made known to IS management, IS is responsive to user needs, top management is knowledgeable about IT, IS often has creative ideas to deploy IT, business plan is made available to IS management (Teo and Ang, 1999), top management selects an appropriate alignment approach to accomplish business objectives and match the internal IS

78

Table 4.3

**Factors Affecting Alignment**

| Authors | Study | Factors affecting alignment |
|---|---|---|
| Pyburn (1983) | Interviews with IS and senior managers from 8 organizations | Style of senior management decision making, volatility of business (and applications development portfolio), complexity of IS organization and management task, and status and physical location of the IS manager |
| Lederer and Mendelow (1989) | Interviews with IS executives in 20 firms | Top management mandate essential for coordinating business plan and IS plan. Alignment is difficult due to: unclear or unstable business mission, objectives, and priorities; lack of communication; absence of IS management from the BP process; and unrealistic expectations and lack of sophistication of user managers |
| Nath (1989) | 62 IS managers and 46 general managers | IS managers identified: education of upper management in IS, upper management commitment to IS, and a strong set of organizational goals and objectives concerning IS<br><br>General managers identified: education of upper management in IS, ability of IS management to keep up with advances in IT, and education of IS management in business goals and objectives |
| Broadbent and Weill (1993) | Case study of 5 banks in Australia | Flexible and issue-oriented strategy formation process, extent and nature of the interaction between business and IS |
| Brown and Magill (1994) | Interviews + surveys of IS and general managers in 6 multidivisional firms | Importance of antecedents varies with the type of structure. Key antecedents: overall organization (e.g., corporate vision, corporate strategy, firm structure, culture-business unit autonomy, strategic IT role, and CIO role) and IS organization (satisfaction with management of technology, satisfaction with management and use of technology, gaps between current and future applications needs, locus of control). External environment (e.g., industry) was not found to be important |
| Ward and Peppard (1996) | Conceptual paper | Culture gap between business and IT in terms of stories and myths, symbols, rituals and routines, control systems, organizational structures, power structures |
| King and Teo (1997) | Matched-pair survey of 157 business and IS planners | Seven benchmark variables (purpose of integration, role of IS function, primary role of IS executive, triggers for developing IS applications, top management participation in ISP, IS executive participation in BP, and the status of IS executive). Three showed weak relationship (performance criteria for IS function, frequency of user participation in ISP, and assessment of new technologies) |
| Teo and King (1997a) | Matched-pair survey of 157 business and IS planners | Organizational characteristics (information intensity of products/services, information intensity of value chain, top management's perceptions of IT importance, technical competence of IS executive) and environmental characteristics (dynamism, heterogeneity, and hostility) were not significant Only business competence of IS executive was significant |

| Source | Method | Findings |
| --- | --- | --- |
| Teo and King (1997b) | Matched-pair survey of 157 business and IS planners | Perceptual differences in BP–ISP alignment may be caused by inherent differences in roles and responsibilities, by the "education gap," "communication gap," and/ or "culture gap" between business executives and IS executives, by the dynamic nature of the evolutionary process of alignment, and by the natural tendency of IS executives to perceive IS processes as more sophisticated than others do |
| Luftman, Papp, and Brier (1999) | Data from business and IT executives from over 500 firms representing 15 industries | Key enablers: senior executive support for IT, IT involved in strategy development, IT understands business, business–IT partnership, well-prioritized IT projects, and IT demonstrates leadership. Key inhibitors: IT/business lack close relationship, IT does not prioritize well, IT fails to meet its commitment, IT does not understand business, senior executives do not support IT, and IT management lacks leadership |
| Peppard and Ward (1999) | Survey of business and IT management in three organizations | Differences in perceptions in terms of values and beliefs, structures and processes, leadership, service quality, and roles |
| Teo and Ang (1999) | Survey of 136 firms in Singapore | Key critical success factors: top management is committed to the strategic use of IT, IS management is knowledgeable about business, top management has confidence in IS department, IS department provides efficient and reliable services, frequent communication between user and IS, IS is able to keep up with advances in IT, business and IS work together to prioritize IS development, business goals and objectives are made known to IS management, IS is responsive to user needs, top management is knowledgeable about IT, IS often has creative ideas to deploy IT, business plan made available to IS management |
| Burn and Szeto (2000) | Survey of 88 firms | Top management selection of appropriate alignment approach to accomplish business objectives, matching the internal IS with external market |
| Hirschheim and Sabherwal (2001) | Case study of 3 firms | Misalignments could be due to organizational inertia, sequential attention to goals, knowledge gaps pertaining to IS and business strategies, split responsibilities (different executives responsible for different aspects of IS strategies), and underestimation of problems |
| Chan (2002) | Case study of 8 firms with high alignment and performance | Informal organization structure more important than formal organizational structure. Other factors include communication and understanding between business and IS executives, linked business and IS missions, priorities, strategies, planning processes, and plans, and line executive commitment to IS issues and initiatives |
| Hussin, King, and Cragg (2002) | Survey of 256 small UK manufacturing firms | IT maturity and CEO software knowledge are related to alignment. CEO involvement and external IT expertise are not significant |
| Chung, Rainer, and Lewis (2003) | Survey of 200 US/ Canadian firms | IT infrastructure flexibility (in terms of connectivity, modularity, and IT personnel) impact alignment. Compatibility (ability to share data) was not significant |

(continued)

Table 4.3 (continued)

| Authors | Study | Factors affecting alignment |
|---|---|---|
| Kearns and Lederer (2003) | Survey of 161 CIOs | Information intensity positively related to alignment |
| Bassellier and Benbasat (2004) | Survey of 109 IT staff in two organizations | Business competence significantly influences the intentions of IT professionals to develop partnerships with their business clients |
| Kearns and Lederer (2004) | Survey of 161 CIOs | Environmental uncertainty and information intensity were positively associated with alignment |
| Broadbent and Kitzis (2005) | Conceptual paper | Four factors important for building business–IT linkages: CIO leadership, executive team that develops informed expectations of IT-enabled enterprise, IT governance, IT portfolio approach |
| Coughlan, Lycett, and Macredie (2005) | Case study of a UK bank | Communication is important for business–IT alignment |
| Lee, Lin and Pai (2005) | Survey of 202 IS executives in large Taiwanese firms | Trading partner's influences, CEO/CIO relationship, Internet-based interorganizational system maturity (significant). Environmental uncertainly (not significant) |
| Scott (2005) | Conceptual paper | Eight dimensions of linkages: understanding IT and corporate planning, CIO is a member of senior management, shared culture and good communications, deep commitment to IT planning by senior management, shared plan goals, deep end-user involvement, joint architecture/portfolio selection, and identity (compatibility) of plan factors |
| Chan, Sabherwal, and Thrasher (2006) | Two studies of business firms and academic institutions | Planning sophistication promotes shared domain knowledge, which, along with prior IS success, facilitates alignment. Alignment is affected by organizational types (business vs. academic) and by business strategy (defenders, prospectors, analyzers). Organizational size affects alignment for business firms but not academic institutions. Mixed results for environmental uncertainty |
| Tan and Gallupe (2006) | Survey of 80 business and IS executives in 6 firms | Higher level of cognitive commonality is positively related to a higher level of business–IS alignment |
| Kearns and Sabherwal (2006/2007) | Survey of 274 senior information officers | Organizational emphasis on knowledge management and centralization of IT decisions affect top managers' knowledge of IT, which facilitates business managers' participation in strategic IT planning and IT managers' participation in business planning, and both of these planning behaviors affect business–IT strategic alignment. Quality of IT project planning and implementation problems in IT projects mediate the relationship between business–IT strategic alignment and business effect of IT |

with the external market (Burn and Szeto, 2000), CEO leadership, an executive team that develops informed expectations about IT, IT governance, and IT portfolio management (Broadbent and Kitzis, 2005).

Research has also examined alignment from the IS management and business management perspectives. The top three factors identified by IS management were: education of upper management in IS, upper management commitment to IS, and a strong set of organizational goals and objectives concerning IS. In contrast, the top three factors identified by general management were: education of upper management in IS, ability of IS management to keep up with advances in IT, and education of IS management in business goals and objectives (Nath, 1989). It appears that although there is agreement on the importance of educating upper management in IS, there is less agreement on other issues. Hence, it is apparent that perceptual differences do exist between business executives and IS executives. These perceptual differences may be caused by inherent differences in roles and responsibilities, by the "education gap," "communication gap," and/ or "culture gap" between business executives and IS executives, by the dynamic nature of the evolutionary process of alignment, and by the natural tendency of IS executives to perceive IS processes as more sophisticated than others do (Teo and King, 1997b). It is therefore important to understand these perceptual differences so that both IS and general management can take appropriate actions to facilitate greater alignment between business and IS.

In addition, antecedents (overall organization, IS organization, IT investment, external environment) associated with different IS organization designs (centralized, decentralized, hybrid, recentralized) have been examined. The importance of antecedents varies with the type of structure, and key antecedents pertain mainly to the overall organization (e.g., corporate vision, corporate strategy, firm structure, culture-business unit autonomy, strategic IT role, and CIO role) and the IS organization (satisfaction with management of technology, satisfaction with management and use of technology, gaps between current and future applications needs, locus of control). External environment (e.g., industry) was not found to be important (Brown and Magill, 1994).

Researchers have also found the following benchmark variables to be associated with different stages (extent) of alignment: purpose of integration, role of IS function, primary role of IS executive, triggers for developing IS applications, top management participation in ISP, IS executive participation in BP, and the status of IS executive. Three benchmark variables showed a weak relationship with the extent of alignment, namely, performance criteria for IS function, frequency of user participation in ISP, and assessment of new technologies (King and Teo, 1997).

Some factors for which significant relationships with alignment were not found include: top management's perceptions of IT importance, technical competence, environmental characteristics (dynamism, heterogeneity, and hostility) (Teo and King, 1997a), CEO involvement, external IT expertise (Hussin, King, and Cragg, 2002), and compatibility (ability to share data) (Chung, Rainer, and Lewis, 2003).

In addition, factors for which there were mixed results include: information intensity (positive relationship for Kearns and Lederer [2003, 2004], and no relationship for Teo and King [1997a]), environmental uncertainty (positive relationship for Kearns and Lederer [2004], and no relationship for Lee, Lin, and Pai [2005]). Some plausible reasons for mixed results include the use of different measurement scales, the relative importance and mix of factors examined, change in relative importance over time, and the contingent nature of some factors. For example, research has found that organizational size affects alignment for business firms but not academic institutions, and the effect of environmental uncertainty on alignment is dependent on the organizational type and business strategy (Chan, Sabherwal, and Thrasher, 2006).

## Inhibitors of Alignment

Instead of examining positive contributors to alignment, other researchers examine ISP problems or general problems that inhibit alignment. Most research tends to focus on facilitators rather than inhibitors of alignment. Research has generally found the following inhibitors: IT/business lack close relationship, IT does not prioritize well, IT fails to meet its commitment, IT does not understand business, senior executives do not support IT, IT management lacks leadership (Luftman, Papp, and Brier, 1999), unclear or unstable business mission, objectives, and priorities, lack of communication, absence of IS management from the BP process, unrealistic expectations and lack of sophistication of user managers, and lack of top management mandate for coordinating business plan and IS plan (Lederer and Mendelow, 1989). Misalignment has been found to be due to some aspects of business and IS strategies changing in different directions, and could be due to organizational inertia, sequential attention to goals, knowledge gaps pertaining to IS and business strategies, split responsibilities (different executives responsible for different aspects of IS strategies), underestimation of problems (Hirschheim and Sabherwal, 2001), culture gap (Ward and Peppard, 1996), and differences in views between business and IT management in terms of values and beliefs, structures and processes, leadership, service quality, and roles (Peppard and Ward, 1999).

## Summary

Facilitators of alignment have been examined more frequently than inhibitors. As such, there is an obvious need for more studies on how inhibitors can be mitigated and managed. It may also be interesting to examine the strengths of the presence/absence of factors as facilitators/inhibitors. In other words, if the presence of a factor facilitates alignment, does its absence inhibit alignment to the same degree?

## CHANGES IN ALIGNMENT OVER TIME

Another stream of research examines how alignment changes over time. Alignment is generally not a steady state but reflects a dynamic model of change (Burn, 1996). In other words, alignment is an emergent and dynamic concept, and organizations often struggle to bring IS and business strategies into alignment. In addition, there are multiple paths toward alignment (Hirschheim and Sabherwal, 2001; Itami and Numagami, 1992; Teo and King, 1997a). The "punctuated equilibrium" model has been found useful in explaining the dynamics of how alignment (defined in terms of fit among business strategy, IS strategy, business structure, and IS structure) evolves over time (Sabherwal, Hirschheim, and Goles, 2001).

In a similar vein, a coevolutionary view of alignment takes into account the dynamic process of mutual change and adaptation of business and IS strategies over time. Under this view, the conditions and outcomes of the business–IS strategy process not only are a function of strategic alignment and structural alignment but also depend on the internal (e.g., attitudes and experiences) and external (e.g., competitive dynamics and technological change) environments in which the firm is operating (Peppard and Breu, 2003). The notion of coevolution can be expanded by conceptualizing alignment as a series of adjustments and adaptations at three levels: individual (alignment between IS infrastructure and users' needs), operational (alignment between organizational and IS structure), and strategic (alignment of IS strategy with business strategy) (Benbya and McKelvey, 2006).

## Summary

It is important to realize that alignment is not a steady state. Changes in organizational and environmental factors can trigger changes in alignment. Hence, it becomes important for firms to take constant action to rectify any misalignment and to enhance alignment between business and IS.

## IMPACT OF ALIGNMENT

Research on the impact of alignment usually attempts to link alignment with performance. In fact, alignment can be viewed as "the capacity to demonstrate a positive relationship between information technologies and the accepted measures of performance" (Strassmann, 1997, p. 3). A summary of research on the impact of alignment is shown in Table 4.4. Because different studies may define and measure alignment differently, the results may not be directly comparable.

### Positive Relationship Between Alignment and Performance

Alignment tends to improve user perceptions of IS performance (Miller, 1993); hence it is perhaps nor surprising that the impact of alignment on performance has generally been found to be positive. For example, the level of alignment between critical business success factors and IT capabilities has been found to be positively associated with perceived IT success as well as organizational performance (Sabherwal and Kirs, 1994). In a similar vein, IS strategic alignment has been found to be a better predictor of IS effectiveness and business performance than business strategy and IS strategy alone (Chan et al., 1997), and the integration of information and IT needs into the planning process has been found to be associated with IT infrastructure capability (Broadbent, Weill, and Neo, 1999).

In addition, BP–ISP alignment was found to have a significant positive relationship with IS contributions to organizational performance and a significant negative relationship with the extent of ISP problems (Teo and King, 1996). A follow-up analysis revealed that higher levels of alignment had a significant inverse relationship with the extent of both ISP process problems and ISP output problems. In addition, alignment was positively related to the extent of IS contributions to organizational performance in terms of return on investment, market share, internal efficiency, sales revenue, and customer satisfaction (Teo and King, 1999).

Another follow-up analysis was done by examining two modes of ISP—reactive and proactive—based on the extent of BP–ISP alignment using King and Teo's (1997) typology. In the typology, the roles of the IS function for stages 1 and 2 are essentially reactive since ISP has negligible influence on business plans and strategies. In contrast, the roles for stages 3 and 4 are essentially proactive since ISP both supports and influences business plans and strategies. Firms operating in the proactive mode were found to have significantly higher status for IS executives, significantly greater perceived IS contributions to organizational performance, and significantly fewer ISP problems than did those operating in a reactive planning mode (King and Teo, 2000). These studies by King and Teo provide empirical evidence of the usefulness and impact of greater BP–ISP alignment. The results also suggest that the notion of IS contributions to organizational performance might be valid only when there is a high degree of alignment between BP and ISP. In a similar vein, another study found that for IS executives, ISP–BP (IS plans aligning with business plans) and BP–ISP (business plans aligning with IS plans) were associated with use of IS-based resources for competitive advantage while for business executives, only ISP–BP were associated with it (Kearns and Lederer, 2000). Further, strategic alignment has been found to be positively

Table 4.4

## Impact of Alignment

| Authors | Study | Impact of alignment |
|---|---|---|
| **Positive relationship** | | |
| Miller (1993) | Case study of aluminum producer | Alignment improved user perceptions of IS performance |
| Sabherwal and Kirs (1994) | Survey of 244 academic institutions | Alignment between critical business success factors and IT capabilities was positively associated with perceived IT success as well as organizational performance |
| Teo and King (1996) | Matched-pair survey of 157 business and IS planners | Alignment had positive relationship with IS contributions to organizational performance and negative relationship with extent of ISP problems |
| Chan et al. (1997) | Survey of 164 financial services/ manufacturing firms | IS strategic alignment is a better predictor of IS effectiveness and business performance than business strategy and IS strategy alone |
| Broadbent, Weill, and Neo (1999) | Quantitative and qualitative data collected from 26 firms in 7 countries | Integration of information and IT in overall planning processes associated with IT infrastructure capabilities |
| Teo and King (1999) | Matched-pair survey of 157 business planners and IS planners | Alignment had negative relationship with the extent of ISP process problems and ISP output problems. Alignment was positively related to the extent of IS contributions to organizational performance in terms of return on investment, market share, internal efficiency, sales revenue, and customer satisfaction |
| Kearns and Lederer (2000) | Matched-pair survey of business and IS executives | IS executive: ISP–BP and BP–ISP associated with use of IS-based resources for competitive advantage. Business executive: Only ISP–BP associated with IS-based resources for competitive advantage |
| King and Teo (2000) | Matched-pair survey of 157 business and IS planners | Proactive alignment mode had higher status for IS executive, greater perceived IS contributions to organizational performance and fewer ISP problems than did those operating in a reactive alignment mode |
| Tallon, Kraemer, and Gurbaxani (2000) | Survey of 304 firms | Alignment is positively associated with perceived payoffs from IT investments |

| | | |
|---|---|---|
| Cragg, King, and Hussin (2002) | Survey of 250 small UK manufacturing firms | Firms with higher IT alignment achieved better organizational performance than firms with low IT alignment |
| Kearns and Lederer (2003) | Survey of 161 CIOs | ISP reflects BP alignment, but BP does not reflect ISP alignment was positively related to the use of IT for competitive advantage |
| Kearns and Lederer (2004) | Survey of 161 CIOs | Alignment was positively associated with the use of IT for competitive advantage |
| Lee, Lin, and Pai (2005) | Survey of 202 IS executives in large Taiwanese firms | Alignment was significantly associated with Internet-based interorganizational system contributions to organizational performance |
| Ness (2005) | Survey of 86 IT executives | Although both IT flexibility and alignment have positive relationships with performance, the effect from IT flexibility is stronger than alignment |
| Kearns and Sabherwal (2006/2007) | Survey of 274 senior information officers | Quality of IT project planning and implementation problems in IT projects mediate the relationship between business–IT strategic alignment and business effect of IT |
| **No relationship** | | |
| Palmer and Markus (2000) | Survey of 80 specialty retailers | No relationship between alignment and business performance |
| **Mixed results** | | |
| Bergeron, Raymond, and Rivard (2001) | Survey of 110 firms | Significant effects were found for mediation, covariation, profile deviation, and gestalts. No effects were found for moderation and matching |
| Sabherwal and Chan (2001) | Two multirespondent surveys of 164 and 62 firms | Alignment seems to influence overall business success in prospectors and analyzers but not in defenders |
| Tallon and Kraemer (2003) | Survey of 63 firms | Positive relationship between alignment and IT payoffs. But result valid up to certain point, beyond which alignment leads to decreased IT payoffs |
| Bergeron, Raymond and Rivard (2004) | Survey of 110 CEOs/managers | Some mixed results but generally, conflictual coalignment patterns of business strategy, business structure, IT strategy, and IT structure will exhibit lower levels of business performance |

(continued)

Table 4.4 *(continued)*

| Authors | Study | Impact of alignment |
|---|---|---|
| Chan, Sabherwal, and Thrasher (2006) | Two studies of business firms and academic institutions | Alignment is positively related to organizational performance. But results more applicable to prospectors and analyzers than to defenders |
| **Alignment as moderator of performance** | | |
| Papp (1999) | Eighteen financial measures based on Fortune's survey of over 500 firms | Partial support for alignment as a moderator of the relationship between industry and financial factor determinants and firm performance |
| Byrd, Lewis, and Byran (2006) | Matched-pair survey of 84 business and IT managers | Alignment as moderator between IT investment and performance |
| Oh and Pinsonneault (2007) | Matched-pair survey 110 CEOs and CIOs | Mixed results depending on choice of performance measures (expense, revenue, and perceived profitability) and assessment of alignment (moderator vs. matching). Moderator approach was found to be better than matching approach in explaining firm performance |

associated with perceived payoffs from IT investments (Tallon, Kraemer, and Gurbaxani, 2000). In other words, firms with higher IT alignment achieved better organizational performance than firms with low IT alignment (Cragg, King, and Hussin, 2002). Alignment was also found to be significantly associated with IIOS contributions to organizational performance (Lee et al., 2005) and the use of IT for competitive advantage (Kearns and Lederer, 2003, 2004).

Other research examined the role of mediating variables between alignment and performance. For example, the quality of IT project planning and implementation problems in IT projects have been found to mediate the relationship between business–IT strategic alignment and the business effect of IT (Kearns and Sabherwal, 2006/2007).

## No Relationship and Mixed Results for Relationship Between Alignment and Performance

Some research has also failed to find a significant relationship between alignment and performance (e.g., Palmer and Markus, 2000). One possible reason is that the way alignment is measured may affect whether significant results are obtained (e.g., Bergeron, Raymond, and Rivard, 2001). Another reason is that the choice of performance measures may also affect the results—for example, it may be easier to relate alignment to cost reduction/savings than to revenue generation as the latter also tend to be affected by other factors such as competition and environmental uncertainty (Oh and Pinsonneault, 2007). Other studies show that alignment has some effect on performance in some situations; for example, alignment seemed to influence overall business success in prospectors and analyzers but not in defenders (Sabherwal and Chan, 2001). In a follow-up study using data from Sabherwal and Chan (2001) and Sabherwal and Kirs (1994), alignment was found to be positively related to organizational performance. While this result holds for prospectors and analyzers, there are mixed results for defenders (since the result was significant for academic institutions but not for business firms) (Chan, Sabherwal, and Thrasher, 2006). In a similar vein, another study found that although conflictual coalignment patterns of business strategy, business structure, IT strategy, and IT structure would generally exhibit lower levels of business performance, there were some mixed results (Bergeron, Raymond, and Rivard, 2004).

Despite the general view that alignment is important, there are some concerns about whether more alignment is better. In a survey of sixty-three firms, although a positive relationship between alignment and IT payoffs was found, this result was valid up to a certain point, beyond which alignment leads to decreased IT payoffs, thereby leading to an "alignment paradox" (Tallon and Kraemer, 2003). This paradox can be explained by the notion that tight fit or alignment might reduce strategic flexibility for firms that compete on a global scale (Jarvenpaa and Ives, 1994). The importance of flexibility is reinforced by a study finding that flexibility has a stronger relationship with performance than alignment (Ness, 2005). It is important to note that IT is often labeled as strategic (or aligned with a strategic plan) in order to secure the necessary IT investments. Consequently, the nature and direction of the alignment between IT and corporate strategy may be unclear (Powell, 1993). Further, while some research has found a positive relationship between alignment and performance, there are many factors that affect performance, and establishing a direct causal link between alignment and performance is often difficult.

## Alignment as a Moderator of Performance

Other research views alignment not as a direct contributor to performance but as a moderator of the relationship between some determinant variable and business performance. For example, earnings per share have a significant effect on overall firm performance when moderated by alignment (Papp, 1999). In a similar vein, strategic alignment was found to be a moderator of the relationship between IT investment and business performance (Byrd, Lewis, and Bryan, 2006). The moderator approach for assessing alignment appears to be better than the matching approach in explaining firm performance (Oh and Pinsonneault, 2007). Other researchers found that factors other than alignment may be more important in affecting performance. For example, although IT flexibility and alignment have positive relationships to performance, the effect from IT flexibility on performance is stronger than that from alignment (Ness, 2005).

## Summary

Past research has generally found evidence of the benefits of alignment. However, how alignment impacts performance may depend on the choice of performance measures, how alignment is assessed, and the nature of the independent variables examined. Hence, the relationship between alignment and performance may be more complex than envisioned as it depends on other factors as well.

## DIRECTIONS FOR FUTURE RESEARCH

In this section, we synthesize the business–IT alignment literature and offer some suggestions for future research.

### Bivariate to Holistic to Process Conceptualization of Alignment

Alignment has moved from bivariate conceptualization (e.g., linking business strategies and IS strategies, business structures and IS structures) to a more holistic conceptualization based on Henderson and Venkatraman's (1993) work. Research has also shown that holistic conceptualization is better than bivariate conceptualization. Further, Van der Zee and De Jong (1999, p. 138) suggest that:

> The continuously growing importance of IT requires organizations to integrate IT decisions with their common planning and decision-making processes at all organizational levels. Trying to align distinct and separate business and IT management processes is just not enough!

Research has also moved forward to incorporate a dynamic perspective emphasizing that alignment is not an event but a process of continuous adaptation and change (Henderson and Venkatraman, 1993). Hence, there are various paths to alignment and there is a constant need to adjust alignment over time as strategies coevolve (Peppard and Breu, 2003).

While there is a trend toward examining alignment processes or various paths to alignment (e.g., Hirschheim and Sabherwal, 2001), it is important to examine in greater detail how business and IS can coevolve and maintain alignment as conditions change. Hence, looking at the dynamics of alignment rather than just the process of alignment would lead to better insights on how to maintain alignment in this increasingly turbulent world. For example, examining cases of how firms that were initially aligned became misaligned and consequently regained alignment would shed some light on the issue of the various steps that firms could take to maintain alignment and correct/minimize misalignment. Future research should also examine the coevolutionary and emergent nature of alignment (Benbya and McKelvey, 2006).

## Internal Factors Affect Alignment More Than External Factors

Researchers have investigated various organizational factors affecting alignment, including IS characteristics (e.g., business knowledge of IS executive, status of IS executive), business characteristics (e.g., top management support, informal organization structure), and relationships between business and IS (e.g., CEO/CIO relationship, communication between business and IS executives). The external environment is generally found to play a lesser role in alignment than the internal environment. While such "variance research" has shed some light on the factors affecting alignment, it is important to move beyond "variance research" to "process research" to examine the interplay among the different variables affecting alignment.

## Trend Toward Integrated Planning

The literature has generally found evidence of the trend toward integrated planning where business planning and IS planning are done concurrently in the same process and at the same time. Teo and King (1997) call it "integrated planning" while Hoque and others (2005) call it "convergence." More research on integrated planning is needed. For example, the balanced business scorecard (which includes four perspectives—financial, customer, business processes, and organizational learning—to assess performance) (Kaplan and Norton, 1996) can be used to facilitate the implementation of an integrated business and IT planning and evaluation process (Van der Zee and De Jong, 1999).

In fact, misalignment is inherent in our current conceptualizations of alignment as there is a time lag due to the "leader–follower" relationship between business (as leader) and IS (as follower) (Smaczny, 2001). Consequently, as long as business strategy and IS strategy are developed separately, it will be very difficult to ensure continuous alignment in a rapidly changing environment. The remedy is to ensure that IS strategy is developed at the same time as business strategy, thereby making alignment inherent in the process of integrated planning rather than attempting to align business and IS separately. Further, a survey that attempts to forecast IT in 2010 found that respondents predicted that "strategy development and execution for both business and IT will become a collaborative effort to deliver enterprise value" (Smith and McKeen, 2006, p. 130). For example, there is no explicit technology strategy at Toyota because it is inherent in their business strategy. Further, Toyota has a very clear understanding of the role technology plays in supporting and enabling business processes (Duvall, 2006). This again points to the trend toward integrated planning. Hence, integrated planning is likely to be more common when IS is viewed as a part of business as highlighted by Sauer and Yetton (1997, p. 53):

> IT needs to become part of the business rather than be treated as something "out there" that needs to be passively aligned with the business. Success will come to those who make IT managers an integral part of defining business opportunities and not simply the builders of other managers' solutions.

## IS Role and Types of Alignment

Since there are various typologies of alignment as well as different roles of IS in different firms, research linking the role of IS to various types of alignment could shed some light on their relationship, and consequently help in devising appropriate strategies to enhance alignment. In other words, the type and nature of alignment often depends on how IS is viewed in the firm. Previous research has examined the type of business strategy (defender, analyzer, and prospector) and alignment (e.g., Chan, Sabherwal, and Thrasher, 2006) but has not linked the role of IS (e.g., as defined by McFarlan and McKenney's [1983] strategic grid) to alignment. It is plausible that the key reason why all firms do not practice integrated planning is that IS is viewed differently in different firms and hence, the importance and need for integrated planning may vary.

**Potential Drawbacks to Alignment**

Alignment theory generally contends that more alignment is better and that alignment leads to better performance. While the conceptual arguments favoring alignment appear logical and most researchers have found support for the positive impact of alignment, some researchers (e.g., Jarvenpaa and Ives, 1993) have found evidence that more alignment is not necessarily better. It would be useful to conduct more research on the alignment paradox (Tallon and Kraemer, 2003) to determine the conditions under which more alignment is good, as well as the conditions under which more alignment could change from good to detrimental. Such research may help to explain some of the mixed findings of the effect of alignment on performance. Further, misalignment can often lead to learning that could result in IS being used in effective but unplanned ways (Ciborra, 1997).

**Need to Examine "Unplanned" Versus "Planned" Alignment**

Previous research has examined factors affecting alignment and the alignment of strategies, structures, and so on. But tinkering, rather than conscious alignment, is responsible for aligned IT applications (Ciborra, 1992). While there are various formal strategic planning methodologies to facilitate alignment (IBM, 1981; Ward and Pepper, 2002), further research is needed on how IS can be "tinkered" with to be aligned to business and leveraged for business transformation and innovation. Encouraging more research on "tinkering" (unplanned) rather than "what to align" (planned) aspects of alignment, would provide new insights that are directly relevant to industry. However, to do so, we need to approach the study of alignment by examining actual cases of how "tinkering" leads to alignment, or specifically, examining actual practices in organizations (Ciborra, 1998).

**Aligning IS to Business Versus How IS Can Transform and Drive the Business**

Given the increasing ubiquity of IS in business operations, the issue facing businesses appears to be less how to align IS to business and more how IS can be used to transform and drive the business. Hence, while aligning IS may be a key issue from the IS executives' perspective, at the practical level, businesses are more concerned with how to leverage IS to streamline and transform business operations and enhance business competitiveness. The status of IS in businesses will be enhanced when IS has improved its credibility by demonstrating how it can contribute to the firm's competitiveness and bottom line.

**ACKNOWLEDGMENTS**

I thank the reviewers and editor for their insightful comments and suggestions.

# REFERENCES

Avison, D.; Jones, J.; Powell, P.; and Wilson, D. 2004. Using and validating the strategic alignment model. *Journal of Strategic Information Systems,* 13, 3, 223–246.

Ball, L., and Harris, R. 1982. SMIS members: a membership analysis. *MIS Quarterly,* 6, 1, 19–38.

Bassellier, G., and Benbasat, I. 2004. Business competence of information technology professionals: conceptual development and influence on IT-business partnerships. *MIS Quarterly,* 28, 4, 673–694.

Benbya, H., McKelvey, B. 2006. Using coevolutionary and complexity theories to improve IS alignment: a multi-level approach. *Journal of Information Technology,* 21, 284–298.

Bergeron, F.; Raymond, L.; and Rivard, S. 2001. Fit in strategic information technology management research: an empirical comparison of perspectives. *Omega* 29, 2, 125–142.

———. 2004. Ideal patterns of strategic alignment and business performance. *Information & Management,* 41, 8, 1003–1020.

Bowman, B.J.; Davis, G.B.; and Wetherbe, J.C. 1983. Three stage model of MIS planning. *Information & Management,* 6, 3, 11–25.

Brancheau, J.C., and Wetherbe, J.C. 1987. Key issues in information systems management. *MIS Quarterly,* 11, 1, 23–45.

Brancheau, J.C.; Janz, B.D.; and Wetherbe, J.C. 1996. Key issues in information systems management: 1994–95 SIM Delphi results. *MIS Quarterly,* 20, 2, 225–242.

Broadbent, M., and Kitzis, E. 2005. Interweaving business-driven IT strategy and execution: four foundation factors. *Ivey Business Journal,* 69, 3, 1–6.

Broadbent, M., and Weill, P. 1993. Improving business and information strategy alignment: learning from the banking industry. *IBM Systems Journal,* 32, 1, 162–179.

Broadbent, M.; Weill, P.; and Neo, B.S. 1999. Strategic context and patterns of IT infrastructure capability. *Journal of Strategic Information Systems,* 8, 2, 157–187.

Brown, C.V. 1997. Examining the emergence of hybrid IS governance solutions: evidence from a single case study. *Information Systems Research,* 8, 1, 69–94.

Brown, C.V., and Magill, S.L. 1994. Alignment of the IS functions with the enterprise: toward a model of antecedents. *MIS Quarterly,* 18, 4, 371–403.

Brown, C.V., and Renwick, J.S. 1996. Alignment of the IS organization: the special case of corporate acquisitions. *Data Base for Advances in Information Systems,* 27, 4, 25–33.

Burn, J.M. 1996. IS innovation and organizational alignment—a professional juggling act. *Journal of Information Technology,* 11, 1, 3–12.

Burn, J.M., and Szeto, C. 2000. A comparison of the views of business and IT management on success factors for strategic alignment. *Information & Management,* 37, 4, 197–216.

Byrd, T.A.; Lewis, B.R.; and Bryan, R.W. 2006. The leveraging influence of strategic alignment on IT investment: an empirical examination. *Information and Management,* 43, 3, 308–321.

Chan, Y.E. 2002. Why haven't we mastered alignment? the importance of the informal organization structure. *MIS Quarterly Executive,* 1, 2, 97–112.

Chan, Y.E., and Huff, S.L. 1993. Strategic information systems alignment. *Business Quarterly,* 58, 1, 51–56.

Chan, Y.E.; Sabherwal, R.; and Thrasher, J.B. 2006. Antecedents and outcomes of strategic IS alignment: an empirical investigation. *IEEE Transactions on Engineering Management,* 53, 1, 27–47.

Chan, Y.E.; Huff, S.L.; Barclay, D.W.; and Copeland, D.G. 1997. Business strategic orientation, information systems strategic orientation, and strategic alignment. *Information Systems Research,* 8, 2, 125–150.

Chandler, A.D. 1962. *Strategy and Structure: Chapters in the History of the Industrial Enterprise.* Boston, MA: MIT Press.

Chung, S.H.; Rainer, R.K., Jr.; and Lewis, B.R. 2003. The impact of information technology infrastructure flexibility on strategic alignment and applications implementation. *Communications of AIS,* 11, 191–206.

Ciborra, C.U. 1992. From thinking to tinkering: the grassroots of strategic information systems. *The Information Society,* 8, 4, 297–309.

———. 1997. De profundis? deconstructing the concept of strategic alignment. *Scandinavian Journal of Information Systems,* 9, 1, 67–82.

———. 1998. Crisis and foundations: an inquiry into the nature and limits of models and methods in the information systems discipline. *Journal of Strategic Information Systems,* 7, 1, 5–16.

Coughlan, J.; Lycett, M.; and Macredie, R.D. 2005. Understanding the business–IT relationship. *International Journal of Information Management,* 25, 4, 303–319.

Cragg, P.; King, M.; and Hussin, H. 2002. IT alignment and firm performance in small manufacturing firms. *Journal of Strategic Information Systems*, 11, 2, 109–132.

Das, S.R.; Zahra, S.A.; and Warkentin, M.E. 1991. Integrating the content and process of strategic MIS planning with competitive strategy. *Decision Sciences*, 22, 5, 953–984.

Dickson, G.W.; Leitheiser, R.L.; Wetherbe, J.C.; and Nechis, M. 1984. Key information systems issues for the 1980's. *MIS Quarterly*, 8, 3, 135–159.

Drazin, R., and van de Ven, A.H. 1985. Alternative forms of fit in contingency theory. *Administrative Science Quarterly*, 30, 4, 514–539.

Duvall, M. 2006. What's driving Toyota? *Baseline*, September, 37–53.

Earl, M.J. 1993. Experiences in strategic information systems planning. *MIS Quarterly*, 17, 1, 1–24.

Ein-Dor, P., and Segev, E. 1982. Organizational computing and MIS structure: some empirical evidence. *MIS Quarterly*, 6, 3, 55–68.

Fiedler, K.D.; Grover, V.; and Teng, J.T.C. 1996. An empirically derived taxonomy of information technology structure and its relationship to organizational structure. *Journal of Management Information Systems*, 13, 1, 9–34.

Goldsmith, N. 1991. Linking IT planning to business strategy. *Long Range Planning*, 24, 6, 67–77.

Hartdog, C., and Herbert, M. 1986. 1985 opinion survey of MIS managers: key issues. *MIS Quarterly*, 10, 4, 350–361.

Henderson, J.C., and Sifonis, J.G. 1988. The value of strategic IS planning: understanding consistency, validity, and IS markets. *MIS Quarterly*, 12, 2, 186–200.

Henderson, J.C., and Venkatraman, N. 1993. Strategic alignment: leveraging information technology for transforming organizations. *IBM Systems Journal*, 32, 1, 4–16.

Henderson, J.C.; Rockart, J.F.; and Sifonis, J.G. 1987. Integrating management support systems into strategic information systems planning. *Journal of Management Information Systems*, 4, 1, 5–24.

Hirschheim, R., and Sabherwal, R. 2001. Detours in the path toward strategic information systems alignment. *California Management Review*, 44, 1, 87–108.

Hong, K.K., and Kim, Y.G. 2002. The critical success factors for ERP implementation: an organizational fit perspective. *Information and Management*, 40, 1, 25–40.

Hoque, F.; Sambamurthy, V.; Zmud, R.; Trainer, T.; and Wilson, C. 2005. *Winning the 3-Legged Race*. Englewood Cliffs, NJ: Prentice Hall.

Hussin, H.; King, M.; and Cragg, P. 2002. IT alignment in small firms. *European Journal of Information Systems*, 11, 2, 108–127.

IBM. 1981. *Business Systems Planning: Information Systems Planning Guide*. GE20–0527–3.

Itami, H., and Numagami, T. 1992. Dynamic interaction between strategy and technology. *Strategic Management Journal*, 13, 119–132.

Ives, B., and Learmonth, G.P. 1984. The information system as a competitive weapon. *Communications of the ACM*, 27, 12, 1193–1201.

Jarvenpaa, S.L., and Ives, B. 1993. Organizing for global competition: The fit of information technology. *Decision Sciences*, 24, 3, 547–580.

———. 1994. Organizational fit and flexibility: IT design principles for a globally competing firm. In C.C. Snow (ed.), *Strategy, Organization Design and Human Resource Management* 3. Greenwich, CT: JAI Press, pp. 1–39.

Jordan, E., and Tricker, B. 1995. Information strategy: alignment with organization structure. *Journal of Strategic Information Systems*, 4, 4, 357–382.

Kanellis, P.; Lycett, M.; and Paul, R.J. Evaluating business information system fit: from concept to practical application. *European Journal of Information Systems*, 8, 1, 65–76.

Kaplan, R.S., and Norton, D.P. 1996. *Translating Strategy into Action: The Balanced Scorecard*. Boston: Harvard Business School Press.

Karimi, J.; Gupta, Y.P.; and Somers, T.M. 1996. The congruence between a firm's competitive strategy and information technology leader's rank and role. *Journal of Management Information Systems*, 13, 1, 63–88.

Kearns, G., and Sabherwal, R. 2006/2007. Strategic alignment between business and information technology: a knowledge-based view of behaviors, outcome, and consequences. *Journal of Management Information Systems*, 23, 3, 129–162.

Kearns, G.S., and Lederer, A.L. 2000. The effect of strategic alignment on the use of IS-based resources for competitive advantage. *Journal of Strategic Information Systems*, 9, 4, 265–293.

————. 2003. A resource-based view of strategic IT alignment: how knowledge sharing creates competitive advantage. *Decision Sciences*, 34, 1, 1–29.

————. 2004. The impact of industry contextual factors on IT focus and the use of IT for competitive advantage. *Information & Management*, 41, 7, 899–919.

Keen, P.G.W. 1993. Information technology and the management difference: a fusion map. *IBM Systems Journal*, 32, 1, 17–39.

Khandelwal, V.K. 2001. An empirical study of misalignment between Australian CEOs and IT managers. *Journal of Strategic Information Systems*, 10, 1, 15–28.

King, W.R. 1978. Strategic planning for management information systems. *MIS Quarterly*, 2, 1, 27–37.

King, W.R., and Cleland, D. 1975. A new method for strategic systems planning. *Business Horizons*, 18, 4, 55–64.

King, W.R., and Teo, T.S.H. 1997. Integration between business planning and information systems planning: validating a stage hypothesis. *Decision Sciences*, 28, 2, 279–308.

————. 2000. Assessing the impact of proactive versus reactive modes of strategic information systems planning. *Omega*, 28, 6, 667–679.

King, W.R., and Zmud, R.W. 1981. Managing information systems: policy planning, strategic planning and operational planning. *Proceedings of the Second International Conference on Information Systems*, Cambridge, MA, 299–308.

Lederer, A.L., and Mendelow, A.L. 1989. Coordination of information systems plans with business plans. *Journal of Management Information Systems*, 6, 2, 5–19.

Lee, G.G.; Lin, H.F.; and Pai, J.C. 2005. Influence of environmental and organizational factors on the success of Internet-based interorganizational systems planning. *Internet Research: Electronic Networking Applications and Policy*, 15, 5, 527–543.

Leifer, R. 1988. Matching computer-based information systems with organizational structures. *MIS Quarterly*, 12, 1, 62–73.

Luftman, J. 2000. Assessing business–IT alignment maturity. *Communications of AIS*, 14, 4, 1–49.

————. 2005. Key issues for IT executives 2004. *MIS Quarterly Executive*, 4, 2, 269–286.

Luftman, J., and Brier, T. 1999. Achieving and sustaining business–IT alignment. *California Management Review*, 42, 1, 109–122.

Luftman, J., and McLean, E.R. 2004. Key issues for IT executives. *MIS Quarterly Executive*, 3, 2, 89–104.

Luftman, J.; Kempaiah, R.; and Nash, E. 2006. Key issues for IT executives. *MIS Quarterly Executive*, 5, 2, 81–99.

Luftman, J.; Papp, R.; and Brier, T. 1999. Enablers and inhibitors of business–IT alignment. *Communications of AIS*, 1, 11, 1–32.

Luftman, J.N. 1996. *Competing in the Information Age-Strategic Alignment in Practice*. New York: Oxford University Press.

Luftman, J.N.; Lewis, P.R.; and Oldach, S.H. 1993. Transforming the enterprise: the alignment of business and information technology strategies. *IBM Systems Journal*, 32, 1, 198–221.

McFarlan, F.W., and McKenney, J.L. 1983. *Corporate Information Systems Management*. Homewood, IL: Richard D. Irwin.

Miller, J. 1993. Measuring and aligning information systems with the organization: a case study. *Information & Management*, 25, 4, 217–228.

Nath, R. 1989. Aligning MIS with business goals. *Information and Management*, 16, 2, 71–79.

Ness, L.R. 2005. Assessing the relationships among IT flexibility, strategic alignment and IT effectiveness: study overview and findings. *Journal of Information Technology Management*, 16, 2, 1–17.

Newkirk, H.E., and Lederer, A.L. 2006a. Incremental and comprehensive strategic information systems planning in an uncertain environment. *IEEE Transactions on Engineering Management*, 53, 3, 380–394.

————. 2006b. The effectiveness of strategic information systems planning under environmental uncertainty. *Information and Management*, 43, 4, 481–501.

Niederman, F.; Brancheau, J.C.; and Wetherbe, J.C. 1991. Information systems management issues in the 1990s. *MIS Quarterly*, 15, 4, 474–499.

Oh, W., and Pinsonneault, A. 2007. On the assessment of the strategic value of information technologies: conceptual and analytical approaches. *MIS Quarterly*, 31, 2, 239–265.

Palmer, J.W., and Markus, M.L. 2000. The performance impacts of quick response and strategic alignment in specialty retailing. *Information Systems Research*, 11, 3, 241–259.

Papp, R. 1998. Alignment of business and information technology strategy: how and why. *Information Management,* 11, 3/4, 6–11.

———. 1999. Business-IT alignment: productivity paradox payoff? *Industrial Management and Data Systems,* 99, 8, 367–373.

Peak, D.C.; Guynes, S.; and Kroon, V. 2005. Information technology alignment planning: a case study. *Information & Management,* 42, 5, 635–649.

Peppard, J., and Breu, K. 2003. Beyond alignment: a coevolutionary view of the information systems strategy process. *Proceedings of the Twenty-Fourth International Conference on Information Systems,* Seattle, WA, 743–750.

Peppard, J., and Ward, J. 1999. "Mind the gap": diagnosing the relationship between the IT organisation and the rest of the business. *Journal of Strategic Information Systems,* 8, 1, 29–60.

Pollalis, Y.A. 2003. Patterns of co-alignment in information-intensive organizations: business performance through integration strategies. *International Journal of Information Management,* 23, 6, 469–492.

Porter, M.E., and Millar, V.E. 1985. How information gives you competitive advantage. *Harvard Business Review,* 63, 4, 149–160.

Powell, P. 1993. Causality in the alignment of information technology and business strategy. *Journal of Strategic Information Systems,* 2, 4, 320–334.

Premkumar, G.; Ramamurthy, K.; and Saunders, C.S. 2005. Information processing view of organizations: an exploratory examination of fit in the context of interorganizational relationships. *Journal of Management Information Systems,* 22, 1, 257–294.

Pyburn, P.J. 1983. Linking the MIS plan with corporate strategy: an exploratory study. *MIS Quarterly,* 7, 2, 1–14.

Rackoff, N.; Wiseman, C.; and Ullrich, W.A. 1985. Information systems for competitive advantage: implementations of a planning process. *MIS Quarterly,* 9, 4, 285–294.

Reich, B.H., and Benbasat, I. 1996. Measuring the linkage between business and information technology objectives. *MIS Quarterly,* 20, 1, 55–81.

———. 2000. Factors that influence the social dimension of alignment between business and information technology. *MIS Quarterly,* 24, 1, 81–113.

Rockart, J.F. 1979. Chief executives define their own data needs. *Harvard Business Review,* 57, 2, 81–93.

Sabherwal, R., and Chan, Y.E. 2001. Alignment between business and IS strategies: a study of prospectors, analyzers, and defenders. *Information Systems Research,* 12, 1, 11–33.

Sabherwal, R., and Kirs, P. 1994. The alignment between organizational critical success factors and information technology capability in academic institutions. *Decision Sciences,* 25, 2, 301–330.

Sabherwal, R.; Hirschheim, R.; and Goles, T. 2001. The dynamics of alignment: insights from a punctuated equilibrium model. *Organization Science,* 12, 2, 179–197.

Sauer, C., and Yetton, P. 1997. *Steps to the Future: Fresh Thinking on the Management of IT-based Organizational Transformation.* San Francisco, CA: Jossey-Bass.

Scott, G.M. 2005. Still not solved: the persistent problem of IT strategic planning. *Communications of the AIS,* 16, 904–936.

Segars, A.H., and Grover, V. 1998. Strategic information systems planning success: an investigation of the construct and its measurement. *MIS Quarterly,* 22, 2, 139–163.

Simmers, C.A. 2002. Aligning Internet usage with business priorities. *Communications of the ACM,* 45, 1, 71–74.

Slaughter, S.A.; Levine, L.; Ramesh, B.; Pries-Heje, J.; and Baskerville, R. 2006. Aligning software processes with strategy. *MIS Quarterly,* 30, 4, 891–918.

Smaczny, T. 2001. Is an alignment between business and information technology the appropriate paradigm to manage IT in today's organizations? *Management Decision,* 39, 10, 797–802.

Smith, H.A., and McKeen, J.D. 2006. IT in 2010: the next frontier. *MIS Quarterly Executive,* 5, 3, 125–136.

Soh, C., and Sia, S.K. 2004. An institutional perspective on sources of ERP package-organization misalignments. *Journal of Strategic Information Systems,* 13, 4, 375–397.

———. 2005. The challenges of implementing "vanilla" versions of enterprise systems. *MIS Quarterly Executive,* 4, 3, 373–384.

Sowa, J.F., and Zachman, J.A. 1992. Extending and formalizing the framework for information systems architecture. *IBM Systems Journal,* 31, 3, 590–616.

Strassmann, P.A. 1997. *The Squandered Computer: Evaluating the Business Alignment of Information Technologies.* New Canaan, CT: Information Economics Press.

Synnott, W.R. 1987. *The Information Weapon: Winning Customers and Markets with Technology.* New York: Wiley.

Tallon, P., and Kraemer, K. 2003. Investigating the relationship between strategic alignment and IT business value: the discovery of a paradox. In N. Shin (ed.), *Creating Business Value with Information Technology: Challenges and Solutions.* Hershey, PA: Idea Group Publishing, pp. 1–22.

Tallon, P.P.; Kraemer, K.L.; and Gurbaxani, V. 2000. Executives' perceptions of the business value of information technology: a process-oriented approach. *Journal of Management Information Systems,* 16, 4, 145–173.

Tan, F.B., and Gallupe, R.B. 2006. Aligning business and information systems thinking: a cognitive approach. *IEEE Transactions on Engineering Management,* 53, 2, 223–237.

Tavakolian, H. 1989. Linking the information technology structure with organizational competitive strategy: a survey. *MIS Quarterly,* 13, 3, 308–317.

Teo, T.S.H., and Ang, S.K. 1999. Critical success factors in the alignment of IS plans with business plans. *International Journal of Information Management,* 19, 2, 173–185.

Teo, T.S.H., and King, W.R. 1996. Assessing the impact of integrating business planning and IS planning. *Information and Management,* 30, 6, 309–321.

———. 1997a. Integration between business planning and information systems planning: an evolutionary-contingency perspective. *Journal of Management Information Systems,* 14, 1, 185–214.

———. 1997b. An assessment of perceptual differences in information systems research. *Omega International Journal of Management Science,* 25, 5, 557–566.

———. 1999. An empirical study of the impacts of integrating business planning and information systems planning. *European Journal of Information Systems,* 8, 3, 200–210.

Van der Zee, J.T.M., and De Jong, B. 1999. Alignment is not enough: integrating business and information technology management with the balanced scorecard. *Journal of Management Information Systems,* 16, 2, 137–156.

Venkatraman, N. 1989. The concept of fit in strategy research. *Academy of Management Review,* 14, 3, 423–444.

Ward, J., and Peppard, J. 1996. Reconciling the IT/business relationship: a troubled marriage in need of guidance. *Journal of Strategic Information Systems,* 5, 1, 37–65.

———. 2002. *Strategic Planning for Information Systems,* 3d ed. Chichester, UK: Wiley.

Watson, R.T.; Kelly, G.G.; Galliers, R.D.; and Brancheau, J.C. 1997. Key issues in information systems management: an international perspective. *Journal of Management Information Systems,* 13, 4, 91–115.

Weiss, J.W.; Thorogood, A.; and Clark, K.D. 2006. Three IT-business alignment profiles: technical resource, business enabler, and strategic weapon. *Communications of the AIS,* 18, 676–691.

Wijnhoven, F.; Spil, T.; Stegwee, R.; and Fa, R.T.A. 2006. Post-merger IT integration strategies: an IT alignment perspective. *Journal of Strategic Information Systems,* 15, 1, 5–28.

Wolf, J., and Egelholf, W.G. 2002. A reexamination and extension of international strategy-structure theory. *Strategic Management Journal,* 23, 2, 181–189.

Zachman, J.A. 1982. Business systems planning and business information control study: a comparison. *IBM Systems Journal,* 21, 1, 31–53.

———. 1987. A framework for information systems architecture. *IBM Systems Journal,* 26, 3, 276–292.

Zviran, M. 1990. Relationship between organizational and information systems objectives: some empirical evidence. *Journal of Management Information Systems,* 7, 1, 65–84.

# CHAPTER 5

# THE ROLE OF DYNAMIC ORGANIZATIONAL CAPABILITIES IN CREATING, RENEWING, AND LEVERAGING INFORMATION SYSTEMS COMPETENCIES

## GANESH D. BHATT

*Abstract: One of the critical questions in information systems (IS) planning and strategy development has been to understand how a firm creates, renews, and exploits IS competencies for business advantage. Drawing from the resource-based view (RBV) of the firm, we show how dynamic organizational capabilities provide necessary mechanisms for creating, renewing, and leveraging IS competencies at the firm level. Dynamic organizational capabilities, which create, renew, and exploit IS competencies, are related, but different in nature. Capabilities that create and renew competencies deal with the characteristics of existing competencies and specific resources that are transformed into competencies, and capabilities that exploit competencies for business advantages pertain to the coordination of functional-level competencies. Dynamic organizational capabilities can help a firm reconfigure and recombine its resources and existing competencies so that each portfolio of competencies is well balanced to provide sustainable advantages.*

*Keywords: IS Competencies, Dynamic Capabilities, IS Strategy, Business Advantages*

Information systems (IS) planning has gone through several eras of change. Traditionally, IS planning was conducted without considering the overall perspective of the business, because the main aim of using systems was to perform back-office service functions. Therefore, the chief concern of IS planning was to recommend those systems that could perform these functions efficiently. In the next stage, the IS planning exercise was performed with an understanding of business plans and strategies. Here, the main concern of IS planning was to support business processes and strategy (King, 1978). In recent years, the process of IS planning has gone through radical changes. Not only is IS planning conducted in conjunction with business planning, but also business plans and strategies are fashioned to leverage the potential of IS. This integration of IS planning with business planning creates opportunities for the firm to specify the IS competencies that it believes best suit its goals and abilities.

As the significance of IS planning has continually grown, so has the need to better understand how information systems lead to business advantage. In the classical perspective, the arguments for competitive advantage were framed under the rubric of industrial organizations. In this perspective, IS may be deployed to raise entry barriers, increase bargaining power with suppliers and customers, offer new products and services, or change the rules of competition (McFarlan, 1984; Porter and Millar, 1985). Based on Williamson's transaction cost theory (TCE), some research studies posited that IS investments between participants are often asset specific, raising the switching cost between customers and suppliers because of the use of specialized resources in the relationship (Clemons and Row, 1991). For example, customers that make asset-specific investments in unique supplier-based IT are subject to switching costs because these specific systems cannot be easily integrated with other suppliers' information technology (IT) resources (Bakos and Treacy, 1986; Feeny and Ives, 1990).

Despite acknowledging the critical roles that IS plays in business strategies, firms in an array of industries are finding that creating "value" from IS has not been easy. The main reasons are attributed to the inability of the firm to develop and leverage IS competencies, since IS applications can often easily be imitated by competitors. Second, unique traditional proprietary interorganization systems between a firm and its trading partners, which were once considered a source of competitive advantage, have gradually shifted toward general-purpose computing platforms—the Internet, Intranets, and Extranets. Third, some firms have been slow to fully appreciate the role of IS in creating competitive advantages, because managers in these firms do not make appropriate changes in organizational infrastructures to effectively exploit IS competencies and to explore new avenues of opportunities for capitalizing on IS resources.

In the past decade or so, following the resource-based view of the firm, scholars have argued that for creating and sustaining business advantage, a firm needs to possess rare, inimitable, and durable IS competencies; yet not much is known about how a firm creates, renews, and exploits these competencies for its business advantage. This gap in the literature is significant, especially in light of the fact that IS planning is now integrated with business planning in many firms. Therefore, the planning for IS competencies can now be done on an integrated basis that is driven by dynamic organizational capabilities, which are made up of cross-functional competencies that the firm possesses or creates.

Although in their study of IS competencies and business performance, Bhatt and Grover (2005) used organizational learning as an antecedent construct of IS competencies and business performance at the firm level, they did not clearly explain the reason for including it. This study extends their research and focuses on the role of dynamic organizational capabilities (organizational learning is considered as an integral component of dynamic organizational capabilities) in creating, renewing, and leveraging IS competencies for business advantages.

In other words, we address the question, "How can firms create, renew, and leverage IS competencies to their advantage?"

Our research is important for business managers as well as academic researchers. By delineating the significance of dynamic organizational capabilities, we show how dynamic organizational capabilities help a firm create, renew, and leverage IS competencies for business advantages.

This research is in line with Henderson and Venkatraman (1993), who have offered a comprehensive model of strategic alignment. However, their study does not specifically analyze how dynamic organizational capabilities help a firm create, renew, and exploit IS competencies for business advantage. This study attempts to fill this gap in the literature and provides an understanding of the role of dynamic organizational capabilities in creating, renewing, and leveraging IS competencies.

We draw from the resourced-based view (RBV) of the firm to build our theoretical base. Following the RBV of the firm, we explain the concept of IS competencies. Next we illustrate how dynamic organizational capabilities help create, renew, and leverage IS competencies for business advantages. Finally, the implications of the dynamic organizational capabilities on functional-level competencies and complementary knowledge are discussed.

## THE RESOURCE-BASED VIEW OF THE FIRM

The RBV argues that competitive advantages are accrued as a result of idiosyncratic, valuable, and inimitable resources and capabilities. This view argues that each organization consists of resources and capabilities that form the basis for accruing rents (Barney, 1991; Rumelt, Schendel, and Teece, 1994). Firms use two complementary mechanisms: resource picking and capability building (Makadok, 2001). Resource-picking mechanisms create economic rents when firms apply superior information and knowledge for acquiring resources. Capability building refers to the ability of firms to build unique capabilities that can leverage their resources (Teece and Pisano, 1994). These capabilities are embedded in business processes, making them comparatively more valuable and inimitable, and, therefore, superior to unembedded resources as determinants of long-term performance.

### Dynamic Organizational Capabilities

In recent years, a number of studies have focused on the dynamic capabilities of firms, because questions are increasingly raised concerning whether the RBV can explain why certain firms gain competitive advantage in complex and unpredictable environments (Teece, Pisano, and Shuen, 1997; Zollo and Winter, 1999). The mere existence of specific resources is not sufficient to sustain competitive advantage, because changing environments often demand new and innovative responses to emerging stimuli. In order to respond appropriately to new stimuli, a firm needs to reconfigure, rearrange, and recombine its resources and its functional-level competencies. This process of reconfiguration, rearrangement, and recombination of resources and functional competencies has led to the concept of dynamic organizational capabilities.

According to Teece, Pisano, and Shuen (1997), dynamic organizational capabilities refer to the processes by which firms reconfigure their resources to gain performance advantages. Dynamic capabilities are critical because they allow a firm to reconfigure and recombine its existing knowledge in such a way as to be able to respond to the challenge of changing environments (Eisenhardt and Martin, 2000). According to Zollo and Winter (2002), one critical dimension of dynamic organizational capability is deliberate learning that offers a perspective of reflection and consequently creates changes in the functional-level competencies.

A dynamic organizational capability can be identified through the ability of a firm (1) to reconfigure and redeploy resources and functional competencies; (2) to anticipate and respond to environmental changes; and (3) to make use of deliberate learning.

The reconfiguration and redeployment of resources and competencies can be undertaken by sharing existing resources and competencies across different business units so that they can be recombined differently (Kogut and Zander, 1992). This process also involves the coordination and integration of functional-level resources and competencies for creating synergies that can be exploited for business advantage. Dynamic organizational capabilities enable a firm to quickly anticipate, identify, and proactively respond to changes in the environment (Galunic and Rodan, 1998).

Deliberate learning involves creating multiple ideas and scrutinizing them throughout the firm. Moreover, learning also provides a way of reflection that leads a firm to understand what works and what does not work (Zollo and Winter, 2002). In a sense, the absorptive capacity of a firm, in conjunction with learning, can create organizational-level changes in the firm (Teece and Pisano, 2001). The absorptive capacity of an organization sensitizes a firm to quickly identify and assimilate new technology across various functional units and thus creates an environment of incremental learning or radical learning (Teece and Pisano, 2001). Cohen and Levinthal (1990) argue that the absorptive capacity consists of identifying, acquiring, assimilating, and exploiting knowledge about resources and opportunities. Firms involved in knowledge-reconfiguration activities possess greater absorptive capacity, and, therefore, can build and renew organizational capabilities sooner than their competitors can. Knowledge-absorptive capacity also facilitates organizational learning to make sense of the continually changing nature of the environment (Slater and Narver, 1995).

## INFORMATION SYSTEMS COMPETENCIES

The IS competencies that are of greatest interest to firms are those IS attributes that cannot easily be imitated by IS units in other firms. In defining IS competencies, researchers have usually paid attention to specific IS units, without focusing on dynamic organizational-level capabilities. For example, according to Mata, Fuerst, and Barney (1995), only managerial IS skills build IS competencies. Ross, Beath, and Goodhue (1996) posit that IS infrastructure flexibility, the business expertise of IS groups (IS business expertise), and the relationship between IS groups and business personnel (relationship infrastructure) constitute IS competencies. Feeny and Willcocks (1998) present a set of nine attributes—IS leadership, business systems thinking, relationship building, architectural planning, making technology work, informed buying, contract facilitation, contract monitoring, and vendor development as IS competencies. Peppard and Ward (2004) view six higher levels of competencies, which can be categorized further into twenty-six attributes. In this chapter, we focus on three attributes of IS competencies as proposed by Ross, Beath, and Goodhue (1996), because they have been empirically supported: IS infrastructure flexibility, IS business expertise, and relationship infrastructure (Bharadwaj, 2000; Bhatt and Grover, 2005).

### IS Infrastructure Flexibility

An IS infrastructure pertains to the arrangement of hardware, software, and networks so that data and applications can be accessed and shared within and between firms (Broadbent, Weill, and St. Clair, 1999). One way to share data and applications is through the use of common standards and rules that must be adopted by firms (Allen and Boynton, 1991).

Because an IS infrastructure can help integrate disparate and geographically distributed systems and make IS applications cost effective in their operations, it becomes essential that a firm make the necessary level of investments and commitment for the development of robust and flexible infrastructures.

### IS–Business Expertise

IS–businesss expertise refers to the extent to which IS groups possess an understanding of business objectives and strategies. Ross, Beath, and Goodhue (1996) argue that high-caliber IS personnel consistently solve business problems and address business opportunities. Thus, IS business expertise lies not only in possessing technical skills but also in understanding business strategies and business goals.

### Relationship Infrastructure

Relationship infrastructure refers to the ability of the IS group to understand business needs and create a partnership with business groups to work together on developing systems that can meet existing and future information needs of the business.

The relationship infrastructure consists of sharing the risk and responsibility of IS applications between IS and business unit management (Ross, Beath, and Goodhue, 1996). Because only business units are in a position to use IS resources effectively in their strategy and everyday work, it is essential that IS and business management work closely to share IS responsibilities and roles (Rockart, Earl, and Ross, 1996).

One major component of the relationship asset is the trust that is developed between IS groups and business units (Nahapiet and Ghosal, 1997). Trust enables knowledge flow and knowledge diffusion between IS groups and business personnel, which is likely to bring greater appreciation for each unit's work, expertise, and roles in the firm.

## RELATIONSHIP BETWEEN DYNAMIC ORGANIZATIONAL CAPABILITIES AND INFORMATION SYSTEMS COMPETENCIES

We emphasize the notion of dynamic organizational capabilities for two reasons. First, having IS competencies offers little value unless these IS competencies are complementary to other functional-level competencies (Clemons and Row, 1991). Second, a firm should be able to exploit a coordinated set of competencies, including IS competencies for business advantages. Dynamic organizational capabilities can help a firm in both of these respects. They help in coordinating various functional-level competencies and in exploiting those competencies for business advantage.

In this context, a dynamic organizational capability can be thought of as the readiness of a firm to understand the value of IS competencies, and consequently, to create, renew, and exploit IS competencies by reconfiguring and assimilating IS resources and existing competencies (Cross, Earl, and Sampler, 1997). Firms are heterogeneous in their dynamic organizational capabilities, since not all firms are equally equipped to create, renew, and exploit IS competencies for business advantage (Johnston and Carrico, 1988). Dynamic organizational capabilities thus refers to an overarching concept that subsumes diverse sets of functional-level competencies and provides the mechanisms necessary to exploit different coordinated sets of competencies for business advantage. As Bhatt and Grover (2005, p. 264) state, "[dynamic organizational capabilities] could be heterogeneous across firms, and thereby also a source of competitive advantage in contemporary environments where awareness and responsiveness buttressed by knowledge activities [are] pivotal."

Dynamic organizational capabilities are of two types. One kind of capability leads a firm to understand and identify IS competencies and acquire those IS resources that it can successfully transform into IS competencies. It must be understood that while dynamic organizational capabilities can help a firm in creating functional-level competencies, the very nature of functional-level competencies, subsequently, begins to shape dynamic organizational capabilities. In other words, the pattern of relationships between dynamic organizational capabilities and functional-level competencies is interactive. In this study, we focus only on the one-way relationship, that is, how dynamic organizational capabilities create, renew, and exploit IS competencies.

In order to transform IS resources into IS competencies, a firm is required to make necessary changes in its organizational infrastructures—processes, organizational structures, employee roles, and their skills—so that acquired IS resources are meshed and integrated with the organizational infrastructures.

Another kind of capability helps a firm to exploit IS competencies in coordination with other functional-level competencies so that their combined effect on business advantage is synergistic.

### How Do Dynamic Organizational Capabilities Create and Renew IS Competencies?

One of the key aspects of dynamic organizational capabilities lies in anticipating the potential of IS competencies. If a firm does not have the ability to anticipate the potential of IS competencies and consequently shape business strategy accordingly, it can find itself unable to capitalize on IS opportunities. Therefore, the requirement for a firm is to understand and anticipate the potential of IS.

This leads to consideration of the relationship of dynamic organizational capabilities with the three IS varieties of competencies: IS infrastructure, IS business expertise, and relationship infrastructure.

### Dynamic Organizational Capabilities and IS Infrastructure

Dynamic organizational capabilities can help a firm in transforming IS resources into IS competencies by way of a flexible IS infrastructure.

A firm usually acquires IS resources—systems, applications, embedded technologies—from the market; but these resources may not be the source of competitive advantage, because competitors can acquire or imitate them easily. If a firm internalizes these resources by meshing and integrating them with appropriate changes in its organizational processes and infrastructures, these resources are transformed into IS competencies. These competencies become unique to each firm, because the way that the IS resources are deployed, configured, and meshed with organizational processes and infrastructures varies greatly from one firm to the next.

So, when firms acquire resources from the market or develop them internally, they often do not provide sustainable advantages because they can easily be imitated by competitors. However, once these resources are internalized within a firm, that is, meshed, coordinated, and integrated with organization infrastructures and practices, they are transformed to functional-level competencies. Creating change across organizational processes and infrastructures is not easy for any firm, because changing human behavior has been always fraught with difficulties.

If a firm creates a collaborative environment for change and motivates and trains its employees in new work processes, technologies, and practices, it can reap the benefit of IS competencies. In this sense, dynamic organizational capabilities play an integral part, especially the way that the firm configures IS resources and creates a readiness to change existing organizational processes and work practices.

Dynamic organizational capabilities also renew IS competencies, that is, create changes in a flexible IS infrastructure. Renewal of competencies becomes quite critical because over time competencies become commodities if they are not continually renewed.

The reconfiguration of resources and existing competencies has been considered an important characteristic of dynamic organizational capabilities. However, not all firms are able to reconfigure their resources and existing IS competencies, because the renewal of competencies depends on the properties of the resources as well as the characteristics of the existing competencies.

Various firms have grown by using legacy systems, which are characterized through islands of databases and networks, developed through patchworks; therefore, reconfiguring, rearranging, and redeploying these resources dynamically is problematic. These systems usually lack flexibility and common standards, and reconfiguration of these systems may be almost impossible. A critical aspect in reconfiguring IS resources lies in the extent to which deployed systems can communicate with other systems to coordinate activities of the firm. By adopting common standards, firms can strengthen their mutual linkages, enhancing their abilities to increase the pace of innovation, which, in turn, can help sustain their competitive advantage.

A flexible IS infrastructure can provide the means necessary for a firm to creatively reconfigure its IS resources so that they are transformed into IS competencies (Bharadwaj, 2000). In this respect, dynamic organizational capabilities become highly dependent on the characteristics of acquired resources and existing competencies.

Being able to meet future business needs and take advantage of emerging technologies from various vendors remains a critical issue for firms, as they seek an information infrastructure that is flexible, adaptable, and portable (Madnick, 1991). In a sense, an IS infrastructure should be both robust in sustaining the current information needs of the business and flexible in meeting the future demands of business through which different IS resources can be reconfigured, recombined, and meshed with organizational processes, infrastructures, and practices. Organizational dynamic capabilities in this situation refer to the ability of the firm to reconfigure IS resources and make appropriate changes in organizational processes, infrastructures, and practices for creating IS competencies.

One characteristic of dynamic organization capabilities is the deliberate learning that allows a firm to make creative changes in its work processes and organizational structures to assimilate complementary resources with IS. A part of this knowledge and skill is determined by the organizational routines that are path-dependent and historically shaped. Therefore, capitalizing on IS resources becomes more dependent on organization-wide complementary resources that are affiliated with IS. Thus, organizational learning becomes a binding mechanism that allows the transformation of IS resources into IS competencies. In addition, deliberate learning can sensitize a firm to reconfigure and recombine IS resources and other functional-level resources in new ways so that they become internalized within the organization.

Thus, the thesis is that the way IS resources are integrated and assimilated with organizational infrastructures depicts the strength of IS competencies. The strength of IS competencies, in turn, determines the extent to which dynamic organizational capabilities can reconfigure IS resources and existing IS competencies in the firm for realizing the potential of IS competencies in a dynamic environment (Bradley, Pridmore, and Byrd, 2006). How the organization is structured around IS resources is likely to determine the intensity and durability of the IS competencies.

### Dynamic Organizational Capabilities and IS-business Expertise

When firms hire IS people from the market, they usually acquire people who possess far more technical knowledge than business acumen. The technical expertise of IS people is thus available to all firms. The dynamic organizational capabilities of a firm can transform these human assets, or resources, into IS competencies. If a firm offers opportunities to its IS personnel to work with line management, or encourages its employees to work in teams, an environment of learning and knowledge sharing can suffuse the IS people's technical knowledge with business knowledge.

Dynamic organizational capabilities play a critical role in this transformation because dynamic organizational capability is characterized by the ability of a firm to rapidly sense and respond to changes in competitive markets. Many business schools have recognized this by increasing the amount of business knowledge that is included in their IS curricula.

The renewal of competencies depends on the properties of the resources as well as the characteristics of the existing competencies. The makeup of the knowledge of IS people is likely to determine the extent to which a firm can reconfigure the technical knowledge of IS people and recombine it with business knowledge. Not all firms possess equal levels of dynamic capabilities to transform technical expertise into a combination of business and IS knowledge. One reason is that many firms still believe in delineating the boundaries of knowledge based on strict specialization. This is most prominent where IS management pays significant attention to the technical expertise of the IS people. Reconfiguring these specialized resources in a firm, where there are clear boundaries across different levels of knowledge, is far more difficult than in a firm that provides its IS personnel the opportunities to work with business personnel (Applegate and Elam, 1992). Dynamic organizational capabilities allow a firm to reconfigure its business and IS knowledge in different combinations to meet its current and future business needs. Not only can IS personnel be teamed up with groups of business personnel, but business personnel can also be teamed up with the groups of IS personnel to facilitate learning about different facets of the business and IS strategies. The rotating of personnel between line management and IS management provides a comprehensive view of organizational practices.

Once IS and line management begin to appreciate each other's contribution to the firm, the pace of mutual learning begins to increase because of the firm's enhanced organizational absorptive capacity (Neo, 1988).

Traditionally, for IS personnel, technical expertise in systems development activities and programming was considered critical. However, over the years, there have been suggestions that argue for IS personnel to get a better understanding of business knowledge because in the present dynamic environment IS personnel are often expected to lead in IS organizations. Several researchers have indicated that business knowledge, technical expertise, and interpersonal skills are all necessary for IS experts (Rockart, Earl, and Ross, 1996; Ross, Beath, and Goodhue, 1996).

Knowing about the business aspects of a firm is considered critical for managing IS resources and competencies. However, it has been well recognized that IS people have traditionally been concerned mostly with acquiring and developing systems that they deemed "fit" for meeting the current business demands of the firm. Presently, with rapid changes in business environments, IS-personnel are expected to propose and develop those systems that not only meet current business demands but also provide sufficient flexibility for the future growth of the business. All of these changes demand that IS people have sufficient knowledge about the business mission, long-term strategies, and goals that a firm wants to achieve. As Clark and others (1997) note, IS groups' business expertise, in combination with IS skills, directly determines the firm's ability to rapidly develop and deploy critical systems that can drive the competitiveness of the firm.

While physical assets and tangible resources can be replicated by competitors, long-term advantage in the market often depends on the expertise of the people in the organization. Firms that have IS groups with superior knowledge about business strategy, competition, and opportunities can continue to leverage them based on their absorptive capacity (Cohen and Levinthal, 1990). This means that if a firm begins with superior knowledge, it is likely to gain further knowledge.

*Dynamic Organizational Capabilities and Relationship Infrastructure*

Firms hire their employees from the market; therefore, acquisition of employees from the market is unlikely to be a unique competency. But once employees in a firm are internalized with an organizational culture that emphasizes collaboration, knowledge sharing, and deliberate learning, a positive and trusting relationship between IS and business people can create IS competencies. Dynamic organizational capabilities play critical roles in creating trust, mutual accountabilities, and mutual responsibilities between IS personnel and business personnel, since internalizing the culture and creating changes in organizational infrastructures, processes, and practices is an important characteristic of deliberate learning.

Since the renewal of competencies depends on the properties of the resources as well as the characteristics of the existing competencies, opportunism and the inability of business people to connect with IS people can have an important effect on dynamic organizational capabilities. In this sense, not all firms possess equal levels of the dynamic capabilities necessary to create a relationship infrastructure between IS and business personnel.

Traditionally, the relationship between IS groups and business people has often been unhealthy. Line management has often accused IS people of providing systems that are either too cumbersome to work with or do not account for their work needs. On the other hand, IS management has often argued that line management does not allocate sufficient budget for the development of systems and that business people routinely change their demands for IS capabilities.

In recent years, a positive and trustworthy relationship between IS personnel and business personnel has come to be considered as crucial. The general conclusion is that a high level of trust between IS personnel and business personnel enables the development of those systems that are flexible and meet the current and future information needs of users. Creating and maintaining trust involves a high degree of mutual readjustment and empathy among various participants. Participants are required not only to understand each other's views but also to facilitate such a process of mutual understanding. Indeed, such a mechanism of creating and maintaining trust is not clearly visible to other parties that are not directly involved in such a relationship.

### How Do Dynamic Organizational Capabilities Leverage IS Competencies?

There are two ways through which the dynamic organizational capabilities of a firm can leverage IS competencies for business advantage: incrementally and radically. In the incremental mode, a firm exploits ongoing operations of existing IS resources and competencies through repeated practice. By preserving project memory, benchmarking with "the best practices" of other companies, sharing organizational knowledge and information among different people working on similar kinds of projects, and reusing commonly used IS modules and templates, a firm can exploit IS competencies incrementally for its competitive advantage.

In the radical mode, a firm attempts to completely overhaul its IS competencies and organizational work practices. These changes can have dramatic improvements in business advantages. However, for leveraging the full potential of IS competencies, firms are required to make large investments in IS resources, work processes, employee training, and organizational structures. Dramatic changes in IS often demand dramatic changes in organizational infrastructures for transforming IS resources into IS competencies. Dramatic changes are risky, because many firms find it difficult to make so many changes simultaneously and thus they fail to leverage the full potential of IS competencies (Worley and Lawler, 2006).

IS competencies are a means, not an end. Although the use of systems is not limited to a specific business unit, the responsibility of developing IS competencies still lies with the IS organization in the firm. Thus, one aim of the firm in leveraging competencies is to coordinate diverse sets of competencies developed at the functional levels. So, to appropriate value from IS, a firm should be able to integrate and synergistically reconfigure diverse sets of competencies across various organizational units that have been integrally tied with IS resources and competencies.

If a firm does not possess the necessary level of dynamic capabilities to coordinate its functional-level competencies, it is unlikely to gain advantages from IS competencies alone. Therefore, a better description of IS competencies should be established on the basis of the firm's capabilities in identifying, creating, and leveraging IS potential. Teece and Pisano (2001) argue that the effectiveness and efficiency of coordination in the firm is directly tied to the dynamic organizational capabilities of the firm. The variations in coordination can have a direct impact on business performance.

Management's role in conceptualizing dynamic capabilities is an important one, since it indicates how consistently IS competencies will be created, renewed, and leveraged for business advantage. To exploit IS competencies, a firm requires the pooling and coordinating of diverse sets of competencies across different business units so that they have synergistic effects on business advantages.

Because of the rapidly changing environment, many of the existing competencies will inevitably become commodities. It therefore becomes imperative that a firm periodically create, develop, and reconfigure new portfolios of resources and competencies. This calls for integration between business demands and IS resources and existing competencies. Often, the integration of business demands and IS resources demands changes in existing business practices and organizational processes for creating business advantages. If a firm does not make changes in its existing practices and routines, it might not be able to exploit the full potential of its IS competencies. Because the process of integration cannot be considered static, it becomes a question of the continued realignment of organizational infrastructures, IS resources, existing IS competencies, and business demands.

## IMPLICATIONS AND CONCLUSION

This chapter shows how dynamic organizational capabilities play critical roles in creating, renewing, and leveraging IS competencies. Dynamic organizational capability is considered as an overarching concept that creates, renews, and exploits competencies. Dynamic organizational capabilities that create and renew functional-level competencies focus on the characteristics of the resources and existing competencies, while dynamic organizational capabilities that exploit competencies focus on coordinating different functional-level competencies for creating value for the firm. The creation and exploitation of IS competencies not only involves renewing the portfolios of existing resources and competencies but also requires discarding those resources and competencies from different portfolios that no longer remain the sources of sustainable advantages. In other words, if a competency becomes a commodity, it no longer must be managed and coordinated with the portfolios of competencies.

Dynamic organizational capabilities are central in continuously creating, renewing, and leveraging IS competencies. Experience, learning, and deliberate changes in some arenas of the firm can play critical roles in assessing the extent to which IS strategy and business strategy in the firm can be aligned for competitive advantage.

Such deliberate exploration of the business environment can also facilitate the ability of a firm to coordinate its IS and other functional-level competencies for competitive advantages. Because organizational environment can have a huge impact on the process of learning—individual as well as organizational—a deliberate exploration of the business environment pushes a firm to understand its dynamic organizational capabilities, and, consequently, take steps to provide appropriate interacting opportunities to its members, so that they can identify the best ways in which IS can be leveraged for business advantages.

Research has also shown that the development of IS skills is usually embedded in specific business practices; therefore, competitive advantages become a function of the assimilation of IS knowledge that is embodied in everyday practices (Bassellier, Horner, and Benbasat, 2001; Mata, Fuerst, and Barney, 1995). Moreover, the agility of a firm to change its business practices and quickly reconfigure its resources and functional-level competencies becomes a predictor of business advantages. In other words, creating business advantages is not a function of a specific set of competencies that are limited to certain business units. Instead, business advantages depend heavily on continuous interaction and communication between IS and other functional personnel so that complementary knowledge and competencies can be creatively shared and recombined. Because the level of dynamic organizational capability is heterogeneous among various firms, only firms that have learned to create, develop, renew, coordinate, and integrate functional level competencies can exploit the potential of IS competencies for their business advantage.

# REFERENCES

Allen, B.R., and Boynton, A.C. 1991. Information architecture: in search of efficient flexibility. *MIS Quarterly,* 15, 4, 435–445.

Applegate, L.M., and Elam, J.J. 1992. New information systems leaders: a changing role in a changing world. *MIS Quarterly,* 16, 4, 469–490.

Bakos, J.Y., and Treacy, M.E. 1986. Information technology and corporate strategy. *MIS Quarterly,* 10, 2, 107–119.

Barney, J.B. 1991. Firm resources and sustained competitive advantage. *Journal of Management,* 17, 1, 99–120.

Bassellier, G.; Horner, B.; and Benbasat, I. 2001. Information technology competence of business managers: a definition and research model. *Journal of Management Information Systems,* 17, 4, 159–182.

Bharadwaj, A.S. 2000. A resource-based perspective on information technology competences and firm performance: an empirical investigation, *MIS Quarterly,* 24, 1, 169–196.

Bhatt, G.D., and Grover, V. 2005. Types of information technology capabilities and their role in competitive advantage: an empirical study. *Journal of Management Information Systems,* 22, 2, 253–277.

Bradley, R.; Pridmore, J.; and Byrd, T. 2006. Information systems success in the context of different cultural types: an empirical investigation. *Journal of Management Information Systems,* 23, 2, 267–294.

Broadbent, M.; Weill, P.; and St. Clair, D. 1999. The implications of information technology infrastructure for business process redesign. *MIS Quarterly,* 23, 2, 159–182.

Clark, C.E.; Cavanaugh, N.C.; Brown, C.V.; and Sambamurthy, V. 1997. Building change-readiness capabilities in the IS organization: insights from the Bell Atlantic experience. *MIS Quarterly,* 21, 4, 425–455.

Clemons, E.K., and Row, M.C. 1991. Sustaining IT advantage: the role of structural differences. *MIS Quarterly,* 15, 3, 275–294.

Cohen, W.M., and Levinthal, D.A. 1990. Absorptive capacity: a new perspective on learning and innovation. *Administrative Science Quarterly,* 35, 128–152.

Cross, J.; Earl, M.J.; and Sampler, J.L. 1997. Transformation of the IT function at British Petroleum. *MIS Quarterly,* 21, 4, 401–423.

Eisenhardt, K.M., and Martin, J. 2000. Dynamic capabilities: what are they? *Strategic Management Journal,* Special Issue, 21, 10–11, 1105–1121.

Feeny, D., and Ives, B. 1990. In search of sustainability. *Journal of Management Information Systems,* 7, 1, 27–46.

Feeny, D.E., and Willcocks, L.P. 1998. Core IS capabilities for exploiting information technology. *Sloan Management Review,* 39, 3, 9–21.

Galunic, D., and Rodan, S. 1998. Resource recombinations in the firm: Knowledge structures and the potential for Schumpeterian innovation. *Strategic Management Journal,* 19, 12, 1193–1201.

Henderson, J.C., and Venkatraman, N. 1993. Strategic alignment: leveraging information technology for transforming organizations. *IBM Systems Journal,* 32, 1, 4–16.

Johnston, H.R., and Carrico, S.R. 1988. Developing capabilities to use information systems strategically. *MIS Quarterly,* 12, 1, 37–50.

King, W.R. 1978. Strategic planning for management information systems. *MIS Quarterly,* 2, 1, 27–37.

Kogut, B., and Zander, U. 1992. Knowledge of the firm, combinative capabilities, and the replication of technology. *Organization Science,* 3, 3, 557–606.

Madnick, S.E. 1991. The information technology platform. In Michael S. Scott Morton (ed.), *In the Corporation of the 1990s: Information Technology and Organizational Transformation.* New York: Oxford University Press, pp. 27–60.

Makadok, R. 2001. Toward a synthesis of the resource-based and dynamic-capability views of rent creation. *Strategic Management Journal,* 22, 5, 387–402.

Mata, F.J., Fuerst, W.L., and Barney, J.B. 1995. Information technology and sustained competitive advantages: A resource-based analysis. *MIS Quarterly,* 19, 4, 487–505.

McFarlan, W. 1984. Information technology changes the way you compete. *Harvard Business Review,* 62, 3, 98–103.

Nahapiet, J., and Ghoshal, S. 1997. Social capital, intellectual capital and the creation of value in the firms. *Academy of Management Best Paper Proceedings,* 35–39.

Neo, B.S. 1988. Factors facilitating the use of information technology for competitive advantage: An exploratory study. *Information & Management,* 15, 4, 191–201.

Peppard, J., and Ward, J. 2004. Beyond strategic information systems: towards an IS capability. *Journal of Strategic Information Systems,* 13 (July), 167–194.

Porter, M.E., and Millar, V.E. 1985. How information gives you competitive advantage. *Harvard Business Review,* 63, 4, 149–60.

Rockart, J.F.; Earl, M.J.; and Ross, J.W. 1996. Eight imperatives for the new IT organization. *Sloan Management Review,* 38, 1, 43–55.

Ross, J.W.; Beath, C.M.; and Goodhue, D. 1996. Develop long-term competitiveness through IT assets. *Sloan Management Review,* 38, 1, 31–45.

Rumelt, R.P.; Schendel, D.; and Teece D. 1994. *Fundamental Issues in Strategy.* Boston, MA: Harvard Business School Press.

Slater, S.F., and Narver, J.C. 1995. Market orientation and the learning organization. *Journal of Marketing,* 59 (July), 63–74.

Teece, D.J., and Pisano, G.P. 1994. The dynamic capabilities of firms: an introduction. *Industrial and Corporate Change,* 3, 3, 537–556.

———. 2001. The dynamic capabilities of firms: an introduction. In G. Dosi, D. Teece, and J. Chytry (eds.), *Technology, Organizations, and Competitiveness.* New York: Oxford University Press, pp. 193–212.

Teece, D.J.; Pisano, G.P.; and Shuen, A. 1997. Dynamic capabilities and strategic management. *Strategic Management Journal,* 18, 7, 509–533.

Worley, C., and Lawler, E. 2006. Designing organizations that are built to change. *Sloan Management Review,* 48, 1, 19–23.

Zollo, M., and Winter, S.G. 1999. From organizational routines to dynamic capabilities. INSEAD R&D Working Papers, 99/48/SM.

———. 2002. Deliberate learning and the evolution of dynamic capabilities. *Organization Science,* 13, 3, 339–351.

# PART II

# THE ORGANIZATIONAL INFORMATION
# SYSTEMS PLANNING PROCESS

# CHAPTER 6

# USING CRITICAL SUCCESS FACTORS IN SETTING INFORMATION TECHNOLOGY AND GENERAL MANAGEMENT RESOURCE PRIORITIES

## JOHN F. ROCKART AND CHRISTINE V. BULLEN

*Abstract: The concept of critical success factors (CSFs) has been in the management lexicon since 1979, when the original Harvard Business Review article introduced the approach. CSFs have been adopted as a management tool by individuals and organizations and embraced by consulting firms as a useful tool for focusing on what is central to helping create success. While the approach has been applied in diverse ways over the years, three primary applications have evolved: defining an individual's information needs, setting priorities for information technology resources, and setting priorities for general management resources. These will be described and highlighted with examples in the following chapter.*

*Keywords: Critical Success Factors (CSFs), Information Systems Resources, Management Resource Planning, Setting Priorities, Strategic Planning*

More than twenty-five years ago, the senior author of this chapter described an approach that would enable executives, given their strategies, to focus on the few things that were most important for the business (Rockart, 1979). Although the initial purpose of the article was to help an executive determine his own information needs, the resulting critical success factors (CSFs) concept has proved to be useful for many diverse purposes. This review, however, will deal only with what we believe to be three of the most significant uses of CSFs. They are:

- Defining an individual's information needs
- Setting priorities for, and justifying, IT resources
- Setting priorities for general management resources

The first two of these have been well described in the literature, and we have laid out the process for dealing with them in an extensive working paper (Bullen and Rockart, 1981). Here we focus on the latter two, the last of which is discussed in this chapter for the first time.

Rockart (1979) defined CSFs as:

> . . . the limited number of areas in which results, if they are satisfactory, will ensure successful competitive performance for the organization. They are the few key areas in which "things must go right" for the business to flourish. (85)

## THE UNDERLYING IDEA

Underlying the idea of critical success factors is the concept of "focus." To choose but three examples from dozens in the literature:

- Some 200 years ago, Baron von Clausewitz's book on warfare identified nine principles. One of these was "concentration of forces." Von Clausewitz wrote that a poor general scatters his forces to all battles while a good general focuses on the few key battles (von Clausewitz, 2004).
- In the 1940s, Juran proposed the 80–20 rule advising management to focus on the "vital few" not the "trivial many" (Juran, 1988). He named it after Vilfredo Pareto, the Italian economist who observed that 20 percent of the people owned 80 percent of the wealth. It has been known as the Pareto principle ever since.
- Peter Drucker, writing in *The Effective Executive,* noted that effective executives determine which tasks are "of priority and which are of less importance" and then focus their time and energy on the former (Drucker, 1993).

To understand their CSFs, managers must step back from the all-too-involving day-to-day issues and think deeply about what is really critical for the future of the organization. Although this sounds simple, it is not. Without careful thought, factors can result that are often superficial, sometimes incorrect, and generally reactive to current pressures.

Given this concept, and its antecedents, we turn to the three major uses. For purposes of this chapter, the first use, which focuses on the individual executive, is discussed primarily to provide a complete description of the evolution of the CSF process.

## AN EXECUTIVE'S INFORMATION NEEDS

In 1978, Larry Gould, then the president of Microwave Associates, was looking for better information to manage his organization. Some 100 reports crossed his desk every month—but he still did not feel that he was well-informed about the company's position—either internally or externally. In a seminal event, Gould, with some coaching, focused in on seven CSFs for the business (Table 6.1). For each CSF, there was a well-thought-through justification. As an example, for "image in the financial markets," Microwave Associates was growing and making acquisitions as it sought to gain leadership in a growth segment of the electronics industry. As is well known, a major factor in effective acquisitions is the organization's price–earnings ratio, which, in turn, depends on its "image in the financial markets."

The resulting CSFs are shown in Table 6.1. In comparing the information required to monitor these CSFs with his existing information, Gould came to a key conclusion. He saw that the information that he had asked for previously, or that had been sent to him, was based heavily either on routine financial data or on previously encountered business issues, many of which would never reoccur. The CSF process, on the other hand, enabled him to step back from the day to day and focus on the fundamentals of the business; the factors that would make or break the organization. The information required was vastly different.

The process developed by the authors to work with Larry Gould became the foundation for the concept that is now well known as the critical success factors process. The remainder of the chapter focuses on this CSF process as it has been used to develop information technology (IT) and general management priorities.

Table 6.1

**Critical Success Factors for Larry Gould, President, Microwave Associates**

1. Image in financial markets
2. Technological reputation with customers
3. Market success
4. Risk recognition in major contracts
5. Profit margin on jobs
6. Company morale
7. Performance to budget on major jobs

*Source:* Rockart (1979, p. 88).

## SETTING PRIORITIES FOR INFORMATION TECHNOLOGY RESOURCES

A second major use of CSFs, starting in the early 1980s, was that of setting priorities for, and justifying, IT applications and infrastructure. Here, the use of CSFs moved from a focus on an individual to the involvement of a management team. Applications of the CSF process in IT and organizational planning—the focus of this discussion—rely on this team approach.

While working with a single individual is both interesting and fruitful, it is reasonably straightforward and avoids the complications of differing opinions (this process is fully described in Rockart, 1979). However, working with a management team is much more complex. The process involves dealing with a sometimes-difficult set of relationships among the leaders of an organization while providing the role of facilitator. Done well, knowledge is developed on both sides. Significant decisions are made and positive action results.

Members of the team go through a three-step process. They are exposed to the CSF concept, determine the organization's CSFs, and, based on these CSFs, think through which IT capabilities are most critical for the organization. Determining the organization's CSFs can be accomplished in a group meeting or by using individual interviews followed by a focusing workshop. The individual interviews require significantly more time but, in our view, provide better insight into the organization. In either case, clarity on what is critical to the business leads to an intelligently focused choice of information resources. These resource decisions are the hardware, software, and systems that can best move the organization forward in its critical areas. (The exact process is the same as that used in setting priorities for top management, which will be much more fully discussed in the next section. The only difference is the end result: IT resource priorities versus organization-wide resource priorities.)

An early example of this approach was at Southwest Ohio Steel (SOS), in 1984. At that time, SOS was one of the top three steel service centers in the United States. SOS purchased steel, processed it to a limited extent, inventoried it, and sold it. At SOS, the use of CSFs went through the three steps noted above, an introductory workshop to acquaint managers with the process, a set of individual interviews, and a "focusing workshop." Following intense discussion in the final workshop, a set of CSFs emerged. They were:

- maintaining excellent supplier relationships
- maintaining or improving customer relationships
- merchandising available inventory to its highest value-added use
- utilizing available capital and human resources effectively and efficiently

Although these may seem simple and straightforward, managers with different functional roles and different lifetime experiences most often do not see things in the same way. This leads to different views as to what is most important for the organization. Talking through these differences, often arguing through them, in the workshop enables the management team to set a clear, jointly agreed-upon view of what is most critical for the organization. As Jacque Huber, then vice president of sales of SOS put it, "the discussion, sharing and agreement was really important. What came out of it was a minor revelation. Jointly seeing it on the blackboard is much more significant than carrying around a set of individually-held ideas which are merely intuitively felt" (Rockart and Crescenzi, 1984, 13).

Given this focus on the business, SOS went on to select and install systems focused on suppliers, customers, inventory, and production scheduling. Earlier they had been urged by a major accounting firm to give priority to installing a new financial system. This was scrapped. The CSF process focused the top management team on the most urgently needed system projects, that is, the ones that had to be in place for the future success of the organization.

Today, Microsoft provides an IT planning and priority-setting process called rapid economic justification (REJ) to allow customers to quantify the business value of IT investments. The REJ process model is a five-step model. Step 1, entitled "Business Assessment," is based on the development of an organization's CSFs. According to Microsoft, the approach has several advantages, two of which are:

- *Rapid Analysis.* The team focuses on how to best help the organization achieve its CSF. They can address only those activities that are likely to have the most impact on the strategies.
- *Alignment.* The team addresses only those activities that have the most impact on the CSF, therefore the proposed solution is more likely to address the needs of the key shareholders. (Microsoft, 2005)

## SETTING PRIORITIES FOR ORGANIZATIONAL RESOURCES

The above process—setting priorities for IT resources—is a special case of setting priorities for general management programs and projects. In the prior case, one works with a selected set of the management team. When the focus is the organization as a whole, one works with the entire management team of that organization, that is, a company, a division, a department, and so on. Between 1985 and the present, we have seen more than a dozen consulting companies (including Ernst & Young, Gemini, a division of PWC and Index Systems [subsequently acquired by CSC]) make use of CSFs to help a management team decide what actions to focus on.

In general, the approach we have used to do this in our work is the three-step process (briefly referred to previously) depicted in Figure 6.1. The process begins with (1) an introductory workshop to enable management to understand the CSF concept and to start thinking about their organization's own CSFs. This is followed by (2) a set of individual interviews with about twenty people including the top management team and a dozen or so other key employees from the lower ranks. These interviews provide the "data" that are used for the development of the "straw man" (a set of interviewer-proposed CSFs for the organization). Development of the straw man from many tens of suggested CSFs is, it should be noted, a process that is far more art than science. Finally, there is (3) a "focusing workshop," usually a day long, which allows management to fully discuss what is critical to the organization.

Three things take place in the focusing workshop. First, there is intense discussion of the suggested CSFs—the straw man. Following this discussion, a consensus is reached on the set of CSFs for the organization. Finally, a set of action programs and projects that will move the organization

Figure 6.1   **The Critical Success Factor (CSF) Process**

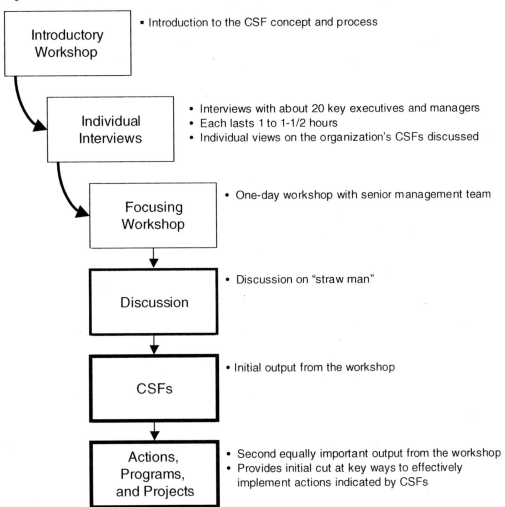

forward in its critical areas is developed. The detailed description of each action program and the implementation process is developed in later meetings. However, if the CSF process has been utilized effectively, top management understanding and buy-in is secure.

The entire process takes place over a one- to two-week time frame. The three parts of the CSF process are discussed in detail below.

**The Introductory Workshop**

The workshop usually consists of a thirty- to forty-five-minute presentation about the CSF concept and the process of the study. Questions are raised and are answered, and the use of examples in this step is valuable. The introductory workshop is designed to involve and gain commitment of the senior management team to the process.

An equally important part of the workshop is the understanding the facilitator gains about the management team. The facilitator is looking for signs among participants of three potential causes of later problems: a failure to understand the process, negativity, or a lack of interest. Failure to understand or accept the importance of CSFs can sometimes happen. Managers with well-defined strategies and operating plans that currently exist as a result of other planning methods in use in the organization may not see the need for an additional process or may be strongly wedded to the products of other planning methods and may resist viewing the business from the CSF perspective. It is critical to note negative behavior, as it is usually the symptom of a deeper concern that must be addressed. In one case, a clearly paranoid manager believed that the study was targeted at him. Disinterest on the part of the chief executive officer (CEO) can also kill a study. In one organization the CEO was in and out of the introductory workshop. Others noted his example and people questioned whether the study should proceed. Although the study did proceed, it was far from successful.

## The Interviews

There are two major approaches to interviewing the management team: as a group or individually. Group interviews are less time consuming and can result in a workable set of CSFs. However, to acquire a deeper understanding of an organization and what should be done to improve effectiveness, we strongly favor individual interviews.

Group interviews of a top management team can suffer because of several factors. First, knowing others will be there to respond, each individual is not required to think deeply about the organization's CSFs prior to the interview. Second, in some organizations, there is a tendency to "follow the leader" as he or she speaks. Third, organizational politics and personal relationships may influence what anyone offers in a group meeting. Finally, much valuable information about what is really critical in the organization often comes from the comments of managers below the top management team. These managers are rarely included in a group interviewing session (and if they are present, they are reluctant to speak because of hierarchical issues).

We usually perform individual interviews of about twenty people, including the whole top management team and a selected set of "up and coming" second-line managers. The value from those below the senior management level is a set of field-level insights into what is going on in the organization.

For individual interviews, we find that people come prepared. Most will have thought about the relevant CSFs during the introductory workshop and the evening before the interview. Time and time again, we find participants arriving at the interview with a set of notes and a clearly defined view of what they believe to be the organization's CSFs. After stating their views, many will ask what the interviewer has heard from others. Making use of this interest, the interviewer can test his or her evolving ideas about the organization's CSFs while being careful to maintain the confidentiality of individual sources.

### Developing the Straw Man

While we do not identify this event as a specific step, it is important to discuss some of the approach that goes into developing the straw-man list of CSFs. The experience and creativity of the facilitator(s) becomes evident in this important aspect of the process.

During the interviews and again while developing the straw man, the facilitator is working with a list of *characteristics* of CSFs (in his or her mind) to ensure that the participants are stretching their thinking and not becoming overly focused on one or a few areas that are at the top of their minds.

Five prime sources of CSFs have been identified through the early work and research (Bullen and Rockart, 1981) and these can be used to delve into areas that may have been overlooked in the subject's initial response:

1.  The industry within which the organization exists—this looks at the general health and direction of the industry and their influences on the manager's organization. For example, if the industry is facing hard times, such as the pharmaceutical industry has been with court cases on drug side effects, the environment of the industry may be a major concern.
2.  Competitive strategy and industry position—this area looks at the organization's position in the industry and competitive positioning factors. For example, the personal computer industry has recently been facing a major re-ordering of competitive positioning. The manager may be focused on how to manage the firm's position in the new marketplace.
3.  Environmental factors—these can be internal or external and describe immediate pressures on the manager's organization. Clearly, this may overlap with some of the other sources of CSFs, but that can help to avoid missing something important.
4.  Temporal factors—these are current issues that may have a short life span. It is important to know if something the interviewee focuses on may be very short term and therefore not critical in determining organizational direction.
5.  Managerial position of the interviewee—there may be factors related to the manager's position and his or her relationships both higher and lower in the managerial hierarchy.

The facilitator can use these five broad areas to be sure the respondent is thinking broadly about the areas that may contain CSFs. It is important that, during the interviews, the facilitator helps to direct, without influencing, the respondent's thinking process. In the effort to create the straw-man list of CSFs, the facilitator can "test" whether the list covers these broad areas or the areas have been consciously rejected as not relevant.

In addition to the five sources, our research revealed two additional ways in which the interviewer can think about whether the subject manager has covered all possible sources of CSFs:

*   Internal versus external issues—sometimes interviewees get "hung up" on the most pressing problem and overlook broader issues. For example, if there are some serious internal politics going on, the subject may not think about the important competitive areas.
*   Monitoring tasks versus building/adapting the business—these two areas can also overshadow each other depending on current happenings. For example, if there is a CEO spearheading a major strategic growth initiative, the subject may not be thinking about ongoing business issues.

Finally, the facilitator can think about a hierarchy of CSFs and whether the interviewee has covered all four levels:

*   Industry
*   Corporate or organization
*   Suborganization (specific unit of the interviewee)
*   Individual (personal CSFs specific to the interviewee)

While the first three levels of the hierarchy above make intuitive sense for areas in which a manager may have CSFs, the last one is less obvious. There are several reasons for seeking very personal CSFs. First, the manager is a person with life pressures. Therefore, it may be important for him or her to express these in the interview process. In a study of the Center for Information Systems Research, one subject was the head of a hospital. In the course of the interview, he said that the support of his wife and family was critical for his success because he had to spend many evenings and weekends at community events and this took him away from his family. While this finding is clearly not something that would become part of the organizational strategy, it does capture an important aspect of how this manager is able to work, which might influence the direction of his efforts.

Second, the individual is the person making managerial decisions in the firm. That person's style and approach to the direction of the organization is important to understand. Important clues on interpreting what the respondent says and how he or she communicates with the other managers may come out of the individual's response to personal CSFs. This understanding can be valuable to the facilitator in the focusing workshop.

Using the guidelines above will help the facilitator to extract meaningful CSFs during the interview step and assist in developing a quality straw-man list of CSFs.

**The Focusing Workshop**

This is the crux of the process. As noted previously, there are three parts to this workshop—discussion, agreement on CSFs, and development of actions.

*Discussion*

No matter how carefully the facilitator has listened and analyzed the interview data, the CSFs presented will not be gratefully accepted by all members of the management team. Even if the facilitator has done a perceptive job, there is bound to be extensive discussion and, sometimes, hostility on the part of some to the suggested CSFs. We have encountered five reasons for this discomfort. First, some of the material is new to some participants and they work hard to question and understand it. Second, in most studies, there are one or more participants whose pet projects, perhaps fundamental to their function, are not on the critical list. Third, there can be a none-too-subtle shift implied by the CSFs in the direction of the organization and, thus, in the power of individuals. For example, in one case, a member of the top management team could clearly see in the discussion that a strategic thrust he had championed would be put on the back burner. Fourth, it is entirely possible that the interviewer may have missed some things that are critical in developing the straw man. Fortunately, the workshop process is designed to correct this failing.

There is one other possibility for real discomfort during the discussion of the straw man. The discussion can lead to major changes in the way that the entire management team views the business. In one study, after much heated discussion, the senior management team realized from their newly developed CSFs that the strategy they had been following was badly flawed. The actions that were critical to that strategy could not be effectively carried out. A competitor was in a much stronger position with regard to these few critical factors. This team spent two extra days rethinking their strategy.

In a more usual situation, the discussion part of the workshop takes four or five hours. But it can run longer.

*Agreement on CSFs*

The next step in the focusing workshop is coming to a consensus to develop agreement and commitment by the management team to the CSFs. This step is the conclusion of an effective discussion.

*Development of Actions and Next Steps*

The development of action plans and next steps is the final step of the workshop. CSFs, no matter how well thought through, are just sets of words. The management team must translate the CSFs into action. We usually ask each member of the group to write down the three or four key actions that the CSFs imply. Each of these is put on the board, aggregating like actions. While the discussion of these actions can take a while, if the CSFs are clear, it is interesting how quickly a set of actions, six to twelve of them in our experience, are agreed upon. In one case it took less than an hour for a management team to agree upon eight actions that they knew would cost several tens of millions of dollars. The stage is thus set for the assignment of leaders for each action program. Detailed action plans, measures for success, accountabilities, and the implications for budgets are usually handled in a later meeting.

**General Management CSFs: An Example**

Senior management of the health care division of a top-twenty insurance company in the late 1980s felt a need to reassess their strategy. One member of the team had attended a lecture on critical success factors and proposed the use of this approach. After some discussion, it was agreed upon. The *introductory workshop* went smoothly. The workshop was concluded in just over an hour and a half. The concept was reviewed briefly. Several questions were asked primarily concerning past experience with the CSF method and comparison with other approaches. The tenor of the session was inquisitive and thoughtful.

Next, fifteen *interviews* were carried out, ten with the senior management team and five with managers reporting to team members. Some interviews were relatively short, taking somewhat less than a half-hour apiece. However, most of the fifteen averaged just under two hours. It was evident that, for these managers, including the vice president who introduced the concept to the organization, this was an extremely important exercise. Each came in with a list of four to seven factors. One had two and a half pages of text backing up each CSF. He left this with the interviewer.

In all, some sixty different CSFs were suggested by the ten team members. About two-thirds of these, however, were statements that, although worded differently were getting at similar concepts and therefore the interviewer was able to compile the sixty CSFs into six "straw man" CSFs (Table 6.2) that would be presented to the management team in the ensuing focusing workshop. For example, the three statements (each suggested by a different interviewee) "we need a new marketing thrust," "the sales people do not have a platform from which to sell," and "we are outgunned on television" were eventually placed under the CSF heading of "improve marketing capabilities"—CSF number 3 in Table 6.2. The other, roughly twenty, suggested CSFs were left off the straw man since they were felt by the interviewers to be either of minor importance or to be statements that applied only to the interviewee's function. It is in this process of sorting out the wheat from the chaff and the eventual wording of the suggested CSFs that the "art" of the CSF process comes into play. A good straw man depends heavily on the knowledge of the interviewer of the industry(ies) in which the organization exists as well as the experience and capability of

Table 6.2

**Critical Success Factors for Health Care Organization**

1. Move quickly from indemnity insurance to managed care
2. Rethink IT capability
3. Improve marketing capability
4. Develop organization "depth chart"
5. Develop new communication department
6. Replace claims software system

the interviewer. In our own work, we have spent hours sorting through a list of possible CSFs to develop the straw man. For some companies, the list quickly becomes apparent. For most, it takes quite a while.

The *focusing workshop* for this company took place in a large conference room. On several sheets of paper on the walls were the six "straw man" CSFs. Each "straw man" CSF had its own sheet of paper with the individual statements that had been compiled into that suggested "straw man" CSF listed under it. These were there so that the management participants could review the logic of the interviewer in determining the suggested CSFs. On two other pieces of paper were the "rejected" potential CSFs.

In this company, as in most others, the initial hour and a half of the workshop was spent with people whose items were on the "rejected" list trying to get their items onto the straw man. In this case, although not always in others, the straw man remained as proposed.

To this point, the atmosphere of the exchange in the room was businesslike, sometimes enlivened by brief bouts of humor as someone tried to force a statement onto the CSF list that was obviously important to the individual, but not to the company. The tenor of the meeting quickly changed, however, when the group began to discuss CSF no. 1: "Move quickly from indemnity insurance to managed care." Everyone agreed that the indemnity insurance process, wherein the insurance company paid all of an insured's medical claims, was a method of insurance that was slowly becoming obsolete as the costs of health care were rising very quickly. Taking its place was "managed care," by which the insurance company, in any of several different forms, limited both patient access to physicians and hospital costs that it would pay. However, the word "quickly" was the flash point. Several team members argued strenuously that the company was moving far too slowly. Several others, however, including the executive in charge of the transition, felt that the pace was correct and that the manner in which the trend to managed care could best be exploited was far from clear. After two and a half hours of vigorous, sometimes harsh debate, the proponents of moving more quickly won out. The CEO, who had sat on the sidelines as the debate ensued, agreed and a task force was set up to work intensively on the issue.

The final three hours of discussion, after lunch, were muted. Each of the five other CSFs was discussed. The exact wording of several was changed although the thrust of each was agreed upon. The group then turned to action plans for each and they were developed. But, it was clear that the major work had been done in the morning.

### Three Other "Interesting" Top Management Resource Planning Cases

Here we briefly present three different CSF cases that highlight various aspects of CSF studies. The first, again, reflects the substantial disagreement that can occur among members of the top management team as they are forced to develop a shared path for the organization. The second notes the fact that divisional CSFs need to fall hierarchically within the organization's CSFs. This is not always beneficial to the suborganization. The third case emphasizes the importance of the CEO in the CSF process.

*Case 1—Consumer Product Company*

The strong disagreement among the members of the top management team noted above is not unusual in focusing workshops. People come into them with different views of the company and the industry and personal agendas. The resulting discussion helps the company to focus but, in some cases, it disrupts some strongly held beliefs of one or more executives. In one consumer product company, the manufacturing executive, clearly the number-two person in the organization, argued at length about the need to fund a new generation of manufacturing equipment. Other executives, however, felt equally strongly that substantial resources needed to be focused on a new logistics information system. The manufacturing executive lost but the discussion was not an easy one.

*Case 2—Division of a Computer Company*

In a division of a computer company, six CSFs were, after much discussion, agreed upon, and action plans for each developed in a seven-hour meeting. However, one CSF and its resultant action plans were rejected at the corporate level of the company. Responsibility for that CSF was placed in a functional organization within the corporate organization. Later events suggested that the transfer of responsibility for the CSF was not a good decision.

*Case 3—The Distracted CEO*

In one other organization, the CEO, noting that his travel schedule kept him from participating, asked his management team to go ahead and carry out the CSF process. The process went smoothly and the team members were extremely satisfied with the results. The resultant CSFs, however, raised issues that the members of the management team felt were greatly important and they had previously attempted to work through with the CEO with little forward movement. The CEO duly sat through the entire focusing workshop, often asking very good questions, and thanked the facilitator at the end. However, no action programs were ever implemented. The management team had one perception of what the company's strategy should be. However, the CEO had his own vision of the thrust of the organization.

While the above three cases are not unusual, the majority of the other senior management engagements that we have carried out, or have reviewed from those done by consulting companies, have produced very good results. To shed insight into the use of the CSF concept, we have presented some of the more interesting cases. They illustrate the key point that management teams are made up of individuals with their own views of the world and biases. CSF discussions affect not only rational approaches to the business but also the desires and beliefs of each manager. This makes these engagements extremely interesting, very useful in pulling together the senior management team, and, often, somewhat stressful for the facilitator!

## THE FUTURE OF THE CSF PROCESS

An idea that became popular in 1979 is still going strong almost thirty years later. A simple process to focus conversations with management and help individuals drill down to the key areas on which they need to focus has shown itself to have staying power, resilience, and flexibility. A Google search of the phrase "critical success factors"—today's litmus test of impact—yields more than three million references, and still growing. There is, of course, a Wikipedia entry for critical success factors (Wikipedia, 2007).

Numerous consulting organizations, academic researchers and others have taken the basic concept of CSFs and adapted and extended it for a variety of uses. Many have employed a different name or phrase in trying to differentiate themselves from the original concept. But like so many simple, straightforward techniques, CSFs have proved their value and endured, delivering results to the organizations that work through the process.

The obvious question is: "what next?" Our prognosis is that managers, consciously or subconsciously, will continue to pursue the notion that finding the critical factors on which to focus is how they will continue to direct and lead their organizations to successful competitive positions. Many managers today refer directly to the CSF concept as they do this. The understanding and acceptance of the process has become widespread and people use the phrase as if it were a generally accepted management principle. We expect the use and extension of the CSF idea to continue to grow and prosper in the coming decades.

## REFERENCES

Bullen, C.V., and Rockart, J.F. 1981. A primer on critical success factors. *MIT Report* (Alfred P. Sloan School of Management, Center for Information Systems Research), no. 69.

Drucker, P.F. 1993. *The Effective Executive.* New York: Harper Business.

Juran, J.M. (ed.). 1988. *Juran's Quality Control Handbook,* 4th ed. New York: McGraw-Hill.

Microsoft. 2005. *Rapid Economic Justification, Enterprise Edition: A Step-by-Step Guide to Optimizing IT Investments That Forge Alliances Between IT and Business.* Redmond, WA: Microsoft Corporation. Available at www.microsoft.com/business/enterprise/value.mspx (accessed on December 12, 2005).

Rockart, J.F. 1979. Chief executives define their own information needs. *Harvard Business Review* 57 (March–April), 81–93.

Rockart, J.F., and Crescenzi, A.D. 1984. Engaging top management in information technology, *Sloan Management Review,* 25, 4, 3–16.

Von Clausewitz, C. 2004. *On War,* trans. Col. J.J. Graham. New York: Barnes and Noble.

Wikipedia. 2007. Critical success factors. Available at http://en.wikipedia.org/wiki/Critical_success_factor.

# CHAPTER 7

# A KNOWLEDGE-BASED VIEW OF INFORMATION SYSTEMS PLANNING AND ITS CONSEQUENCES

## Review and Propositions

RAJIV SABHERWAL, RUDY HIRSCHHEIM, AND ANAND JEYARAJ

*Abstract: Prior research has argued, and empirically shown, that one of the primary objectives of information systems (IS) planning is the alignment between business and IS strategies. Moreover, lack of shared knowledge among business and IS executives is considered a major inhibitor of IS planning. However, the role of knowledge management (KM) processes in IS planning, and in aligning business and IS strategies, has not been examined. This chapter seeks to address this gap in the prior literature by providing a knowledge-based view of IS planning. More specifically, it focuses on five KM processes (direction, internalization, exchange, combination, and socialization) to examine their effects on specific domain knowledge and shared knowledge, and alignment. The KM processes may be classified into three types: knowledge substitution, which includes direction; knowledge transfer, which includes exchange and internalization; and knowledge synthesis, which includes socialization and combination. We further argue that knowledge substitution, transfer, and synthesis processes have little, moderate, and considerable effects, respectively, on shared knowledge. Prior literature on KM and IS planning is used to develop some initial research propositions. Three case studies provide further insights into IS planning, and help develop a model of the knowledge-based view of IS planning. Some implications of this emergent model for future research and practice are examined.*

*Keywords: Information Systems, Knowledge Management, Planning, Alignment, Business Performance*

Information systems (IS) researchers have long examined the role of IS planning in organizations (Earl, 1993; King, 1978). IS planning has shifted attention from its focus on operational aspects in developing applications portfolios to the more strategic aspects in satisfying, or even informing, business goals (Blumenthal, 1969; Ward, Griffiths, and Whitmore, 1990). Prior literature on IS planning has clarified the role and scope of IS planning, uncovered a variety of conditions for IS planning, and examined the consequences of IS planning (Grover and Segars, 2005; King and Teo, 2000; Lederer and Sethi, 1996; Sabherwal, 2006; Segars and Grover, 1998; Silva and Hirschheim, 2007). However, this literature: (a) implicitly assumes but does not explicitly examine the role of knowledge or knowledge mechanisms in IS planning, and (b) generally disregards the consequences of IS planning from a knowledge perspective, due to (a) above.

Knowledge has been recognized as a crucial element of IS planning. For instance, prior research has pointed out the distinctive knowledge bases possessed by top managers and IS managers, and how such knowledge bases eventually result in performance efficiencies and gains (Kearns and Lederer, 2003; Lederer and Sethi 1988). Further, researchers have pointed out the importance of involving knowledgeable IS managers in the strategic planning process as well as having IS managers elicit business knowledge possessed by top managers (Kearns and Sabherwal, 2006; Lederer and Sethi, 1988; Vitale, Ives, and Beath, 1986). However, the role of knowledge has typically been assumed in prior research.

IS planning is known to have significant organizational effects. Prior literature describes how IS planning may lead to strategic IS alignment and eventually to performance. IS planning, which should involve both business and IS managers, may help achieve strategic IS alignment as both business and IS managers arrive at a shared understanding of the business and IS plans (Kearns and Sabherwal, 2006). Further, strategic IS alignment has been found to impact business performance (Sabherwal and Chan, 2001; Chan, Sabherwal, and Thatcher, 2006). However, these explanations about linkages between business and IS planning, or between business and IS strategies, have rarely been presented from a knowledge-based perspective.

Seeking to address this limitation, this chapter provides a knowledge-based explanation of IS planning and its consequences, in which knowledge and its related mechanisms are modeled explicitly. It draws upon the knowledge management (KM) literature (e.g., Conner and Prahalad, 1996; Grant, 1996a, 1996b) to explain: (a) the mechanisms by which organizations may realize IS planning; and (b) the consequences of such IS planning mechanisms within organizations.

The next two sections describe the theoretical foundations for the chapter, and introduce the research model. Data collection and analysis methods are described next. The subsequent two sections describe the empirical cases and the emergent model of IS planning. The chapter concludes with a discussion of its implications and limitations.

## INFORMATION SYSTEMS PLANNING: A KNOWLEDGE-BASED VIEW

IS planning and its scope have evolved over the years. Early conceptualizations of IS planning focused largely on developing portfolios of IS applications (Blumenthal, 1969; McFarlan, 1971). Later treatments focused on planning for specific IS projects, including the development strategy, the goals of the system, and the priorities for selecting system functions (Ein-Dor and Segev, 1978). More recent definitions have recognized the strategic nature of IS planning (Ward, Griffiths, and Whitmore, 1990). For instance, strategic IS planning is defined as the identification of a portfolio of computer-based applications that will enable an organization to execute its business plans and achieve its business goals (Lederer and Sethi, 1996).

Prior literature has extensively examined strategic IS planning. Different approaches to IS planning have been suggested earlier. Pyburn (1983) distinguished between a written-formal planning system and a personal-informal planning system, where the former was a structured top-down approach while the latter was an adaptive bottom-up approach. Earl (1993) described five different approaches to IS planning: business-led, method-driven, administrative, technological, and organizational, of which the organizational approach, a hybrid of structured and unstructured styles, seemed most effective. Segars and Grover (1998) demonstrated that a mix of rational and adaptive approaches was more conducive to IS planning. King and Teo (2000) examined the reactive and proactive modes of IS planning, and found that proactive modes of IS planning, which referred to a two-way interaction between business and IS groups, were more effective. A formal and comprehensive approach to IS planning may be more successful than an informal and incremental approach in turbulent and uncertain environments (Newkirk and Lederer, 2006; Salmela,

Figure 7.1   **Knowledge-Based View of Information Systems (IS) Planning**

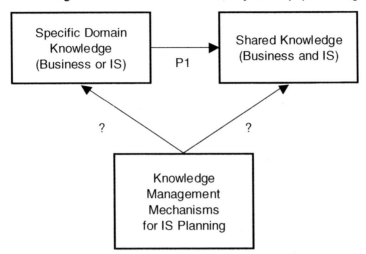

Lederer, and Raponen, 2000). However, extant literature is virtually silent on the mechanisms underlying IS planning. While the foregoing provides a good description of the different approaches to IS planning, there is really no description of the mechanisms by which organizations achieve or engage in IS planning.

The knowledge-based view of IS planning (Figure 7.1) presented in this chapter argues that knowledge management mechanisms associated with IS planning facilitate the specific domain knowledge as well as the shared knowledge of business and IS professionals, and the shared knowledge, in turn, produces the effects that have hitherto been associated with IS planning. Thus, the knowledge-based view of IS planning comprises three distinct components: *specific domain knowledge, shared knowledge,* and *knowledge management mechanisms for IS planning,* the descriptions and the relevant literatures for which are presented in the following subsections. Since IS planning is linked to synergies between business and IS executives (Chan, Sabherwal, and Thatcher, 2006; King and Teo, 2000; Sabherwal and Chan, 2001; Teo and King, 1997), the knowledge-based view assumes that IS planning is achieved using specific domain knowledge and shared knowledge possessed by top managers and IS managers.

**Specific Domain Knowledge**

Individuals in organizations possess specific knowledge (Demsetz, 1988) related to their roles and functions within the organization. In general, specific knowledge is applicable and valid only to that domain in which the individuals perform their duties, may not be known to or appreciated by individuals working in other domains, and is accumulated over time (Devin and Kozlowski, 1995). In the context of this study, specific domain knowledge has two dimensions: *top managers' knowledge of business* and *IS managers' knowledge of IS,* each relating to a major stakeholder in IS planning. Prior research has demonstrated how top managers, but not IS managers, are more knowledgeable about the business, including environments, strategies, and goals (Rockart, 1979), and how IS managers, but not top managers, are more knowledgeable about IS architectures, capabilities, and functions (Vitale, Ives, and Beath, 1986). Specific domain knowledge of both top managers and IS managers are crucial, as the absence of such knowledge may be detrimental to IS planning. For instance, top managers' knowledge of the business strategies as well as the IS managers' knowledge of the IS applications may both be important for IS planning; the lack of such mutual knowledge may lead to deficiencies in IS planning (Lederer and Mendelow, 1988; Vitale, Ives, and Beath, 1986).

## Shared Knowledge

Nelson and Cooprider (1996) developed the construct of "shared knowledge," which they define as "an understanding and appreciation among IS and line managers for the technologies and processes that affect mutual performance" (p. 411). Reich and Benbasat (1996) defined a similar construct of "shared knowledge" as "the ability of IT and business executives, at a deep level, to understand and be able to participate in the other's key processes and to respect each other's unique contribution and challenges" (p. 86). In the context of this study, shared knowledge has two dimensions: *top managers' knowledge of IS* (Bassellier, Reich, and Benbasat 2001; Vitale, Ives, and Beath, 1986) and *IS managers' knowledge of business* (Boynton and Zmud, 1987). Prior literature has emphasized that shared knowledge between top managers and IS managers might facilitate IT decision making (Ranganathan and Sethi, 2002), and aid the definition and verification of requirements, resource allocation, and mutual understanding (Lederer and Mendelow, 1988). Different approaches such as participation of IS managers in strategy formulation, having an IS team recreate the business goals through interviews with top managers, and so on, have been used to build shared knowledge (King, 1978; Vitale, Ives, and Beath, 1986), with the recognition that shared knowledge is vital to establish a common ground for understanding business strategies and developing relevant information systems.

Specific domain knowledge provides the foundation for shared knowledge. When specific domain knowledge is high, that specific domain knowledge can be used to develop shared knowledge, but when specific domain knowledge is low, it will be much more difficult to build shared knowledge (Kogut and Zander, 1992; Nahapiet and Ghoshal, 1998). This is consistent with Grant's (1996a, 1996b) view that common knowledge includes common pools of specialized knowledge.

> *Proposition 1:* The level of specific domain knowledge is positively associated with the level of shared knowledge.

## Knowledge Management Processes

Knowledge includes explicit knowledge and tacit knowledge (Polanyi, 1966). Explicit knowledge can be expressed in numbers and words and shared formally and systematically in the form of data, manuals, and the like. Tacit knowledge, which includes insights, intuitions, and hunches, is difficult to express, formalize, and share. Based on the KM literature (e.g., Alavi and Leidner, 2001; Conner and Prahalad, 1996; Grant, 1996a, 1996b), we identified five KM processes—direction, exchange, internalization, combination, and socialization. Organizations often use a KM process, *direction,* in which an individual with specialized knowledge guides the action of another without transferring the underlying knowledge (Grant, 1996a). This maintains the advantages of specialization and avoids the difficulties inherent in transferring tacit knowledge. In contrast, *exchange* is used to transfer explicit knowledge (Grant, 1996b). It often relies on externalization,[1] or the conversion of tacit knowledge into explicit form through techniques that help to express ideas as words, concepts, visuals, metaphors, analogies, and narratives (Nonaka and Konno, 1998). *Internalization* is the conversion of explicit knowledge into tacit knowledge. Learning by doing, on-the-job training, learning by observation, and face-to-face meetings are some illustrative internalization processes (Nonaka, 1994). *Combination* helps to integrate explicit knowledge of group members, but the new knowledge generated through combination often transcends the group (Nonaka and Konno, 1998). Combination involves the conversion of explicit knowledge into more complex sets of explicit knowledge (Nonaka, 1994). Finally, *socialization* is the synthesis of tacit knowledge across individuals, usually through joint activities rather than written or verbal instructions (Nonaka, 1994). For example, by transferring ideas and images, apprenticeships help newcomers to see how others think.

Each of the above KM processes can directly or indirectly facilitate learning by individuals, and this learning could be in the areas of either business or information systems. We propose that specific domain knowledge and shared knowledge can be developed using KM processes. However, we are not aware of any study of the effects of the five KM processes on specific domain knowledge of IS and business executives or the shared knowledge between IS and business executives. Therefore, we did not propose a priori research propositions regarding how KM processes affect specific domain knowledge and shared knowledge. Instead, we used the cases to develop propositions related to these relationships.

It has been argued that mutual understanding between business and IS executives facilitates alignment (Boynton and Zmud, 1987; Earl, 1989). More specifically, greater business knowledge among IS managers enhances their understanding of the business plans (Lederer and Mendelow, 1987), enabling them to consider business plans during IS planning (Earl, 1989). Similarly, more IT-knowledgeable top management is likely to participate more during IS planning (Lederer and Mendelow, 1987; Bassellier, Reich, and Benbasat, 2001). Shared knowledge also facilitates alignment by improving links between business and IS planning and communication between business and IS executives (Reich and Benbasat, 2000).

*Proposition 2:* Shared knowledge is positively related to strategic IS alignment.

## STRATEGIC INFORMATION SYSTEMS ALIGNMENT

Strategic IS alignment has been defined as "the degree to which the IT mission, objectives and plans support and are supported by the business mission, objectives and plans" (Reich and Benbasat, 1996, p. 56). To examine *business strategy,* we used the popular typology of defenders, analyzers, and prospectors (Miles and Snow, 1978), which combines elements of both corporate-level strategy (i.e., which products and markets to compete in) and business-level strategy (i.e., how to compete in a particular industry). *IS strategy* is examined in terms of the ways in which information systems are being sought to impact the organization. The five strategic thrusts (low cost, differentiation, growth, alliance, and innovation) identified by Wiseman (1988) and studied by several authors (e.g., Neumann, 1994; Sabherwal, Hirschheim, and Goles, 2001), are used for this purpose. Recognizing that differentiation, growth, alliance, and innovation are not mutually exclusive (Sabherwal and King, 1991), and that a firm may not consider IS as strategic (e.g., Brown and Magill, 1998), four situations were considered: nonstrategic IS; low cost IS strategy; differentiation, growth, innovation, or alliance IS strategy; and a combination of low cost and differentiation/growth/innovation/alliance IS strategy.

Prior literature (e.g., Brown, 1997; Brown and Magill, 1998; Sabherwal and Chan, 2001; Segev, 1989) helped identify the IS strategy best aligned to each business strategy. By offering high quality but standard products at low prices, the *defender* seals off a stable and narrow niche in its industry. Stressing operational efficiency and scale economies, it does not generally seek new opportunities, and rarely makes major adjustments in its technology. The *low cost IS strategy* is best suited for this business strategy. The *prospector* is the defender's opposite. Continuously seeking new opportunities, it is the creator of change in its market. It invests heavily in environmental scanning

Figure 7.2  **The Initial Model**

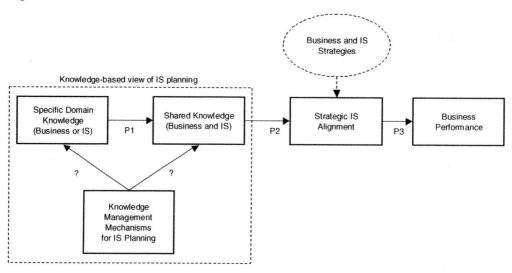

and research and development. Its desire for flexibility and innovativeness reduces controls and operational efficiency. This business strategy is best aligned with a *differentiation, growth, innovation, or alliance IS strategy.* Combining the strengths of the other two types, the *analyzer* seeks to simultaneously minimize risk and maximize growth opportunities. It maintains a stable domain of core products, but also seeks new opportunities. It does not usually initiate new products, but often quickly follows the prospector with competitive, and occasionally better, products. Thus, it does not create change, but does not avoid change either. This strategy is best aligned with a *combination of low cost and differentiation/growth/innovation/alliance IS strategy.* There is low alignment between all business strategies and nonstrategic IS (King, 1978).

Alignment between business and IS strategies facilitates business and IS success (King, 1978). Greater alignment indicates that the firm has a clear vision of, and plan for, addressing critical areas (Lederer and Mendelow, 1989), and so IS may be expected to make a greater contribution to the business performance (Sabherwal and Chan, 2001). Strategic IS literature suggests that alignment heightens awareness and use of IS (Segars and Grover, 1998), increases the firm's ability to realize its goals and objectives (Lederer and Mendelow, 1989), and thereby helps improve business performance (King, 1978; Sabherwal and Chan, 2001; Wiseman, 1988).

*Proposition 3:* Strategic IS alignment is positively related to business performance.

Figure 7.2 shows the theoretical model depicting the relationships among the knowledge-based view of IS planning, strategic IS alignment, and business performance.

## RESEARCH METHODS

### Data Collection

To pursue our research objectives, we studied three organizations in some detail. A qualitative approach based on case studies was selected due to: (a) the paucity of prior empirical research on the knowledge-based view of IS planning; (b) the desire to understand the impact of KM processes on specific domain knowledge and shared knowledge; (c) the need to understand the thinking behind the major decisions made along the way; and (d) the sensitive nature of the data needed (Benbasat, Goldstein, and Mead, 1987; Yin, 1984). At the same time, we wanted to examine strategic IS alignment in some different contexts. The case sites were selected based on access to senior executives, interestingness of the issues encountered over time, and diversity of firm size, industry, and issues. To maintain confidentiality, the names of all companies and individuals are disguised. We use the pseudonyms Alpha, Beta, and Gamma to represent the three companies. Their nature is summarized in Table 7.1. Gamma is international, with considerable presence in the United States, Alpha is located in United States, and Beta is Australian. Beta and Gamma are large, while Alpha is small. One major subsidiary of Gamma, Sub-G, provides consulting and IS services to external organizations and other subsidiaries of Gamma. Gamma's IS group was a major portion of Sub-G.

In each case,[2] IS planning and strategic IS alignment were retrospectively studied through multiple intensive interviews with executives from different backgrounds and at various hierarchical levels, and examination of company documents. We asked the informants to focus on major events but encouraged them to expand their comments into specific aspects of the company's business and IS conditions. In total, thirty interviews, lasting about forty-seven hours, were conducted with twenty-five informants. Each interview was tape-recorded and transcribed. Additional notes were taken when needed.

## Data Analysis

Given our research objectives, we were interested in the changes over time in the business and IS strategies and KM processes. We tried to produce more general explanations (Eisenhardt, 1989) through "analytic generalization" (Yin, 1984), where theoretical concepts and patterns are generalized. In each case, we examined changes over time through rigorous analysis involving four broad steps, as described below.

First, we conducted *an initial analysis of the transcripts.* Each transcript was read carefully, and comments on the events and explanations for those events were highlighted. The interviewee remarks were linked to business strategy and IS strategy, and to the relationship between them. In each case, periods of major changes and the intervening periods of relatively little change were identified.

Second, we conducted a more formal interpretation of the transcripts to *segment the interview data.* Three raters participated in this step. Each case was assigned to two raters, such that each rater independently read the transcripts for two cases. Two different perspectives were thus used for each case to minimize the likelihood of missing something important. To facilitate consistent interpretation, the raters used a common set of definitions of the research constructs, and the same form to code transcripts. Using electronic versions of the transcript-coding form and the transcripts, each rater performed several "copy" and "paste" commands to move segments of the transcripts to one of the columns of the form. The raters also indicated the perceived nature of each comment on this electronic form. The comment could concern business or IS strategy, business or IS performance, a factor that may have triggered a major change, or some important change in alliances or internal personnel.[3] The form also indicated, for each comment, its location on the transcript, the approximate date to which it was relevant, and any links to other comments.

Next, we used these segments of interview data to *analyze the research constructs.* This was done in three steps. First, the electronic forms containing the interpretations for all the transcripts

Table 7.1

## The Cases

| | Alpha | Beta | Gamma |
|---|---|---|---|
| The company | Independent equipment leasing firm | Diversified business units including financial services, property services, capital investments | Exploration, production, refining, and marketing of petroleum products. |
| Location | United States | Australia | Multinational; significant presence in United States |
| Size | For the period examined, net worth ranged from $25 million to $100 million and number of employees ranged from 90 to 275 | Annual revenue of about $2 billion | Annual revenue of over $20 billion |
| Key aspects of strategic IS management | Rapid increase in internal systems to facilitate corporate turnaround | Outsourcing of IT activities and acquisition of 35 percent share in the IT vendor | Creation of a separate IS subsidiary with freedom to seek external contracts |
| No. of interviewees | 5 | 7 | 13 |
| No. of interviews | 5 | 9 | 16 |
| Case periods | 1985 to 1995 | 1980 to 1997 | 1990 to 1998 |
| Interview periods | January–February 1996 | April 1996; July 1997 | February–April 1996; June–July 1997; April 1998 |
| Interviewees | • Chief financial officer<br>• Senior vice president (Operations)<br>• Vice president (Accounting)<br>• Vice president (Marketing)<br>• The former IS director | • Corporate chief financial officer<br>• Corporate CIO<br>• IT manager, later promoted to CIO<br>• New IT manager (brought in after outsourcing arrangement began)<br>• IT director for Financial Services<br>• IT director for Property Services<br>• IT project manager (who reports to IT director for Property Services) | • President and CEO of SUBSID<br>• Six of the nine individuals, including customer support managers, directly reporting to Sub-G's CEO (one of these six individuals is the current CEO)<br>• Six IT line of business managers |

for each case were combined in a spreadsheet. These spreadsheets were quite large, with the one for the simplest case, Alpha, having 310 rows. Each spreadsheet was sorted based on the nature of, and the time period related to, each comment. To facilitate this, an additional column was created based on a combination of the rater's interpretation of the nature of the comment, and the related time period (in terms of the early, middle, and later stages of the case study period). This step helped us to decontextualize the interviewee comments out of the original interview, and recontextualize them by assembling all comments (in each case) about a particular aspect (e.g., the defender strategy initially pursued by Gamma). Second, the printouts of the three sorted spreadsheets were used to identify the business/IS strategies and performance. This helped us to describe the changes over time in alignment. Third, the comments related to changes in business/IS structure and comments that had been marked as "others" were examined with special attention to words related to KM (we conducted an electronic "find" for all comments containing: "know," "ignore," "ignorant," "aware," "understand," "recognize," "educate," "education," "learn," "teach," and "train").[4] The remaining comments were then read to identify any others related to KM. Overall, in this step, we identified comments about: (a) KM processes; (b) knowledge of business and IS/IT (these were then used to assess shared knowledge, i.e., business executives' IS/IT knowledge and IS executives' business knowledge, and specific domain knowledge, i.e., business executives' business knowledge and IS executives' IS/IT knowledge); and (c) relationship between KM and alignment. This step was critical in explaining the changes in alignment using knowledge considerations. Thus, we examined each research construct based on several interviewee comments. Each case description includes some illustrative quotes.

Finally, we *examined the relationships among research constructs in light of the emergent theoretical model.* KM processes, business and IS strategies, alignment, and business performance, were viewed together for each period and within each case, in light of the initial model. Changes in the research constructs over time were examined by comparing across the various time periods for each case.

## EMPIRICAL CASES

### Case Study 1: Alpha

Started in 1976 as an equipment sales firm, Alpha became an independent equipment lessor in 1983. Its net worth grew from US$25 million to $100 million from 1986 to 1996. The case focused on the events before, during, and after a turnaround, which the company went through from late 1989 to 1992.

*Period 1—1985 to October 1989*

Until late 1989, Alpha employed a *prospector* strategy, seeking rapid growth by aggressively pursuing new products. It operated without controls, standards, or concern for proper records. It devoted little attention to IS, which was viewed as *nonstrategic,* almost as a distraction. Alpha consequently had little useful information for planning and control. Its *business performance suffered* during this phase, as it did not adapt to changes in its business environment. For example, a tax reform in 1986 repealed certain tax benefits applicable to the leasing business. But Alpha continued to operate as it did before the tax reform. It failed to recognize the sharp decline in mainframe computer prices due to the advent of personal computers. In October 1989, Alpha realized it was in trouble.

*Knowledge-based View*

During this period, Alpha's IS group was small and centralized. Isolated from the business functions, it provided *direction* to the users regarding what to do with IS, without seeking their input or educating them about IT applications. There was a *low level of specific domain knowledge* as business and IS personnel seemed to operate on a limited base of knowledge: business personnel did not consider changes in their environment and IS personnel only provided direction on using IS. Consequently, there was a *low level of shared knowledge,* as business and IS personnel lacked understanding of IS and business issues, respectively. According to the individual who later became the IS director, "a lot of people in the trenches didn't know what they (IS personnel) were doing." The lack of shared knowledge was consistent with non-integration across functional areas, which operated as "little fiefdoms" (chief financial officer) and the *low level of alignment* between business and IS strategies.

*Period 2—October 1989 to August 1992*

Following the recognition of the financial troubles, David Garcey was hired as senior VP (Operations) in October 1989. Several senior executives, mainly from Garcey's previous company, were hired in April–June 1990. In 1990, Alpha had a debt of $100 million and equity of $60 million. As it incurred further losses, debt/equity ratio quickly rose to about three to one. In August 1990, Alpha was "put in the workout" (VP, Accounting) by its lender banks. It now had to do monthly compliance reports. Recognizing the seriousness of the situation, the entrepreneurs hired Rick Moon, a banker, as chief executive officer (CEO). The former IS director characterized this as "fighting bankers with a banker." Soon after Moon arrived, the business strategy shifted to *defender.* Alpha stopped growing and started cutting costs. A business plan was prepared in January 1991. A few months later, a transaction review committee was created to monitor sales deals. This committee met daily to approve bids, credits, and major sales. Moon primarily focused on cutting costs, firing fifty people in December 1990 and another twenty a little later. In August 1991, the board decided not to renew Moon's contract, and named Garcey as president.

Garcey quickly instituted clear lines of reporting. Also, the changes in top management and business strategy were accompanied by major changes in IS. Recognizing the importance of IS, Moon had hired Adrian as the new IS director, which was followed by the hiring of some other IS executives. Adrian told Garcey that he wanted to stop some of the ongoing IS activities and focus on the major ones, and introduced some new KM mechanisms. Following these changes, business executives actively sought opportunities to use IT to enhance efficiency and reduce costs. This *low cost* IS strategy was followed by *improved business performance* toward the end of this phase. Detailed standards were set up by early 1992, and most of the databases were cleaned up by May 1992. Alpha reported profits in April 1992. The banks gave Alpha a one-year extension in August 1991, and then a thirty-month extension in August 1992, allowing it to keep a certain formula amount of cash flows to invest in new business.

*Knowledge-based View*

During this period, there was a *high level of specific domain knowledge* due to Garcey's appointment as the new senior VP (Operations), Moon's appointment as the new CEO, Adrian's appointment as the new IS director, the various committees that were put in place for interaction among business personnel, and the hiring of several new IS personnel. The daily meetings of the transaction review committee allowed for KM mechanisms such as *socialization* and *combination.*

Adrian instituted several KM mechanisms to better integrate business and IS knowledge. First, he moved four IS employees to user areas. These individuals regularly met with others in their area, played a major role in local IS decisions, and communicated weekly with Adrian. This use of local IS personnel helped achieve *socialization and combination,* as these individuals and the business personnel worked together to identify ways of using IS to address the business needs.

> Senior VP (Operations): "We also put in place programming staff and a support staff—what we called a support staff—somebody to interface with the users."

Second, Adrian constituted an "interactive advisory committee," which helped in IS planning, and supported *socialization and combination* at the strategic level. He also instituted mechanisms to facilitate the *exchange* of explicit knowledge. These included carefully selected liaison persons and release of information on IS activities, for example, through "MIS Releases" explaining "what we're changing, what's important to everybody in the company," and so on (IS director). The transaction review committee's frequent meetings also supported *socialization* by enabling people from business and IS to work with each other. Moreover, with Garcey's support, Adrian and other senior executives started "cross-training" across various areas, including IS. This facilitated *internalization*—of IS knowledge by business executives and of business knowledge by IS personnel—as they worked with people from the other areas.

> Chief Financial Officer: "Senior management meets every day and reviews every single deal. We get input from marketing . . . from our Asset Management Group . . . from IS."

> Adrian: "Everybody had an appreciation for everybody else's jobs. We did a lot of cross training—programmers would work with users, IS managers would sit with accountants so we could understand their systems. . . . It was . . . a lot of sharing of knowledge."

Together, the above processes promoted sharing and synthesis of tacit and explicit knowledge concerning business and IS. There was consequently an increase in *shared knowledge* as business and IS personnel started to better understand each other's areas. This effect of KM processes on shared knowledge is illustrated by the above comment as well as the following remarks.

> VP (Accounting): "I made her (accounting manager) a liaison with the IS Department . . . to make sure that we could develop the systems we needed, we needed somebody who understood accounting but who could also talk to the IS people. So, I put her in that area and it worked out very well. She could explain to them what was needed."

> Adrian: "That was the greatest savior—getting them in the trenches with the users because they brought back things like, 'Mike, you should see what they do to cook a deal.' Well, let's change it. It's not right. It's not efficient. Change it."

There was a considerable increase in the IS personnel's knowledge of business. But business executives' knowledge of IS showed a moderate increase. They better understood the role IS could play at Alpha (e.g., in cutting costs), but they did not learn about underlying IT and left IS decisions to Adrian.

*Period 3—August 1992 to 1995*

Following the turnaround, central IS staff was trimmed toward the end of 1992, down to two people, with the individual departments assuming responsibility for various IS functions. The IS personnel in various departments now operated independently of the central IS group. Vendors were hired for IS maintenance, but no mechanisms were established to learn from them. Adrian left the IS group, but continued on at Alpha, becoming "quasi-advisory" to IS. Another individual took over as head of IS, but was not given the title of IS director. Moreover, David Garcey brought sales under his direct control in 1994, and started emphasizing growth. Along with the traditional leasing of computer equipment, Alpha began leasing other kinds of equipment (e.g., forklifts and trucks). The belief was that the back office had been taken care of, and so the front office needed attention. With the business strategy reverting to *prospector,* controls and IS began being ignored again. The IS budget was lowered to $300,000. Having made a strategic contribution to the turn-around, IS was now *nonstrategic* again.

*Knowledge-based View*

There was a *low level of specific domain knowledge* as the IS function was downsized (including Adrian, the IS director), and business personnel attempted to expand and grow the organization's business without fully understanding the problems in the back office. Most KM mechanisms were discarded. The one or two IS personnel in some departments no longer reported to the central IS group, which had only two people. The interactive IS advisory committee also became inactive as there was no IS director. Alpha had reverted to a situation where IS was maintaining existing systems and providing some *direction* to business about the use of these systems. Adrian disagreed with these ongoing changes, and in late 1995, decided to leave Alpha. The IS group's business knowledge decreased considerably as the senior IS personnel who understood the business issues departed and the mechanisms providing exchange of business knowledge were discarded. Business personnel did not understand the emergent IT, as mentioned earlier, and their awareness of IT's strategic potential also decreased with the IS advisory committee becoming dormant. Consequently, IS and business personnel no longer had a good understanding of what the other group was doing.

This *reduction in shared knowledge* was accompanied by a shift to earlier business and IS strategies—prospector and nonstrategic, respectively. *Strategic IS alignment* was consequently *low* as well. Some senior executives were concerned that the nonstrategic nature of IS could come back to haunt them by adversely affecting *business performance* in the future.

> Chief financial officer (CFO): "It's like you're on a little curve. Right now, the IS group is on the downside of that curve. But at some point we are going to pay for that, too; for only having two people in IS."

Senior management's warnings about Alpha's long-term future proved correct. Alpha's net earning per share started declining from 1997. Deteriorating performance has culminated in its being delisted from NASDAQ and eventually being made inactive. While we are reluctant to say that Alpha's inability to achieve strategic alignment was the sole cause, we believe it did contribute to the company's current crisis.

**Case Study 2: Beta**

Beta is a diversified Australian company with annual revenue of about US$2 billion and after-tax profits of over US$250 million. Its businesses include financial, property, and capital services, and investments. This case focused on events before, during, and after a major change, in which

Beta outsourced its IS activities to a multinational IS vendor and obtained an equity holding in the vendor's Australian unit.

*Period 1—1980 to 1993*

Pursuing a *prospector* strategy, Beta grew considerably from 1980 to 1993 by entering new areas through acquisitions. One major acquisition was a large integrated financial services firm in 1985. Consistent with its growth by acquisition, Beta included several business units, which differed vastly in the technologies used. According to an IT manager, IS "had been historically much underfinanced." Several IS executives indicated that the total money invested on IS was tightly maintained but the IS resources were used inappropriately, with too much expenditure on maintaining old systems. IS was thus considered *nonstrategic,* reflecting *a low level of alignment* with the prospector strategy.

*Knowledge-based View*

Each business unit had a separate IS group. Due to the diversity of the business units and the technologies used, there was no synergy between the business units or the IS groups within the business units. This resulted in a *low level of specific domain knowledge.* The IS activities were driven by "the techies," with little input from the business side according to a senior business executive. There was considerable *direction* from IS toward business about the systems to be developed.

> A business executive: "We had no discipline in making strategic decisions on IT. We had no role in those decision processes in terms of business value to be returned. Often they were being driven very much by emotion . . . 'if you don't do this the world will come to an end.'"

Even in the strategic steering committee, the discussions were primarily about IS expenditures without understanding the possible synergies between business and IS. Business and IS executives lacked knowledge of each other. The following comments illustrate the lack of *shared knowledge:*

> IT director (Financial Services): "The steering committee used to sit down and approve major projects and in my judgment approve them on inadequate information."

> An IS executive: "IT has been responsive to business needs, but we haven't had a map at the back to say, okay they have these business needs."

By 1990, Beta was facing *major business problems,* especially in growth. This was attributed partly to the low alignment; Beta's information systems did not help to identify growth opportunities, and Beta did not seek opportunities to grow using IT. Recognizing the problems, the CEO, Steve Avery, engaged a large consulting firm in 1990 to catalog areas for future growth. The report identified the IT industry as a key growth area.

*Period 2—1993 to October 1995*

As several international companies started moving into Australia, Beta sought to reduce costs due to the threat from them. Its business strategy consequently shifted to *analyzer.* Beta sought to acquire a stake in the IS industry through an alliance with a major IS provider. IS now became strategic to: (a) generating external revenues through a stake in an IS company; and (b) significantly reducing business costs. Thus, IS strategy was to simultaneously seek *low cost and growth/alliance*, reflecting a *high level of alignment* with the analyzer strategy. Beta initiated negotiations with a global IS vendor in early 1993, but stopped them in late 1993. Then in early 1994, a global IS vendor approached Beta about a possible joint venture, which Beta found attractive. As part of the agreement, Beta would have a 35 percent stake in this new Australian company, and Beta would outsource all of its IS to the new company. The joint-venture company went online on October 1, 1994.

*Knowledge-based View*

Beta's dealings (for joint ventures and outsourcing) with the global IS vendor allowed it to appreciate the importance of IT but did not directly increase its own internal pool of business or IT knowledge as there was no indication of KM mechanisms for knowledge transfer. This resulted in a *low level of specific domain knowledge.*

Based on the consultant's report and several other external sources of information, the CEO clearly recognized (*internalization*) the importance of IT in achieving a 35–40 percent expense reduction. Having gained a better understanding of IT and its strategic potential, he explicitly stated his views to the corporate chief information officer (CIO) and other senior executives (*direction*).

> IT director (Property Services): " . . . outsourcing was directly determined by the CEO. With his traveling around the world, he was learning very rapidly about IT. He decided that he would never move Beta into thinking about IT unless he did something bluntly. I believe it was his strategy or tactic to just say, 'guys, you'll never change so I'm gonna change you.'"

*Shared knowledge,* especially business executives' knowledge of IT, increased at the corporate level, but this was not paralleled within the divisions. No KM mechanisms supporting exchange, internalization, socialization, or combination had been established for the divisions. Business executives' knowledge of IS/IT was expected to increase due to the vendor's inputs, but this did not happen.

> IT director (Financial Services): "We see ourselves as leaders in IT in the future, and expected a global IT provider to give us a lot of input at low cost on what the international best practices are today in terms of systems and processes. . . . So far they haven't delivered."

*Business performance* improved moderately, but problems quickly surfaced. The main problem was how to take the user requirements and fit them into the overall service structure of the outsourcing contract. Corporate executives had established the new alliance, and the historically independent business units had little input in the matter. The vendor's contract was ill defined, and the business units' needs and expectations were poorly understood. Inadequate definition of service levels was exacerbated by the fact that in transitioning Beta's IS personnel to the vendor, only the former IS director of financial services was retained, and even he left in June 1995. There was really no one from Beta to handle IS from June 1995.

*Period 3—October 1995 to 1997*

In light of the problems in implementing the IS strategy, several changes were made starting with the hiring of a corporate CIO in October 1995. New IS directors were hired for each business unit.[5] IS management was now shared by Beta and the business units; each unit's own people now managed its part of the contract. These individuals were charged with translating business unit needs into IS services that the vendor could deliver. *Strategic IS alignment* continued to be *high,* with an *analyzer* strategy and IS being used to simultaneously seek *low cost and growth/alliance.*

*Knowledge-based View*

The hiring of corporate CIO and IS directors for business units enhanced the internal pool of IS knowledge, indicating a *high level of specific domain knowledge.* Increased attention was given to knowledge integration across business and IS personnel, at corporate as well as business unit levels. A "culture of communication" between IS and business personnel was developed (*exchange and socialization*), for example, through a number of "road shows" to get the users to learn about IS (*internalization*). The steering committees within divisions also actively started examining IT in detail, and in relation to business issues (*combination and socialization*).

> IT director (Financial Services): "We are increasing the communications structure. Once we have established a culture of communication, we'll be in a position to properly communicate where we are and where we are going. In the meantime, I am spending a lot of my time getting around the various groups. To listen to their thinking in terms of what they should be expecting. People worry about response times, they worry about all those hard measures and they are not worrying about the real important issues. So I try to talk to them to get people to think it's worth it. There are lots of good things."

> IT director (Financial Services): "In the business planning and budgeting process the chief executives of the lines of business are very much involved, especially in their IT strategy and planning. Not in the nitty gritty but in the identification of where you want to take the business, the sort of improvements we need to become competitive."

These changes increased *shared knowledge* at the divisional level. Users and IS personnel gained more knowledge of IT and business issues, respectively.

> IT director (Property Services): "The users are now more aware. They are starting to ask more intelligent questions now."

The problems in implementing the business and IS strategies were reduced as a result of the increased IS knowledge, and improved knowledge integration, within the divisions. This led to a *high level of alignment.* There was also greater confidence about the future impact of IT on *business performance.*

> IT director (Financial Services): "We are establishing a process for prioritizing where we spend money and build our plans for the future, being very much driven by the business."

> IT director (Property Services): "The place has turned around in a very short period of time, it is now focusing on a business point of view."

**Case Study 3: Gamma**

Gamma is the U.S. subsidiary of an international organization performing the exploration, production, refining, and marketing of petroleum products. It has revenues of over $20 billion and more than 15,000 employees. It went through a major reorganization, which was announced on January 1995, and created several independent units, including one, Sub-G, whose major focus was on IS. This case is discussed in three parts: the events at Gamma from 1990 to April 1993, and from April 1993 to September 1995, and the events at Sub-G from January 1995 to April 1998. The overlap from January 1995 to September 1995 occurs because during this period Gamma's IS strategy was changing while Sub-G was preparing its own strategy.

*Gamma from 1990 to April 1993*

Until April 1993, Gamma had a centralized business structure. Gamma had followed a *defender* strategy, maintaining its territory through low costs but not seeking opportunities for growth. The IS group played a *nonstrategic* role. Gamma's *business performance* in the early 1990s also deteriorated, especially relative to other energy firms. The energy industry was becoming increasingly competitive, partly due to protracted low oil prices in the late 1980s and early 1990s, and Gamma did not seem prepared for this change.

*Knowledge-based View*

IS management was performed by a central IS group, which was perceived as telling business people what to do rather than listening to their needs. IS supported the business areas but was "less business oriented and more technology focused" (line of business manager, Technology Services). Moreover, the company used "the classic central control of an IT organization. I set the rules and you follow the rules" (customer support manager, Professional Firms). This period was characterized by a *low level of specific domain knowledge* as the central IS group only provided direction and the business personnel only maintained their ground without influx of additional knowledge.

   *Direction* from the IS group was not accompanied by internalization, socialization, or other KM processes. Business and IS groups believed that they knew their respective areas best. They operated within their own domains without acquiring much knowledge of the other area. There was thus a *low level of shared knowledge* between business and IS. The level of shared knowledge was also low across business areas, and Gamma had a tendency to reinvent the wheel. For example, instead of using existing external knowledge bases and vendors, oil rigs and drilling platforms were designed and built in-house, from scratch. Continued success had apparently caused a complacent and inflexible culture.

> General manager (Business Development), speaking in 1996: " . . . the problem with our IT function, and I used to be one of them so I am talking about myself too, we always thought when it came to IT we knew more about what the business needed than the business itself."

IS did not play much role in reducing business costs, as required for the Defender strategy. *The low level of alignment* was consistent with the low level of shared knowledge. That IS had not enabled, or even targeted, reduction of business costs, contributed to Gamma's margins being below that of its competitors.

> Customer support manager (Oil Products): "While everybody else was scrambling we had managed to stay the course. Unfortunately, we were staying a course that wasn't fit for the

world in which we were heading, and when we got there in 1988–89–90, we found that we were ill prepared for that world."

### Gamma from April 1993 to September 1995

A new president and CEO, Paul Hill, was hired in April 1993. He commissioned a thorough evaluation of the company's mission and structure by an external consultant. Based on this consultant's recommendations, Hill and four executive VPs mandated a radical shift in business strategy and corporate philosophy in February 1994. Gamma's business strategy shifted toward *analyzer* with greater attention to market conditions and growth opportunities. Correspondingly, the corporate philosophy shifted from the centralized "command and control" structure to what they called "federal governance" (a customer support manager).[6] Decision making was moved to the lowest organizational level that had the information needed for the decision,[7] and "urgency combined with 80 percent success replaced the prior focus on 100 percent success without urgency" (an IT manager).

With the corporate transformation on January 1, 1995, each subsidiary became independent with profit and loss responsibility. One subsidiary, Sub-G, employed about 1,800 people, including about 800 in IS, and the rest in financial and accounting services and distribution channel management. Sub-G's mission was to provide these services to Gamma subsidiaries and also on the open market to organizations unrelated to Gamma (including other firms in the energy industry). Sub-G's corporate siblings were free to seek IS services outside. Sub-G had an existing revenue base in excess of $300 million, mainly from other Gamma subsidiaries. Gamma was now aiming to reduce business and IS costs through anticipated efficiencies from market competition. It also expected increased revenues from Sub-G. There was thus a clear shift in IS strategy, toward both *low cost and growth*. This IS strategy suited the Analyzer strategy, reflecting an *increase in alignment*. There were indications of improvements in both *business performance* of Gamma and perceived IS performance.

> Sub-G's president and CEO: "Before we started Sub-G, I got some feedback (from peers). A few of my colleagues would come and tell me IT didn't work. The criticism of IT was more common before we set up the company (Sub-G) than it is now."

### Knowledge-based View

Top management at Gamma included a leadership council and a larger leadership group, including senior executives from the various subsidiaries. Similarly, each subsidiary's leadership group and council included one or more representatives from Gamma. Sub-G's board included the CEO and three other senior executives from Gamma, but not the heads of the other business units (to avoid conflict of interest). Sub-G's CEO was one of the fourteen members of Gamma's leadership council. IS decisions were pushed into the business units, and a CIO was appointed for each unit. These led to an *increase in specific domain knowledge* within Gamma. Several mechanisms for *socialization, exchange, and combination* were introduced, including "strategic positioning studies," "strategy challenge sessions," and "decision circles" (line of business manager, Technology Services). These mechanisms, as well as the leadership council and the leadership forum for Gamma and each subsidiary, provided valuable forums for face-to-face discussions by business and IS executives.

Customer support manager (Oil Products): "They (other business units) were willing for me to come and sit in on what they call their strategy challenge session. They went over each one of their strategies and the various options that they had and allowed me to sit on a couple of teams with the customers where they work on things like new product development and business performance . . ."

Customer support manager (Exploration and Production): "You try to get the right people in a room and say 'here's the business problem; here's what's happening; what's the right answer?' and it requires compromise and work."

The introduction of the above KM mechanisms led to an *increase in the level of specific domain knowledge* as well as *shared knowledge*. Business executives became better aware of the potential as well as the pitfalls of IT. This was also necessitated by their increased responsibility for IS.

General manager (Business Development): " . . . the businesses are now going to feel good about it because they own it (information technologies and systems)—it's their decision."

*Sub-G from January 1995 to April 1998*

Following the major upheaval, the subsidiaries fine-tuned internal structures and strategies. Sub-G's senior executives spent nine months assessing strengths, weaknesses, market, and competition, and completed the strategic plan in September 1995.

Customer support manager (Exploration and Production): "One of the first things we did as a new company was say: 'Hey, we need to rework and rethink our strategy.' . . . We went through a strategy exercise. Some of it was introspection: 'what is it that you do well, what are your competencies?' Some of it was looking outward: 'does anybody care, is there a market for the things you do well, what is there a market for?' . . . That process took about 6 months."

Sub-G started with a *prospector* strategy, seeking to obtain external business not only from systems development but also from selling surplus IS capacity and IS-related infrastructure. Moreover, IS strategy shifted toward *differentiating* Sub-G from its competitors and enabling business *growth*. Sub-G also had good industry knowledge and the ability to do oil and gas accounting at about half the industry cost. There was a *high level of alignment* between this IS strategy and the prospector business strategy.

Free to go elsewhere for IS services, Gamma's other business units started investigating such possibilities. But this worked well for Sub-G; the search for an external vendor led to a better appreciation of the value of Sub-G among the other subsidiaries of Gamma. Their assessments of Sub-G's performance improved as well, going up by five percentage points in 1997 in terms of overall satisfaction level. The customer support manager (Exploration and Production) remarked: "Some people went off the reservation. . . . Now they are saying 'gee, it cost a whole lot more to do it that way and it's not quite as good.'"

*Knowledge-based View*

To pursue its Prospector strategy, Sub-G's structure was changed from centralized cost centers to a matrix structure including twenty-one lines of businesses. Sub-G created the position of general manager (or GM) (Business Development) to seek external contracts, made a customer support manager responsible for each of the Gamma customers, and appointed a CIO who was responsible for deciding about the systems to be used internally by Sub-G's lines of businesses. This resulted in a *high level of specific domain knowledge*. However, the CIO and the GM (Business Development) also played an important role in each other's area of primary responsibility, providing one way of sharing knowledge of external business opportunities and internal IS/IT.

> President and CEO: "I also see (the CIO) serving an important role with regard to the offering we make to customers. It's kind of a dual role. . . . If we are focusing on an external customer, or internal customer, I see his advice as very important."

> GM (Business Development): "I have to be really careful that I don't get so bogged down in working internal strategies that we never develop any external business."

There was considerable discussion of business and IS issues among people with expertise in the two areas. Sub-G used circles, wherein individuals with knowledge of various business and IT areas would discuss issues without having to make any decisions. These circles, which differed from triangles in which decisions were made, promoted knowledge integration through *socialization and combination.*

> VP of Operations: "The circle is a unique environment. We actually try not to make a decision (in the circle), you can't make decisions quickly in a group of 40 people."

Due to the dual roles played by the CIO and the general manager (Business Development), and the use of decision circles and other dialogue mechanisms (which were present at both Gamma and Sub-G) to promote socialization and combination, the *shared knowledge* increased. Consequently, even the IS personnel "began to learn to manage things like a business and not like technical people" (customer support manager, Professional Firms). As Sub-G's IS personnel developed a better understanding of the business opportunities, they recognized that internal information systems and superior IS skills, including advantages in subsurface IT and infrastructure processing (e.g., massive parallel processing for seismic data), could help in differentiating Sub-G and enabling its growth. There was thus an *increase in alignment.*

> Line of business manager (Technology Services): "We used the notion of councils or groups of people, usually large groups that are really too ponderous to make decisions but they are not designed to make decisions, they are information sharing, they are used to help develop the alignment that you were talking about early, getting everybody on the same page."

Despite this alignment, Sub-G initially encountered poor *business performance* due to difficulties in implementing its prospector strategy. The established attitudes within Sub-G inhibited dealing with the new emphasis on revenue enhancement. Sub-G personnel also had to make a transition from treating their Gamma customers as a captive audience to treating them as free-market customers.

> Customer support manager (Professional Firms): "From an IS standpoint, I still think we have a lot of arrogance. . . . I still think converting ourselves from telling people the answer to being consultants, I don't think we know how to do that."

Sub-G was now competing for both existing and new business with large competitors eager to get a foothold in the energy industry. It had no track record in the external market. The competitors' strengths were in areas where Sub-G was weak, including deal making and relationship building. To overcome these knowledge gaps, Sub-G started hiring commissioned salespersons for the first time in company history.

> VP (Operations): "We lack competencies around the kind of deal-making and analysis that goes with these . . . service industry deals. So there is a whole area of developing the deal, closing or analyzing the deal, pulling together the right kind of proposal, knowing that you have got to live with some of these deals for five to ten years. How do you handle that?"

To further draw upon external pools of business knowledge, Sub-G decided to seek a strategic alliance with an IS vendor. In May 1997, Sub-G obtained a $100 million project from another Gamma subsidiary. Sub-G was conducting this project along with an external vendor. In addition to the business from the Gamma companies, Sub-G obtained several external projects, ranging from $100,000 to over $5 million. Its revenues for 1996 were about $350 million and $430 million in 1997. By April 1998, Sub-G had continued making changes along three basic lines. The biggest change was the merger of Sub-G, a U.S.-based entity, with other similar subsidiaries of Gamma's global parent to form a single IS and business services subsidiary supporting all the business units of the global company. Its market focus had shifted from providing services to the general energy industry toward gaining a larger share of Gamma's parent company's business. The new organization's share varied widely between business units, but overall it had captured only 20 percent of the global parent's available business in the areas where it provided service. The second major change involved further consolidation of Sub-G's lines of business, first from twenty-one to thirteen and then to four. The organizational structure had evolved into a three-dimensional matrix based on Sub-G lines of business, geographical regions, and the business units of Gamma's global parent. This structure supported face-to-face interactions among business and IS executives, and enabled *socialization and combination,* globally as well as within each country. Finally, Sub-G continued to increase its reliance on external pools of business knowledge. Sub-G was acquiring new skills in marketing and relationship management, but with a slight twist. It was still hiring individuals with expertise in these areas, and expecting that they "not only could go out and sell but could begin to train the rest of us" (general manager, Business Development). However, it was also exploring several strategic partnerships to enhance its competencies and market attractiveness. A new executive position responsible for "Strategic Relation Planning" on the same level as the CFO and CIO, reporting directly to the CEO, was created to oversee these partnerships.

## THE EMERGENT MODEL

Table 7.2 summarizes the changes that occurred in the three cases. For simplicity, we refer to the three periods in Alpha as A1, A2, and A3. Similarly, B1, B2, and B3, and G1, G2, and G3, are used for Beta and Gamma. We next use the cases to develop the propositions constituting the emergent model. However, it is important to note that although the emergent model and the underlying propositions are consistent with prior literature, they are directly based on three case studies. Therefore, they would need to be empirically tested in future research.

### The Relationship Between Specific Domain Knowledge and Shared Knowledge (P1)

The empirical cases provided support for the expected benefits from specific domain knowledge, that is, business executives' knowledge of business and IS executives' knowledge of IS. The

Table 7.2

**Summary of Cases**

| Period | Alpha | | | Beta | | | Gamma | | |
|---|---|---|---|---|---|---|---|---|---|
| | A1 | A2 | A3 | B1 | B2 | B3 | G1 | G2 | G3 |
| | 1985 to October 1989 | October 1989 to August 1992 | August 1992 to 1995 | 1980 to 1993 | 1993 to October 1995 | October 1995 to 1997 | 1990 to April 1993 | April 1993 to September 1995 | Sub-G: January 1995 to April 1998 |
| Subsequent short-term business performance | Good | Good | Good | Good | Fair | Good | Poor | Good | Poor |
| Subsequent long-term business performance | Poor | Fair | Too early to tell, ominous | Poor | Fair | Too early to tell, optimism | Fair | Good | Too early to tell |
| Business strategy | Prospector | Defender | Prospector | Prospector | Analyzer | Analyzer | Defender | Analyzer | Prospector |
| IS strategy | Nonstrategic | Low cost | Nonstrategic | Nonstrategic | Low cost and growth/ alliance | Low cost and growth/ alliance | Nonstrategic | Low cost and growth | Differentiation and growth |
| Strategic IS alignment | Low | High | Low | Low | High | High | Low | High | High |
| Business knowledge of business | Low | High | Low | Low | Low | High | Low | High | High |
| IS knowledge of IS | Moderate | High | Low | Low | Moderate | High | Moderate | High | High |
| Specific domain knowledge | Low | High | Low | Low | Low | High | Low | High | High |
| Business knowledge of IS | Low | Moderate | Low | Low | Moderate | High | Low | High | High |

*(continued)*

143

Table 7.2 (continued)

| Period | Alpha | | | Beta | | | Gamma | | |
|---|---|---|---|---|---|---|---|---|---|
| | A1 | A2 | A3 | B1 | B2 | B3 | G1 | G2 | G3 |
| | 1985 to October 1989 | October 1989 to August 1992 | August 1992 to 1995 | 1980 to 1993 | 1993 to October 1995 | October 1995 to 1997 | 1990 to April 1993 | April 1993 to September 1995 | Sub-G: January 1995 to April 1998 |
| IS knowledge of business | Low | High | Low | Low | Moderate | High | Low | High | High |
| Shared knowledge | Low | High | Low | Low | Moderate | High | Low | High | High |
| **Knowledge management mechanisms** | | | | | | | | | |
| Direction | * | | * | * | * | | * | | |
| Exchange | | * | | | * | * | | * | * |
| Internalization | | * | | | * | * | | | |
| Combination | | * | | | | * | | * | * |
| Socialization | | * | | | | * | | * | * |
| **Potential factors explaining change from previous period** | | | | | | | | | |
| Change in internal pool of business knowledge | | New CEO | | | | | | New CEO | Seeking new skill sets |
| Change in internal pool of IS/IT knowledge | | New IS director | Departure of IS director | | Departure of key IS executives | Hiring of new IS executives | | | |
| Change in external pool of business knowledge | | Banks' knowledge | Banks' reduced inputs | | Consultant's report | | | Consultant's report | |
| Change in external pool of IS/IT knowledge | | | | | | | | | Alliances |

*Indicates the presence of the type of KM mechanism shown in the row.

cases revealed that, in addition to its other benefits (e.g., greater ability to implement business or IS strategy), specific domain knowledge provides the foundation for shared knowledge. When specific domain knowledge is high, that specific domain knowledge can be used to develop shared knowledge, but when specific domain knowledge is low, it will be much more difficult to build shared knowledge (Kogut and Zander, 1992; Nahapiet and Ghoshal, 1998). This is consistent with Grant's (1996a, 1996b) view that common knowledge includes common pools of specialized knowledge. For example, when Alpha hired Adrian and other senior IS personnel in A2, IS executives' IS knowledge (specific domain knowledge) at Alpha increased, facilitating IS knowledge among business executives (shared knowledge) as well.

## The Effects of KM Processes on Specific Domain Knowledge and Shared Domain Knowledge (Emergent)

The cases indicate a positive association between KM processes, other than direction, and specific domain knowledge. Not all of the nine situations had exemplars of the other KM mechanisms (exchange, internalization, socialization, and combination) for specific domain knowledge; but where these mechanisms appeared, the association to specific domain knowledge was positive. For instance, in B3 and G3, the newly appointed business and IS personnel enhanced the pool of specific domain knowledge. Beta (in B3) and Gamma (in G3) also initiated different interactions among the business and the IS personnel within the organization, thus paving the way for several KM mechanisms, including exchange, combination, and socialization, which eventually led to a high level of specific domain knowledge. However, in A1 (at Alpha), there were minimal interactions among the business and IS personnel within the organization, which resulted in a low level of specific domain knowledge.

Overall, the following pattern may be seen in Table 7.2 with respect to the relationship between KM mechanisms and specific domain knowledge. Specific domain knowledge was low in all four situations (A1, A3, B1, G1) where direction was the only mechanism used. In contrast, specific domain knowledge was high in all four situations (A2, B3, G2, G3) where combination and socialization mechanisms were used. Exchange and internalization seemed to be in between direction and combination/socialization: specific domain knowledge was high in all four situations (A2, B3, G2, G3) where exchange and/or internalization were used along with combination and socialization mechanisms, but low in the only situation (B2) where exchange and/or internalization were used along with direction.

The cases also indicate a positive association between KM processes and shared knowledge. As may be seen from Table 7.2, some KM processes were used in each of the nine situations. However, the differences in the types of KM processes seemed to affect the level of shared knowledge, with direction not appearing to facilitate shared domain knowledge. We found a pattern in terms of the relationship between KM mechanisms and shared domain knowledge that resembles the above pattern for the relationship between KM mechanisms and specific domain knowledge. Shared domain knowledge was low in all four situations (A1, A3, B1, G1) where direction was the only mechanism used. On the other hand, shared domain knowledge was high in all four situations (A2, B3, G2, G3) where combination and socialization processes were used. Finally, shared domain knowledge was high in all four situations (A2, B3, G2, G3) where exchange and/or internalization were used along with combination and socialization processes, but moderate in the only situation (B2) where exchange and/or internalization were used along with direction.

In the light of the above, and based on the prior KM literature, the five processes were grouped into three types—knowledge substitution, transfer, and synthesis.

*Knowledge Substitution Processes*

Direction seemed to be related to low specific domain knowledge and low shared knowledge (A1, A3, B1, G1). Direction involves transfer of instructions but not knowledge, and has been called knowledge substitution (Conner and Prahalad, 1996). Direction facilitates efficiency through specialization (Demsetz, 1988), and may therefore be expected to have a low effect on shared knowledge.

*Knowledge Transfer Processes*

In B2, exchange and internalization were used, but not the other three KM processes. Shared knowledge was moderate in this case. Specific domain knowledge seemed to depend on direction (associated with low level of specific domain knowledge) and combination/socialization (associated with high level of specific domain knowledge), with exchange and internalization not having any clear effect of their own. This may be because exchange and internalization involve knowledge transfer across individuals, but they do not directly create new knowledge.[8] These processes may therefore be expected to have a moderate effect on specific domain knowledge and shared knowledge (Grant, 1996a, 1996b; Nahapiet and Ghoshal, 1998). They may be used to separately transfer business knowledge or IS/IT knowledge, but they do not help to combine these types of knowledge.

*Knowledge Synthesis Processes*

In all four situations where socialization and combination were used (A2, B3, G2, G3), both specific domain knowledge and shared knowledge were high, although these situations also benefited from exchange (A2, B3, G2) and internalization (A2, B3). Interview transcripts and prior KM literature suggest that socialization and combination make a significant contribution to KM by helping to integrate prior knowledge (tacit knowledge or explicit knowledge, respectively) to create new knowledge (Nonaka, 1994). Thus, socialization and combination facilitate the synthesis of business and IS/IT knowledge to produce synergistic benefits. They may also enable the synthesis of different areas of business knowledge to produce new business knowledge or the synthesis of different areas of IS/IT knowledge to produce new IS/IT knowledge. They apparently have the greatest impact on both specific domain knowledge and shared knowledge. This is consistent with Nonaka and Konno's (1998) view that innovative organizations typically use combination and socialization to develop new concepts that are created and adopted at both the organizational and interorganizational level. Reich and Benbasat also seem to agree with the effects of socialization and internalization:

> Creating an environment in which shared knowledge can grow may entail actions such as physically moving IT people into business units, making industry (non-IT) reading, course work, and conference attendance mandatory, and sending IT people on regular trips to visit sales offices and customers . . . (Reich and Benbasat, 2000, p. 107)

Based on the above theoretical arguments and the empirical patterns in the case studies, we propose the following propositions.

### The Relationship Between KM Processes and Specific Domain Knowledge (P4A)

a. The use of *direction* for KM is associated with a low level of specific domain knowledge;

b.  the use of *exchange* and *internalization* for KM is associated with a moderate level of specific domain knowledge; and

c.  the use of *socialization* and *combination* for KM is associated with a high level of specific domain knowledge.

### The Relationship Between KM Processes and Shared Knowledge (P4B)

a.  The use of *direction* for KM is associated with a low level of shared knowledge;

b.  the use of *exchange* and *internalization* for KM is associated with a moderate level of shared knowledge; and

c.  the use of *socialization* and *combination* for KM is associated with a high level of shared knowledge.

### The Relationship Between Shared Knowledge and Alignment (P2)

Proposition 2, suggesting a positive association between shared knowledge and alignment, was supported in all situations. But it received moderate support in B2. Further examination of B2 revealed that shared knowledge was high at the corporate level, but low at the business-unit level. Alignment was assessed at the corporate level, and a high level of alignment was consistent with the high level of shared knowledge at that level.

### The Relationship Between IS Alignment and Business Performance (P3)

A high level of alignment was associated with good business performance in periods A2, B3, and G2. A low level of alignment was associated with poor business performance in G1. These situations are consistent with Proposition 3, which is also moderately supported in A1, A3, B1, B2, but not in G3. Simply based on these observations, it seems that there is a fair degree of support for Proposition 3. However, when we examined the situations where Proposition 3 was not well supported, the interview transcripts revealed the following caveats.

In three (A1, A3, B1) of the four situations where Proposition 3 received only moderate support, alignment had the expected effect on long-term business performance but not on short-term business performance. For example, in A1, the low alignment did not adversely affect Alpha's business performance in the short term, but it produced serious negative consequences in the long term. This indicates that *the effects of alignment might occur over time*. The other two situations where Proposition 3 received moderate (B2) or no (G3) support highlight *the importance of the ability to implement business and IS strategies*. In G3, Gamma was pursuing mutually aligned business and IS strategies, but it did not possess the necessary competencies for implementing them. It was trying to build those competencies through hiring and alliances. Similarly, in B2, well-aligned business and IS strategies had been developed by corporate executives, but the business units lacked the expertise needed to implement the IS strategy.

### The Effect of Business Performance on Specific Domain Knowledge and Shared Knowledge in IS Planning (Emergent)

We also observed other situations resembling the above example of increase in specific domain knowledge due to the hiring of senior IS executives at Alpha. When Adrian stepped down as IS director and later left Alpha, there was a drop in both specific domain knowledge and shared knowledge. Similarly, the departure of key IS executives at Beta (in B2) reduced shared knowledge, despite the increase in IS knowledge of corporate business executives. The situation improved when new senior IS executives were hired in B3. Changes in specific or shared knowledge were also influenced by external sources, including alliances (G2, G3), consultants' reports (B2, G2), and banks (A2, A3). The hiring of new individuals (including a new CEO in A2 and G2) and the changes in knowledge obtained through external sources were, in turn, apparently triggered by changes in business performance. Variations in business performance seem to lead to changes in specific domain knowledge and shared knowledge through turnover, external influences, and other possibilities that our cases might not have revealed.

> *Proposition 5A:* Changes in business performance may lead to changes in the levels of specific domain knowledge.
>
> *Proposition 5B:* Changes in business performance may lead to changes in the levels of shared knowledge.

## The Effect of Business Performance on the KM Processes in IS Planning (Emergent)

Moreover, as evident from Table 7.2 and the case descriptions, changes also took place in the KM processes. The changes in personnel, external relationships, and so on, which followed improvement or deterioration in business performance, led to the introduction of certain new KM mechanisms or to the discarding of some existing ones. For example, following deterioration in business performance, the new IS director at Alpha, Adrian, introduced several KM mechanisms in A2. These mechanisms demanded executives' time and attention, and were discarded in A3, when improving business performance was followed by Mike's departure. We therefore suggest the following propositions concerning the effects of changes in business performance. These propositions are consistent with the argument that moderate, single-loop learning is more likely in stable situations, while revolutionary, double-loop learning is more common during reorientation following major performance problems (Argyris, 1982).

> *Proposition 6:* Changes in business performance may lead to changes in KM processes.

Figure 7.3 summarizes the emergent model. Alignment between business and IS strategies is proposed to facilitate business performance (Proposition 3, or P3). Alignment depends on shared knowledge (P2), which in turn depends on KM processes (P4B) and specific domain knowledge (P1). Specific domain knowledge depends on KM processes as well (P4A). Moreover, improvement or deterioration in business performance produces changes in specific domain knowledge (P5A), shared knowledge (P5B), and KM processes (P6). These changes occur through personnel changes, shifts in alliances, and so on, following performance changes. Although developed from the cases, this model is consistent with the prior KM literature, as indicated for the above research propositions. P1 to P4 represent relationships within the short-term, and are posited as associations, whereas P5 and P6 represent relationships over the longer term, and are posited as causal effects.

The emergent model helps in understanding the cases. At Alpha, A1 involved low strategic alignment, which was consistent with the low level of shared knowledge (P2) associated with the reliance on direction for KM (P4B). The low alignment hurt business performance (P3), as Alpha continued growing without building essential systems. The company ended up close to

Figure 7.3  **The Emergent Model**

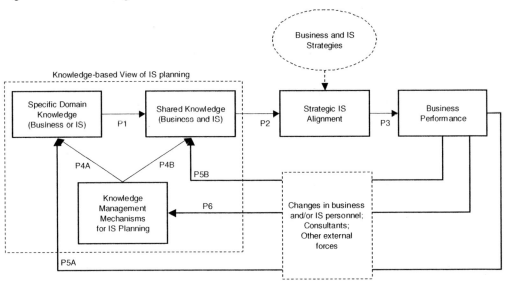

bankruptcy. The situation changed drastically from A1 to A2, due to several factors, including deteriorating business performance, the consequent pressure from the banks, and top-management changes (including quick changes in CEO and the hiring of the IS director). Pools of business and IS knowledge, including both specific (P5A) and shared knowledge (P5B), changed due to these personnel changes. KM mechanisms were also transformed, mainly due to the thrust from Garcey and Adrian (P6). New knowledge transfer and synthesis mechanisms were introduced, enhancing shared knowledge (P4B). Strategic IS alignment increased (P2), as business and IS strategies changed to defender and low cost, respectively. The increased alignment, in turn, improved business performance (P3). But once performance improved and the banks relaxed their controls, another set of major changes ensued, moving Alpha back to a situation resembling A1. The position of IS director was discontinued and the IS staff was trimmed, significantly eroding IS knowledge (P5A). Moreover, most of the knowledge sharing and synthesis mechanisms introduced in period 2 were discarded (P6). The central IS group was small and isolated from the business groups, and shared knowledge between business and IS reduced again (P4B, P1, P5B). Following the reduction in shared knowledge, business and IS strategies reverted to prospector and nonstrategic, respectively, with low alignment between them (P2). Although the company was still performing well, concerns were expressed about its long-term future (P3), and the focus on sales without controls resurfaced.

At Beta, during B1, the use of direction was accompanied by low levels of shared knowledge (P4B), alignment (P2), and performance (P3). The consulting firm, an important external pool of business and IS knowledge, provided recommendations that resulted in improved knowledge integration at the corporate level but not at the divisional level. This resulted in increased IS knowledge among the top business executives (P5B), greater alignment (P2), and improved business performance in B2 (P3). But the lack of knowledge integration at the divisional level was exacerbated by the reduction in the IS staff (reduced internal pool of IS knowledge) (P5A), which constrained shared knowledge (P4B) and performance. This was addressed by hiring the corporate CIO and IS directors for the divisions, enhancing the internal pool of IS knowledge (P5A), followed by the institution of several mechanisms for integrating business and IS knowledge within business units and across corporate and business unit levels (P6). Consequently, specific domain knowledge (P4A), shared knowledge (P4B, P1), alignment (P2), and business performance (P3) all increased in B3.

At Gamma, G1 involved the use of direction, low level of shared knowledge (P4B), low alignment (P2), and poor performance (P3). Gamma's business performance was deteriorating due to its failure to react to the new environment (reduced prices, increased competition). The situation changed in G2 following the hiring of a new CEO (change in the internal pool of business knowledge) and then the recommendations from the consulting firm (an external pool of business knowledge) (P5A). This change in the business knowledge led to Gamma's reorganization, which produced changes in KM processes (P6) through the use of socialization, combination, and exchange, among business and IS executives. These changes, in turn, improved specific domain knowledge (P4A), shared knowledge (P4B), alignment (P2), and performance (P3). In G3, Sub-G also benefited from these KM processes (P4A). However, its lack of business knowledge, with respect to marketing, deal making, negotiations, and so on, initially limited its business performance, despite the high level of alignment. In response, Sub-G drew upon external pools of business knowledge through hiring and alliances (P5A). Short-term business performance seemed to have improved as a result of these changes.

## CONCLUSIONS

This chapter began with two broad research questions, concerning: (a) the knowledge mechanisms underlying IS planning, and (b) the impacts of the knowledge-based IS planning. Three detailed case studies were conducted. Individually, each case provides some insights into these research questions, as examined in the case descriptions. Taken together, the cases contribute to our understanding of IS planning (and its knowledge underpinnings) and its consequences relating to strategic IS alignment and business performance. These conclusions were presented in the form of the propositions and the emergent model in the previous section. The insights developed in this chapter advance our understanding of IS planning and its impacts in several ways.

First, we proposed a knowledge-based view of IS planning that comprised three distinctive aspects: specific domain knowledge possessed by business as well as IS personnel, shared knowledge across business and IS personnel, and knowledge mechanisms that facilitate specific domain knowledge and shared knowledge. Though knowledge has been implicitly assumed in prior research, our model explicitly modeled knowledge in the context of IS planning.

Second, each case found broad support for the initial propositions for the knowledge-based view of IS planning. A number of KM mechanisms were used over time in each case, and they affected the level of specific domain knowledge of business and IS as well as shared knowledge between business and IS. Moreover, greater shared knowledge was associated with greater alignment, which is consistent with the literature. Greater alignment was, in turn, associated with better business and IS performance in seven of the nine situations observed in the cases.

Third, alignment turns out to be a more complex notion than the literature suggests. As shown in the case studies, organizations move in and out of alignment for many reasons. Alignment is not a one-shot proposition where an organization moves into alignment and then stays there forever. Also, unconditional statements about the universal value of alignment are called into question. Prior research evidence on the effect of alignment has been based on statistical analysis of survey data. The use of detailed cases indicated that while this is generally true, there are some situations in which a high level of alignment may not lead to good performance. Most notably, even well-aligned business and IS strategies will not produce good performance if they cannot be effectively implemented due to the lack of requisite specialized knowledge. In both the situations where the expected relationship between alignment and performance was not found, the explanation seemed to lie in problems in implementing the strategies.

Fourth, the cases provide insights into changes in knowledge related to IS planning and alignment over time. Each case involved change in shared knowledge, due to changes in KM processes and specific domain knowledge, that is, the pools of business and IS knowledge being integrated. Both KM processes and knowledge pools were affected by changes in the organization's external alliances and in its business and IS personnel. The alliances and personnel, in turn, seemed to depend on performance, with poor performance leading to hiring or seeking help from external consultants. Managers making decisions about personnel changes and consulting arrangements should find it useful to consider such direct or indirect impacts of these decisions on specific domain knowledge, shared knowledge, alignment, and performance.

Finally, the chapter provides insights into the KM mechanisms that can be used by business and IS executives. A variety of examples have been described in the three cases, and these examples should be useful to firms trying to enhance shared knowledge. More specifically, we believe that KM processes have a direct impact on strategic alignment, and Table 7.3 offers a summary of this impact. This table focuses on KM processes and their relationship to strategic alignment. When business and IS personnel only provide direction, there is no knowledge integration, and strategic IS alignment is low. Unidirectional knowledge integration, which is either IS-led or business-led, adopts exchange and internalization, and typically yields moderate strategic alignment. Lastly, knowledge integration that is mutual (business and IS leadership) embraces combination and socialization, and yields high strategic alignment. This suggests that organizations should focus on the adoption of combination and socialization processes to achieve strategic alignment. They should provide opportunities for IS and business unit personnel to transfer from one group to the other, develop appropriate career paths for individuals who choose such opportunities, offer mentoring to those who wish to learn new ideas and skills, and support creative "out of the box" thinking.

The above conclusions from this study should be considered in light of the study's *limitations*. First, the findings are based on only three organizations, albeit of different sizes and from different industries. Second, the cases were studied mainly through retrospective interviews during one to three visits at fairly close points in time. Third, to prevent the model from becoming unduly complex, we excluded the potential effects of shared knowledge on KM processes or their relationship with alignment. Finally, we collected and used extensive qualitative data, but did not use any quantitative measures of knowledge, KM processes, alignment, or performance. Consequently, although our conclusions are rooted in rigorous analysis of considerable qualitative evidence, they have not been tested through quantitative measures.

The chapter also has several *implications for future research*. First, it is an initial step toward understanding the knowledge explanations of IS planning. By examining the cases, individually and in comparison with each other, in light of the a priori knowledge-based model of IS planning, the chapter helps in understanding IS planning and its consequences. Although we cannot rule out alternative explanations, the emergent model provides one possible explanation for the knowledge-based view of IS planning. Future research should empirically test these findings, using additional cases and multistage surveys.

Second, the findings for Proposition 3 suggest that large-sample studies investigating the effect of alignment on business performance might find it useful to examine how this effect changes with different time lags between alignment and performance measures. Moreover, such studies might benefit from statistically controlling for differences in the firms' abilities to implement business and IS strategies.

Table 7.3

**Knowledge Management Mechanisms in IS Planning and Strategic Alignment**

| Knowledge management | Type of knowledge exchanged | Knowledge management mechanisms | | | | | |
|---|---|---|---|---|---|---|---|
| | | Category of KM processes | Explicit knowledge | Tacit knowledge | Specific domain knowledge | Shared domain knowledge | Strategic IS alignment |
| Nonintegration | None | Knowledge substitution | Direction | Direction | Low or high | Low | Low |
| Unidirectional IS-led (IS → Business) | IS/IT | Knowledge transfer | Exchange and internalization | Exchange | High specific IS knowledge, low or high specific business knowledge | Moderate | Moderate |
| Business-led (Business → IS) | Business | | | | High specific business knowledge, low or high specific IS knowledge | | |
| Mutual (Business ↔ IS) | IS/IT and Business | Knowledge Synthesis | Combination | Socialization | High | High | High |

Finally, this chapter contributes to the KM literature by proposing a model of the way in which changes in business performance may both follow and lead to changes in KM processes. Future KM research may examine the generalizability of the proposed model by examining it for other areas of knowledge.

In conclusion, this chapter has attempted to advance our understanding of IS planning from a knowledge perspective. It has offered one possible explanation of the ways in which organizations may engage in IS planning, with implications for strategic IS alignment and business performance. We hope that this chapter provides an initial step toward understanding a knowledge-based view of IS planning and how the underlying knowledge mechanisms eventually impact organizational performance.

## ACKNOWLEDGMENTS

We are grateful to Tim Goles for his assistance in collecting and interpreting some of the data used in this chapter. We are also indebted to the numerous interviewees at the three companies for their valuable time and insights.

## NOTES

1. Externalization and exchange are closely intertwined, and we include externalization within exchange.

2. Some additional details about these cases are available in Sabherwal, Hirschheim, and Goles (2001).

3. A few comments, which did not concern these aspects, were marked as "may be important."

4. This also identified comments that contain these pieces of text, for example, "*know*ledge," "*aware*-ness," and "*learn*ing."

5. However, the property services division brought its own IS director on board before the financial services division.

6. A similar "federal governance" model of IS management was discussed by Zmud, Boyton, and Jacobs (1986).

7. Gamma also departed from its earlier de facto policy of lifelong employment.

8. Socialization enables the transfer of tacit knowledge, and creates new knowledge. It is discussed in knowledge synthesis.

## REFERENCES

Alavi, M., and Leidner, D. 2001. Knowledge management and knowledge management systems: conceptual foundations and research issues. *MIS Quarterly*, 25, 1, 107–136.

Argyris, C. 1982. How learning and reasoning processes affect organizational change. In P.S. Goodman et al. (eds.), *Change in Organizations: New Perspectives on Theory, Research and Practice*. San Francisco: Jossey-Bass, 47–86.

Bassellier, G.; Reich, B.H.; and Benbasat, I. 2001. Information Technology competence of business managers: a definition and research model. *Journal of Management Information Systems*, 17, 4, 159–182.

Benbasat, I.; Goldstein, D.K.; and Mead, M. 1987. The case research strategy in studies of information systems. *MIS Quarterly*, 11, 3, 368–386.

Blumenthal, S.C. 1969. *Management Information System: A Framework for Planning and Control*. Englewood Cliffs, NJ: Prentice-Hall.

Boynton, A.C., and Zmud, R.W. 1987. Information technology planning in the 1990's: directions for practice and research. *MIS Quarterly*, 11, 1, 59–84.

Brown, C.V. 1997. Examining the emergence of hybrid IS governance solutions: evidence from a single case site. *Information Systems Research*, 8, 1, 69–94.

Brown, C.V., and Magill, S.L. 1998. Reconceptualizing the context-design issue for the information systems function. *Organization Science*, 9, 2, 176–194.

Chan, Y.E.; Sabherwal, R.; and Thatcher, J.B. 2006. Antecedents and outcomes of strategic IS alignment: an empirical investigation. *IEEE Transactions on Engineering Management*, 53, 1, 27–47.

Conner, K., and Prahalad, C.K. 1996. A resource-based theory of the firm: knowledge versus opportunism. *Organization Science*, 7, 5, 477–501.

Davenport, T.H., and Prusak, L. 1998. *Working Knowledge: How Organizations Manage What They Know.* Boston: Harvard Business School Press.

Demsetz, B.H. 1988. The theory of the firm revisited. *Journal of Law, Economics and Organization*, 4, 141–161.

Devin, D. J., and Kozlowski, S. W. 1995. Domain-specific knowledge and task characteristics in decision making. *Organizational Behavior and Human Decision Processes*, 64, 3, 294–306.

Earl, M.J. 1989. *Management Strategies for Information Technology.* New York: Prentice Hall.

———. 1993. Experiences in strategic information systems planning. *MIS Quarterly*, 17, 1, 1–24.

Eisenhardt, K.M. 1989. Building theories from case study research. *Academy of Management Review*, 14, 4, 532–550.

Grant, R.M. 1996a. Prospering in dynamically-competitive environments: organizational capability as knowledge integration. *Organization Science*, 7, 4, 375–387.

———. 1996b. Toward a knowledge-based theory of the firm. *Strategic Management Journal*, 17, 109–122.

Grover, V., and Davenport, T. 2001. General perspectives on knowledge management: fostering a research agenda. *Journal of Management Information Systems*, 18, 1, 5–18.

Grover, V., and Segars, A.H. 2005. An empirical investigation of stages of strategic information systems planning: patterns of process design and effectiveness. *Information & Management*, 42, 5, 761–779.

Hirschheim, R., and Sabherwal, R. 2001. Detours in the Path toward strategic information systems alignment: paradoxical decisions, excessive transformations, and uncertain turnarounds. *California Management Review*, 44, 1 (Fall), 87–108.

Kearns, G.S., and Lederer, A.L. 2003. A resource-based view of strategic IT alignment: how knowledge sharing creates competitive advantage. *Decision Sciences*, 34, 1, 1–29.

Kearns, G.S., and Sabherwal, R. 2006. Strategic alignment between business and information technology: a knowledge-based view of behaviors, outcome, and consequences. *Journal of Management Information Systems*, 23, 3, 129–162.

King, W.R. 1978. Strategic planning for management information systems. *MIS Quarterly*, 2, 1, 27–37.

King, W.R., and Teo, T.S.H. 2000. Assessing the impact of proactive versus reactive modes of strategic information systems planning. *Omega*, 28, 6, 667–679.

Kogut, B., and Zander, U. 1992. Knowledge of the firm, combinative capabilities and the replication of technology. *Organization Science*, 3, 3, 383–397.

Lederer, A.L., and Mendelow, A.L. 1987. Information resource planning: information systems managers' difficulty in determining top management's objectives. *MIS Quarterly*, 13, 3, 388–399.

———. 1988. Convincing top management of the strategic potential of information systems. *MIS Quarterly*, 12, 4, 525–534.

———. 1989. Coordination of Information Systems Plans with Business Plans. *Journal of MIS*, 6, 2, 5–19.

Lederer, A.L., and Sethi, V. 1988. The implementation of strategic information systems planning methodologies. *MIS Quarterly*, 12, 3, 445–461.

———. 1996. Key prescriptions for strategic information systems planning. *Journal of Management Information Systems*, 13, 1, 35–62.

Miles, R.E., and Snow, C.C. 1978. *Organizational Strategy, Structure, and Process.* New York: McGraw-Hill.

Nahapiet, J., and Ghoshal, S. 1998. Social capital, intellectual capital, and the organizational advantage. *Academy of Management Review*, 23, 2, 242–266.

Nelson, K.M., and Cooprider, J.G. 1996. The contribution of shared knowledge to IT group performance. *MIS Quarterly*, 20, 4, 409–432.

Neumann, S. 1994. *Strategic Information Systems: Competition through Information Technologies.* New York: Macmillan.

Newkirk, H.E., and Lederer, A.L. 2006. The effectiveness of strategic information systems planning under environmental uncertainty. *Information & Management*, 43, 4, 481–501.

Nonaka, I. 1994. Dynamic theory of organizational knowledge creation. *Organization Science*, 5, 14–37.

Nonaka, I., and Konno, N. 1998. The concept of "ba": building a foundation for knowledge creation. *California Management Review,* 40, 3, 40–54.

Polanyi, M. 1966. *The Tacit Dimension.* Garden City, NY: Doubleday.

Pyburn, P. 1983. Linking the MIS plan with corporate strategy: an exploratory study. *MIS Quarterly,* 7, 2, 1–14.

Reich, B.H., and Benbasat, I. 1996. Measuring the linkage between business and information technology objectives. *MIS Quarterly,* 20, 1, 55–81.

———. 2000. Factors that influence the social dimension of linkage between business and information technology objectives. *MIS Quarterly,* 24, 1, 81–113.

Rockart, J. 1979. Chief executives define their own data needs. *Harvard Business Review,* 57, 2, 81–92.

Sabherwal, R. 2006. Seeking strategic information systems alignment: facilitators, obstacles, and consequences. *Cutter Benchmark Review,* 6, 11, 5–13.

Sabherwal, R., and Chan, Y.E. 2001. Alignment between business and IS strategies: a configurational approach. *Information Systems Research,* 12, 1, 11–33.

Sabherwal, R., and King, W.R. 1991. Towards a theory of strategic use of information resources: an inductive approach. *Information and Management,* 20, 3, 191–212.

Sabherwal, R.; Hirschheim, R.; and Goles, T. 2001. The dynamics of alignment: insights from a punctuated equilibrium model. *Organization Science,* 12, 2, 179–197.

Salmela, H.; Lederer, A.L.; and Raponen, T. 2000. Information systems planning in a turbulent environment. *European Journal of Information Systems,* 9, 1, 3–15.

Sauer, C., and Yetton, P. 1994. The dynamics of fit and the fit of dynamics: aligning IT in a dynamic organization. *Proceedings of the Fifteenth International Conference on Information Systems,* 41–50.

Segars, A.H., and Grover, V. 1998. Strategic information systems planning success: an investigation of the construct and measurement. *MIS Quarterly,* 22, 2, 139–163.

Segev, E. 1989. A systematic comparative analyses and synthesis of two level strategic typologies. *Strategic Management Journal,* 10, 487–505.

Silva, L., and Hirschheim, R. 2007. Fighting against windmills: strategic information systems and organizational deep structures. *MIS Quarterly,* 31, 2, 327–354.

Teo, T.S.H., and King, W.R. 1997. Integration between business planning and information systems planning: an evolutionary-contingency perspective. *Journal of Management Information Systems,* 14, 1, 185–214.

Vitale, M.; Ives, B.; and Beath, C. 1986. Identifying strategic information systems' process. *Proceedings of the Seventh International Conference of Information Systems.* San Diego, December, 265–276. Available at http://aisel.aisnet.org/.

Ward, J.; Griffiths, P.; and Whitmore, P. 1990. *Strategic Planning for Information Systems.* Hoboken, NJ: Wiley.

Wiseman, C. 1988. *Strategic Information Systems.* Homewood, IL: Irwin.

Yin, R.K. 1984. *Case Study Research: Design and Method.* Beverly Hills, CA: Sage.

Zmud, R. W., Boynton, A. C., and Jacobs, G. C. 1986. The information economy: a new perspective for effective information systems management. *Data Base,* 18, 1, 17–23.

# CHAPTER 8

# STRATEGIC ALIGNMENT

## Highly Valued, but Elusive in Practice

### CHRISTINE V. BULLEN AND JERRY N. LUFTMAN

*Abstract:* *Strategic alignment is fundamental for creating effective information technology (IT) strategies. The concept consistently tops the lists made by both IT managers and the top business managers of the organization. Therefore it is clear that the value of strategic alignment is understood at the highest management levels. The challenge appears to be in successfully managing all six enablers of strategic alignment to continuously increase the level of alignment within an organization. The chapter provides a full description of the history and process of strategic alignment and provides guidelines for improving alignment as part of the strategic planning process in organizations.*

*Keywords:* *Alignment, Enablers and Inhibitors, Information Technology, IT, Planning, Strategic Alignment, Strategy, Top Management*

The effective management of information technology (IT) organizations in the dynamic business and technical environment of the twenty-first century demands that senior IT managers be proactive with senior functional (e.g., marketing, R&D, finance) managers to develop IT and business strategies that are aligned. IT and business management must be continuously aware of the opportunities to transform the firm by leveraging technology. This is especially true if the firm is to sustain competitive advantage. The process for developing strategy must demonstrate the opportunity for IT to enable or drive business strategy, and operational effectiveness and efficiency. Strategic alignment is the key framework for creating effective IT strategies. Alignment addresses both how IT is in harmony with the business and how the business should or could be in harmony with IT.

Strategic alignment is often described but rarely defined. The accurate definition is: the process by which the top management of an organization closely weaves together IT strategy and business strategy to ensure that IT is enabling and driving the business goals and objectives. Strategic alignment is often described as "linking" IT strategy and business strategy. This is not accurate because linking suggests that the strategies are developed independently and then synchronized in some way. Strategic alignment requires that both potential business strategies and potential IT strategies are examined at the same time to devise the overall strategy that will drive the business toward the vision incorporated in its goals and objectives.

## ENABLERS AND INHIBITORS TO ALIGNMENT

One of the most important missions for information technology (IT) management in the twenty-first century is to be *architects* of aligning business and IT. The metaphor of architecture is useful

Table 8.1

**Enablers and Inhibitors to Alignment**

| | Enablers | Inhibitors |
|---|---|---|
| 1 | Senior executive support for information technology (IT) | IT and business lack close relationships |
| 2 | IT involved in strategy development | IT does not prioritize well |
| 3 | IT understands the business | IT fails to meet commitments |
| 4 | Business–IT partnership | IT does not understand business |
| 5 | Well-prioritized IT projects | Senior executives do not support IT |
| 6 | IT demonstrates leadership | IT management lacks leadership |

because IT strategy is *not* just about technology—it is about the purposeful creation of *integrated* environments that leverage human skills, business processes, organizational structures, and technologies to transform the competitive position of the business.

As architects of alignment, IT management plays a pivotal role as they have a responsibility to consider the organization across functional and process boundaries internally and externally to include customers/clients and partners. Many of these extended collaborative relationships are evolving toward wikinomics (Tapscott and Williams, 2006) because of the complex nature of the stakeholder networks forming in today's marketplace.

It is important to understand that alignment is about the evolution of a relationship between business and IT, and how the organization can leverage information technology. Alignment is a process that is enabled or inhibited by a number of factors that are experienced every day. Recent research into the factors that enable or inhibit alignment based on survey responses from senior business and IT managers show that there are six key enablers to alignment as well as six corresponding inhibitors to alignment (Table 8.1). Several of the attributes that enable alignment also show up in the inverse as inhibitors to alignment. The enablers and inhibitors identified in the original research have not changed, as the research continues.

Achieving and sustaining alignment requires conscious attention and focus by IT and functional management to enhance the enablers of alignment and minimize alignment's inhibitors. Alignment is a consequence of sound practices and evolving human relationships that embrace mutual understandings of goals, value, culture, and capabilities that leverage the development of strategies that can ultimately co-adapt to changing circumstances.

## THE STRATEGIC ALIGNMENT MODEL

The strategic alignment model was proposed by researchers at the MIT Sloan School Center for Information Systems Research (CISR) in 1991 (Henderson and Venkatraman, 1991). It resulted from work with organizations examining how the effectiveness of IT within an organization could be improved. Building on a history of research focused on the importance of scanning, interpretation, and action in the process of creating strategy, Henderson and Venkatraman proposed the model in the context of developing strategy for IT. They propose "IT strategic planning is not an activity that occurs after key strategic business choices are made (a traditional view of functional planning), but is a concurrent activity that allows the potential of emerging technology to directly influence the strategic direction of the firm" (Henderson and Venkatraman, 1991, p. 73). They argue "what determines a manager's inclination to persist or reorient the firm's use of IT is linked to how top managers perceive the nature of, and the relationships among, critical factors surrounding both the business and IT realms of the organization" (Henderson, Thomas, and Venkatraman, 1992, pp. 4–5).

The strategic alignment model was proposed as a model for conceptualizing and directing the strategic management of information technology: "the inability to realize value from IT investments is, in part, due to the lack of *alignment* between the business and IT strategies of organizations" (Henderson and Venkatraman, 1993, p. 4). There are two fundamental assumptions underlying the model: "One, economic performance is directly related to the ability of management to create a *strategic fit* between the position of an organization in the competitive product-market arena and the design of an appropriate administrative structure to support its execution; and Two, strategic fit is inherently dynamic. The choices made by one business enterprise will over time evoke imitative actions, which necessitate subsequent responses. Thus strategic alignment is not an event but a process of continuous adaptation and change" (ibid., pp. 4–5).

## TWO FUNDAMENTAL ASPECTS

The concept of strategic alignment is based on two fundamental assumptions—strategic fit and functional integration. In this section strategic fit will be discussed in detail.

### Strategic Fit

Strategic fit is the concept that any strategy must address both how to position the firm in the external marketplace as well as determine how to devise the best internal structure to carry out this strategy. The external domain is concerned with those strategic choices and decisions that relate to:

1. *The scope of the firm's business*—its customers, products, markets, and competitors. For some organizations, the scope in all respects is very broad, e.g., GE, which is in many product/service areas in consumer, commercial, and government marketplaces. GE competitors are everywhere. An example of a broad market, but more narrow in scope is Toyota, with a global marketplace in the car and truck product area. Toyota's competitors are other major automobile manufacturers and, to some extent, financial service firms offering car loans and leases.

2. *The distinctive competencies* include both the core competencies and critical success factors that provide competitive advantage. Core competencies are those activities that differentiate the organization from its competitors. Critical success factors describe those activities the organization must do to succeed.

One example is USAA, a financial services firm focused on current and former members of the U.S. Armed Forces. USAA's unparalleled knowledge of its policyholders and its ability to integrate this customer knowledge across its product lines to provide seamless and reliable service to policyholders at all times are distinctive competencies. USAA has the ability not merely to respond to, but to *anticipate* customer needs thanks to their distinctive competence in the use of technology.

3. *The governance of the firm*—business governance covers a wide range of choices that are made to determine the way an organization is managed with a focus on the issue of ownership. Governance defines the fundamental how and who process regarding strategies and plans, make/buy decisions, and overall management decision making.

Governance is becoming increasingly important as companies pursue alliances and partnerships to obtain additional competencies and capabilities for competitive advantage. For example, Ford

Motor Company is aggressively pursuing alliances with "pop culture" through Internet portals such as Yahoo! and AOL to boost their online car sales and the popular TV show *American Idol* to reach a younger marketplace.

Governance also includes the respective regulatory considerations that organizations must comply with.

These external concerns are reflected in the business strategy quadrant of the strategic alignment model (Figure 8.1) (Henderson and Venkatraman, 1993).

In contrast, the internal domain, reflected in the organizational infrastructure quadrant of the strategic alignment model, is concerned with choices and decisions that determine the internal arrangements of the firm and are required to execute the business strategy:

1. *Administrative (organizational) structure*—the decisions that define the roles, responsibilities, and authority structure, for example, whether the firm has chosen a functional, matrix, decentralized, process-based, geographic, networked (wikinomics-based), or some form of federated/hybrid organizational structure. There is a great deal of literature addressing types of organizational structures that can be useful in understanding the implications of various designs (Daft, 2001; Robbins, 1990).

2. *Critical business processes*—the architecture of its "salient" business activities or tasks; that is, those activities that are most relevant to a firm's identity (e.g., marketing, R&D, manufacturing, logistics). The identification of which processes are truly salient (and which are merely background processes) can determine a company's ability to successfully implement strategy (Keen, 1997). Salient processes often define a company to its marketplace, for example, FedEx's absolute promise to deliver packages by 10 A.M. the next day or Wal-Mart's focus on efficiency to provide the lowest prices on every product, every day.

3. *Human resource skills*—the acquisition and development of the capabilities (experience, competencies, etc.) of the people required to manage and operate the firm's key business activities. It is important to anticipate whether a new business strategy will require new skills or conflict with the traditional values and norms of the organization.

**Functional Integration**

A firm's competitors will eventually imitate any strategic choice, thereby rendering temporary any competitive advantage, whether this is obtained from a specific product or service or from a specialized technology or suite of applications. From an IT management perspective, strategic fit implies the need for the organization to develop and sustain capabilities that leverage IT to generate sustainable competitive advantage. Strategic fit also implies that IT management cannot make "strategic bets" on any one particular technology or application, as this might lower barriers to competitive imitation. An effective IT strategy is dynamic; it must not merely accept change, it must embrace the fact of change.

Business literature and research persuasively argue that to achieve *sustainable* economic performance, the fit and ability to quickly adapt between the strategic dimensions of external positioning and internal arrangement is essential.

**FUNCTIONAL INTEGRATION**

A second and equally important dimension of strategic alignment is the concept of functional integration. Ideally, the choices made in the IT strategic domain will shape and/or support the

Figure 8.1   The Strategic Alignment Model

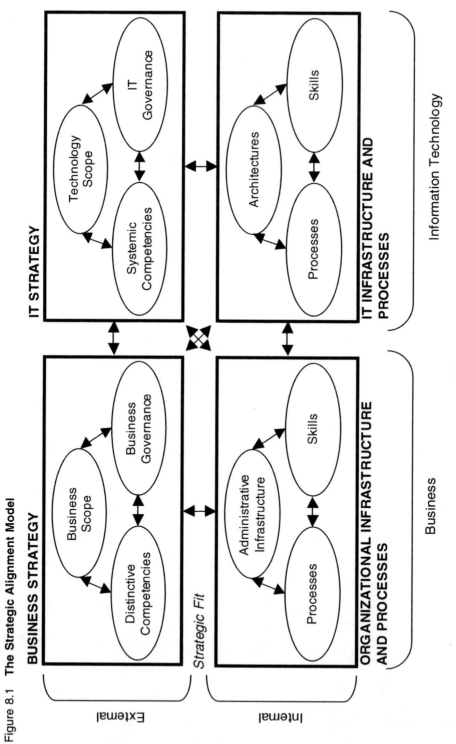

*Source:* Henderson and Venkatraman (1993).

business's strategic choices. Given the potential of IT to offer competitive business advantage, the linkage among the externally focused choices made by IT management and the strategic choice made by senior business management needs to be explicitly accounted for. In the strategic alignment model, the linkage between the IT strategy domain and the business strategy domain is called *strategic integration.*

In similar fashion, the internal domains of business and IT need to be integrated such that the capabilities of the IT infrastructure support the requirements and expectations of the business's organizational structure and processes. This level of linkage is called *operational integration.*

Figure 8.1 illustrates the strategic alignment model and the relationships among the domains of strategic fit and functional integration. Ideally, any IT strategy planning process needs to take into account both these dimensions.

An important aspect of enabling the best functional integration is enhancement of the relationship between IT management and business management. This process is described in another research effort from Henderson (1990) on creating strategic partnerships within organizations. The primary approach in this research is to understand the determinants of partnership in order to manage them to the successful goal of a positive working relationship between IT and business.

## STRATEGIC ALIGNMENT MATURITY

Organizations often fail to successfully execute strategic objectives. Research into this issue hypothesized that an organization's ability to successfully implement strategy is related to the level of strategic alignment between IT and the business (Luftman, 2000). A model of alignment maturity emerged from this research and consists of two major categories (see also Luftman et al., 2004, pp. 68–84): the strategic alignment maturity criteria (shown in Figure 8.2) and the strategic alignment maturity summary (shown in Figure 8.3).

The six components shown in Figure 8.2 are each evaluated individually (total of forty-seven criteria) to determine a maturity level. This is done by a team of IT and business executives, and results in a rating of one, two, three, four, or five for each of the six areas. The discussions associated with determining each rating are themselves of value in understanding the current maturity level and in recognizing a need to improve the maturity level. An overall score is converged on (using the model as a descriptive tool) by IT and business executives, and followed by the identification of a plan created to reach a higher level of maturity (using the model as a prescriptive tool).

The six criteria are described below:[1]

- Communications—Creating the effective exchange of ideas and having a clear understanding of what it takes to ensure successful strategies
- Competency/value measurements—Devising metrics that demonstrate the value of the IT organization to the business function (IT dashboard) that are tied to clear rewards and penalties
- Governance—Ensuring that the appropriate business and IT participants formally discuss and review the priorities and allocation of IT resources
- Partnership—Developing the relationship between IT and the business function to a level of trust resulting in a sharing of the role of defining business strategies
- Scope and architecture—Providing a flexible infrastructure that enables business processes and strategies
- Skills—Developing careers that support the dynamic environment of the organization, including the ability to leverage innovation and support business strategy.

Figure 8.2   **Strategic Alignment Maturity Criteria**

| COMMUNICATIONS | COMPETENCY/VALUE MEASUREMENTS | GOVERNANCE |
|---|---|---|
| • Understanding of business by IT<br>• Understanding of IT by business<br>• Inter/Intra-organizational learning/education<br>• Protocol rigidity<br>• Knowledge sharing<br>• Liaison(s) effectiveness | • IT Metrics<br>• Business metrics<br>• Balanced metrics<br>• Service-level agreements<br>• Benchmarking<br>• Formal assessments/ reviews<br>• Continuous improvement | • Business strategic planning<br>• IT strategic planning<br>• Reporting/organization structure<br>• Budgetary control<br>• IT investment management<br>• Steering committee(s)<br>• Prioritization process |

## SIX IT BUSINESS ALIGNMENT MATURITY CRITERIA

| PARTNERSHIP | SCOPE AND ARCHITECTURE | SKILLS |
|---|---|---|
| • Business perception of IT value<br>• Role of IT in strategic business planning<br>• Shared goals, risk, rewards/penalties<br>• IT program management<br>• Relationship/trust style<br>• Business sponsor/ champion | • Traditional, enabler/driver, external<br>• Standards articulation<br>• Architectural integration: Functional organization; Enterprise; Interenterprise<br>• Architectural transparency, agility, flexibility<br>• Managing emerging technology | • Innovation, entrepreneurship<br>• Cultural locus of power<br>• Management style<br>• Change readiness<br>• Career crossover<br>• Education, cross-training<br>• Social, political, trusting interpersonal environment |

The summary shown in Figure 8.3 indicates the five conceptual levels of strategic alignment maturity:[2]

1. Initial/ad hoc—Business and IT are not aligned or harmonized
2. Committed process—The organization has committed to becoming aligned
3. Established focused process—Strategic alignment maturity is established and focused on business objectives
4. Improved/managed process—The concept of IT as a "value center" is reinforced
5. Optimized process—Business and IT strategic planning is integrated and co-adaptive.

Companies with higher level of alignment maturity tend to demonstrate higher levels of success (e.g., Revenues, productivity). A detailed description of how to determine the ratings can be found in Luftman and colleagues (2004, 2007).

## KEY ISSUES FOR INFORMATION TECHNOLOGY EXECUTIVES

The executive board of the Society for Information Management has conducted a yearly survey among its members (primarily executives in charge of the information technology function) to identify their top concerns in three broad areas: key management concerns, application and tech-

Figure 8.3 **Strategic Alignment Maturity Summary**

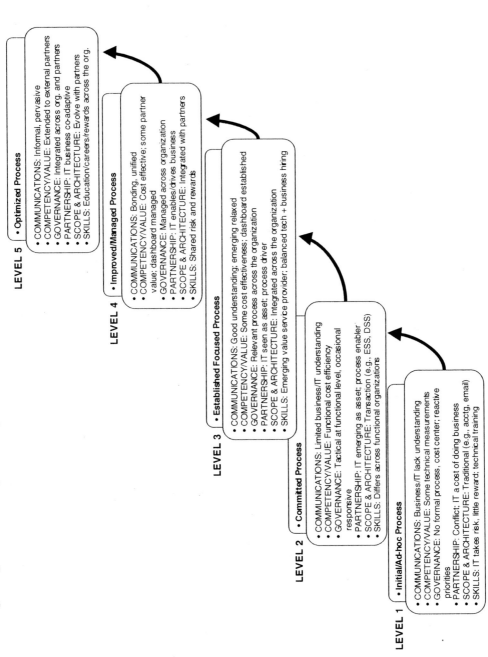

**LEVEL 5** • Optimized Process

- COMMUNICATIONS: Informal, pervasive
- COMPETENCY/VALUE: Extended to external partners
- GOVERNANCE: Integrated across org. and partners
- PARTNERSHIP: IT business co-adaptive
- SCOPE & ARCHITECTURE: Evolve with partners
- SKILLS: Education/careers/rewards across the org.

**LEVEL 4** • Improved/Managed Process

- COMMUNICATIONS: Bonding, unified
- COMPETENCY/VALUE: Cost effective; some partner value; dashboard managed
- GOVERNANCE: Managed across organization
- PARTNERSHIP: IT enables/drives business
- SCOPE & ARCHITECTURE: Integrated with partners
- SKILLS: Shared risk and rewards

**LEVEL 3** • Established Focused Process

- COMMUNICATIONS: Good understanding; emerging relaxed
- COMPETENCY/VALUE: Some cost effectiveness; dashboard established
- GOVERNANCE: Relevant process across the organization
- PARTNERSHIP: IT seen as asset; process driver
- SCOPE & ARCHITECTURE: Integrated across the organization
- SKILLS: Emerging value service provider; balanced tech + business hiring

**LEVEL 2** • Committed Process

- COMMUNICATIONS: Limited business/IT understanding
- COMPETENCY/VALUE: Functional cost efficiency
- GOVERNANCE: Tactical at functional level, occasional responsive
- PARTNERSHIP: IT emerging as asset; process enabler
- SCOPE & ARCHITECTURE: Transaction (e.g., ESS, DSS)
- SKILLS: Differs across functional organizations

**LEVEL 1** • Initial/Ad-hoc Process

- COMMUNICATIONS: Business/IT lack understanding
- COMPETENCY/VALUE: Some technical measurements
- GOVERNANCE: No formal process, cost center; reactive priorities
- PARTNERSHIP: Conflict; IT a cost of doing business
- SCOPE & ARCHITECTURE: Traditional (e.g., acctg, email)
- SKILLS: IT takes risk, little reward; technical training

Table 8.2

**Strategic Alignment Maturity Data 2006**

| Strategic alignment criteria | Average rating by IT and business management (out of 5.0) |
|---|---|
| Partnership* | 3.21 |
| Scope and architecture* | 3.21 |
| Governance | 3.17 |
| Communications | 3.11 |
| Value metrics | 2.93 |
| Skills | 2.91 |
| **Overall average** | **3.09** |

*Indicates same rating.

nology developments, and IT–business alignment. Five earlier studies looking at the key issues facing IT management had been carried out since 1980. In all but one of these studies over more than a twenty-year period, IT–business alignment ranked in the top nine concerns. And since 2003, IT–business alignment has been number one. This raises the interesting question of whether alignment has failed to improve and why this is taking so long.

The primary answer to this question appears to be that top IT management tends to focus on improving one or two of the areas shown in Table 8.1, the enablers and inhibitors. So while an improvement in, for example, "senior executive support for IT" but not in "IT understanding the business" will appear to be increasing alignment, in fact it is only a small step in the right direction. The IT executive will become focused on ensuring that one enabler is maintained, but lose focus on the other five enablers. The result is that IT executives may end up doing the same thing over and over, believing they are increasing strategic alignment, when, in fact, they are only improving one enabler.

To succeed in strategic alignment, all six enablers must be managed to reach higher levels of maturity and ensure the role of IT in business strategy. The alignment maturity assessment evaluates all six components.

The most recent SIM-sponsored survey (Luftman and Kempaiah, 2008) again indicates the high level of importance ascribed to strategic alignment by both business and IT management. Of the twenty-two issues rated by management, IT and business alignment is number one. Table 8.2 shows the average ratings for each of the strategic alignment maturity criteria. They are arranged in order, with the highest level of maturity first.

These results serve to underscore both the importance of strategic alignment and the distance still to be covered before true strategic alignment is achieved. There is no single silver bullet—a combination of all six components must be focused on.

In the following section, we describe an analysis process that is designed to help focus the strategic planning effort in order to improve alignment.

## STRATEGIC ALIGNMENT AS PART OF THE STRATEGIC ANALYSIS PROCESS

In addition to understanding the organization's alignment maturity level, to achieve the goal of being aligned, management must also follow a strategic analysis process that includes looking at business and IT opportunities throughout the many elements of the strategy formulation process.

Figure 8.4 shows an overview of the strategic analysis process. It contains eleven elements, each of which can be used to examine both IT and business characteristics to identify areas of opportunity that can be formulated into business strategies.

## Phase 1

Phase 1 of the analysis process consists of three elements: Understanding the As-Is situation of the organization, the strategic alignment maturity assessment, and the stakeholder analysis. The strategic alignment maturity assessment was described earlier. The stakeholder analysis is a technique that is well understood and there are many approaches to carrying out this element (see, e.g., MindTools. com, 2007). The results of these two elements will identify areas in which maturity can be increased and in which there are potential weaknesses to be included in the super SWOT analysis (to be described). The As-Is element is an assessment including a section on the business and one on IT. The As-Is element and its partner, the To-Be element, are both well-recognized techniques used as part of a strategic planning exercise (a template for As-Is and To-Be is provided in Appendix 8.1). The primary purpose of the As-Is is to create a baseline of key aspects of the organization and will help to identify both strengths and weaknesses in the current organization in both business and IT areas.

## Phase 2

Phase 2 consists of three elements working together to identify potential strategies for the organization.

### Ansoff Product/Service Market Matrix

This model focuses on an organization's present and future products/services and markets to examine ways to grow, using existing and future products/services and considering existing markets and new markets (Ansoff, 1965). This model is used in the strategic analysis process to identify opportunities for the organization. (These opportunities will be the set from which viable ones will be moved along to the super SWOT model.) The result is a four-quadrant matrix that is well known and described in the literature.

In each of the quadrants it is important to consider both incremental opportunities, that is, conservative step-wise changes, as well as radical ones, describing significant departures from the organization's traditional comfort zones.

In Figure 8.5 the traditional Ansoff model is enhanced by indicating typical areas in which to seek opportunities in each quadrant. These opportunities are not limitations of what can happen in each quadrant, but rather ideas to spark creative thinking.

In the northwest quadrant "market penetration" organizations should seek opportunities to grow their market share in the current markets with their current products/services through: (1) marketing that may educate their customers to better understand or appreciate their products; (2) incentive programs to increase acquisition of the product; (3) minor enhancements that may make the product more attractive; or (4) information technology employed in ways to increase the attractiveness of the product to the existing marketplace.

The expansion of the southwest quadrant, "market development" indicates a few ways to describe a "market" and thus help surface opportunities for current products/services in new markets: (1)

166

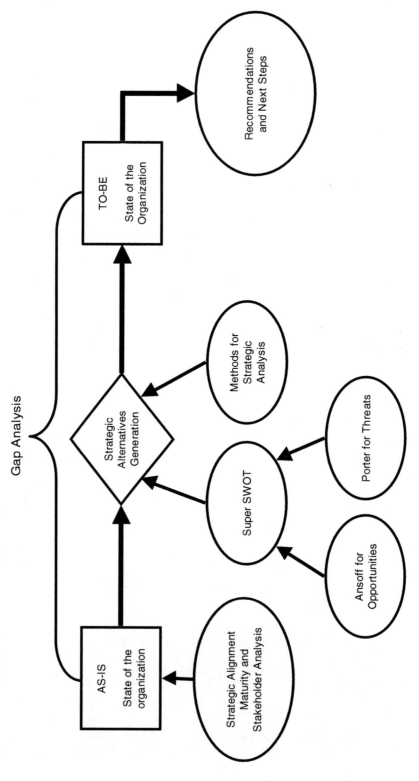

Figure 8.4  Overview of the Strategic Analysis Process

Figure 8.5   **Ansoff Expanded**

|  | Existing<br>Products/Services | New<br>Products/Services |
|---|---|---|
| **Existing Markets** | Market Penetration<br>Opportunities<br><br>• Marketing<br>• Incentives<br>• Enhancements<br>• IT related | Product Development<br>Opportunities<br><br>• Add services to product<br>• Related product/service<br>• Redesign<br>• Co-branding<br>• IT related |
| **New Markets** | Market Development<br>Opportunities<br><br>• Geographic<br>• Demographic<br>• Brick vs. Click<br>• Social/choice | Diversification Opportunities<br><br>• New market may determine<br>  product/service evolution<br>• Radically new approach<br>• Totally different business<br>• IT related |

the geographic market is the one most commonly thought about; (2) the demographic market is an important market differentiator for consumer products, particularly in light of the "graying" population and changing ethnic populations; (3) brick vs. click refers to the differences between operating in a physical marketplace versus the digital world; (4) social/choice prompts thinking about the customer's voluntary choices, such as environmental impact.

"Product development," the northeast quadrant, where the question is asked how the organization might develop new products/services to serve its existing markets, is expanded to include: (1) adding services to an existing product, such as providing satellite radio in new cars; (2) moving into a related product or service area, for example, offering a credit card, as Amazon.com has done; (3) redesigning products based on improvements or correction of flaws; (4) entering into co-branding agreements to create an improved image; (5) changing or improving the product with the use of information technology, for example, GPS systems in cars.

Finally, "diversification" covers the opportunities to develop new products/services for new marketplaces and is the location for truly innovative ideas as all the existing rules can be broken—invent new products/services, enter new markets; it is possible that the new market, if it is the digital market, will help to define the new product.

This element of the strategic analysis process helps to guide thinking about new opportunities that can lead to new business strategies. By focusing on IT-related opportunities in each quadrant, the process is guided toward improving strategic alignment for the organization.

*Porter's Five Competitive Forces That Determine Industry Profitability*

The opposite side of seeking opportunities is uncovering threats. The Porter model (Porter, 1979) can be used to investigate threats beyond the traditional view of those posed by industry competitors.

The five forces in the title refer to the boxes in Appendix 8.2, Figure 8A.2 within the circle. These are the original market forces that Porter described where competition and bargaining power can be used to threaten an organization's position in the marketplace. Each force should be evaluated as to its competitive threat, for example, low, medium, or high. The Porter five force model is well known and described in the literature. A brief explanation is supplied in Appendix 8.2.

In addition to the five central forces, Porter identified six more as shown outside the circle. These forces are somewhat self-explanatory but must be understood and measured along with the central five forces in terms of the nature of the threats and their strength. These threats can then be moved on to the super SWOT analysis

*Super SWOT*

The SWOT analysis has been used for a long time in strategic analysis (Humphrey, 2004), but the basic listing of factors in the strengths, weaknesses, opportunities, and threats categories has never been tied to other methods to improve the generation of the ideas. The strategic analysis process described here used other elements to provide a structure for surfacing factors in these four categories: (1) Ansoff focuses on identifying opportunities, (2) Porter is used to understand threats, (3 and 4) strengths and weaknesses are uncovered by doing the As-Is, strategic alignment maturity assessment, stakeholder analysis and can also come out of Ansoff and Porter.

One of the fundamental values contributed by this analysis process is to help structure thinking and thereby provide a greater opportunity for creativity and innovation along with maintaining a focus on IT to enhance the alignment process.

A significant improvement to the simple SWOT analysis is the super SWOT (Wikipedia, 2007). You will see in Figure 8.6, that the super SWOT is derived by organizing the four simple SWOT categories in such as way as to create intersecting quadrants.

The external quadrants can be compared with each other to help structure thinking to uncover strategies. This technique provides a valuable tool for deriving strategies that follow logically from the four key areas of SWOT.

The intersecting quadrants can be understood as follows:

1. The intersection of strengths and opportunities creates the SO strategies quadrant where the management should use organizational strengths to pursue opportunities that can provide competitive advantage.
2. Strengths and threats intersect to form the ST strategies quadrant where the organizational strengths can be used to avoid threats.
3. The WO strategies quadrant is the result of comparing how to overcome weaknesses by taking advantage of opportunities.
4. The last quadrant, WT strategies, looks at how to generally minimize threats and overcome weaknesses.

Each item shown in a quadrant should begin with an action verb, for example, create, derive, plan, enact, acquire, partner. The resulting statement will be a specific strategy that can be considered in the group of alternatives that are developed in Phase 4 of the analysis process. It is in this phase that the important stage of filtering through the large quantity of ideas that have been generated begins and the most valuable directions emerge. It should be noted that weaknesses are always internal to the organization and threats are always external to the organization. This can cause some confusion and the lists should be tested to be sure this rule is carried out. It is also important to test each inter-

Figure 8.6  **Super SWOT**

| **Super SWOT<br>Company XYZ** | **Strengths**<br><br>List strengths | **Weaknesses**<br><br>List weaknesses |
|---|---|---|
| **Opportunities**<br><br>List opportunities | **SO STRATEGIES**<br><br>Use strengths to take<br>advantage of opportunities | **WO STRATEGIES**<br><br>Overcome weaknesses by<br>taking advantage of<br>opportunities |
| **Threats**<br><br>List threats | **ST STRATEGIES**<br><br>Use strengths<br>to avoid threats | **WT STRATEGIES**<br><br>Minimize weaknesses<br>and avoid threats |

secting quadrant to see if there are IT-related strategies that should be included. The super SWOT is one of the key ways to examine whether business and IT strategies are aligned.

## Phase 3

Phase 3 consists of one element—additional methods and models. This element is used to introduce tools to help focus on a particular area of the organization to identify additional strengths, weaknesses, opportunities, and threats. A vast array of managerial literature covers approaches to understanding a variety of aspects of an organization ranging from information technology, to product management, to leadership and strategy formulation. At least 180 well-regarded methods and models can be considered by anyone undertaking the strategic analysis process. These include well-known classic models such as the balanced scorecard, the BCG (Boston Consulting Group) matrix, and the delta model, and newer approaches such as the open innovation model and B-webs. This element allows those involved with this process to be creative and discover strategic possibilities that may have been overlooked.

## Phase 4

Phase 4 covers the generation of strategic alternatives or options that are feasible to consider for the organization to pursue. Prior to this phase, a draft To-Be may have been generated based on the analysis process to that point or based on a vision that the individuals undertaking this analysis have for the organization. However, it is in this process of clearly stating potential strategies and enhancing each with a list of the pros and cons that the analysis process begins to coalesce around the end goal of specific directions for the organization. It is critical in this phase to ensure that IT strategies are being considered in concert with all of the business strategies. This is an important element in building strategic alignment.

These alternatives are derived from the previous elements and most directly from the super SWOT where specific strategies are created in each of the intersecting quadrants.

## Phase 5

The last phase consists of finalizing the To-Be with the vision that has emerged from the process and choosing the alternatives that will become the recommendations to enact the vision. The number of recommendations should be manageable because implementing any single strategy requires a major effort. Each recommendation should be justified with a cost/benefit tradeoff discussion (the precursor to a true cost/benefit analysis) and must be provided with a list of next steps. This last element, "next steps," is important as it shows the actions that must be taken immediately to launch the new strategy (a template for next steps is provided in Appendix 8.3).

## FUTURE

The concept of strategic alignment has endured as a critical element in the management of the modern organization. Confusion concerning how to obtain and maintain strategic alignment has persisted partly because managers do not understand how to monitor and balance the enablers and inhibitors of alignment. No doubt, some of this is due to the increasingly complex role of the top-level managers in the IT function. However, it has always been important and is becoming imperative for alignment to succeed. Information technology pervades every function in an organization to a greater or lesser extent. As the new generation of managers enters the workforce, this will increase because they have been raised with a multitude of information technology tools at their fingertips. They are comfortable with and dependent on the technologies and will demand them in the business environment.

The analysis process described here will support the creation of strategic alignment in organizations and help to ensure the harmony of IT and business in the organizations of coming decades.

The role of the top management of the IT function (chief information officer; CIO) has been described in many ways. The chart in Figure 8.7 looks at the roles the CIO can play and compares the strategic attitude with the proactive nature of the CIO (Polanksy, 2007).

This figure suggests that the CIO has choices in how he or she interacts in the organization. The ideal is to be concerned about competitive positioning, that is, by being "strategic" and to play a leadership role by being "proactive." This role has evolved over time. The early days of IT were focused on supporting the business and providing the foundation for growth.

This phase was followed by a cost-cutting period as organizations reacted to the investment required to build an IT infrastructure. Fortunately, the next period was one involving recognition of the value of IT to products and services of the organization and providing the CIO with the opportunity to begin playing a more strategic role in the firm's direction.

This last role, proactive, strategic, and a driver for business strategy is where the best organizations are today. The future for the CIO is described by Polansky (2007) as "game changer." The

Figure 8.7 **The Twenty-first Century CIO**

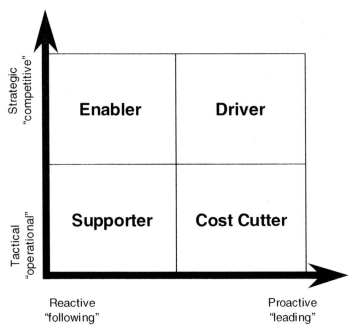

CIO as game changer works with the senior management of the organization to provide innovation in the business model itself. This is the ultimate goal of strategic alignment, and organizations that allow the CIO to be a game changer will reap the value that information technology can provide in the essence of the organization itself.

## APPENDIX 8.1. AS-IS/TO-BE

Figure 8A.1 is a useful template for the As-Is and To-Be analysis because the side-by-side depiction makes for easy comparison.

## APPENDIX 8.2. PORTER COMPETITIVE FORCES

Figure 8A.2 is provided as an in-depth description of the two Porter models to demonstrate how they can be used to determine threats as part of the analysis process.

The first step uses the five force model represented inside the circle in the figure.

- Industry competitors—the box in the center represents the "known" threat, for example, the traditional competitors who create rivalry in the industry. While this is an important force, it is also one that is carefully studied and planned for. However, it is important to understand the relative competitive positions of each rival and the strength of the threat posed by them. The remaining four forces are more vague in terms of how they might be creating threats.
- Threat of substitutes—substitutes are not products from rival firms, but rather products outside the immediate industry that can be substituted for the organization's product. A simple

Figure 8A.1  **As-Is/To-Be—Business**

Page 1

| | AS-IS | TO-BE |
|---|---|---|
| | Business Strategy | |
| Business Scope | Products and Services | Products and Services |
| | Customers/Clients | Customers/Clients |
| | Competitors | Competitors |

Page 3

| | AS-IS | TO-BE |
|---|---|---|
| | Business Infrastructure | |
| Org. Structure | (Can show organization chart on separate page) | |
| Key Processes | | |
| Human Resources | | |

Page 2

| | AS-IS | TO-BE |
|---|---|---|
| | Business Strategy | |
| Distinctive Competencies | | |
| Business Governance | Internal Decisions<br><br>Regulatory<br><br>Partners | Internal Decisions<br><br>Regulatory<br><br>Partners |

example is the threat of cable TV to broadcast TV. Another example is the threat of the sales of digital books to the sales of physical books.

- Buyer power—buyer power has traditionally depended on the concentration of buyers in an industry. For example if there are many suppliers and one buyer, the buyer has extraordinary power. Some place Wal-Mart in this category with respect to its suppliers. However, in this era of infinite access to product information on the Internet, all buyers, including the end consumer, have become more savvy and able to bargain and choose with considerable power.
- Supplier power—supplier power is related to the degree of dependence an organization has on its suppliers. An interesting example to consider here is Dell Computers. Dell does not manufacture anything; rather, it assembles parts that are manufactured by many others to produce its product. Dell is totally dependent on the quality of the parts, on the prices charged by the suppliers, and on their reliability in supplying the part when Dell needs it to build its products in the "just-in-time" world of its business.

Figure 8A.2    **The Competitive Forces that Determine Industry Profitability**

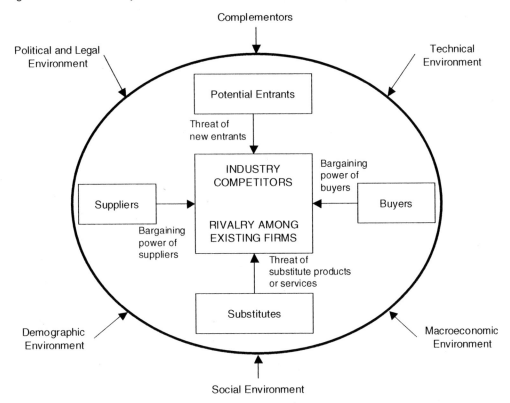

The second step is to use the six additional forces represented outside the circle in the figure.

- Political and legal environment represents any internal or external threats that may arise due to politics (internal management politics or external national politics) and legal issues (regulatory matters, local and national laws, etc.)
- Complementors involves looking at complementary products and services and determining whether there is any exposure to threats from their association with your products or services. For example, when an organization engages a celebrity spokesperson, there is a complementary relationship. However, if that spokesperson becomes engaged in illegal or immoral activities, the relationship will become a threat and is no longer a useful complementary relationship.
- Technical environment requires an examination of the technologies used in the process of delivering an organization's products and services. These technologies encompass manufacturing technologies as well as information technologies.
- Demographic environment accounts for the factors related to the demographics of an organization's customers. Demographics represent what a customer is, for example, age, ethnicity. Threats may be related to an organization's focus on a target market to the exclusion of other markets. For example, organizations are beginning to recognize the large "graying" population, however, this population has been ignored in the past and that act has endangered some markets.

Figure 8A.3  **Next Steps**

| # | Description of Step | Assigned to | Target Date | Issues |
|---|---------------------|-------------|-------------|--------|
| 1 | Market Recommendations | VP of IT | 1 month | VP time and budget |
| 2 | Secure Sponsorship | VP of IT | 2 months | VP time, top management time, cost/benefit analysis budget |
| 3 | Create a Prototype | Project Team | 3 months | Staff time and budget allocation |
| 4 | | | | |

*Note:* You must have a set of Next Steps for each Recommendation.

• Social environment accounts for factors related to customer choices. As opposed to demographics, which are related to what someone is, the social environment is related to what someone chooses to be, for example, environmentally concerned, anti-agribusiness, anti-smoking. Examining these areas can uncover potential threats to an organization.
• Macroeconomic environment covers the general economic environment at the time of the analysis. Externally this may relate to consumer price index, spending patterns, and cost of natural resources. Internally, this factor can be used to focus on budget issues.

An important aspect of using the Porter models is to assign a rating to each factor that indicates its level of importance. Usually low, medium, or high provides enough information to rate a factor's importance in the strategic analysis process.

## APPENDIX 8.3 NEXT STEPS

Figure 8A.3 is useful for summarizing Next Steps in the analysis process. Each recommendation that results from the analysis will have its own set of next steps. Some cells are filled in to provide examples of the information in the template.

## NOTES

1. A more in-depth discussion of the criteria can be found in Luftman (2000).
2. The five levels of maturity in this model are based on the model developed in the mid-1980s at the Software Engineering Institute at Carnegie Mellon University, which is called the Capability Maturity Model for software (CMM) (available at www.sei.cmu.edu/cmm/).

## REFERENCES

Ansoff, H.I. 1965. *Corporate Strategy: An Analytical Approach to Business Policy for Growth and Expansion.* New York: McGraw-Hill.
Daft, R.L. 2001. *Organization Theory and Design,* 7th ed. Cincinnati, OH: South-Western College Publishing.
Henderson, J.C. 1990. Plugging into strategic partnerships: The critical IS connection. *Sloan Management Review,* 31, 3 (Spring), 7–18.

Henderson, J.C., and Venkatraman, N. 1991. Understanding strategic alignment. *Business Quarterly,* 55, 3 (Winter), 72–78.

———. 1993. Strategic alignment: leveraging information technology for transforming organization. *IBM Systems Journal,* 32, 1, 4–16.

Henderson, J.C.; Thomas, J.B.; and Venkatraman, N. 1992. Making sense of IT: strategic alignment and organizational context. MIT Center for Information Systems Research Working Paper, no. 247 (October).

Humphrey, A.S. 2004. SWOT analysis. Available at www.businessballs.com/swotanalysisfreetemplate.htm (accessed on August 13, 2008).

Keen, P.G.W. 1997. *The Process Edge: Creating Value Where It Counts.* Boston: Harvard Business School Press.

Luftman, J. 2000. Addressing business–IT alignment maturity. *Communications of the Association for Information Systems,* 4, 14 (December), 1–51.

Luftman, J., and Kempaiah, R. 2008. Key issues for IT executives 2007. *MIS Quarterly Executive,* 7, 2 (June), 99–112.

Luftman, J.; Bullen, C.; Liao, D.; Nash, E.; and Neumann, C. 2004. *Managing the Information Technology Resource: Leadership in the Information Age.* Upper Saddle River, NJ: Pearson Education.

Luftman, J. and Kempaiah, R. 2007. An update on business-IT alignment: "A line" has been drawn. *MIS Quarterly Executive,* 6, 3, (September), 165–177.

MindTools.com. 2007. Stakeholder analysis: winning support for your projects. Available at www.mindtools.com/pages/article/newPPM_07.htm (accessed on August 13, 2008).

Polansky, M. 2007. Presentation to Executive CIO Roundtable. Sponsored by the Advisory Council, Premier Event Management, Stevens Institute of Technology, April 13.

Porter, M.E. 1979. How competitive forces shape strategy. *Harvard Business Review,* March/April.

Robbins, S.P. 1990. *Organization Theory: Structure, Design, and Applications,* 3d ed. Englewood Cliffs, NJ: Prentice Hall.

Tapscott, D., and Williams, A. 2006. *Wikinomics: How Mass Collaboration Changes Everything.* New York, NY: Portfolio Penguin Group (USA).

Wikipedia. 2007. SuperSWOT. Available at http://simple.wikipedia.org/wiki/SuperSWOT (accessed on August 13, 2008).

CHAPTER 9

# INFORMATION TECHNOLOGY BUDGETING

## Planning's Evil Twin

### HEATHER A. SMITH AND JAMES D. MCKEEN

**Abstract:** *Planning and budgeting should be a matched set of practices that work together to implement an organization's information technology (IT) plans. Unfortunately, today's IT budgeting practices are more like IT planning's "evil twin"—out to undermine planning wherever possible. Asking many IT managers about budgeting elicits much caustic comment. There is widespread disenchantment among IT leaders who feel much of the effort involved is not only artificial and time consuming but also ineffective, and often works counter to strategic intentions. This chapter examines the challenges IT managers face in developing and monitoring their budgets. It presents the findings of a day-long focus group of senior IT managers from a variety of industries, and places the issues discussed within a larger context. It first describes our data collection methodology and then looks at key concepts in IT budgeting to establish what they mean for IT managers and how they can differ between IT organizations. It next explores why budgets are an important part of the management process. Following this, the chapter examines the elements of the IT budget cycle. Finally, it identifies some recommended practices for improving IT budgeting. It concludes that the IT budgeting process is a critical linchpin between many different organizational stakeholders: finance and IT; business units and IT; corporate strategy and IT; and between different internal IT groups, and plays a key role in implementing strategic and operational plans and controlling costs.*

**Keywords:** *Information Technology Budget, Information Technology Planning, Information Technology Strategy, Information Technology Effectiveness, IT Processes, IT Operations Costs, IT Capital Expenses, IT Budgeting Tools, IT Budgeting Methodology*

"If done well, a budget is the operational translation of an enterprise's strategy into costs and planned revenue" (Buytendijk, 2004). As such, planning and budgeting should be a matched set of practices that work together to implement an organization's information technology (IT) plans. Unfortunately, today's IT budgeting practices are more like IT planning's "evil twin"—out to undermine planning wherever possible. "Budgeting is a very negative process at our firm," one IT manager told us. "And it takes way too long." Asking many IT managers about budgeting elicits much caustic comment. Apparently, there are significant disconnects between the ideal and real worlds of IT budgeting, which leads to widespread disenchantment among IT leaders who feel that much of the work involved is both artificial and overly time consuming.

Others agree. While there has been little research done on IT budgeting per se (Hu and Quan, 2006; Kobelsky et al., 2008), there appears to be broad, general consensus that the budgeting processes of many corporations are broken and need to be fixed (Buytendijk, 2004; Hope and Fraser, 2003; Jensen, 2001; McKeen and Smith, 2008). There are many problems. First, budgeting takes too long and consumes too much managerial time. One study found that budgeting is a protracted process taking at least four months and consuming about 30 percent of management's time (Hope and Fraser, 2003). Second, most budgeting processes are no longer effective or efficient. They have become disconnected from business objectives and plans, as well as slow and expensive (Buytendijk, 2004). Third, rigid adherence to the numbers has been found to stifle innovation and discourage front-line staff from taking responsibility for performance (Hope and Fraser, 2003; Norton, 2006). And fourth, while many researchers have studied how organizations choose between strategic investment opportunities, studies show that all too often, the budgeting process undercuts management's strategic intentions, causing significant frustration among managers at all levels (McKeen and Smith, 2008; Norton, 2006; Steele and Albright, 2004).

Finally, the annual budgeting cycle can cast business plans "in concrete" at a time when companies need to be flexible and agile. This is particularly true in IT. "Over time, . . . IT budgeting processes [have] become institutionalized. As a result, IT investments [have] become less about creating competitive advantages for firms [and] more about following organizational routine and creating legitimacy for management as well as organizations" (Hu and Quan, 2006, p. 85). Now that senior business leaders have at last recognized the strategic importance of IT (Smith and McKeen, 2003), and IT has become many firms' largest capital expenditure (Koch, 2006), a hard look at how IT budgets are created and spent is clearly called for.

To explore these questions and the challenges that IT managers face in developing and monitoring their budgets, the authors convened a day-long focus group of senior managers from fifteen different companies in a variety of industries. This chapter presents the findings of this focus group, placing the issues discussed within a larger context. It first describes our data collection methodology and then looks at key concepts in IT budgeting to establish what they mean for IT managers and how they can differ between IT organizations. It next explores why budgets are an important part of the management process. Following this, the chapter examines the elements of the IT budget cycle. Finally, it identifies some recommended practices for improving IT budgeting.

## RESEARCH METHODOLOGY

Due to the exploratory nature of this research, we decided to use focus group methodology. While focus group methodology can be used for both exploratory and confirmatory research (Stewart and Shamdasani, 1990), it is particularly well suited for exploratory research. The methodology is widely employed in various disciplines as a qualitative research technique (Morgan, 1996). It entails a process of obtaining possible ideas or solutions to a problem from a group of participants through discussion (Stewart and Shamdasani, 1990). What constitutes focus groups is still debated in the literature but "most researchers seem to agree on at least a few characteristics: they should consist of a relatively small group of people (usually 7–12), led by a moderator, discussing a particular topic for 90–120 min" (Eason, Easton, and Belch, p. 719). The main advantage of the methodology is based on the kind of data it generates. Krippendork (1980) differentiates between *emic* data (i.e., that which arises in a natural or indigenous form) and *etic* data (i.e., that which represents the researcher's imposed view of the situation). While pure forms of data are rarely obtained in practice, focus group data are much more emic. As a result, focus groups are extremely useful in obtaining general background information about a topic, generating research hypotheses for further research, stimulating new ideas, learning what and why individuals think about the phenomenon of interest, and interpreting previously obtained quantitative results (Bellenger, Bernhardt, and Goldstucker, 1976; Higgenbotham and Cox, 1970).

Senior IT managers from fifteen different organizations were invited to attend a full-day focus group. Focus group participants represented consulting, manufacturing, insurance, banking and financial, government, retail, telecommunications, automotive, and pharmaceutical institutions. In preparation for this meeting, we asked them to consider a number of questions about their IT budgeting process. Specifically, they were asked about how their process functioned and what worked well and what did not. Additional questions addressed how their firms used IT budgets to support IT planning, specifically to manage demand, achieve flexibility, accomplish *enterprise* strategies, and upgrade infrastructure.

The participants were also asked to bring any corporate documents that they considered relevant to the topic. The discussion was moderated by one of the authors while the others recorded the discussion independently. The authors actively pushed for clarification of discussions and prompted participants to share actual experiences of specific events within their organizations in order to make arguments and concepts as concrete as possible. The participants were forthcoming with examples to support their observations of organizational phenomena. The research also relied on data collected from the participating organizations' Web sites. Further, while analyzing the data, e-mail and telephone communications were also conducted with a few participants in order to get more details and clarification on some of their responses. Our findings are based on an analysis of the focus group discussion in juxtaposition with the published literature. Our goal was to let practice inform theory and vice versa.

## KEY CONCEPTS IN INFORMATION TECHNOLOGY BUDGETING

Before looking at how budgeting is actually practiced in IT organizations, it is important to understand what a budget *is* and *why* an effective IT budgeting process is so important, both within IT and for the enterprise as a whole. Current organizational budgeting practices emerged in the 1920s as a tool for managing costs and cash flows. Present-day annual fixed plans and budgets were established in the 1970s to drive performance improvements (Hope and Fraser, 2003). Since then, most organizations have adhered rigidly to the ideals of this process, in spite of much evidence of their negative influence on innovation and flexibility (Hope and Fraser, 2003). These problems are clearly illustrated by the impact this larger corporate fiscal management process has on IT budgeting and the problems IT managers experience in trying to make their budget processes work effectively. The concepts and practices of the corporate fiscal world bear little similarity to how IT actually works. As a result, there are clear discontinuities between these two worlds.

These gaps are especially apparent in the differences between the fiscal view of IT and the functional one. Fiscal IT budgets[1] are broken down into two major categories: *capital expenditures* and *operating expenses,* although what expenditures go into each is highly variable. In the focus group, there was wide variation in how organizations handle their capital budgets, and hence, what types of IT expenses get allocated to each category. In accounting, capital budgets are utilized to spread large expenses (e.g., buying a building) over several years, while operating expenses cover the annual cost of running the business. The distinction between these two concepts gets very fuzzy however, when it comes to IT.

Generally speaking, all IT organizations want to capitalize as much of their spending as possible because it makes their annual costs look smaller. However, chief information officers (CIOs) are limited in what types of IT expenditure they can capitalize by both organizational and tax policy. It is the chief financial officer (CFO) who, through corporate financial strategy, establishes what may be capitalized and this, in turn, determines what IT can capitalize in its fiscal budget and what it must consider operating expense. In the focus group, some firms capitalized project development, infrastructure, consulting fees, and full-time staff, while others capitalized only major technology purchases.

How capital budgets are determined and the degree to which they are scrutinized also varies widely. There was no evidence that this varied by industry or some other contextual factor. Some firms allocate and prioritize IT capital expenses out of a corporate "pot," and others manage IT capital separately. Typically, capital expenses appear to be more carefully scrutinized than operating expenses, but not always. It was a surprise to all participants in the focus group how different types of expenses are handled in each firm and the wide degree of latitude allowed for IT costs under "generally accepted accounting principles." In fact, there are few accepted accounting principles when it comes to IT spending (Koch, 2006). As a result, researchers should use caution in relying on measures of the amount of capital spent on IT in firms or industries.

It is within this rather fuzzy *fiscal* context that the structure and purpose of *functional* (or working) IT budgets must be understood because these accounting concepts do not usually correspond exactly to how IT managers and researchers view IT work and how they plan and budget for it. In contrast to how fiscal IT budgets are designed, IT managers, according to the focus group, plan their spending using two somewhat different categories: *operations costs* and *strategic investments:*

• *Operations costs.* This category consists of what it costs to "keep the lights on" in IT. These are the expenses involved in running IT like a utility. Operations involves the cost of maintenance, computing and peripheral functions (e.g., storage, network), and support, regardless of how it is delivered (i.e., in-house or outsourced). This category can therefore include both operating and capital costs. Between 50 percent and 90 percent of a firm's IT budget (average 76 percent) is spent in this area, so the spending involved is significant (Gruman, 2006). In most firms, there is constant pressure on the CIO to continually reduce operations costs year on year (Smith and McKeen, 2006).

• *Strategic investment.* The balance of the IT budget consists of the "new" spending, that is, on initiatives and technology designed to deliver new business value and achieve the enterprise's strategic objectives. Because of the interactive nature of IT and business strategy these days, this part of the IT budget can include a number of different types of spending such as: business improvement initiatives to streamline processes and cut costs, business-enabling initiatives to extend or transform how a company does business, business opportunity projects to test the viability of new concepts or technologies and then scale them up, and sometimes, infrastructure (Smith, McKeen, and Singh, 2007). Because spending in this area can include many different kinds of expense, for example, full-time and contract staff, software and hardware, some parts of the strategic investment budget may be considered capital expenses, while others are classified as operating costs.

Another fuzzy fiscal budgeting concept is *cost allocation,* that is, the process of allocating the cost of the services IT provides to others' budgets.[2] The cost of IT can be viewed as a corporate expense, a business unit expense, or a combination of both, so the way in which IT costs are allocated can have a significant impact on what is spent in IT. For example, a majority of focus group companies allocate their operating expenses to their business units' operating budgets—usually using a formula based on factors such as the size of the business unit and its previous year's spending. Similarly, strategic expenses are typically allocated on the basis of which business unit will benefit from the investment. However, in today's IT environment, focus group members stated that the real world process of cost allocation is less than effective for a number of reasons.

While many strategic IT investments today involve the participation of more than one business unit, budgeting systems still tend to be designed around the structure of the organization (Norton, 2006). This leads to considerable artificiality in allocating development resources to projects, which in turn can lead to dysfunctional behavior, such as lobbying, games, nonsupportive cross-functional work, and the inability to successfully implement strategy (Buytendijk, 2004; Norton, 2006). "We don't fund corporate projects very well," admitted one manager whose company allocates all costs to individual business units.

Allocations can also lead to operational inefficiencies. "The different allocation models tend to lead to 'gaming' between our business units," said another. "Our business unit managers have no control over their percentage of operating costs," explained a third. "This is very frustrating for them and tends to be a real problem for some of our smaller units." Because of these allocations, some business units may not be willing to share in the cost of new hardware, software, or processes that would lead to reduced enterprise costs in the longer term. This is one of the primary reasons why so many IT organizations end up supporting several different applications all doing the same thing, explained focus group members. Furthermore, sometimes, when senior managers get disgruntled over their IT expenses, this method of allocating operations costs can lead to their cutting of IT operational spending in ways that have little to do with a cost-effective way of running IT. For example, one firm's management slashed its hardware and software replacement budget, which resulted in significant additional IT staff time required to support old equipment, additional downtime for the firm, and several extra months added to the testing and quality assurance effort needed before new applications could be implemented. While IT managers have done some work educating their chief executive officers (CEOs) and CFOs about what constitutes effective cost cutting (e.g., appropriate outsourcing, adjusting service levels), the fact remains that most business executives still do not understand or appreciate the factors that contribute to the overall cost of IT. As a result, allocations can lead to a great deal of angst for IT managers at budget time as they try to justify each expense and business managers try to "nickel and dime" each expense category (Koch, 2006).

As a result of all this fuzziness, modern IT budgeting practices do little to give business leaders confidence that IT spending is both effective and efficient (Gruman, 2006). And the challenges IT managers face in making the real world of IT spending fit into contemporary corporate budgeting practices are significant.

## THE IMPORTANCE OF INFORMATION TECHNOLOGY BUDGETS

Ideally, budgets are a key component of corporate performance management. They are also a subset of good governance processes in that they enable management to understand and communicate what is being spent and where. Ideally, therefore, a budget is more than a math exercise; it is "a blueprint for fiscally sound IT and business success" (Overby, 2004). Effective *IT* budgeting is important for many reasons, but two of the most important are:

1. *Fiscal discipline.* As overall IT spending has risen, senior business leaders are paying much closer attention to what IT costs and how its budgets are spent. In many organizations, there is still a great deal of skepticism that IT budgets are used wisely so reducing spending, or at least the operations portion of the budget, is now considered a key way for a CIO to build trust with the executive team (Gruman, 2006). Demonstrating an understanding and appreciation of the realities of business finance has become a significant part of IT leadership (Goldberg, 2004) and the ability to create and monitor a budget is therefore "table stakes" for a CIO (Overby, 2004).

In the focus group it was clear that senior executives are using the budgeting process to enforce tougher rules on how IT dollars are spent. Some organizations have centralized IT budgeting in an effort to better understand what is being spent; others are making the link between reducing operations spending and increasing investment in IT as a reason for introducing new operations disciplines (e.g., limiting maintenance, establishing appropriate support levels). Still others have established tighter requirements for business cases and monitoring returns on investment. In particular, most of the focus group organizations also use their IT budgets to manage and limit demand. "Our IT budget is capped by our CEO," stated one focus group manager. "And it's always less than the demand." Using budgets in this way, while likely effective for the enterprise, can cause problems for CIOs in that they must in turn enforce spending disciplines on business unit leaders.

Finally, budgets and performance against budgets are a key way of holding IT management accountable for what it spends, both internally to the leadership of the organization and externally, to shareholders and regulatory bodies. Improperly used, budgets can distort reality and encourage inappropriate behavior (Hope and Fraser, 2003; Jensen, 2001). However, used responsibly, they can be "a basis for clear understanding between organizational levels and can help executives maintain control over divisions and the business" (Hope and Fraser, 2003, p. 4). Research is beginning to show that there is a positive relationship between good IT budgeting practices (i.e., using IT budgets to manage demand, make investment decisions, and govern IT) and overall company performance (Kobelsky et al., 2008; Overby, 2004).

2. *Strategy implementation.* Budgets are also the "real world" of implementing IT strategy, linking the long-term goals of the organization and their short-term execution through the allocation of resources to activities. Unfortunately, research shows that the majority of organizations do not link their strategies to their budgets, which is why so many have difficulty making strategic changes (Norton, 2006). This is particularly true in IT, according to the focus group. As one manager complained, "no one knows what we're doing in the future. Therefore, our goals change regularly and at random." Another noted, "The lines of business pay little attention to IT resources when they're establishing their strategic plans. They just expect IT to make it happen."

Budgets can affect IT strategy implementation in a number of ways. First, *where* IT dollars are spent determines the impact IT can have on corporate performance. Clearly, if 80 percent of IT expenditures is going to operations and maintenance, IT can have less strategic impact than if this proportion is 20 percent lower. Second, *how* discretionary IT dollars are spent is important. For example, some companies decide to invest in infrastructure while others do not; some will choose to "bet the company" on a single large IT initiative while others will choose more focused projects. In short, the outcome of how a company chooses between investment opportunities is reflected in its budgets (Steele and Albright, 2004).

Third, the budgeting process itself reflects and reinforces the ability of strategic decision making to have an impact. Norton (2006) states that because budget processes are inherently biased toward the short term, in many organizations operational needs will systematically preempt strategic ones. In IT, the common practice of routinely allocating a fixed percentage of the IT strategic budget to individual business units, makes it almost impossible to easily reallocate resources to higher priority projects at the enterprise level or in other business units. In addition, several focus group members noted that their siloed budgeting processes make it difficult to manage the cross-business costs of strategic IT decisions.

Overall, budgets are a critical element of most managerial decisions and processes and are used to accomplish a number of different purposes in IT: compliance, fiscal accountability, cost reduction, business unit and enterprise strategy implementation, internal customer service, delivery of business value, and operational excellence, to name just a few. This, in a nutshell, is the reason why IT budgeting is such a complex and challenging process.

Figure 9.1    **A Generic Information Technology (IT) Planning and Budgeting Process**

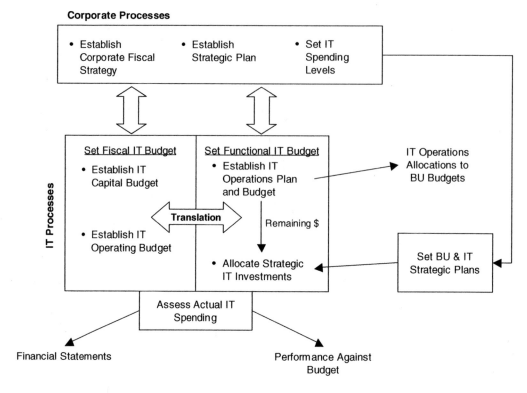

## THE INFORMATION TECHNOLOGY PLANNING AND BUDGET PROCESS

Today's IT budgets are used in so many different ways and serve so many stakeholders, it is no wonder that the focus group concurred that the whole process of IT budgeting is "painful" and "artificial" and could use some serious improvement. Figure 9.1 illustrates a generic and simplified IT planning and budgeting process that is consistent with most of the processes used in the focus group. This section outlines the steps involved in putting together an IT budget utilizing some of the key concepts presented above.

### Corporate Processes

These three activities set the corporate context within which IT plans and budgets are created.

*Establish Corporate Fiscal Policy*

This process is usually so far removed from the annual budget cycle that IT leaders may not even be aware of its influence or the wide number of options in the choices that are made (particularly around capitalization). Corporate fiscal policies are not created with IT spending in mind, but as noted above, can significantly impact how a fiscal IT budget is created and the levels of scrutiny under which certain kinds of expenses are placed. A more direct way that corporate fiscal policies affect IT is in company expectations around the return on investment for IT projects. Most focus group companies now have an explicit expected return rate for all new projects that is closely monitored.

*Establish Strategic Plan*

Conversely, IT budgeting *is* directly and continuously affected by many corporate strategic goals. The process of establishing IT and business unit strategies occurs within the context of this overall plan. In some organizations, there is tight integration between enterprise, business unit, and IT strategic planning; in others, these are more loosely coupled, informal and iterative. However, in almost none of the focus group companies was there a provision for enterprise funding for enterprise IT initiatives. Thus, corporate strategic plans are typically broken down into business unit budgets. As one focus group manager explained, "first our executives decide our profits and then the business units decide how to achieve them and then IT develops a plan with the business unit. . . . We still don't do many corporate projects."

*Set IT Spending Levels*

Establishing how much to spend on IT is the area that has been most closely studied by researchers, although it was not much mentioned in the focus group. This is a complex process, influenced by many external and internal factors. *Externally,* firms look to others in their industry to determine the level of their spending (Hu and Quan, 2006). In particular, companies frequently use benchmarks with similar firms to identify a percentage of revenue they should be spending on IT (Koch, 2006). Unfortunately, this approach can be dangerous for a number of reasons. First, it can be a strong driver in inhibiting competitive advantage and leading to greater similarities between firms in an industry (Hu and Quan, 2006). Second, this metric tells management nothing about how well its money is being spent (Koch, 2006). Third, it does not address IT's ability to use IT strategically (Kobelsky et al., 2008).

A second and increasingly strong external driver of IT spending is the regulatory environment within which a firm operates. Legislation, standards and professional practices are all beginning to affect what IT can and cannot do and how its work is done (Smith and McKeen, 2006). These in turn, affect how much is spent on IT and where it is spent (Hu and Quan, 2006). Other external factors that have been shown to affect how much money is spent on IT, include:

- *Number of competitors*—more concentration in an industry reduces the amount spent.
- *Uncertainty*—more uncertainty in a business's external environment leads to larger IT budgets.
- *Diversification of products and services*—firms competing in more markets will tend to spend more on IT (Kobelsky et al., 2008).

Internal factors affecting the size of the IT budget include:

- *Affordability*—a firm's overall performance and cash flow will influence how much discretion it has to spend more on IT.
- *Growth*—growing firms tend to invest more in IT than mature firms.
- *Previous year's spending*—firm spending on IT is unlikely to deviate significantly year over year (Hu and Quan, 2006; Kobelsky et al., 2008).

## IT Processes

These are multilevel and complex and frequently occur in parallel with each other.

### Set Functional IT Budget

This budget documents spending as it relates to how IT organizations *work,* that is, what is to be spent on IT operations and how much is available to be spent on strategic investments. As noted above, the operations budget is relatively fixed and contains the lion's share of the dollars, and therefore, requires much less planning. In spite of this, there are a number of machinations that IT managers must go through annually to justify this expenditure. Most IT organizations are still seen as cost centers, so obtaining budget approvals is often a delicate ongoing exercise of relationship building and education to prevent inappropriate cost cutting (Koch, 2006). Once the overall IT operations budget has been established, there is still the challenge of allocating it to the individual business units, which, given the complexity of today's shared technical environment, is often a fixed or negotiated percentage of the total. Business units can resent these allocations, over which they have no control and at best, they are viewed as a "necessary evil." In organizations where the IT operations budget is centralized, IT managers have a better opportunity to reduce expenses year over year, by introducing standards, streamlining hardware and software, and sharing services. However, in some focus group companies, operations budgets are decentralized into the business units and then aggregated up into one IT budget. This approach makes it considerably more difficult for IT managers to implement effective cost reduction measures. However, even in those firms that are highly effective and efficient, the relentless pressure from executives to do more with less makes this part of the annual budgeting process a highly stressful activity.

Allocating the funds remaining to strategic investments is a completely separate process in which potential new IT projects are cost justified and prioritized through strategic IT planning. Companies have many different ways of doing this and most focus group companies appear to be in a transition phase between methods of prioritization. Traditionally, IT organizations have been designed to parallel the organization structure and new development funds have been allocated to business units on the basis of some rule of thumb. For example, each business unit might be allotted a certain number of IT staff and dollars to spend on new development (based on a percentage of overall revenue) that would remain relatively stable over time. More recently, however, with greater integration of technology, systems and data, there has been a recognition of the cross-business costs of new development and of the need for more enterprise spending to address these. Increasingly, therefore, organizations are moving to plan and prioritize some or all new development at the enterprise level, thereby removing fixed allocations of new development resources from the business units.

However it is determined, the strategic portion of the functional IT budget also involves staffing the initiatives. This introduces yet another level of complexity in that, even if the dollars are available, appropriate IT resources must also be available to be assigned to particular projects to address the organization's cost-cutting requirements. Thus, undertaking a new project not only involves cost justification and prioritization, it also requires the availability of the right mix of skills and types of staff. For example, one focus group company is required to use fixed percentages of full-time, contract, and offshore staff in its projects. Almost all focus group companies prefer to use a mix of employees and contract staff in their development projects, in order to keep overhead costs low. As a result, creating new IT development budgets often involves a complementary exercise in staff planning.

*Set Fiscal IT Budget*

A second, parallel stream of IT budgeting, involves establishing the *fiscal* IT budget, which the CFO uses to implement the company's fiscal strategy and provide financial reports to shareholders and regulatory and tax authorities. This is seen largely as a "translation" exercise by IT managers in the focus group, where the functional IT budget is reconstituted into the operating and capital spending buckets. Nevertheless, it represents an additional "hoop" through which IT managers must jump before their budgets can be approved. In some companies, capital funding is difficult to obtain and must be cost justified against an additional set of financial criteria. In one focus group company, IT capital expenditures had to be prioritized against all other corporate capital expenses, for example, buildings, trucks. "This is a very challenging exercise," said the manager involved. In other firms, CFOs are more concerned about increasing operating expenses. In either case, this is an area where many IT managers set themselves up for failure by failing to speak the language of finance (Girard, 2004). Because most IT managers think of their work in terms of operations and strategic investments, they fail to understand some of the larger drivers of fiscal strategy such as investor value and earnings per share. To get more "traction" for their budgets it is therefore important for IT leaders to better translate what IT can do for the company into monetary terms (Girard, 2004). To this end, many focus group companies have begun working more closely with their companies' finance staff and are seeing greater acceptance of their budgets as a result.

## Assess Actual IT Spending

At the other end of the IT planning and budgeting process is the need to assess actual IT spending and performance. A new focus on financial accountability has meant that results are more rigorously tracked than in the past. In many focus group companies, finance staff now monitors business cases for all new IT projects, thus relieving IT of having to prove the business returns on what is delivered. Often, the challenge of finding the right resources for a project or unexpected delays means that not all of the available development budget is spent in a fiscal year. "We typically tend to spend about 85 percent of our available development budget because of delays or resourcing problems," said one manager. Hitting budget targets *exactly* in the strategic investment budget is therefore a challenge, and current IT budgeting practices typically do not allow for much flexibility. On one hand, they can create a "use it or lose it" mentality—since if money is not spent in the fiscal year it will disappear. "This leads to some creative accruals and aggressive forecasting," said the focus group. On the other hand, IT managers who want to ensure there is *enough* money for key expenditures create "placeholders," that is, approximations of what they think a project will cost, and "coffee cans," that is, unofficial slush funds, in their budgets. The artificial timing of the budget process, combined with the difficulties of planning and estimation and reporting complexity, all mean that incentives for accurate reporting of what is spent can get distorted, said participants. As a result, another disconnect is created between the ideal and the real worlds of IT budgeting.

## INFORMATION TECHNOLOGY BUDGETING PRACTICES THAT DELIVER VALUE

Although there is general agreement that current budgeting practices are flawed, there are still no widely accepted alternatives. Within IT itself, according to the focus group, companies seem to be experimenting with ways to "tweak" budgeting to make it (a) easier and (b) more effective. Participants agreed that the following five practices have proved to be useful in this regard:

## Appoint an IT Finance Specialist

Many focus group companies now have a finance expert working in IT or on staff with the CFO working *with* IT. "Getting help with finance has really made the job of budgeting easier," said one manager. "Having a good partnership with finance, helps us to leverage their expertise," said another. Financial specialists can help IT managers to understand their costs and drivers in new ways. Within operations, they can assist with cost and value analysis of services and infrastructure (Gruman, 2006) and also manage the "translation" process between the functional IT budget and the fiscal IT budget. "Finance helps us to understand depreciation and gives us a deeper understanding of our cost components," a manager noted. Finance specialists are also being used to build and monitor business cases for new projects, often acting as brokers between IT and the business units. "They've really helped us to better articulate business value. Now they're in charge of ensuring that the business gets the benefits they say they will, not IT." The improving relationship between finance and IT is making it easier to gain acceptance of IT budgets. "Having dedicated IT finance people is great since this is not what IT managers want to do," said a focus group manager.

## Use Budgeting Tools and Methodologies

About half of the members of the focus group felt they had effective budgeting tools for such things as asset tracking, rolling up and breaking down budgets into different levels of granularity and reporting. "We have a good, integrated suite of tools," said a manager "and they really help." Because budgets serve so many different stakeholders, tools and methodologies can help "slice and dice" the numbers many ways, dynamically enabling changes in one area to be reflected in all other areas. Those who did not have good or well-integrated tools found that there were gaps in their budgeting processes that were hard to fill. "Our poor tools lead to disconnects all over the place," said a participant. Good links to the IT planning process are also needed. Ideally, tools should tie budgets directly to corporate strategic planning, resource strategies, and performance metrics, enabling a further translation between the company's accounting categories and hierarchy and its strategic themes and targets (Norton, 2006).

## Separate Operations from Innovation

While most IT managers mentally separate these two IT activities, in practical terms, maintenance and support, in particular, are often mixed up with new project development. This happens especially when IT organizations are aligned with and funded by the business units. Once IT funds and resources are allotted to a particular business unit, rather than to a strategic deliverable, it is very difficult to reduce these allocations, said the focus group. There appears to be growing agreement that operations (including maintenance) must be fully financially separated from new development in order to ensure that the costs of the first are fully scrutinized and kept under control, while focus is kept on increasing the proportion of resources devoted to new project development (Dragoon, 2005; Girard, 2004; Gruman, 2006; Norton, 2006). Repeatedly, focus group managers told stories of how their current budget processes discourage accuracy. "There are many disincentives built into our budgeting processes to keep operational costs down," said one manager. Separating operations from innovation in budgets provides a level of visibility in IT spending that has traditionally been absent and that helps business unit leaders better understand the true costs of delivering both new systems and ongoing services.

## Adopt Enterprise Funding Models

While it is still rare to find organizations that provide corporate funding for enterprise-wide strategic IT initiatives, there is broad recognition that this is needed (Norton, 2006). Only one focus group company had a formal process of enterprise funding established, although others noted "if it's a corporate priority, it somehow gets the funding." The conflict between the need for truly integrated initiatives and traditional siloed budgets frequently stymies innovation, frustrates behavior designed for the common good, and discourages accountability for results (Hope and Fraser, 2003; Norton, 2006; Steele and Albright, 2004). It is therefore expected that more organizations will adopt enterprise funding models for at least some IT initiatives over the next few years. Similarly, decentralized budgeting for core IT services is declining, due to the cost-savings opportunities available from sharing these. While costs will likely continue to be charged back to the differing business units, the current best practice is for IT operation budgets to be developed at an enterprise level.

## Adopt Rolling Budget Cycles

Focus group members agreed that IT plans and budgets need attention more frequently than once a year. While not used by many companies, utilizing an eighteen-month rolling plan that is reviewed and updated quarterly appears to be a more effective way of budgeting, especially for new project development (Hope and Fraser, 2003; Smith, McKeen, and Singh, 2007). "It is very difficult to plan new projects a year in advance," said one focus group manager. "Often we are asked for our 'best estimates' in our budgets. The problem is that once they're in the budget, they are then viewed as reality." The artificial timing of budgets and the difficulty of estimating the costs of new projects are key sources of frustration for IT managers. Rolling budget cycles, when combined with integrated budgeting tools, should better address this problem, while still providing the financial snapshots needed by the enterprise on an annual basis.

## CONCLUSION

Although IT budget processes have been largely ignored by researchers, they are a critical linchpin between many different organizational stakeholders: finance and IT; business units and IT; corporate strategy and IT; and between different internal IT groups. Not surprisingly therefore, IT budgeting is much more complex and difficult to navigate than it would first appear. This chapter has outlined some of the challenges faced by IT managers trying to juggle the realities of dealing with both IT operations and strategic investments while meeting the differing needs of their budget stakeholders. Surprisingly, there are very few guidelines for IT managers in this area. Each organization appears to have quite different corporate financial policies, which in turn drive different IT budgeting practices. Nevertheless, IT managers do face many common challenges in budgeting. Although other IT practices have benefited from focused management attention in recent years, such as prioritization and operations rationalization, budgeting has not as yet been targeted in this way. However, as business and IT leaders begin to recognize the key role that budgets play in implementing strategic and operational plans and controlling costs, it is hoped they will make a serious effort to address the real world budgeting problems faced by IT.

## NOTES

1. Because IT organizations usually prepare two separate types of budgets, we have distinguished between them in this chapter. The fiscal IT budget refers to the budget prepared for the CFO, while the functional IT budget refers to the spending plan used by IT managers themselves.

2. Allocations can be either theoretical or "real" dollars, in which case they are known as chargebacks. There is no agreement in companies about the effectiveness of chargebacks so we have taken no position on their utility in dealing with IT budgeting challenges.

## REFERENCES

Bellenger, D.N.; Bernhardt, K.L.; and Goldstucker, J.L. 1976. *Qualitative Research in Marketing.* Chicago: American Marketing Association.

Buytendijk, F. 2004. New way to budget enhances corporate performance measurement. Gartner, Inc., Resource Id #423484, January 28.

Dragoon, A. 2005. Journey to the IT promised land. *CIO Magazine,* April 1.

Eason, G.; Easton, A.; and Belch, M. 2003. An experimental investigation of electronic focus groups. *Information and Management,* 40, 717–727.

Girard, K. 2004. What CIOs need to know about money. *CIO Magazine* (Special Money Issue), September 22. Available at www.cio.com.

Goldberg, M. 2004. The final frontier for CIOs. *CIO Magazine* (Special Money Issue), September 22. Available at www.cio.com.

Gruman, G. 2006. Trimming for dollars. *CIO Magazine,* July 1. Available at www.cio.com.

Higgenbotham, J.B., and Cox, K.K. 1970. *Focus Group Interviews: A Reader.* Chicago: American Marketing Association.

Hope, J., and Fraser, R. 2003. Who needs budgets? *Harvard Business Review,* 81, 2 (February), 2–8.

Hu, Q., and Quan, J. 2006. The institutionalization of IT budgeting: empirical evidence from the financial sector. *Information Resources Management Journal,* 19, 1 (January–March), 84–97.

Jensen, M. 2001. Corporate budgeting is broken—let's fix it. *Harvard Business Review,* 79, 11 (November), 95–101.

Kobelsky, K.V., Richardson, R.; Smith, H.A.; and Zmud, R. 2008. Determinants and consequences of firm information technology budgets. *Accounting Review* (forthcoming).

Koch, C. 2006. The metrics trap . . . and how to avoid it. *CIO Magazine,* April 1. Available at www.cio.com.

Krippendork, K. 1980. *Content Analysis: An Introduction to Its Methodology.* Beverly Hills, CA: Sage.

McKeen, J.D., and Smith, H.A. 2008. *IT Strategy in Action.* Englewood Cliffs, NJ: Pearson Prentice Hall.

Morgan, L. 1996. Focus groups. *Annual Review of Sociology,* 22, 129–152.

Norton, D. 2006. Linking strategy and planning to budgets. *Balanced Scorecard Report,* 8, 3 (May) (Harvard Business School Publishing).

Overby, S. 2004. "Tips from the budget masters." *CIO Magazine* (Special Money Issue), September 22. Available at www.cio.com.

Smith, H.A., and McKeen, J.D. 2003. Developing and delivering on the IT value proposition. *Communications of the Association of Information Systems,* 11, 25 (April), 438–450.

———. 2006. IT in 2010: the next frontier. *MISQ-Executive,* 5, 3 (September), 125–136.

Smith, H.A.; McKeen, J.D.; and Singh, S. 2007. Developing IT strategy for business value. *Journal of Information Technology Management,* 18, 1 (June), 49–58.

Steele R., and Albright, C. 2004. Games managers play at budget time. *MIT Sloan Management Review,* 45, 3 (Spring), 81–84.

Stewart, D.W., and Shamdasani, P.N. 1990. *Focus Groups: Theory and Practice.* Thousand Oaks, CA: Sage.

# CHAPTER 10

# SOME DOS AND DON'TS OF STRATEGIC INFORMATION SYSTEMS PLANNING

## GEORGE PHILIP

**Abstract:** *Given the dynamic and constantly changing business environment, there is considerable debate about the value of conducting strategic planning for information systems (IS). Despite the divergent views, the author and many others are convinced that such planning is an essential and critically important activity for all organizations. In this chapter a distinction is made between planning for operational efficiency and planning for strategic advantage. The former is achieved through exploitation strategies and the latter through exploration strategies. The main focus, however, is on the identification and discussion of eight principles for successful planning for IS. Two case studies were conducted to see if these principles are followed by real world organizations. Based on the evidence, it is suggested that a detailed written plan is not always an essential requirement for successful and effective use of technology.*

**Keywords:** *Operational Efficiency, Strategic Planning for IS, Exploitation Strategy, Exploration Strategy, Role of CIO, Implementation Strategy, IS Strategy*

## INTRODUCTION TO STRATEGIC INFORMATION SYSTEMS PLANNING

Strategic information systems planning (SISP) is defined as "the process of identifying a portfolio of computer-based applications that will assist an organization in executing its business plans and realizing its business goals" (Hartono et al., 2003). More specifically the aims of SISP are: (1) to establish symbiosis between information systems and business objectives; (2) to outperform rivals; (3) to manage information resources effectively; and (4) to develop an information technology (IT) infrastructure and a portfolio of prioritized applications consistent with the information vision of the organization. Unsurprisingly, then, this issue has consistently been ranked among the top ten issues in almost all IT surveys of organizations in the past two decades or so (Brancheau, Janz, and Wetherbe, 1996; Brown, 2004). For example, a survey conducted in December 2004 in the United States showed that, of the top ten IT issues facing firms, strategic planning for IT emerged as the fourth issue (Maltz and DeBlois, 2005). The importance of planning is emphasized by many others as well: "Improving strategic planning within the realm of information technology management is consistently identified by top corporate executives as a critical competitive issue" (Segars and Grover, 1999). This is not to say that there is now universal agreement about the need to develop strategic plans (more on this later).

The first section of this chapter looks at the planning methods employed by organizations and the conflicting views about the value of conducting strategic planning. The next section describes eight principles (dos and don'ts) for successful planning, and the following one analyzes whether these principles are followed by real world organizations. The chapter ends with a short conclusions section.

## IS Planning Methods

Historically the majority of strategic planning methods have taken a top-down business-led approach (Premkumar and King, 1994) to bring about alignment between information systems (IS) strategy and business strategy. An extensive review of the literature, however, will reveal that, depending on the focus of the planning exercise, planning methodologies for IS generally fall into two broad categories—impact and align methodologies (Booth and Philip, 2005; Lee and Gough, 1993). Thus, if the focus of an organization is to gain competitive advantage through the use of IT, then impact methodology is to be used, and this methodology was very popular in the 1980s and 1990s when there was a great deal of exuberance and euphoria concerning the strategic/competitive use of IT. Examples of impact methodologies include: Ives and Learmonth's (1984) customer resource life cycle, Porter's value chain analysis (Porter 1985), and Wiseman's (1985) strategic option generator. There is a question mark, however, over the value of all of them since most of the evidence has been anecdotal rather than based on a systematic study of a large number of small and medium-size enterprises (SMEs) and multinationals. Moreover, while they can help managers to identify strategic opportunities, they cannot provide any advice concerning the specific ways in which technology may be used. Also they do not address the issue of *sustainable* advantage.

The align methodology, on the other hand, seeks to establish symbiosis between IS strategy and business objectives (Reich and Benbasat, 2000). There are a range of align methodologies available. These include those emanating from the major consulting firms, such as Coopers & Lybrand (now PricewaterhouseCoopers), Andersen Consulting (Lederer and Gardiner, 1992), IBM (Business Systems Planning methodology), Information Engineering (Martin, 1989), and Total Information Systems Management (Osterle, Brenner, and Hilbers, 1993). The proliferation of methods is itself open to criticism, and is seen by many as symptomatic of an immature and disorganized research community, with individual researchers working to advance their own agendas at the expense of the advancement of the community/tradition as a whole (Booth and Philip, 2005). Tukana and Weber (1996, p. 737), for instance, argue that researchers have "focused too much on introducing new items onto the IS planning agenda. Too little work has been undertaken, on the other hand, to understand, improve and predict IS planning behaviors." Lehmann (1993) also makes a similar point and, in his view, researchers have so far succeeded in creating "not so much a framework than a body of tribal knowledge."

Be that as it may, an illustration of how these two methodologies relate to organizations is shown in Figure 10.1. The starting point for most organizations would be stage 1, where, using align methodology, the organization tries to achieve operational efficiency with a focus on internal functions. The primary purpose is to achieve alignment between business needs and IT systems and it may also include the integration of all the disparate information systems to enable a seamless flow of information within the firm. This may be followed by stage 2, when some firms might spot an external opportunity or threat for the competitive/strategic use of IT and then design an IT system (using impact methodology) to support this application. Initially, the new system is unique to the firm and may give the first mover (left upper quadrant) some serious initial strategic advantage. However, this position can be sustained only if the IT system is constantly updated and repositioned as shown in stage 3. This may be achieved through business process reengineering (BPR), redefinition of external relationships/network, business diversification, or the development

Figure 10.1    **Information Systems (IS) Strategic Planning Stages: From Operational Efficiency to Unsustainable Strategic Advantage**

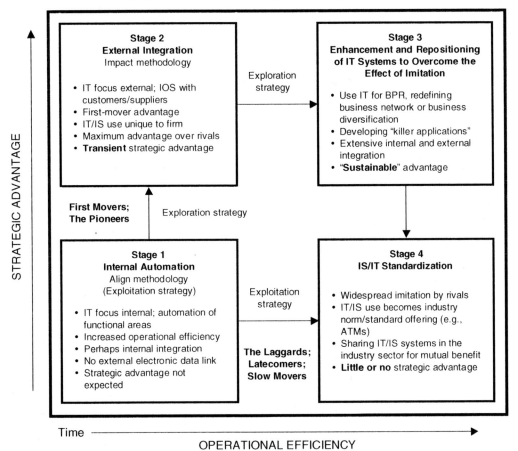

of "killer applications" (Downes and Mui, 1998). For example, the Sabre system of American Airlines (Martin et al., 2005) was able to provide significant competitive advantage over a longer period of time because it was constantly updated and enhanced from being a simple seat inventory management system to a system capable of supporting multilayer pricing strategy and sophisticated revenue management facilities. (Sabre is now an independent company.) In the real world, unfortunately, the fact is that most of the IT systems will sooner or later be copied or imitated by rivals, so any advantage will be reduced and most businesses are likely to end up in the bottom right hand quadrant in stage 4 (as competitive casualties) with increased operational efficiency (Carr, 2004b; Philip and Booth, 2001;). So, what was once unique to a particular company will soon become a standard offering within its industry sector (Philip, 2007). A well-known example is automated teller machines (ATMs), which initially gave significant competitive advantage to Citibank, but are now commonplace in the financial sector. Finally, with the passage of time and perhaps with increased pressure from their industry sector, some organizations may move slowly, but directly, from stage 1 to stage 4 for increased operational efficiency.

Clearly, as shown in Figure 10.1, organizations have two primary expectations of IS: (1) improved operational efficiency and (2) sustainable competitive advantage. Also, in order to sustain advantage, organizations need to continuously enhance and reposition their IT systems. As Galliers (2001) observed recently: "IS strategy should also be seen as being on-going and processual, crucially dependent on learning from 'below,' from tinkering and improvisation, and from the emergent and unintended consequences of strategic decisions, as well as from the more deliberate, designed and codified ICT 'solutions' that have been implemented." The implication clearly is that an IS strategy should have both an exploitation strategy and an exploration strategy enabled by a facilitative sociotechnical environment (Galliers, 2001).

*Exploitation Strategy (Align Methodology)*

This strategy adopts an analytical/methodical approach to IS development. The system may be developed internally or purchased from an external vendor (e.g., ERP systems). The purpose of exploitation strategy is to improve operational efficiency and effectiveness and it generally goes through two stages: (1) a top-down analysis to clarify business needs with a view to identifying appropriate information system requirements, and (2) a bottom-up evaluation of existing information systems to study their effectiveness and also to identify gaps in, contribution and vulnerability of, existing information systems. The aim is to establish symbiosis/alignment between information systems and business needs. One of the early examples of a methodology for doing this is IBM's Business Systems Planning (BSP).

*Exploration Strategy (Using Impact Methodology)*

While exploitation strategy takes a structured, analytical, evaluative, and methodical approach to IS development, the nature of the beast is quite different in exploration strategy, which is about identifying opportunities for the innovative use of IT. While structured approaches can give some signposting for the innovative use of IT, they alone are not sufficient to nurture the creative talents of individuals within the organization. Exploration strategy specifically seeks to encourage and promote innovation and creativity and thereby achieve competitive or strategic advantage for the business. This will involve the use of unconventional approaches such as tinkering and improvisation to unleash the creative potential of bright sparks and visionaries in the organization. Individuals and/or teams might come up with fresh ideas and the feasibility of these ideas has to be tested by creating a prototype. Such experimentation/exploration must be encouraged, despite the possibility of its becoming costly, and may, in the majority of cases, need to be abandoned after the initial feasibility study. This should not involve harsh criticism or loss of face of individuals/ teams. Impact methodologies are part and parcel of any exploration strategy.

In summary, then, exploitation strategies, which take a methodical approach, are concerned with improving operational efficiency whereas exploration strategies, which make use of experimentation and prototyping, are meant to provide competitive/strategic advantage for the business. Both of these strategies are essential for a balanced SISP process.

A great deal of work has also been done in the past couple of decades to understand the success factors of many of the strategic planning efforts. These include: organizational issues (Lederer and Sethi, 1991), resource issues (Tukana and Weber, 1996), effectiveness of the planning methods used and the actual relevance of the plan, and, more importantly problems associated with implementing the plans themselves (Tukana and Weber, 1996). Many researchers (Galliers, 2001; Teo and Ang, 2001) have also argued for an ongoing process of evaluation and review and the consideration of implementation as a critical issue. These calls are not always heeded and the reality is that, many

IS planning decisions/documents, rather than being proactively implemented, are left to gather dust on the shelf or in many instances implemented only partially.

Another fundamental problem is that many still question the value of conducting strategic planning. For them, strategic planning is inappropriate/ineffective for responding to the modern fast-changing business world because, by the time plans are developed and implemented, business requirements will have changed (and/or technology moved on), rendering the plans obsolete. As Slater (2002) has observed, many CIOs "have apparently responded to the forces of chaos by throwing in the towel on strategic planning." His view resonates with that of Bensaou and Earl (1998), who point out that a lot of (Western) companies have abandoned the idea of a long-term IS planning process altogether. Also a more recent survey (Slater, 2002) in the United States has shown that 39 percent of the respondents had no formal IT strategy at all. Some would go even further to suggest that the emergence of the Internet marks the death knell for strategies and strategic plans. Porter disagrees strongly: "In our quest to see how the Internet is different, we have failed to see how the Internet is the same. While a new means of conducting business has become available, the fundamentals of competition remain unchanged. The next stage of the Internet's evolution will involve a shift in thinking from e-business to business, from e-strategy to strategy. Only by integrating the Internet into overall strategy will this powerful new technology become an equally powerful force for competitive advantage" (Porter, 2001). Carr (2004a) sides with Porter and points out that the difficulty in sustaining a competitive position, because of the speed of imitation by rivals, actually strengthens rather than weakens the need for strategic planning. "As buyers become more powerful and business processes and systems more homogeneous, only the strategically astute companies will be able to rise above the competitive free-for-all." He cites the success of Dell and Wal-Mart, which, despite the acquisition of sophisticated IT systems by competitors, are able to maintain their competitive position primarily through astute business and IT plans and strategies. Slater (2002) believes that such chaotic times "make it more necessary than ever for the CIO to routinely take a strategic view." Varon (2000) agrees with Slater: " Strategic planning is more important today than ever before, and it is the very speed of change in today's business climate which makes it so." The case for conducting strategic planning is therefore well argued. The unanswered question, however, is: how should organizations go about conducting successful strategic planning? In this chapter we attempt to identify several dos and don'ts for success. More specifically, eight principles for successful strategic planning are identified from the prior literature (Bensaou and Earl, 1998; Ferranti, 2001; Gordon, 2002; Hartono et al., 2003; Lederer and Sethi, 1998; Slater, 2002; Varon, 2000), and case examples from organizations of contrasting size and structure that report effective IS planning efforts are described. This chapter also emphasizes the need for planning to be an ongoing activity and that IT systems that are planned and developed must be continuously repositioned and enhanced to enjoy long-term sustainable advantage.

In the next section, each of the eight principles is described in more detail. This is followed by an examination of the IS planning practices in two firms that focus on using IS to achieve specific business operational goals. A cross comparison of the planning practices of the two companies in the light of these principles is also carried out to determine whether they are valid in the real world of business.

## DOS AND DON'TS OF SUCCESSFUL INFORMATION SYSTEMS PLANNING

"Competitive advantage through information technology" used to be the slogan used by many academics and consultants in trying to respond to all of the business ills of the 1980s and 1990s.

Undoubtedly, information systems have the potential to provide significant strategic advantage, but organizations should bear in mind that IS planning for operational efficiency can be as important and productive as planning for competitive advantage. As shown in Figure 10.1, given its ubiquitous presence, the use of IT has become a strategic imperative for all organizations. Long-term plans (say, three to five years) were appropriate for a static world and not for the highly dynamic business and IT environment of today. The IT strategic plan (formal or informal) for operational efficiency will instead focus more on addressing how IT enables business processes rather than trying to plot an inflexible course for IS for the long term. This point is also highlighted by Bensaou and Earl (1998) in their study of Japanese companies, where IT investment benefit is validated in terms of operational efficiency measures rather than the fulfillment of a long-term grand plan.

### Principle 1: Business and IS Strategies to Be Developed Jointly and Concurrently

There is considerable debate in the academic literature on the issue of business/IS alignment. As yet, no one has come up with a universal methodology for achieving it. However, there is significant consensus that business planning should not be done in isolation. Indeed, it has to be done in conjunction with IT plans and both plans need to be developed collaboratively by a team consisting of business-focused managers and technology-focused IS professionals. Clearly, the implication is that, when writing an IT strategic plan, chief information officers (CIOs) should not wait until the business plan is formulated. CIOs should be active participants in the development of both strategies. In a case study of Hewlett-Packard, Feurer and others (2000) makes the point that a sequential approach to alignment is not effective and that "a better approach is one in which strategies, processes, technologies and actions are defined and aligned concurrently." Similarly, Goldsmith (1991) advocates the development of IS strategy during the same process and at the same time as business strategies if organizations are to derive maximum advantage from IT systems.

The reality in many organizations, however, is that they have no formal business planning process, let alone an IS strategic planning process. In fact a recent survey by the Cutter Consortium (Slater, 2002) confirmed that almost a third of respondents did not have a formal business plan—that is, a written plan. Perhaps a *detailed written* plan is not always essential as long as both parties—business-savvy managers and IT specialists—are well informed about the corporate aims and objectives and participate in the informal planning process to understand how technology can help the organization in realizing them (Philip, 2007).

### Principle 2: Commitment and Visionary Leadership from Top Management Are Crucial

Unfortunately, IT tends to have a polarizing effect on the majority of senior managers, either frightening or dazzling them (Davenport, 1994). The former do their best to ignore the technology, while the latter are likely to become "prisoners" of their own technological fixation, with the result that technology is advocated for its own sake, with very little attention paid to the people within the organization who will have to face the IT-related upheavals (Booth and Philip, 2005). As one IT manager told us: "They (business managers) have a fear of technology and don't really appreciate the issues. They realize that technology, for reasons that they don't fully appreciate, is absolutely fundamental, although if they had the choice they'd rather do without it." Such attitudes are not uncommon.

Most organizations will have many competent and committed IT staff but they have to be led, managed, and organized in ways that fully use their creative energies. Senior executives must be proactive in providing leadership, vision, coordination, and making sure that resources are made available at the appropriate stages of the planning and implementation processes. A number of studies have confirmed this point (Basu et al., 2002; Lederer and Sethi, 1992a, 1992b; Teo and King, 1996). For example, Teo and Ang's (2001) study of a number of companies in Singapore found that one of the major IS planning problems is the lack of support from senior managers in the three stages of planning, namely, launching, development, and implementation. It is not unusual to come across bottlenecks during the implementation of plans, and it is the responsibility of senior managers to take whatever steps are needed to move the plan forward.

A clear example of visionary leadership is illustrated in the case of FedEx. According to *Fortune*, FedEx is the second most admired company in America, due largely to the partnership and efforts of its chief executive officer (CEO) and CIO. Indeed the CIO, Rob Carter, is at "the strategic heart of what makes FedEx successful." The IT budget of the company is $ 1 billion and the CEO, Fred Smith, "completely believes in the importance of infotech." (O'Brien and Marakas, 2007/8, 443).

### Principle 3: 360 Degree Listening and Communication

Listening and communication are the two critical elements in SISP. Before developing the plans, it is important to listen to the views of employees at all levels, and once the plan is prepared it should be communicated to all employees so that there is a shared vision of the role that IS can play in the organization. Both IT staff and senior business managers should engage in top-down and bottom-up listening with regard to the impact and role of technology in the organization. Communicate to everyone as much as possible about everything as often as possible, preferably face to face rather than electronically. "Management by e-mail" is not always an effective way to win employee commitment to and support of strategic plans. Indeed, a major reason for IS planning failure is the lack of involvement of end users and business managers in the process (King and Teo, 2000; Teo and Ang, 2001). Obviously, those who are close to the business are in a better position to provide valuable feedback on the performance of existing systems as well as to identify gaps in information systems. These inputs are invaluable in making better prioritization decisions. Such user participation (Feurer et al., 2000) and consultation with employees can also create a sense of belonging and empowerment. The success of the planning approach is thus as much about fostering an appropriate culture as anything else.

Listening must be accompanied by effective communication of the information vision to all stakeholders of the organization, focusing particularly on how technology can significantly improve business performance. Lack of communication (Teo and Ang, 2001) can result in employees' serious resistance to the implementation of a strategic plan and the accompanying changes. Moreover, listening and communication should not be restricted to internal employees. It should include all stakeholders of the organization—suppliers, customers, distributors, and so on. This means creating an organizational culture that proactively supports constructive engagement and information sharing between all levels of the organization and its external stakeholders.

### Principle 4: Develop a High-Level Plan with Broad Principles, Not Specific Actions

If a written IT plan is produced, ensure that it is easily understood and digested by ordinary business managers and that it is not unnecessarily long and loaded with technical details. The plan should be high-level enough to allow changes in implementation details without rewriting the whole document. Business managers are busy bodies and drowning them in too many details can only put them off. As one manager commented:

> On a three-year document all you're doing is highlighting where you want to get to: the road that you take may vary. As long as you've got the view of where you want to go in the longer term then the road that you take will define the nature of the business.

Another manager, who is convinced that strategic planning is one way to impose some order on the unpredictability of the external environment, said:

> I think that even though it is an unpredictable world, you have got to have a sense of direction. It's no use gliding down the stream, saying "I hope this takes me somewhere nice."

Dividing the strategic plan into two sections is one way of addressing this issue: one describing applications or solutions for business units in nontechnical terms and the other providing information on infrastructure requirements, software upgrades, and so on (Slater, 2002). In this way, if they choose, representatives from other departments can focus on solutions and not the architecture. However, it does not always follow that the IT strategic plan supports the company's business strategy. This is because if the IT strategy is based on current requirements alone, then the company is unwittingly trying to achieve market parity rather than market dominance. Given that an IT strategy should be about creating business value, one could argue in favor of merging the IT strategic plan and the business strategic plan into a single document because they should lay out general directions at a strategic level rather than set out specific actions. Therefore, the underlying strategy remains the same but the execution of the plan can be easily modified.

## Principle 5: Identification and Exploitation of Opportunities

Opportunities are the raw materials for innovation, and their identification and exploitation should become the rhythm of organizational life. "The strategy of successful firms is adaptive and opportunistic" (Kay, 1993 p.4). Consequently strategic planning should not be regarded as an exclusively rational and deliberate activity—analytical, structured, and methodical. Organizations should not rely solely on the "design school" approach (Mintzberg, 1990, 1994a, 1994b, 1994c) to planning. Opportunistic strategy formulation (Hackney and Little, 1999) can bring about significant benefits to the organization. Earl (1996) makes a similar point: "planning techniques are not (always) the answer." Varon (2000) also recommends that it is important to keep the IS strategic plan general. While it is crucial to examine how different IT projects relate to the strategic plan, enterprising individuals/ teams should have the freedom to come up with new ideas for the innovative use of IT.

Downes and Mui (1998) go further, suggesting that traditional strategic planning based on "predict and plan" is inappropriate and that what is required now is a "digital strategy" involving experimentation and quick response. Pencil-and-paper–based strategic planning is too slow for the digital age. Instead organizations must spot opportunities for the development of "killer applications"—"applications that utterly decimate existing categories or create whole new ones"— through the rapid prototyping route rather than the methodical approach adopted by traditional planners. Decreasing costs and the ubiquitous presence of technology make it easy to test ideas through working prototypes rather than through prolonged document-based strategy development and analysis. Downes and Mui (1998) outline two ways to identify opportunities for proceeding down the digital strategy route. The first one is through "learning encounter workshops" and the second is through "technology study tours." The former involves organizing brainstorming sessions for a group of senior executives/managers. The session starts by showing them case studies of technology use by their competitors in order to spark fresh and radical ideas to achieve a quantum leap over their rivals through the far superior use of technologies. The second way (study tour) involves visiting a number of start-up companies by a team consisting of senior executives and IT professionals to observe emerging technologies that are currently in embryonic form. The authors cite the example of companies developing advanced video games. Such a peek into future technologies can help to open the eyes of executives and IT managers to the nature of the competitive threat around the corner. Simon Nixon, the co-founder of one of the major price comparison Web sites in the UK, Moneysupermarket.com, for instance, makes the point that he spends 20 percent of his time looking at his competitors' sites because he recognizes that "nothing stands still in this industry. In the Internet age, change happens in a heartbeat" (Higgins, 2007, p. 86).

An example of a company that has developed killer applications is Google. It has stolen a march on its nearest rivals Yahoo!, MSN, and Time Warner in the Internet search engine field by developing a better way to index and rank Web pages. Their PageRank system uses a complex mathematical algorithm to identify how many other influential sites are linked to a particular page. By identifying well-connected pages, they are able to provide much better and more relevant search results for users. It is no wonder that Google has emerged as the most popular search engine, capturing almost 60 percent of all Web searches in the United States and three out of four of all searches carried out in the rest of the world.

### Principle 6: Plans Should Not Be Cast in Stone

Planning should not be regarded as an event but a journey. While IT strategic planning should take a long-term view, the plan should be reviewed preferably twice a year by a team consisting of business managers and IT personnel. Indeed the IT strategic plan should include contingency plans and provision for ongoing reviews (Salmela and Spil, 2002). Contingency plans for the longer and shorter term need to be worked out in advance in consultation with the business people. This helps to cement business alignment and support and allows the CIO to anticipate weaknesses in the budget.

Businesses should also engage in environmental scanning, technology forecasting, and scenario planning (Teo and Ang, 2001) to anticipate the implications of technological developments on the horizon and to be agile in responding effectively to potential threats (or opportunities) to the business. Increasingly, there is a worrying trend among businesses to rely solely on external vendors for advice on emerging technological developments, and it is not uncommon for software houses to hype the capability of IT products (Fearon and Philip, 2005) on the market.

### Principle 7: CIOs Should Think Outside the Technical Box and Be Technology Scouts and Interpreters

Silo mentality is no good for effective planning. CIOs have to take a leading position in the continued development of the IS plan. IT professionals should start thinking "outside the technical box" and be prepared to move from the comfort zone to the awkward zone. They should open themselves up to new ideas and ways of conducting business using technology. Above all, they should have the political and persuasive skills to knock down "walls" in a way that is acceptable to the organization. Nowadays in most large corporations CIOs are invited to take part in the planning process, and, in many cases, they are part of the executive board so that they are fully aware of the corporate aims and business objectives. In all of the above principles, CIOs, quite apart from their normal IT responsibilities (Rockart, Earl, and Ross, 1996), have at least two critical roles to play (Booth and Philip, 2005; Gordon, 2002). First, CIOs need to play the role of technology scout within organizations because of the need to match the company's vision with the incessant technological changes. They also need to ascertain the right time and right opportunity for making the right investments in new technologies. A scout should have foresight and not get bogged down in the immediate problem, and should be able to analyze objectively the implications of new technology for the business in the medium and long term. Sometimes this reconnaissance mission can also identify new business opportunities and discover better ways of serving customers, and the CIO needs to keep an eye out for such opportunities. As the CIO of FedEx (Rob Carter) said recently: "We have a philosophy—it came out of the Marine Corps—from the early days that says, 'Move, communicate and shoot.' . . . We have an innovation team that does nothing but look for new opportunities to come out of the gate with something that'll be a whack on the side of the head to them" (O'Brien and Marakas, 2007/8, p. 443).

The second role of the CIO is that of technology interpreter. This means being fluent in two languages—the business language and the language of technology. The CIO should know how to bridge the gap between IT and business operations and be able to explain the potential applications of technology in nontechnical terms to business managers. It is advisable that exploration of the potential of emerging IT is undertaken by a group of dedicated people (Benamati and Lederer, 2001) rather than by the CIO alone. The importance of scouting (technology forecasting) and interpreting the implications of new technology is also emphasized by other researchers (Teo and Ang, 2001).

### Principle 8: Essential to Have an Implementation Strategy

According to Hartono and colleagues (2003), one of the major causes of SISP failure is the lack of understanding and emphasis on implementation issues. Plans are likely to remain and gather dust on the shelf unless there is an effective implementation strategy (Earl, 1993; Lederer and Sethi, 1992a, 1992b; Teo and Ang, 2001; Teo and King, 1996). In order to address this problem Hartono and his colleagues (2003) have come up with a "comprehensive and parsimonious set of factors or practices that predict implementation" and suggest that they "may help planners and researchers better understand implementation." It is highly desirable for the plan to be read by all key stakeholders. The skill set of employees should also come under scrutiny. Implementation can fail if the organization lacks employees with the appropriate expertise. Plans must proactively be put into practice under the supervision of a project champion and any problems at the implementation stage must be sorted out to derive maximum benefit from the plans. As Hartono and colleagues (2003) point out: "too often organizations fail to implement the recommendations from a SISP study." An implementation strategy should therefore form an integral part of any strategic planning process.

Having described the eight principles, it is pertinent to investigate whether these principles are practiced in real world business organizations.

### DETAILS OF EMPIRICAL WORK

This investigation has taken a case study approach to collect data. More specifically it involved interviewing a number of stakeholders from two different companies in the UK—one an SME and the other a multinational. These case sites were selected because they are very successful companies and have a good track record in exploiting IT to support their business objectives. It was also important to observe whether there was any variation in planning approaches based on size and organizational structure, since collaborative processes (such as those espoused for IS planning) can differ greatly in very large versus small firms. They also represent two different industrial sectors—one where IT is a means to analyze and market data (service organization), and another, where technology itself is the product (manufacturing company). Interviews with senior managers lasted for one to two hours. All interviews were taped and later transcribed. The data from interviews and other sources were analyzed manually to investigate the relevance of each of the main principles of SISP for the companies, and data were cross-referenced from different sources to get multiple perspectives on how the process was carried out in the two companies.

### Company A (SME)

This company is the world's leading provider of marketing intelligence for the automotive industry. In terms of customer base, the company has every major car manufacturer in the world as a customer, whether at a global headquarter level, a pan-European level, or the level of local importers and daughter companies. It has approximately 200 employees spread over 40 countries worldwide gathering local market data and another 120 employees located in the UK. The company has a turnover of £24 million and is wholly owned by its chairman who set the company up nearly twenty-five years ago.

Data are collected for all vehicles in the market in terms of prices and specifications; around 600 features of each vehicle are collected and entered into a database. The data are presented in such a way that they enable customers to do a comparative analysis. The database is very complex because there are lists of standard specifications and additional features of vehicles that can be bought. These features have rules: for example, a customer can purchase air conditioning without a sunroof or if he wants an airbag he must also purchase air conditioning. All of these logics must be built into the system so that the user can get a full picture of the features and specifications of an automobile he or she is interested in.

The primary use of IT is to improve operational efficiency. Investment in IT is written off as an expense and there are no assets shown for technology. IT is used on a large scale to manage internal functions such as accounts, communication—that is, e-mail—tracking of customers, and business processes. It originally made use of Lotus Notes as a means of sharing information with customers as well as staff. The IT organization's activities revolve around developing technology, providing support services, and performing documentation activities. Thus, IT is viewed as necessary to support business processes rather than as a strategic weapon. This approach to IT investments is in line with Bensaou and Earl's (1998) findings on Japanese corporations, where "IT projects are not assessed primarily by financial metrics; audits and formal approval for investment are rare. Instead, because operational performance goals drive most IT investments, the traditional metric is performance improvement, not value for money."

### Company B (multinational)

Company B is a Canadian telecommunications company that was created over a century ago. It delivers networking and communication services and infrastructure to customers worldwide. With revenues of $11 billion in 2003, versus $31 billion in 2000, the company was part of the telecom decline during the early part of this decade. Currently, 35,000 people are employed in 62 countries around the world; one of its UK sites employing approximately 900 employees was chosen for the present study.

Until three years ago the IT function had a decentralized governance structure but it has become more centralized recently for economic and efficiency reasons. The IT budget at present is around 4–5 percent of turnover. According to the IS manager, there are business plans that are primarily financial plans. For example, the head of the company in Europe has a plan that ascertains which opportunities are going to be targeted in the next three to six months. There is also a supply chain plan that covers inventory, lead times, and so on for the next three, six, and nine months. The IS manager makes a distinction between a strategic plan that looks ahead between eighteen months and two years and an operating plan that states what is to be achieved over the next six months. He says that there needs to be a connection between these two documents and the operating plan should "sit on top" of the strategic plan. Around 50 percent of its activities are outsourced; the external vendor performs the operational side of activities and the internal staff is responsible for the engineering and management activities. As in company A, the main thrust of IS use is largely to improve operational efficiencies through the redesign of business processes rather than to adhere to a long-term rigid strategic plan.

*Principle 1. Business and IS Strategies to Be Developed Jointly and Concurrently*

*Company A.* There is no detailed written business or IS strategy document; however, there is an informal strategic plan for IS, and these plans are developed jointly by business managers and IT professionals. As the CEO mentioned, the business strategy and IS strategy have a mutually reinforcing influence on his company. They have an "away day" every year to develop strategic plans for business and the IS strategy is a part of the business plan. Those involved with strategy formulation are: the CEO and director of the e-Services Division, the chief financial officer, the director of the Automotive Division, director of the Data Division, and a director of Field Operations.

The business strategy of the company is described by the CEO as being a collection of the strategic intentions of the company. However, they found that between 1999 and 2001, "There were so many changes going on in the business that we were moving strategically fairly rapidly. Mainly because of the boom that occurred in the early days of the Web, we were trying to move a little bit faster than the more, if you like, steady state that you get from a strategy document," according to the CEO. He feels that the company is now in a more stable environment in terms of its business processes and the marketplace is more stable and established. The IT strategy is part of the business plan, "There are clear strands of business intentions, each of which require technology or are formulated around the capabilities of technology." What comes first, the technology or the business strategy, can vary because, "The capabilities of the technology color the way we think about the business, so it's not black and white. They reinforce each other."

*Company B.* At the time of our study, the company had no formal written business strategy, but it was in the process of formalizing this task. This was something that was to some extent prompted by the employees of the company who stated in employee surveys that they wanted to know more about the strategy of the company. Strategy is formulated at a high level in the company and there are approximately twelve different priorities that follow from this. At the European level, the European head of the company along with the heads of Sales, Enterprise, Supply Chain, R&D, HR, and IS form a cabinet, and these priorities are shared among these people. The main themes therefore are generated globally so this cabinet is involved in implementing and exploiting the global programs. The IS manager states that the company strategy (not in a documentary form) is formulated first, then the IS strategy follows from it—not exactly the way recommended in the literature (the two should be done concurrently). The strategic plan for IS is, however, developed with the joint participation of both business and IT managers. For example, the IT manager is part of the executive board and he is asked regularly to update senior managers about the impact of IT on their business. In fact 30 percent of the CIO's time is spent in sales and the rest in IT.

*Principle 2: Commitment and Visionary Leadership from Top Management Are Crucial*

*Company A.* This company is owned solely by one person and the owner is also the CEO. The company was built up over a period of twenty-five years and has a turnover well in excess of £24 million. Consequently, it is not surprising to find that the CEO and other senior managers are providing visionary leadership in the use of IT. Initially, car specification data were mailed to manufacturers, and later it was made available on disk (CDs). With the emergence of the Internet all the data are now available on a Web site for use by authorized customers. The CEO acknowledges that data are increasingly becoming a commodity on the Internet; others could set up similar car specification databases and consequently the company has to be at the forefront for exploiting the power of IT in analyzing and formatting data and thus providing better value to their customers. The Internet is like a bubbling cauldron, and in the absence of visionary leadership, the company could be swallowed up.

*Company B.* This is a multinational company with headquarters based in Canada, and, given the constant turmoil and competition in the telecom industry sector, it has to keep its eyes on the ball at all times. Considerable emphasis is placed on visionary leadership and the commitment of senior managers in exploiting the full potential of IT. Senior managers from headquarters regularly visit branches around the world to encourage employees and to ensure continued support and leadership to take the company forward. This is also evident from the fact that the CIO is a member of the Executive Board and is asked to make frequent presentations on how IT can support their business objectives.

*Principle 3: 360 Degree Listening and Communication*

*Company A.* Given that this is a small company most of the listening and communication with employees is informal. This is also in line with the devolved governance structure for IT. For instance, the company does not have a CIO as such; instead, since 2000, IT experts have been devolved into business units and there is no formal IT representation at board level. His reasoning for devolution is that managers of business units are the ones who are most seriously motivated to ensure that the systems work well, "Not just technology but including technology." Devolution of IS to business units is in fact a good practice advocated by Earl (1996) in his "organizational approach" to IS planning. As far as its external stakeholders (e.g., customers) are concerned, the company is very proactive in listening and communication. Thus, the CEO relies more on listening to the requirements of his customers and being made aware of changes in the way people make decisions to guide the direction of the company and is less reliant on, "Being an ingenious businessman." The company has a solid customer base and it is in a "virtual circle" situation where the industry understands what it does and there is a free flow of feedback on the requirements of the automotive industry. This allows it to learn more about the marketplace and, in turn, the ability to develop additional products and services.

*Company B.* Listening and communication is very systematic in this multinational company. This takes the form of a forum for IS managers to meet with employees in all units of the company (Europe) on a three- to six-month basis to explain to them what is being planned and also to solicit their views and suggestions through informal and formal (employee satisfaction survey) means. To ensure alignment between the business and IS strategies, the IS manager believes that the most important criterion is "Being close to the key people in the business." As detailed above, the IS manager is part of a cabinet in Europe. There is a cabinet meeting once a month and the IS manager attends about once every two months. During the latest cabinet meeting, the IS manager was allotted thirty minutes to talk about, "Running the company on its own products." He holds the opinion that the IS organization knows the themes that are important at a business level, and he is aware of the areas that are being invested in and areas of the market that the company is targeting.

With regard to testing whether employees are following the IS strategy, the CIO meets with all the local IS employees every three months and the IS manager also meets face to face with all the IS employees in Europe every six months. The IS organization carries out employee satisfaction surveys from the IS perspective, and recently recorded an 84 percent satisfaction rate in Europe. Open-ended questions are used to find out what is being done well and where improvements could be made. The company is currently introducing a CIO award (a small financial reward) for a number of teams that have performed well in the past quarter.

Strong links are also built up with external stakeholders (customers and suppliers) through listening and communication. There are people who work with the channel partners from an e-business perspective and account teams who focus on each customer. The IS manager explains that there are around 130 different channel partners in Europe, and there are channel forums that act as user groups. These meet twice a year and people who work for the IS manager on the e-business side attend these meetings. One person is responsible for coordinating all the rollouts in Europe and the IS manager considers him as much a businessperson as an IT person. All the key stakeholders are present for conference calls and this is managed very tightly because if a certain tool is not working for a week, for example, then revenue targets are missed. The company benchmarks itself against competitors in terms of e-business activities and also gathers feedback from its channel partners.

### Principle 4: Develop a High-Level Plan with Broad Principles, Not Specific Actions

*Company A.* Given that there is no detailed written strategy document, this is not a serious problem. During the annual "away day" managers agree on broad principles rather than becoming bogged down in too many details. As the CEO says, sometimes "there are the usual guesses, you have to toss a coin up in the air and make a decision." He gives the example that some business processes are based around desktop technology and others around Web technology, and says they are currently trying to decide how much of the desktop technology might be supplied by Web technology in future. This exemplifies the type of question the company is trying to address, which drives the strategic intentions of the business.

*Company B.* The plans are deliberately designed to be general in scope. Plans are reviewed regularly to respond to the changing business requirements. For example, according to the IS manager, the IS plan is currently driven more by six-month priorities than by a grand plan for the next five years. He explains that, "We're continually churning, every month your results will change, your results will move, to some extent your strategy, not at a high level, at a detailed level, moves and changes, and you need to be flexible." Other things that influence the IS plan are technology evolution, how much there is to invest, and the operation of the internal function of IS.

### Principle 5: Identification and Exploitation of Opportunities

*Company A.* A company such as this one cannot survive in the Internet age without the use of technology. As data have become a commodity on the Internet, the only way to survive is to improve the quality and presentation of data and thereby differentiate your product from competitors. A manager said: "Technology plays a very large part in our business because most of the services that we provide are based around technology." The bulk of the company's activity is based around data collection, processing, and detecting changes in the market and responding to them quickly. What the company delivers to its customers is in the form of databases and systems so, "An enormous amount of value is added to the basic data by technology." The technology that the company uses is highly targeted to the type of activities and the processes that the car manufacturers are involved in and the data provided allow customers to chart their competitive position. However the CEO states, "I'm not very interested in making a company driven by technology, technology really has to be the servant to the business processes that we want." In other words, "investment in IT follows a logic of strategic instinct rather than strategic alignment" (Bensaou and Earl, 1998). He has found it to be the other way around in the past and it has not been very successful. As one of the managers points out, "I am more concerned about what the marketplace is demanding in terms of services and seeing how technology can support that . . . I'm just cautious about being led by technology."

Technology allows the company to increase its business substantially because its customers are looking for answers to their questions in the fastest time possible and in the most accessible format possible. The CEO comments, "If (customers) can get the report they need to produce once a month and they can do it by pressing one button and behind that button there's a whole range of technological capabilities, that's exactly what I want." Indeed the devolved IT facilities of the company encourage the emergence of opportunistic ideas for exploitation using technology.

*Company B.* While a methodical approach to system development is used to improve operational efficiency, this company does not blindly follow the "design school" approach to planning. For instance, it has a very strong R&D department that constantly experiments with ideas for more effective use of IT systems. In fact, it runs most of its telecommunication infrastructure and IT systems using its own products. The CIO is often asked to make presentations at cabinet meetings concerning better use of IT systems. As indicated earlier, the company carries out employee satisfaction surveys regularly from the IS perspective. They are also encouraged to make suggestions and offer ideas for more innovative and creative use of IT systems.

## *Principle 6: Plans Should Not Be Cast in Stone*

*Company A.* The relatively small size of the company means that it is not hard to make changes to any plan as the situation demands. However, in the absence of written strategies, it is difficult to find formal evidence of frequent review processes or contingency planning in the company. As mentioned elsewhere, senior managers have an annual off-site meeting to consider the possible consequences of changes in the business environment and how to respond to those changes using IT.

*Company B.* Although the company has no scenario planning, it has a policy of frequent review of projects and contingency planning. With respect to planning for e-business projects, the IS manager feels that the company has the foundation in place and there is a clear view of what needs to be achieved in the next twelve to eighteen months in terms of e-business. A business case is prepared for each project and reviewed internally from an architectural, technical, and cost-resourcing perspective within the IS organization. From an architectural perspective, it must be ascertained that it fits into the overall systems architecture. From a technology perspective, constraints must be taken into account as to the middleware being used, the portal technologies being employed, and so on. From a resourcing perspective, it must be ascertained that the funds are available to complete the project within the company, by the IS partner company, or by a third party.

*Principle 7: CIOs Should Think Outside the Technical Box and Be Technology Scouts and Interpreters*

*Company A.* This company has no formal CIO; it has a devolved governance structure for IT. Thus, information professionals/business managers of the various divisions (e.g., Data Division, Automotive Division, Marketing, etc.) are responsible for proactively identifying and exploiting the potential of emerging technologies and have more recently developed a Web-based service to market data on car specifications on a global basis. With regard to the role of technology interpreter, the CEO relies on one or two, "technology people who have a reasonable business sense as well," so he can talk to them in terms of technology and what needs to be done, and they give an answer that is, "a very practical business answer not just a technology answer." The CEO appreciates this because he believes that, in the past, he has fallen into the trap of services or products that were developed because it was technically possible and not because they were driven by business needs or market pull.

*Company B.* This company has a well-resourced IT department headed by a CIO. It has IS managers who are business savvy and experts in technical matters and as a result are able to make the best use of current technology. These managers also act as technology scouts and interpreters to benefit from emerging technologies as well. For example, the CIO pointed out that he acts as a technology interpreter for the company in that he supports both the sales and the R&D functions. He gives the example that the company has moved in the past three years toward running on its own products; the IS organization takes the lead product, puts it into the networks to test it, and then gives feedback to the R&D organization.

*Principle 8: Essential to Have an Implementation Strategy*

*Company A.* The hands-on approach to everything decided by the CEO ensures the effective and rapid implementation of the agreed-upon plans. The company is in the business of collecting, analyzing, and marketing data/information about automobile specifications on a global basis. This has to be done at great speed for the benefit of customers, namely, car manufacturers around the world. Consequently, the company is always anxious to implement the most appropriate technology for data analysis, database creation, and marketing of the data on a global basis using both conventional and Internet technology.

*Company B.* There is strong evidence in this company that the IS plan is *proactively* put into practice. For example, all IS plans are prioritized and reviewed on a regular basis and the CIO also proactively promotes the strategy by having regular meetings with employees at local and European levels.

**Cross Comparison of the Two Case Study Companies**

A comparison of the strategic-planning approaches of the two companies is shown in Table 10.1. Neither company had a *detailed written* business strategy at the time of this study. However, both companies hold annual off-site meetings of managers to discuss and agree on strategic plans for the businesses. Another similarity is that both of them follow largely an *exploitation* rather than an exploration strategy with a view to enhancing operational efficiency (as opposed to competitive advantage). While the emphasis is on operational efficiencies, given the emergence of the Internet, increasingly more effort is directed toward the competitive use of technology.

Table 10.1

## Comparison of the Two Companies Vis-à-Vis the Eight Principles

| Eight principles | Company A | Company B |
|---|---|---|
| 1 Business and IS strategies to be developed jointly and concurrently | Informal approach to strategy development. No *written* business or IS strategy; but annual "away day" to discuss and develop both. This has a mutually reinforcing influence on the company | No detailed written strategies. CIO is member of the executive board and asked to update business managers regularly on IT matters. Joint meeting between business and IS managers. Thirty percent of CIO's time spent in sales and the rest in IT |
| 2 Commitment and visionary leadership from top management are crucial | CEO is also the owner and is very proactive and supportive of the use of technology | Strong support from headquarters in Canada and local leadership, including use of its own IT products in running the company |
| 3 360 degree listening and communication | Small size means listening and communication are informal. Evidence of significant consultation with customers (car manufacturers) | Formal and informal. Done extensively. CIO meets with employees in every unit on a three- to six-month interval to explain plans and get their views and suggestions |
| 4 Develop a high-level plan with broad principles, not specific actions | Given that there are no detailed written plans, this is not a serious issue | Given that there are no detailed written plans, this is not a serious issue; but moving toward more formal written strategy |
| 5 Identification and exploitation of opportunities | Adaptive and opportunistic approach to strategy. IT functions decentralized with each unit having the freedom to take an opportunistic approach | Adaptive and opportunistic approach to strategy. Both formal and informal planning methods used—such as running the company using its own IT products |
| 6 Plans should not be cast in stone | Flexible; but no explicit evidence of reviewing plans | IS plans are prioritized and reviewed on a regular basis |
| 7 CIOs should think outside the technical box and be technology scouts and interpreters | No CIO. IT devolved. Each unit to act as scouts and interpreters | CIO's main role is to act as a scout and technology interpreter. He supports both sales and R&D functions. Company's whole telecom infrastructure built using its own products, thanks to the efforts of the IT department and R&D |
| 8 Essential to have an implementation strategy | CEO takes a hands-on approach to implementing plans. Strong evidence that the "informal plans" are proactively implemented | CIO and other managers are very proactive in implementing plans |

The IT governance structures for the two companies are entirely different: company A has a devolved infrastructure while company B has opted for a centralized infrastructure. Company B, given its large size, seems to have a better-resourced IT organization compared with company A. Both companies have IS professionals who are well informed about business objectives and about how to make the best use of current technology to support business processes. These managers also act as technology scouts and interpreters to benefit from emerging technologies.

Given the small size of company A, no *formal* top-down and bottom-up listening and communication take place internally, but there is extensive consultation/engagement with their external stakeholders (e.g., car manufacturers). Similarly, no formal procedure for frequent review of IT plans or contingency plans exists in Company A, but in Company B this is done very systematically. Company B appears to follow almost all eight principles with slight variations. For example, business strategy is developed first, followed by IS strategy, rather than developing them concurrently (Principle 1).

## CONCLUSIONS

This chapter began by identifying the two main planning approaches to IS: impact and align methodologies. The former is needed if the purpose is to achieve strategic advantage and the latter is used to ensure that information systems are there to support business needs. These two approaches are complementary. A matrix (see Figure 10.1) was used to illustrate how these two methodologies evolve through the four stages from operational efficiency to unsustainable competitive advantage. It was shown that, in the absence of continued repositioning and enhancement of IT systems, any advantage gained will be unsustainable.

This chapter also examined the current debate about whether or not strategic planning is useful. Despite the highly volatile and dynamic business environment, it is argued that the need to conduct SISP is stronger than ever. Indeed, eight principles for successful IS strategic planning have been identified from the published literature to determine whether there is a match between academic theories (principles) and corporate practice. To do this, two successful companies, very different in size, were chosen to examine whether these principles are followed in practice. Both companies lacked a *detailed written* business or IS strategy document, suggesting that successful IS planning for operational efficiency does not depend on a written document if the business objectives are clear. With regard to the eight individual principles, six are followed by Company A and all eight are practiced by Company B (see Table 10.1).

We also established the need for both exploitation strategies and exploration strategies (see, e.g., Galliers, 2001). While exploitation strategies are best when operational efficiencies are sought, exploration strategies are important for promoting innovation and creativity to generate and sustain significant competitive advantage. It is proposed that Principles 1–4, 6, and 8 are important for effective exploitation strategies, while Principles 5 and 7 are central for exploration strategies. While improving operational efficiency is the main concern in both case study companies, increasingly attention is turning toward the use of IT for strategic advantage. Consequently, both companies fall into the two left-hand quadrants (bottom and top) of the matrix in Figure 10.1.

This study is based on the experience of just two companies. Further research should examine a larger sample of companies to establish whether these eight principles are indeed critical for successful strategic planning for IS, and should possibly include the identification of other best practices. Our research and other recent surveys (Slater, 2002) suggest that current research emphasizing the need for formally written business and IS strategies may require reassessment.

# REFERENCES

Basu, V.; Hartono, E.; Lederer, A.L.; Sethi, V. 2002. The impact of organizational commitment, senior management involvement, and team involvement on strategic information systems planning. *Information and Management,* 39, 6, 513–524.

Benamati, J., and Lederer, A.L. 2001. Rapid information technology change, coping mechanisms and emerging technologies group. *Journal of Management Information Systems,* 17, 4, 183–202.

Bensaou, M., and Earl, M. 1998. The right mindset for managing information technology. *Harvard Business Review* (September–October), 119–128.

Booth, M.E., and Philip, G. 2005. Information Systems Management: role of planning, alignment and leadership. *Behaviour and Information Technology,* 24, 5, 391–404.

Brancheau, J.C; Janz, B.D; and Wetherbe, J.C. 1996. Key issues in information systems management: 1994–95 SIM Delphi Results. *MIS Quarterly,* 20, 2, 225–242.

Brown, I.T.J. 2004. Testing and extending theory in strategic information systems planning through literature analysis. *Information Resources Management Journal,* 17, 4, 20–48.

Carr, N.G. 2004a. The corrosion of IT advantage: strategy makes a comeback. *Journal of Business Strategy,* 25, 5, 10–15.

———. 2004b. *Does IT Matter? Information Technology and the Corrosion of Competitive Advantage.* Boston: Harvard Business School Press.

Davenport, T. 1994. Saving IT's soul: human-centered information management. *Harvard Business Review,* 72, 2, 119–131.

Downes, L., and Mui, C 1998. The end of strategy. *Strategy and Leadership,* 26, 5, 4–9.

Earl, M.J. 1993. Experiences in strategic information systems planning. *MIS Quarterly,* 17, 1–24.

———. 1996. Information systems strategy. . . . why planning techniques are not the answer. *Business Strategy Review,* 7, 1, 54–67.

Fearon, C., and Philip, G. 2005. Managing expectations and benefits: a model for electronic trading and EDI in the insurance industry. *Journal of Information Technology,* 20, 3, 177–186.

Ferranti, M. 2001. Gartner align thyself. *CIO Magazine,* November 15. Available at www.cio.com/article/30687/Gartner_Found_to_Be_Lacking_in_IT_Business_Alignment (accessed on August 16, 2006).

Feurer, R.; Chaharbaghi K.; Weber M. and Wargin J. 2000. Aligning strategies, processes, and IT: a case study. *Information Systems Management,* 17, 1, 23–34.

Galliers, R.D. 2001. Rethinking information systems strategy: towards an inclusive strategic framework for business information systems management? Paper presented at the EGOS Colloquium, Lyon, France.

Gordon, M. 2002. How to succeed in strategic planning. *CIO Magazine,* March 15. Available at www.cio.com/article/30948/How_to_Succeed_in_Strategic_Planning (accessed on August 16, 2006).

Goldsmith, N. 1991. Linking IT planning to business strategy. *Long Range Planning,* 24, 6, 67–77.

Hackney, R., and Little, S. 1999. Opportunistic strategy formulation for IS/IT planning. *European Journal of Information Systems,* 8, 2, 119–125.

Hartono, E; Lederer, A.L; Sethi, V.; and Zhuang, Y. 2003. Key predictors of the implementation of strategic information systems. *DATA BASE for Advances in Information Systems,* 34, 3, 41–53.

Higgins, Ria. 2007. A life in the day of Simon Nixon, Internet entrepreneur. *Sunday Times Magazine* (UK) (October), 86.

Ives, B., and Learmonth, G.P. 1984. The information system as a competitive weapon. *Communications of the ACM,* 27, 12, 1192–1201.

Kay, J. 1993. *Foundations of Corporate Success.* Oxford: Oxford University Press.

King, W.R., and Teo, T.S.H. 2000. Assessing the impact of proactive versus reactive modes of strategic information systems planning. *Omega,* 28, 6, 667.

Lederer, A.L., and Gardiner, V. 1992. Strategic information systems planning. The method/1 approach. *Information Systems Management,* 9, 3, 13–20.

Lederer, A.L. and Sethi, V. 1991. Critical dimensions of strategic information systems planning. *Decision Sciences,* 22, 1, 104–119.

———. 1992a. Meeting the challenges of IS planning. *Long Range Planning,* 25, 2, 69–80.

———. 1992b. Root causes of strategic IS planning implementation problems. *Journal of Management Information Systems,* 9, 1, 25–45.

———. 1998. Seven guidelines for strategic information systems planning. *Information Strategy,* 15, 1, 23–29.

Lee, G.G., and Gough, T. 1993. An integrated framework for information systems planning and its initial applications. *Journal of Information Technology,* 8, 4, 227–240.

Lehmann, H. 1993. Core competence and learning alliances: the new face of information management? *Journal of Information Tech*nology, 8, 4, 149–174.

Maltz, L., and DeBlois, P.B. 2005. Top ten IT issues 2005. *Educause Review,* 40, 3, 14.

Martin, J. 1989. *Information Engineering. Book 1, Introduction.* Englewood Cliffs, NJ: Prentice Hall.

Martin, E.W.; Brown, C.V.; DeHayes, D.W.; Hoffer, J.A.; Perkins, W.C. 2005. *Managing Information Technology,* 5th ed. Englewood Cliffs, NJ: Prentice Hall.

Mintzberg, H. 1990. The Design School: Reconsidering the basic premises of strategic management. *Strategic Management Journal,* 11, 3, 171–195.

———. 1994a. Rethinking strategic planning part II: new roles for planners. *Long Range Planning,* 27, 3, 22–30.

———. 1994b. Rethinking strategic planning part I: pitfalls and fallacies. *Long Range Planning,* 27, 3, 12–21.

———. 1994c. The fall and rise of strategic planning. *Harvard Business Review,* 72, 1, 107–114.

O'Brien, J.A., and Marakas, G.M. 2008. *Management Information Systems,* 8th ed. Boston: McGraw-Hill/ Irwin.

Österle, H.; Brenner, W.; and Hilbers, K. 1993. *Total Information Systems Management: A European Approach.* Chichester, UK: Wiley.

Philip, G. 2007. IS planning for operational efficiency. *Information Systems Management,* 24, 3, 247–264.

Philip, G., and Booth, M.E. 2001. A new six "S" framework on the relationship between the role of information systems (IS) and competencies in "IS" management. *Journal of Business Research,* 51, 3, 233–247.

Porter, M.E. 1985. *Competitive Advantage: Creating and Sustaining Superior Performance.* New York: Free Press.

———. 2001. Strategy and the Internet. *Harvard Business Review,* 79, 3, 63–78.

Premkumar, G., and King, W.R. 1994. Organizational characteristics and information systems planning: an empirical study. *Information Systems Research,* 5, 2, 75–109.

Reich, B.H., and Benbasat, I. 2000. Factors that influence the social dimension of alignment between business and IT objectives. *MIS Quarterly,* 24, 1, 81–113.

Rockart, J.F.; Earl, M.J.; and Ross, J.W. 1996. Eight imperatives for the new IT organization. *Sloan Management Review,* 38, 43–55.

Salmela, H., and Spil, T.A.M. 2002. Dynamic and emergent information systems strategy formulation and implementation. *International Journal of Information Management,* 22, 6, 441–460.

Segars A.H., and Grover, V. 1999. Profiles of strategic information systems planning. *Information Systems Research,* 10, 3, 199–232.

Slater, D. 2002. Mistakes: strategic planning Don'ts (and Do's). *CIO Magazine,* June 1. Available at www.cio.com/article/31106/Mistakes_Strategic_Planning_Don_ts_and_Dos_ (accessed on August 16, 2006).

Teo, T.S.H., and Ang, J.S.K. 2001. An examination of major IS problems. *International Journal of Information Management,* 21, 6, 457–470.

Teo T.S.H., and King, W. 1996. Assessing the impact of integrating business planning and IS planning. *Information and Management,* 30, 309–321.

Tukana, S., and Weber, R. 1996. An empirical test of the strategic grid model of information systems planning. *Decision Sciences,* 27, 4, 735–765.

Varon, E. 2000. Be nimble, be quick. *CIO Magazine,* June 15. Available at www.cio.com/archive/061500/nimble_sidebar1.html (accessed on August 16, 2006).

Wiseman, C. 1985. *Strategy and Computers: Information Systems as Competitive Weapons.* Homewood, IL: Dow Jones-Irwin.

# CHAPTER 11

# STRATEGIC INFORMATION SYSTEMS PLANNING

## The Search for an Optimal Level

### HENRY E. NEWKIRK, ALBERT L. LEDERER, AND CIDAMBI SRINIVASAN

*Abstract: Strategic information systems planning (SISP) remains a critical issue for senior business and information systems executives, but both too little and too much SISP might prove ineffective. Hypotheses test the proposed relationship between SISP comprehensiveness and SISP effectiveness in five planning phases. They predict a nonlinear, inverted-U relationship, thus suggesting the presence of an optimal comprehensiveness level. A postal survey of 1,200 U.S. information systems executives produced 161 usable responses. An extensive validation of constructs followed. The statistical analysis supported the hypothesis in a strategy implementation planning phase, but not in four other SISP phases. Managers may benefit from the formal finding that both too much and too little implementation planning may impede SISP success. Future investigators should research reasons that the hypothesis was supported for that phase, but not the others.*

*Keywords: Strategic Information Systems Planning, Strategic Information Systems Planning Success, Nonlinear Relationship*

Due to today's highly competitive global marketplace, planning for information systems (IS) has become essential to the realization of business performance from investment in information technology (Byrd, Lewis, and Bryan, 2006). Such information systems do not happen by chance, and planning gives organizations the opportunity to align their new systems with their business strategies in anticipation of predicted competitive, technological, and other environmental changes. Researchers have, however, asserted that both too little and too much strategic information systems planning (SISP) can be disadvantageous to such organizations (Earl, 1993; Newkirk, Lederer, and Srinivasan, 2003; Premkumar and King, 1991; Raghunathan and Raghunathan, 1991; Sambamurthy, Zmud, and Byrd, 1994).

Too little SISP could fail to produce sufficient understanding of the external competitive environment, the internal organizational environment, and emerging information technologies (Premkumar and King, 1991; Raghunathan and Raghunathan, 1991). This could produce poorly conceived strategic alternatives and inappropriate choices of them. The new investments proposed in the SISP effort plan could thus fail to enable the organization to respond to its challenges. Implemented investments would more likely fail to serve the organization as well as they should.

Too much SISP would demand too much time. The competitive environment, the internal organizational environment, and emerging information technology would change and make the plan obsolete before it could even be implemented (Min, Suh, and Kim, 1999; Sambamurthy,

Figure 11.1   **Strategic Information Systems Planning (SISP) Success and Comprehensiveness**

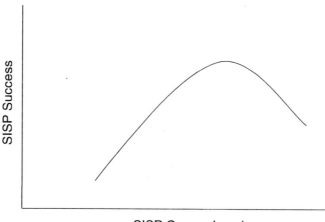

Zmud, and Byrd, 1994). Too much planning would slow the organization down in reacting to those changes, and once again, the plan would fail to enable the organization to address its challenges. Instead, according to contemporary observers, planning must be "agile," meaning able to react with speed and surprise (Sambamurthy, Bharadwaj, and Grover, 2003) and "artful," meaning agile to the point of "planning for creativity and innovation, planning for serendipity, and [even] planning not-to-plan" (Baskerville, 2006, p. 114).

This research investigates the relationship between comprehensiveness and effectiveness in five SISP planning phases. SISP research typically investigates linear relationships, but this research tests a nonlinear, inverted-U relationship between the constructs that suggests an optimal level of SISP practice. Figure 11.1 shows this relationship. The objective of the study was thus to test whether such a level exists. Subsequent sections explain the comprehensiveness and effectiveness constructs, and the rationale for the basis of their measurement in the study.

## THE COMPREHENSIVENESS OF THE SISP PROCESS

SISP is the process of determining a portfolio of computer-based applications to help an organization achieve its business objectives (Lederer and Sethi, 1988). It is a complex set of specific, interrelated activities. It can be viewed as a set of defined activities, and hence the current research examines the extent to which it is practiced—that is, its comprehensiveness—in terms of those activities. Prior research has often considered its comprehensiveness, but has rarely decomposed it into its specific activities (McFarlan, 1971; McLean and Soden, 1977; Premkumar and King, 1991; Raghunathan and Raghunathan, 1991; Segars and Grover, 1999). It has, instead, usually examined SISP in terms of broad characteristics or general behaviors.

According to Fredrickson and Mitchell (1984), comprehensiveness in planning such as SISP has been formally defined as "the extent to which an organization attempts to be exhaustive or inclusive in making and integrating strategic decisions" (p. 402). Seven broad behaviors illustrate comprehensiveness in strategic planning: (1) the thorough canvassing of a large number of alternatives; (2) the surveying of a full set of objectives; (3) the careful weighing of what management already knows about the costs and risks of each possible outcome; (4) the intensive searching for new information relevant for each alternative; (5) the considering of any new information or expert judgment; (6) the reconsidering of the consequences of all alternatives before choosing one; and (7) the making of detailed provisions for implementing the selected course of action (Janis and Mann, 1977). These behaviors represent strategic business planning well, and are thus relevant to planning in general and to strategic information systems planning as an example of planning, but they are not specific to the heavily IS-oriented SISP.

SISP, nevertheless, like other similar forms of planning, can also be performed more or less comprehensively (Baker, 1995; Sambamurthy, Venkatraman, and Desanctis, 1993). SISP comprehensiveness has been illustrated in assessments of critical characteristics of SISP. Examples of such characteristics include top management involvement, user involvement, and the employment of IS planning and IS resources (Premkumar and King, 1992). (Presumably, the more prevalent such characteristics are the greater comprehensiveness is.) Other examples of SISP characteristics include the analysis of the organization, anticipated changes in the external environment, solutions to potential resistance during the implementation, project relevance to the business plan, responsibility for implementation, and the clear presentation of the issues of implementation (Gottschalk, 1999a).

SISP comprehensiveness is often contrasted to SISP incrementalism, and elucidation of incremental planning can help explain comprehensive planning (Newkirk and Lederer, 2006a; Salmela and Spil, 2002). SISP incrementalism is based on the organizational learning theory of Argyris and Schoen (1978), which asserts that organizations learn and adapt as a result of their learning. Incremental planning takes a more gradual approach with emphasis on informal contacts, face-to-face communications, personal experiences and judgments, and experimentation (Ciborra, 1994; Pyburn, 1983; Sambamurthy, Zmud, and Byrd, 1994).

Comprehensiveness has also been viewed as one of six broad SISP dimensions (with formalization, focus, flow, participation, and consistency as the other five) (Segars, Grover, and Teng, 1998). Segars, Grover, and Teng (1998) represented comprehensiveness with items focused on the concepts of exhaustiveness, decision making, and integration from Fredrickson and Mitchell's (1984) definition. The comprehensiveness dimension as well as the other five dimensions show how SISP can be practiced more or less extensively although they fail to tap the specific activities comprising SISP.

SISP has been described in terms of three IS resources planning activities associated with the assets that serve as the major targets of the planning (Newkirk and Lederer, 2007): technical resources planning activities (i.e., planning activities associated with application software, systems software, hardware, and network communications), personnel resources planning activities (i.e., planning activities related to more people-oriented concerns such as technical training, end-user computing, facilities, and the personnel themselves), and data security planning activities (i.e., planning activities associated with protecting the organization from unwanted intrusion and recovering from such intrusion if and when it occurs) (Doherty and Fulford, 2006; Harris, 1995). However, they were also very general activities, not tied to the tasks in the SISP process.

SISP has also been viewed in terms of five different general approaches (Earl, 1993). The approaches have been referred to as business-led (i.e., planning focused on the enterprise), method-driven (i.e., focused on the planning technique), administrative (i.e., focused on the available resources), technology (i.e., focused on the information systems model), and organizational (i.e., focused on learning), and have gained credence from an assessment of the extent of the rationality and adaptability of the planning process (Doherty, Marples, and Suhaimi, 1999; Earl, 1993; Grover and Segars 2005; Segars and Grover, 1999). Such assessment has demonstrated that SISP comprehensiveness can be viewed in terms of rationality and adaptability, although those two constructs, again, do not tap the specific activities of SISP.

SISP comprehensiveness has also been described in terms of the extent to which SISP identifies the cause of major planning problems, generates alternatives, and evaluates particular actions. Although it has been shown to predict effective planning in that context (Sambamurthy, Zmud, and Byrd, 1994), such a depiction of SISP considers only a small number of its activities.

An examination of seventy-one prescriptions, deemed potential predictors of successful SISP, further demonstrated that it could be carried out more or less comprehensively (Lederer and Sethi, 1996). However, the characterization of SISP as a set of suggestions for performing it well, rather than as a set of actual tasks, provides a skewed view of it.

Finally, SISP has been described in terms of phases and the specific activities within them (Mentzas, 1997; Newkirk and Lederer, 2006b). The phases and activities represent the components of the planning process, each having its own objectives, participants, preconditions, products, and techniques. The phases and activities can be applied to describe an organization's efforts to be comprehensive in its SISP process. For example, the strategy formulation phase includes identifying new business processes, new information technology (IT) architectures, specific new projects, and the priorities for the new projects. The extent to which an organization can carry out each phase and activity permits the assessment of SISP comprehensiveness.

Table 11.1 shows the phases and activities. Strategic awareness entails the organizing and initiating of the planning process in an organized manner with sufficient top management support. Situation analysis is the analyzing of the internal and external environments in which the planned information systems will be expected to contribute. Strategy conception is the imagining of various possible information systems that might be implemented. Strategy formulation is the choosing and prioritizing of the specific information systems that will be implemented. Strategy implementation planning is the planning of the activities necessary to ensure that the new information systems are actually placed into production and used. These phases form the basis for the assessment of SISP comprehensiveness in the current research because they reflect specific actions and they tap the full range of the SISP effort.

## SISP SUCCESS

Researchers developed an early theoretical construct of planning system success in the area of strategic business planning (Venkatraman and Ramanujam, 1987). Its two dimensions of multiple, scaled items were distinct, but interrelated: the extent of fulfillment of key objectives and the improvement in the capability of the planning system. The source of the dimensions was Cameron and Whetten's (1983) strategic management study identifying goal-centered, comparative, normative, and improvement-in-judgment perspectives. Venkatraman and Ramanujam based their extent of fulfillment of key objectives on the goal-centered perspective and their improvement in the capability of the planning system on the improvement-in-judgment perspective. Venkatraman and Ramanujam validated the measurement properties of the model using an empirical test. However, because the dimensions described strategic business planning rather than strategic information systems planning, they were inappropriate for the current research.

Raghunathan and Raghunathan (1994) later adapted the Venkatraman and Ramanujam model of fulfillment of key objectives and goal-centered dimensions to SISP by employing items specific to information systems planning. They did so in response to the recent importance given to IS planning, the lack of an empirical model in the IS literature to measure SISP success, and the usefulness of developing such a model to guide future research related to SISP. The new SISP

Table 11.1

## Information Systems (IS) Planning Phases and Activities

| | |
|---|---|
| Planning the IS planning process (i.e., strategic awareness) | Determining key planning issues |
| | Defining planning objectives |
| | Organizing the planning team(s) |
| | Obtaining top management commitment |
| Analyzing the current environment (i.e., situation analysis) | Analyzing current business systems |
| | Analyzing current organizational systems |
| | Analyzing current information systems |
| | Analyzing the current external business environment |
| | Analyzing the current external information technology (IT) environment |
| Conceiving strategy alternatives (i.e., strategy conception) | Identifying major IT objectives |
| | Identifying opportunities for improvement |
| | Evaluating opportunities for improvement |
| | Identifying high-level IT strategies |
| Selecting strategy (i.e., strategy formulation) | Identifying new business processes |
| | Identifying new IT architectures |
| | Identifying specific new projects |
| | Identifying priorities for new projects |
| Planning strategy implementation (i.e., strategy implementation planning) | Defining change management approach |
| | Defining action plan |
| | Evaluating action plan |
| | Defining follow-up and control procedure |

*Source:* Mentzas (1997).

success model demonstrated strong support through statistical tests and other key measurement criteria. The adaptation of a theoretically supportable model made a significant contribution to IS research by identifying construct measurement issues.

A more recent instrument developed for measuring SISP success used the same two constructs, but decomposed them into four dimensions (Segars and Grover, 1998). Three of these were alignment, analysis, and cooperation. They represented the extent of fulfillment of key objectives (and thus Cameron and Whetten's [1983] goal-centered approach) (Venkatraman and Ramanujam, 1987).

Alignment refers to the results of the linkage of IS and business strategy (Baets, 1992; King, 1978; Henderson, Rockart, and Sifonis, 1987; Henderson and Venkatraman, 1993). It improves top management's understanding of the importance of information systems as well as IS management's understanding of business objectives. It thus encourages senior business executives to furnish managerial leadership and financial resources for the development of new information systems to support the firm's objectives rather than for the development of those that merely continue current patterns of organizational usage.

Analysis concerns the results of the examination of the internal operations of the organization (Boynton and Zmud, 1987; Brancheau, Schuster, and March, 1989; Hackathorn and Karimi, 1998). It helps planners to better understand the firm's existing business processes and procedures, IT, and power structure for the purpose of learning how the firm can use IT to compete via an integrated architecture of databases and applications.

Cooperation refers to the outcomes of the agreement about development priorities, implementation schedules, and management responsibilities (Henderson, 1990). Planners use it to ensure that key managers and users support the SISP process and content. Cooperation can establish a partnership between managers, users, and information systems developers, and thereby avoid conflicts that might put SISP implementation at risk.

The fourth dimension, capabilities, represented the improvement in the potential of the planning system (and thus the improvement-in-judgment approach) (Cameron and Whetten, 1983; Venkatraman and Ramanujam, 1987). The adapting of the planning process over time represents a key element of planning effectiveness. Thus, the organizational learning experienced through SISP would result in greater ability to align IS with business strategies, to analyze internal operations, to promote cooperation within the organization, to anticipate internal and external changes, and to adapt to unexpected changes.

The constructs were chosen to form the basis for the assessment of SISP success in the current research because they provided a more detailed and broader assessment of the fulfillment of key objectives. Each construct was thus represented by a set of scaled items, and the four sets of items form the basis for the assessment of SISP success in the current research. The constructs and items appear in Table 11.2.

## THEORY DEVELOPMENT

SISP research typically investigates linear relationships between SISP characteristics and outcomes. It assumes and often confirms the simple hypothesis that more planning leads to more success. For example, greater IS planning sophistication predicted greater IS success in colleges and universities (Sabherwal, 1999). IS planning dimensions predicted IS planning effectiveness as assessed by IS executives (Raghunathan and Raghunathan, 1991). Characteristics of strategic IS plans predicted the extent of plan implementation (Gottschalk, 1999a). Finally, alignment between business strategy and IS strategy was significantly associated with the outcome of perceived business performance in a study of pairs of chief executive officers (CEOs) and IS executives (Sabherwal and Chan, 2001).

At the same time, more SISP might not always be more successful. The purpose of this research was to test whether a nonlinear, inverted-U relationship describes the effect of SISP comprehensiveness on SISP success.

In organizations practicing greater comprehensiveness (i.e., those with more planners spending more time and effort on the planning process), planners could spend more time and effort better identifying issues and objectives, assembling a more capable planning team, and convincing top management to be committed to the planning process (i.e., strategic awareness). Planners could spend more time and effort listening to management, users, and others while developing a better understanding of the internal and external environments (situation analysis). Planners could take more time and feel less pressure as they imagine more, new information systems (strategy conception). Planners could spend more time and effort assessing the various results of the new information systems and make more careful choices of new information systems (strategy formulation). Planners could more carefully develop implementation plans with greater attention to key issues (strategy implementation planning).

Thus, increased comprehensiveness of more planners with more resources would thus lead to better planning teams, better analysis of the environments, better options for new systems, better choices of such systems, and better implementation plans, all of which would lead eventually to improved performance. However, at some point in increased comprehensiveness (i.e., with too many planners

Table 11.2

## Success Measures

| | |
|---|---|
| **Alignment** | Understanding the strategic priorities of top management |
| | Aligning information systems (IS) strategies with the strategic plan of the organization |
| | Adapting the goals/objectives of IS to changing goals/objectives of the organization |
| | Maintaining a mutual understanding with top management on the role of IS in supporting strategy |
| | Identifying information technology (IT)-related opportunities to support the strategic direction of the firm |
| | Educating top management on the importance of IT |
| | Adapting technology to strategic change |
| | Assessing the strategic importance of emerging technologies |
| **Analysis** | Understanding the information needs of organizational subunits |
| | Identifying opportunities for internal improvement in business processes through IT |
| | Improving understanding of how the organization actually operates |
| | Developing a "blueprint" that structures organizational processes |
| | Monitoring internal business needs and the capability of IS to meet those needs |
| | Maintaining an understanding of changing organizational processes and procedures |
| | Generating new ideas to reengineer business processes through IT |
| | Understanding the dispersion of data, applications, and other technologies throughout the firm |
| **Cooperation** | Avoiding the overlapping development of major systems |
| | Achieving a general level of agreement regarding risks/tradeoffs among system projects |
| | Establishing a uniform basis for prioritizing projects |
| | Maintaining open lines of communication with other departments |
| | Coordinating the development efforts of various organizational subunits |
| | Identifying and resolving potential sources of resistance to IS plans |
| | Developing clear guidelines of managerial responsibility for plan implementation |
| **Capabilities** | Ability to identify key problem areas |
| | Ability to identify new business opportunities |
| | Ability to align IS strategy with organizational strategy |
| | Ability to anticipate surprises and crises |
| | Ability to understand the business and its information needs |
| | Flexibility to adapt to unanticipated changes |
| | Ability to gain cooperation among user groups for IS plans |

*Source:* Segars and Grover (1998).

spending too much time and effort on the planning process), coordinating greater planning efforts with more planning outputs by so many planners over so much time would become much more difficult to manage. The excessive effort—although well intended—could delay the conclusion of the planning process to a point where the environment changes, and top management and key users begin to lose their commitment. Such excessive planning could thus render plans of less use or even obsolete before they are implemented, resulting in deterioration rather than improvement in performance.

With excessive comprehensiveness, planners could thus bog down in identifying key issues and objectives, delay in assembling a planning team, and thereby lose any initial management enthusiasm and commitment (strategic awareness). Planners might develop an excellent understanding of the internal and external environments (situation analysis), but due to delays, the environment would change so extensively that it would no longer be relevant when the time to imagine, choose, or implement new systems arrived. Planners might take more time to imagine more new information systems (strategy conception), to assess their various outcomes, and to make more careful choices (strategy formulation), but again, the environment might change and management interest might be lost. Planners might more carefully develop implementation plans (strategy implementation planning), but again, the lengthy duration of the process might make the plans obsolete before they are implemented. In effect, too much comprehensiveness in any of the phases might lead to reduced performance.

Figure 11.1 shows how initially increased comprehensiveness might lead to improved performance, but also eventually lead to reduced performance. Such an inverted-U-shaped curve is, in fact, illustrated by the widely known law of diminishing returns. The law states that the assignment of one unit of input to a process results in an increase to the total output. The marginal output is the extra output added by one unit of input, while holding other factors constant (Samuelson, 1976). The marginal output of that unit adds positively to the process and the total output increases at a rising rate. However, as additional units are added to the process, the marginal output begins to decline and the total output begins to rise at a declining rate. At this point, increasing returns give way to decreasing returns and total output continues increasing (McGuigan, Moyer, and Harris, 1996). As more units are added to the process, the marginal output of each unit becomes zero and the total output levels off. At this point, the total output is at its optimal level. The marginal output then becomes negative and the total output starts to decline. As more and more input is added to the process, the total output further declines (Sichel and Eckstein, 1974).

The assertion that too much planning in general and too much SISP in particular can be detrimental is, in a sense, supported by advocates of incremental planning. Mintzberg and Waters (1985), for example, advocated general business planning that they described as "emergent" because it incorporates the notion of strategic learning, which enables the organization to review and adjust plans to adapt to environmental changes. Advocates of incremental SISP similarly recommend planning in which IS plans are simpler, continuously reviewed to adapt to changed circumstances, more loosely integrated with the overall strategy of the organization, developed by fewer individuals, and more reliant on personal experience and judgment (Ciborra, 1994; Earl, 1993; Pyburn, 1983; Sambamurthy, Venkatraman, and Desanctis, 1994; Vitale, Ives, and Beath, 1986).

Sethi and King (1999) pointed out that nonlinear relationships have received little consideration in IS research. The authors of the current study were able to identify only two with any relevance to SISP. However Ang and colleagues (1999) in the first study, relying on evidence that learning was nonlinear (Argote, Beckman, and Epple, 1990; Auer and Reponen, 1997; Baloff, 1971; Givons and Horsky, 1990; Goold, 1996; Little, 1979; Yelle, 1979), tested the nonlinear effect of organizational and implementation variables on IS planning benefits. Although Ang and colleagues (1999) found significant nonlinear relationships among some important characteristics of SISP (i.e., IS sophistication, communications, culture, technology forecasting, top management support, and firm size) and the benefits, they did not examine the specific activities of the planning process. Furthermore, they did not examine the relationships as inverted-U functions, but simply as nonlinear ones. The results suggested that at higher levels of IS sophistication, competitiveness stagnates and may even decrease. The authors reasoned that bureaucratic bottlenecks, overly formal rules, and procedures may delay the organization's response to environmental changes.

Such bottlenecks might stem from the need to coordinate too many IS planners performing too many lengthy and detailed tasks.

Another study examined the nonlinear effect of three broad behaviors—organizational commitment, senior management involvement, and team involvement—on the achievement of SISP objectives (Basu et al., 2002). Senior management involvement predicted the dependent variable in a positive manner whereas only organizational commitment predicted it in an inverted-U relationship.

The current study examines the notion of an optimal level of SISP in the context of five phases (Mentzas, 1997). For example, the situation-analysis phase involves analyzing current business systems, current organizational systems, current information systems, and current external business and IT environments. Conceivably, planners could do too many or too few of these activities. Likewise, planners could do too much or too little in terms of the activities in the other phases. Thus, the following hypotheses are proposed:

> H1. As comprehensiveness in the strategic-awareness phase of SISP increases, SISP success increases until it (success) reaches a maximum; as SISP comprehensiveness continues to increase, SISP success decreases.
> H2. As comprehensiveness in the situation-analysis phase of SISP increases, SISP success increases until it (success) reaches a maximum; as SISP comprehensiveness continues to increase, SISP success decreases.
> H3. As comprehensiveness in the strategy-conception phase of SISP increases, SISP success increases until it (success) reaches a maximum; as SISP comprehensiveness continues to increase, SISP success decreases.
> H4. As comprehensiveness in the strategy-formulation phase of SISP increases, SISP success increases until it (success) reaches a maximum; as SISP comprehensiveness continues to increase, SISP success decreases.
> H5. As comprehensiveness in the strategy implementation planning phase of SISP increases, SISP success increases until it (success) reaches a maximum; as SISP comprehensiveness continues to increase, SISP success decreases.

## METHODOLOGY

This research gathered data via a field survey of IS executives. The instrument operationalized two constructs, strategic IS planning comprehensiveness and strategic IS planning success. Each used five-point Likert scales.

The comprehensiveness construct measured five planning phases and the activities within each. The items, derived from Mentzas (1997) and used by Mirchandani and Lederer (2008), appear in Table 11.1. Appendix 11.1 shows them as they were in the survey.

The success construct measured the extent to which the organization fulfilled its IS objectives of alignment, analysis, and cooperation and the extent to which IS capabilities improved over time. It used the success items from Segars and Grover (1998) in Table 11.2. Appendix 11.2 shows the items as they appeared in the survey.

### Pilot Test

Five IS executives were asked to participate in a pilot test, and they all agreed. Four had the title of chief information officer (CIO) and one had the title of director of Information Services. Their experience ranged from seventeen to thirty-eight years. They worked in a variety of industries.

Each completed the survey in the presence of the senior author in about seventeen minutes. Afterward, they were asked for feedback. They commented on the contents, length, and overall appearance of the instrument. Changes from each of the first four were integrated into the survey before the next interview. The fifth resulted in no change to the survey.

## Data Collection

A sample of IS executives was randomly selected from the *Directory of Top Computer Executives* (Applied Computer Research Inc., 1999). The survey was sent to 1,200 executives. A total of 220 returned it for a response rate of 18 percent. Fifty-nine sent only demographic data and stated that they had not participated in an organization's SISP. The remaining 161 surveys were used in the analysis.

## DATA ANALYSIS

Respondents in this study were employed in a variety of industries, well educated, and experienced. Fifteen percent of them worked in manufacturing, 12 percent in finance, 11 percent in insurance, and the remainder in other industries. Ninety-three percent held a four-year college degree while 68 percent had some postgraduate school and 50 percent had completed an advanced degree. They also had an average of twenty-one years of IS experience. They had been employed by their current companies for an average of fourteen years.

The most common scope of the planning was the entire enterprise. The most common planning horizon was three years. Organizations in this study used substantial IS resources. The average number of IS employees was 853 and the average IS budget was $131 million.

The means and standard deviations of the IS planning activities and IS planning success measures are given in Tables 11.3 and 11.4. The greatest effort appears to have gone into strategy conception (3.91) and the least into strategy implementation planning (3.31). The greatest success appears in alignment (3.73) and the least in analysis (3.46).

### Common Method Variance and Analysis of Potential Response Bias

The most knowledgeable person in the organization to assess SISP activities and success as defined in this study is typically the CIO (Premkumar and King, 1992). Most SISP research uses a single subject to assess SISP activities and success (Gottschalk, 1999a; Lederer and Sethi, 1996; Raghunathan and Raghunathan, 1991; Sabherwal, 1999). Nevertheless, Harman's single-factor test was used to check for common method variance (Schriesheim, 1979), a problem that can account, at least in part, for a relationship between similar measures (Podsakoff and Organ, 1986; Podsakoff et al., 2003). The assumption of the test is that, if a substantial amount of variance exists in the data, a single factor will emerge from an exploratory factor analysis of all the variables accounting for most of the variance. However, the results of that analysis revealed twelve factors with eigenvalues greater than 1 and no single factor explained most of the variance (i.e., they ranged from 2 percent to 33 percent). These results are consistent with the absence of significant systematic variance common to the measures.

A time-trend extrapolation test examined nonresponse bias (Armstrong and Overton, 1977). Its assumption is that nonrespondents resemble late ones more than early ones. With the first 25 percent as early respondents and the last 25 percent as surrogates for nonrespondents, a multivariate analysis of variance of the fifty-one variables indicated no significant differences (Wilks's lambda

Table 11.3

**Information Systems (IS) Planning Activities**

| Variable | Item | Mean | S.D. |
|---|---|---|---|
| **Strategic awareness (F1)** | | 3.80 | 0.75 |
| Determining key planning issues | ACT11 | 3.87 | 0.88 |
| Defining planning objectives | ACT12 | 3.84 | 0.81 |
| Organizing the planning team(s) | ACT13 | 3.74 | 0.91 |
| Obtaining top management commitment | ACT14 | 3.79 | 1.02 |
| **Situation analysis (F2)** | | 3.55 | 0.75 |
| Analyzing current business systems | ACT21 | 3.71 | 0.92 |
| Analyzing current organizational systems | ACT22 | 3.51 | 1.01 |
| Analyzing current information systems | ACT23 | 3.76 | 0.87 |
| Analyzing the current external business environment | ACT24 | 3.33 | 0.98 |
| Analyzing the current external IT environment | ACT25 | 3.43 | 1.02 |
| **Strategy Conception (F3)** | | 3.91 | 0.71 |
| Identifying major information technology (IT) objectives | ACT31 | 4.04 | 0.77 |
| Identifying opportunities for improvement | ACT32 | 3.96 | 0.77 |
| Evaluating opportunities for improvement | ACT33 | 3.66 | 0.87 |
| Identifying high-level IT strategies | ACT34 | 3.97 | 0.87 |
| **Strategy Formulation (F4)** | | 3.74 | 0.70 |
| Identifying new business processes | ACT41 | 3.43 | 0.91 |
| Identifying new IT architectures | ACT42 | 3.70 | 0.96 |
| Identifying specific new projects | ACT43 | 3.99 | 0.82 |
| Identifying priorities for new projects | ACT44 | 3.82 | 0.98 |
| **Strategy Implementation Planning (F5)** | | 3.31 | 0.76 |
| Defining change management approach | ACT51 | 3.20 | 0.98 |
| Defining action plan | ACT52 | 3.63 | 0.85 |
| Evaluating action plan | ACT53 | 3.30 | 0.87 |
| Defining follow-up and control procedures | ACT54 | 3.11 | 0.93 |

$= 0.98$; $p = 0.17$). This finding is consistent with the absence of nonresponse bias.

**Validation of SISP Comprehensiveness Construct**

The strategic IS planning comprehensiveness activities construct contained five phases, each with four or five activities. This study used the phases to represent the latent factors of this construct. Their internal consistency was calculated via Cronbach's alpha, and ranged from 0.77 to 0.86, thus exceeding the minimally required 0.70 level (Nunnally, 1978).

*Confirmatory Factor Analysis*

Confirmatory factor analysis (CFA) was performed on the detailed items of the construct using requirements that the comparative fit index (CFI), robust comparative fit index (RCFI), and non-normed fit index (NNFI) be 0.90 or higher, the Satorra-Bentler chi-square divided by degrees of freedom (SB $\chi^2$

Table 11.4

## Information Systems (IS) Planning Success Measures

| Variable | Item | Mean | S.D. |
|---|---|---|---|
| **Alignment (F1)** | | 3.73 | 0.54 |
| Understanding the strategic priorities of top management | AL1 | 3.97 | 0.79 |
| Aligning IS strategies with the strategic plan of the organization | AL2 | 3.85 | 0.77 |
| Adapting the goals/objectives of IS to changing goals/objectives of the organization | AL3 | 3.84 | 0.81 |
| Maintaining a mutual understanding with top management on the role of IS in supporting strategy | AL4 | 3.70 | 0.81 |
| Identifying information technology (IT)-related opportunities to support the strategic direction of the firm | AL5 | 3.80 | 0.79 |
| Educating top management on the importance of IT | AL6 | 3.59 | 0.85 |
| Adapting technology to strategic change | AL7 | 3.64 | 0.75 |
| Assessing the strategic importance of emerging technologies | AL8 | 3.47 | 0.83 |
| **Analysis (F2)** | | 3.46 | 0.59 |
| Understanding the information needs of organizational subunits | AN1 | 3.61 | 0.85 |
| Identifying opportunities for internal improvement in business processes through IT | AN2 | 3.61 | 0.84 |
| Improving understanding of how the organization actually operates | AN3 | 3.63 | 0.76 |
| Developing a "blueprint" that structures organizational processes | AN4 | 3.13 | 0.96 |
| Monitoring internal business needs and the capability of IS to meet those needs | AN5 | 3.30 | 0.76 |
| Maintaining an understanding of changing organizational processes and procedures | AN6 | 3.30 | 0.88 |
| Generating new ideas to reengineer business processes through IT | AN7 | 3.53 | 0.84 |
| Understanding the dispersion of data, applications, and other technologies throughout the firm | AN8 | 3.56 | 0.90 |
| **Cooperation (F3)** | | 3.56 | 0.66 |
| Avoiding the overlapping development of major systems | C01 | 3.94 | 0.95 |
| Achieving a general level of agreement regarding risks/tradeoffs among system projects | C02 | 3.55 | 0.86 |
| Establishing a uniform basis for prioritizing projects | C03 | 3.35 | 0.95 |
| Maintaining open lines of communication with other departments | C04 | 3.73 | 0.83 |
| Coordinating the development efforts of various organizational subunits | C05 | 3.43 | 0.88 |
| Identifying and resolving potential sources of resistance to IS plans | C06 | 3.39 | 0.88 |
| Developing clear guidelines of managerial responsibility for plan implementation | C07 | 3.56 | 0.90 |
| **Capabilities (F4)** | | 3.71 | 0.50 |
| Ability to identify key problem areas | CA1 | 3.84 | 0.62 |
| Ability to identify new business opportunities | CA2 | 3.70 | 0.72 |
| Ability to align IS strategy with organizational strategy | CA3 | 3.93 | 0.84 |
| Ability to anticipate surprises and crises | CA4 | 3.38 | 0.77 |
| Ability to understand the business and its information needs | CA5 | 3.90 | 0.68 |
| Flexibility to adapt to unanticipated changes | CA6 | 3.53 | 0.81 |
| Ability to gain cooperation among user groups for IS plans | CA7 | 3.68 | 0.78 |

/ *df*) ratio be 2.0 or lower, the standardized root mean square residual (RMR) be 0.10 or less, and the root mean square error of approximation (RMSEA) be 0.08 or less (Browne and Cudeck, 1993; Gefen, Straub, and Boudreau, 2000; Hatcher, 1994). The initial CFA results did not meet those criteria. However, after dropping two items (ACT24 and ACT33 due to high covariances with other items), results showed that the measurement model for the construct provided an acceptable fit to the data.

*Convergent Validity*

The standardized factor loadings ranged from 0.54 to 0.90 and the *t*-statistics were significant at $p < 0.001$. These results supported convergent validity for the strategic IS planning comprehensiveness construct.

*Discriminant Validity*

This study used the chi-square difference test, confidence interval test, and variance extracted test to assess discriminant validity of the construct. After setting pairwise correlations among the constructs to 1, the chi-square differences between the standard measurement model and the revised measurement models were significant at $p < 0.001$. These results supported discriminant validity for the construct. Moreover, none of the intervals calculated for the construct included 1.0, thus indicating that the confidence interval test also supported discriminant validity for the construct.

Discriminant validity is also demonstrated if the square root of the variance extracted estimates for two factors are greater than the correlation between the factors (Fornell and Larcker 1981). The variance extracted test provided mixed support for discriminant validity. That is, the correlation between F3 and F4 was greater than the square root of the variance extracted estimate for F4. However, in general the analyses confirmed the validity of the construct.

**Validation of SISP Success Construct**

Thirty detailed items measured the success construct. Eight measured alignment, eight measured analysis, seven measured cooperation, and seven measured capability. Cronbach's alpha ranged from 0.79 to 0.87, and was thus above the minimally accepted level.

*Confirmatory Factor Analysis*

The NNFI was not within the acceptable range of the initial CFA. After dropping one item (AL8), the fit indices were above the acceptable level.

*Convergent Validity*

The standardized factor loadings ranged from 0.50 to 0.76 and the *t*-statistics were significant at $p < 0.001$. These results supported the convergent validity for the construct.

*Discriminant Validity*

After setting pairwise correlations among the constructs to 1, the chi-square differences between the standard measurement model and the revised measurement models were significant ($p < 0.001$). Moreover, the confidence intervals calculated for the construct did not include the value 1.0. Thus, both tests supported discriminant validity for the construct.

Table 11.5

**Linear Regression of Phases on Success**

|  | Linear parameter estimate | P value | t value |
|---|---|---|---|
| Strategic awareness | 0.219 | 0.0001** | 5.23 |
| Situation analysis | 0.087 | 0.02* | 2.32 |
| Strategy conception | 0.097 | 0.04* | 2.04 |
| Strategy formulation | 0.096 | 0.04* | 2.04 |
| Strategy implementation planning | 0.163 | 0.0001** | 4.41 |

$*p < 0.05; **p < 0.0001.$

The variance extracted test provided mixed support for discriminant validity. The correlations between F1 and F2, F1 and F4, and F3 and F4 were greater than the square root of both variance extracted estimates for the respective factors. Also, the correlations between F2 and F3 and between F2 and F4 were greater than the square root of one variance extracted estimate for the respective factors. However, in general, the analysis confirmed the validity of the construct.

*A Conventional Analysis of the Effect of Comprehensiveness on Success*

Rather than simply assume the conventional linear interpretation of the effect of SISP comprehensiveness on SISP success, this research first tested it. A multiple linear regression using the SAS software package confirmed that the relationship of the five phases to SISP success was significant ($F = 59.64$, $df = 158$, $p = 0.0001$, $R^2 = 0.66$). Table 11.5 shows that all five phases were significant at the 0.05 level or greater. All five variance inflation factors were less than 10 (with the highest at 2.19), thus suggesting that multicollinearity was not a problem. Evidence of heteroscedasticity was not present.

## HYPOTHESES TESTING

Segmented regression analysis was applied for testing H1 through H5 (Hudson, 1966). The analysis consists of dividing the range of the independent variable into segments at a change-point and fitting a regression model (either linear or polynomial) for each segment so that the full model is continuous in the independent variable. The segments could be data dependent or predetermined. Segmented regression analysis, although computationally intensive, permits efficient modeling of a nonlinear relationship effectively capturing its local behavior. However, because Hudson's (1966) approach would have excessively complicated the combining of the five hypotheses into a single model due to possible statistical dependence between the phases, five separate models would be run.

Segmented regression analysis is suitable for empirically testing H1 through H5. A two-segment regression model, that is, a linear one followed by a quadratic one, can be applied to each hypothesis. The curve in Figure 11.1 shows such a combination of linear (on the left) and quadratic (on the right) functions. A segmented regression analysis would provide evidence to support a hypothesis if the slope of the linear model in the initial segment is significant and positive, and the coefficient of the quadratic term in the second segment is significant and negative (as illustrated in a formula below).[1]

Following this reasoning, a regression model consisting of two segments, a linear one followed by a quadratic one, was fitted for each phase. The segments were determined by choosing an optimal cut-off value, $X^{**}$, in the range of the independent variable for each phase. $X^{**}$ was the value for which $SSE(X^{**}) \leq SSE(X^*)$ for all $X^*$, where a two segment linear-quadratic regression model was fitted with $X^*$ as the cut-off and the residual (or error) sum of squares $SSE(X^*)$ of the fitted model was numerically computed. Thus, the optimal cut-off is data dependent and corresponds to the best-fitting two-segment, linear and quadratic regression models (i.e., those with least residual sum of squares).

The analysis of the relationship of the two variables in each hypothesis used the SAS software package. The relationship below the cutoff was expected to be a conventional linear one, while the relationship above the cutoff was expected to assume a concave inverted-U quadratic function. The regression analysis procedure of the SAS software package estimated the parameters of this quadratic function:

$$S = a + b_1 * C + b_2 * C^2 + \varepsilon$$

Where:

$S$, SISP success
$C$, SISP comprehensiveness
$a$, intercept
$b_1$ and $b_2$, coefficients
$\varepsilon$, random error term.

Based on the calculus, a negative $b_2$ significantly different from zero would confirm the inverted-U relationship predicted in the hypothesis.

The regression analysis confirmed a positive linear relationship for four of the five phases: strategic awareness ($p < 0.0001$), situation analysis ($p < 0.0001$), strategy conception ($p < 0.05$), and strategy implementation planning ($p < 0.0001$).

The analysis also showed an inverted-U relationship for strategy implementation planning. The value of $b_2$ was negative and the $t$-statistic was significantly different from zero ($p < 0.05$). $F$ tests for the strategy implementation planning linear ($F = 20.59$) and quadratic ($F = 12.11$) models were both significant. Thus, the analysis supported H5 (but not the other hypotheses). Table 11.6 shows the details of these tests. (Evidence of heteroscedasticity was not present.)

## DISCUSSION

First, the preliminary analysis of the conventional, linear relationship between the phases and success showed that all of the phases were significant at the 0.05 level or better. That is, more strategic awareness, situation analysis, strategy conception, strategy formulation, and strategy implementation planning all lead to greater planning success.

As Table 11.5 indicates, the strongest effect was for strategic awareness with $p < 0.0001$ ($t = 5.23$). Thus, greater effort at planning the planning project—that is, determining key planning issues, defining planning objectives, organizing the planning team(s), and obtaining top manage-

Table 11.6

**Hypothesis Testing**

| Phase | Cut-off | Function | Coefficient estimate (standard error) | P value | t value | Df | $R^2$ |
|---|---|---|---|---|---|---|---|
| Strategic awareness | 4.1 | Linear | 0.45 (.06) | 0.0001** | 7.44 | 106 | 0.34 |
| | | Quadratic | −0.03 (.79) | 0.97 | −0.04 | 50 | 0.26 |
| Situation analysis | 4.1 | Linear | 0.37 .06 | 0.0001** | 5.85 | 122 | 0.22 |
| | | Quadratic | −1.30 (.96) | 0.19 | −1.35 | 34 | 0.30 |
| Strategy conception | 3.1 | Linear | 0.35 (.21) | 0.11 | 1.68 | 21 | 0.12 |
| | | Quadratic | −0.17 (.11) | 0.13 | −1.52 | 134 | 0.36 |
| Strategy formulation | 3.2 | Linear | 0.30 (.13) | 0.03* | 2.28 | 47 | 0.10 |
| | | Quadratic | −0.01 (.17) | 0.96 | −0.05 | 108 | 0.23 |
| | 3.6 | Linear | 0.34 (.08) | 0.0001** | 4.54 | 98 | 0.18 |
| Strategy implementation planning | | Quadratic | −0.60 (.29) | 0.04* | −2.08 | 57 | 0.30 |

$*p < 0.05; **p < 0.0001.$

ment commitment produces the greatest planning success. Given the well-recognized importance of top management commitment, this finding is not surprising.

The second strongest effect was for strategy implementation planning with the same level of significance ($t = 4.41$). Thus, greater effort at implementing the plan—that is, defining the change management approach, defining the action plan, evaluating the action plan, and defining follow-up and control procedures is similarly a powerful predictor of planning success. Given the all-too-often failure of plan implementation, this finding is not surprising.

Both strategy conception (identifying major IT objectives, identifying opportunities for improvement, evaluating opportunities for improvement, and identifying high-level IT strategies) and strategy formulation (identifying new business processes, identifying new IT architectures, identifying specific new projects, and identifying priorities for new projects) were significant predictors of planning success, but at the lowest level ($p < 0.05$). Such findings suggest that the phases, although critical within the planning process, are not as potent in producing the desired outcomes of planning. They indicate that the choice of the strategy is not as important as the firm's initiation of the planning process and the implementation of whatever is planned.

In other words, the data strongly supported the simplistic view that more SISP is better. They also provided some insights into the relative predictiveness of the phases.

A closer look at the data in terms of the analysis of the inverted-U relationship between comprehensiveness and success found support for the strategy implementation planning phase (i.e., the activities of defining the change management approach, defining the action plan, evaluating the action plan, and defining the follow-up and control procedure) but not the other four phases. In other words, as comprehensiveness in that phase of SISP increases, SISP success increases until it (success) reaches a maximum; as SISP comprehensiveness in that phase continues to increase, SISP success decreases. This finding is consistent with the expectations illustrated by the law of diminishing returns (Samuelson, 1976).

The finding is especially interesting because the failure to implement strategic information systems plans has perhaps attracted more attention than any other SISP problem (Gottschalk, 1999a, 1999b, 1999c). Plan implementation failure is common (Earl, 1993; Ward and Griffiths, 1996) and the lack of implementation often leaves firms quite dissatisfied with their SISP initiatives (Galliers, 1994; Premkumar and King, 1994). In fact, a majority of senior IS executives have classified the "difficulty to secure top management commitment to implement the IS plan" and "ignoring the IS plan once it has been developed" as major IS planning problems (Teo and Ang, 2001, p. 461). The lack of responsibility for the implementation and the lack of user involvement during the implementation have been identified as the strongest inhibitors to strategy implementation (Gottschalk, 1999a). Researchers have thus suggested that management fails to focus its SISP efforts on implementation issues (Min, Suh, and Kim, 1999).

In a sense, the findings of the current study may be consistent with this view that management fails to focus such efforts on implementation in that management might in some cases spend too much time and effort on the tasks presumed necessary for implementation whereas in other cases it spends too little time and effort on those tasks. Perhaps management simply does not know the appropriate level of SISP necessary for the essential tasks of successful implementation.

Moreover, the strategy implementation planning construct had the lowest average score (meaning that planners perform it less than the other phases). This may further underscore the problems of planning the implementation of information systems strategies.

This research failed to support the inverted-U for the other SISP phases. The failure to find a statistically significant relationship must always be treated with hesitation. The effect may be present, but the investigation did not detect it. However, in contrast to the significant finding for strategy planning implementation, the failure to support inverted-U in the other four phases could be deemed consistent with the assertion that strategic information systems planners do not overdo their efforts in them. In other words, in their actual practice of strategic awareness, situation analysis, strategy conception, and strategy formulation, planners do not reach that optimal level after which performance would decline.

## IMPLICATIONS FOR PRACTICE AND RESEARCH

The practical implication of support for the strategy implementation planning hypothesis is that planners may do too much or too little of such planning. Too little could produce implementation plans with insufficient detail to permit their successful execution. Too much could complicate, delay, or otherwise impede implementation. Support for the hypothesis confirms concerns about the difficulty of implementing strategic information systems plans.

The support for the hypothesis thus suggests that planners be careful to evaluate how much of that particular SISP activity they should perform. It further suggests that then they do neither too much nor too little of it.

Future researchers should investigate strategy implementation planning more extensively. The construct did follow the inverted-U curve as theoretically predicted and such a finding provides a meaningful warning to planners. However, the finding raises many questions: Can researchers identify an optimal level of planning describable in practical terms? How would planners know that they were adhering to such a level? In other words, can researchers provide guidance that is more meaningful than the simple recognition that both too little and too much strategy implementation planning can be suboptimal as shown by the Likert scales in this study?

Perhaps a closer examination of the subtasks holds the answers to such questions. Perhaps the activities of defining the change-management approach, defining the action plan, evaluating the action plan, and defining the follow-up and control procedure differ from one another in the optimal level of each. Perhaps qualitative case research, where investigators can ask more detailed and probing questions, would help to find answers.

Future researchers should also try to explain why the data did not support more of the inverted-U hypotheses. Perhaps the reason is that planners simply do not overdo their efforts in the strategic awareness, situation analysis, strategy conception, and strategy formulation phases. Perhaps, on the other hand, researchers can find characteristics specific to each phase explaining the lack of support for its hypothesis.

However, the theoretical bases for the other hypotheses are fairly strong. It seems conceivable that planners may still overdo efforts in them, and thus future research might continue to investigate them using different methodological approaches.

The hypotheses in the current research describe a quadratic function. However, they could also describe other functions. Future researchers could thus test alternative curves.

This research used primarily medium to large companies in a variety of different industries to investigate the relationships among the constructs. Future researchers could investigate the relationships among them by gathering data from small companies. Perhaps smaller companies are more vulnerable to doing both too little and too much planning.

Future researchers could also investigate specific industries. SISP in companies from the more information-intensive finance industry, for example, might differ from SISP in the less information-intensive manufacturing sector. Perhaps, industry influenced the outcome of the hypothesis testing in this study.

## CONCLUSION

One challenge to performing effective SISP involves determining the extent to which organizations should practice planning. Survey research with strategic information systems planners tested five related hypotheses and found support for one of them. In doing so, the research made the following contributions.

It provided further validation for an existing measure of SISP success (Segars and Grover, 1998). The instrument offers considerable potential for future use. The current research demonstrated its validity and reliability.

It validated an activities-related measure of SISP comprehensiveness (Mentzas, 1997). Future research can use this measure with some degree of confidence based on the current research.

It provided partial support for the hypotheses. It thus illustrated the law of diminishing returns in the context of information systems research. Because information systems are so critical to organizations today, because efforts to implement strategic information systems plans have failed too often, and because too much or too little time and effort on planning offer intuitive explanations for such failure, the study more importantly provided a rationale for future research to continue the investigation and to discover why that support was merely partial.

Finally, although the study furnished only partial support, it provided some empirical basis to encourage strategic information systems planners to be wary of too much or too little SISP. Perhaps, additional attention to the possibility of too much or too little SISP in the implementation planning phase can enable them to improve their planning efforts.

## APPENDIX 11.1. RELEVANT COMPREHENSIVENESS ITEMS FROM THE INSTRUMENT

### SISP Comprehensiveness

Please mark the number to indicate the extent to which the organization conducted each of the following five phases and their related tasks during its SISP efforts:

|   |   | No extent | | | Great extent | |
|---|---|---|---|---|---|---|
| 1 | Planning the IS planning process | 1 | 2 | 3 | 4 | 5 |
|   | Determining key planning issues | 1 | 2 | 3 | 4 | 5 |
|   | Defining planning objectives | 1 | 2 | 3 | 4 | 5 |
|   | Organizing the planning team(s) | 1 | 2 | 3 | 4 | 5 |
|   | Obtaining top management commitment | 1 | 2 | 3 | 4 | 5 |
| 2 | Analyzing the current environment | 1 | 2 | 3 | 4 | 5 |
|   | Analyzing current business systems | 1 | 2 | 3 | 4 | 5 |
|   | Analyzing current organizational systems | 1 | 2 | 3 | 4 | 5 |
|   | Analyzing current information systems | 1 | 2 | 3 | 4 | 5 |
|   | Analyzing the current external business environment | 1 | 2 | 3 | 4 | 5 |
|   | Analyzing the current external IT environment | 1 | 2 | 3 | 4 | 5 |

| 3 | Conceiving strategy alternatives | 1 | 2 | 3 | 4 | 5 |
| | Identifying major IT objectives | 1 | 2 | 3 | 4 | 5 |
| | Identifying opportunities for improvement | 1 | 2 | 3 | 4 | 5 |
| | Evaluating opportunities for improvement | 1 | 2 | 3 | 4 | 5 |
| | Identifying high level IT strategies | 1 | 2 | 3 | 4 | 5 |
| 4 | Selecting strategy | 1 | 2 | 3 | 4 | 5 |
| | Identifying new business processes | 1 | 2 | 3 | 4 | 5 |
| | Identifying new IT architectures | 1 | 2 | 3 | 4 | 5 |
| | Identifying specific new projects | 1 | 2 | 3 | 4 | 5 |
| | Identifying priorities for new projects | 1 | 2 | 3 | 4 | 5 |
| 5 | Planning the strategy implementation | 1 | 2 | 3 | 4 | 5 |
| | Defining change management approach | 1 | 2 | 3 | 4 | 5 |
| | Defining action plan | 1 | 2 | 3 | 4 | 5 |
| | Evaluating action plan | 1 | 2 | 3 | 4 | 5 |
| | Defining follow-up and control procedures | 1 | 2 | 3 | 4 | 5 |

## APPENDIX 11.2 RELEVANT SUCCESS ITEMS FROM THE INSTRUMENT

### SISP Success

Please mark the number to indicate the extent to which the organization fulfilled each of the following objectives of alignment, analysis, and cooperation from its SISP efforts:

| | Entirely unfulfilled | | | | Entirely fulfilled |
| --- | --- | --- | --- | --- | --- |
| *Alignment objectives* | | | | | |
| Understanding the strategic priorities of top management | 1 | 2 | 3 | 4 | 5 |
| Aligning IS strategies with the strategic plan of the organization | 1 | 2 | 3 | 4 | 5 |
| Adapting the goals/objectives of IS to changing goals/objectives of the organization | 1 | 2 | 3 | 4 | 5 |
| Maintaining a mutual understanding with top management on the role of IS in supporting strategy | 1 | 2 | 3 | 4 | 5 |
| Identifying IT-related opportunities to support the strategic direction of the firm | 1 | 2 | 3 | 4 | 5 |
| Educating top management on the importance of IT | 1 | 2 | 3 | 4 | 5 |
| Adapting technology to strategic change | 1 | 2 | 3 | 4 | 5 |
| Assessing the strategic importance of emerging technologies | 1 | 2 | 3 | 4 | 5 |
| *Analysis objectives* | | | | | |
| Understanding the information needs of organizational subunits | 1 | 2 | 3 | 4 | 5 |

| Identifying opportunities for internal improvement in business processes through IT | 1 | 2 | 3 | 4 | 5 |
| Improved understanding of how the organization actually operates | 1 | 2 | 3 | 4 | 5 |
| Development of a "blueprint" which structures organizational processes | 1 | 2 | 3 | 4 | 5 |
| Monitoring of internal business needs and the capability of IS to meet those needs | 1 | 2 | 3 | 4 | 5 |
| Maintaining an understanding of changing organizational processes and procedures | 1 | 2 | 3 | 4 | 5 |
| Generating new ideas to reengineer business processes through IT | 1 | 2 | 3 | 4 | 5 |
| Understanding the dispersion of data, applications, and other technologies throughout the firm | 1 | 2 | 3 | 4 | 5 |

*Cooperation objectives*

| Avoiding the overlapping development of major systems | 1 | 2 | 3 | 4 | 5 |
| Achieving a general level of agreement regarding the risks/tradeoffs among system projects | 1 | 2 | 3 | 4 | 5 |
| Establishing a uniform basis for prioritizing projects | 1 | 2 | 3 | 4 | 5 |
| Maintaining open lines of communication with other departments | 1 | 2 | 3 | 4 | 5 |
| Coordinating the development efforts of various organizational subunits | 1 | 2 | 3 | 4 | 5 |
| Identifying and resolving potential sources of resistance to IS plans | 1 | 2 | 3 | 4 | 5 |
| Developing clear guidelines of managerial responsibility for plan implementation | 1 | 2 | 3 | 4 | 5 |

Please indicate the extent to which the following SISP capabilities improved over time within the firm:

|  | Much deterioration | | | | Much improvement |
| --- | --- | --- | --- | --- | --- |
| Ability to identify key problem areas | 1 | 2 | 3 | 4 | 5 |
| Ability to identify new business opportunities | 1 | 2 | 3 | 4 | 5 |
| Ability to align IS strategy with organizational strategy | 1 | 2 | 3 | 4 | 5 |
| Ability to anticipate surprises and crises | 1 | 2 | 3 | 4 | 5 |
| Ability to understand the business and its information needs | 1 | 2 | 3 | 4 | 5 |
| Flexibility to adapt to unanticipated changes | 1 | 2 | 3 | 4 | 5 |
| Ability to gain cooperation among user groups for IS plans | 1 | 2 | 3 | 4 | 5 |

## NOTE

1. The authors originally subjected the entire data set for each phase to the conventional quadratic analysis, but found that the large number of lower success values in each planning phase dampened the curvilinear

effect for the higher success values. Hence the segmented approach—which connected the straight line and curvilinear models into a single model—was adopted and is reported.

## REFERENCES

Ang, J.S.K; Quek, A.; Thompson, S.H.T.; and Lui, B. 1999. Modeling IS planning benefits using ACE. *Decision Sciences,* 30, 2 (Spring), 533–561.

Applied Computer Research Inc. 1999. *Directory of Top Computer Executives.* Phoenix, AZ.

Argote, L.; Beckman, S.L.; and Epple, D. 1990. The persistence and transfer of learning in industrial settings. *Management Science,* 36, 2, 140–154.

Argyris, C., and Schoen, D. 1978. *Organizational Learning: A Theory of Action Perspective.* Reading, MA: Addison-Wesley.

Armstrong, J.S., and Overton, T.S. 1977. Estimating nonresponse bias in mail surveys. *Journal of Marketing Research,* 14 (August), 396–402.

Auer, T., and Reponen, T. 1997. Information system strategy formation embedded into a continuous organizational learning process. *Information Resources Management Journal,* 10, 2, 32–43.

Baets, W. 1992. Aligning information systems with business strategy. *Journal of Strategic Information Systems,* 1, 4, 205–13.

Baker, B. 1995. The role of feedback in assessing information systems planning effectiveness. *Journal of Strategic Information Systems,* 4, 1, 61–80.

Baloff, N. 1971. Extension of the learning curve: some empirical results. *Operations Research Quarterly,* 22, 4, 329–340.

Baskerville, R.L. 2006. Artful planning. *European Journal of Information Systems,* 15, 2, 113–115.

Basu, V.; Hartono, E.; Lederer, A.L.; and Sethi, V. 2002. The impact of organizational commitment, senior management involvement, and team involvement on strategic information systems planning. *Information and Management,* 39, 6 (May), 513–524.

Boynton, A.C., and Zmud, R.W. 1987. Information technology planning in the 1990's: directions for practice and research. *MIS Quarterly,* 11, 1 (March), 59–71.

Brancheau, J.C.; Schuster, L.; and March, S.T. 1989. Building and implementing an information architecture. *Database,* 19, 2, 9–17.

Browne, M., and Cudeck, R. 1993. Alternative ways of assessing model fit. In K.A. Bollen and J.S. Long (eds.), *Testing Structural Equation Models.* London: Sage, pp. 136–162.

Byrd, T.A.; Lewis, B.R.; and Bryan, R.W. 2006. The leveraging influence of strategic alignment on IT investment: an empirical examination. *Information & Management,* 43, 3, 308–321.

Cameron, K.S., and Whetten, D.A. 1983. Some conclusions about organizational effectiveness. In K.S. Cameron and D.A. Whetten (eds.), *Organization Effectiveness: A Comparison of Multiple Models.* New York: Academic Press, pp. 261–277.

Ciborra, C. 1994. The grassroots of IT and strategy. In C. Ciborra and T. Jelassi (eds.), *Strategic Information Systems: A European Perspective.* Chichester, UK: Wiley, pp. 3–24.

Doherty, N.F., and Fulford, H. 2006. Aligning the information security policy with the strategic information systems plan. *Computers & Security,* 25, 1, 55–63.

Doherty, N.F.; Marples, C.G.; and Suhaimi, A. 1999. The relative success of alternative approaches to strategic information systems planning: an empirical analysis. *Journal of Strategic Information Systems,* 8, 263–283.

Earl, M.J. 1993. Experiences in strategic information systems planning. *MIS Quarterly,* 17, 1 (March), 1–24.

Fornell, C., and Larcker, D.F. 1981. Evaluating structural equations models with unobservable variables and measurement error. *Journal of Marketing Research,* 18, 1, 39–50.

Fredrickson, J.W., and Mitchell, T.R. 1984. Strategic decision processes: comprehensiveness and performance in an industry with an unstable environment. *Academy of Management Journal,* 27, 2, 399–423.

Galliers, R.D. 1994. Strategic information systems planning: myths, reality and guidelines for successful implementation. In R.D. Galliers and B.S.H. Baker (eds.), *Strategic Information Management.* Oxford: Butterworth-Heinemann, pp. 129–147.

Gefen, D.; Straub, D.W.; and Boudreau, M. 2000. Structural equation modeling and regression: guidelines for research practice. *Communications of the AIS,* 4, 7, 1–78.

Givons, M., and Horsky, D. 1990. Untangling the effects of purchase reinforcement and advertising carryover. *Marketing Science,* 9, 2, 171–187.

Goold, M. 1996. Learning, planning, and strategy. *California Management Review,* 38, 4, 100–102.

Gottschalk, P. 1999a. Implementation predictors of strategic information systems plans. *Information & Management,* 39, 77–91.

———. 1999b. Strategic information systems planning: the IT strategy implementation matrix. *European Journal of Information Systems,* 8, 2 (June), 107–118.

———. 1999c. Implementation of formal plans: the case of information technology strategy. *Long Range Planning,* 32, 3, 362–372.

Grover, V., and Segars, A.H. 2005. An empirical evaluation of stages of strategic information systems planning: patterns of process design and effectiveness. *Information & Management,* 42, 5 (July), 761–779.

Hackathorn, R.D., and Karimi, J.A. 1998. Framework for comparing information engineering methods. *MIS Quarterly,* 12, 2 (June), 203–220.

Harris, A.L. 1995. Information technology planning in manufacturing industry: an empirical study. *International Journal of Computer Applications in Technology,* 8, 1/2, 12–20.

Hatcher, L. 1994. *A Step by Step Approach to Using the SAS System for Factor Analysis and Structural Equation Modeling.* Cary, NC: SAS Institute.

Henderson, J.C. 1990. Plugging into strategic partnerships: the critical IS connection. *Sloan Management Review,* 31, 7–18.

Henderson, J.C., and Venkatraman, N. 1993. Strategic alignment: leveraging information technology for transforming organizations. *IBM Systems Journal,* 32, 1, 4–16.

Henderson, J.C.; Rockart, J.F.; and Sifonis, J.G. 1987. Integrating management support systems into strategic information systems planning. *Journal of Management Information Systems,* 4, 1, 5–24.

Hudson, D.J. 1966. Fitting Segmented Curves Whose Join Points Have to Be Estimated. *Journal of the American Statistical Association,* 61, 316 (December), 1097–1129.

Janis, I.L., and Mann, L. 1977. *Decision Making: A Psychological Analysis of Conflict, Choice, and Commitment.* New York: Free Press.

King, W.R. 1978. Strategic Planning for Management Information Systems. *MIS Quarterly,* 2, 1, 27–37.

Lederer, A.L., and Sethi, V. 1988. The implementation of strategic information systems planning methodologies. *MIS Quarterly,* 12, 3 (September), 445–461.

———. 1996. Key prescriptions for strategic information systems planning. *Journal of Management Information Systems,* 13, 1 (Summer), 35–62.

Little, J.D. 1979. Aggregate advertising models: the state of the art. *Operations Research,* 27, 4, 629–667.

McFarlan, F.W. 1971. Problems in planning the information system. *Harvard Business Review,* 42, 2, 75–89.

McGuigan, J.R.; Moyer, C.R.; and Harris, F.H.B. 1996. *Managerial Economics.* Minneapolis/St. Paul: West.

McLean, E.R., and Soden, J.V. 1977. *Strategic Planning for MIS.* New York: Wiley.

Mentzas, G. 1997. Implementing an IS strategy: a team approach. *Long Range Planning,* 10, 1, 84–95.

Min, S.K.; Suh, E.H.; and Kim, S.Y. 1999. An integrated approach toward strategic information systems planning. *Journal of Strategic Information Systems,* 8, 4, 373–394.

Mintzberg, H., and Waters, J.A. 1985. Of strategies, deliberate and emergent. *Strategic Management Journal,* 6, 3 (July–September), 257–272.

Mirchandani, D.A., and Lederer, A.L. 2008. The impact of autonomy on information systems planning effectiveness. *Omega, the International Journal of Management Science,* 36, 5 (October), 789–807.

Newkirk, H.E., and Lederer, A.L. 2006a. Incremental and comprehensive strategic information systems planning in an uncertain environment. *IEEE Transactions on Engineering Management,* 53, 3 (August), 380–394.

———. 2006b. The effectiveness of strategic information systems planning under environmental uncertainty. *Information and Management,* 43, 481–501.

———. 2007. The effectiveness of strategic information systems planning for technical resources, personnel resources, and data security in environments of heterogeneity and hostility. *Journal of Computer Information Systems* (Spring), 34–44.

Newkirk, H.E.; Lederer, A.L.; and Srinivasan, C. 2003. Strategic information systems planning: too little or too much? *Journal of Strategic Information Systems,* 12, 3, 201–228.

Nunnally, J. 1978. *Psychometric Theory.* New York: McGraw-Hill.

Podsakoff, P.M., and Organ, D.M. 1986. Self-reports in organizational research: problems and prospects. *Journal of Management,* 12, 4, 531–543.

Podsakoff, P.; MacKenzie, S.; Lee, J-Y.; and Podsakoff, N. 2003. Common method biases in behavioral research: a critical review of the literature and recommended remedies. *Journal of Applied Psychology,* 88, 5, 879–903.

Premkumar, G., and King, W.R. 1991. Assessing strategic information systems planning. *Long Range Planning,* 24, 5, 41–58.

———. An empirical assessment of information systems planning and the role of information systems in organizations. *Journal of Management Information Systems,* 9, 2 (Fall), 99–125.

———. 1994. The evaluation of strategic information systems planning. *Information and Management,* 26, 327–340.

Pyburn, P.J. 1983. Linking the MIS plan with corporate strategy: an exploratory study. *MIS Quarterly,* 7, 2, 1–14.

Raghunathan, B., and Raghunathan, T.S. 1991. Information systems planning and effectiveness: an empirical analysis. *Omega,* 19, 2/3, 125–135.

———. 1994. Adaptation of a planning system success model to information systems planning. *Information Systems Research,* 5, 3 (September), 326–340.

Sabherwal, R. 1999. The relationship between information systems planning sophistication and information systems success: an empirical assessment. *Decision Sciences,* 30, 1 (Winter), 137–167.

Sabherwal, R., and Chan, Y.E. 2001. Alignment between business and IS strategies: a study of prospectors, analyzers and defenders. *Information Systems Research,* 12, 1, 11–33.

Salmela, H., and Spil, T.A.M. 2002. Dynamic and emergent information systems strategy formulation and implementation. *International Journal of Information Management,* 22, 441–460.

Sambamurthy, V.; Bharadwaj, A.; and Grover, V. 2003. Shaping firm agility through digital options: reconceptualizing the role of IT in contemporary firms. *MIS Quarterly,* 27, 2, 237–263.

Sambamurthy, V.; Venkatraman, S.; and Desanctis, G. 1993. The design of information technology planning systems for varying organizational contexts. *European Journal of Information Systems,* 2, 1, 23–35.

Sambamurthy, V.; Zmud, R.W.; and Byrd, T.A. 1994. The comprehensiveness of IT planning process: a contingency approach. *Journal of Information Technology Management,* 5, 1 (November), 1–10.

Samuelson, P.A. 1976. *Economics.* New York: McGraw-Hill.

Schriesheim, C. 1979. The similarity of individual-directed and group-directed leader behavior descriptions. *Academy of Management Journal,* 22, 345–355.

Segars, A.H., and Grover, V. 1998. Strategic information systems planning success: an investigation of the construct and its measurements. *MIS Quarterly* (June), 139–163.

———. 1999. Profiles of strategic information systems planning. *Information Systems Research,* 10, 3 (September), 199–232.

Segars, A.H.; Grover, V.; and Teng T.C. 1998. Strategic information systems planning success: planning system dimensions, internal coalignment, and implication for planning effectiveness. *Decision Sciences,* 29, 2 (Spring), 303–345.

Sethi, V., and King, R. 1999. Nonlinear and noncompensatory models in user information satisfaction measurement. *Information Systems Research,* 10, 1 (March), 87–97.

Sichel, W., and Eckstein, P. 1974. *Basic Economic Concepts.* Chicago: Rand McNally.

Teo, T.S.H., and Ang, J.S.K. 2001. An examination of major IS problems. *International Journal of Information Management,* 21, 457–470.

Venkatraman, N., and Ramanujam, V. 1987. Planning system success: a conceptualization and an operational model. *Management Science,* 33, 6 (June), 687–705.

Vitale, M.R.; Ives, B.; and Beath, C.M. 1986. Linking information technology and corporate strategy: an organizational view. *Proceedings of the Seventh International Conference on Information Systems.* San Diego, CA, 265–274.

Ward, J., and Griffiths, P. 1996. *Strategic Planning for Information Systems.* Wiley Series in Information Systems. Chichester, UK: Wiley.

Yelle, L.E. 1979. The learning curve: historical review and comprehensive survey. *Decision Sciences,* 10, 2, 302–329.

# CHAPTER 12

# THE ROLE OF ORGANIZATIONAL LEARNING IN STRATEGIC INFORMATION SYSTEMS PLANNING IN UNCERTAIN ENVIRONMENTS

SAMUEL OTIM, VARUN GROVER, AND ALBERT H. SEGARS

**Abstract:** *Improving strategic planning within the realm of information technology management is consistently identified by top corporate executives as a critical competitive issue. This study attempts to take a major step in conceptualizing the strategic information systems planning (SISP) process and examining its effectiveness. Two profiles of SISP process and four of SISP effectiveness are developed conceptually and supported with empirical analysis. The six dimensions of SISP process identified in the previous literature are grouped into radical and incremental profiles both conceptually and empirically based on the patterns they display. Similarly, the four dimensions of SISP effectiveness from prior literature are grouped into fit and fitness profiles, from which four types of organizations emerge based on their performance along these two dimensions. The results suggest that a radical approach to SISP consists of high comprehensiveness, high formalization, creativity focus, bottom-up flow, high participation, and high consistency while an incremental approach exhibits the opposite emphases along these dimensions. For SISP effectiveness, empirical analysis supported four types of organizations (adaptive, learning-impaired, alignment-impaired, and planning-impaired). Adaptive organizations are adept at balancing exploration and exploitation and they achieve high levels of both fitness and fit. Other organizations are impaired in either one or both dimensions. Thus, organizations need to think in terms of both fit and fitness if they are to align their business–IT plans and thereby avoid long periods of underperformance. Since the competitive environment is continually evolving, they should consider fit as requiring constant monitoring and regular updating, rather than intermittent interventions.*

**Keywords:** *Strategic Planning, Planning Effectiveness, Environmental Uncertainty, Organizational Learning, Fit, Fitness*

The pervasiveness of information technology (IT) and the increasing pressure on organizations to leverage their IT resources make strategic information systems planning (SISP) an important consideration. SISP refers to the process of developing an information systems (IS) portfolio that will support the organization's business plans, needs, and goals (Reich and Benbasat, 2000; Venkatraman, 1989a). SISP is vital in achieving business-IT alignment, which enables an organization to exploit IT capabilities to transform business processes and ultimately influence business performance. While much has been written about SISP, most studies focus on planning content, with particular interest in the methods and measurement of alignment between business and information systems strategies. The focus on "fit" or alignment between business strategies and IT strategies has overlooked the issue of how to sustain this harmony between business and IT in a rapidly changing environment (Hirschheim and Sabherwal, 2001). Consequently, the difficulties in achieving and sustaining alignment in dynamic settings as well as the organizational aspects of SISP have not been sufficiently addressed. In order to gain insight into planning effectiveness, it is important to examine the planning process and the evolution of planning as a learning system.

Organizational and environmental contexts are often identified as the key determinants of characteristics and planning effectiveness (Newkirk and Lederer, 2006; Wang and Tai, 2003). While organizational context may be important, rapid advances in open networks and IT capabilities are substantially increasing environmental complexity and uncertainty (Chi et al., 2005). These advances are changing the structure of industries, ushering in new business models, initiating new businesses, and, as a result, continuously shaping and reshaping the business environment (Porter, 2001). Therefore, environmental conditions play a critical role in the SISP process since changes in technology, competitors, customers, government, and vendors can greatly influence both the direction and pace of a firm's strategic use of IS, and the value of new systems (Chi et al., 2005; Choe, 2003).

Some empirical studies explicitly incorporating various dimensions of the environment report interesting but mixed results. Grover and Segars (2005) find that both environmental uncertainty and IT diffusion have differential effects across SISP stages, supporting their contention that SISP should be an adaptive system that responds to increasing environmental uncertainty and increasing IT diffusion. Newkirk and Lederer (2006) tested the effect of incremental versus comprehensive SISP on planning effectiveness in environments of varying uncertainty. Their findings suggest that planners should expect comprehensive SISP to be less effective as changeability and unpredictability increase, but more effective as competition increases. Chi and colleagues (2005) found that while the planning horizon and enterprise versus division-level SISP had no effect on the extent of environmental assessment, top management initiation and IS department participation in business planning significantly influenced the extent of environmental assessment. Furthermore, they found support for the hypothesis that the extent of environmental assessment is positively associated with achievement of SISP objectives.

Given the lack of consistency in empirical findings, it is important to develop a consistent framework that recognizes the effect of environmental influences on SISP. Based on process-oriented frameworks, early studies by Sullivan (1985) and Sabherwal and King (1995) suggest that planning systems vary along a continuum from completely rational to completely adaptive. Subsequent studies by Segars and Grover (1998, 1999) found that systems that exhibit process characteristics of both rationality and adaptability tend to be more successful. However, the rational-adaptive characterization of SISP process is problematic because adaptability does not exclude rationality and vice versa. Every SISP process necessarily incorporates some elements of both rationality and adaptability. Therefore, a SISP process needs to be characterized by the degree to which it has more of one element than the other. For instance, Newkirk and Lederer's (2006) conceptualization of the SISP process as either incremental or comprehensive is a useful categorization of the approaches to the SISP process.

Our focus in this chapter is on the role of organizational learning in the SISP process in uncertain environments. In developing our framework, we first discuss the process dimensions of SISP identified in the literature. We then adapt Newkirk and Lederer's (2006) categorization of the SISP process and buttress it in our analysis using the theoretical concepts of incremental and radical innovation (Dewar and Dutton, 1986), and exploration and exploitation in organization learning (March, 1991). We then map out the dimensions of SISP process onto our framework.

# DIMENSIONS OF THE STRATEGIC INFORMATION SYSTEMS PLANNING PROCESS

Earlier studies within the area of strategic management focused on identifying and examining the dimensions of the planning process and their emergent structure or profile across organizations (e.g., Chakravarthy, 1987; Chakravarthy and Doz, 1992; Fredrickson and Iaquinto, 1989; Hart, 1992; Kukalis, 1991; Ramanujam and Venkatraman, 1987; Venkatraman, 1989a; Venkatraman and Prescott, 1990). A parallel line of inquiry has taken place within IS research with investigation of the general design characteristics of SISP, emergent profiles of planning, and differences in effectiveness among profiles (e.g., Byrd, Sambamurthy, and Zmud, 1995; Das, Zahra, and Warkentin, 1991; Earl, 1993; Grover and Segars, 2005; Pyburn, 1983; Raghunathan and Raghunathan, 1989; Sabherwal and King, 1995; Sambamurthy, Venkatraman, and Desanctis, 1993; Segars and Grover, 1999; Segars, Grover, and Teng, 1998; Teo and King, 1997). Through qualitative and empirical analyses, these literature streams suggest six broad dimensions of the planning process that are independent of a particular method and yet manifest across a variety of organizational and environmental contexts. These dimensions are comprehensiveness, formalization, focus, flow, participation, and consistency. Below, we briefly discuss the salient characteristics of these planning dimensions. Table 12.1 summarizes these SISP process dimensions.

## Comprehensiveness

Comprehensiveness is recognized as a multifaceted construct (Janis and Mann, 1977; and subsequent studies, e.g., Segars, Grover, and Teng, 1998), consisting of the following characteristics:

1. the thorough canvassing of a wide range of alternatives;
2. the surveying of a full range of objectives;
3. the intensive searching for information to evaluate alternative actions;
4. the objective evaluating of information, or expert judgment regarding alternative actions;
5. the reexamining of the positive and negative consequences of all known alternatives; and
6. the making of detailed plans, including consideration of contingencies for implementing a chosen action.

One of the major challenges organizations face is how to allocate the required managerial time and financial resources and to balance the benefits of the extensiveness of solution search with the costs of narrow or limited solution search. It seems that environmental context might have an influence on the degree of organizational comprehensiveness in the SISP process (Chi et al., 2005; Grover and Segars, 2005; Newkirk and Lederer, 2006).

## Formalization

Formalized planning processes systemize information collection, analysis, and dissemination, thus facilitating the identification and storage of strategic issues. Systemization of information collection, analysis, and dissemination produces information-related efficiency gains, which translate into an organizational capacity to consider a greater number of strategic issues. However, formalization may reduce the flexibility needed to quickly cull unimportant issues, or implement resolved issues. Thus, striking the balance between structure and rapid resolution of strategic issues is a

Table 12.1

**Process Dimensions of Strategic Information Systems Planning**

| Dimension | Description | Descriptors | Supporting literature |
|---|---|---|---|
| Comprehensiveness | The extent to which an organization attempts to be exhaustive in making and integrating strategic decisions | Comprehensive vs. limited | Das, Zahra, and Warkentin (1991), Grover and Segars (2005), Lederer and Sethi (1996), Sabherwal and King (1995), Sambamurthy, Zmud, and Byrd (1994), Segars and Grover (1999), Segars, Grover, and Teng (1998) |
| Formalization | The existence of structures, techniques, written procedures, and policies that guide the planning process | Formal vs. informal | Das, Zahra, and Warkentin (1991), Earl (1993), Grover and Segars (2005), Lederer and Sethi (1996), Sabherwal and King (1995), Premkumar and King (1992), Segars and Grover (1999), Segars, Grover, and Teng (1998) |
| Focus | The degree of balance between creativity and control orientations inherent within the strategic planning system | Creativity vs. control | Byrd et al. (1995), Grover and Segars 2005), Lederer and Sethi (1996), Sabherwal and King (1995), Segars and Grover (1999), Segars, Grover, and Teng (1998) |
| Flow | The locus of authority (i.e., the role played by corporate and divisional managers) in the initiation of the planning process | Top-down vs. bottom-up | Byrd, Sambamurthy, and Zmud (1995), Grover and Segars (2005), Pyburn (1983), Segars and Grover (1999), Segars, Grover, and Teng (1998) |
| Participation | The breadth of involvement of different organizational constituencies in the strategic planning process | Broad vs. narrow | Byrd, Sambamurthy, and Zmud (1995), Das, Zahra, and Warkentin (1991), Grover and Segars (2005), Lederer and Sethi (1996), Sabherwal and King (1995), Segars and Grover (1999), Segars, Grover, and Teng (1998) |
| Consistency | The frequency of planning activities or cycles, and evaluation/ revision of strategic choices | High vs. low | Byrd, Sambamurthy, and Zmud (1995), Grover and Segars (2005), Sabherwal and King (1995), Segars and Grover (1999), Segars, Grover, and Teng (1998) |

*Source:* Adapted from Grover and Segars (2005).

challenge that ought to be addressed by formalization (Reich and Benbasat, 1996). On one hand, formalization should provide adequate structure for identifying a wide variety of opportunities to support strategy and create new strategic opportunities. On the other hand, it should facilitate the rapid resolution of strategic issues to fit environmental conditions (Chi et al., 2005, Earl, 1993; Lederer and Sethi, 1996; Sabherwal and King, 1995).

**Focus**

Although this is often conceptualized as the balance between creativity and control, related notions of innovation and integration are often addressed (Segars and Grover, 1999). An innovative orientation nurtures creativity through systematic search for opportunities and/or threats in the competitive environment (Byrd, Sambamurthy, and Zmud, 1995; Lederer and Sethi, 1996; Sabherwal and King, 1995). The organization then assesses its resource capabilities for opportunity exploitation and threat response. An integrative orientation, on the other hand, tends to focus more on control through coordination and integration of corporate activity. This orientation pertains to controlled diffusion of assets within the organization and is often tied to budgetary systems related to resource allocation and cost performance measures (Byrd, Sambamurthy, and Zmud, 1995; Segars, Grover, and Teng, 1998). An integrative approach is more internally oriented and seeks to leverage an organization's existing resources for competitive actions.

**Flow**

Flow addresses the locus of control or decision rights pertaining to the SISP process, which can be either "top-down" or "bottom-up." The top-down planning flow originates from top management to lower levels of the organization and is characterized by limited participation of lower-level managers in the initiation of the strategic planning process (Chakravarthy, 1987; Segars and Grover, 1999; Segars, Grover, and Teng, 1998). This approach often relegates lower-level managers to the role of plan execution and systems implementation. Bottom-up planning flow is from lower-level managers to top management. It entails high levels of involvement of lower-level managers in the initiation of strategic planning. This planning approach is diffuse, with ideas and proposals coming from several operational and functional managers. Top management orchestrates and integrates the various planning proposals from business units into an overall plan for the organization. Top-down and bottom-up planning flow have similarities with centralized and decentralized IS governance modes, respectively (e.g., see Weill, 2004).

**Participation**

While planning flow addresses the location of SISP planning initiation in the organizational hierarchy, participation is concerned with the breadth of involvement of organizational members in strategic planning (narrow versus broad). Narrow participation profiles entail little involvement or interaction among various functional or operational managers in the SISP process. It is often associated with a "top-down" planning flow (Byrd, Sambamurthy, and Zmud, 1995; Earl, 1993) and is suitable when: (1) lower-level managers lack business or "strategic" knowledge, (2) the number of strategic issues considered in formulating the strategic plan is low, and (3) the issues are stable. In such an environment, the participation of many managers is not necessary and may in fact thwart the examination of alternatives and the reaching of a decision about them (Byrd, Sambamurthy, and Zmud, 1995; Eisenhardt, 1989; Lederer and Sethi, 1996). In contrast, broader participation profiles include many planning participants from a variety of functional and operational areas. It is often associated with a "bottom-up" planning flow and is necessary when environmental uncertainty is high (Das, Zahra, and Warkentin, 1991; Sabherwal and King, 1995).

Table 12.2

**Dimensions of Environmental Uncertainty**

| Dimension | Description | Descriptors | Supporting Literature |
|---|---|---|---|
| Dynamism | The rate and unpredictability of environmental change | High vs. low | Aldrich (1979), Cyert and March (1963), Dess and Beard (1984), Newkirk and Lederer (2006), Starbuck (1976) |
| Complexity | The diversity and interdependencies in environmental factors | More vs. less | Aldrich (1979), Child (1972), Duncan (1972), Newkirk and Lederer (2006), Starbuck (1976), Tung (1979) |
| Munificence | The availability of resources and degree of competition in the external environment | Munificent vs. hostile | Aldrich (1979), Cyert and March (1963), Dess and Beard (1984), Newkirk and Lederer (2006), Starbuck (1976) |

### Consistency

This may be conceptualized in terms of the frequency of planning activities or cycles and evaluation/revision of strategic choices. When SISP is done infrequently, the time frames of strategic plans and planning cycles are likely to be longer (e.g., year to year, or once every six months), and this is sometimes achieved through sporadic face-to-face meetings (Byrd, Sambamurthy, and Zmud, 1995; Earl, 1993; Pyburn, 1983). This is appropriate when strategic issues surrounding IS are relatively few and stable (Premkumar and King, 1994; Sabherwal and King, 1995). However, if this is not the case, then a continuous planning process with frequent meetings, constant communication among planning participants, and frequent assessment and revision of strategic direction are necessary to achieve SISP effectiveness (Das, Zahra, and Warkentin, 1991; Premkumar and King, 1994; Sabherwal and King, 1995). Consistency in SISP process is likely to be important in environments with high levels of uncertainty.

### ENVIRONMENTAL UNCERTAINTY AND ORGANIZATIONAL LEARNING

Uncertainty is the lack of fit between information availability and information requirements for decision making (Daft and Weick, 1984; Galbraith, 1977). In the context of SISP, uncertainty represents the lack of information on which to create IS plans (Newkirk and Lederer, 2006). Uncertainty can be reduced through the acquisition of more information and because of this, Daft and Weick (1984) argued that the main task of the organization is to collect and act upon information from its environment. Thus, constant organizational learning is required in order to resolve uncertainty.

As shown in Table 12.2, environmental uncertainty is commonly conceptualized to consist of three dimensions: dynamism, complexity, and munificence (Dess and Beard, 1984). *Environmental dynamism* creates uncertainty because managers lack full knowledge about environmental change due to rapid and unpredictable changes (Newkirk and Lederer, 2006).

*Complexity* refers to the heterogeneity, diversity, and interdependencies of environmental factors and components (Child, 1972; Duncan, 1972; Tung, 1979). *Heterogeneity* refers to the relative differentiation or variety of environmental factors and components. *Diversity* encompasses the number of factors and components in the environment that must be taken into consideration in decision making, goal setting, and goal attainment. *Interdependencies* comprise the degree of interdependence among environmental factors and components and relate to the problem of manageability of the task environment (Tung, 1979). Complexity can occur in customer behaviors, product lines, and the nature of competition (Miller and Friesen, 1983; Sahberwal and King, 1992; Teo and King, 1997). In addition to lack of full knowledge of the decision environment, complexity also leads to equivocal interpretations of the environmental conditions and outcomes by the various stakeholders (Daft and Weick, 1984).

*Munificence* refers to the degree of benevolence or hostility of the environment. It pertains to both resource availability and degree of competition in the external environment (Miller and Friesen, 1983; Newkirk and Lederer, 2006). Uncertainty arises when managers lack knowledge about the availability of resources and about their competitors.

Organizational theorists emphasize that organizations must adapt to their environment if they are to remain viable (Duncan, 1972). All three dimensions of environmental uncertainty outlined above potentially affect how well organizations use SISP to achieve their objectives. Dynamism implies that SISP plans may easily be rendered obsolete due to rapid and unpredictable changes in the environment. Due to complexity, it may be hard to reach consensus on SISP outcomes in a timely manner because a lot of information needs to be processed and yet this problem is exacerbated by equivocal interpretations of available information. Less munificent (or hostile) environments entail resource scarcity and competitive pressures that make it hard for managers to fully incorporate resource planning or anticipate all competitive actions during the SISP process.

## THE COALIGNMENT OF SISP PROCESS DIMENSIONS

Coalignment is the structure of multiple process dimensions that act collectively as components of a common system, contingent upon the degree of environmental uncertainty (Grover and Segars, 2005; Segars, Grover, and Teng, 1998). Coalignment is related to the concept of fit (Umanath, 2003; Venkatraman, 1989b) and provides greater insight into systems of planning by examining profiles of collective dimensions under different conditions of environmental uncertainty. Several such profiles exist in the literature, including that of Earl (1993), Pyburn (1983), Sabherwal and King (1995), Segars, Grover, and Teng (1998), and Sullivan (1985). A key lesson to be learned about SISP effectiveness from the previous studies is that profiles incorporating aspects of both rationality and adaptability are more effective. Despite this insight, there are a couple of limitations with these studies. First, how the dimensions are conceptualized needs to be redefined. Distinguishing SISP processes as either rational (structured) or incremental (adaptable) implies that rational processes do not adapt at all. They indeed adapt, albeit slowly, and it is more useful to characterize SISP profiles in terms of the degree of adaptation. Second, prior studies develop SISP profiles without explicit treatment of environmental uncertainty. Our analysis explicitly takes into account environmental uncertainty in the development of SISP profiles. As shown in Table 12.3, we reconceptualize SISP profiles in terms of the degree of adaptation and relate these profiles to environmental conditions in which they might be more successful.

We evoke the concept of incremental and flexible (or radical) strategies, which mirrors the concept of radical and incremental innovation (Dewar and Dutton, 1986) and March's (1991) concept of exploration and exploitation in organizational learning. These concepts do not imply the lack of adaptation in one dimension, but rather the difference in the degree of adaptation, being gradual or incremental and less pronounced in one dimension, and rapid or radical and more pronounced in the other dimension. Incremental strategies or plans gradually introduce changes

Table 12.3

**Strategic Information Systems Planning (SISP) Approaches and Coalignment of Process Dimensions**

| SISP approach | Environmental conditions | Coalignment of process dimensions | | | | | |
|---|---|---|---|---|---|---|---|
| | | Comprehensiveness | Formalization | Focus | Flow | Participation | Consistency |
| Incremental | Low dynamism, less complexity, munificent | Low | Low | Control | Top-down | Low | Low |
| Radical | High dynamism, more complexity, hostile | High | High | Creativity | Bottom-up | High | High |

in existing strategies or plans. An incremental SISP process parallels March's (1991) concept of exploitation and includes such things as selection and refinement of existing plans, implementation, execution, and efficiency focus. This approach is suitable for environments with low dynamism, less complexity, and high munificence. Since plans are changed gradually, changes tend to be ad hoc and plans themselves tend to be less comprehensive, less formalized, low in participation and consistency, control-oriented, and tending to flow top-down from senior executives.

Radical strategies or plans on the other hand, are associated with March's (1991) concept of exploration, which is captured by terms such as search, variation, risk taking, experimentation, flexibility, discovery, and innovation. A radical SISP process is suitable for environments with a high degree of uncertainty characterized by high dynamism, more complexity, and low munificence (i.e., great hostility). The high degree of environmental uncertainty requires comprehensive information processing in order to resolve uncertainty. Thus, the SISP process tends to be very comprehensive, requiring high participation and bottom-up flow. Due to the extent of participation, a high level of formalization is also required to streamline the process and coordinate the efforts of the various stakeholders. In order to adapt to changing environmental conditions, the focus is on creativity, and high environmental dynamism implies that the SISP process must be done very consistently (with a high level of frequency or continuously) in order for strategic information systems plans to remain relevant.

## DIMENSIONS OF STRATEGIC INFORMATION SYSTEMS PLANNING EFFECTIVENESS

Using the perspectives of "goal fulfillment" and "improvement in capabilities" as theoretical underpinnings, Segars and Grover (1998) did an extensive review of the IS literature to identify various SISP objectives and any underlying dimensions that provide structure to them. Iterative classifications using a panel of experts led to the identification of four broad dimensions that are reflective of SISP effectiveness: alignment, analysis, cooperation, and improvement in capabilities. These dimensions are summarized in Table 12.4 and are briefly discussed below.

### Alignment

This is the degree to which the information technology mission, objectives, and plans support and are supported by the business mission, objectives, and plans (Reich and Benbasat, 1996). This definition conceptualizes alignment as a state or an outcome (Chan et al., 1997). Reich and Benbasat (2000) point out the duality in alignment, consisting of intellectual dimension (the existence of a high-quality set of interrelated businessIT plans) and social dimension (commitment of the organizational managers to the business and IT mission, objectives, and plans). Thus, the determinants of alignment are likely to be processes, such as communication and planning. Alignment engenders the acquisition and deployment of information technology (IT) that is harmonious with the organization's business needs rather than just existing patterns of IT use within and across organizations.

### Analysis

This is the process by which IS planners seek to identify better ways of operating and competing through the use of information technology (Segars and Grovers, 1998). By focusing on examining how information is used within the organization in light of the developments in the organization's

Table 12.4

**Dimensions of Strategic Information Systems (IS) Planning Effectiveness**

| Dimension | Description | Supporting literature |
|---|---|---|
| Alignment | The close linkage of the IS strategy with business strategy | Grover and Segars (2005), Segars and Grover (1998, 1999), Segars, Grover, and Teng (1998) |
| Analysis | A concerted effort by IS planners to better understand the organization's internal processes, procedures, and technologies | Grover and Segars (2005), Segars and Grover (1998, 1999), Segars, Grover, and Teng (1998) |
| Cooperation | A general agreement among IS planners concerning development priorities, implementation schedules, and managerial responsibilities | Grover and Segars (2005), Segars and Grover (1998, 1999), Segars, Grover, and Teng (1998) |
| Improvement in capabilities | The enhancement in strategic IS planning capabilities as a result of organizational learning | Grover and Segars (2005), Segars and Grover (1998, 1999), Segars, Grover, and Teng (1998) |

*Source:* Adapted from Grover and Segars (2005).

environment, analysis should enable the IS planners to uncover critical development areas and build the needed architecture of integrated systems across the functional boundaries of the organization. This should be a consequence of deep insight emanating from the analysis of the organization's processes, procedures, and technologies.

## Cooperation

This pertains to the general level of agreement among different organizational subgroups concerning IS development priorities, development standards, implementation schedules, decision rights, IT use, and managerial responsibilities. Cooperation is essential in order to reduce potential disagreements and conflict among key coalitions and bases of power within the organization, which ultimately undermine the success of the SISP process. Cooperation may be achieved by creating partnerships between IS and user groups in order to ensure SISP effectiveness (Segars and Grover, 1998).

### Improvement in Capabilities

The organizational learning and adaptation mechanisms should result in an improvement in the SISP process over time. This will be reflected in better analysis and insights into the organization's processes and technologies, higher cooperation and partnership among functional managers and user groups, and better alignment of business and IS strategies (Segars and Grover, 1998).

## PROFILES OF SISP EFFECTIVENESS: FIT AND FITNESS

A profile is related to the systems approach to the concept of fit (Umanath, 2003; Venkatraman, 1989b), whereby fit is viewed as holistic configurations or gestalts of interdependencies among

Table 12.5

**Profiles of Strategic Information Systems Planning (SISP) Effectiveness**

| | Dimensions of SISP effectiveness | | | |
| --- | --- | --- | --- | --- |
| SISP effectiveness profile | Alignment | Analysis | Cooperation | Improvement in capabilities |
| Fit | High | Low | Low | Low |
| Fitness | Low | High | High | High |

factors simultaneously subjected to multiple contingencies. Therefore, SISP profiles refer to the relative positions of organizations with respect to the configurations of the dimensions of SISP effectiveness defined above. Like SISP process dimensions, we suggest two profiles of SISP effectiveness: fit and fitness. These are presented in Table 12.5.

Referring to March's (1991) concept of exploration and exploitation in organizational learning, fit is more closely associated with exploitation while fitness closely pertains to exploration. "Fit" refers to a profile that is reflected by a pattern of SISP effectiveness dimensions that create overall alignment of business and IS strategies. It is a pattern that reflects the exploitation of IS for business advantage under current environmental conditions. We argue that the "fit" profile with its focus on alignment will be high on the alignment dimension only. It is the planning outcome that is a hand-off from the exploration process and reflects decision making by a few managers to achieve quick alignment. However, the fit profile is low on the other three dimensions. Extensive analysis typical of exploratory learning undermines the immediate attainment of fit required to exploit IT capabilities for current business opportunities. In this case, simple analysis is necessary in order to achieve expedited exploitation of business opportunities. Fit is also low on cooperation because expeditious exploitation of business opportunities means that decisions may be vested upon those where the opportunity lies. Furthermore, since this profile is low on analysis, it is also low on improvement of capabilities because limited analysis undermines the learning process needed to achieve improvement in capabilities over time.

"Fitness" is a pattern of SISP effectiveness dimensions most closely associated with the organization's capacity to learn and change to fit new circumstances. Fitness is necessary in order to attain sustained (long-term) business IS alignment in turbulent environments. Since the focus of fitness is on learning, extensive analysis is performed and hence this profile is high on analysis. However, extensive analysis implies that in the short run the degree of alignment between IS and business strategies may be low since fitness involves experimenting with new ideas. Effective learning requires high cooperation and since learning endows the organization with the ability to adapt SIS plans to new environments, fitness is also associated with high levels of improvement in capabilities over time.

Rather than focus our subsequent analysis on the two distinct profiles of fit and fitness, there is a growing recognition that organizations need to coevolve IT and the business (Agarwal and Sambamurthy, 2002). In order to coevolve IT and business in uncertain environments, organizations need both fit and fitness since they need to continuously learn to maintain the *fitness* required to *fit* changing environmental circumstances. In order to achieve this, organizations need a balance between exploitation and exploration activities as March (1991) vividly put:

> Adaptive systems that engage in exploration to the exclusion of exploitation are likely to find that they suffer the costs of experimentation without gaining many of its benefits. They

**Figure 12.1   Interactions Between Fit and Fitness Profiles of Strategic Information Systems Planning Effectiveness**

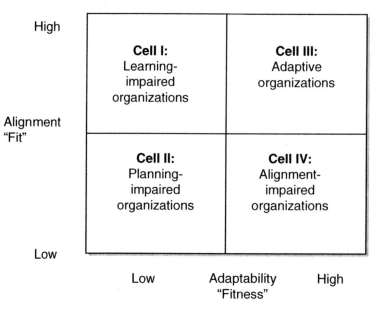

exhibit too many undeveloped new ideas and too little distinctive competence. Conversely, systems that engage in exploitation to the exclusion of exploration are likely to find themselves trapped in suboptimal stable equilibriums. As a result, maintaining an appropriate balance between exploration and exploitation is a primary factor in system survival and prosperity (March, 1991, p. 71).

Therefore, we focus our analysis on the interactions of these two profile dimensions as shown in Figure 12.1. Organizations in *Cell I* are *learning-impaired* and are likely to be trapped in what March (1991) called suboptimal (and temporary) equilibriums. Since they are high on fit, the focus is on alignment of IT and business plans. However, their limited attention to learning implies that they lack the adaptability or fitness needed to maintain congruence with changing environmental conditions. Ultimately, the alignment between IT and business plans and strategies will be eroded as environmental circumstances change. Organizations in *Cell II* are *planning-impaired* since they are weak on both fit and fitness. The planning process is underdeveloped and hence these organizations lack the capacity to streamline IT and business strategies in order to achieve the required alignment. Furthermore, they also lack the organization learning capability needed to attain fitness or adaptability to changing environmental conditions. Organizations in *Cell III* are the *adaptive* ones that have achieved a balance between exploration and exploitation. These organizations have high learning capabilities that endow them with the fitness needed to adapt to changing environmental circumstances. They also have the ability to leverage knowledge and experience from the learning process to align IT and business strategies (i.e., they are high on fit or alignment). Finally, the organizations in *Cell IV* are *alignment-impaired* organizations since they are engaged in too much learning and exploration with little leveraging of the learning outcomes to achieve congruence between business and IT strategies.

In summary, achieving SISP effectiveness can be conceptualized as consisting of the organization's ability to learn effectively given changing environmental conditions (fitness), and its ability to leverage knowledge gleaned from learning to align businessIS strategies under new conditions (fit). To be adaptive, organizations must continuously learn to maintain the *fitness* required to *fit* changing environmental circumstances.

## METHODOLOGY

### Data

The subsequent empirical analysis in this chapter is based on a data set used in prior published work by the authors (Grover and Segars, 2005; Segars and Grover, 1998, 1999; Segars, Grover, and Teng, 1998). The data were collected from a field survey using the East Edition of *The Directory of Top Computer Executives* as a sampling frame. The directory contains the names, titles, addresses, and phone numbers of top computer executives in the eastern half of the United States. From this, a sample of 600 firms in the private sector was chosen at random. The questionnaire used in the survey had items that measured dimensions of the SISP planning process and effectiveness, planning stages, environmental uncertainty, and IT diffusion. The response rate was 43.5 percent for a total of 253 usable responses (readers may refer to the authors' published work cited above for details on the measurement scale and survey implementation).[1]

### Deriving Configurations of SISP Process and Effectiveness Dimensions

Our aim is to use empirical analysis to extract profiles of SISP process dimensions and SISP effectiveness dimensions suggested in the fourth and sixth sections, respectively. While several multivariate statistical approaches can be employed to develop groupings (profiles) across a series of variable measures, cluster analysis is typically utilized to examine patterns in complex variables across organizations (Segars and Grover, 1995, 1999). Although several clustering algorithms exist, Ward's minimum variance criterion was chosen for this analysis based on past practice and its accuracy in identifying clusters in several simulation studies (Punj and Stewart, 1983). The clustering criterion of this technique is minimization of total within-group sums of squares. It employs agglomerative hierarchical clustering whereby objects (in the present case, firms) are iteratively assigned to clusters (or groups) based on how similar they are to existing members across all measures of the strategic planning process. As the clustering algorithm progresses, it eventually joins all objects into a specified number of clusters. While the optimal number of clusters to extract is sometimes an empirical issue, based on the profiles proposed in the fourth and sixth sections, we extract two clusters for SISP process dimensions and four clusters for SISP effectiveness dimensions (based on Figure 12.1).

### Post Hoc Analysis

Since cluster analysis does not incorporate the environmental uncertainty measure, further analysis was done to examine the effect of environmental uncertainty on SISP process profiles. After cluster analysis, based on cluster membership of each case, it was coded "1" if it belonged to the "radical" cluster (profile) and "0" otherwise. Binary logistic regression analysis was performed relating this new dichotomous variable to environmental uncertainty measures. The specific logistic regression equation estimated was of the form specified below:

Table 12.6

**Strategic Information Systems Planning Profiles: Means and Standard Deviations of Planning Process Dimensions**

|  |  | Radical ($n = 90$) | Incremental ($n = 163$) |
|---|---|---|---|
| Comprehensiveness | Mean | 18.99 | 10.55 |
|  | S.D. | 2.24 | 4.94 |
| Formalization | Mean | 21.42 | 12.10 |
|  | S.D. | 2.06 | 4.91 |
| Focus | Mean | 12.35 | 8.35 |
|  | S.D. | 1.17 | 2.26 |
| Flow | Mean | 14.71 | 8.96 |
|  | S.D. | 1.72 | 2.73 |
| Participation | Mean | 21.53 | 12.20 |
|  | S.D. | 1.89 | 4.13 |
| Consistency | Mean | 23.46 | 12.05 |
|  | S.D. | 2.04 | 4.59 |

$$\ln\left(\frac{p}{1-p}\right) = a + bX$$

where

$p$ is the probability of a "1" and
$X$ is the environmental uncertainty measure.

In order to facilitate the interpretation of the results, $\ln(p\,/\,1{-}p)$ can be conveniently expressed as the log(odds), where the odds of being a "1" (in this case, radical profile) can be derived for a given value of the explanatory variable, $X$ (environmental uncertainty in this case).

## RESULTS AND DISCUSSION

### SISP Planning Profiles

Table 12.6 presents the results of cluster analysis using planning process dimensions. The number of cases for the radical profile is 90 (35.6 percent) and for the incremental profile, 163 (64.4 percent). This indicates that a larger proportion of the organizations in the sample are using an incremental approach to SISP. This is not surprising since many organizations are often reluctant to introduce radical and disruptive changes. Instead, they prefer to introduce changes gradually (or incrementally). However, a potential risk of the incremental approach to SISP is that organizations might lock themselves into suboptimal eqilibriums. Included in Table 12.6 are the mean factor scores and standard deviations of the six process dimensions of SISP across the two profiles. As

Figure 12.2  **Strategic Information Systems Planning Process Profiles**

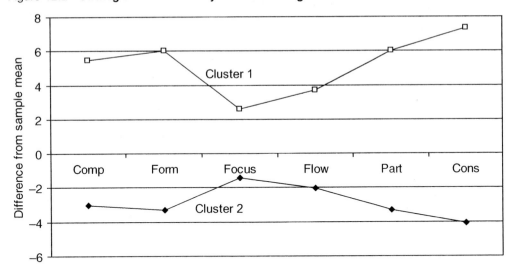

*Notes:* Cluster 1 = radical approach; Cluster 2 = incremental approach; Comp = Comprehensiveness; Form = Formalization; Part = Participation; and Cons = Consistency.

conceptualized, the mean factor scores across the six dimensions of SISP are higher for the radical profile relative to the incremental one. These results imply that relatively fewer organizations in the sample tend to use an SISP approach that is more comprehensive, more formal, more focused on creativity than on control, has a greater emphasis on bottom-up flow, is associated with higher levels of participation in the SISP process, and is more consistent (frequent) in terms of planning activities (i.e., the radical approach).

Figure 12.2 also depicts the two SISP process profiles determined in cluster analysis. These results represent profile deviations from the overall sample means for the six dimensions of SISP. Profile deviation is one of the approaches used to examine the concept of fit in empirical analysis (Venkatraman, 1989b). The two profiles represent deviations from the "average" profile for the entire sample. As can be seen from Figure 12.2, profile 1 (radical approach) is relatively higher on all six dimensions than profile 2 (incremental approach).

Table 12.7 presents the results of the logistic regression using the log(odds) on environmental uncertainty. The estimated coefficient for environmental uncertainty of 0.253 is statistically significant ($p < 0.01$), which translates to an odds ratio of 1.288 (odds ratio = exp($B$)). The odds ratio of 1.288 implies that organizations are 1.288 times more likely to use the radical approach to SISP as environmental uncertainty increases. Since the odds ratio is fairly close to 1, these results imply that organizations are more or less equally likely to use either the radical or incremental approach as environmental uncertainty increases. It may be that organizations need to be ambidextrous (i.e., using both approaches) in order to achieve SISP effectiveness in uncertain environments.

**SISP Effectiveness Profiles**

The results from cluster analysis using SISP effectiveness dimensions are presented in Table 12.8. Nearly half of the cases (123 or 48.62 percent) fall under *Cell III* of Figure 12.1 (*adaptive* organizations). This is encouraging since it implies that nearly half of the organizations in the sample have the capacity to

Table 12.7

**Logistic Regression Results**

| Variable | B | S.E. | Wald | df | Sig. | Exp(B) |
|---|---|---|---|---|---|---|
| Environmental uncertainty | 0.253 | 0.050 | 26.035 | 1 | 0.000 | 1.288 |
| Constant | −3.689 | 0.636 | 33.658 | 1 | 0.000 | 0.026 |

−2 log likelihood = 298.616; Cox and Snell $R^2$ = 0.114; Nagelkerke $R^2$ = 0.157.

Table 12.8

**Means and Standard Deviations of Strategic Information Systems Planning Effectiveness Dimensions Across Profiles**

| Dimension | Statistic | Planning-impaired organizations | Learning-impaired organizations | Alignment-impaired organizations | Adaptive organizations |
|---|---|---|---|---|---|
| Alignment | Mean | 10.23 | 18.14 | 14.85 | 23.37 |
|  | S.D. | 3.19 | 3.16 | 2.95 | 2.95 |
| Analysis | Mean | 6.36 | 14.25 | 20.70 | 21.87 |
|  | S.D. | 2.37 | 2.70 | 3.10 | 3.42 |
| Cooperation | Mean | 9.88 | 14.13 | 19.06 | 29.10 |
|  | S.D. | 2.05 | 3.09 | 3.34 | 2.81 |
| Improvement | Mean | 8.77 | 11.19 | 17.70 | 27.47 |
|  | S.D. | 2.59 | 2.96 | 2.93 | 3.25 |
| Number of cases |  | 45 | 39 | 46 | 123 |
| % of total |  | 17.79 | 15.41 | 18.18 | 48.62 |

adapt the SISP process as environmental conditions change. These organizations are high on both fit and fitness (i.e., across all four dimensions of SISP effectiveness). Also the means of the factor scores reported in Table 12.8 are higher across all SISP effectiveness dimensions for adaptive organizations. The *alignment-impaired* organizations (*Cell IV* of Figure 12.1) are high on analysis, cooperation, and improvement in capabilities. However, they seem to be defined mainly by the analysis dimension since there was a significant positive difference from the "average" profile only in the analysis dimension of alignment-impaired organizations. Alignment-impaired organizations focus mainly on fitness at the expense of fit. While these organizations are also high in cooperation and improvement in capabilities (as conceptualized for the fitness profile in Table 12.5), these levels are not high enough relative to the average profile. Hence alignment-impaired organizations have negative profile deviations for these dimensions. *Learning-impaired organizations* (*Cell I* of Figure 12.1), on the other hand, focus mainly on alignment or "fit" and therefore they are high only in the alignment dimension. These organizations are learning-impaired because compared with adaptive organizations, they are low on analysis, cooperation, and improvement in capabilities. Analysis and cooperation are critical in the learning process required to achieve fitness. Finally, *planning-impaired* organizations (*Cell II* of Figure 12.1) are low on all dimensions compared with other organizations. These organizations may be planning-impaired because they view planning as a process rather than as a strategic exercise.

**Figure 12.3    Deviations of Organizational Profiles for Strategic Information Systems Planning Effectiveness Dimensions**

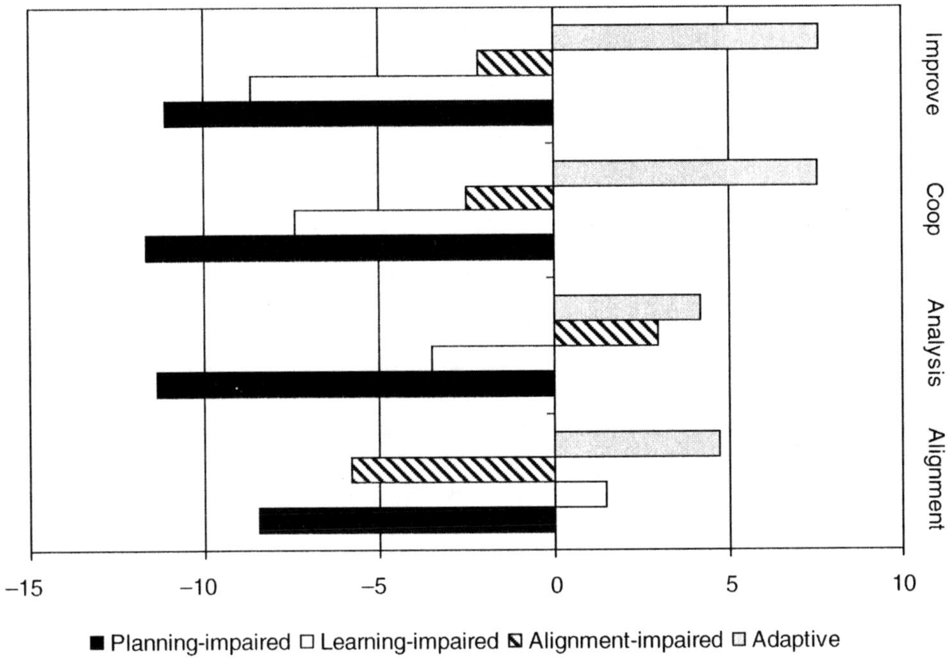

■ Planning-impaired □ Learning-impaired ◨ Alignment-impaired □ Adaptive

Figure 12.3 reinforces the patterns observed in Table 12.8 discussed above. As can be seen from Figure 12.3, adaptive organizations have positive deviations from the average profile for all four dimensions of SISP effectiveness. Learning-impaired organizations have a positive deviation only for the alignment dimension, while alignment-impaired organizations have a positive deviation only for the analysis dimension. The planning-impaired organizations have negative deviations across all four dimensions of SISP effectiveness.

## Discussion

The results largely support conceptualized profiles of both SISP process and SISP effectiveness. The *learning school* discussed by Segars and Grover (1999) is useful in discussing the pattern of results reported above. This school views strategic planning as comprised of knowledge acquisition and application. Thus, the main task of strategic planning entails knowledge creation, acquisition, and transfer in order to modify IT-based initiatives to achieve congruence with changing environmental conditions. The fundamental tenet of planners within the learning school is that strategy emerges as a result of formal and continuous reconciliation of ongoing initiatives throughout the organization and associated opportunities within the competitive context. Institutionalizing the gathering and transfer of knowledge creates a learning organization committed to continuous planning in order to better identify avenues of innovation and adaptation needed for effective competition. An ongoing superstructure of planning activity helps in the reconciliation of the evolving strategic planning processes. In order to achieve this, the activity of planning is distributed to all levels of the organization, with orchestration by senior management. The learning school resembles Earl's (1993) "organizational" approach to SISP.

In line with March's (1991) concept of exploration in organizational learning, planning behavior within the learning school seems best described as an eclectic blend of systematic problem solving, strategic experimentation, formal reconciliation, and efficient knowledge transfer. Teams consisting of IS staff and members of other functional areas employ scientific methods for data collection and analysis in order to generate fact-based scenarios of current IT needs and the effectiveness of past planning efforts in meeting organizational needs. The insights gleaned from this practice are used to continuously refine priorities as well as improve the process for strategic planning. This is complemented by the process of experimentation, which involves a deliberate process of acting, determining what works, reconciling, and retaining desired actions. It is important to note that the effectiveness of the learning school depends on efficient transfer of knowledge, which ensures that the right people get the right knowledge at the right time. In case of explicit knowledge, organization portals and knowledge repositories are often utilized for knowledge dissemination. The ultimate outcome of the learning activities is the coevolution of strategy and implementation activities sustained by a shared consensus for action.

The above description better describes the *adaptive organizations* profile of Figure 12.1 and Table 12.8. The adoption of a learning philosophy tends to result in a profile of planning activity that is extremely adaptive to changing organizational and environmental conditions. Constant evaluation of planning outcomes and planning processes tends to produce high levels of alignment between business and corporate strategy as well as improvement in planning over time. Structured problem solving and experimentation through the use of cross-functional teams tend to produce high levels of understanding regarding organizational processes and also to create coalitions of support for new IS initiatives.

Furthermore, consistent with the pattern of the six dimensions of SISP process for the *radical* profile, high levels of comprehensiveness reflect the extensive efforts of learning that firms exert to acquire knowledge. This knowledge can take the form of skills, insights, or innovative relationships that aid the organization in better understanding the competitive and technological environment. High levels of formalization and a creativity focus reflect the need to structure problem solving and yet allow a degree of creativity that engenders novel solutions to problems. Furthermore, broader participation implies that strategies can emerge from top-level executives as well as from a collective group of individuals throughout the hierarchy. In turn, emergent strategies tend to develop in many conventional and nonconventional ways as individuals or coalitions interact, mutually adjust, learn from each other, conflict, and eventually develop consensus. Therefore, process dimensions of broad participation and high consistency seem necessary for supporting the institutional availability and reconciliation of strategic knowledge.

Why then do all organizations not follow the learning school? A possible answer could be that the learning school requires enormous amounts of financial and time resources for the planning effort. For instance, performance assessment requires substantial amounts of managerial time, and experimental planning requires finances, despite lack of assurance of success. Perhaps organizations not following this school ought to rationalize their investments in learning in real options logic since even though they may not have an immediate payoff, they can create opportunities for the future and also offer managerial flexibility. The most important metric of success seems to be continuous improvement through a process of formalized benchmarking and controlled experimentation, rather than just cost considerations.

Less successful organizations in terms of SISP effectiveness seem to be following other schools of thought. Those using the *incremental* approach to the SISP process seem to be following the political school discussed by Segars and Grover (1999). This school represents strategic planning with limited formal structure, participation, or reconciliation. The central theme of this school tends to be strategy making through bargaining and negotiation. Power and political means are used to achieve a desired outcome. Therefore, the primary role of the planner is that of a negotiator or broker between organizational interests. However, more often than not, the development of deliberate strategies is difficult (Segars and Grover, 1999). This is primarily due to the tendency among planners to dispute rather than share strategic perspectives. The convergence of actions into patterns that are characteristic of the learning school is also difficult because the bargaining process is haphazard, rewarding different strategic players at different times. However, consistent with firms identified by Earl (1993) as following an "administrative approach," successful strategic plans may emerge from the political school, usually in the aftermath of a power struggle.

Since it is parochial in nature, the process structure of the political school reinforces the beliefs and behaviors of the key planning participants. High levels of comprehensiveness and formalization are not required because planning issues arise primarily through the informal opinions and impressions of key organizational players. Since political capital rather than financial capital is an important driver within this school, narrow participation, a control focus and very little consistency are found in the process structure. The philosophy and planning structure behind the political school support IS managers as they gather opinions and negotiate acceptable courses of action. Various conversations and known opinions held by key organizational coalitions are documented, as is often done in the systems analysis process.

Generally low levels of success are associated with all measures of planning effectiveness for the firms following the political school. *This is consistent with the planning-impaired organizations cluster.* Constant bargaining thwarts alignment of the IS function with the larger strategic goals of the organization and the initiation of efforts to systematically analyze the business and its strategic needs. In turn, project development and management tend to be a series of reactions to power bases inside and outside the IS function. This phenomenon generates allies as well as pockets of resistance that can reduce cooperation with strategic initiatives and divide rather than unite organizational constituencies. However, on occasion, political maneuvering can be very effective in removing well-entrenched forms of resistance and may be vital in securing funding and other forms of organizational support for IS initiatives. Overall, a climate of politics-based strategic planning typically results in planning outcomes far below those desired, as the parochial interests of departments and individuals are placed above those of the company in developing and prioritizing strategic IS-based initiatives.

The incremental approach and other profiles of SISP effectiveness also have some elements of the design and planning schools. In the design school, the fundamental tenet is that strategic planning is a conceptual process in which a strategic visionary analyzes and then reconciles organizational capabilities with competitive opportunity. The design school places greater emphasis on decision-making speed to quickly identify and launch innovative and adaptive technological initiatives. Therefore, rather than seeking to create a set of detailed plans and implementation priorities, the desired outcome of the planning process is typically a vision statement that serves as a guide for the organizational effort. In essence, the design school operates in the realm of visions, concepts, and invention. Planning is vested in the hands of a few visionaries, and correspondence among different organizational members and documentation of planning efforts tend to be informal. This is consistent with the *learning-impaired* organizations cluster.

In line with an *incremental* approach to SISP, the design school is associated with moderate levels of comprehensiveness, formality, and creativity, top-down flow focus, and moderate levels of participation and consistency. Strategy emerges mainly through intuition, experience, and informal knowledge of corporate events. Furthermore, the design school with its top-management orientation tends to result in strategic actions that are well aligned with larger organizational goals and objectives. However, its potential downside is that the tendency to oversimplify very complex planning issues may miss emerging complexities in the organizational and/or external environment (learning-impaired organizations).

In sum, the underlying beliefs of the design school suggest that top executives "know best" and should therefore be charged with charting the strategic direction of the IS organization. Thus, the senior planner assumes the role of a visionary. Furthermore, the underlying structure of planning reflects a top-down flow of executive strategy making that is neither based on finding optimal courses of action nor overly confined by policy and procedure. While these initiatives provide a context for realizing alignment, they tend to be centered on business rather than technology issues and may sacrifice detailed understanding of business processes and technologies.

Strategic planning within the planning school is a controlled, conscious, and formalized process decomposed into distinct steps, each delineated by checklists and supported by known tools and techniques. In contrast to the broad vision statements that characterize the outcomes of the design school, detailed sets of objectives, budgets, tasks, and operating plans emerge from the strategic planning activities of the planning school. However, the planning school is associated with less than satisfactory levels of alignment and cooperation. The planning school seems to define the *alignment-impaired* organizations. Since a significant amount of organizational resources (time, money, and training) are devoted to planning activities within the planning school, it implicitly promotes activity planning and tends to resemble the overall corporate budgeting process. Due to its activity planning orientation, a primary drawback of this highly rational philosophy is that planning activity may become dysfunctional due to complexity. In addition, the velocity of planning cycles can become inordinately slow, resulting in reactive rather than proactive strategic actions. To alleviate these problems, the organization may resort to *incremental* strategy by benchmarking off from previous plans. Furthermore, in contrast to the design school, the senior planner tends to approve rather than create strategic plans. The outcome of these planning exercises is a comprehensive set of activities and benchmarks that reflect strategic intent and provide guidance to the implementation efforts of the IS organization.

## IMPLICATIONS

The results of this analysis suggest that planning profiles are distinguishable across dimensions of the SISP process as well as across dimensions of SISP effectiveness. Now that reliance on IT has increased to the level where a lack of IT agility and responsiveness can create a competitive disadvantage, the traditional alignment frameworks and models that focus on "fit" only are ineffective. In order to attain sustained businessIT alignment in turbulent environments, organizations also need to attain "fitness"—the capacity to learn and change to fit new circumstances. The outcomes of SISP effectiveness may be rooted in whether organizations are following the radical or incremental approach to the SISP process. Figure 12.4 provides further categorization of organizations based on their SISP effectiveness.

On the top right quadrant of Figure 12.4, organizations that score high on both fit and fitness dimensions are able to achieve *coevolutionary adaptation* of businessIT strategies to achieve congruence with changing environmental conditions. This is where all organizations should aspire to be. Organizations in this quadrant score high on fitness because they are proactive about organizational learning and have mechanisms in place that facilitate the learning process. This is not just a measurement of how much learning they do, it is about how well they do it (effectiveness). Furthermore, they do not learn just for the sake of learning—these organizations actively embrace learning outcomes and enthusiastically look for ways to adapt strategic IS plans. Since

Figure 12.4    **Profiles of Organizations Based on Their Performance on Fit and Fitness**

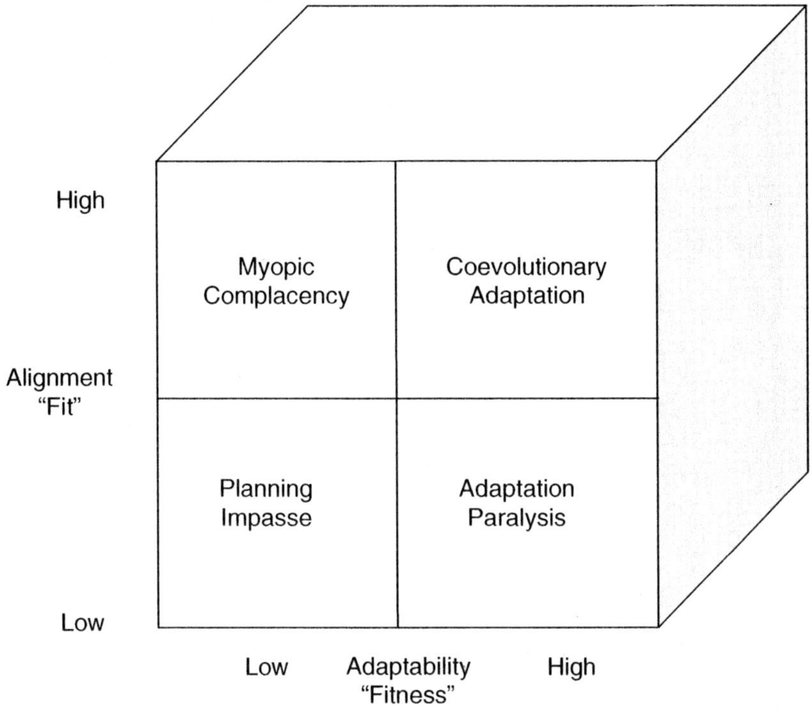

they are proactive about maintaining businessIT alignment in changing circumstances, they also have high levels of fit.

What differentiates organizations in the bottom-right quadrant of Figure 12.4 is that while they engage in active learning and attain levels of fitness as high as those for organizations in the top-right quadrant, they fail to leverage their learning to adapt strategic IS plans to maintain businessIT congruence in changing environmental conditions. These organizations suffer from *adaptation paralysis* even though they are actively engaged in learning. This may be a case of "strategic drift," trying anything without some overarching objective—almost like "hope" as a strategy. This may be an outcome of two factors. First, these organizations may be engaged in too much exploratory learning and thus do not take time to synthesize learning initiatives into action-able strategic IS plans (or by the time they synthesize actionable outcomes, change has already taken place). The implication here is that these organizations ought to balance learning initiatives and synthesis of learning outcomes. Otherwise, by engaging in "rapid-fire" exploratory learning, they may be doing too much of a good thing. Second, these organizations may be suffering from adaptation paralysis because they do not have the organizational buy-in or acceptance to act on learning outcomes. The culprits here are often lack of a strong and clear management directive to implement change and an organizational culture that is defensive rather than open. There may also be too many stakeholders with conflicting agendas or one naysayer who has not been dealt with appropriately and who derails the effort. Or it may just be a case of organizational disconnect because the learning unit is separate from the planning unit. What happens typically is that the organization gets bogged down in the learning process and loses sight of the ultimate goal. The result: learning for the sake of learning. The implication here is that to leverage their learning, organizations need commitment to change and to nurture organizational culture and structure that is conducive to and supportive of change.

Organizations in the top-left quadrant of Figure 12.4 are in a state of *myopic complacency.* They have strategic IS planning capabilities that work well in static environments. As a result, while they have a high level of fit, it is transient since they have not invested heavily in learning. Should environmental conditions change, they do not have the fitness required to rapidly adapt to fit the new circumstances. Ultimately, environmental turbulence will tend to push them to the bottom-left quadrant since they will lose their high level of fit too. The advice for these organizations is not to be complacent in their current situation, as changing environmental circumstances will erode the fit between their business and IT strategies. They need to begin investing in organizational learning so that they can maintain fitness to enable them to adapt to change.

The organizations in the final bottom-left quadrant of Figure 12.4 are plagued with *planning impasse.* They have neither the fit nor the fitness that might help alleviate the planning problem. This may be the outcome of an immature and ad hoc planning system that lacks the adaptability needed in turbulent environments. These organizations may be viewing planning as a process rather than a strategic exercise. They face a tougher challenge since they need to develop capabilities simultaneously in the two dimensions of fit and fitness.

## CONCLUSION

This study attempts to take a major step in conceptualizing the SISP process and examining its effectiveness. Two profiles of both SISP process and SISP effectiveness are first developed conceptually and then supported with empirical analysis. The six dimensions of the SISP process identified in the previous literature are grouped into radical and incremental profiles both conceptually and empirically based on the pattern they display. Similarly, the four dimensions of SISP effectiveness from prior literature are first grouped into fit and fitness profiles, from which four types of organizations emerge based on a two-by-two interaction between the fit and fitness profiles. The patterns from conceptual analysis are supported by empirical results.

Overall, this analysis has made it possible to generate a broader understanding of planning process and effectiveness profiles. The results suggest that the process for strategic IS planning may be conceptualized as highly comprehensive, formalized, based on creativity, bottom-up, participative, and consistent. It may also be conceptualized as exhibiting the opposite extremes. Considered together, these lines of inquiry strongly suggest that effective planning approaches tend to emphasize emergent/learning/evolutionary process structures. Such structures may be in stark contrast to traditional planning within organizations. With the current competitive environment characterized by rapid change, the strong recognition of the strategic potential of IT, high opportunity, high expectations, rapid technological obsolescence, and global competitive pressure, the implications of these results are important for fostering robust knowledge gathering and effective forging of strategic intent.

Thus, organizations need to think in terms of both fit and fitness if they are to realign their businessIT plans and thereby avoid long periods of underperformance. Since the competitive environment is continually evolving, they should consider fit as requiring constant monitoring and regular updating, rather than intermittent interventions. The terms *fit* and *fitness* imply that success in dealing with rapidly changing environments is not solely about an organization's aim to align its business and IT strategies (fit), but also about its ability to learn and adapt to changing circumstances (fitness). Reinforcing March's (1991) suggestion, *maintaining an appropriate balance between exploration and exploitation is a primary factor in organizational survival and prosperity.*

## NOTE

1. The data set for this analysis was reproduced using Monte Carlo methods by sampling from a normal distribution using our knowledge of the mean and standard deviation reported in the authors' published work. We proceeded with our analysis after confirming all of the previously published results to ensure that our data generation process does not bias the pattern of results.

## REFERENCES

Agarwal, R., and Sambamurthy, V. 2002. Principles and models for organizing the IT function. *MIS Quarterly Executive,* 1, 1, 1–16.

Aldrich, H.E. 1979. *Organizations and Environments.* Englewood Cliffs, NJ: Prentice Hall.

Byrd, T.A.; Sambamurthy, V.; and Zmud, W.R. 1995. An examination of IT planning in a large, diversified public organization. *Decision Sciences,* 26, 49–73.

Chakravarthy, B.S. 1987. On tailoring a strategic planning system to its context: some empirical evidence. *Strategic Management Journal,* 8, 517–534.

Chakravarthy, B.S., and Doz, Y. (eds.) 1992. Strategy process: managing corporate self-renewal. *Strategic Management Journal,* 13 (Special Summer Issue), 26–39.

Chan, Y.E.; Huff, S.L.; Barclay, D.W.; and Copeland, D.G. 1997. Business strategy orientation, information systems orientation and strategic alignment. *Information Systems Research,* 8, 2, 125–150.

Chi, L.; Jones, K.G.; Lederer, A.L.; Li, P.; Newkirk, H.E.; and Sethi, V. 2005. Environmental assessment in strategic information systems planning. *International Journal of Information Management,* 25, 253–269.

Child, J. 1972. Organization structure, environment and performance: the role of strategic choice. *Sociology,* 6, 1–22.

Choe, Jong-Min. 2003. The effect of environmental uncertainty and strategic applications of IS on a firm's performance. *Information & Management,* 40, 4, 257–268.

Cyert, R.M., and March, J.G. 1963. *A Behavioral Theory of the Firm.* Englewood Cliffs, NJ: Prentice Hall.

Daft, R.L., and Weick, K.E. 1984. Toward a model of organizations as interpretation systems. *Academy of Management Review,* 9, 2, 284–295.

Das, S.R.; Zahra, S.A.; and Warkentin, M.E. 1991. Integrating the content and process of strategic MIS planning with competitive strategy. *Decision Sciences,* 22, 953–984.

Dess, G., and Beard, D. 1984. Dimensions of organizational task environment. *Administrative Science Quarterly,* 29, 1, 52–73.

Dewar, R.D., and Dutton, J.E. 1986. The adoption of radical and incremental innovations: an empirical analysis. *Management Science,* 32, 11, 1422–1433.

Duncan, R.B. 1972. Characteristics of organizational environments and perceived environmental uncertainty. *Administrative Science Quarterly,* 17, 3, 313–327.

Earl, M.J. 1993. Experiences in strategic information systems planning. *MIS Quarterly,* 17, 1–24.

Eisenhardt, K.M. 1989. Making fast strategic decisions in high-velocity environments. *Academy of Management Journal,* 32, 543–576.

Fredrickson, J.W., and Iaquinto, A.L. 1989. Inertia and creeping rationality in strategic decision processes. *Academy of Management Journal,* 32, 516–542.

Galbraith, J. 1977. *Designing Complex Organizations.* Reading, MA: Addison-Wesley.

Grover, V., and Segars, A.H. 2005. An empirical evaluation of stages of strategic information systems planning: patterns of process design and effectiveness. *Information & Management,* 42, 761–779.

Hart, S.L. 1992. An integrative framework for strategy-making processes. *Academy of Management Review,* 17, 327–351.

Hirschheim, R., and Sabherwal, R. 2001. Detours in the path toward strategic information systems alignment. *California Management Review,* 44, 1, 87–109.

Janis, I.L., and Mann, L. 1977. *Decision-Making.* New York: Free Press.

Kukalis, S. 1991. Determinants of strategic planning systems in large organizations: a contingency approach. *Journal of Management Studies,* 28, 143–160.

Lederer, A.L., and Sethi, V. 1996. Key prescriptions for strategic information systems planning. *Journal of Management Information Systems,* 13, 35–62.

March, J.G. 1991. Exploration and exploitation in organizational learning. *Organization Science,* 2, 1 (Special Issue: Organizational Learning: Papers in Honor of [and by] James G. March), 71–87.

Miller, D., and Friesen, P.H. 1983. Strategy-making and the environment: the third link. *Strategic Management Journal*, 4, 3, 221–235.

Newkirk, H.E., and Lederer, A.L. 2006. Incremental and comprehensive strategic information systems planning in an uncertain environment. *IEEE Transactions on Engineering Management*, 53, 3, 380–394.

Pollalis, Y.A. 2003. Patterns of co-alignment in information-intensive organizations: business performance through integration strategies. *International Journal of Information Management*, 23, 469–492.

Porter, M. 2001. Strategy and the Internet. *Harvard Business Review*, 79, 3, 63–78.

Premkumar, G., and King, W.R. 1994. Organizational characteristics and information systems planning: an empirical study. *Information Systems Research*, 5, 75–109.

Punj, G., and Stewart, D.W. 1983. Cluster analysis in marketing research: review and suggestions for application. *Journal of Marketing Research*, 20, 134–148.

Pyburn, P.J. 1983. Linking the MIS plan with corporate strategy: an exploratory study. *MIS Quarterly*, 7, 1–14.

Raghunathan, B., and Raghunathan, T.S. 1989. Relationship of the rank of information systems executive to the organizational role and planning dimensions of information systems. *Journal of Management Information Systems*, 6, 111–126.

Ramanujam, V., and Venkatraman, N. 1987. Planning system characteristics and planning effectiveness. *Strategic Management Journal*, 8, 453–468.

Reich, B.H., and Benbasat, I. 1996. Measuring the linkage between business and information technology objectives. *MIS Quarterly*, 20, 453–468.

———. 2000. Factors that influence the social dimension of alignment between business and information technology objectives. *MIS Quarterly*, 24, 1, 81–113.

Sabherwal, R., and King, W.R. 1992. Decision processes for developing strategic application for information systems: a contingency approach. *Decision Sciences*, 23, 4, 917–943.

———. 1995. An empirical taxonomy of the decision-making processes concerning strategic applications of information systems. *Journal of Management Information Systems*, 11, 1, 177–214.

Sambamurthy, V.; Venkatraman, S.; and DeSanctis, G. 1993. The design of information technology planning systems for varying organizational contexts. *European Journal of Information Systems*, 2, 23–35.

Sambamurthy, V.; Zmud, W.R.; and Byrd, T.A. 1994. The comprehensiveness of IT planning processes: a contingency approach. *Journal of Information Technology Management*, 5, 1–10.

Segars, A.H., and Grover, V. 1995. The industry level impact of information technology: an empirical analysis of three industries. *Decision Sciences*, 26, 337–368.

———. 1998. Strategic information systems planning success: an investigation of the construct and its measurement. *MIS Quarterly*, 22, 139–163.

———. 1999. Profiles of strategic information systems planning. *Information Systems Research*, 10, 3, 199–232.

Segars, A.H.; Grover, V.; and Teng., J.T.C. 1998. Strategic planning for information systems: the coalignment of planning system design and its relationship with planning system success. *Decision Sciences*, 29, 2, 303–340.

Starbuck, W.H. 1976. Organizations and their environments. In M.D. Dunnette (ed.), *Handbook of Industrial and Organizational Psychology*. Chicago: Rand McNally, pp. 1069–1123.

Sullivan, C.H. 1985. Systems planning in the information age. *Sloan Management Review*, 26, 3–12.

Teo, T.S.H., and King, W.R. 1997. Integration between business planning and information systems planning: an evolutionary-contingency perspective. *Journal of Management Information Systems*, 14, 1, 185–214.

Tung, R.L. 1979. Dimensions of organizational environments: an exploratory study of their impact on organizational structure. *Academy of Management Journal*, 22, 4, 672–693.

Umanath, N.S. 2003. The concept of contingency beyond "It depends": Illustrations from IS research stream. *Information & Management*, 40, 551–562.

Venkatraman, N. 1989a. Strategic orientation of business enterprises: the construct, dimensionality, and measurement. *Management Science*, 35, 942–962.

———. 1989b. The concept of fit in strategy research: toward verbal and statistical correspondence. *Academy of Management Review*, 14, 3, 423–444.

Venkatraman, N., and Prescott, J.E. 1990. Environment-strategy coalignment: an empirical test of its performance implications. *Strategic Management Journal*, 11: 1–23.

Wang, E.T.G., and Tai, J.C.F. 2003. Factors affecting information systems planning effectiveness: organizational contexts and planning systems dimensions. *Information & Management*, 40, 287–303.

Weill, P. 2004. Don't just lead, govern: how top-performing firms govern IT. *MIS Quarterly Executive*, 3, 1, 1–17.

# PART III

## INFORMATION SYSTEMS INVESTMENT PLANNING

CHAPTER 13

# INFORMATION SYSTEMS PLANNING

## The Search for Potential Value

MICHAEL J. DAVERN

*Abstract:* The search for projects of potential value is the first step in information systems planning. It is also one of the most challenging. In this chapter, six cases, drawn from a range of studies over the past decade, are examined to illustrate success and failure in finding, creating, recognizing, and acting on potential value. Reflecting on each case, specific insights into the search for potential value are identified. Issues of organizational capital are shown to be critical, as is the need to "experiment" and take managed risks to gather information on value potential. The metaphor of real options is used to synthesize the various reflections and insights into the search for potential value in information systems planning.

*Keywords:* Business Value of IT, Potential Value, Real Options, Complementary Investments

Information systems planning logically begins by identifying what projects to pursue. It is a search for projects of potential value. The potential value of an information systems project is a measure of the opportunity offered by a project. For example, the potential value of a customer relationship management system is driven by the opportunity it provides to increase market share and consequently profitability. Potential value is a measure of the capacity of a project to deliver value, across a range of levels of analysis (business process, firm, market) in both tangible and intangible forms (Davern and Kauffman, 2000). In practice, this value may not always be fully realized. Conversion contingencies (Kauffman and Weill, 1989), such as critical complementary investments (Brynjolfsson and Hitt, 1998; Brynjolfsson, Hitt, and Yang, 2002; Brynjolfsson and Yang, 1997; Davern and Kauffman, 2000) in user training and process redesign, can definitively affect whether potential value is realized or not. But these are matters of implementation that can be planned for once it is established that a project has sufficient potential value to warrant further investigation and investment. The search for potential value is the starting point in planning an organization's portfolio of information systems projects.

The search for potential value raises several questions of interest to both researchers and practitioners:

1. How does a business find, create, or recognize potential value?
2. Why do some businesses fail to recognize or act on the potential value in a project?
3. How can decision makers plan their portfolio of projects to assist in finding high potential value projects?

There is no "silver bullet" for solving the problem of the search for potential value. Indeed, we should hardly expect one, given the lack of a "silver bullet" for the relatively more structured task of developing software solutions for which the potential value has already been established (Brooks, 1987). Like most difficult organizational problems, the search for potential value does not have a "solution" per se. Rather, it requires an organization to put in place a process that will hopefully lead to the resolution of the problem. As Smith (1989, p. 967) notes, the prescriptive value of a model of problem solving "comes less from saying 'Do this next,' and more from saying 'Do this in this way.'" The approach adopted in this chapter is to address the "problem" of the search for potential value as thus similarly process focused (i.e., the "way" to search for potential value). To this end, six illustrative cases are examined to provide insight into questions 1 and 2 above. The insights are then synthesized together using the lens of real options analysis, to address question 3 above.

## ILLUSTRATING THE SEARCH FOR POTENTIAL VALUE—SIX CASES

The cases have been selected from organizations studied in an ongoing program of related research over the past ten years (e.g., Davern and Kauffman 1998, 2000; Davern, Mantena, and Stohr, 2008; Davern and Wilkin, 2004, 2006, forthcoming; Davern, Stagnitti, and Ferguson, 2006; Parkes, 2004; Parkes, Davern, and Pan, 2007). They have been specifically selected as exemplifying different scenarios in the search for potential value: *finding potential value, believing in potential value, creating potential value, selling potential value, denying potential value,* and *missing out on potential value.* These different scenarios are by no means intended to be exhaustive or comprehensive, rather the objective here is to illustrate the variety of ways in which an organization can succeed or fail in the search for potential value (thereby providing insight into questions 1 and 2 above). Furthermore, the goal is not to precisely categorize or label each case, but rather to provide valid interpretations of a range of cases that are illustrative of the variety of scenarios that occur as organizations search for potential value.

In each case, the relevant data sources are identified and the implications for practice are discussed. Where appropriate, the reader is referred to the relevant full study or studies for details of data collection methods and bases for the summary descriptions presented here. Pseudonyms have been employed to protect the confidentiality of the organizations.

### Case 1—Alpha: Finding Potential Value

*Organization*

Alpha was a subsidiary of a large multinational conglomerate (Alpha has since been broken up and sold to partners in the various countries in which it operated). Alpha was an independent information technology (IT) sales and service company, originally set up to support the conglomerate. Alpha subsequently expanded to become a value-added reseller of computer equipment and technology services to corporate customers.

*Data Source*

Data for this case were obtained from individual interviews and discussions with the chief information officer (CIO) of Alpha, the senior business analyst, the senior technical analyst, and the principal external consultant on the project described below.

*Case Description*

In the mid-1990s Alpha faced a highly competitive market. The CIO of Alpha was looking to data warehousing as a foundation for business intelligence tools to combat the increased competition. However, Alpha's CIO faced a problem common to large infrastructure projects, namely, how to justify the potential value of the project. As is typical of infrastructure projects, much of the value lay in the analytic applications that could be built on top of the data warehouse infrastructure. The potential value of the data warehouse was contingent on the applications that could take advantage of it, but assessing the potential value of the applications relied on the existence of the data warehouse.

Alpha resolved the problem by finding value in the data warehouse itself. Alpha's clients were large multidivisional corporations, and Alpha organized its sales teams around the different divisions of its clients. This ensured that Alpha's sales and service staff understood well the client's domain of application, rather than simply the technology. It also reflected Alpha's heritage as an outgrowth of an internal group of a multidivisional conglomerate. This structure had resulted in disparate databases supporting different sales divisions. As a value-added reseller of computer equipment, Alpha was eligible for sizable rebates from manufacturers based on the volume of equipment Alpha sold to each customer. However, because of the disparate databases and different sales divisions, Alpha was unable to substantiate the volume of equipment from any given manufacturer sold to the many different divisions of a given customer, and thus obtain the rebates. The introduction of a data warehouse offered the potential to integrate the necessary information. Alpha would then be able to claim the valuable rebates, which were expected (and later proved) to exceed the cost of developing the data warehouse. Alpha had been successful in *finding* this nonobvious potential value of the project.

*Implications for Practice*

The case of Alpha illustrates the importance of looking for indirect sources of value. There may be sufficient potential value in the side benefits of a project to justify it. The challenge here is that indirect benefits are often difficult to identify a priori. For example, Lucas (1999) makes this very point with respect to the sale of airline reservation systems to travel agents—a huge benefit that was not originally envisioned in the development of computerized reservation systems.

**Case 2—Beta: Believing in Potential Value**

*Organization*

Beta is a health maintenance organization of around 10,000 employees, and over 650,000 insured members. Based in the United States, the company has been in operation for some fifty years.

*Data Source*

The data for this case were obtained from interviews with the CIO and the principal consultant on the project described below.

*Case Description*

Like Alpha, Beta was seeking the benefits of a large-scale data warehousing project to integrate the many disparate data systems in the organization. The size of the project required approval from Beta's board of directors. The project was a nontrivial outlay for an organization operating in an industry almost obsessed with cost control. As a health maintenance organization, Beta had a board of directors heavily composed of experienced and qualified medical practitioners. Thus, the executive decision makers considering the data warehousing project also had substantial "frontline" experience with the day-to-day operations of the organization (i.e., the delivery of health care services). This gave Beta executives a rare insight into how the integrated data warehouse would support the management and operations of the organization. With their experience from the frontline, Beta executives were, in the words of the data warehousing consultant advising on the project, able to "see the vision" of the potential benefits of the project. Consequently, there was relatively little in the way of formal (financial) justification of the project—Beta decision makers quite simply *believed* in the potential value it offered.

### Implications for Practice

Beta's case illustrates the potential of user involvement not simply in the development of systems, but also ex ante in understanding the value that they provide. It reinforces the notion that the value is not in information technology per se but in the application of information technology in a given task domain.

### Case 3—Gamma: Creating Potential Value

### Organization

Gamma is an alliance of over thirty public hospitals and health care providers in a regional area of Australia covering 60,000 square kilometers. Gamma was formed in the late 1990s to aid in the development of the effective and efficient use of IT by alliance members.

### Data Source

Gamma is the industry partner in a large-scale multiyear government-funded academic research project assessing the economic and quality of care impacts of video conferencing in health care (Davern, Stagnitti, and Ferguson, 2006). The case description draws on notes from numerous meetings held between Gamma and the research team, as well as internal reports to Gamma management, external reports to funding agencies, and survey and machine log data of usage of the video-conferencing technology.

### Case Description

In 2005, Gamma began a rollout of a "virtual services" project, which sought to use video-conferencing technology over an existing broadband network to improve patient care and service delivery in the rural and regional areas covered by Gamma members (Davern, Stagnitti, and Ferguson, 2006). It was thought that the technology would allow greater access to a broader range of health services without the need for travel (either by patient or health practitioner). Gamma members had substantial vehicle fleets and health practitioners were required to travel extensively throughout its rural catchment. The total cost of the two-year rollout was budgeted at nearly AUD$3 million, of which roughly one-third was provided by Gamma members and two-thirds were to be provided by a state government technology infrastructure grant. Interestingly, in the sixty-two-page justification for government funding, there was very little quantifiable estimate of benefits. The quantifiable benefits that were described were either practically unmeasurable and/or based on pure supposition rather than any detailed analyses. As an example, 50 percent improvement in patient well-being was one such target, but there was no uniformly applied measure of patient well-being. Transport costs savings of 30 percent were also suggested, but no basis was provided for the estimate.

In discussions with the chief information officer of Gamma (who championed the project) it was apparent that Gamma viewed the project as an "experiment" that would be subject to ex post assessment of benefit. Indeed, Gamma collaborated with a university research team to provide consultation and reporting in relation to this ex post assessment (Davern, Stagnitti, and Ferguson, 2006). Initially, it appeared that Gamma was adopting a "build it and they would come" mentality. For example, the technology rollout was almost complete before Gamma began to work with alliance members to define the organizational processes of how the technology was to be put to use. However, a deeper analysis revealed that the CIO of Gamma was working well beyond a "build it and they would come" approach. Rather, the CIO was pushing a "build it and we will make them come" approach. This was evidenced by his active lobbying of the chief executive officers of alliance members to have them reduce their vehicle fleets by at least 10 percent within the first full year of the benefits assessment. This would drive usage of the technology and ensure that there were sufficient early economic benefits deriving from the project to justify it ex post. Gamma's CIO essentially created a self-fulfilling prophecy. While the project planning lacked robust assessment of potential, the lobbying actions of the CIO sought to create potential value for the technology. The CIO sought to build the need, not just roll out the technology itself.

*Implications for Practice*

Gamma's case provides an example of an "experimental" justification of potential value, followed by active management to create value. It was clearly difficult to assess a priori the potential value of Gamma's virtual services project. However, the high potential upside on success is evidenced by the willingness of not just Gamma to fund the project but also of external competitive grant agencies (both for the technology infrastructure and for a research team to study the rollout [Davern, Stagnitti, and Ferguson, 2006]). Having justified the potential upside of the "experiment," Gamma's CIO took action to ensure the project-generated value. Gamma's CIO did more than just manage the IT elements of the project, he also effectively managed the stakeholders who were in a position to extract value from the project. While the project is not yet complete, initial evidence suggests the "experiment" was a resounding success. Detailed analysis of machine logs of call traffic and survey responses from users reveals an average estimated cost saving in transport-related costs of nearly AUD$500,000/year (per the research team's internal reports to Gamma).

### Case 4—Delta: Selling Potential Value

*Organization*

Delta is an Australian public sector organization with over 1,400 employees. While under government regulation and funding, Delta functions largely autonomously.

*Data Source*

Delta was the subject of a full-blown case study on the project described below. Data were obtained from both survey and extensive interviews with Delta staff and an external consultant on the project (Parkes, 2004; Parkes, Davern, and Pan, 2007).

## Case Description

By the late 1990s, like many similar public sector organizations, Delta was being pressured by the government to adopt a more commercial approach to its management and operations. As a result, Delta found that its financial systems were increasingly inadequate for the demands that were being placed on the organization. However, the AUD$1.5 million cost of upgrading the existing enterprise resource planning (ERP) system posed a financial challenge (Parkes, 2004; Parkes, Davern, and Pan, 2007). Government funding cuts were occurring and Delta was in the middle of difficult collective salary negotiations with its largely unionized workforce. Delta knew it needed the upgrade but it also knew it needed to show more immediate returns. The potential value of the upgrade was evident, but the gains were longer term.

To resolve their dilemma Delta management took a novel approach. Rather than try to cut back or delay the required upgrade, Delta took the bold step of incorporating a workflow project into the upgrade. This workflow project, while expanding the overall upgrade, offered the potential to deliver the required immediate returns. In essence, the workflow project was used as a tangible and more immediate demonstration of the potential value of the upgrade. It was contemporaneously a worthwhile project in its own right and a vehicle for *selling* the potential value of the larger project. Despite the challenging context of implementation (e.g., financial pressures due to funding cutbacks and salary negotiations), the workflow system proved a success. As recently described by a senior Delta employee, the system was successfully used throughout Delta for six years until it was superseded by a change in the underlying ERP system that provided its own integrated workflow system (Parkes, Davern, and Pan, 2007).

## Implications for Practice

Delta demonstrates the value of bundling projects with more immediate value, together with those that have longer-term value. In this case, the workflow system provided the necessary immediate returns to justify proceeding with the "related" ERP project for which the returns were less immediate.

## Case 5—Sigma: Denying Potential Value

### Organization

Sigma is an international upper-upscale chain of hotels each of several hundred rooms and extensive conference and dining facilities. It is a mix of franchised, managed, and chain-owned sites each operating with a large degree of autonomy. Sigma has sixteen hotels in the chain, located in major destinations in North America. The company has been in operation for over sixty years.

### Data Source

Data for this case included extensive discussions with senior management both at Sigma headquarters and at a number of individual hotels. Daily data on key performance indicators such as revenue and occupancy were provided for a two-year period of intensive study (Davern, Mantena, and Stohr, 2008).

### Case Description

Like many in the hotel industry, Sigma's head office management were actively investigating IT-enabled revenue management. Revenue management involves forecasting market demand by segment and employing price discrimination to maximize revenue. Judicious pricing is used to handle short-term fluctuations in demand given fixed capacity. Such is the potential of revenue management that one systems vendor even guarantees a 4 percent increase in revenues on implementation of its system (Davern and Kauffman, 2000).

Despite the marketing claims of vendors, assessing the potential value of a revenue management system for Sigma was problematic. To assess the potential value of a revenue management system, Sigma needed to examine the quality of current decision making and thus the available opportunity for improving revenue management. However, the only data collected on relevant performance metrics by location were in spreadsheets posted to a central Lotus Notes database. Since there was no formal system, and given the relative autonomy of each location, the spreadsheet data for each site were often incomplete or inconsistently recorded. Even with this data in hand, assessing the quality of revenue management decision making was challenging. It required the development of a new methodology (see Davern, Mantena, and Stohr, 2008) to distinguish performance due to superior managerial decision making from random fluctuations due to uncontrollable market conditions (i.e., to distinguish good management from luck, and bad management from misfortune).

The two sites with the most complete records were also, somewhat unsurprisingly, the sites that headquarters believed to be the best performers. Consequently, any analysis of revenue potential on these two sites was likely to have understated the potential for improvement, and thus the potential value of revenue management systems to the chain. In fact, the research project indicated that revenue could be improved by at least 5 percent, even if only obvious mistakes in revenue management decision making were corrected (Davern, Mantena, and Stohr, 2008). Given relatively low variable costs, even a small percentage increase in revenue has a significant impact on bottom-line performance. Thus, for example, a single hotel with annual revenues of, say, $5 million (a 180-room hotel, averaging around 75 percent occupancy and $100/room) could make an extra $250,000/year. To put this in proportion, a market leader spent roughly $1 million to *develop* a chain-wide revenue management system in the late 1990s. Even with this potential, Sigma has failed for several years to initiate a revenue management system implementation project. In large part this is due to Sigma's organizational structure. The relatively autonomous management were resistant to interventions from headquarters, believing they understood how to manage their specific hotel more effectively without the aid of a formal system. They remained unconvinced of the potential value, believing more in their own managerial skill (despite evidence to the contrary). In essence, Sigma was *denying* the potential value of a revenue management system.

*Implications for Practice*

Prior research has revealed that to maximize return from IT investments requires investments in complementary assets, so-called organizational capital (Brynjolfsson and Hitt, 1998; Brynjolfsson, Hitt, and Yang, 1997 2002). Such organizational capital would include processes, human intellectual capital, and organizational structure. Sigma's case suggests that appropriate "organizational capital" is often necessary for the firm even to see the potential value of a project, let alone realize it. In Sigma's case, this is evidenced by the autonomy of individual hotel management (organizational structure), and an apparent lack of managerial insight into true performance (human intellectual capital), leading to the denial of the potential value of a revenue management system.

## Case 6—Omega: Missing Out on the Potential Value

*Organization*

Omega is a chain of 165 independently owned holiday parks operating as an alliance under a common brand name and with common quality standards. Omega is thus at the opposite end of the accommodation spectrum to Sigma. It caters predominantly to backpackers, campers, and owners of caravans, motor homes, and recreational vehicles.

*Data Source*

Data for the Omega case were collected as part of a multiyear research collaboration with Omega (Davern and Wilkin, 2004, 2006, forthcoming). Specifically, this entailed extensive site visits, including electronic recording of observations of the operation of information systems at individual Omega parks, and extensive interactions with individual park owners and managers, as well as Omega's senior management and board of directors itself.

*Case Description*

By early 2004 Omega and its competitors in the low end of the accommodation sector had begun to seriously consider embracing revenue management. In part, this reflected the natural development of participants in the industry from small family-run concerns to more actively managed businesses. By building onsite cabin accommodation, parks had also begun to compete directly with the budget motel/hotel accommodation. This provided greater potential revenue and a consequent need for more sophisticated business practices.

In an effort to develop appropriate business practices and systems, Omega opened its business to a research team with expertise in revenue management and direct experience in park operations and management (Davern and Wilkin, 2004). From the outset, the potential for introducing revenue management practices was obvious. In a board level discussion of revenue management potential, one director and park owner realized that with only a few simple changes in pricing strategy he could boost revenues by AUD$70,000 in one two-week peak period. The problem was that individual park operators lacked the skills and processes to implement comprehensive revenue management practices without system-based support (Davern and Wilkin, 2006).

As an "experiment," a simple data-tracking system was developed that could provide improved information about demand. Despite the fact that the software was made available at no cost to Omega park operators, the uptake was quite low. Omega has subsequently shifted its focus away from revenue management systems and essentially placed projects in the area in the "too hard" basket for the foreseeable future.

With Omega, the problem was not in recognizing the potential value: the problem was envisaging and planning how to realize that value. The relatively low levels of management and technology expertise hampered the situation. Operationally, staff tended to "work around" even existing systems, thus diminishing a lot of the managerial value that they were intended to deliver (Davern and Wilkin, 2004, forthcoming). Omega thus lacked both the expertise and the financial resources to develop a full-blown custom system, and as yet the market has not provided anything suitable off the shelf for Omega's market segment. As a result, Omega is currently *missing out* on the potential value, despite being well aware of the extent to which the potential benefits exceed the potential costs.

Table 13.1

**Insights into the Search for Potential Value**

| Case | Scenario | Practical insight illustrated |
|------|----------|-------------------------------|
| Alpha | Finding potential value | Look for indirect sources of potential value. |
| Beta | Believing in potential value | Involve those with user experience in assessing potential value. |
| Gamma | Creating potential value | Experiment, and actively create value. |
| Delta | Selling potential value | Bundle projects appropriately to sell the whole. |
| Sigma | Denying potential value | Organizational capital is needed to identify potential value. |
| Omega | Missing out on potential | Organizational capital is needed to act on identified potential value. |

*Implications for Practice*

Like Sigma, Omega illustrates the importance of organizational capital in the search for potential value. In this case Omega can see the potential value, but does not have the intellectual capital (in terms of both IT and management skills) to develop appropriate system solutions. In part, this is also hampered by the organizational structure of Omega; Omega itself has largely just been a marketing alliance and thus does not have the necessary governance structures to mount a large systems development project.

## A PROBLEM FOR PLANNING: THE SEARCH FOR POTENTIAL VALUE

Each of the cases yields insight into the search for potential value (see Table 13.1). In considering the six cases as a whole the burning question is how can an organization ensure that it is able to recognize potential value and begin taking planned actions to realize the potential (i.e., question 3 above)? Alpha and Beta were uncommon situations. It is unusual for an infrastructure project like Alpha's data warehouse to have potential value in and of itself. Similarly, it is rare for executive decision makers to have the extent of frontline experience, as was the case with Beta. However, both cases suggest that a fundamental issue is the availability of firsthand information about the domain of application to facilitate the search for potential value of a project. In Beta's case, the executives had firsthand knowledge of frontline operations (and thus the potential impact of the project). In Alpha's case, as a value-added reseller of computer equipment, it was essentially in the business of establishing the potential value of IT infrastructure as part of its sales pitch. Finding potential value for an IT project was a core competency in Alpha's business model (indeed it was what motivated the disparate domain-focused sales teams in the first place). By contrast, Gamma and Delta both illustrate creative management: experimentation and marketing to demonstrate project value, as opposed to specific knowledge advantages. Thus, it seems that decision makers either need good firsthand knowledge of the front line of the application domain, or must be willing to take risks and put "spin" on a project to get it off the ground.

The problem is dealing with what are clearly risky projects from an ex ante perspective. How can decision makers carefully and strategically plan high-potential value-information systems projects when faced with a lack of information and risky projects? How can firms acquire relevant information about potential returns when faced with legitimate concerns about the risks the projects would likely entail? The problem, as demonstrated in Sigma and Omega, is one of organizational capital. The question then is: What processes can be put in place for the organization to improve its likelihood of success in the search for potential value, in the context of a lack of information and risky projects?

Even without financial estimates, it is obvious that risky projects are unlikely to be pursued. Indeed, conventional investment analysis techniques such as net present value by design penalize projects with higher risk (by imposing a higher risk-adjusted discount rate on future cash flows). Yet from a strategic perspective, taking risks provides an organization with the opportunity to learn and adapt—increasingly important factors in the competitive and flatter global marketplace (Davern, 2007; Davern, Ferguson, and Pinnuck, 2005; Freidman, 2005).

Consider the case of Gamma. The virtual services project was clearly undertaken essentially as an "experiment." There was a belief that the project could potentially deliver substantial value, but also recognition of the risk that it might not. The justification for the project was a strategic one, rather than one focused on immediate returns. If the project was a success, it would radically change the operations of Gamma and its member health care providers. The risk was great but the upside potential was also very great. The purpose of this "experiment" was to gather information on the likelihood of success. Indeed, the government funding of the project was based on the possibility that if it worked then Gamma's project could form the model for a large-scale replication across the state. What is required then is a process that encourages decision makers to take a strategic perspective, and recognize the upside potential of risky projects, while appropriately managing the inherent risks.

## PLANNING FOR POTENTIAL: A REAL OPTIONS PERSPECTIVE

Real options analysis provides a lens from which this strategic perspective may be obtained. In Smith's (1989) terms, it provides an approach, a "way" of addressing the problem of the search for potential value. The concept of real options is derived from that of financial options in the securities markets. However, the goal in this chapter is to use real options more as a metaphor or "lens" for understanding potential value rather than as a computational tool for calculating value. Nonetheless, to facilitate understanding of the application of real options in information systems, a brief illustration of financial options is now discussed.

### A Financial Options Example

A call option is a financial contract that gives the holder the right but not the obligation to buy a financial asset (e.g., a stock) at a predetermined price (the strike or exercise price) until some expiration date in the future. Table 13.2 provides an illustrative example of a financial call option.

As the example in Table 13.2 illustrates, buying options provides a far better potential return on investment. In part, this is because the option price is always substantially less than the underlying stock price. However, the option has an expiration date. More interestingly, however, the riskier the underlying stock (i.e., the more volatile the price), the more valuable the option, because there is a greater likelihood that the option will be "in the money" (i.e., the stock price will exceed the exercise price). Thus, from an options perspective, risk has value. It is important to note that options allow not only speculation about future possible gains but also the ability to hedge a position and protect against the risk of a price decline. The essence of an option is that it allows a relatively small investment to be made based on expectations of possible outcomes, with

Table 13.2

**A Financial Options Example**

| | |
|---|---|
| Scenario | Suppose you have an expectation that stocks in ABC company currently trading at $100 will rise to $120 within six months. |
| Choice 1: Buy the stock | • You buy 1,000 shares of stock at $100, for an investment of $100,000 and hold for six months. |
| | • If the stock price falls to $80, you lose $20,000. |
| | • If the stock price rises to $120, you make $20,000. |
| Choice 2: Buy options on the stock | • You buy 1,000 options with an exercise price of $110 at $1 each, for a total investment of $1,000. |
| | • If the stock price falls to $80, you do not exercise the option and lose the $1,000 option cost. |
| | • If the stock price rises to $120, you can exercise the option, buy the shares at $110, and effectively sell them in the market at $120, making $9,000 net of your option cost. |

the ability to expand the investment or drop it completely at a later date, once further information has been obtained (e.g., as the market movement becomes evident over time).

**Real Options in Information Systems**

Many information systems projects have option-like characteristics. Consider the data warehousing projects at Alpha and Beta. Much of the value lay not with the data warehouse itself but with the follow-on applications that could then be built. Analogous to financial options on stocks, these projects create "real options" for future actions in regard to IT projects. This may be the option to expand or replicate a project (such as the virtual services project at Gamma), to abandon a project should it not prove fruitful, or an option to "wait and learn" (Kambil, Henderson, and Mohsenzadeh, 1993).

The application of real options analysis to understanding investments in information systems projects has been an area of growing research interest (Bardhan, Bagchi, and Sougstad, 2004; Benaroch, 2002; Fichman, 2004; Fichman, Keil, and Tiwana, 2005). It also certainly has not been without debate (Benaroch and Kauffman, 1999).[1] Pragmatically, it has been viewed as the application of rather complex mathematical approaches to future cash flows that are themselves, at best, fuzzy estimates. Despite such criticisms, it remains useful as a metaphor or lens, providing a strategic perspective for planning information systems without the need to resort to any financial mathematics.

By analogy to financial options, a real option can be characterized as:

a. a relatively small-scale investment
b. in a risky project
c. with the opportunity to gather information about whether a larger project is likely to deliver value or not (i.e., akin to observing the direction in which the stock price moves).

More formally, the use of real options analysis requires that three preconditions be met (Dixit and Pindyck, 1994; Fichman, 2004):

1. Uncertainty in potential payoff
2. Irreversibility of the cost of the project
3. Managerial flexibility in structuring the project

A key notion in real options analysis is that it takes managerial flexibility as a given (in contrast to the traditional net present value analysis, which typically assumes a static plan of future cash flows). The real options project is an experiment. It is designed to discover the potential of a project. A primary goal of a real options project is to preserve the opportunity to embark on a full project, should observation and time reveal sufficient potential value to warrant further investment and action. Applying the real options lens to the earlier cases yields several interesting insights into possible management actions.

## Applying the Real Options Strategic Lens

In the case of Gamma (creating potential value), the virtual services project was clearly embarked upon as a strategic option. All parties concerned implicitly took a real options perspective and viewed the project as an experiment that may or may not succeed, but certainly one that was strategically important to take. In the case of Gamma, however, we see that managerial action is not restricted simply to deciding whether to ramp up or wind down the project based on the revealed potential value. Rather, managerial action can actually create potential value. It is important to note that first Gamma had to take the step to embark on the project before it could build the need and create potential value. Gamma members could not reduce their vehicle fleets without an alternative solution, as this would have reduced service, which in the rural health care sector would have led to a public outcry. The lesson here is both the value of the strategic real options perspective (i.e., an experiment), and the approach to actively creating value rather than simply waiting to realize potential that may or may not be present.

In a similar vein, Delta (selling potential value) embarked on a small project, the workflow system, to provide clear evidence of the potential value of the larger ERP project. From a technical perspective, the workflow project did not provide an option for proceeding with the ERP upgrade. However, from a financial and managerial perspective it did provide such an option. It made the ERP upgrade possible by demonstrating the potential value of the larger project to which it was attached. The Delta case also illustrates the distinction between a simple pilot project and a strategic options-driven project. Often, pilot projects are tests to ensure that the ultimate implementation goes well—to refine the design and implementation procedures of a project that has already been justified. In contrast, a real options-based project is a strategic experiment. While some pilot projects may be "experimental," their focus is on assessing the value of the project itself. In contrast, a real options-based project is focused on the value of the options it creates. In the case of Delta, the demonstrated immediate returns from the workflow project made the option of the larger ERP upgrade possible, not technically, but in terms of acceptability to key stakeholders. The workflow project clearly was not a "pilot" for the ERP upgrade, but it made pursuing the upgrade an organizationally acceptable *option*.

Sigma (denying potential value) faced a situation where many decision makers were denying the potential value of a revenue management system. In this case, the challenge for Sigma was to keep the option of a revenue management system viable with the view to ultimately exercising the option as the organization learned from the option experience. Sigma could thus pursue project(s) advancing revenue management practices, rather than trying to implement a whole system (e.g., following Omega's efforts with the demand tracking system). This changes the situation from making a business case for a comprehensive system for the whole hotel chain, to making a case for a small-scale strategic "experiment" at a single location of some aspect of IT-enabled revenue management. Interestingly, the worst-performing hotel is likely to have the greatest potential for improvement (the greatest option value). Yet the leading performer would likely be the most willing to innovate and also most likely to have the necessary organizational capital (culture and commitment) to succeed.

In the case of Omega (missing out on potential value), the project of the demand data tracking system is an implicit attempt to pursue a real option. As with Delta, this was not so much an option from a technical perspective as from a financial and managerial perspective. It provided the opportunity to clearly demonstrate potential value broadly across the entire Omega chain of holiday parks. It also provided the opportunity to try to develop awareness, skills, and processes for IT-enabled revenue management. Omega failed to act on the option it had created because of a lack of the organizational capital required to exercise the option. As an alliance of independent operators, Omega did not have a heavily resourced central headquarters. Nor had the central headquarters traditionally served a major role in anything other than marketing. It would seem that the complementary assets (intellectual capital, organizational structure) were simply not in place to realize the potential value. This was true both for Omega as an alliance and for the individual independently owned and managed holiday parks within Omega.

The Omega case demonstrates that real options are not always exercised. Whether this is due to a lack of requisite resources or a lack of evidence of potential value, the results are the same: the investment in the initial option is lost. However, this should not necessarily be viewed as a failure. Just as with financial options, investment in information systems projects as implicit real options can be based on speculation about potentials and/or hedging against potential losses. A large part of the motivation for Omega was to protect itself from competitors who they believed were also looking at developing systems for revenue management. Exploring options in IT-enabled revenue management was thus as much about hedging against a market risk as it was about betting on a potential gain. In this regard, the strategic application of the real option lens provides a means for managing risk. It is akin to providing an insurance policy. A small investment now can protect against uncertain changes in the future. However, just as with an insurance policy, if the situation you are insuring against does not eventuate (e.g., you do not crash your car), you still lose the cost of the insurance (i.e., your car insurance premium is not refunded). Fortunately for Omega, its competitors have similarly been unable to make inroads into IT-enabled revenue management.

The question of whether or not to invest in a risky IT project is typically framed as why should we invest? From the real options "insurance" perspective, the question becomes what might happen if the firm does not? Indeed, this logic is routinely applied in battles over technology standards. Consider the recent battle between high-definition DVD and Blu-ray DVD formats. A number of manufacturers and movie studios were hedging, and producing in both formats, when it was clear that one format would dominate. The manufacturers and movie studios simply did not want to bear the risk of being late to the market for whichever format ended up dominating. They may have backed one format more than another, but they recognize the significant value in preserving the option to pursue the other format. Similarly, in the cases described above, we saw the importance of valuing projects on the basis of their ability to preserve options or create options.

## SUCCESS AND FAILURE: PLANNING TO MANAGE RISK

The six cases above demonstrate a variety of ways in which potential value can be found, believed, created, sold, denied, and lost in planning information systems projects. Information systems projects tend to be inherently risky. But without taking risks, experimentation can never occur. Adopting the lens of real options analysis provides a means for strategically planning a portfolio of risky information systems projects. It provides the opportunity for experimenting to learn of the potential value of a project, or to create or demonstrate potential value. While it may not always lead to the discovery and realization of potential value, it provides a means for conceptualizing the planning of projects and managing the inherent risk. In practice this requires a portfolio of projects, some speculative, some hedging, but all focused on discovery of potential value.

## ACKNOWLEDGMENTS

Funding for part of this work was provided by the Australian Research Council Linkage Grant LP0774949. The support of collaborators on the various projects described herein, in particular Alison Parkes, and cooperating organizations from the work on which the cases are drawn is gratefully acknowledged.

## NOTE

1. Theoretically the application of a valuation model, such as the Black-Scholes option pricing model, to information systems projects has been questioned. Specifically, the Black-Scholes model was derived on the assumption of the presence (for hedging purposes) of a market for the underlying asset on which the option exists, but in the case of risky information systems projects, no such market exists.

## REFERENCES

Bardhan, I.; Bagchi, S.; and Sougstad, R. 2004. Prioritizing a portfolio of information technology investment projects. *Journal of Management Information Systems,* 21, 2, 33–60.
Benaroch, M. 2002. Managing information technology investment risk: a real options perspective. *Journal of Management Information Systems,* 19, 2, 43–84.
Benaroch, M., and Kauffman, R.J. 1999. A case for using real options pricing analysis to evaluate information technology project investments. *Information Systems Research,* 10, 1, 70–86.
Brooks, F.P. 1987. No silver bullet: essence and accidents of software engineering. *Computer,* 20, 4, 10–19.
Brynjolfsson, E., and Yang, S. 1997. The intangible costs and benefits of computer investments: evidence from the financial markets. *Proceedings of the Eighteenth International Conference on Information Systems.* Atlanta, GA, December 15–17, 1997. Available at www.AISeL.aisnet.org.
Brynjolfsson, E., and Hitt, L. 1998. Beyond the productivity paradox. *Communications of the ACM,* 41, 8, 49–55.
Brynjolfsson, E.; Hitt, L.; and Yang, S. 2002. Intangible assets: computers and organizational capital. *Brookings Papers on Economic Activity,* 1, 138–199.
Davern, M.J. 2007. Information-driven markets. Paper presented at the University of Melbourne Malaysian Alumni Seminar Series, Kuala Lumpur, Malaysia, May 25.
Davern, M.J., and Kauffman, R.J. 1998. The limits to value of decision support systems. Paper presented at the Tenth Workshop on Information Systems and Economics, New York, December 11–12, 1998. Extended abstract available at http://is-2.stern.nyu.edu/~wise98/pdf/five_b.pdf.
Davern, M.J., and Kauffman, R.J. 2000. Discovering potential and realizing value from information technology investments. *Journal of Management Information Systems,* 16, 4, 121–143.
Davern, M.J., and Wilkin, C.L. 2004. Innovation with Information Systems: an appropriation perspective. *Proceedings of the Fourteenth Australasian Conference on Information Systems,* Hobart, Tasmania, December 1–4, 2004. Available at AISeL.aisnet.org.
———. 2006. Managerial control in small-to-medium enterprises: the role of accounting information systems. *Proceedings of the Second Annual Asia/Pacific Research Symposium on Accounting Information Systems,* June 20, 2006. Program and abstract available at http://www.sigasys.org/asiapacificsymposium/2006/2nd%20Asia%20Pacific%20AIS%20Program%20.2006.pdf.

————. Forthcoming. Evolving innovations through design and use. *Communications of the ACM*.

Davern, M.J.; Ferguson, C.; and Pinnuck, M. 2005. The pervasiveness of information and communication technology: its effects on business models and implications for the accounting profession. *Australian Accounting Review,* 15, 3 (Supplement), 44–55.

Davern, M.; Mantena, R.; and Stohr, E. 2008. Diagnosing decision quality. *Decision Support Systems,* 45, 1 (April), 123–139.

Davern, M.J.; Stagnitti, K.E.; and Ferguson, C. 2006. *Modelling the Adoption and Use of Virtual Services Technologies for Rural and Regional Healthcare: Economic and Quality of Care Perspectives.* Australian Research Council Funded Linkage Grant Project #0774949.

Dixit, A., and Pindyck, R. 1994. *Investment Under Uncertainty.* Princeton, NJ: Princeton University Press.

Fichman, R. 2004. Real options and IT platform adoption: implications for theory and practice. *Information Systems Research,* 15, 2, 132–154.

Fichman, R.; Keil, M.; and Tiwana, A. 2005. Beyond valuation: "options thinking" in IT project management. *California Management Review,* 47, 2, 74–96.

Friedman, T.L. 2005. *The World Is Flat: A Brief History of the Twenty-First Century.* New York: Farrar, Straus, and Giroux.

Kambil, A.; Henderson, J.; and Mohsenzadeh, H. 1993. Strategic management of information technology investments: an options perspective. In R.D. Banker, R.J. Kauffman, and M.A. Mahmood (eds.), *Strategic Information Technology Management: Perspectives on Organizational Growth and Competitive Advantage.* Hershey, PA: Idea Group Publishers, pp. 161–178.

Kauffman, R.J., and Weill, P. 1989. An evaluative framework for research on the performance effects of information technology investment. *Proceedings of the Tenth International Conference on Information Systems.* Boston: ACM. Dcember 4–6, 1989. Available at AISeL.aisnet.org.

Lucas, H.C.J. 1999. *Information Technology and the Productivity Paradox: Assessing the Value of Investing in IT.* New York: Oxford University Press.

Parkes, A. 2004. A case study of workflow implementation success factors. *Proceedings of the Fifteenth Australasian Conference on Information Systems.* Hobart, Australia, December 1–4, 2004. Available at AISeL.aisnet.org.

Parkes, A.; Davern, M.; and Pan, G. 2007. Implementing workflow systems: a case study of an Australian public sector organization. Working Paper, Department of Accounting and Business Information Systems, University of Melbourne.

Smith, G.F. 1989. Defining managerial problems: a framework for prescriptive theorizing. *Management Science,* 35, 8, 963–981.

# CHAPTER 14

# PLANNING TECHNOLOGY INVESTMENTS FOR HIGH PAYOFFS

A Rational Expectations Approach to Gauging Potential and Realized Value in a Changing Environment

YORIS A. AU, KIM HUAT GOH, ROBERT J. KAUFFMAN, AND FREDERICK J. RIGGINS

*Abstract:* *The importance of distinguishing between potential and realized value for information technology (IT) investments has been recognized by senior managers and information systems (IS) researchers since some time in the 1980s, when it became apparent that not all IT investments were likely to achieve equivalent levels of return on investment (ROI). This chapter explores a new perspective for potential and realized value, specifically noting the importance that rational expectations of IT strategic planners and investment managers play in conditioning decision making by senior managers. The key insights that we offer are as follows: (1) Since organizational, operational, and market contexts will tend to vary around different kinds of IT investments, it is only natural that such heterogeneity in outcomes should be reflected in the different expectations of the managers who make the investments; (2) with this in mind, it should also be apparent that understanding heterogeneity in both potential and realized value should be a matter of arriving at an appropriate set of expectations, based on the acquisition of relevant updated information over time that will permit adaptive learning to occur on the part of senior managers; (3) no matter what the process is that enables managers to update their expectations (and achieve rational expectations in the process about their IT investments), the planning process that leads to new estimates of the payoffs from specific IT investments should be tuned to encourage the tracking of a trajectory of values for potential value. This view is analogous to what an investor would do in tracking the value of stocks held in an investment portfolio, subject to value changes based on a variety of forces that are likely to affect the future cash flows of the firm and the present value of its growth opportunities. We develop this IT investment planning perspective in terms of the underlying theory and offer a number of new conceptual and methodological ideas that will enable managers to think through their IT investment processes with a more effective understanding of the rational expectations that are likely to be inherent in them.*

*Keywords:* *Adaptive Learning, Business Value, Investment Evaluation, IT Investments, Planning Perspective, Potential Value, Rational Expectations Theory, Realized Value*

# INTRODUCTION

Senior managers have long recognized the important distinction between the potential value of their information technology (IT) investments and the realized value that is actually observed to accrue in the context of firm operations in different industries. Since the 1990s, information systems (IS) researchers have incorporated the notion into formal models and analyses. Davern and Kauffman (2000, p. 122) argue that it is appropriate, "both *ex ante* and *ex post*, to compare the potential value of an IT project and its realized value. Furthermore, analyzing the potential value of an IT investment, in addition to related expenditures, is useful both for researchers developing theories of IT value creation and for practitioners who must evaluate IT projects and strategies."

## Potential and Realized Value Assessments Are Necessary in Managing Technology Investments

We have observed the necessity for making these kinds of assessments in many different contexts where technology investments are impacted over time by a variety of forces that are endogenous and exogenous to the firm. Senior managers are hard-pressed to find the time to fully surface all of the relevant information, suffer from bounded rationality, and sometimes fail to place enough emphasis on the value of information. Some of the most immediately obvious forces can be identified in settings such as commercial banking, air travel services, Internet-based selling, and e-commerce infrastructure services.

In commercial banking, for example, in the 1980s, Clemons and McFarlan (1986) and Banker and Kauffman (1988) asked whether telecommunication investments for electronic banking networks were a "hook up or lose out" value proposition. They wondered whether e-banking had the capability to enable firms to create unique competitive advantage, and, on that basis, appropriate value from the marketplace. Similar arguments were made by Duliba, Kauffman, and Lucas (2001) in the context of airline reservation systems in support of airline competition for higher market shares at the city-pair route level, and higher load factors, well-controlled operating costs, and greater profits at the aggregate national level. More recently, we have seen growth toward increasing transparency in products and prices of airline firms and the related reservation-making travel intermediaries (Granados, Gupta, and Kauffman, 2006). The potential value of the underlying technologies that support the industry's operations seems tremendous. However, to some extent, the technologies have also eroded the capacity of airline firms to control price competition and lock in their own profitability (Granados, Gupta, and Kauffman, 2007).

A similar conclusion can be reached for firms involved in financial markets, especially the stock market and the market for fixed income securities (Bloomfield and O'Hara, 1999; Granados, Gupta, and Kauffman, 2005, 2006). With greater market transparency, we have seen changes in investors' capabilities to acquire knowledge of market prices and be more effective in trading and investing, as was predicted earlier in the 1990s (Hasbrouck, 1995). For additional materials that may be useful for expanding on some of the themes discussed in this chapter for undergraduate, MBA and executive audiences, the interested reader should see: Benaroch and Kauffman (1999, 2000); Benaroch and colleagues (2007); Clemons (1991, 2007); Clemons and Gu (2003); Devaraj and Kohli (2000, 2002, 2003); Han, Kauffman, and Nault (2004); Kauffman and Wang (2002); and Saloner and Spence (2002).

**The Value of IT Investments in the Marketplace**

The same can be said in the contexts of Internet-based selling and e-commerce infrastructure services provision. Although there are quite a few notable examples of outstanding profitability in a "blue ocean" marketplace (Kim and Mauborgne, 2005) involving transformed business opportunities for nearly uncontested entry in network technology-based entrepreneurship (e.g., Amazon, Travelocity, Google, Digital River, Akamai, YouTube, etc.), not everything has turned out the way knowledgeable industry analysts expected (Burnham, 1999). Recall such names as Mobshop and Mercata in group-buying on the Internet (Kauffman and Wang, 2001, 2002), Priceline and Expedia in air travel and hospitality services reservation-making (Granados, Gupta, and Kauffman, 2005), I2 and Ariba in Internet-based procurement services (Day, Fein, and Ruppersberger, 2003), and many others that have since failed or strategically morphed their business models to be only shadows of their earlier forms when they entered the market as entrepreneurial ventures (Kauffman, Miller, and Wang, 2006). It is clear from these examples that the potential value of the firms' IT investments was diminished by a variety of forces: the inappropriateness of the Internet channel for transaction making in a product or service, the lack of competitive immediacy for some Internet-based sellers in the presence of everyday discounters such as Wal-Mart and BestBuy, and the "deep pockets" and latent competitive capabilities of long-time industry players. The coalition of airlines behind Orbitz. com, or the capacity of Sotheby's and Christie's to bring their prowess in collectibles auctions to the Internet come to mind, for example. Today, companies such as Amazon and Travelocity are faced with formidable and capable competitors, proving that the technological innovations that drove their development and initial valuations are not long-term barriers to entry for other firms. As a result, we have observed—as we should have expected—the migration and movement in the value of their underlying technology-based competencies for the marketplace (Kauffman and Li, 2005).

**Evaluation and Planning Need to Be Aligned with Effective IT Strategy for Changing Environments**

These observations motivate us to work toward aligning planning perspectives for IT investments with the realities of a changing environment that inflict severe pressures on the operations and organizational capabilities that different kinds of IT investments create. This is true for traditional firms that invest in IT to support their operations, as well as e-commerce firms that are exploring the latest technologies for data mining and recommender systems, to other firms that use technology to transform the marketplace that exists around them (Burnham, 1999). In all of these instances, one thing is certain: the technological and competitive business world will not be static. Instead, the changes and the perceived impacts on the organizations that are affected should evolve over time—exhibiting *volatility* in their *variance* and *returns,* from the point of view of finance professionals and IT value researchers.

In one of the most well-referenced articles in the IS literature on changes in value depending on different estimates of the variance of the expected costs and payoffs, Dos Santos (1991) offered the first meaningful recognition and illustration of the role of the volatility of costs and revenues in identifying the differential payoffs of IT. Implicit in his view, as many have come to understand today, is that cost and benefits flows are stochastic in time with respect to IT investments. As a result, based on observations as time passes, one should be able to track the trajectory of the costs and the benefits, and determine whether they match the forecast levels of volatility when the investment decision was made initially, or if they fall outside the confidence interval of the original forecast. More recently, Schwartz and Zozaya-Gorostiza (2003) and Kauffman and Li (2005) have formalized the assessment of the volatility of IT value and its fundamental drivers by using stochastic analysis in the context of real options models related to prospective IT investments. Although the modeling treatments in each are somewhat different from what Dos Santos used—the asset-for-asset exchange model of Margrabe (1978)—the strategic intuition hardly improves on Dos Santos's (1991) early conceptualization.

## IT Investment Value Volatility Requires New Perspectives in Senior Management Decision Making

As of late 2008, it is fair to say that the spate of research that Dos Santos's (1991) work spawned in the IS field, supported by the many works in financial economics (Dixit and Pindyck, 1994) and strategy (Kogut and Kulatilaka, 1994; Kulatilaka and Venkatraman, 2001) that appeared, has now reached a point of relative maturity. Real options methods have been proposed for use in both conceptual (e.g., Fichman, Keil, and Tiwana, 2005) and modeling terms (e.g., McGrath and MacMillan, 2000; Taudes, 1998). They have also been embedded in other game-theoretic models (Dai, Kauffman, and Riggins, 2007; Zhu and Weyant 2003), and successfully applied (Benaroch, 2001; Benaroch and Kauffman, 1999, 2000) and evaluated (Gustafson and Luft, 2002; Taudes, Feurstein, and Mild, 2000). Nevertheless, Sougstad and Bardhan (2008) and Kauffman and Sougstad (2007) suggest that there is ample room for innovation in the development of trajectory metrics that enable an analyst to gauge the impacts of changing risk over time. Their modeling insights suggest that it is possible to establish value trajectories and risk bounds in a portfolio of IT assets that can be evaluated based on preset probabilities that a given cost or revenue flow stays within a given limit.

The volatility of IT value requires senior managers to update their expectations of the payoffs, and to think of their portfolio of IT investments as a set of market assets, even though they will never be traded or priced by others outside the firm (Au and Kauffman 2001, 2003, 2005). Indeed, this is our core insight: senior managers within the firm ought to be sensitive to the impacts of a variety of market forces that act on IT investments which have already been made, as well as on those that are under review, and whose estimates for potential value can be flexibly updated to match new information as it is acquired.

In this general context, we will discuss the rationale for developing a planning perspective that considers potential value and realized value more explicitly. We believe that it will provide MBA students, technology planners, and senior executives with stronger tools and a more effective roadmap for translating their expectations into meaningful assessments of the changing value of their planned and implemented IT investments. We are especially interested in laying out some key concepts that will guide their thinking. One key concept involves the *drift or migration of potential value over time*, in terms of preinvestment potential value, when the details of the investment are not well understood, and in terms of postinvestment potential value, when the payoff outcome can be affected by various factors (Dos Santos, 1991; Kauffman and Li, 2005; Schwartz and Zozaya-Gorostiza, 2003). They include: the commitments of senior managers, the success of the implementation effort, the vagaries of the marketplace and interfirm competition, emerging technologies that substitute for or entirely replace the functionality of prior technologies, and changing patterns of business and consumer use of the technologies.

## New Concepts Are Needed to Create the Basis for More Effective Managerial Understanding

We will discuss such concepts as the *role of market consensus*, the development of *rational expectations* among senior managers for IT payoffs, the *potential value trajectory*, and the related modeling ideas to provide a quantitative basis that pulls these concepts together into a useful tool set. At present, most technology strategists understand the basis for making effective high-level assessments of the forces that impinge on the business value of IT. We have seen this in the work of Clemons and his coauthors, and some others. Some examples include: the *move-to-the-middle theory* (Clemons, Reddi, and Row, 1993); the role of *functionality risk* in strategic systems design and *chunkification strategies* in determining the value outcomes of decomposable large-scale IT investments (Aron, Clemons, and Reddi, 2005; Clemons, 2007); the impacts of *information exploitation* (Clemons and Hitt, 2004; Han, Kauffman, and Nault, 2004), and most recently, the effects of *informational asymmetries* in the context of the technological transformation of electronic markets (Clemons, 2007).

The dual roles of risk and return are increasingly well understood in IS research. In addition to Clemons, Reddi, and Row's (1993) move-to-the-middle revelations, today we know much more about the volatility-driven risks from the underlying investments in IT that firms make which give rise to digital options (Amram and Kualtilaka, 1999; Benaroch, Lichtenstein, and Robinson, 2006; Dewan, Gurbaxani, and Chi, 2004; Hunter, Kobelsky, and Richardson, 2004; Kauffman and Mohtadi, 2004; Sambamurthy, Bharadwaj, and Grover, 2003). We also have a much better understanding of the time-varying risk–return relationship relative to the volatility of IT investments in a portfolio analysis context (Bardhan, Sougstad, and Bagchi, 2004; Cummings, 2002; Hoffman, 2003; Jeffery and Leliveld, 2004; Kauffman and Sougstad, 2007; Luehrman, 1998).

Josefek and Kauffman (1997) and Clemons and Gu (2003) have also pointed out the difficulties and risks that strategic IT investments pose. Time and expectations of value become critical in an anticipated or potential sense, and also in terms of the accrual and realization of value. Wait too long—so the usual story often goes—and the opportunities to appropriate value vanish with the result that your best people leave to seek opportunities elsewhere. Move too soon, and you may not get it right, in spite of the satisfaction that comes with organizational learning. Enter late and join the competitive fray, but also face the risk of possibly losing the opportunity to capture value, as your key competitor achieves near-monopoly market power relative to the technology innovation—for example, Apple with iPods, and Skype with VoIP in the past several years (Kauffman and Wu, 2006). Timing, then, is critical; yet it is equally critical to balance the speed of action with the risks that a firm faces before all of the competitive facts of the technology, the market, and consumer and firm behavior relative to the IT investment become known (Clemons and Gu, 2003).

## Why Rational Expectations Shape Managerial Decisions about IT Investment Value

Rational expectations about the range of possible outcomes from an IT investment on the part of senior managers become especially important in such strategic managerial contexts. The term *rational expectations* was coined by the economist John Muth (1961), more than forty-five years ago. Since Muth's early musings on rational expectations, other researchers in economics and finance have developed these ideas much further, creating a strong theoretical basis for a generation of foundational thinking that has influenced the development of macroeconomic policy, the management of campaigns for political candidates, and even the conduct of military operations. Some examples include Frydman (1982), Sargent (1993), and Sargent and Wallace (1976).

Muth argued that agents in an economy form their expectations of relevant future outcomes (e.g., price levels or interest rates) on the basis of the "true" structural model of the economy in which they make their decisions. He also viewed the agents' expectations as being the same as the predictions of the relevant economic theory: what they think will be the best-informed interpretation of what is likely to occur in the future. A similarly compelling idea was put forth by Nerlove (1958), who posited that agents learn over time, and that the extent to which they learn adds flexibility to their expectations about potential outcomes that rational expectations alone would not predict under the same circumstances. These ideas have many applications in real life, including the formation of consumer expectations of gas prices for their cars, mortgage interest rates related to their house purchases, the likelihood of finding a well-paying job, and so on. The perspective reflects the feedback loops that tie the expectations of one agent to the expectations of another (and another and another, etc.).

Lohmann (2000) aptly characterizes this perspective in the title of an article on common knowledge and information cascades: "I know you know he or she knows we know you know they know." We tie this into Nerlove's view of adaptive expectations, since a change in any agent's perspective in this is likely to affect the sentiments of the others. British pop psychologist R.D. Laing (1970) expressed these concepts exceptionally well too, outside the context of economic theory, in his poetic descriptions of psychological rational expectations in human relationships in his "new age" psychology book called *Knots*.

Nobel laureate in economics, Herbert Simon (1957), further enriched this dialogue on the theory of agent decision making in contexts where information sharing is possible. He argued that all managers are subject to bounded rationality, and as a result, no matter how much information a senior manager or policymaker is able to acquire, there will still be issues related to the person's inability to process all of it, or to comprehend what it means, such that boundedly rational decision making necessarily will be fraught with discrepancies and characterized by disagreements among agents that can only be resolved as they compare what they know over time.

**Research Questions**

With these observations on this extraordinary body of theoretical knowledge in mind, we will explore the following research questions in this chapter:

- How can we leverage the theories of rational expectations, adaptive learning, and bounded rationality to create a new theoretical synthesis that will inform senior management perspectives on the potential and realized value of IT investments?
- To what extent do rational expectations and adaptive learning provide a basis for describing and analyzing the expected value trajectories of new technology investments over time?
- How should the insights from the theory inform decision making related to strategic planning for technology adoption, investment, and business value outcomes? How do market perceptions and information sharing among agents tie in? What is likely to come out, as a result, for private intrafirm and heterogeneous interfirm assessments of value?
- How do these newly available theoretical perspectives provide a basis to think creatively about methodological innovations to support rational expectations-based evaluations in IT strategic planning and investment evaluation? What new and valuable ideas flow from this relative to some of the classical problems in the IT value literature, especially related to IT investment decisions under uncertainty (e.g., standards, network externalities, optionality, adoption rate, market saturation, etc.).

**Plan of the Chapter**

The remainder of this chapter is structured in six sections. The next section explores some of the current and basic thinking that we have brought to our research on IT planning and evaluation for investments. It examines the role of incomplete information, uncertainty, and risk in this area, and further develops our views on potential value and realized value. We also discuss information sharing and the role of "cheap talk" in the formation of estimates for technology value. The third section provides additional background on the rational expectations and adaptive learning perspectives, and attempts to identify factors that will affect rational expectations in technology investment decision contexts. It also considers how rational expectations support a somewhat different conceptualization of the role of risk and uncertainty in decision making, and uses these insights as a basis to formulate a conceptual model for planning in IT investments. The fourth section further develops our arguments about rational expectations-based technology investment decision making, and explores the process that leads to a market-wide consensus for investments, something that is especially relevant for technologies subject to network effects. The penultimate section extends the discussion, by providing some new concepts and suggestions for analysis tools that will aid IT investment managers to improve their decision-making practices. Our conclusion section offers a discussion of the contributions and limitations of our work, as well as encouragement to our readers to try to put these new ideas to work, and to influence best practices in industry for IT investment planning and assessment.

## WHY EFFECTIVE TECHNOLOGY INVESTMENTS ARE CHALLENGING TO MAKE

We next consider the impetus for the planning perspectives that we offer in greater detail, by focusing on the role of incomplete information and the extent to which it impedes decision making for IT investments by creating uncertainty about the payoffs that are likely to occur. We first discuss the sources of uncertainty and risk in technology investment decision making, including technology, consumers, organization and management, IT investment performance, stakeholder considerations, standards, market competition, and financial issues. These risks impact IT investment decision makers' sense of the relationship between potential and realized value. To change their perception, it is helpful to obtain additional information to diminish uncertainty so that there is greater clarity about the payoffs associated with an investment. The observations that we make in this section provide a foundation for our subsequent consideration of why rational expectations theory is useful in characterizing the technology investment decision-making behavior we have observed in our field study research, and why an appropriate planning approach for IT investments needs to incorporate some consideration of information sharing for uncertainty reduction.

### Sources of Uncertainty and Risk

Incomplete information constitutes one of the more difficult issues for senior managers who are charged with IT investment decision making. At one level, the firm ought to be risk-neutral in terms of its evaluation of IT assets, since it will make many decisions over time and many technologies that hold considerable promise (as well as unknown risks) will not be considered. We can point to a number of reasons why senior managers who are involved in technology investment decisions feel they have incomplete information. The same reasons also explain why the information that they have changes over time, complicating their understanding of the value of their investment decisions.

### Technology

One issue involves *technology and innovation uncertainties,* which are probably the first source that most people would consider beyond their control and, sometimes, even beyond their ability to effectively predict what developments are to come. Benaroch (2001) refers to these as *technology investment risks*. Technology vendors have different and often unknown capabilities to deliver on their promises and value propositions. They are significantly affected by competition in the market, their ability to hold on to key staff, the emergence of new technologies that substitute for what they offer, and their own profitability outcomes. The performance of Digital Equipment Corporation (DEC) in the 1980s and early 1990s comes to mind, for example. After a period when the firm was a league leader in mid-tier minicomputer solutions, the market shifted to higher-end PC-based servers and other solutions in which DEC had no real competitive advantage. Technology and innovation uncertainties often give rise to *functionality risks,* as prior technology investments may no longer be able to serve current needs and functionality requirements.

## Consumers

The success and payoffs that come from technology projects are also typically influenced by *consumer acceptance in the marketplace,* which gives rise to *market acceptance risks.* Senior managers are rarely able to perfectly predict the speed and degree of consumer acceptance, and so it often occurs that the growth of the user-installed base cannot be accurately forecasted. A goal that is set out often is to achieve "critical mass" in the marketplace, such that there is some certainty going forward that a particular technology or software application will continue to be demanded. For example, we have seen this with Apple Macintosh PCs relative to Microsoft Windows-compliant PCs over the years; Apple has always managed to maintain its viability in installed base, although its future prospects have often been uncertain and its market share has been small. Other technological innovations, on the other hand, have not lived up to the high hype of market expectations, including the e-money plays on the Internet, Beenz and Flooz, IBM's OS/2, Steve Jobs's NeXT computers, and e-books (Haskin, 2007).

## Organization and Management

A third issue is the *stability of organizational structure* and the extent of *commitment of senior managers* of the firm. In the first instance, many events can lead an organization to change its structure and governance. At the extreme end is a merger or an acquisition, resulting in full reconsideration of the likely value flows and expected costs of a large-scale IT investment. When this occurs, it is normally necessary for the management team to reappraise its commitment. At the other end of the spectrum is the importance that senior managers in a strategy-stable, structure-stable organization can have by acting as project champions and promoters of the adoption and usage of new systems and technology investments. When things do not go right, it usually becomes apparent that technology investment projects are subject to ongoing *organizational risks.*

## IT Investment Performance

A fourth issue is the performance of IT investments in support of business processes. In some instances, the value flows from implementing IT in support of business processes are relatively immediate. In other cases, there may be a considerable lag time that occurs before value is produced. This period of diminished value flows is called the *value latency period,* which has been extensively explored by a number of different IS researchers, including Deveraj and Kohli (2000), Goh and Kauffman (2005), and Kauffman and Wu (2006). Current thinking suggests that very large-scale IT investments typically take a longer period of time to pay off—up to several years—and they are subject to many sources of *value latency risk.* In other cases, the barriers to achieving value are more associated with *implementation risks,* for example, not providing enough resources for training, leaving behind application bugs and usability problems, or failing to get all of the elements of the systems analysis correct.

## Stakeholders

A fifth issue is the degree of the relevant stakeholders' support for higher payoffs from an IT investment. Different stakeholders create different kinds of uncertainties and risks. For example, in procurement-related settings, the success of an IT implementation is often based on what Devaraj and Kohli (2003) have called the "missing link": the degree of actual usage by stakeholders involved with the deployed systems. Similar arguments apply regarding usage of systems that support trade services in international banking, where systems integration capabilities make it possible to achieve highly productive transactional support for trade services and the related banking business partners. The stakeholders can be of numerous kinds, including external stakeholders such as buyers and suppliers, and other industry and technology partners. They also can include internal business partners such as financial and accounting managers, or product design and development, and manufacturing operations staff members. In all of these cases, IT implementations are subject to a variety of *relational risks* that come up in principal–agent relationships.

## Standards

Another concern that results in uncertainty is what happens over time with respect to technology standards and technology-led network externalities in the marketplace. Much research suggests that the key difficulty managers face is to figure out whether and when a particular technology will become a standard in the marketplace. In the absence of certainty about future outcomes, the best they will be able to do is to make informed predictions, probably based on common knowledge and shared expectations across the marketplace. For example, we have seen this with Bluetooth, the Wi-Fi family of 802.11 standards, WiMax, and more recently with RFID (radio frequency identification) chips and readers. We have also recently had experience with electronic bill presentment and payment (EBPP) systems and technologies, where it has required the broad consensus of a number of different stakeholders before standard solutions gain the confidence of the marketplace (Au and Kauffman, 2003). The primary risks that managers face related to uncertainty include the *adoption timing risk* of being too early or late and incurring higher costs as a result, and the *lock-in risk* of being stranded with the wrong choice of standard as the market's sentiments shift to a different standard.

## Competition

When new IT investments support products and services whose performance is determined in the marketplace, competitive factors give rise to significant uncertainties and *competitive risks.* The firm's investments are subject to *strategic entry risk* by major competitors in general, as well as the *preemption risk* of earlier entry by a competitor when the firm has its own entry in the works for a technology product or service area. Kauffman and Wu (2006) have recently studied such developments for large-scale IT investments in mass storage e-mail services by competitors, Google and Yahoo!, where the competition has seemed like a timing game in near-duopoly form. Other examples include the race to bring photo-sensors to market on digital single lens reflex (D-SLR) cameras that are larger and larger—from 4 megapixels to 8 megapixels to 10.2 megapixels for image capture now (Stensvold, 2007), and in the near future up to 13.5 and 16.7 megapixels, according to *Digital Photographer* magazine (2007a, 2007b). Additional uncertainties arise with technology-based products that are associated with different technology generations, an *obsolescence risk*.

*Financial Issues*

All IT investments that are planned to occur over multiple periods (e.g., quarters or years) are subject to uncertainties that relate to the availability of scarce financial capital in the firm, and to being able to consistently obtain the funding commitments from the chief financial officer's office. These *funding risks* often shape the decisions that senior managers make about how to plan and structure IT investments, so as to do as much as possible to ensure that they will be viable on a continuing basis. As a result of funding risks, and some of the other issues that we have discussed above, managers often think in terms of the real options that are embedded in their technology investments, including the option to defer investment, reduce scale, increase scale, shift the emphasis development, or abandon a project entirely (Benaroch, 2001; Benaroch Jeffery, Kauffman, and Shah, 2007).

Table 14.1 summarizes and describes the different sources of risk and uncertainty. These additional observations that we have made and their relationships to different kinds of risks that arise further prompt us to explore how to specifically incorporate the consideration of incomplete information into managerial thinking related to IT investment planning. This is why information sharing and exchange among senior IS managers can play an important role in diminishing their uncertainty. They enable them to find a basis for a shared understanding of developments related to the variety of uncertainties and risks that they face.

**Potential Versus Realized Value of Investments**

The IT value-conversion process (Kauffman and Weill, 1989) is impacted by firm-specific, market-related factors and other factors we have discussed that are dynamic in nature (Benaroch, 2001). Stochasticity in these factors causes greater variability in the value trajectory of IT investments and leads to higher risks in the investment. Information about the key risks is important for managers to assess and predict the possible inaccuracies in their estimation of potential and realized value. Incomplete information leads to greater uncertainty and exacerbates the risk profile of the IT investment. Potential value and realized value of an IT investment are constantly changing due to risk exposure of the IT investment and this dynamic process. (See Figure 14.1 for a theoretical illustration.) The potential value for a given level of IT investment is represented by the dotted curve that measures the upper bound of output produced. The realized value is represented by the solid curve at or below the potential value curve. This figure shows that shifts in both the potential value and realized value can occur due to changes in the risk exposures experienced by the IT investment.

Since the potential value of IT investments is constantly updated by changes in the underlying risk factors, the curve representing the estimation of potential value should shift whenever new information is introduced into the estimation function. The shift of this potential value curve is likely to be substantial in the early phases of IT system investment, where high variability and unpredictability of project progress prevails. As time passes, the movement of potential value will usually become more stable and come closer to its final position as realized value. The realization

Table 14.1

**Sources of Risk, Uncertainty, and Incomplete Information**

| Source | Comments |
| --- | --- |
| Technology and innovation, vendor risks | Technology changes and emerging innovations are continuous in the marketplace, but the timing of their introduction is unknown. Vendors behind the technologies are of key concern, especially their willingness to support the chosen technology and their strategic commitment to a vision that is in line with the investor's needs relative to the technology. |
| Consumer acceptance | Consumers exhibit different rates of adoption and acceptance of technology-based products and services, depending upon the market segment in which the products and services are introduced. |
| Management support, organization | Senior management commitment to a technology project and stability of organizational structure and strategy intent are similarly critical, but often they cannot be guaranteed. |
| Operational and business process performance | Operational performance of a newly implemented technology is subject to a period of "work out" and refinement, so that it is possible to achieve maximum productivity and organizational performance with respect to it in different business and organizational processes. |
| Stakeholder support | Stakeholder acceptance of the technology implementation that occurs around an investment is also crucial, but may not be locked in prior to when the investment occurs. Stakeholders (e.g., buyers and suppliers, financial and accounting managers, industry and technology partners) have different goals in principal–agent terms, and the extent to which they have an incentive to support a given technology investment is not always clear. |
| Standards and externalities | Standards are either in question or stabilized for a period of time until the next major technology change occurs. For this reason, it is natural for managers to express uncertainty about how network externalities will develop in the marketplace, and what standard will become dominant. |
| Competition and entry | The firm faces external risks and uncertainties in addition to changing technology, especially the uncontrollable actions of major competitors who may roll out similar technology-based products and services, and other unexpected new competitors who may leap-frog the competition by introducing innovative new processes and products that diminish the value of the existing ones. |
| Financial issues | Most organizations experience significant demand on their base of capital for all kinds of projects and uses—in addition to those that require capital commitment for technology investment projects. As a result, most organizations must endure periods of "scale-back" or "deferral" of additional necessary investments and the restructuring of large-scale IT investments, creating additional uncertainty for initial investments. |

of IT value occurs predominantly after the implementation and is not instantaneous due to value latency involving possible factors such as learning discontinuities, organizational inertia, and user resistance. We do not expect actual realized value to match estimated potential value in all instances; instead, managers will be interested in the reasons why they do not end up matching one another.

The value trajectory shifts throughout the lifecycle of an IT investment. This calls for greater understanding and objective assessment of the phenomenon. Accepting that the value flow process is dynamic allows managers to arrive at current and informed decisions about the IT investment

Figure 14.1    **Impact of Changes in Risk Exposure on Potential and Realized IT Investment Value**

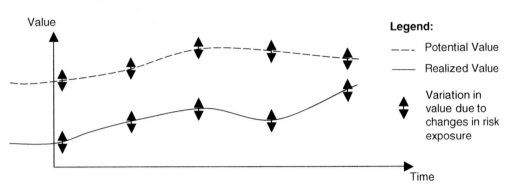

*Note:* This figure is a theoretical illustration of the potential and realized value of an IT investment and does not represent any specific empirical result. Both the potential value and realized value of IT can drift upward or downward over time, depending on the organizational, environmental, technological, and competitive forces that affect the risk exposure of the investment.

and implementation process. Managers should estimate the ever-changing potential value over time by basing it on updated expectations of the IT investment payoff, enabling them to better realize the value through additional effort in making value-related treatments such as complementary investments, training, and revised deployments.

## Information Sharing for the Reduction of Uncertainty

As managers face the risks outlined above that arise from incomplete information, they will seek ways to engage in information sharing and information gathering to minimize these risks. For example, a manager considering a technology investment may seek to reduce uncertainty by gaining a better understanding of what other relevant parties are likely to do in the future. This includes understanding the plans of vendors who may change their support for the technology, competitors who may choose to adopt a different technology, partners who may have different timing expectations of adoption, or senior management who may or may not be supportive in the future. Second, managers may seek information from others to gain a better understanding of the technology and its capabilities in terms of the future viability of a given technology, the evolutionary track of its functionality over time, the likelihood that benefits will be realized in a reasonable amount of time, or which factors must be in place to shorten the latency period to realize benefits sooner. Finally, managers considering technology investments may try to gather information to gain a better understanding of what others believe the future state of the world might be, such as what other seemingly unrelated projects may be on the planning horizon that may drain resources, the possibility of a merger or acquisition that may impact the decision, or the overall future economic climate that may necessitate scaling back investments in the new technology. Such information sharing and information gathering are ways of diminishing incomplete information, thereby minimizing unnecessary risks and controlling for uncertainty about the future.

Farrell and Rabin (1996) point out three ways that information sharing may occur between parties that might inform decision making. First, it is well known in economics that various forms of *economic institutions* can convey information to managers, such as competitive markets that adjust prices based on supply and demand. Second, on a smaller scale, *signaling* may occur between parties based on their actions or announcements that can convey information about intended future actions (Spence 1973, 1974). The third way, as proposed by Farrell and Rabin (1996), is through informal communication they call "cheap talk." *Cheap talk* is represented by costless, nonbinding, and nonverifiable messages between parties that may occur in a variety of settings such as through e-mails, telephone conversations, discussions at industry conferences, hallway chat at technology conventions, or even discussions on the golf course. Although this type of communication may be easy to dismiss as meaningless, research has shown that parties often have an incentive to provide truthful information in such situations lest they come to be regarded as untrustworthy in the future or find themselves inadvertently committed to unmanageable situations later (Kim, 1996). As managers come into contact with others they engage in information sharing and information gathering that they can use to update their expectations of future events regarding the possible actions of others, the potential of the technology, and future states of the environment. Along with more formal mechanisms such as economic institutions and signaling, we can see that cheap talk is a valuable way of sharing information to inform technology investment decision making.

## THE RATIONAL EXPECTATIONS PERSPECTIVE: DEVELOPMENT

We next provide background on the theories of rational expectations and adaptive learning, and identify factors that will affect rational expectations in technology investment decision contexts, on the basis of our earlier discussion of why technology investments are challenging to make and involve decision-making uncertainty. We discuss how the rational expectations theory supports perceptions of variation over time in the value trajectory of IT investments. We then use these insights as a basis to formulate a conceptual model for planning in IT investments. In contrast to the more general observations that we offered in the previous section on why IT investment decision making is complex, here we develop a more focused theoretical perspective on why the decision-making process is in harmony with adaptive learning about the likely payoffs on the part of managers. Our discussion culminates in a proposal for IT investment planning that takes into account rational expectations, factors affecting the perceived risks, and managerial uncertainty, which brings together elements of the prior section and the present section of this chapter.

### Rational Expectations and Adaptive Learning

Muth's (1961) rational expectations hypothesis (REH) basically states that economic agents form their expectations based on the "true" structural model of the economy in which their decisions are made. In our case, economic agents are the managers that make IT investment/adoption decisions. The REH claims that managers' subjective expectations of economic variables are the same as the mathematical conditional expectation of those variables. It considers subjective expectations on average as equal to the variables' true values, and this is a central tenet of the theory. The theory is relevant in the IT planning context because it assumes that managers act rationally in circumstances of economic uncertainty and make efficient use of all available information and their understanding of the model governing the market. Muth (1961) further maintained that from a purely theoretical perspective, there are good reasons for assuming rationality. One of them is because it is a principle that is applicable to all dynamic problems that fit the descriptions of IT planning.

The REH is based on two key assumptions: (1) economic agents form their expectations based

Table 14.2

**Definitions for Primary Terms and Concepts from Rational Expectations Hypothesis**

| Term | Definition |
|---|---|
| Rational expectations hypothesis (REH) | A theory formulated by Muth (1961) that suggests that economic agents form their expectations on the basis of the "true" structural model of the economy in which their decisions are made, and that on average, these expectations are essentially the same as the predictions of the relevant economic theory. |
| Bounded rationality | Recognizes the limited cognitive capacity of humans in decision making when they face problem complexity under the constraints of time and lacking information (Schwartz and Zozaya-Gorostiza, 2003). |
| Adaptive learning | Framework based on REH. Assumes that economic agents know the true equilibrium structural relations of the economy but—due to bounded rationality—are not allowed to learn the actual values of the parameters in the equilibrium relations (Muth, 1961). |
| Rational expectations equilibrium (REE) | Equilibrium condition characterized by three features: all markets clear at equilibrium prices; every agent knows the relationship between equilibrium prices and private information of all other agents; and the information in equilibrium prices is exploited by all agents in making inferences about private information of others (Muth, 1961). |

on a given set of information and will fully utilize all of the information available; and (2) economic agents somehow know the stochastic process that generates the rational expectations equilibrium (REE) condition. The second assumption is what makes the REH unique. However, this assumption is often considered too strong since it requires economic agents to have full knowledge of the structure of the relevant models and their parameter values. Simon (1957) argued that economic agents have bounded rationality since they have limited cognitive resources and capabilities that often make it hard for them to process all available information and come up with the correct decision quickly. Another challenge is that all of this information may not be available to the managers, at least not initially. Considering these limitations, Sargent (1993) suggested an alternative notion, *adaptive learning*, in which agents are assumed to be willing and able to update their expectations about relevant parameter values on the basis of newly received information. Consequently, in order for the rational expectations theory to work, the managers should be allowed some time to obtain and process all available information. Table 14.2 includes definitions for the primary terms and concepts that are drawn from rational expectations theory.

In IT investment and adoption planning, the rational expectations and adaptive learning theory can be used to explain the phenomenon of drift or migration of potential value over time described in the previous section. The fluctuation is due to the fact that boundedly rational managers may not be able to determine the true potential value of a new technology right away, although they will be able to do so over time. These managers must continue to collect new information about the technology from all available sources and update their expectations about the technology's potential value accordingly. The REH and adaptive learning perspectives can help us foresee the process through which some of the "wait and see" issues will be worked out as the capabilities of a new technology expand. In fact, we expect managers to be rational expectations planners, taking advantage of new information as it comes from the variety of players that have entered the market with hopes to profit from it. Consequently, they will continue to follow the development of the new technology and only make a full commitment to adopt when the time is right.

A critical component in the rational expectations-based perspective of IT investment and adoption planning is the alignment of expectations. The rational expectations and adaptive learning theories suggest that managers observe the environment and try to align their expectations with those of the other managers before making an IT investment and adoption decision. The alignment is done through the exchange of information among managers. It should occur intraorganizationally (among chief executive officers, chief information officers, and other managers within the same organization), as well as interorganizationally (among managers from different companies). The alignment is necessary to confirm each manager's own expectations about the potential value of the technology being considered. Any new developments may alter each manager's expectations and result in a new level of alignment.

The alignment process may take some time during which we can expect no major decision to be made. This may explain the current adoption status of Blu-ray and HD-DVD, two competing high-capacity optical disc storage technologies backed by various computer and consumer electronics manufacturers. Blu-ray is Sony's standard and backed by Dell, Hewlett-Packard, Hitachi, LG Electronics, Matsushita Electric Industrial (Panasonic), Mitsubishi Electric, Philips Electronics, Pioneer Electronics, Samsung Electronics, Sharp, TDK, and Thomson Multimedia. On the other hand, HD-DVD is supported by Toshiba, NEC, Sanyo, Memory-Tech, and Microsoft (which is also supporting HD-DVD in its next version of Windows).

Although it got an early start and had powerful backers, Blu-ray was not able to quickly win the market. In fact, it later found itself having to compete with HD-DVD, which was introduced to the market about three years later in 2006. During the first three years on the market, boundedly rational managers were not able to reach the equilibrium point of adoption because new information about the new technology (i.e., Blu-ray) kept coming in, causing the managers to repeatedly adjust their expectations about the potential value of the technology. This was made worse by the fact that there were a lot of rumors about the potentially competing technology, HD-DVD. Although Blu-ray offered more capacity, HD-DVD was cheaper due to the fact that it carries the same basic structure as the current DVD, making converting existing manufacturing lines into HD-DVD lines simpler and more cost-effective. Consequently, it took more time for managers to decide on any particular technology. This explains why some major studios, such as Paramount Pictures, DreamWorks, Warner Bros., and New Line Cinemas, have been essentially neutral in the battle of the two technologies. Recent sales figures show that Blu-ray discs have outsold HD-DVD discs during the first quarter of 2007 by a 70–30 margin, according to market research conducted by *Home Media Magazine* (McGoughey, 2007), indicative of an upcoming technological winner.

## Factors Affecting Rational Expectations in Technology Investment Decisions

Different kinds of factors are likely to be influential in affecting the development of technology value in light of their impacts on the formation of rational expectations. The IT investment and adoption scenario that we described above assumes similar levels of risk-averseness among managers. The assumption may not always hold, however, since managers may take actions under different degrees of uncertainties. For example, managers of a firm may decide to invest in an emerging technology early to secure the first-mover advantage. Although Shapiro and Varian (1999) maintained that first-mover advantage can be powerful and long lasting for firms that can establish an installed base before the competition arrives, the advantage can be short-lived or even fail to materialize if early entrants are unable to maintain their dominance. This implies higher degrees of uncertainties and risks. The impact of risk aversion and perceived reliability of information was analyzed by Chatterjee and Eliashberg (1990). They found that lower risk aversion and greater perceived reliability of information imply earlier expected adoption. Another reason for adopting early is because a firm has a vested interest in the technology. In the Blu-ray vs. HD-DVD case, some major movie studios such as Columbia Pictures and MGM, have long decided to adopt Blu-ray simply because these companies are owned by Sony Corp., the company that created and now sells the technology.

Another factor that may affect the formation of rational expectations is the degree of information sharing among managers. Without a full degree of information sharing, some managers will be unaware of the plans of other managers. This, of course, will inhibit the formation of rational expectations because when it is very costly to share information, it will be very costly for managers to reach a shared understanding of the potential value of a technology. Consequently, the rational expectations and adaptive learning theory will work best when information sharing is costless or nearly costless, such as we have seen with cheap talk. When information transmission costs become somewhat greater, it may be in the interest of some managers and their firms to subsidize the diffusion of relevant information.

*Self-fulfilling expectations* can also interfere with the formation of rational expectations. Merton (1957, p. 477) maintains that a *self-fulfilling prophecy* is a phenomenon that occurs when "a false definition of the situation evoking a new behavior . . . makes the original false conception come true. This specious validity of the self-fulfilling prophecy perpetuates a reign of error." Once an expectation is set, even if it is not accurate, people will tend to act in ways consistent with that expectation. Any new and emerging technology goes through a phase of over-enthusiasm or hype, and unrealistic projections due to a flurry of well-publicized activities by technology vendors and supporters. During this phase, it is possible that some managers may prematurely reach a consensus on the potential value of the technology and make technology investment decisions based on the consensus. Thus, it is very important for the managers to be aware of this initial phase so as not to fall into the trap of a false sense of security in thinking they have done the best possible job in the technology potential-value assessment. Managers should be able to gauge these factors during a technology investment planning process to the extent that they can filter this "noise" that can potentially distort the real potential value.

## Rational Expectations, Risks, and Uncertainties: A Model for Planning

In decision making under uncertainty, managers begin with certain expectations about future events and modify these expectations as new information and insights are gained from interactions and information sharing with other relevant parties. The rational expectations and adaptive learning theory implicitly maintains that managers will be able to minimize the gap between potential value and realized value if they recognize the dynamic nature of the various factors and underlying risks that together determine the value of the technology. Managers who acknowledge that there is great uncertainty associated with any new technology will allow themselves enough time to assess the potential value of the technology. Through multilateral interactions with the other stakeholders, cheap talk, and other market-based information-sharing mechanisms (e.g., industry and technology conferences), managers will repeatedly update their predictions about the potential value of the technology until they reach a consensus with respect to potential value, which should be a better prediction of the realized value.

What is needed is a means for understanding how these expectations translate into specific decisions and actions. It should explain several issues related to decision making and investment decisions under uncertainty. For example, to what extent can we assume that the manager's expectations about the future accurately reflect the best guess about future events? How does the manager formally update these expectations as new information is gathered? How might different managers arrive at decisions to adopt the same technology that ultimately resembles clustered adoption by the marketplace? These and other issues are formally dealt with in the theories of rational expectations and adapted learning, and their extensions.

To this end, we develop a model for technology adoption and investment planning, based on the key concepts we have discussed and taking advantage of these theoretical perspectives. The diagram in Figure 14.2 is a representation that suggests a set of planning actions based on our perspective. The actions include an initial assessment of the technology being considered. This is preceded by the initial information-gathering process through interactions with other stakeholders, cheap talk, and market-based information sharing. The rational expectations and adaptive learning perspective recognizes the managers' bounded rationality and the fact that they may have access to dissimilar information, causing information asymmetry. Consequently, our model suggests that each manager should wait some time and collect more information through the same previous mechanisms.

After this waiting period, the managers should reassess the potential value of the technology using the newly acquired information, which includes the other stakeholders' assessments. If there is any change in the assessment, the managers should return to the waiting period and gather more information. The process repeats until there is no more change in the assessment, signifying the reaching of a consensus on the potential value of the technology. At this point, the managers may proceed with the actual technology adoption and investment, if the consensus potential value of the new technology is greater than its cost.

## RATIONAL EXPECTATIONS IN TECHNOLOGY INVESTMENTS: APPLICATION

In this section, we further develop our arguments about rational expectations-based technology investment decision making, based on the model introduced earlier. We also explore the process that leads to a market-wide consensus for investments, something particularly relevant for a technology that exhibits strong network effects.

### The Role of Rational Expectations in Technology Investment Planning

As our model in Figure 14.2 shows, the rational expectations and adaptive learning theory suggests that managers will invest a reasonable amount of time to gather all relevant information from all possible sources and process the information optimally to learn about the potential value of a new technology. This implies that managers do not simply follow what others have done, although they may learn from the experience of others. This is different from the concept of *herd behavior* (Bikchandani, Hirshleifer, and Welch, 1992, 1998), where a manager follows the action of another manager and ignores his or her own information. *Herding* or *groupthink* defies a basic assumption of economic behavior, namely, that decision makers as economic agents do the best they can with the information they have.

The practical implication of the rational expectations and adaptive learning perspective is that managers should not make any major IT investment decision before they feel comfortable with their knowledge about the technology. This is important to keep in mind: the pace at which IT

Figure 14.2    **Rational Expectations and Adaptive Learning IT Investment/Adoption Planning Model**

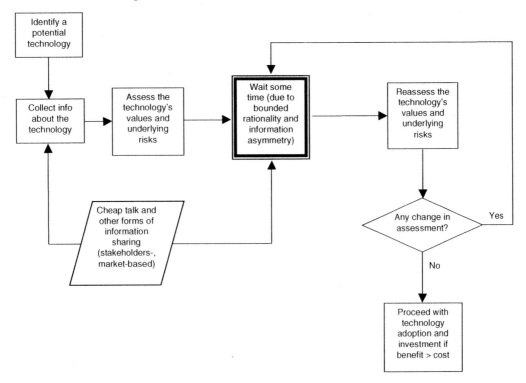

evolves can lead to errors caused by rushing into investing in the latest technology to stay ahead of the competition or, at least, to avoid being left behind. Rushing often leads to disastrous results, as the trend for most new and emerging technologies is to go through the phase of inflated expectations when unrealistic projections occur. This causes any estimates to involve high levels of variance in terms of costs, benefits, and risks.

Determining how long to wait and how much new information to collect before reassessing the new technology is key in our model. The amount of waiting time should be determined based on how fast the new technology develops its presence in the market and how costly the information about the new technology is. Bhattacharya, Chatterjee, and Samuelson (1986) revealed that costly information acquisition may lead to an infinite delay in the adoption of a profitable new technology. This is an important consideration in our model and it serves as the rationale for our assumption that managers will gather information about the technology from different sources, including cheap talk, which can and often does matter, since even a limited common interest may make it meaningful (Farrell and Rabin, 1996). Other low-cost information sharing and transmission among managers can occur through their participation in industry conferences, the development of technology via vendor-supported pilot projects, and increasingly widespread knowledge of the technological innovations. The presence of these sometimes costless and usually low-cost information sources can prevent an infinite delay in the adoption of a profitable new technology. Our model is consistent with Jensen (1988a), who found that if information costs are positive but sufficiently small, the optimal policy for a firm may be represented by the process of "wait, buy new information, wait, buy new information, adopt."

Our model requires managers to repeatedly wait and reassess the technology's value and underlying risks, until there is no more change in the assessment. As we have discussed, the main reason for the waiting and reassessment approach is that managers have bounded rationality, which can mean either limited access to information or limited ability to process the available information, or both. Consequently, our model suggests that a manager's ability to collect and make the most of the information plays a key role in the IT investment and adoption decision-making process. The impact of a manager's capacity to obtain and evaluate information is analyzed by Jensen (1988b), who demonstrates that a greater information capacity entails not only faster learning but also a more rigorous adoption criterion, which tends to make firms adopt later. Furthermore, Thijssen and colleagues (2001) study adoption timing when costless new information arrives according to a Poisson stochastic process, to capture the intensity of information arrival. They show that the firm will choose to wait for even more signals as new information arrives faster.

The main challenge in any technology investment and adoption decision-making process is to identify the timing of investment and adoption, which, according to our model, is the time when new information does not change a manager's assessment of the new technology any further. In the rational expectations and adaptive learning theory's terminology, it is the time when the rational expectations equilibrium point is reached. The theory suggests that this timing occurs when all managers involved in the information exchange and cheap talk reach a consensus on their assessments on the value and risks of the technology. At this point, all acts of learning are complete, in the sense that there is no more incentive on the part of managers to change their assessments. This implies that managers can actually leverage cheap talk to identify timing of investment and adoption by constantly exchanging their assessments.

## Rational Expectations and Market-Wide Consensus on Technology Value

The ideas related to market-wide consensus can be exemplified using RFID adoption and implementation. Although RFID technology holds great promise in areas that range from national security to aggregate supply-chain management for corporations to specific consumer applications (e.g., smart shopping carts in supermarkets), several main issues continue to challenge the use of the technology (Curtin, Kauffman, and Riggins, 2007). In the pharmaceutical industry, for instance, a recent study indicates RFID adoption has been slower than expected, despite several leading pharmaceutical companies' positive experiences in testing it as well as encouragement from the U.S. Food and Drug Administration (FDA) to investigate the technology (*RFID Journal*, 2007). The pharmaceutical market is actually a perfect incubator for RFID applications because it has high-value products and high volumes, making it easier to justify investment and to recognize economies of scale. The market is also compliance-driven, which means that it is possible to impose adoption timelines by creating a sense of urgency for the technology. However, the industry must agree on several issues before widespread adoption can occur. The issues include which frequency to use, whether there are standards for sharing data and for integrating data with back-end systems (Roberti, 2006). All these require consensus among all stakeholders in the industry. Once these issues are resolved and consensus is reached, a domino effect will most likely follow, since the pharmaceutical value chain is heavily integrated with the consumer packaged goods, retail, and health care supply chains.

RFID is an example of technology that relies on network effects to thrive, and the rational expectations and adaptive learning perspective works particularly well with this kind of technology. This is because a manager with rational expectations that considers a technology with network effects will make sure that the other managers will also adopt the same technology; otherwise, the manager faces the risks of being stranded. *Stranding* occurs when only one or two managers decide to adopt the technology and the others decide not to, eliminating the chance for the adopters to realize the expected network benefits. We maintain that to avoid such risks, managers will choose to adopt the technology at about the same time, that is, when they learn that all managers are ready to adopt. We call this phenomenon *clustered adoption* (Au and Kauffman, 2003, 2005). This requires that managers continuously monitor the perceptions of the other managers on the potential value of the technology and adjust their own accordingly. This causes migration in perceptions on potential value over time. Managers might begin with different value expectations due to different information and capabilities that they possess but over time will adjust their perceptions and expectations. And since they have a mutual goal of getting the most benefit from the technology based on the common understanding that most of the benefit will come from network effects, managers will actually try to share as much information as possible and find the cheapest way to do so.

The need for managers to reach a consensus creates interesting dynamics in the IT investment and adoption decision-making process. Managers must now monitor each other's actions and perhaps take signals from each other before making a technology investment and adoption decision. They should be aware, however, that there may be some exceptions to the rational expectations and adaptive learning technology adoption process. This is because, along with this process, some managers may decide to conduct a pilot test, and some may even decide to adopt early before a consensus is reached. We can argue that an early technology adoption or investment decision is based more on risk-taking behavior than rational expectations. In other words, managers who are more averse to risk will still make a decision later when enough information has become available and has been processed appropriately and, more important, a consensus has been reached. This demonstrates the need for managers to assess the risk tolerance of others who influence their decision-making process.

## MANAGING POTENTIAL-TO-REALIZED VALUE TRAJECTORIES: AN EXTENSION

The theoretical model discussed previously suggests that managers should expect to see the phenomenon of drift or migration of technology value over time. In this section, we discuss a methodology that managers can use to better manage the value trajectory of their technology investments. We discuss how this perspective can be extended to treat settings in which technology investment planners and managers wish to manage the value trajectory for potential-to-realized value.

### Market-Wide Consensus vs. Potential Value of Technology Investment

To better manage the value trajectory of technology investments, managers must first have a methodology or a tool that enables them to objectively measure the potential and realized value of an IT investment. In this section, we discuss a new methodology proposed by Goh and Kauffman (2006) that applies at the industry level, involving a production economics-based *potential value measurement model* (hereafter PVMM). The methodology uses the *Malmquist productivity index* to chart the potential and realized value of investments in U.S. industries. The Malmquist productivity index is a nonparametric measure introduced by Caves, Christensen, and Diewert (1982) that determines the details of efficiency changes over time by economic units. The specification of this measurement model is flexible and can be generalized to measure the potential and realized value of firm-level, business-process, and other activity-level IT investments. To apply this methodology, the user needs to have historical technology investment data, along with information on other factors of production and measures of the technology investment output. These include benefits such as process improvement data, cost savings information, and evidence of revenue gains. Based on the historical data, PVMM permits the analyst to construct an upper boundary on the potential value, which further enables the gap between the realized value and potential value to be assessed.

The model is designed to handle multiple technology production inputs and multiple outputs. This is helpful because the benefits of technology often occur in different forms in various areas in the organization. Since the outputs do not have to be aggregated to a common measure (e.g., aggregate revenues or transactions), this facilitates a more accurate and informative estimation of the technology's potential value. The potential value of technology investments changes in accordance with new information made available to the manager. PVMM can assess technology investments across multiple time periods, so that with each successive time period new investment and performance data will update and re-plot the boundary of potential value. The constant update of this boundary of potential value is useful to managers as it reflects the dynamic nature of value conversion, hence providing realistic estimation to match investors' expectations.

PVMM has various uses for technology investors including: (1) estimating and updating expected value of the existing project, (2) evaluating additional and complementary investment, and (3) post hoc assessment of managerial investment decisions. The use of this model for estimating existing projects is straightforward and involves the direct application of existing available investment data, as described in the previous paragraph. In the remainder of this section, we focus on describing the use of this model for evaluating additional investment. The model allows the user to obtain estimates of potential value for the impending investments, and this facilitates users in better evaluating the project in its planning and implementation stages. Potential value projection is essential as it can be readily used as a gauge to assess additional complementary technology investment based on prior expectations. Technology investments often occur in stages and some key information that investors need is the projected potential benefits of the investment and how additional investment will complement and augment the potential value of existing investments in subsequent time periods. This information, however, is not readily and sufficiently estimated using conventional financial valuation techniques such as return on investment (ROI) or net present value (NPV) (Devaraj and Kohli, 2002). Conventional financial valuation techniques focus mainly on cash flow and are unable to incorporate the risk profile, intangible benefits, and stochasticity of IT investments.

PVMM is appropriate for this purpose, as by design, it decomposes the value-conversion process for multiple time periods into (1) the change in potential value and (2) the change in realized value. In multiple time periods where subsequent technology investments are being made, one expects the value conversion process to shift. This shift can be measured by either the change of potential value—where subsequent investments provide greater (or lesser) option value, or a change in realized value—where subsequent investments are more (or less) readily absorbed into the organizational processes to realize its benefit along the value trajectory curve. By populating the measurement model with historical data that contain key parameters of technology investments made at multiple stages, the measurement model breaks down the shift in the value-conversion process at each stage of technology investment. Managers are able to observe the projected change in potential or realized value from one investment project to another to make a more informed decision about additional investment at different stages of the corporate IT plan. We next discuss the use of this measurement perspective for *post hoc* assessment of the quality of managerial decisions.

**Managerial Decisions and the Realization of Technology Investment Value**

Managerial performance is reflected by how well decisions are made in light of the information available and how these decisions are subsequently translated into firm performance. Technology investments are usually made based on prior beliefs and expectations about the payoff. An effective investment decision-making process involves accurately weighing the potential benefits against the projected costs of investment to obtain an objective assessment of the investment plan. Having a model such as PVMM that measures the potential and realized value of IT investments serves not only as a forecasting tool but also as a *post hoc* quality assessment tool for managerial decisions. There are two ways to use PVMM for quality assessment on managerial decisions. First, the model can be used to measure the precision of the decision that is made (i.e., a decision assessment). Second, it can be used to assess the effectiveness of the actions of the decision in terms of resulting in payoffs for the firm (i.e., an action assessment).

Decision assessment involves evaluating the variance between managers' predicted potential value and actual potential value of the investment. In Text Box 14.1, we provide a more precise description of how this assessment can be conducted using our modeling approach, PVMM. In this context, an action assessment involves evaluating the effectiveness of the managerial actions that follow throughout the cycle of investment for value realization. This assessment is performed mainly at the end of the implementation phase and can be extended to multiple time periods after the implementation is completed due to lags in the flow of the value payoffs.

When the implementation is completed, the realized value of the investment at that point is not likely to match the potential value, for the technology needs time to be fully absorbed in the organization's business processes to achieve its maximum ability to create value. Similar to what we would do when we assess an IT investment decision, we compute the potential value of the investment at the end of implementation using PVMM, and compare this value against the realized value at various points in time after completion. The realized value in this case is measured using identical metrics and the gap between the potential and realized value signals the effectiveness of managerial actions in managing the implementation process to yield the realized value of the investment.

## CONCLUSION

In this chapter, we have sought to provide some new ideas for how IT investment planning might be approached with a rational expectations planning perspective in mind. We have also made an effort to show how this perspective can be applied in practice, through its application in typical settings and through the introduction of some important concepts that help to structure senior managers' thinking.

### Contributions

Our primary contribution to academic research is to provide a theoretical synthesis that relates rational expectations to concepts of potential and realized value of IT investments. In this case, the rational expectations and adaptive learning theories recognize the gap in the potential and realized value, and explain how such a gap can be minimized given sufficient time. We also illustrate how the rational expectations hypothesis can be operationalized and implemented using production economic techniques, as a basis for exploring the payoffs of IT investments. Although this is a first step toward creating a synthesis of these two different theoretical paradigms, our effort is

**TEXT BOX 14.1**

**DECISION ASSESSMENT USING THE POTENTIAL VALUE MEASUREMENT MODEL (PVVM)**

We now provide a detailed illustration of our potential value measurement model (PVVM). We begin by assuming that the original managerial estimation of potential value is based on some other means of evaluation outside the scope of PVMM. For the purposes of this discussion, we will assume these estimates are based on some kind of heuristics for the assessment of IT value (e.g., order of magnitude of returns, Delphi assessments among a group of stakeholders, or individual "guesstimates," etc.). The assessment can occur in all stages throughout the entire lifecycle of the investment. In the planning stage, the investment decision is made based on initial expectations and estimation of the potential benefits. We capture this initial heuristic-based estimate with the notation V for value in $V_{Planning}^{Heuristic}$. The subscript Planning represents the planning phase and the superscript Heuristic represents the evaluation heuristic that is used.

As the IT investment moves into the implementation stage, managers will have a greater sense of the technology in terms of its progress in implementation by the rate of its adoption and the functionality benefits that support value creation. Based on this latest information, they can heuristically update their projection of potential benefits, $V_{Implementation}^{Heuristic}$, with the subscript Implementation representing the implementation phase. At completion, managers will be fully informed of the technology's capabilities, the organizational resistance or acceptance that has been experienced, and the qualities and influence of the business environment in which the technology is operating. This will permit them to update $V_{Implementation}^{Heuristic}$ to the final estimation of potential value, $V_{Completion}^{Heuristic}$, with the subscript Completion representing the completion phase of the investment cycle. To compare the accuracy of these heuristic-based estimates, we use PVMM to compute the potential value of the investment at the time of completion, VPVVM. Estimates for VPVVM should consist of performance metrics that are identical to the measures used to measure the value in the planning, implementation, and completion phases. The variances between VPVVM and each of the prior managerial estimates will be quality indicators of the managerial investment decision. Overall, smaller variances tend to suggest higher decision quality, with managerial forecasts being highly reflective of the actual situation. One expects the variance to be larger for estimates in the early planning stages than when the investment is completely implemented, as we have seen in other research (e.g., on software development metrics in Banker, Kauffman, and Kumar, 1993; Banker et al., 1994).

Thus, it should be the case that:
$\left| V^{PVMM} - V_{Planning}^{Heuristic} \right| > \left| V^{PVMM} - V_{Implementation}^{Heuristic} \right| > \left| V^{PVMM} - V_{Completion}^{Heuristic} \right|$. By definition, a positive variance in value, $V^{PVVM} > V^{Heuristic}$, for any of the heuristics indicates that the PVMM estimate is higher than the managerial estimate; a negative variance indicates the opposite. The presence of a negative variance suggests suboptimal decision making as managers are overestimating the potential value of the IT investment at different phases of investment. Although a positive variance may seem to be beneficial to the organization, in fact, it suggests that the managers may have adopted a risk-averse stance—and hence the lower estimation of value potential—and are making suboptimal decisions for the firm by missing out on investment opportunities. This may be symptomatic of underinvestment in IT, a common problem where there are risks and uncertainties, information asymmetries, agency problems, and incomplete contracts between business partners (Han, Kauffman, and Nault, 2004).

important in establishing a meaningful conceptual understanding of the theoretical underpinnings for rational expectations in IT investments. We highlight a model for measuring the potential and realized value of IT that helps extend the IS literature on IT value measurement. We also incorporate economic theory and management science methods that offer particular leverage for understanding this complex problem. We show how the application of this model will facilitate future research by enabling researchers to better understand the gap between the potential and the realized value of IT investments.

In this chapter, we have illustrated some ways in which a measurement model can be used by practitioners for future technology planning, and to assess current initiatives and evaluate past investments. This will aid practitioners in making optimal investment decisions and better planning and implementing their technology initiatives. We draw practitioners' attention to the ways that information can shape their expectations about investment payoffs and how new information is likely to affect the value trajectory for their IT investment alongside existing investments. By highlighting this process in our writing, we hope to establish a more in-depth understanding in senior managers' minds about the nature of the IT value-conversion process. Finally, we have suggested and described various practical applications for the use of a *potential value measurement system* for practitioners. We hope this proposal will spawn new and valuable ideas related to the management of technology investments under conditions of uncertainty.

## Limitations

Our objective in this chapter has been to showcase some newly available theoretical and methodological perspectives that will serve to stimulate discussion among IS researchers and senior managers who are charged with making IT investment decisions. Although we have not presented empirical support in this chapter—instead, leaving that for future research—this does not undermine the usefulness of the ideas that we have proposed. We have covered some of the relevant empirical literature in this domain on behalf of the reader, and we hope that this will encourage more empirical research on IT investment and evaluation practices from the rational-expectations point of view.

In discussing the applications of PVMM, we suggest using historic investment data on technology investments, which may be difficult to acquire by firms that have limited prior experience in technology implementation. Despite this operational limitation, the benefits of the measurement system should not be overlooked. We believe that this application is still well-suited for software vendors and consulting firms that have access to large amounts of past investment data and have an interest in further developing it into a rational expectations-based forecasting tool.

## ACKNOWLEDGMENTS

We would like to acknowledge input we received on these IT investment planning ideas from a variety of sources, including faculty and doctoral colleagues at the University of Texas at San Antonio, the University of Minnesota, Arizona State University, the Workshop on IS and Economics, INFORMS Conference on IS and Technology, and the Hawaii International Conference on System Sciences. Bill King and two anonymous reviewers also offered useful suggestions on improving this chapter. Yoris Au thanks the College of Business of the University of Texas at San Antonio for generous support. Rob Kauffman thanks Donna Sarppo and the MIS Research Center, and the W.P. Carey Chair at Arizona State University for partial support. Fred Riggins thanks 3M Corporation for research funding through their 2005–2006 and 2006–2007 faculty fellowships.

## REFERENCES

Amram, M., and Kulatilaka, N. 1999. *Real Options: Managing Strategic Investment in an Uncertain World.* Cambridge: Harvard Business School Press.

Aron, R.; Clemons, E.K.; and Reddi, S.P. 2005. Just right outsourcing: understanding and managing risk. *Journal of Management Information Systems,* 22, 2, 35–56.

Au, Y.A., and Kauffman, R.J. 2001. Should we wait? network externalities and electronic billing adoption. *Journal of Management Information Systems,* 18, 2, 47–64.

———. 2003. What do you know? rational expectations and information technology investment. *Journal of Management Information Systems,* 20, 2, 49–76.

———. 2005. Rational expectations and information technology adoption. *Information Systems and E-Business Management,* 3, 1, 47–70.

Banker, R.D.; Isakowitz, T.; Kumar, R.; and Zweig, D. 1994. Tools for repository management. In P. Geriner (ed.), *Analytical Methods for Software Engineering Economics II.* New York: Springer-Verlag, 117–138.

Banker, R.D., and Kauffman, R.J. 1998. Strategic contributions of information technology: an empirical study of ATM networks. In *Proceedings of the Ninth International Conference on Information Systems,* Minneapolis, MN, December, 141–150.

Banker, R.D.; Kauffman, R.J.; and Kumar, R. 1993. Tracking the life cycle trajectory: metrics and measures for controlling productivity of computer aided software engineering (CASE) development. In J. Keyes (ed.), *Handbook on Software Productivity.* New York: McGraw-Hill, 263–296.

Bardhan, I.R.; Sougstad, R.; and Bagchi, S. 2004. Prioritization of a portfolio of information technology projects. *Journal of Management Information Systems,* 21, 2, 33–60.

Benaroch, M. 2001. Option-based management of technology investment risk. *IEEE Transactions on Engineering Management,* 48, 4, 428–444.

Benaroch, M., and Kauffman, R.J. 1999. A case for using real options pricing analysis to evaluate information technology project investments. *Information Systems Research,* 10, 1, 70–86.

———. 2000. Justifying electronic network expansion using real option analysis. *MIS Quarterly,* 24, 2, 197–225.

Benaroch, M.; Jeffery, M.; Kauffman, R.J.; and Shah, S. 2007. Option-based risk management: a field study of sequential IT investment decisions. *Journal of Management Information Systems,* 24, 2, 103–140.

Benaroch, M.; Lichtenstein, Y.; and Robinson, K. 2006. Real options in IT risk management: an empirical validation of risk-option relationships. *MIS Quarterly,* 30, 2, 827–864.

Bhattacharya, S.; Chatterjee, K.; and Samuelson, L. 1986. Sequential research and the adoption of innovations. *Oxford Economic Papers,* 38 (Supplement), 219–243.

Bikchandani, S.; Hirshleifer, D.; and Welch, I. 1992. A theory of fads, fashion, custom, and cultural change as informational cascades. *Journal of Political Economy,* 100, 5, 992–1026.

———. 1998. Learning from the behavior of others: conformity, fads and informational cascades. *Journal of Economic Perspectives,* 12, 3, 151–170.

Bloomfield, R., and M. O'Hara. 1999. Market transparency: who wins and who loses? *Review of Financial Studies,* 12, 1, 5–35.

Burnham, B. 1999. *How to Invest in E-Commerce Stocks.* New York: McGraw-Hill.

Caves, D.W.; Christensen, L.R.; and Diewert, W.E. 1982. Multilateral comparisons of output, input, and productivity using superlative index numbers. *Economic Journal,* 92, 365, 73–86.

Chatterjee, R., and Eliashberg, J. 1990. The innovation diffusion process in a heterogeneous population: a micromodeling approach. *Management Science,* 36, 9, 1057–1079.

Clemons, E.K. 1991. Evaluating strategic investments in information systems. *Communications of the ACM,* 34, 1, 22–36.

———. 2007. An empirical investigation of third-party seller rating systems in e-commerce: the case of buySAFE. *Journal of Management Information Systems,* 24, 2, 43–71.

Clemons, E.K., and Gu, B. 2003. Justifying contingent information technology investments: balancing the need for speed of action with certainty before action. *Journal of Management Information Systems,* 20, 2, 11–48.

Clemons, E.K., and Hitt, L.M. 2004. Poaching and the misappropriation of information: transaction risks of information exchange. *Journal of Management Information Systems,* 21, 2, 87–107.

Clemons, E.K., and McFarlan, W. 1986. Telecom: hook up or lose out. *Harvard Business Review,* 64, 4, 90–97.

Clemons, E.K.; Reddi, S.P.; and Row, M.C. 1993. The impact of information technology on the organization of economic activity: the "move to the middle" hypothesis. *Journal of Management Information Systems,* 10, 2, 9–35.

Cummings, J. 2002. IT portfolio management. *NetworkWorld,* April 1.

Curtin, J.; Kauffman, R.J.; and Riggins, F.J. 2007. Making the "MOST" out of RFID technology: a research agenda for the study of the adoption, usage and impact of RFID. *Information Technology and Management,* 8, 2 (June), 87–110.

Dai, Q.; Kauffman, R.J.; and March, S. 2007. Valuing information technology infrastructures: a growth options approach. *Information Technology and Management,* 8, 1, 1–17.

Davern, M., and Kauffman, R.J. 2000. The value of decision technologies: discovering potential and realizing value. *Journal of Management Information Systems,* 16, 4, 121–144.

Day, G.S.; Fein, A.J.; and Ruppersberger, G. 2003. Shakeouts in digital markets: lessons from B2B exchanges. *California Management Review,* 45, 2, 131–150.

Devaraj, S., and Kohli, R. 2000. Information technology payoff in the healthcare industry: a longitudinal study. *Journal of Management Information Systems,* 16, 4, 41–67.

———. 2002. *The IT Payoff,* 1st ed. Upper Saddle River, NJ: Prentice Hall.

———. 2003. Performance impacts of information technology: is actual usage the missing link? *Management Science,* 49, 3, 273–289.

Dewan, S.; Gurbaxani, V.; and Chi, C. 2004. Investigating the risk–return relationship of information technology investment: firm-level empirical analysis. Paper presented at the 2004 Annual Meeting of the American Accounting Association, Orlando, FL, August 8–11.

*Digital Photographer.* 2007a. Kodak vs. Kodak: Which 13.5MP DSLR takes the sharpest prints? April. Available at www.digiphotomag.com/issues/current.html (accessed on June 28, 2007).

———. 2007b. Canon EOS 1D2 Mark II: A 16.7MP CMOS image sensor, extensive professional controls and full-frame capture put this DSLR at the top of the heap. April. Available at www.digiphotomag.com/issues/current.html (accessed on June 28, 2007).

Dixit, A., and Pindyck, R. 1994. *Investment under Uncertainty.* Princeton, NJ: Princeton University Press.

Dos Santos, B. 1991. Justifying investment in new information technologies. *Journal of Management Information Systems,* 7, 4, 71–89.

Duliba, K.; Kauffman, R.J.; and Lucas, H.C. Jr. 2001. Appropriation and value of airline computer reservation systems. *Organization Science,* 12, 6, 702–728.

Farrell, J., and Rabin, M. 1996. Cheap talk. *Journal of Economic Perspectives,* 10, 3, 103–118.

Fichman, R.; Keil, M.; and Tiwana, A. 2005. Beyond valuation: options thinking in IT project management. *California Management Review,* 47, 2, 74–96.

Frydman, R. 1982. Towards an understanding of market processes: individual expectations, learning, and convergence to rational expectations equilibrium. *American Economic Review,* 72, 4, 652–668.

Goh, K., and Kauffman, R.J. 2005. Toward a theory of value latency for IT investments. In R. Sprague (ed.), *Proceedings of the Thirty-eighth Hawaii International Conference on Systems Science,* Island of Hawaii, HI. Los Alamitos, CA: IEEE Computer Society Press.

———. 2006. An industry-level analysis of the potential and realized value of IT. In D. Straub and S. Klein (eds.), *Proceedings of the Twenty-seventh International Conference on Information Systems,* Milwaukee, WI, December 10–13.

Granados, N.F.; Gupta, A.; and Kauffman, R.J. 2005. Transparency strategy in Internet-based selling. In K. Tomak (ed.), *Advances in the Economics of Information Systems.* Harrisburg, PA: Idea Group.

———. 2006. The impact of IT on market information and transparency: a unified theoretical framework. *Journal of the Association for Information Systems,* 7, 3, 148–178.

———. 2007. IT-enabled transparent electronic markets: the case of the air travel industry. *Information Systems and E-Business Management,* 5, 1, 65–91.

Gustafson, N., and Luft, J. 2002. Valuing strategic flexibility in information technology investments: when do subjective valuation and real options analysis differ? Working paper, Eli Broad School of Business, Michigan State University, East Lansing.

Han, K.; Kauffman, R.J.; and Nault, B.R. 2004. Information exploitation and interorganizational systems ownership. *Journal of Management Information Systems,* 21, 2, 109–135.

Hasbrouck, J. 1995. Trade and quote transparency: principles and prospects for the year 2000. In R.A. Schwartz (ed.), Global *Equity Markets: Technological, Competitive, and Regulatory Challenges.* New York: Irwin Professional, 218–226.

Haskin, D. 2007. Don't believe the hype: the 21 biggest technology flops. *Computerworld,* April 4. Available at www.computerworld.com/action/article.do?command=viewArticleBasic&articleId=9012345 (accessed on June 28, 2007).

Hoffman, T. 2003. Balancing the IT portfolio. *Computerworld,* February 10.

Hunter, S.; Kobelsky, K.; and Richardson, V.J. 2004. Information technology and the volatility of firm performance. Working paper 4449–03, Sloan School of Management, MIT, Cambridge, MA, March.

Jeffery, M., and Leliveld, I. 2004. Best practices in IT portfolio management. *Sloan Management Review,* 45, 3, 41–49.

Jensen, R. 1988a. Information cost and innovation adoption policies. *Management Science,* 34, 2, 230–239.

———. 1988b. Information capacity and innovation adoption. *International Journal of Industrial Organization,* 6, 3, 335–350.

Josefek, R.A., and Kauffman, R.J. 1997. Dark pockets and decision support: the information technology value cycle in efficient markets. *Electronic Markets,* 7, 3, 36–42.

Kauffman, R.J., and Li, X. 2005. Technology competition and optimal investment timing: a real options perspective. *IEEE Transactions on Engineering Management,* 52, 1, 15–29.

Kauffman, R.J.; Miller, T.; and Wang, B. 2006. Understanding the survival of Internet firms. *First Monday,* 11, 7 (July). Available at www.firstmonday.org (accessed on May 28, 2007).

Kauffman, R.J., and Mohtadi, H. 2004. Proprietary and open systems adoption: a risk-augmented transactions cost perspective. *Journal of Management Information Systems,* 21, 1, 137–166.

Kauffman, R.J., and Sougstad, R. 2007. Value-at-risk in IT services contracts. In R. Sprague (ed.), *Proceedings of the Fortieth Hawaii International Conference on Systems Science,* Island of Hawaii, HI. Los Alamitos: IEEE Computing Society Press.

Kauffman, R.J., and Wang, B. 2001. New buyers' arrival under dynamic pricing market microstructure: the case of group-buying discounts on the Internet. *Journal of Management Information Systems,* 18, 2, 157–188.

———. 2002. Bid together, buy together: on the efficacy of group-buying models in Internet-based selling. In P.B. Lowry, J.O. Cherrington, and R.R. Watson (eds.), *Handbook of Electronic Commerce in Business and Society.* Boca Raton: CRC Press, 99–137.

Kauffman, R.J., and Weill, P. 1989. An evaluative framework for the performance effects of investments in information technology. In *Proceedings of the Tenth International Conference on Information Technology,* Boston, MA, December 4–6, 377–388.

Kauffman, R.J., and Wu, P. 2006. Optimal launch timing for new technology products with firm launch cost heterogeneity and value latency. Paper presented at the 2006 INFORMS Conference on Information Systems and Technologies, Pittsburgh, PA, November 4–5.

Kim, J. 1996. Cheap talk and reputation in repeated pretrial negotiation. *RAND Journal of Economics,* 27, 4, 787–802.

Kim, W.C., and Mauborgne, R. 2005. *Blue Ocean Strategy: How to Create Uncontested Market Space and Make the Competition Irrelevant.* Boston: Harvard Business School Press.

Kogut, B., and Kulatilaka, N. 1994. Options thinking and platform investments: investing in opportunity. *California Management Review,* 36, 4, 52–71.

Kulatilaka, N., and Venkatraman, N. 2001. Strategic options in the digital era. *Business Strategy Review,* 12, 4, 7–15.

Laing, R.D. 1970. *Knots.* London: Penguin.

Lohmann, S. 2000. I know you know he or she knows we know you know they know: common knowledge and the unpredictability of informational cascades. In D. Richards (ed.), *Political Complexity: Non-Linear Models of Politics.* Ann Arbor: University of Michigan Press, 137–173.

Luehrman, T.A. 1998. Strategy as a portfolio of real options. *Harvard Business Review,* 76, 5, 89–99.

Margrabe, W. 1978. The value of an option to exchange one asset for another. *Journal of Finance,* 33, 1, 177–186.

McGoughey, J. 2007. Blue-ray leads HD DVD in high def wars. *Associated Content,* April 23. Available at www.associatedcontent.com/article/223961/bluray_leads_hd_dvd_in_high_def_wars.html (accessed on June 28, 2007).

McGrath, R.M., and MacMillan, I. 2000. Assessing technology projects using real options reasoning. *Research Technology Management,* 43, 4, 35–49.

Merton, R.K. 1968. *Social Theory and Social Structure,* Enlarged Edition. New York: Free Press.

Muth, J.F. 1961. Rational expectations and the theory of price movements. *Econometrica*, 29, 3, 315–335.

Nerlove, M. 1958. Adaptive expectations and cobweb phenomena. *Quarterly Journal of Economics*, 72, 3, 227–240.

*RFID Journal*. 2007. Pharma RFID adoption still slow. April. Available at www.rfidjournal.com/ article/ articleview/3264/1/1/ (accessed on June 4, 2007).

Roberti, M. 2006. RFID is poised for widespread adoption. *RFID Journal*, December. Available at www. rfidjournal.com/article/articleview/2863/1/2/RFID (accessed on June 28, 2007).

Saloner, G., and Spence, A.M. 2002. *Creating and Capturing Value: Perspectives and Cases on Electronic Commerce*. New York: Wiley.

Sambamurthy, V.; Bharadwaj, A.; and Grover, V. 2003. Shaping agility through digital options: Reconceptualizing the role of information technology in contemporary firms. *MIS Quarterly*, 27, 2, 237–263.

Sargent, T.J. 1993. *Bounded Rationality in Macroeconomics*. Oxford: Oxford University Press.

Sargent, T.J., and Wallace, N. 1976. Rational expectations and the theory of economic policy. *Journal of Monetary Economics*, 2, 2, 169–183.

Schwartz, E.S., and Zozaya-Gorostiza, C. 2003. Investment under uncertainty in information technology: acquisition and development projects. *Management Science*, 49, 1, 57–70.

Shapiro, C., and Varian, H.R. 1999. *Information Rules: A Strategic Guide to the Network Economy*. Boston: Harvard Business School Press.

Simon, H.A. 1957. *Models of Man*. New York: Wiley.

Sougstad, R., and Bardhan, I. 2008. Empirical advances in analyzing information technology investment portfolios: leveraging the log-transformed binomial model. In R.J. Kauffman and P.A. Tallon (eds.), *Economics, Information Systems, and Electronic Commerce Research: Empirical Research*, Volume 13, *Advances in Management Information Systems*. Armonk, NY: M.E. Sharpe.

Spence, A.M. 1973. Job market signaling. *Quarterly Journal of Economics*, 87, 3, 355–374.

———. 1974. *Market Signaling: Informational Transfer in Hiring and Related Screening Processes*. Boston: Harvard University Press.

Stensvold, M. 2007. Complete D-SLR system guide: with 10 companies offering D-SLRs today, there's something for everyone. *PCPhoto*. Available at www.pcphotomag.com/buyerrsquos-guides/cameras/ complete-d-slr-system-guide.html (accessed on June 28, 2007).

Taudes, A. 1998. Software growth options. *Journal of Management Information Systems*, 15, 1, 165–185.

Taudes, A.; Feurstein, M.; and Mild, A. 2000. Options analysis of software platform decisions: a case study. *MIS Quarterly*, 24, 2, 227–244.

Thijssen, J.J.J.; van Damme, E.E.C.; Huisman, K.J.M.; and Kort, P.M. 2001. Investment under vanishing uncertainty due to information arriving over time. Discussion paper (Int. rep. 2001–14) (February), Tilburg University, Netherlands.

Zhu, K., and Weyant, J. 2003. Strategic decisions of new technology adoption under asymmetric information: a game-theoretic model. *Decision Sciences*, 34, 4, 1–33.

# CHAPTER 15

# INFORMATION TECHNOLOGY INVESTMENT PLANNING

## Anticipating Social Subsystem Costs and Benefits

SHERRY D. RYAN

**Abstract:** *The costs and benefits associated with organizational employees can be consider-able when new IT is acquired. Therefore, it is important that decision makers consider these social subsystem issues when planning for new information systems. Using sociotechnical systems theory as the theoretical lens, this chapter discusses various categories of these costs and benefits, when organizations are likely to consider them, and how organizations grapple with costs and benefits that are difficult to quantify. The chapter also describes the ways that these issues are incorporated into IT planning and decision processes and the characteristics of organizations that are most likely to consider these employee-related costs and benefits.*

**Keywords:** *IT Investment Decisions, Decision-making Processes, Intangible Costs and Benefits, IT Assessment, Sociotechnical Systems*

Worldwide spending in information technology (IT) is predicted to reach $10.7 billion by 2009 (Perera, 2007). Justifications for these investments often rely on anticipated return on investment (ROI). Yet executives frequently struggle with how to incorporate costs and benefits associated with their employees in the implementation and postimplementation phases of IT adoption. Previous research has shown that these costs and benefits can be significant (e.g., He, 2004; Williams, 2006), and ignoring or undervaluing them may lead to inaccurate assumptions about the true expenses and returns of the IT under consideration. This can lead to less than optimal decisions or technology choices that do not provide the anticipated yields.

This chapter discusses the importance of IT investment costs and benefits that result from employees' task interdependencies, expertise, judgments, and decisions. Consistent with the tenets and terminology of sociotechnical systems (STS) theory (Herbst, 1974), we label these social subsystem costs and benefits. Our discussion will first briefly review the underlying principles of sociotechnical systems theory (STST). Next, we will describe the types of social subsystem costs and benefits that organizations sometimes consider. Third, we will examine when firms are likely to consider social subsystem costs and benefits in their IT planning processes followed by a discussion of the importance of social subsystem issues relative to other factors. We include in this discussion how organizations wrestle with the less quantifiable or intangible forms of social subsystem costs and benefits. We also describe the ways that these issues are incorporated into

IT planning and decision processes. Finally, we discuss the characteristics of firms that are most likely to consider social subsystem costs and benefits.

## PRINCIPLES OF SOCIOTECHNICAL SYSTEMS THEORY

STST has its roots in open systems theory. In open systems theory, the term "open" implies that the components receive input from the environment and "system" describes the interaction of components with one another. With sociotechnical systems (STS), linear and mechanistic thinking are replaced by system thinking—a way of thinking that recognizes the interaction among components and the importance of the whole (Kofman and Senge, 1993).

STS assumes that organizations are made up of people (the social subsystem) using tools, techniques, and procedures (the technical subsystem) to produce goods or services valued by customers (part of the organization's external environment). How well the social and technical subsystems are designed with respect to one another and with respect to the demands of the external environment determines to a large extent how effective the organization will be (Pasmore, 1988). Many researchers have embraced the STS approach by applying the concepts to IS topics such as system analysis and design (Effken, 2002), software project risk analysis (Wallace, Keil, and Rai, 2004), corporate responsibility and business ethics (Johnson, 2006), and development of group support systems (Herrmann et al., 2004).

"Joint optimization" is a key STS principle. Unlike technological determinism, STS is widely recognized for promoting the joint evaluation of both social and technical subsystems of any organizational system. Organizations can perform optimally when social subsystem and technical subsystem are both designed to fit each other (Pasmore, Petee, and Batrian, 1986). In this interdependent relationship, even small problems in fit can often create large systemic impacts. Therefore, an intervention in one subsystem will almost certainly have an impact on the other subsystem. Suboptimization will occur when only the social or the technical subsystem is emphasized (Trist, 1981).

These STS principles have also been applied to the IT investment process, so that the anticipated payoffs of the IT adoption can be gauged more clearly and accurately (Ryan and Harrison, 2000; Ryan, Harrison, and Schkade, 2002). When a decision is made to acquire a new IT, the STS principle of interdependency implies that the effects of the new IT carry through both the technological and social subsystems. Likewise, the effects in both subsystems have associated costs and benefits. Decision makers who neglect the social subsystem and evaluate only the benefits and costs associated with the technological subsystem ignore crucial portions of the valuation issue. The expenses associated with a particular IT investment may be much greater than anticipated as a result of the unrecognized social subsystem costs.

## SOCIAL SUBSYSTEM COSTS AND BENEFITS CONSIDERED BY SOME ORGANIZATIONS

When planning for new IT, organizations do take into account, to varying degrees, the costs and benefits associated with the social subsystem. The literature is replete with admonitions to incorporate these into the planning and decision process, yet there is a gap between prescriptive wisdom and actual practice (Ryan, Harrison, and Schkade, 2002). Table 15.1 shows the social subsystem benefits and costs that are often described in the literature. Each cost or benefit is discussed below. Decision makers should be aware of these costs and benefits and incorporate them into their information systems (IS) planning process.

Table 15.1

**Social Subsystem Benefits and Costs Considered in the Information Technology Planning Process**

| Social subsystem benefits | Social subsystem costs |
|---|---|
| Improved productivity | Training |
| Enhanced quality | Learning curve |
| Improved decision-making ability | Change management |
| Labor savings | Loss of power or control |
| Increased customer orientation | Increased job dissatisfaction and loss of morale |

## Social Subsystem Benefits

Information system-related social subsystem benefits include improved productivity, enhanced quality, improved decision making ability, labor savings, and increased customer orientation. These are considered by decision makers in varying degrees.

### Improved Productivity

A majority of companies consider employee productivity improvement when analyzing the value of IT investments, however, few quantify productivity improvement (*eWeek*, 2006). Productivity is viewed by firms in several different ways. First, it is conceived of in the traditional sense, where outputs increase, while the level of resources or inputs remains constant (Hitt and Brynjolfsson, 1996). Improved productivity is also viewed in terms of the value of activities that organizational members perform. By reducing the number of routine tasks individuals must perform, and allowing employees to concentrate on higher value tasks, the organization is able to leverage individual competencies for its advantage. However, many chief information officers (CIOs) are skeptical of this latter view in that it is difficult to assess whether employees will actually engage in higher level tasks. If they do so, how to evaluate the alternative use of time remains a question (Ryan and Harrison, 2000).

### Enhanced Quality

Another potential benefit of an IT implementation considered by some firms is the improvement in the quality of work. Quality can be assessed by the decrease in the number of defects or the creation of a superior product. IT interventions that assist in this area are those that allow employees to investigate more innovative, cost-effective options. A method sometimes used to measure quality improvement is the determination of the cost of quality (COQ). The COQ index translates process improvements into monetary terms. The first component is the price of nonconformance, or what it costs to produce goods or services that do not meet internal and external customer requirements. It is used to measure all forms of process waste such as handling customer complaints, scrap, rework, and so on. The second component is the price of conformance, or the discretionary activities that an organization takes to prevent nonconformances. These activities include education, audits, and so on. Many firms, however, that do consider quality payoffs do so solely as an intangible benefit (Ryan and Harrison, 2000).

*Improved Decision-Making Ability*

A variance, used in sociotechnical systems literature, refers to an unplanned divergence from standards or procedures that are caused by the condition of materials used or the normal state of technical procedures (Trist, 1981). Key variances significantly impact the productivity of an organization or the quality of life of its organizational members. By controlling variances nearer to their origins, problems in other parts of the system can be circumvented. This approach can save the organization considerable time, money, and energy.

IT can provide information about variances, but it can also provide information useful in other types of decision-making activities. An IT intervention can facilitate employee or managerial decision making by providing information about core activities. Although the specifics of core activities vary, depending on the type of organization, general categories of activities might include strategic planning, management control, opportunity recognition, and operational control. Decision making is facilitated by information systems that augment the capabilities for compilation, analysis, and presentation of data.

IT can also contribute to organizational effectiveness by helping organizational members to manage uncertainty. By providing closer-to-the-source information that indicates that variances may be occurring and empowering employees to participate in correcting variances, the service, quality of products, and work can be improved and decisions can be made more quickly. IT enables more efficient transfer of knowledge so that these variances can be spotted. This, in turn, allows the organization to be more agile in recognizing and responding to environmental conditions and variances within the organizational system.

While improved decision-making ability, either in the timeliness or accuracy of choices made, has been discussed in the normative literature, Ryan and Harrison (2000) found that only 17 percent of the executives in their sample included this benefit in their decision-making process. Because it is difficult to quantify, many executives exclude improved decision-making ability from their consideration.

*Labor Savings*

The actual decrease in the number of employees or total hours worked in a firm as a result of the implementation of technology is considered to be labor savings. It is fairly easily quantified in terms of payroll and can be included in a formal cost/benefit analysis.

Only 15 percent of the decisions in Ryan and Harrison's (2000) study took labor savings into consideration. While it was somewhat surprising that more companies did not consider this quantifiable benefit, most organizations focused not on downsizing or eliminating personnel as a result of IT implementation, but rather on "doing more with less." That is, they incorporated a productivity improvement assessment rather than a labor savings calculation in their investment decision process.

*Increased Customer Orientation*

Certain types of IT encourage employees to become more customer service oriented, focusing on the needs and preferences of customers. Customer relationship management (CRM) software is a prime example, which seeks to enhance corporate revenues and increase value through understanding and satisfying the individual customer's needs (Liu, 2007). CRM systems enable organizations to manage their customers and to monitor their behavior, but more important, to build customer loyalty. To obtain benefits, however, the software implementation must be undergirded by unambiguous corporate strategic direction, process changes in daily work tasks, and a new mindset of employees.

Some firms indirectly measure the increased customer orientation of their employees by changes in customer satisfaction. In fact, one study of IT business executives showed that 77 percent of the respondents use customer satisfaction as a technique to analyze the value of IT investments (*eWeek*, 2006). Other research substantiates the notion that there is a correlation between improved customer-oriented and positive outcomes such as a study in the U.S. banking industry, which reported that banks that develop a customer-oriented strategy obtain higher profits (Lamparello, 2000).

## Social Subsystem Costs

Decision makers often consider training costs as they plan for information systems. However, other social subsystem costs are those such as learning curve costs, change management, employee perceptions of loss of power or control, and increased job dissatisfaction and loss of morale. These are discussed below.

### Training

In Ryan and Harrison's (2000) study, training costs were the most frequently cited social subsystem consideration by executives making an IT investment decision (59 percent). As technology continues to be interwoven throughout organizational work, tighter integration of activities and functions occurs. Technology facilitates rapid speed and real-time response, yet it also brings more costly consequences of errors and breakdowns. In an environment where activities are tightly linked, and where the costs of errors are high, a labor force that does not understand the IT system they use and thus cannot respond to potential problems is very costly. Therefore, training of employees on the IT systems they use is essential.

Emphasis on technical skill development is consistent with STST. Since the social and technological subsystems are interrelated, changes that occur in one subsystem impact operations in the others. When considering the cost of an IT investment, one must consider the cost of training users to leverage the technology effectively. Yet, by implementing the technology and not training, the organization may incur even greater costs.

While training costs are often incorporated into the planning and decision-making process, when budgets become tight, training expenditures are often the first to be omitted. Alternatives to formal training classes are often considered. For example, departments might designate a "super user" to help others in a department learn a new IT system or handle problems as they occur. Decision makers may also carefully evaluate the ease of use and help facilities within an application program to attempt to minimize the amount of formal training required. However, failing to plan for or underestimating training requirements can lead to ineffective IT use, and thus, the anticipated payoffs will not be obtained.

### Learning Curve

Closely related to but conceptually distinct from training costs are learning curve costs. Training costs are associated with the training vendor, materials, and other purchases from external sources. Learning curve costs are the temporary decrease in productivity or quality of employee work during the initial stage of learning a new technology or a new process that is facilitated by technology. Different technologies have different learning curves. One danger is that organizations may abandon a technology prior to realizing the benefits that would occur later in the learning curve. Ryan and Harrison's (2000) study showed that in only 14 percent of the IT decisions did decision makers consider the time period when the employees learn and become competent with an IT system.

*Change Management*

Change management was identified by Grover and colleagues (1995) as a critical success factor for projects that reengineer business processes. Technology-induced change must be anticipated, managed, and communicated to all parties involved. Failure to do so can lead to resistance and, potentially, suboptimization or failure of the IT.

Lewin's (1951) theory of change provides a generic three-step process of change that entails (1) "unfreezing" old habits, (2) "moving" to the new ways of doing things, and (3) "refreezing" or solidifying new procedures and methods. Top management commitment to change and to the specific project must be evident, setting the tone to cultivate acceptance. Yet, to truly move organizational members through the three-step change process, personnel affected by IT-induced change must be informed about why changes were necessary, what benefits the changes bring to them personally and organizationally, and be trained to develop the new requisite skills (May and Kettelhut, 1996). Despite its critical importance, in only seventeen percent of the IT investment decisions in Ryan and Harrison's study (2000) did executives consider the costs of change management. That is, only a small percentage of the executives interviewed evaluated costs associated with planning, overseeing, and communicating information to the end users about IT-induced change.

*Loss of Power or Control*

IT can provide information to lower levels of employees, thus enabling or empowering employees for action. However, this is not the case for all technologies that are implemented. Abdul-Gader and Kozar (1995) discuss computer powerlessness as the feeling that the computer is dominating the individual. This occurs when individuals perceive that they do not have control over their work processes or work outcomes, and rather, that computer system holds the control. It may also occur if employees feel they have lost their sense of identity to uniquely contribute to the work process (May and Kettelhut, 1996). One classic example of an IT implementation that resulted in a feeling of loss of power was the store management information system in the Mrs. Field's Cookies Company. This system tracked the financial progress of each cookie store and scheduled the details of daily activities within the store, including minute details such as the number of cookies that should be baked each hour (Cash et al., 1994). While the intent of the system was to free store managers to concentrate on sales, some associated the implementation of this system with a lack of trust, resulting in a sense of power loss.

*Increased Job Dissatisfaction and Loss of Morale*

The degree to which the implementation of an IT results in increased job dissatisfaction is a function of an individual's subjective evaluation of how the IT has changed the work environment. Work tasks may also change as the result of IT implementation. For example, manual tasks may be automated, requiring employees to acquire different skill sets. Some employees may resist

Figure 15.1    **Social Subsystem Disruption Continuum**

| | Incremental Change | Radical Change |
|---|---|---|
| **Type I:** Information Systems Core (e.g., computer-aided software engineering tools) | | |
| **Type II:** Administrative Core (e.g., accounts payable system) | | |
| **Type III:** Technical Business Core (e.g., material requirements planning system) | | |

*Social Subsystem Disruption*

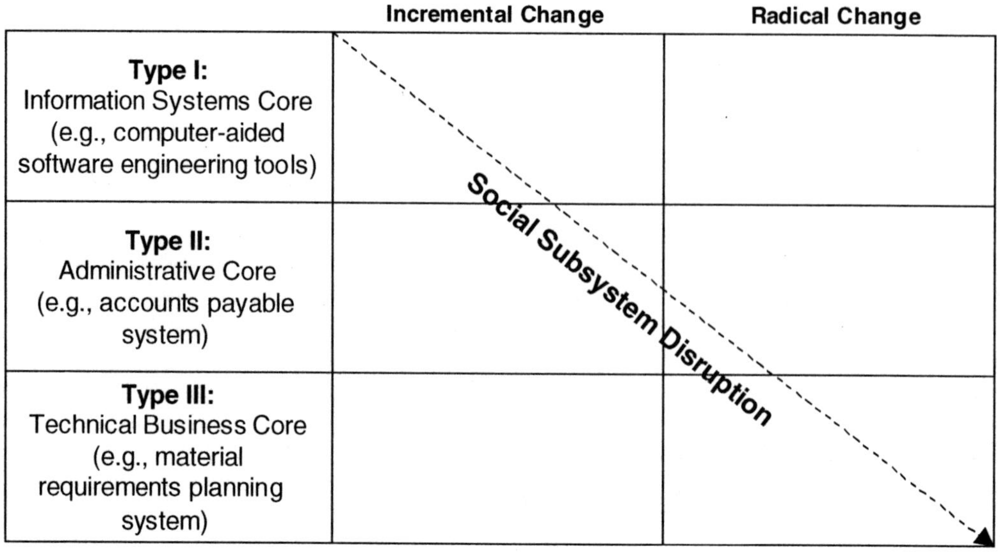

*Source:* Ryan and Harrison (2002).

this change and become dissatisfied. However, if the implementation is managed properly, these IT implementations can result in satisfied employees and significant productivity gains for the organization. Job dissatisfaction has been related to important organizational outcomes such as absenteeism, turnover, and filing of grievances (Griffeth, Hom, and Gaertner, 2000). Therefore, the impact of IT on employee satisfaction should not be ignored.

## SOCIAL SUBSYSTEM DISRUPTION

Decision makers pay more attention to these social subsystem issues when the IT that is being considered will significantly disrupt core business processes. The degree of disruption is jointly determined by the type of IT innovation being considered and the degree of change it will induce. Ryan and Harrison (2000) created a two-dimensional framework by combining Swanson's (1994) tri-core model of IS innovation types on one dimension and the degree of work process change on the other dimension. Based upon interview data and later confirmed by a broad-based survey (Ryan, Harrison, and Schkade, 2002), they suggested that a single continuum, entitled "social subsystem disruption," traversed this two–dimensional framework. This social subsystem disruption continuum implies that all IT investments do not produce the same degree of disturbance, and therefore, consideration of social subsystem costs and benefits will (and should) also vary (see Figure 15.1).

For example, in the upper left-hand corner of the framework, Type I—Information Systems Core investments, such as replacing a printer, would induce little or no work process changes for users. At the other extreme, in the lower-right hand corner of the framework, implementing a Type III—Technical Business Core investment such as an enterprise resource planning (ERP) system would cause great disruption in the social subsystem because the tools and the processes by which everyday tasks are accomplished would be radically altered.

Despite the increased focus on them as the potential for social subsystem disruption grows, there is evidence that consideration of these issues is still inadequate (Ryan and Harrison, 2000). One of the main reasons identified for major IT implementation failures is the end users' reluctance to embrace newly implemented IT systems (Nah, Tan, and Teh, 2004). Even when core business processes are expected to change radically, decision makers fail to consider many employee-related costs and benefits.

## THE IMPORTANCE OF SOCIAL SUBSYSTEM ISSUES RELATIVE TO OTHER FACTORS

Financial/economic justification is considered a key component in the IT investment-decision process where costs and benefits are estimated as dollar amounts (*U.S. Banker*, 2006). Today's chief executive officers are demanding that IT departments become more adept at demonstrating the business value of IT projects. Yet many companies are "still wed to ineffective ROI practices" and only about 60 percent of executives believe that the business metrics they use accurately assess the value of their IT investments (*CIO Insight*, 2006). ROI and cost–benefit analysis are the most frequently used types of economic assessments for IT with common techniques for measuring business value also including payback time and return on assets (*U.S. Banker*, 2006).

When comparing the importance that decision makers placed upon social issues as compared with financial or technical issues, Ryan and Gates (2004) found that decision makers considered financial decision criteria the most important, followed by technical issues, then employee-related issues. Financial quantification is appealing because alternatives are relatively easy to compare. When emphasis is placed on financial justification as the principal decision criterion, decision makers often ignore or discount costs or benefits that are intangible (Parker, Benson, and Trainor, 1988).

Technical issues were also considered more important than social subsystem issues. The costs and benefits associated with technical aspects, like a hardware upgrade or a new software package tend to be more tangible, and therefore, easier to quantify (Ryan and Harrison, 2000). Some technical subsystem costs and benefits (e.g., degree of integration with current infrastructure) might be semitangible. However, few technical subsystem costs and benefits are completely intangible.

From the STS perspective, the emphasis on the technical subsystem and its consideration as more important than the social subsystem indicates a lack of systemic thinking. Both need to be jointly optimized to achieve maximum organizational system performance.

### Explicit Versus Implicit Consideration of Costs and Benefits

The inclusion of intangible costs and benefits in the decision process is difficult due to the lack of methodologies. One problem is that intangibles are often obscure and qualitative in nature. Hinton and Kaye (1996, p. 52) state, "with any IT investment there may be a number of outcomes which are 'hidden' from the decision maker. This involves the qualitative ramifications of the investment which the decision maker either overlooks or chooses to ignore or, for one reason or another, fall beyond the boundaries established by existing investment approaches."

While the majority of weight in IT decisions is given to tangible or quantifiable calculations, there is increasing pressure to place value on intangible or soft benefits. In a recent survey, 64 percent of the respondents said that their company places too little value on the intangible benefits of IT (*eWeek*, 2006). Decision makers often avoid formally incorporating social subsystem benefits and costs when making an IT investment decision because they are intangible, or difficult to measure. Yet, evidence exists that decision makers consider employee-related costs and benefits, at least on some occasions (Ryan and Harrison, 2000).

Although social subsystem issues may not be formally included in the decision process, they may be informally or implicitly considered at some level. Explicit consideration could be equated to quantification, yet this perspective is narrow. Research has shown that even large companies do not always make their decisions strictly on the basis of quantification techniques (*eWeek,* 2006).

When investigating these issues, Ryan and Gates (2004) used a broader definition where explicit referred to "clearly developed or formulated," and implicit referred to "implied, tacitly understood, rather than expressly stated." When surveying IT executives they found a significant difference between implicit and explicit consideration of social subsystem issues. Of the social subsystem costs and benefits evaluated, decision makers gave significantly more implicit consideration to productivity, learning curve, and change management. That is, they "thought about," "considered," or "mulled over" these issues, but were less likely to engage in specific, observable or manifest actions such as "calculating," "forecasting," or "projecting" costs and benefits associated with them. Training was also considered to a greater degree implicitly when the IT under consideration would cause significant process disruption in the environment.

Some methods have been proposed to assist with the incorporation of intangible costs and benefits in the IS planning and decision process. For example, Borenstein and Bentecourt (2005) proposed a multicriteria decision-making model for justifying IT investments that incorporated operational, tactical, and strategic criteria. Within the operational category, a human resources criterion, which aimed to "identify the IT influence on the human element in the organization," was included (Borenstein and Bentecourt, 2005, p. 7). The model was implemented with the Analytic Hierarchy Process Method using the Team Expert Choice™ software.

Another method for incorporating intangibles into the investment decision is to look for related algorithms in the same cost or benefit area (Keen, 2003). For example, while a formula calculating the value of improved customer orientation based on increased gross revenue might be too uncertain, an alternative formula based on a reduction in customer turnover and the cost of replacing a lost customer may be more acceptable.

## WAYS THAT SUBSYSTEM COSTS AND BENEFITS ARE INCORPORATED INTO INFORMATION TECHNOLOGY PLANNING AND DECISION PROCESSES

Despite the difficulties decision makers have incorporating social subsystem cost and benefit information in their decision process, these issues should not be ignored because they are realized in the implementation and postimplementation phases of an IT project (Ryan, Harrison, and Schkade, 2002; Irani and Love, 2000/2001). Information can be gathered from both internal and external sources. Methods commonly used are shown in Table 15.2.

### Internal Sources

The most common method of gathering social subsystem cost and benefit information is from functional managers (Ryan and Harrison, 2000). Managers who supervise employees in the areas where the proposed IT will be introduced are often called upon to assess issues, such as the degree of process change the new IT will cause, the ease or difficulty the employees will have learning and adapting to the IT, and the overall impact it will have on quality and productivity.

While formal end-user involvement in the IT planning and decision process has been discussed

Table 15.2

**Sources of Social Subsystem Costs and Benefit Information**

| *Internal sources* | *External sources* |
|---|---|
| Discussions with functional managers | Vendors—(if the decision is a "buy" not a "make" decision) |
| Formal end-user involvement | Reference sites |
| • Requirements meetings | Customers or suppliers |
| Task forces | Trade shows, conferences, association meetings |
| • Prototyping | Consultants |
| • Impact analysis | Information on the Internet |
| Informal conversations with the end user | Magazines/trade journals |
| | Government regulations |

extensively in the normative literature, in practice, these techniques are performed in only about one-quarter of the IT decisions (Ryan and Harrison, 2000). As with other types of functional requirement gathering processes, formal end-user involvement in requirements meetings, such as joint application development sessions, planning sessions, or individual interviews are common. Especially in the context of enterprise resource planning decisions, task forces, or cross-functional project teams are often used. While prototyping or pretesting can also yield valuable insights, the focus is often on the determination of functional requirements rather than the assessment of social subsystem-related costs and benefits. Informal conversations with end users are also used to assess what the impact of new technology will be.

## External Sources

Vendors can be a major source of social subsystem cost and benefit information if the decision is a "buy" not a "make" decision. Vendors can supply productivity improvement estimates, training costs, and potential labor savings, but not less tangible costs and benefits that deal with the specific interaction between the organizational context and the proposed technology.

A valuable source from which to gather social subsystem cost and benefit information is a reference site. Some vendors supply lists of customer references that use the particular technology under consideration. When decision makers visit these sites, they are able to see the IT system at work within its organizational context. While the specific assessment of how the IT will affect their firm must be made, discussing various issues with the reference-site representatives can provide valuable insight. For example, a representative from a reference site might say, "We thought it would take three months to train our employees on this system, but in reality, our users were not fully proficient in using the system for six months." A vendor may be able to tell a prospective customer what their system is supposed to do or the benefits that should be derived, but these might be nothing more than a marketing ploy. By seeing the IT system, as it was implemented in an actual work situation, valuable insights can be gained and a more realistic evaluation can be made.

A firm's customers or suppliers that have the IT under consideration provide similar, or even more valuable, insights than those of the official vendor-recommended reference sites. If the relationship is good between the firm and a customer or supplier that uses the prospective IT, honest and less-guarded information might be exchanged.

Trade shows, conferences, and association meetings are other venues by which cost and benefit information can be obtained. At user group meetings, representatives from various firms may share their experiences, both positive and negative. At such meetings, participants have been known to express concerns about the things they do not like. This can provide indications of the degree to which users are satisfied with the IT. Testimonials of benefits and problems can help organizations formulate a more accurate idea of what the costs and benefits will be.

Consultants, especially those who have had implementation experience with the proposed IT, can often make valuable assessments of the product's benefits or pitfalls. Other sources of cost and benefit information may come from information on the Internet, magazines or trade journals, and even governmental regulations.

### Determination of Social Subsystem Costs and Benefits: Potential Actions and Critical Costs and Benefits

Figure 15.2 contains a flow chart denoting possible actions and critical social subsystem costs and benefits that decision makers can use to begin to assess social subsystem costs and benefits. This flowchart is not meant to replace a comprehensive implementation plan.

On the left-hand side of the flow chart is the social subsystem disruption continuum (see also Figure 15.1). This continuum implies that evaluating social subsystem costs and benefits is more critical for some types of IT investment decisions. A joint consideration of innovation type and degree of anticipated change is needed. The possible actions and critical social subsystem costs and benefits to consider listed on the flow chart are cumulative.

### 1. Initial Assessments

The first action is to determine the type of IT under consideration. Even if the IT is a Type I Information Systems Core intervention that is unnoticeable to end users or induces very little disruption, functional managers should be kept informed.

The IT implementation may affect the speed with which end-user tasks are accomplished, as in the case of changing the networking architecture or upgrading servers. In these cases, productivity improvement benchmarks should be considered to help better assess the productivity improvement. Potential social subsystem issues to consider are productivity, improved decisions due to the timeliness with which they can be made, and labor savings. Although in some cases the impact may be marginal, in others the change may bring significant financial payoffs.

### 2. Task Procedure Changes

If the task procedures by which the users conduct their daily job tasks are altered, providing an overview of changes in features is helpful. An assessment should also be made as to the degree of training required. Vendors can assist in making this determination.

If task procedures change significantly, the assessments for the critical social subsystem costs and benefits reviewed in the previous step, productivity, improved decision-making ability, and labor savings, may need to be revisited or evaluated in more detail. Also, quality of work, learning curve, and change management costs should be considered. To gauge these, decision makers may want to visit reference sites where the IT under consideration is already installed. Business area managers as well as technical managers and employees should be included in the visit. Information can be obtained regarding the length of time it took for the users to learn and become productive using the new technology, their change in productivity once they became proficient in the new IT, the impact

Figure 15.2    Determination of Social Subsystem Costs and Benefits: Potential Actions and Critical Costs and Benefits

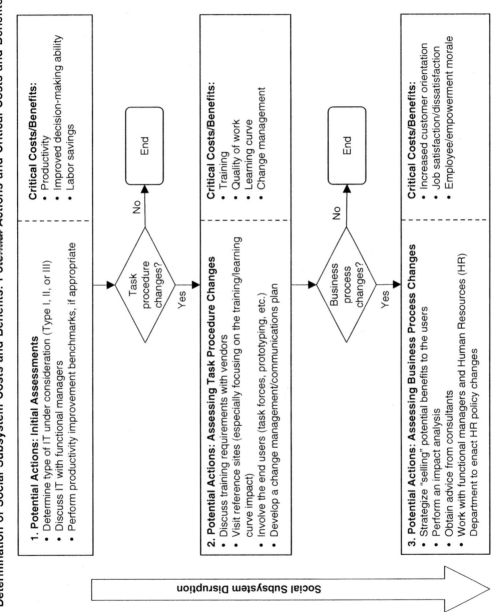

on their work quality, and any issues related to the resistance of the changes by end users. Additional input can be gathered internally from end users through informal conversations, and, more formally, through involving them in requirements meetings, task forces, or prototyping of the competing choices. User input into the formulation and customization of the IT is also desirable (Kendall and Kendall, 2008). Change management costs are also significant when the IT change will significantly alter users' tasks. The managerial time expenditure of creating and executing a change management and communications plan is rarely considered when evaluating new IT, yet can be significant.

*3. Business Processes Changes*

A business process has been defined as "a set of logically related tasks performed to achieve a defined business outcome" (Davenport and Short, 1990, p.12). The way in which individual tasks are completed may change, but the business process may stay the same. However, when business processes are radically changed, there is great social subsystem disruption. The decision maker should be aware of the social subsystem considerations previously discussed, especially revisiting change management and communication issues as well as additional employee-related concerns, such as increased customer orientation, job satisfaction/dissatisfaction, and employee empowerment and morale.

When end users see the need for new IT, change is met with less resistance than if they do not see the value in the new IT (Venkatesh et al., 2003). Decision makers can strategize with first-line managers on how to "sell" the new technology to the users, stressing the rationale for why changes are beneficial, the usefulness of the new procedures, and the system's ease of use.

For major business process changes, an impact analysis should be part of the planning and evaluation of the new IT. Through methods such as interviews and observation, the processes that are going to be impacted and the degree of the impact can be determined. Often, firms solicit advice and help from consultants.

Human resources (HR) policy changes can be important to IT success. For example, changing compensation plans to reward productivity and behaviors made possible by new business processes can encourage users to embrace the new IT system. The effort, time, and expense of making HR policy changes may be significant.

The flowchart in Figure 15.2 highlights social subsystem costs and benefits and methods for gathering them across the full range of the social subsystem disruption. While not every possible social subsystem cost or benefit is listed, the flowchart can serve as a useful starting point for recognizing significant social subsystem costs and benefits. As a result, these anticipated costs and benefits can be brought into initial decisions about making a major IT investment.

## THE TYPES OF FIRMS MORE LIKELY TO CONSIDER SOCIAL SUBSYSTEM COSTS AND BENEFITS

Research has shown that firms doing a more thorough job of evaluating employee-related costs and benefits are differentiated from others in terms of their organizational culture and firm strategy (Ryan, Harrison, and Schkade, 2002). Specifically, firms with a continuous learning culture do a better job overall of assessing social subsystem costs and benefits, regardless of what type of IT is being considered or what degree of social subsystem disruption is induced. Firms that recognize the importance of IT from a strategic perspective also do a more thorough job of assessing social subsystem costs and benefits, but only when disruption is high. These characteristics are discussed in more detail below.

## Continuous Learning Culture

Organizational learning is a critical factor for success in today's competitive environment (Chen et al., 2003). Learning organizations are characterized by a "continuous-learning culture," that is, a culture that supports and values constant learning (Tracey, Tannenbaum, and Kavanagh, 1995). Such organizations are able to achieve superior results through creating, acquiring, and communicating knowledge and modifying their behavior in accordance with knowledge acquired (King, 2001).

Consistent with STS, learning organizations place a high priority on employee knowledge acquisition and usage. As such, these firms intentionally manage the collective knowledge, skills and abilities possessed by their employees. They provide learning opportunities for their employees, use learning to reach goals, and link individual performance with organizational performance (Rowden, 2001). Research has established a direct, positive connection between organizational culture and consideration of social subsystem costs and benefits (Ryan, Harrison, and Schkade, 2002). Traditional firms, without such a learning culture, pay significantly less attention to social subsystem issues. Thus, a firm's organizational culture provides a possible explanation for the differential between prescriptive theory and the disappointing results of failed implementations.

From an STS perspective, learning organizations have developed a culture that appreciates the mutual interdependency of the technical and social subsystems. They place a higher priority on and expend more thought and effort in determining the social consequences of an IT investment than other firms, regardless of the level of social subsystem disruption. Thus, organizations with continuous learning cultures recognize the STS principle of joint optimization such that all technology interventions have at least some degree of social consequences.

## Firm Strategy

Firms that embrace the strategic relevance of IT also spend more time and effort evaluating social subsystems costs and benefits, but only under conditions of high social subsystem disruption (Ryan, Harrison, and Schkade, 2002). Therefore, when an IT investment is being considered that will radically change the everyday activities of employees, firms that understand the strategic relevance of IT are more likely to spend additional time and effort considering the social subsystem issues because they can impact the anticipated payoff of the investment. When the IT investment decisions are expected to have minimal disruptive effects on the social subsystem, firms tend to treat social costs and benefits similarly—with a low level of effort at gathering or evaluating employee-related issues, regardless of how important the role of IT is in their competitive position.

Therefore, firms most susceptible to ignoring or overlooking important employee-related issues, even when the IT implementation will induce radical disruption in the environment, are those firms that do not place a high value on the current and future strategic relevance of IT. When strong reverberations or disruptions are anticipated, only those firms with more strategic objectives for their IT heighten their sensitivity to end-user issues when making the IT investment decision.

## CONCLUSION

Social subsystem costs and benefits are realized when an IT is acquired, yet they are often inadequately considered or omitted when evaluating IT investment alternatives. Therefore, to more accurately and thoroughly evaluate IT payoffs, these social subsystem costs and benefits must be incorporated into IT investment decisions. The more social subsystem disruption the IT under consideration will induce (characterized as a combination of innovation type and degree of change in work flow), the more consideration IT decision makers should give to the associated costs and benefits. We have described the costs and benefits that decision makers incorporate into their decision process and the ways in which they gather that information. Our flowchart of proposed actions and social subsystem costs and benefits can aid decision makers as they plan their IT evaluation strategies. By formally recognizing social subsystem costs and benefits, the anticipated IT payoff is less at risk of encountering unanticipated issues that arise in the implementation or postimplementation phase of a project.

## REFERENCES

Abdul-Gader, A.J., and Kozar, K.A. 1995. The impact of computer alienation on information technology investment decisions: an exploratory cross-national analysis. *MIS Quarterly,* 19, 4, 535–558.

Borenstein, D., and Bentecourt, P.R.B. 2005. A multi-criteria model for the justifying of IT investments. *Infor,* 43, 1, 1–21.

Cash, J.I. Jr.; Eccles, R.G.; Nohria, N.; and Nolan, R.L. 1994. *Building the Information-Age Organization: Structure, Control, and Information Technologies.* Boston: Irwin.

Chen, J.Q.; Lee, T.D.; Zhang, R.; and Zhang, J. 2003. System requirements for organizational learning. *Communications of the ACM,* 46, 12, 73–78.

*CIO Insight.* 2006. Demonstrating ROI will remain a struggle. *CIO Insight,* p. 39.

Davenport, T., and Short, J. 1990. The new industrial engineering: information technology and business process redesign. *Sloan Management Review,* 31, 4, 11–27.

Effken, J.A. 2002. Different lenses, improved outcomes: a new approach to the analysis and design of health-care information systems. *International Journal of Medical Informatics,* 65, 1, 59–74.

*eWeek.* 2006. ROI: not all it's cracked up to be. *eWeek,* 23, 50, 40–44.

Griffeth, R.W.; Hom, P.W.; and Gaertner, S. 2000. A meta-analysis of antecedents and correlates of employee turnover: update, moderator tests, and research implications for the next millennium. *Journal of Management,* 26, 3, 463–488.

Grover, V.; Jeong, S.R.; Kettinger, W.J.; and Teng, J.T.C. 1995. The implementation of business process reengineering. *Journal of Management Information Systems,* 12, 1, 109–144.

He, X. 2004. The ERP challenge in China: a resource-based perspective. *Information Systems Journal,* 14, 2, 153–167.

Herbst, P.G. 1974. *Socio-Technical Design: Strategies in Multidisciplinary Research.* London: Tavistock.

Herrmann, T.; Hoffmann, M.; Kunau, G.; and Kai-Uwe Loser, G. 2004. A modelling method for the development of groupware applications as socio-technical systems. *Behaviour & Information Technology,* 23, 2, 119–135.

Hinton, M., and Kaye, R. 1996. Investing in information technology: a lottery? *Management Accounting* (London), 74, 10, 52.

Hitt, L.M., and Brynjolfsson, E. 1996. Productivity, business profitability, and consumer surplus: three different measures of information technology value. *MIS Quarterly,* 20, 12, 121–141.

Irani, Z., and Love, P.E.D. 2000–2001. The propagation of technology management taxonomies for evaluating investments in information system. *Journal of Management Information Systems,* 17, 3, 161–177.

Johnson, D.G. 2006. Corporate excellence, ethics, and the role of IT. *Business & Society Review,* 111, 457–470.

Keen, J. 2003. Don't ignore the intangibles. *CIO,* 16, 22, 40–41.

Kendall, K.E., and Kendall, J.E. 2008. *Systems Analysis and Design,* 7th ed. Upper Saddle River, NJ: Prentice Hall.

King, W.R. 2001. Strategies for creating a learning organization. *Information Systems Management,* 18, 1, 12–20.

Kofman, F., and Senge, P. 1993. Communities of commitment: the heart of learning organizations. *Organizational Dynamics,* 22, 2, 4–23.

Lamparello, D. 2000. Doing more for the right customers. *Bank Systems and Technology,* 37, 1, R10–R11.

Lewin, K. 1951. *Field Theory in Social Science.* New York: Harper and Row.

Liu, H. 2007. Development of a framework for customer relationship management (CRM) in the banking industry. *International Journal of Management,* 24, 1, 15–32.

May, D., and Kettelhut, M.C. 1996. Managing human issues in reengineering projects: a case review of implementation issues. *Journal of Systems Management*, 47, 1, 4–11.

Nah, F.F.; Tan, X.; and Teh, S.H. 2004. An empirical investigation on end-users' acceptance of enterprise systems. *Information Resources Management Journal*, 17, 3, 32–53.

Parker, M.M.; Benson, R.J.; and Trainor, H.E. 1988. *Information Economics: Linking Business Performance to Information Technology.* Englewood Cliffs, NJ: Prentice Hall.

Pasmore, W.A. 1988. *Designing Effective Organizations: The Sociotechnical Systems Perspective.* New York: Wiley.

Pasmore, W.; Petee, J.; and Batrian, R. 1986. Sociotechnical systems in health care: a field experiment. *Journal of Applied Behavioral Science*, 22, 3, 329–339.

Perera, D. 2007. Remote access. *Government Executive*, 39, 7, 63–64.

Rowden, R.W. 2001. The learning organization and strategic change. *SAM Advanced Management Journal*, 66, 3, 11–17.

Ryan, S.D., and Gates, M.S. 2004. Inclusion of social subsystem issues in IT investment decisions: an empirical assessment. *Information Resources Management Journal*, 17, 1, 1–18.

Ryan, S.D., and Harrison, D.A. 2000. Considering social subsystem costs and benefits in IT investment decisions: a view from the field on anticipated payoffs. *Journal of Management Information Systems*, 16, 4, 11–40.

Ryan, S.D.; Harrison, D.A.; and Schkade, L.L. 2002. Information technology investment decisions: when do costs and benefits in the social subsystem matter? *Journal of Management Information Systems*, 19, 2, 85–127.

Swanson, E.B. 1994. Information systems innovation among organizations. *Management Science*, 40, 9, 1069–1086.

Tracey, J.B.; Tannenbaum, S.I.; and Kavanagh, M.J. 1995. Applying trained skills on the job: the importance of the work environment. *Journal of Applied Psychology*, 30, 2, 239–252.

Trist, E. 1981. The sociotechnical perspective. In Andrew Van de Van and William Joyce (eds.), *Perspectives on Organization Design and Behavior.* New York: Wiley, pp. 57–69.

*U.S. Banker.* 2006. Second annual bank ROI study. 2006. *U.S. Banker*, 116, 2–3.

Venkatesh, V.; Morris, M.G.; Davis, G.B.; and Davis, F.D. 2003. User acceptance of information technology: toward a unified view. *MIS Quarterly*, 27, 3, 425–478.

Wallace, L.; Keil, M.; and Rai, A. 2004. How software project risk affects project performance: an investigation of the dimensions of risk and an exploratory model. *Decision Sciences*, 35, 2, 289–321.

Williams, P. 2006. Poor IT implementation costs companies billions. *Finance Week*, February 8, 9.

CHAPTER 16

# OPTION-BASED MANAGEMENT OF RISK IN INFORMATION SYSTEMS PLANNING

MICHEL BENAROCH

**Abstract:** *The operative elements in both the traditional and the sense-and-respond approaches to information systems (IS) planning are information technology (IT) investments. There is growing agreement that effective management of risk within and across IT investments requires careful planning and informed judgments on how much and what forms of flexibility to incorporate into the investments. To place this endeavor on a solid economic foundation, a growing body of IS research uses real options theory to conceptualize and value different forms of flexibility and the risk mitigation strategies they enable in terms of real options. A framework embodying the main ideas underlying this research is called option-based risk management (OBRiM). OBRiM is one of several approaches using real options to configure investments so as to control risk and add value, but its fundamental advantages are its metrics for calibrating risk and its structured approach to identifying which real options to use for given risks. The logic of OBRiM and its underlying theory has been validated empirically in two different contexts. And OBRiM itself has been applied successfully in a field study setting to a large-scale data-warehousing project at a major airline. While our review of this body of research confirms and demonstrates the relevance of option-based risk management to IT investment planning and management, it also highlights important implications for research and practice and reveals challenges requiring additional research. Perhaps the most important implications are that IS work on real options provides a solid economic basis for improving IT risk management practices, it opens new venues for investigating a host of behavioral and economic issues relating to IS planning, and it can be linked with mean-variance theory for the purpose of managing portfolios of interrelated IT investments.*

**Keywords:** *IT Investment, Risk, Risk Management, Real Options*

## INTRODUCTION

> Ultimately, planning is about control: we seek, by decisions that we make today, to improve future circumstances. The enemy of planning, of course, is uncertainty. Although this fact is sometimes suppressed, strategic planners are often faced with massive and ubiquitous uncertainty in many dimensions. (Davis, 2002, p. 1)

The growing need to manage uncertainty has been a major change driver in the area of information systems (IS) planning (Applegate, Austin, and McFarlan, 2003; Voloudakis, 2005). Traditionally, IS planning is seen as a linear multiyear effort largely driven by the business side. It starts with a long-term strategic planning step, followed by tactical and operational planning steps aimed at project-based execution of the strategic plan. A common criticism is that, in times of fast-paced change, taking a year to articulate a plan and several years to implement the plan is too risky. On one level, the IS organization is often perceived as being nonresponsive and a barrier to change, because information technology (IT) implementation occurs late in the planning effort and in supporting the firm's strategic plan. On a more fundamental level, business and IT planners typically suppress uncertainty and optimize against some image of the future. For these reasons, the traditional view of IS planning has been discredited to the point where most organizations have significantly cut back on strategic planning of the bureaucratic and optimization-oriented variety (Mintzberg, 1993).

An alternative emerging view is just-in-time IS planning with sense-and-respond strategy making. In this view, upon sensing changes in customer demand, shifting technology or other unforeseen events, a firm's response is to use experiments to test hypotheses about uncertain aspects of the future (e.g., demand for new products, cannibalization of channels, whether customers can self-serve). Fichman (2004) explains that an *experiment* can be: a research project carried out in isolated test-beds apart from current service operations, a provisional (or pilot) project that allows a detailed evaluation of technology, or a larger baseline implementation of a full standard service. Rapid execution of experiments requires having an agile and responsive IT infrastructure (Baskerville, Mathiassen, and Pries-Heje, 2005; Overby, Bharadwaj, and Sambamurthy, 2006). A successful experiment can be scaled up and rolled out, leading to major organizational and infrastructural changes or to more incremental process-improvement initiatives. Such forms of experimentation enable systematic learning for resolving uncertainties over time and fine-tuning resource allocations in response to internal and external conditions (Kulatilaka and Ciriello, 2005).

Moving beyond differences between these two divergent IS planning views (Sambamurthy, Zmud, and Byrd, 1994; Newkirk, Lederer, and Srinivasan, 2003), recall that the operative vehicles in both views are IT projects or IT investments. IT managers tell us that a critical aspect of IS planning is the development of a risk management plan for each IT project (Benaroch, Lichtenstein, and Robinson, 2006). This aspect involves decisions about: resource allocation across projects, methods to be deployed for organizational changes (e.g., process enhancements, reengineering) and for technical infrastructure migration (e.g., rehosting vs. rearchitecting of data), IT implementation strategies (e.g., make vs. buy vs. outsource) and plans (e.g., phased with interim deliverables, pilot with full-scale follow-up), and so on. Such decisions can be more crucial under the sense-and-respond view. Since a company can have a steady stream of experiments providing follow-up investment opportunities, which refer to directly succeeding projects that can almost be regarded as a single flow of activities, risk must be managed across many interdependent projects that are not centrally planned and coordinated.

There is growing agreement that affective IT risk management requires careful planning and informed judgments on how much, and what forms of, flexibility to incorporate into IT investments and portfolios of IT investments. This endeavor rests on the recognitions that: risk has monetary consequences, flexibility adds value but can also add cost, and all these competing tendencies affect the net value of an IT investment. IT managers may, as a rule, use these recognitions to build flexibility into IT projects with some intuitive sense. But, lack of adequate ways to quantify risk and value flexibility preclude the possibility of augmenting this endeavor with solid economic or engineering practices.

In recent years, however, new theoretical foundations have emerged that enable the development of coherent ways to measure the monetary consequences of risk and to conceptualize and value flexibility in terms of the risk management strategies it enables. Perhaps the best example is real options theory (Amram and Kualatilaka, 1999; Trigeorgis, 1996). Conceptually speaking, a *real option* is a choice that IT managers implicitly hold (e.g., deferring an investment) or deliberately make possible through some effort and cost (e.g., building a prototype). Such a choice amounts to having the flexibility to adjust the course of an IT project for the purpose of avoiding downside consequences of risk and/or exploiting upside opportunities. *Real options theory* is concerned mainly with the conceptualization and valuation of different forms of flexibility, or real options, in the context of capital investment decision making.

This chapter discusses the application of real options theory to the management of IT investment risk in IS planning. IS research has applied this theory to problems ranging from the evaluation and management of IT projects embedding various real options (Benaroch and Kauffman, 1999, 2000; Dai, Kauffman, and March, 2006; Panayi and Trigeorgis, 1998; Kualatilaka, Balasubramanian, and Strock, 1999; Taudes, 1998; Taudes, Feuerstein, and Mild, 2000; Zhu, 1999) to optimal investment strategies when faced with competing technology innovations (Fichman, 2004; Grenadier and Weiss, 1997; Kauffman and Li, 2005). Much of this research has increasingly shifted its perspective to the role of real options in IT risk management. One important end product is the *option-based risk management* (OBRiM) framework (Benaroch, 2002). OBRiM helps managers to choose which real options to use to configure (or structure) an IT investment and build into it the right amount and forms of flexibility for optimally controlling risk and maximizing value. OBRiM is one of several approaches, including sequential statistical decision analysis and dynamic programming (Clemons and Gu, 2003)[1] that can be used to configure investments so as to control risk. However, the fundamental advantages of OBRiM are its metrics for calibrating risk and its structured approach to identifying which real options managers ought to use for given risks (Benaroch, et al., 2007). Furthermore, the logic of OBRiM and its underlying theory has been validated empirically in the context of IS project escalation (Tiwana, Keil, and Fichman, 2006) and IT investment risk management in general (Benaroch, Lichtenstein, and Robinson, 2006). Hence, OBRiM's logic appears to be consistent with managers' intuitions about how different forms of flexibility (options) ought to be used in risk management. Yet, other empirical research shows that managers cannot adequately value flexibility (options) based on intuition alone (Busby and Pitts, 1997; Jägle and Howell, 1996; Tiwana, et al., 2007). It therefore seems that IT managers' natural intuition about flexibility and its value can be supplemented by the OBRiM framework and its quantitative tools from real options theory.

Whether the logic of OBRiM is viable and adds value in practice is something that can be established only by applying the framework in real-world settings. We are already seeing the use of this logic in academic settings for a greater range of problems and contexts (e.g., Kauffman and Kumar, 2007), and we are starting to see applications in real-world practitioner settings as well (e.g., Bräutigam, Esche, and Mehler-Bicher, 2003). A good example, which we review later, is an evaluative field study of OBRiM applied to a data-warehousing project at a major airline (Benaroch, et al., 2007). It is found that OBRiM enables IT executives to configure the target IT investment so that the value of the data-warehousing project can be maximized by managing its risk. Moreover, interviews with senior technology executives reveal the areas where OBRiM's overall power lies: more accuracy in risk analysis, support of proactive IT investment planning, and simplification of the real-options thinking.

While this growing body of research demonstrates conceptually and empirically the relevance of option-based risk management to IT investment management and IS planning, it also highlights the implications it could have for research and practice and reveals challenges that require additional research. Perhaps the most important implication is that IS work on real options can and ought to span various aspects of risk management in IS planning. On one level, it provides the basis for improving IT risk management practices at the single investment level and opens a useful venue for investigating a host of behavioral and economic issues relating to IS planning. At another level, its scope can be expanded to portfolios of interrelated IT investments and linked with mean-variance theory. This would enable conceptualizing and visualizing the affects of OBRiM on a collection of interrelated IT investments and also provide a theoretical basis for developing an optimization-oriented approach to managing IT investment portfolios and their risk. However, the challenges that still need to be overcome are numerous. They range from those concerning operationalization of OBRiM (e.g., estimation of IT risk factors and volatilities for real options) to those concerning its organizational adoption and implementation for regular use (e.g., ensuring exercise of options, financial training of IT managers).

To summarize, this chapter advocates using real options to manage risk in IS planning. It first reviews notions such as IT risk and real options, laying down the foundations necessary to develop our core arguments. It then presents the OBRiM framework, discusses empirical testing of OBRiM's logic, and describes an application of OBRiM to a large-scale and risky data-warehousing project. This discussion overlooks many option-related details so that our core arguments can be further developed and voiced from a higher-level IT investment planning and management perspective, but the reader is pointed to other work offering comprehensive discussions of missing details. The chapter concludes with a broader discussion and assessment of the growing body of work on real options and IT risk management, its important implications on research and practice, limitations that still need to be overcome, and some thoughts on the next steps this work could take.

## INFORMATION TECHNOLOGY RISK, REAL OPTIONS, AND RISK MANAGEMENT

### IT Investment Risk

The way IT investment risk is defined and conceptualized has changed markedly in recent years (Alter and Sherer, 2004). Traditionally, IS research defines risk in terms of negative outcomes; for example, a lack of skilled analysts could lead to poor system design (Barki, Rivard, and Talbot, 1993; Boehm, 1989). Nowadays, however, IS research increasingly embraces the notion that risk can also have positive consequences; for example, high customer acceptance rates can present follow-up opportunities (Benaroch, 2002; Fichman, 2004). This change in view is consistent with the way other disciplines, such as finance and management science, define risk as the downward or upward *variation* in the outcome expected from pursuing an investment opportunity.

The sources of risk are *risk factors*, characteristics of an IT investment or its contextual environment, which can impact the degree of variation in expected investment outcome. IS risk research has identified many different risk factors (Alter and Sherer, 2004). Some arise during software development—such as personnel skills, application complexity, and continuous stream of requirement changes (Boehm, 1989). Some relate more broadly to IS implementation—for example, technology newness, organizational environment, user involvement, top management commitment, and conflict between user departments (Keil, et al., 1998). And others pertain generally to investment financial success—for example, project funding uncertainties, unstable business environment, customer acceptance, supplier adoption, and competitive duplication (Clemons, 1991).

Analogous to the way finance research talks about risk, different IT risk factors can be categorized as firm-specific and firm-independent (see Figure 16.1). *Firm-specific IT risks* are due to factors endogenous to the firm. They fall into two subcategories. Software development risk factors relate to the firm's technical capabilities and investment characteristics, and they affect the ability to build the system underlying an investment. Organizational risk factors determine

322

Figure 16.1    **Classes of Information Technology (IT) Investment Risks**

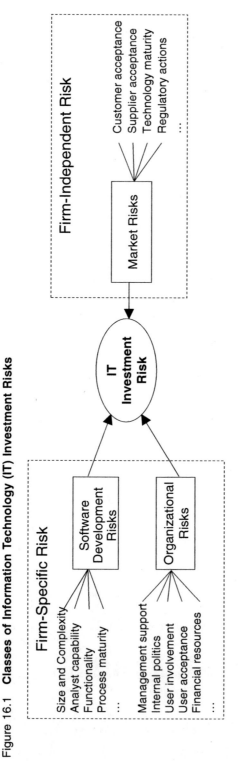

*Source:* Ryan and Harrison (2002).

how well an IT investment fits its internal development and operating environment, and they affect the firm's ability to realize the IT investment fully and successfully. *Firm-independent risks* are due to exogenous factors affecting all firms that consider, or have already made, the same IT investment. They could be the result of uncertainty about customer demand for the product or service yielded by a target investment, potential regulatory changes, unproven capabilities of a target technology, the emergence of a cheaper or superior substitute technology, and so on. These risk factors may affect the firm's ability to obtain the full expected investment benefits even if the underlying system has been realized successfully.

## Risk Management and Real Options

When the value *V* of an investment is uncertain, its distribution has a nonzero variance (see Figure 16.2A). Exposure of the investment to more risk factors normally widens the distribution of *V*, something that follows from our earlier definition of risk. The embedding of real options in the investment has the effect of beneficially changing the distribution of *V* asymmetrically (see Figure 16.2A). To understand this central notion, we can look at the role played by financial options in managing financial investment risk.

Financial risk management is about designing investment positions that protect the investor against losses due to, and/or generate profits from exploiting, well-defined risks (Hull, 1993). Given an "exposed" position containing some underlying asset *V* (e.g., stock), a "covered" position can be created by purchasing and/or selling financial options on *V* and adding them to the exposed position. A financial option on asset *V* is a side-bet on *V*'s future value between the option seller and the option buyer.[2] Figures 16.2B and 16.2C show the value functions of the most basic covered positions created by buying a put or a call option on *V* (ignoring option cost), respectively, and the beneficial effect of these options on the distribution of *V*. The way both options work in all covered positions is simple—the buyer and the seller of an option on *V* hold different beliefs about the (uncertain) behavior of *V*, and so they create a side-bet on the future value of *V* by trading the option. In this sense, options are vehicles for trading specific risks across investors that perceive those risks differently.

The analogy with managing capital investment risk is straightforward. The value of an exposed position parallels the so-called *passive* NPV ($NPV^P$) of a capital investment, the options added to the exposed position parallel real options embedded in the investment, and the value of the covered position parallels the so-called *active* NPV ($NPV^A$) of the investment:

$$active \text{ NPV}^A = passive \text{ NPV}^P + value \text{ } of \text{ } embedded \text{ } options$$

With this said, there is an important difference between financial options and real options. The value of financial options stems from the ability of two economic agents to trade risk when they hold different perceptions over how *V* will evolve. By contrast, the value of real options stems from the presence of managerial flexibility that allows changing the course of a capital investment *V* when risk materializes. This is why the active $NPV^A$ seeks to account for the value of managerial flexibility in relation to rational interventions that management can apply to favorably change traits of an investment project (timing, scale, scope, etc.) as uncertainties unfold. Financial capital budgeting research has shown that managerial flexibility can be conceptualized and valued as real options, as it permits taking actions that can change the distribution of investment value asymmetrically (Trigeorgis, 1996). Hence, using real options, risk is managed mostly "internally," through exploitation of managerial flexibility embedded in the investment. Another basis for the

Figure 16.2  **Effects of Uncertainty and Option-based Risk Management on Investment Value**

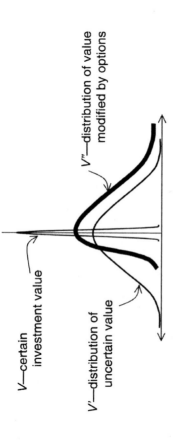

*V*—certain investment value

*V'*—distribution of uncertain value

*V''*—distribution of value modified by options

**A.** Effects of uncertainty and real options on the distribution of investment value

- - - - option value added to position

———— value of "exposed" position

━━━━ value of "covered" position

☐ avoided/enhanced outcomes

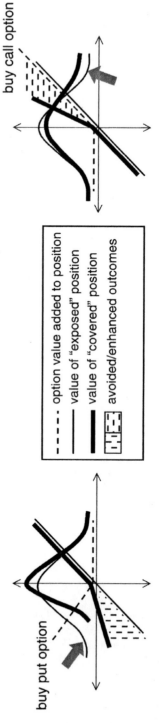

buy call option

**C.** Adding to an exposed position a call option can enhance good fluctuations in *V*

buy put option

**B.** Adding to an exposed position a put option can cancel out bad fluctuations in *V*

value options added will be discussed later, based on mean-variance theory and portfolio management concepts from finance.

## IT Research on Real Options

Early IT research on real options uses this recognition to establish the importance of managerial flexibility in the valuation of risky IT investments (Benaroch and Kauffman, 1999). The approach it follows is simple: given an IT investment that is exposed to known risks and is already embedding managerial flexibility needed to respond to the risks, conceptualize the flexibility as real options (defer, pilot, stage, etc.) and use formal option pricing models to quantify the value that flexibility adds in relation to risk (e.g., Benaroch and Kauffman, 2000; Taudes, Feuerstein, and Mild, 2000). Benaroch and colleagues (2007) offer references to studies that use this approach to examine the effect of various types of real options in connection with specific risks. It also offers a definition of the different real option types discussed in IT research, namely: defer, explore (pilot, prototype), stage, change scale, outsource, lease, and strategic growth. Overall, although this early work has no direct link with IT risk management, it does recognize that the value of flexibility and real options is driven by the presence of risk.

Later IT research on real options has looked at the link between flexibility, real options, and IT risk management. Flexibility is a crucial success factor in IS development, as it enables deployment of risk countermeasures contingent on the materialization of risk (Avison et al., 1995). On this ground, real options theory was used to justify certain IT project management practices relating to risk (Kim and Saunders, 2002; Kumar, 2002). Real options theory has also been proposed as a sound theoretical basis for managing software development risk from an economic perspective (Boehm and Sullivan, 2000). This proposal coincides with the fact that software engineering research identifies certain risk mitigation strategies that map directly to real options, for example, prototyping and abandonment (Boehm, 1989).

Building on these ideas, the option-based risk management (OBRiM) framework more explicitly expands the scope of real options theory to IT risk management (Benaroch, 2002). OBRiM starts with the recognition that flexibility is not inherent in any risky investment and instead must be proactively built into the investments in a way that can add value. On this ground, OBRiM offers a comprehensive way to link the management of different risks with the forms of flexibility afforded by different options. It helps a decision maker to find the most cost-effective combination of real options, or forms of flexibility, to embed in an IT investment in order to control risk and maximize value. Empirical support for OBRiM's underlying motivation and objectives has been found recently in a study that sought to explain IS project escalation using real options theory:

> While our research shows that managers are quite open to placing a value on real options . . . , this will be of little practical consequence unless mechanisms are put in place to make real options salient in practice—and then used appropriately. These mechanisms include augmenting project planning to include an active search for opportunities to embed real options, employing techniques that realistically value real options, implementing project management practices to continuously track the evolving value of options, and committing to actually exercising options when appropriate. (Tiwana, Keil, and Fichman, 2006, p. 383)

## OPTION-BASED RISK MANAGEMENT

The idea underlying the OBRiM framework can be summarized as follows. To track the goal of maximizing investment value, a good manager must size up relevant risks and proactively build flexibility into the investment to the extent that the flexibility is expected to add value. The manager thereafter has to continually evaluate new information about the risks and, if necessary, take corrective actions within the bounds of flexibility built into the investment.

OBRiM operationalizes this idea based on real options theory (Benaroch, 2002). Aiming to optimize the balance between risk and value, and considering the cost of building flexibility, OBRiM prescribes four steps that supplement the "base case" analysis traditionally used to compute the passive $NPV^P$ of a target IT investment and its sensitivity to risk (see Figure 16.3).

1. *Risk analysis.* Risks affecting the target investment are identified.
2. *Map risks to options.* The identified risks one seeks to control dictate the choice of which real options (forms of flexibility) to consider embedding in the IT investment. Some real options act as risk mitigation strategies in themselves (e.g., prototyping, abandonment [Boehm, 1989]), while others simply create the flexibility needed to deploy more granular risk mitigation steps (e.g., deferral enables reducing risk due to restrictive regulation by providing time to lobby for a regulatory change [Benaroch and Kauffman, 2000]). Respectively, OBRiM offers a menu of risk-option mappings prescribing which options permit controlling the risks present.
3. *Design investment configurations.* The options chosen for the specific risks present permit structuring the investment in different ways. Therefore, embedding different combinations of the options in the investment generates different alternative investment configurations.
4. *Pick the best configuration.* Different combinations of options affect the investment value differently, because each may allow controlling the same risks to varying degrees and may have a different associated cost. Therefore, an economically superior configuration is found by using formal option pricing models to compute the active $NPV^A$ for each investment configuration.

Overall, these steps enable configuring an IT investment using the most cost-effective combination of real options designed to control risk and to add maximum value.

While the logic underlying the OBRiM framework may have a natural appeal, researchers and practitioners condition the benefits of applying this logic in practice on the answer to three questions.

First, is OBRiM's logic consistent with the thinking of managers in IT investment management decision making? This question applies primarily to the risk–option mappings OBRiM offers in support of step 2, since these mappings must be valid for the framework's prescriptions about what options to use to be valid. Initial supporting evidence to that extent has arrived recently in the context of IS project escalation (Tiwana, Keil, and Fichman, 2006) and more specifically in the context of OBRiM's risk–option mappings (Benaroch, Lichtenstein, and Robinson, 2006). The next section elaborates on this important issue.

Second, do managers need to apply OBRiM's logic formally or can they just keep it to the intuitive level? The answer is apparent from empirical evidence about managers' limited ability to value the flexibility that options afford. Decision makers' intuition was found to agree with the qualitative prescriptions of real options theory, but their subjective option valuations differ from formal option valuations (Busby and Pitts, 1997; Jägle and Howell, 1996; Tiwana et al., 2007). This is especially so with regard to the effect of risk on the value of deferral options (Bjornstad et al., 2001; Sirmans and Yavas, 2001), growth options (Howell and Jägle, 1997, 1998), and abandonment and staging options (Tiwana, Keil, and Fichman, 2006). In this light, formal ap-

Figure 16.3   **Steps in the Option-based Approach to Managing Information Technology Investment Risk**

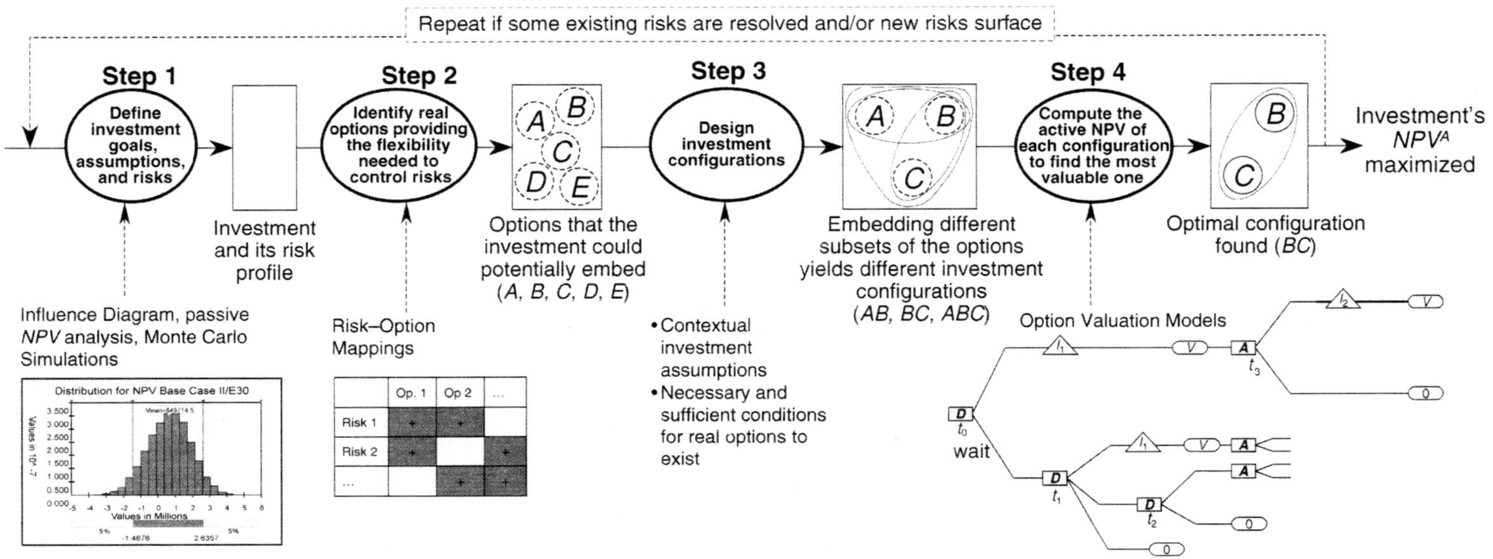

*Source:* Adapted from Benaroch (2002).

plication of the OBRiM framework is necessary to supplement IT managers' intuition about the value of flexibility that options afford. In other words, if managers are to enhance their current IT investment management practices, they will also have to rely on the formal quantitative real option tools that provide OBRiM with its ability to economically evaluate risk and flexibility and to optimally manage their tradeoffs.

Third, does OBRiM and its logic work when applied formally and in real-world settings? Answering this question is difficult because it requires showing that OBRiM is usable and adds value when applied by practitioners to realistic IT investments. As we explain later, a small first step in this direction has been taken by a recent evaluative field study that offers rather encouraging results (Benaroch et al., 2007). With this said, it is clear that more work is needed to address this question effectively.

## EMPIRICAL VALIDATION OF OBRiM'S RISK–OPTION MAPPINGS

A principle tenet of OBRiM is that the specific risks one seeks to control should dictate the choice of which specific options to embed in a target investment. It respectively offers a set of prescriptive risk–option mappings for making this choice. The mappings are shown in Table 16.1: cells marked with a "+" indicate that a certain option is suitable for controlling a specific risk. These mappings were originally posited based on purely theoretical and normative rationales.

A recent study has empirically established the validity of OBRiM's posited risk–option mappings (Benaroch, Lichtenstein, and Robinson, 2006). This study tested whether these mappings correspond well with the intuitions and practices that experienced IT managers use in risk management. The research site was a large Irish financial services organization (IFSO) with 2,500 employees and revenues of €3 billion in 2003. IFSO was deemed suitable for the study because it has a critical mass of large IT projects and because of its sophisticated IT risk management practices.

IFSO operates a dedicated Project Investment Department (PID) responsible for evaluating every proposed IT investment and ensuring that its business case includes an adequate risk management plan. IT investment sponsors build a business case for each proposal and submit it to PID. The business case is a comprehensive document including: the project description, resources required, benefits and financial plans, and a risk management plan. The last segment was the target of the analysis aimed at validating OBRiM's risk–option mappings. Based on the mitigations the risk management plan used to address specific IT risks, the study examined whether the managers systematically relied on the presence of, or made decisions that create, forms of flexibility (or options) that make those mitigations feasible. Establishing this link between risks, respective mitigations, and their enabling options was one way to examine whether OBRiM's risk–option mappings are observed in practice. It is important to note that IFSO's IT managers were not relying on any real options model or framework at the time of the study.

A sample of fifty of IFSO's IT projects was identified and data about them was obtained as follows. Data about the risks affecting each project were obtained directly from the complete risk assessment originally developed for the project as part of its business cases. Risk items in the assessment were matched against risk items in the IT literature, and confirmatory factor analysis was used to extract risk factors paralleling OBRiM's risk categories. Data about the specific mitigations planned for controlling project risks was collected through structured interviews with managers in PID. These risk mitigations were coded and used to establish the real options present in each project. Finally, logistic regression was used to test the relationship between the risk factors identified and the real options present in projects exposed to these risks.

Benaroch, Lichtenstein, and Robinson's (2006) results show that the majority of OBRiM's

Table 16.1

## Information Technology Investment Risks Mapped to Real Options That Can Control Them

| Risk area | Risk factor (opportunity) | Explore | | | | Exit (switch-use) | Contract development | Outsource | Lease | Expand (growth) |
| | | Defer | Pilot | Proto-type | Stage/incremental development | | | | | |
|---|---|---|---|---|---|---|---|---|---|---|
| **Monetary risks:** | | | | | | | | | | |
| Costs | Firm cannot afford the project (unacceptable financial exposure) | | + | | | | | | | |
| | Development or operational costs may not remain in line with projected benefits | + | | + | + | + | + | + | + | |
| Benefits | Poor estimation, no process to harvest benefits, and so on | + | + | | | | | | + | |
| **Project execution risks:** | | | | | | | | | | |
| Project | Staff lacks needed skills and experience | + | | + | + | | | + | | |
| | Project is too large or too complex | | + | + | + | | + | + | + | |
| | Lack of architectural stability or compliance, inadequate implementation infrastructure | + | | + | + | | + | | + | |
| Function | Inadequate design (e.g., system does not do what is expected of it, performance shortfalls) | + | | + | + | | + | + | + | |
| | Problematic requirements (stability, completeness, etc.) | + | + | + | + | | + | | | |
| Organization | Uncooperative internal parties | + | | | + | + | | | + | |
| | Parties slow to adopt the application | | + | | + | + | + | | + | |
| Competition | Competition's response eliminates the firm's advantage | + | + | | | + | + | | + | |

(continued)

Table 16.1 (continued)

| Risk area | Risk factor (opportunity) | Option | | | | | | | | |
|---|---|---|---|---|---|---|---|---|---|---|
| | | Explore | | | Stage/ incremental development | Exit (switch-use) | Contract development | Outsource | Lease | Expand (growth) |
| | | Defer | Pilot | Proto-type | | | | | | |
| Environment | Competitive preemptive action | + | + | | | | | | | |
| | Low customer/supplier/partner demand/ adoption/usage | + | + | | + | + | + | | + | |
| | Demand exceeds expectations (follow-up opportunities exist) | + | + | | | | | | | + |
| | Demand/usage may overwhelm the application | + | + | | | + | + | | + | + |
| | Unanticipated action of regulatory bodies | + | | | | + | | | + | |
| Technology | Application may be infeasible with the technology considered, or the technology is immature | + | | + | + | + | | + | + | |
| | The introduction of a new superior implementation technology may render the application obsolete | + | | | | + | | | + | |

Source: Adapted from Benaroch (2002).
+ Shows which option can be used to control which risk.

proposed risk–option mappings are found in practice, and equally important, that the majority of mappings *not* proposed by OBRiM are *not* found. More specifically, mappings were over six times more likely to be found where predicted by OBRiM than where not predicted. These results offer strong empirical support to the theorized rationales linking the way specific IT risks are managed with specific real options. They clearly show that a higher level of specific risks for which mitigations were planned is associated with an increased presence of specific options that facilitate deployment of those mitigations. In essence, the intuitions and practices that IT managers used to construct risk management plans appear to correspond well with OBRiM's risk–option mappings. Of course, it could be that the reason support was not found for some mappings is that IFSO's managers did not formally subscribe to the real-options thinking, although these managers' natural intuitions seem to match this thinking considerably.

The fact that these empirical results rest on data from a single organization, however, can impact their generalizability. While using a single research site controls for exogenous differences in firm and industry characteristics that might confound a similar study spanning multiple firms, the research site's sophistication of IT risk management practices is an important distinct capability that may limit the findings to organizations having a similar capability. In this light, conducting similar studies in organizations with different profiles could determine whether the findings extend to other kinds of organizations. There is reason to believe that other organizations exhibit the same level of reliance on real options in managing IT risk. For example, the number of options in IFSO's projects sample is comparable to the number of options that Kenneally and Lichtenstein (2002) found in the IT portfolio of a manufacturing firm with no visibly distinct IT risk management practices.

## ASSESSMENT OF OBRiM'S APPLICATION IN PRACTICE

The viability of the OBRiM framework in a real-world setting has recently been assessed using an evaluative field study involving interviews with senior managers, collection of data from multiple firms, and additional modeling and analysis (Benaroch et al., 2007). Among the main research questions the study sought to answer are: Does OBRiM produce investment structures (configurations) that managers find adequate for controlling uncertainty? And, is it feasible to evaluate these investment structures using financial real option models?

The evaluative field study of OBRiM was conducted in the context of a complex *data mart consolidation* (DMC) project aimed at producing an *enterprise data warehouse* (EDW). (Benaroch et al., [2007] offers a detailed discussion of this context and associated terminology.) Support for the study was provided by Teradata, a leading provider of data warehousing and analytic customer relationship management (CRM) solutions, in cooperation with a major airline (hereafter, Global Airline) considering a DMC investment. Global Airline hoped to consolidate ten existing data marts and enhance its CRM capabilities. These data marts fall into four clusters based on a similarity of their technology platform and relatedness of their business functions.

A DMC project includes two main phases. *Rehosting* physically migrates data and processes (queries, scripts, programs) into the EDW without really changing the data models underlying the data marts. *Rearchitecting* develops an integrated enterprise data model and reengineers the data before they are moved into the EDW. Rearchitecting can yield significant performance improvements by enabling a firm to harness the full value of integrated enterprise data, but it makes DMC much more risky and adds 60 to 75 percent more time and cost compared with rehosting alone.

A DMC project can offer substantial benefits but it also involves significant risk. The benefits include: immediate IT costs savings (e.g., lower total cost of ownership of a single-vendor data platform), improved data and analytical capabilities for business decision making (e.g., a firm-wide "view of the truth," hot reload of data), and follow-up investment opportunities (e.g., in integrated analytic CRM). The risks could be attributed to business and organizational factors (e.g., organizational politics over data control, management support in relocating data mart support staff, user involvement in developing a unified data model) as well as to technical and technology factors (e.g., quality of source data, team's skills and experience, development tools and processes).

In this light, planning the project implementation so as to manage risk is crucial. Lacking experience with DMC projects, Global Airline decided to outsource the project to Teradata as a way to transfer some of the risks to the vendor (for whom the risks are less significant). Even then, base cases analysis shows that risk management is still necessary. The base case analysis considered two cases. One involves *rehosting all data marts at once*. This "big bang" approach offers scale economies and earlier cost savings from IT personnel reductions, but it is risky because full investment commitment must be made despite uncertainties. Another base case involves *rehosting and rearchitecting all data marts at once*. The benefits and drawbacks of this approach are similar, but they are accented by the rearchitecting effort. The expected passive *NPVs* for both base cases are positive, especially if an integrated analytical CRM solution is added. Yet, sensitivity analysis using Monte Carlo simulations shows significant variability (risk) in all cases, with about a 40 percent chance for a negative *NPV.*

To improve on these results, OBRiM's four steps are applied so as to optimally configure a DMC project. These steps determine how many data marts to target, whether to just rehost or also rearchitect, whether to follow a big-bang or incremental approach, whether to include CRM deployment, and so on. They identify which real options ought to be used to provide the forms of flexibility needed to manage risk from an economic perspective.

- *Step 1:* Risk analysis reveals that the risk factors affecting the DMC project are due to uncertainty over the quality data, user participation, senior management support, changes in end-user skill requirements, and user adoption. (Recall that some other risks are transferred to the outsourcing vendor, for example, lack of data warehousing skills and project complexity.)
- *Step 2:* The risks identified are mapped to specific real options providing the forms of flexibility needed to control them. This is done based on OBRiM's empirically validated risk–option mappings (Table 16.1). Only four viable options are found: *staging, piloting, contraction (changing scale)*, and *growth*.
- *Step 3:* More than fifteen plausible investment configurations are designed, each embedding a different combination of viable options that is consistent with context-related assumptions. Table 16.2 shows four sample configurations, denoted C1–C4, where C4 is a hybrid of C1 and C3. Evaluating a hybrid configuration is harder but it eliminates the need to evaluate separately each of the simpler configurations it subsumes.
- *Step 4:* A configuration that maximizes value is found by computing for each configuration its active $NPV^A$. Options were valued using a multioption nested pricing model (Benaroch, Shah, and Jeffery, 2006a). Most model parameters are estimated based on data used for the "base case" analysis. The volatility (risk) of the options' underlying assets, however, is estimated using Monte Carlo simulations with risk factor estimates obtained from proprietary data about Teradata's experience with past clients and using a framework for measuring customer centricity (Benaroch et al., 2007).

OBRiM's evaluation results are quite revealing. Investment configurations involving only rehosting are found to have low valuations, in part, because CRM benefits are low without rearchitecting. Investment configurations involving rearchitecting have much higher valuations only when an

Table 16.2

**Sample Plausible Alternative Configurations for Global Airline's DMC Investment**

| No. | Investment configuration | Risks (opportunities) they can control |
|---|---|---|
| C1 | Pilot / Full scale follow-up; Rehost cluster I; Rehost clusters II, III, IV | *Pilot* rehost of the first cluster of data marts and a follow-up rehost of the remaining clusters contingent on the success of the pilot effort. The pilot would enable resolving uncertainty about IT personnel displacement and the quality of data sources. |
| C2 | Stage + abandon …; Growth; Rehost cluster I; Rehost II; Rearch. II; Rehost III; Rearch. III, IV; Rehost IV; Integrated CRM | *Staged* rehost and rearchitect followed by contingent customer relationship management (CRM) deployment, where the staged rehost effort could resolve uncertainty about IT personnel displacement and quality of data sources, and the staged rearchitect effort could additionally resolve uncertainty about end-user participation. |
| C3 | Pilot / Full scale follow-up; Growth; Rehost + rearchitect I; Rehost + rearchitect rest (II, III, IV); Integrated CRM | *Pilot* rehost and rearchitect I with a full-scale follow-up followed by contingent CRM deployment, where the *pilot* could resolve risk due to IT personnel displacement, quality of data sources, and end-user involvement. |
| C4 | Pilot / Contract / Full scale follow-up; Growth; Rehost + rearchitect I; Rehost rest (II, III, IV); Rehost + rearchitect rest (II, III, IV); Integrated CRM | Hybrid configuration of C3 and C1. It is similar to C3, with one difference: if the pilot effort reveals that end-user involvement is low, it is possible to contract the scope of the DMC effort so that the remaining data mart clusters are only rehosted. |

□ Decision node/Option

333

integrated CRM solution is deployed. Most important, the value that option-based risk management adds to these configurations is substantial. Although staging and piloting options increase the DMC cost and thus lower the passive $NPV^P$ of an investment configuration, they are found to add value equaling two to four times the size of the passive $NPV^P$. The CRM growth option is found to add another one to two times the value of the passive $NPV^P$. In particular, when CRM deployment is contingent on the outcome of rehosting and rearchitecting, the CRM growth option adds much more value because the management of risk in rearchitecting also permits resolving most of the CRM implementation risks.

The evaluative application of OBRiM in the data mart consolidation context enabled managers at Teradata and Global Airline to reach an important conclusion—OBRiM *does* produce information essential to the development of an economically rational risk management plan for DMC projects. This information enables Teradata's clients to reduce the overwhelming implementation risk that DMC investments carry with them, by considering alternative implementation choices and their tradeoffs in terms of different risk, reward, and cost components. It enables the long-term strategic value of such large-scale IT investments to be best understood and valued relative to the different implementation alternatives and real growth options they create. At a somewhat higher level, the main benefits of OBRiM that technology executives identified in the context of Global Airline's study include: simplification of the complexities of real options, accuracy and rigor in risk analysis of IT investments, support of proactive planning, and results that correspond well to real-world experience on DMC investments. It is also worth noting that, while the Global Airline field study reflects the experience of applying OBRiM in only one real-world context, this context is representative of many large-scale IT investments. Hence, there is reason to believe that the lessons drawn about OBRiM's viability and strengths generalize to other complex IT investments.

## WHERE TO GO FROM HERE?

Having reviewed and assessed the growing body of work on real options in IT risk management, the next sections broaden the discussion to the main implications of this work for research and practice as well as to challenges that still need to be overcome. One implication that is of central concern relates to how the scope of this work can be extended to include portfolios of IT investments. This implication could be far reaching considering that IS planning is also about choosing IT investments, building IT capabilities and assets for effective execution of investments, and managing the risks of these two elements in a way that maximizes the IT portfolio value.

### OBRiM's Strengths

There is growing empirical evidence that the logic of the OBRiM framework and its underlying theory could be of great importance to IT investment management and planning. Benaroch, Lichtenstein, and Robinson's (2006) Irish study confirms the theorized link between the risk management practices of experienced IT project managers and the presence of real options. Furthermore, Tiwana, Keil, and Fichman (2006) find IT managers' behavior in relation to IS project escalation to be consistent with OBRiM's logic. These findings indicate that managers do rely intuitively on OBRiM's logic in choosing which options to embed in IT investments. Yet, we cannot forget other empirical evidence showing that managers can neither value accurately nor act objectively on the flexibility afforded by various option types (Bjornstad et al., 2001; Howell and Jägle, 1998; Tiwana, Keil, and Fichman, 2006; Tiwana et al., 2007). Hence, without adequate aids for valuing different forms of flexibility, managers can plan and design flexibility into IT investments only in some intuitive sense.

The OBRiM framework can supplement IT managers' natural intuitions about real options and enable them to approach IT risk management and IT investment planning from an *economic optimization* perspective. The framework uses real option concepts and quantitative tools to provide managers with the ability to better assess risk and its monetary consequences. This is critical since IT project managers were observed to improperly evaluate risks before prioritizing them for management attention (Schmidt et al., 2001). OBRiM also uses solid economic principles to help managers in planning the exact amount and forms of flexibility to design into IT projects. As such, OBRiM can yield practical economic insights concerning which risk mitigations to pursue in order to effectively address the risks most worth controlling. And it can do so while recognizing that proactively created real options have a cost and their value is usually nonadditive. OBRiM's application to Global Airline's IT investment case clearly demonstrates the significant value that the framework can add in developing economically justified risk management plans for IT investments.

## OBRiM's Challenges

With this said, many challenges surrounding the adoption of OBRiM for regular use are becoming evident. We summarize the main research challenges here and refer the reader to a fuller discussion of these and other challenges in (Benaroch et al., 2007). It is important to note, however, that the research challenges extend well beyond the scope of the framework into areas we discuss below.

1. *Risk estimation.* There is a need for improved metrics and methods for obtaining firm-specific estimates for IT risk factors and volatilities for real options. This need is more acute when using financial option models that impose strong assumptions but can accept and work with more reliable benchmark- and market-driven risk estimates.
2. *Identifying plausible growth options.* Research on the business impact of IT investment has shown the importance of growth options, but an important question remains open: What approach is adequate in determining which growth options to consider for a specific IT investment?
3. *Gaps between OBRiM's underlying theory and practice.* Some of the risk mitigations regularly used by IT project managers cannot be accounted for by any of the real option types that OBRiM prescribes (Benaroch, Lichtenstein, and Robinson, 2006). Reconciling this gap is an interesting issue for future research (Benaroch and Goldstein, 2006).
4. *Ensuring optimal exercise of proactively created real options.* Exercising of options in a timely and rational manner, or lack thereof, is a concern that was raised explicitly by technology executives (Benaroch et al., 2007) and reinforced by empirical findings about the behavior of IT managers in IS project escalation (Tiwana, Keil, and Fichman, 2006).
5. *IT managers' training in financial and real options concepts.* Insufficient financial training is a major challenge apparent from difficulties IT managers have in fitting real option concepts with risk management practices (Benaroch, Lichtenstein, and Robinson, 2006), from observations made by technology executives (Benaroch et al., 2007), and from an empirical study of factors affecting the adoption of IT portfolio management practices (Jeffery and Leliveld, 2004).

The direct implications of these challenges are three. First, more research is needed on some fundamental issues surrounding the operationalization of OBRiM. Second, organizations ought to formally adopt the OBRiM framework if they are to fully realize its benefits, something that was shown to hold in the context of using a real options approach to manage R&D projects (Kumaraswamy, 1998). Third, even if the first two points are addressed, more research is needed to assess whether the benefits of full adoption of OBRiM would add sufficient value to outweigh the costs (effort and time) associated with regular use of OBRiM in practice.

## Broadening the Scope of Option-Based Risk Management

Interpreting the objective of OBRiM and its effect from the perspective of mean-variance theory suggests that the logic of OBRiM can and ought to be extended to the management of risk across portfolios of interdependent IT investments. In mean-variance theory, the notion of efficient frontier is central to the management of investment portfolios (Elton and Gruber, 1995). For financial portfolios of tradeable assets, there is a *market-determined efficient frontier* that represents all portfolios yielding the maximum return allowable by capital markets for different levels of risk.[3] A portfolio (i.e., an asset or combination of assets in different proportions) that lies below the efficient frontier represents a poor investment in the sense that its expected rate of return is too low for its level of risk. To move such a portfolio to the efficient frontier, investors can use diversification. Diversification is the selection of assets that are not highly correlated so that the portfolio is protected against excessive exposure to any single source of risk without necessarily lowering the expected return.

For portfolios of IT investments that are not necessarily tradable, there is no market-determined efficient frontier and instead we need to talk about the *firm-specific efficient IT frontier* that every firm has. This frontier is determined by the firm's IT capabilities (assets), organizational capabilities, and IT investment and sourcing opportunities available within the bounds of its business strategy. Bad IT investment choices and weak IT assets (e.g., poor execution and risk management capabilities) may mean that IT investments in the portfolio lie below the firm's efficient IT frontier. By contrast, good investment choices and improved use of strong IT assets (e.g., competent planning, execution, and risk management capabilities) could move IT investments and the portfolio itself toward the frontier. This thinking fits well with the way the OBRiM framework helps to manage risk at the level of a single IT investment by using real options to structure the investment and create managerial flexibility. Managing intrainvestment IT risk in this fashion increases the *passive NPV$^P$* by adding valuable flexibility, yielding the *active NPV$^A$*, and it normally also lowers risk. As seen in Figure 16.4, this amounts to moving an investment (or a portfolio) that starts at point A to some point between A' and A" on the frontier, or even to moving the frontier itself. The latter affect is most visible when an investment is structured so as to create growth options. Growth options corresponding to future investment opportunities enable the extraction of more value from the investment and therefore shift the investment up toward the efficient frontier. Growth options corresponding to new IT assets that open up new investment opportunities not currently available to the firm can, in addition, push up the frontier itself; this is often the case with investments in IT infrastructure (e.g., IT staff training, software process maturity improvements) and in IT assets (e.g., creating a unified enterprise data model).

While the potentially far-reaching implications of this realization remain to be explored, we can highlight two main ones here. At a more intuitive and strategic decision-making level, one important implication is the ability to conceptualize and visualize the affects of OBRiM in the context of a single IT investment as well as a portfolio of IT investments. At a more formal and optimization-oriented decision-making level, another implication is the availability of a solid theoretical basis for managing risk at the aggregate portfolio level by means of explicitly modeling cross-investment risk dependencies. Bardhan, Bagchi, and Sougstad (2004) have taken first

**Figure 16.4  Effect of Real Options on the Firm's Efficient Information Technology Frontier**

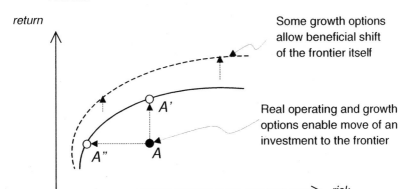

steps toward modeling such situations for an IT portfolio of interrelated e-commerce investments. Although these authors do not model risk and the value of flexibility as direct functions of risk factors, like OBRiM advocates, it may be possible to adapt their approach to the conceptual structure on which OBRiM rests.

In summary, expanding the scope of OBRiM's thinking to portfolios of interrelated IT investments opens another important dimension for future work. It could provide the basis for improving risk management practices in IS planning of IT investment portfolios as well as open a useful venue for investigating a host of behavioral and economic issues relating to IS planning. These additional potential benefits of OBRiM and its underlying theory offer a stronger motivation to explore the challenges surrounding the applications of OBRiM in practice and its adoption for regular use.

## CONCLUSION

IS research on real options has come a long way, especially in areas relating to IT investment risk management and planning. In particular, important progress has been made by finding strong empirical support for the core logic of the option-based approach to risk management and its underlying theory. Also important is the successful application of this framework to a large-scale IT investment in real-world settings and the favorable reaction of technology executives to this application. Perhaps the most important practical implication of this body of findings is that organizations stand to benefit from formally adopting the OBRiM framework. The findings have important implications for research as well.

In spite of these exciting prospects, there are still limitations to this body of research and areas for additional development effort remain. They include, for example, empirical results that could be tainted by the fact that they rest on small sample sizes and data coming from a single organization. Replicating the kinds of studies discussed in this chapter but in organizations with varied profiles could determine whether the findings to date generalize across business contexts. Likewise, additional field and case studies on the use of OBRiM in real-world settings could tell us more about both its practical value and its strengths and weaknesses. In this regard, we also highlighted an important direction for future research that could expand the scope of this work and its applicability to portfolios of interrelated IT investments.

## NOTES

1. Clemons and Gu's (2003) interpretation of a real option is slightly more restrictive than ours. They characterize IT investments bearing real options as *strategy-enabling partial investments* that create the possibility, not the obligation, to undertake certain future investments when conditions become known and requirements become clear. The initial partial investments are therefore seen as creating *strategic options*, and completion of the future contingent investments can be seen as *exercising* the strategic options. Hence, they consider a real option to be an investment made to preserve flexibility and to accelerate subsequent choices, without requiring an expensive full commitment.

2. The basic financial options are *calls* and *puts*. A *European call* (*put*) gives its holder the right to buy (sell) $V$ for an agreed-upon exercise price, $X$, at a fixed expiration date, $T$. For example, a "January 2008 call" on Microsoft stock with a $120 exercise price allows its holder to buy Microsoft shares for $120 on January 15, 2008. This call is worth exercising only if the value of a Microsoft share on January 15 exceeds $120. Hence, the payoff functions of a call and a put on expiration are $C = \max(0, V - X)$ and $P = \max(0, X - V)$, respectively. Unlike a European option, an *American option* can be exercised anytime before it expires. As is well known (Hull, 1993), the current value of a call, $C$, feeds mainly on the volatility (variability) of the underlying asset's value, $\sigma$, and its time to maturity, $T$. The higher $\sigma$ is, or the longer $T$ is, the higher $C$ is.

3. The efficient frontier can be visualized as a curved line in a two-dimensional space, with the axes being risk and return (Elton and Gruber, 1995). If two assets can be included in a portfolio, $A$ and $B$, the exact shape of the frontier will depend on the correlation between these assets' returns. This correlation measures the extent to which returns on $A$ and $B$ are sensitive to changes in uncertain factors reflecting the state of the economy (e.g., inflation). Exposure to one or more of these factors creates risk, or uncertainty about the expectation that a future return will occur, measured by the volatility (variability) of an asset's return. This is why these factors are also called risk factors.

## REFERENCES

Alter, S., and Sherer, S.A. 2004. A general, but readily adaptable model of information risk. *Communications of the Association for Information Systems,* 14, 1–28.
Amram, M., and Kulatilaka, N. 1999. *Real Options: Managing Strategic Investment in an Uncertain World.* Boston: Harvard Business School Press.
Applegate, L.; Austin, R.; and McFarlan, W.F. 2003. *Corporate Information Strategy and Management,* 6th ed. New York: McGraw-Hill.
Avison, D.E.; Powell, P.L.; Keen, P.; Klein, J.H.; and Ward, S. 1995. Addressing the need for flexibility in information systems. *Journal of Management Systems,* 7, 2, 43–60.
Bardhan, I.; Bagchi, S.; and Sougstad, R. 2004. Prioritizing a portfolio of information technology investment projects. *Journal of Management Information Systems,* 21, 2, 33–60.
Baskerville R.; Mathiassen, L.; and Pries-Heje, J. 2005. Agility in fours: IT diffusion, IT infrastructures, IT development and business. In R. Baskerville, L. Mathiassen, J. Pries-Heje, and J. De Gross (eds.), *Business Agility and Information Technology Diffusion.* New York: Springer, pp. 3–10.
Barki, H.; Rivard, S.; and Talbot, J. 1993. Toward an assessment of software development risk. *Journal of Management Information Systems,* 10, 2, 203–225.
Benaroch, M. 2002. Managing information technology investment risk: a real options perspective. *Journal of Management Information Systems,* 19, 2, 45–86.
Benaroch, M., and Goldstein, J. 2006. An integrative economic optimization model to IS development risk management. *Proceedings of the 12th Americas Conference on Information Systems,* Acapulco, Mexico, August 4–6. Available at ais.bepress.com/amcis2006/68/ (accessed on August 2, 2008).
Benaroch, M., and Kauffman, R.J. 1999. A case for using real options pricing analysis to evaluate information technology project investment. *Information Systems Research,* 10, 1, 70–86.
———. 2000. Justifying electronic banking network expansion using real options analysis. *MIS Quarterly,* 24, 2, 197–225.
Benaroch, M.; Lichtenstein, Y.; and Robinson, K. 2006. Real options in IT risk management: an empirical validation of risk-option relationships. *MIS Quarterly,* 30, 2, 827–864.
Benaroch, M.; Shah, S.; and Jeffery, M. 2006a. On the valuation of multi-stage IT investments embedding nested real options. *Journal of Management Information Systems,* 23, 1 239–261.

Benaroch, M.; Jeffery, M.; Kauffman, R.J.; and Shah, S. 2007. Option-based risk management: a field study of sequential IT investment decisions. *Journal of Management Information Systems*, 24, 2, 103–141.
Bjornstad, D.; Brewer, P.; Cummings, R.; and McKee, M. 2001. An experimental test of the options theory of investment and the bad news principle. Working paper, Oak Ridge National Laboratory, Tennessee.
Boehm, B.W. 1989. *Software Risk Management*. Washington, D.C.: IEEE-CS Press.
Boehm, B.W., and Sullivan, K. 2000. Software economics: a roadmap. International Conference on Software Engineering, *Proceedings of the Conference on The Future of Software Engineering*, Limerick, Ireland, June 8, 321–343.
Bräutigam, J.; Esche, C.; and Mehler-Bicher, A. 2003. Uncertainty as a key value driver of real options. Fifth Conference on Real Options: Theory Meets Practice, Washington, D.C., July 9–10. Available at www.realoptions.org/papers2003/BraeutigamUncertainty.pdf (accessed on May 2, 2007).
Busby, J., and Pitts, C. 1997. Real options in practice: an exploratory survey of how finance officers deal with flexibility in capital appraisal. *Management Accounting Research*, 8, 2, 169–186.
Clemons, E.K. 1991. Evaluation of strategic investments in information technology. *Communications of the ACM*, 34, 1, 22–34.
Clemons, E.K., and Gu, B. 2003. Justifying information technology investments: balancing the need for speed of action with certainty before action. *Journal of Management Information Systems*, 20, 2, 11–48.
Dai, Q.; Kauffman, R.J.; and March, S. 2006. Valuing information technology infrastructures: a growth options approach. *Information Technology and Management*, 7, 4, 109–130.
Davis, P.K. 2002. Strategic planning amidst massive uncertainty in complex adaptive systems: the case of defense planning. *InterJournal*, Complex Systems section, 375. Available at www.rand.org/about/contacts/personal/pdavis/strategic.html (accessed on August 2, 2008).
Elton, J.E., and Gruber, M.J. 1995. *Modern Portfolio Theory and Investment Analysis*. Hoboken, NJ: Wiley.
Fichman, R.G. 2004. Real options and IT platform adoption: implications for theory and practice. *Information Systems Research*, 15, 2, 132–154.
Grenadier, S.R., and Weiss, A.M. 1997. Investment in technological innovations: an option pricing approach. *Journal of Financial Economics*, 44, 3, 397–416.
Howell, S.D., and Jägle, A. J. 1997. Laboratory evidence on how managers intuitively value real growth options. *Journal of Business Finance & Accounting*, 24, 7 & 8, 915–935.
Howell, S.D., and Jägle, A.J. 1998. The evaluation of real options by managers: a potential aspect of the audit of management skills. *Managerial Auditing Journal*, 13, 6, 335–352.
Hull, J.C. 1993. *Options, Futures, and Other Derivative Securities*, 2d ed. Englewood Cliffs, NJ: Prentice Hall.
Jägle, A.J., and Howell, S.D. 1996. Evidence on how managers intuitively value real growth options: a laboratory study. Working Paper Series, Centre for Business Research, Manchester Business School, University of Manchester, June.
Jeffery, M., and Leliveld, I. 2004. Best practices in IT portfolio management. *Sloan Management Review*, 45, 3, 41–49.
Kauffman, R.J., and Kumar, A. 2007. Modeling network decisions under uncertainty: countervailing externalities and embedded options. In R. Sprague (ed.), *Proceedings of the Fortieth Hawaii International Conference on Systems Science*, Kona, HI. Los Alamitos, CA: IEEE Computer Society Press, 3484–3493.
Kauffman, R.J., and Li, X. 2005. Technology competition and optimal investment timing: a real options perspective. *IEEE Transactions on Engineering Management*, 52, 1, 15–29.
Keil, M.; Cule, P.E.; Lyytinen, K.; and Schmidt, R.C. 1998. A framework for identifying software project risks. *Communications of the ACM*, 41, 11, 76–83.
Kenneally, J., and Lichtenstein, Y. 2002. The optional value of IS projects: a study of an IS portfolio at a multinational manufacturer. *ECIS '2002, Tenth European Conference on Information Systems*, Gdansk, Poland, June 6–8. Available at is2.1se.ac.uk/asp/aspecis/20020155.pdf (accessed on August 2, 2008).
Kim, Y.J., and Sanders, L.G. 2002. Strategic actions in information technology investment based on real option theory. *Decision Support Systems*, 33, 1, 1–11.
Kulatilaka, N., and Ciriello, J. 2005. *Shaping the Future Through Experimentation: Dr. Moulton's Evolving Cone of Possibilities*. Boston University Institute for Leading in a Dynamic Economy.
Kulatilaka, N.; Balasubramanian, P.; and Strock, J. 1999. Using real options to frame the IT investment problem. In L. Trigeorgis (ed.), *Real Options and Business Strategy: Applications to Decision-Making*. London: Risk Books, pp. 155–224.
Kumar, R.L. 2002. Managing risks in IT projects: an options perspective. *Information and Management*, 40, 1, 63–74.

Kumaraswamy, A. 1998. An organizational real-options perspective of firms' R&D: empirical evidence. *Second Annual Conference on Real Options: Theory Meets Practice,* Chicago, June.

Mintzberg, H. 1993. *The Rise and Fall of Strategic Planning.* New York: Free Press.

Newkirk, H.; Lederer, A.; and Srinivasan, C. 2003. Strategic information systems planning: too little or too much? *Journal of Strategic Information Systems,* 12, 3, 201–228.

Overby, E.; Bharadwaj, A.; and Sambamurthy, V. 2006. Enterprise agility and the enabling role of information technology. *European Journal of Information Systems,* 15, 2, 120–131.

Panayi S. and Trigeorgis L. 1998. Multi-stage real options: The cases of information technology infrastructure and international bank expansion. *Quarterly Review of Economics and Finance,* 38, 675–692.

Sambamurthy, V.; Zmud, R.W.; and Byrd, T.A. 1994. The comprehensiveness of IT planning process: a contingency approach. *Journal of Information Technology Management,* 5, 1, 1–10.

Schmidt, R.; Lyytinen, K.; Keil, M.; and Cule, P. 2001. Identifying software project risks: an international Delphi study. *Journal of Management Information* Systems, 17, 4, 5–36.

Sirmans, C.F., and Yavas, A. 2001. Real options: experimental evidence. Working paper 310, Center for Real Estate, University of Connecticut, Storrs, CT, December.

Taudes, A. 1998. Software growth options. *Journal of Management Information Systems,* 15, 1, 165–185.

Taudes, A.; Feuerstein, M.; and Mild, A. 2000. Options analysis of software platform decisions. *MIS Quarterly,* 24, 2, 227–243.

Tiwana, A.; Keil, M.; and Fichman, R.G. 2006. Information systems project continuation in escalation situations: a real options model. *Decision Sciences,* 37, 3, 357–391.

Tiwana, A.; Wang, J.; Keil, M.; and Ahluwalia, P. 2007. The bounded rationality bias in managerial valuation of real options: theory and evidence from IT projects. *Decision Sciences,* 38, 1, 157–181.

Trigeorgis, L. 1996. *Real Options.* Cambridge, MA: MIT Press.

Voloudakis, J. 2005. Hitting a moving target: IT strategy in a real-time world. *Educause Review,* 40, 2, 44–55.

Zhu K. 1999. Evaluating Information Technology Investment: Cash Flows or Growth Options. *Proceedings of the 11th Workshop on Information Systems Economics (WISE'99),* Charlotte, NC, September 11–12.

# CHAPTER 17

# CREATING BETTER ENVIRONMENTS FOR INFORMATION SYSTEMS DEVELOPMENT PROJECTS

JUN HE

**Abstract:** *Information systems development (ISD) researchers have long recognized the importance of creating better environments for ISD teams. However, existing discussions of the effects of environmental characteristics remain largely conceptual in the ISD literature, and the mechanisms through which these factors influence ISD processes and eventually shape the productivity of ISD project teams have not been empirically examined in a thorough manner. To fill the gap, this study proposes an integrative model to investigate the impacts of six environmental characteristics that have been suggested as important in the literature and tests their effects on team productivity, operationalized as team performance and system quality. Team cognition is proposed as a mediating mechanism that transfers the effects of environmental factors into ISD productivity outcomes. The results provide useful evidence on which environmental factors operate through the team cognition mediator and which do not, and generally support the pragmatic approach of "smaller is better" for ISD project teams to achieve overall development success. Implications for future research are discussed, and guidelines for ISD practice are also provided.*

**Keywords:** *Information Systems Development, Development Environment, Team Cognition, Team Performance*

## INTRODUCTION

Issues in improving the efficiency and effectiveness of information systems development (ISD) projects have received the attention of information systems (IS) researchers since the early era of the use of computers in business (e.g., Edstrom, 1977; Garrity, 1963; McFarlan, 1971; Swanson, 1974). The importance of the topic cannot be overestimated, given the continuing high rate of ISD project failures and the resulting losses to organizations (Klein, Jiang, and Tesch, 2002).

To achieve ISD success, researchers have proposed various approaches to better manage the development process, including the selection and use of innovative development methods (Hardgrave, Wilson, and Eastman, 1999; Nerur, Mahapatra, and Mangalaraj, 2005; Sircar, Nerur, and Mahapatra, 2001), user participation in development projects (DeBrabander and Edstrom, 1977; Ives and Olson, 1984; Markus and Mao, 2004), conflict management (Robey, Smith, and Vijayasarathy, 1993), risk management (Barki et al. 2001; Dillon, Pate-Cornell, and Guikema, 2005), team communication (Brodbeck, 2001; Mantei, 1981), team coordination (Faraj and Sproull, 2000; Kraut and Streeter, 1995; Nidumolu, 1995), and project leadership (Faraj and Sambamurthy, 2006; Zhang and Faerman, 2007).

The research and practitioner literature suggests that project planning conducted prior to development work is a critical element for successful ISD projects (Ginzberg, 1981b; Robey and Markus, 1984). Three general strategies have been widely applied to planning in order to enhance the likelihood of the success of ISD projects: one strategy focuses on the design of project complexity, another focuses on the design of project teams, and the third focuses on the creation of favorable development environments.

## Designing Projects with Feasible Complexity

ISD projects are inherently complex because they deal with both technological issues and organizational factors that are largely beyond the project team's control (Murray, 2000; Xia and Lee, 2004). Evidence shows that unrealistic expectations for ISD projects are likely to lead to development failure (Ginzberg, 1981a). Pursuing ISD success will be wishful thinking if the complexity is not well understood and if user requirements are set at levels that have little chance of achievement (Glass, 1999). Thus, planning ISD projects with feasible complexity is suggested as an effective strategy for ISD teams to achieve success.

Even after the scope of an ISD project is determined in the initial project definition stage (Ginzberg, 1981a), pressures still exist among ISD stakeholders to drive up the complexity of the ISD process.

> From the IT side, there is interest in using new development software; in moving to more sophisticated operating systems, communications techniques, and hardware; or trying new development methods. Within the senior management group, there is an interest in improving the organization's competitive position within its industry, in taking advantage of an opportunity to move to a higher level of customer service, and, often, in an assumed ability to reduce expense. (Murray, 2000, p. 30)

Therefore, the literature suggests that the planning of project complexity not be restricted to the early stages of the ISD process. For example, Chiang and Mookerjee (2004) suggest the dynamic management of expectations based on ongoing analysis of system requirements throughout the development process. Similarly, Benbya and McKelvey (2006) propose a coevolutional approach to ISD that allows for flexibility in managing complexity with evolving user requirements and needs.

## Designing Project Teams

ISD is intellectual work that requires knowledge and skills from various domains (Curtis, Krasner, and Iscoe, 1988). ISD project teams may be purposively constructed to leverage the specialized expertise of individual team members. Klein, Jiang, and Tesch (2002) classified the knowledge and skills needed for a successful ISD team as: technical expertise (being familiar with systems development methods, procedures, and tools), end-user expertise (being able to acquire and articulate accurate user requirements), and sociopolitical expertise (being aware of, and able to balance, the distribution of power among stakeholders). Ideally, an ISD project team is staffed so that both the levels and the distribution of knowledge possessed by the team members match those required for the successful completion of the project (Walz, Elam, and Curtis, 1993). However, the formation of an ISD team is usually contingent on the availability of people (Faraj and Sproull, 2000). Thus, forming an ISD team with the best "mix" of the most capable members is likely to be a significant challenge.

In addition, the potential of having diverse knowledge and expertise on an ISD team cannot be fully realized if team members do not collaborate on common project objectives through knowledge coordination (Faraj and Sproull, 2000) and teamwork (Hoegl and Gemuenden, 2001). Thus, the design of successful ISD project teams needs to address intrateam coordination. Jiang, Klein, and Discenza (2002) discussed preproject partnering as a strategy to induce collaboration among ISD developers. He, Butler, and King (2007) investigated the effects of familiarity among team members on team formation, and found that initial levels of interpersonal knowledge facilitated the formation and development of team cognition, especially during early stages of the ISD process. Other individual factors, such as the developers' mindset regarding the development methods (Armstrong and Hardgrave, 2007) and developers' job status (e.g., contract versus permanent [Ang and Slaughter, 2001]), may also influence coordination in ISD teams.

## Creating Favorable Environments for ISD Projects

Another general strategy for achieving ISD success is to provide ISD project teams with favorable development environments. The importance of environmental influences to the success of ISD projects has long been recognized by IS researchers (e.g., Garrity, 1963; Mason and Mitroff, 1973). The contingency theory of IS (Weill and Olson, 1989) articulates that contextual factors will affect various aspects of the development process and ultimately will affect performance outcomes at system and organizational levels. DeLone and McLean (1992) suggest that taking account of factors such as "the organizational strategy, structure, size, and environment of the study organization; the technology; and the task and individual characteristics of the system being studied" (p. 88) in the design of ISD environments.

Much research on the impacts of the ISD environment is still exploratory in nature, featuring profile analysis that describes the patterns of different characteristics (e.g., Biehl, 2007; Rockart and Hofman, 1992; Wastell and Sewards, 1995) or simple correlations between project environmental characteristics and project success (e.g., Palanisamy, 2005; Raymond, 1990).

The mechanisms through which environmental factors affect project success are also not well studied. For example, management support has long been recognized as a critical environmental factor that helps ISD project teams to obtain needed resources and to overcome political obstacles (Jarvenpaa and Ives, 1991; Kwon and Zmud, 1987; Leonard-Barton and Deschamps, 1988; Sharma and Yetton, 2003), but the effect of management support is typically studied as a simple main effect. "This approach neither reflects the richness of the theory (regarding the complex relationship between management support and ISD success), nor provides a good description or explanation of the relationship" (Sharma and Yetton, 2003, p. 534). Given the existence of various guidelines for creating favorable environments for ISD projects in the prescriptive literature (e.g., Biehl, 2007; Corbin, 1991; Rockart and Hofman, 1992), empirical research has lagged behind the other approaches in assessing and explaining the effects of environmental factors on ISD outcomes.

## OBJECTIVE AND CONCEPTUAL MODEL OF THE STUDY

To fill this gap, this study investigates the impact of various ISD environmental characteristics on the productivity of ISD teams. Viewing ISD processes as cognitive in nature, we propose team cognition, the collective mental models that guide team members' activity and behavior, as the mediating mechanism that translates the effects of environmental characteristics into ISD productivity outcomes.

Figure 17.1 depicts the conceptual model of the study. Team characteristics, task characteris-

Figure 17.1  **Original Model Showing Constructs and Measures**

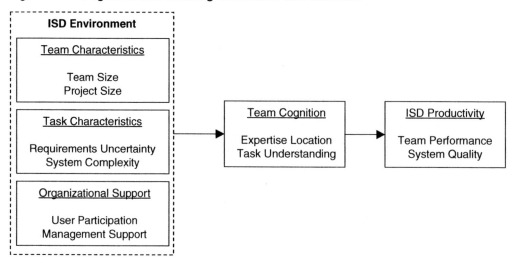

tics, and organizational support are shown to influence team cognition, as a mediator, in affecting ISD productivity.

The conceptual model of Figure 17.1 integrates some widely examined environmental factors (i.e., team characteristics, task characteristics, and organizational support) from the literature as predictors, "team cognition" as a mediator, and "ISD productivity" as outcomes. The objective of the study is to test the predictive value of the ISD environmental characteristics on the left, as mediated, on ISD productivity.

## CONTINGENCY APPROACHES TO THE STUDY OF ISD ENVIRONMENTS

The importance of project environments to ISD success has its theoretical roots in the contingency approach to the study of organizations (Kast and Rosenzweig, 1973; Szilagyi and Wallace, 1980) and of information systems (Weill and Olson, 1989). The contingency approach in organizational research focuses on the interplay between the internal attributes of an organization (e.g., structure and orientation) and its relevant external environment (Lawrence and Lorsch, 1967). According to the theory, certain organizational patterns work differently under various circumstances. Thus, managers and business owners should select appropriate organizational designs and plans based on the examination of their environmental conditions. Such adaptation, often studied in terms of the fit between an organizational structure and various environmental variables, is argued to be an important predictor of organization performance (Duncan, 1973; Lawrence and Lorsch, 1967).

One attraction of contingency theory is that it provides "a framework . . . of research on the complex functional relationships between management and situational variables" (Luthans and Stewart, 1977, p. 183). This is particularly true in the field of information systems where there is a need to organize knowledge from non-IS areas (Tait and Vessey, 1988). Much evidence of the effects of environmental factors on ISD outcomes has been obtained from studies with other research foci. Weill and Olson (1989) have theorized this approach in their proposal for a general contingency theory in IS research, in which environmental variables (e.g., size, environment, technology, task, etc.) influence IS variables (e.g., implementation and development of an ISD project), which in turn affect performance outcomes (e.g., ISD success and organizational performance).

One criticism of the contingency approach is that its common focus on the special fit between organization structures and certain environmental attributes will lead target organizations to be studied in a restricted fashion (Schreyögg, 1980). This is evidenced in the study of ISD environments. The literature has accumulated evidence regarding the effects of environmental factors on ISD performance. But, much of the evidence is fragmented among many narrowly defined research contexts. There is a lack of integrative research regarding the extent to which the underlying mechanisms of ISD environments influence the performance of ISD processes.

## EXPLICATION OF THE CONSTRUCTS AND HYPOTHESES

Following the left-to-right pattern of the model of Figure 17.1, we now consider ISD environmental characteristics as predictors, team cognition as a mediator, and ISD productivity as the dependent constructs as well as hypotheses related to the mediator and dependent constructs.

### ISD Environmental Characteristics as Predictors

ISD project environmental characteristics, as shown in Figure 17.1, consist of "team characteristics," "task characteristics," and "organizational support."

*Team Characteristics*

ISD projects are typically complex and dynamic, and involve unstructured tasks (Brodbeck, 2001; Kraut and Streeter, 1995). When a project exceeds the capacity of an individual, a team is created and social processes interact with cognitive and motivational processes in the performance of technical work (Curtis, Krasner, and Iscoe, 1988). Team characteristics, which reflect the scale, resources, expectations, and goals of a project, may facilitate or hinder ISD performance. Thus, the ISD literature suggests various team characteristics, including team size and project size as important predictors of the productivity of ISD teams.

Team size refers to the number of members working on an ISD project team; project size reflects the overall complexity of development effort in terms of the required time, resources, and/or lines of codes that need to be programmed. The two factors together reflect the scope of ISD projects (Barki, Rivard, and Talbot, 1993). Compared with small projects, projects that are large in scope are more difficult to complete successfully, and suffer more project failures (Curtis, Krasner, and Iscoe, 1988).

Team size and project size are closely related, but methodologically distinct. From a measurement perspective, team size is an objective measure of the number of team members, while project size is perceptual in nature,[1] and is often best measured by the relative scale of a project in comparison with an average project in an organization (Barki, Rivard, and Talbot, 1993, 2001; Yetton et al., 2000).

*Task Characteristics*

"Task characteristics" as shown in Figure 17.1 are made up of requirements uncertainty and system complexity. Requirements uncertainty refers to the ambiguity and uncertainty that surround the business requirements of a system, and system complexity refers to the ambiguity and uncertainty that surround the practice of system development. The two factors reflect the difficulty of developing systems in terms of the business context and technology context, respectively.

In situations where requirements uncertainty is high, system developers will find it difficult to work out solutions to satisfy user needs. Even with high levels of user participation, system developers may feel frustrated if: (1) the business context is very difficult to comprehend (Lucas, 1982; Rowen, 1990); in some cases, even the users may not have a clear understanding of the application domain at the beginning of a project (Benbya and McKelvey, 2006; Walz, Elam, and Curtis, 1993); (2) there exists a diverse or unknown user group (especially for Web-based ISD projects) (Kautz, Madsen, and Norbjerg, 2007); (3) information requirements fluctuate during the development process because of the dynamics in the external business environment (Nidumolu, 1995); (4) information requirements fluctuate due to changing internal requirements (McKelvey, 1999); or (5) there are various possible solutions but their consequences are not well understood, so that the selection of the most appropriate one for a target system is more an art than a science.

Similarly, in situations where technological complexity is high, problems will often arise in the analysis and specification of the system (Tait and Vessey, 1988). In such instances, ISD project teams must devote more time and effort to clarifying technical issues during the development process. High levels of system complexity are often caused by the use of complex or state-of-the-art technology (Murray, 2000; Zmud, 1980) or by a lack of understanding and training of people on the technology (McKeen, Guimaraes, and Wetherbe, 1994). System complexity causes technical risk or uncertainty in ISD processes (Nidumolu, 1995; Zmud, 1980), and composes an important dimension of the risk profile for ISD project teams to manage in order to achieve high performance and deliver quality products (Barki, Rivard, and Talbot, 1993, 2001).

*Organizational Support*

Most ISD projects are resource intensive and cannot be accomplished without significant support from the organization (Sharma and Yetton, 2003). The efforts to achieve development success should not be restricted within the boundary of the project team. As ISD projects "must be aligned with company goals and are affected by corporate politics, culture, and procedures" (Curtis, Krasner, and Iscoe, 1988; p. 1269), help from stakeholders is needed during the development process. Typically, support from organizations comes from potential users and senior management.

The necessity of having users participate in developing a system is widely studied through the construct "user participation," which is defined as "the behaviors and activities that the target users or their representatives perform in the systems development process" (Barki and Hartwick, 1989, p. 59). One important mode of user participation is to recruit user representatives for the ISD project team to work on a formal and regular basis (Brodbeck, 2001; Barki and Hartwick, 1994; Hartwick and Barki, 2001; Ives and Olson, 1984).

The practice of user participation is expected to help ISD teams achieve overall development success with enhanced user satisfaction and increased system quality (Ives and Olson, 1984; Markus and Mao, 2004). The common reasoning is that through user participation, ISD teams acquire valuable practical knowledge from users about the business domain that the system is to support (Howcroft and Wilson, 2003; Ravichandran and Rai, 1999; Swanson, 1974). This should result in higher quality systems that meet user requirements, "which in turn will cause frequent system use and user satisfaction" (Hwang and Thorn, 1999, pp. 233–234).

Management support is another commonly suggested organizational factor in determining team performance. Support from management reflects the symbolic commitment of the organization to the project, and helps ISD project teams acquire important resources (e.g., sufficient budget and a flexible schedule) and to overcome political obstacles when support from other business units or departments is needed (Markus, 1983). Since restricted resources are a contributor to many ISD failures (Eid-Dor and Segev, 1978), management support should help ISD teams to better achieve overall development success (Sharma and Yetton, 2003). This has been evidenced in previous studies about the design and development of various types of information systems, such as decision support systems (Guimares, Igbaria, and Lu, 1992; Igbaria et al., 1997), data warehouses (Wixom and Watson, 2001), and global information systems (Biehl, 2007).

## Team Cognition as a Mediating Mechanism

Team cognition refers to the mental models collectively held by a group of individuals that enable them to accomplish tasks by acting as a coordinated unit. Team cognition functions as the mental template that is imposed on information environments to give them form and meaning, providing a cognitive foundation for action (Walsh, 1995).

The concept of team cognition has been proposed as a powerful explanatory mechanism for understanding interactions on effective teams (Cannon-Bowers, Salas, and Converse, 1993; Cooke et al., 2000; Klimoski and Mohammed, 1994). For a team to exchange and process information and knowledge among team members requires both time and cognitive resources (MacMillan, Estin, and Serfaty, 2004). Team cognition enables members to formulate accurate teamwork and taskwork predictions (Cannon-Bowers, Salas, and Converse, 1993; Katz and Tushman, 1979), adapt their activities and behaviors in a collaborative way, and thereby increase overall team effectiveness (Cannon-Bowers and Salas, 2001; Lewis, 2004). Without well-formed team cognition, team members will not be able to efficiently share knowledge and information, coordinate each other's activities, resolve conflicts, or negotiate agreed-upon solutions (Cannon-Bowers and Salas, 2001; Jackson, May, and Whitney, 1995; Walsh, 1995).

The need for team members to develop collective and mutually adjusted mental models is well recognized in the ISD literature. For example, Kraut and Streeter (1995) discuss the necessity for team members to form a common view of the software development task, such as "what the software they are constructing should do, how it should be organized, and how it should fit with other software systems already in place or undergoing parallel development" (p. 69), so that team members can efficiently mesh their activities and coordinate their work.

Faraj and Sproull (2000) discuss the importance of knowing members' knowledge and expertise within ISD teams. Recently, Ren, Carley, and Argote (2006) and He, Butler, and King (2007) further articulated that shared awareness of expertise location and shared understanding of the task are the two most important elements of team cognition for ISD teams to facilitate member activities and behaviors in a coordinative and productive fashion.

Team cognition is shown in Figure 17.1 to be assessed in terms of "Expertise Location" and "Task Understanding."

### Expertise Location

Expertise location refers to the common awareness of each team member's specialized knowledge and unique expertise. Such a shared awareness of the distribution of knowledge and expertise plays a key coordinative and integrative function on ISD teams (Faraj and Sproull, 2000). By knowing others' knowledge and expertise, team members are able to anticipate, rather than simply react to, each other's behavior, thus improving team efficiency by executing ISD tasks in a coordinative fashion (Moreland and Myaskovsky, 2000). In addition, through such awareness, team members have an improved ability to access one another's specialized expertise, resulting in an expanded pool of knowledge and expertise for decision making and problem solving (Hollingshead, 1998, 2001). In such instances, team tasks are more likely to be assigned to the people who are most capable of performing them, thereby improving team effectiveness and avoiding redundancy of effort (Hollingshead, 2001; Moreland and Myaskovsky, 2000).

Expertise location is formed mainly through cognitive interactions among team members, such as training together (Hollingshead, 1998; Liang, Moreland, and Argote, 1995), observing and monitoring (Moreland, 1999), and team communication (MacMillan, Estin, and Serfaty, 2004; He, Butler, and King, 2007). These information- and knowledge-processing activities will naturally facilitate a better understanding of each other's knowledge and expertise and lead to the development of shared aware-ness of expertise location on the team (He, Butler, and King, 2007). Environmental characteristics that reflect the scale, resources, expectations, and goals of the project, will inevitably influence the development process and the interactions among team members (Weill and Olson, 1989). Generally, the more sophisticated a project environment is, the more cognitive obstacles are likely to exist for the ISD team members to overcome (Katz and Tushman, 1979).

*Team and Project Size Effects on Expertise Location*

Team size and project size are two indicators used in this research to assess the overall size of a project. The prescriptive literature has suggested "smaller is better" as a pragmatic approach for ISD project teams to control project complexity and reduce coordination difficulty within the team (Curtis, Krasner, and Iscoe, 1988; Murray, 2000). When there are many people working on a large project, and the scope of the project reflected by the required time and resources is extensive, the distribution of knowledge and expertise in the team may be an overly big picture for team members to form and comprehend.

> H1:   Team size has a negative effect on expertise location.
> H2:   Project size has a negative effect on expertise location.

*Requirements Uncertainty and System Complexity Effects on Expertise Location*

This research assesses the business and technical aspects of ISD projects via the constructs of require-ments uncertainty and system complexity. If the development process is overwhelmed with complicated business or technical issues, team members may have to struggle to comprehend these issues before searching for knowledge and expertise to bring to bear on problems. For example, adding required features or changing the requirements of a project, and using new or unfamiliar technologies, often require project developers to exert more time and effort, sometimes beyond their cognitive capabilities, to cope with the increased complexity of the project (Murray, 2000). Limited or inaccurate understand-ings of these development issues are likely to mislead the search for relevant knowledge and expertise, therefore hindering the development of shared understanding of expertise location in the team.

> H3:   Requirements uncertainty has a negative effect on expertise location.
> H4:   System complexity has a negative effect on expertise location.

*User Participation and Management Support Effects on Expertise Location*

Developing ISD projects may be constrained or enhanced by organizational contexts (Curtis, Krasner, and Iscoe, 1988; Weill and Olson, 1989). This research assesses two organizational factors, user participation and management support. User participation reflects support from the user group; it is effective in clarifying user requirements and providing the ISD project team with the needed application domain knowledge (Ives and Olson, 1984; Markus and Mao, 2004), and therefore helps to reduce the overall complexity of the project. With many application-related issues (e.g., existing practices, procedures, dependent systems, and potential users and their special needs) being understood and system requirements being clarified, the knowledge and expertise available in the team can be recognized and brought to bear on problems (Curtis et al., 1993; Faraj and Sproull, 2000). Similarly, support from the management group helps the ISD project team gain access to a variety of resources, both financial and intellectual, that may be needed to cope with problems in the development process (Markus, 1983; Sharma and Yetton, 2003). In addition, institutional theory suggests that perceived support from management helps increase team members' commitment to certain activities favored by the organization (Purvis, Sambamurthy, and Zmud, 2001), such as encouraging and formalizing debates on key development issues as a mechanism to acquire and share knowledge within the team (Walz, Elam, and Curtis, 1993). Thus, the development of expertise location is expected to benefit from help from the two relevant stakeholder groups.

H5: User participation has a positive effect on expertise location.
H6: Management support has a positive effect on expertise location.

*Task Understanding*

Task understanding characterizes the degree to which members share an understanding of a focal ISD project. Mutually shared understanding of a focal task, including the involved procedures, sequences, actions, and strategies, helps team members form common explanations and expectations of the task, and in turn, coordinate activities in a harmonious and efficient fashion (Cannon-Bowers, Salas, and Converse, 1993; Levesque, Wilson, and Wholey, 2001). This element of team cognition is particularly important for ISD teams. As various people work together on a complex ISD project, they need to "negotiate a mutually agreed upon solution and means of achieving it" (Levesque, Wilson, and Wholey, 2001, p. 136) to prevent the development process from being a frustrating and time-consuming experience. The shared understanding on development issues enables team members to interpret cues in a similar manner, to make compatible decisions, and to take appropriate joint action (Klimoski and Mohammed, 1994; Mohammed and Dumville, 2001). When such understanding exists, the need for interpersonal communication is typically reduced, allowing team members to spend more time on executing various ISD tasks and less effort on negotiating for coordinative activities (MacMillan, Estin, and Serfaty, 2004; Mathieu et al., 2000).

*Team and Project Size Effects on Task Understanding*

As is the case for expertise location, the development of task understanding is affected by team process and interactions (He, Butler, and King, 2007; Levesque, Wilson, and Wholey, 2001; Mathieu et al., 2000), upon which environmental factors are argued to exert great influence.

Team size and project size are expected to negatively affect the development of task understanding in the ISD project team. People involved in the ISD project bring different perspectives to address development issues (Klein, Jiang, and Tesch, 2002; Murray, 2000). With increased team size, the development of shared understanding on the project task tends to be hindered by the increased effort toward narrowing initially diverse views on different developmental issues.

Similarly, increased project size requires more team members, time, and effort to cope with the scope of the project (Murray, 2000), thus increasing the difficulty of forming a common understanding on development issues.

H7:   Team size has a negative effect on task understanding.
H8:   Project size has a negative effect on task understanding.

*Requirements Uncertainty and System Complexity Effects on Task Understanding*

The business and technical complexity of the project also adds difficulty to the development of task understanding in the ISD project team. The more complicated the project is, the more difficulty system developers will experience in learning about project details. Imperfect understanding of the project often results in conflicting views on key development issues (Curtis et al., 1993), and therefore requires more cognitive efforts for team members to achieve consensus (Kraut and Streeter, 1995). Thus, the development of task understanding may suffer from high complexity of the project that is reflected in requirements uncertainty on the business aspects, and system complexity on the technological aspects.

H9:   Requirements uncertainty has a negative effect on task understanding.
H10: System complexity has a negative effect on task understanding.

*User Participation and Management Support Effects on Task Understanding*

Learning the details of a project will be easier when help from relevant stakeholders is available. The aforementioned benefits of user participation and management support to the development of expertise location can also be applied to the development of task understanding. Application domain knowledge brought to the team through user participation helps the ISD project team to understand and clarify system requirements and other application-related issues. Management support helps the team to access needed resources, remove political obstacles, and improve team morale for more cooperative interactions among team members. Thus, the development of a common understanding on various development issues is expected to be easier for teams with high levels of user participation and management support than for teams with low levels.

H11: User participation has a positive effect on task understanding.
H12: Management support has a positive effect on task understanding.

## Team Performance and System Quality as the Dependent Variables: ISD Productivity Hypotheses

In this study, team performance and system quality are considered as two indicators of the productivity of ISD teams.

*Team Performance*

In the ISD literature, team performance is often defined as the extent to which an ISD project team "is able to meet established quality and cost and time objectives" (Hoegl and Gemuenden,

2001, p. 438). Team performance is an important indicator of IS project success (Jones and Harrison, 1996), and reflects the immediate goals that an ISD project team pursues. In this study, the "quality" aspect of team performance is taken to be the quality of its actions, such as its operating efficiency and its interactions with people outside the team rather than the quality of the system, which is taken as a derivative outcome measure.

Team cognition is expected to have direct positive effects on team performance in that it helps direct members' activities and behavior in a collaborative way (Cooke, Kiekel, and Helm, 2001). In terms of the two elements of team cognition specified in this study, expertise location helps enhance team performance by: (1) improving coordination by assigning tasks to the right people; (2) facilitating cooperation even if task assignments are unclear; and (3) matching problems with people who are most likely to solve them (Moreland and Myaskovsky, 2000). In the ISD literature, the positive effect of expertise location on team performance has been supported by empirical evidence (e.g., Faraj and Sproull, 2000; He, Butler, and King, 2007).

> H13: The level of expertise location is positively associated with the level of team performance.

Task understanding is also expected to positively affect team performance in that the formation of shared understanding on the focal project encourages more knowledge utilization activities among team members (Klimoski and Mohammed, 1994; Mohammed and Dumville, 2001). This is particularly apparent in ISD teams, where the existence of different knowledge domains may trigger communication obstacles caused by the use of different terminologies or jargons (Abdul-Gader and Kozar, 1990). The shared understanding of development issues will make it "unnecessary to construct understanding from scratch each time similar stimuli are encountered" (Vandenbosch and Higgins, 1996, p. 200), therefore facilitating effective teamwork and enhancing the performance of ISD teams.

> H14: The level of task understanding is positively associated with the level of team performance.

## System Quality

System quality is another key indicator of ISD success. System quality is typically measured in terms of ease-of-use, functionality, reliability, flexibility, data quality, portability, integration, and importance of the system that is produced by the team, as distinguished from the quality of the team's efforts and its intermediate work products (DeLone and McLean, 2003). System quality assesses the quality of IS projects produced by ISD teams, and therefore can be considered a consequence of team performance. High levels of team performance often lead to high quality systems, which are the products of successful teamwork. It is unlikely that quality systems would be associated with low levels of team performance, although it is conceivable that successful teamwork might produce unsuccessful systems.

> H15: A high level of team performance is associated with a high level of system quality.

The hypotheses are graphically summarized in the research model of Figure 17.2. Signs indicate whether the individual effects are expected to be positive or negative.

Figure 17.2   **Graphical Research Model and Hypotheses**

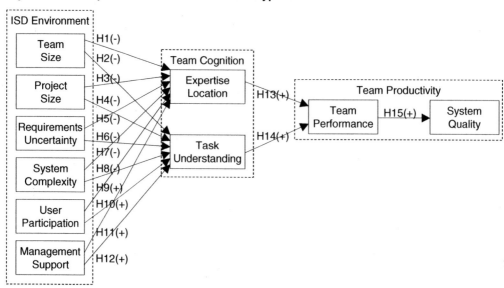

## RESEARCH METHOD

The research method is described in terms of survey design and procedure, measures, and data collection.

### Survey Design and Procedure

A field survey was conducted to test the research model. We designed a two-stage, team-level survey to collect data from ISD teams that had recently completed their projects. Target respondents included system developers, user representatives, and IS managers.

In the first stage, invitation letters explaining the purpose and the procedures of this research were sent to IS senior managers. The purpose was to get management support for the study. In the second stage, those managers who agreed to have their organizations participate received survey packages including: (1) survey instructions, (2) a questionnaire for user representatives, and (3) a questionnaire for system developers. The survey instruction asked the senior manager to identify a recent ISD project and to distribute the questionnaires to the project team members according to their roles in the project. Managers were also asked to answer a few questions concerning the "demographics" of the selected project. An Internet version of the survey with the same set of questions was also developed. A link to the online survey was provided in both the invitation letter and survey package letter for the convenience of respondents.

If no response was received from someone who agreed to participe within two weeks, a reminder e-mail was sent to the contact person. After a reexplanation of the research purpose, the contact was asked to forward the linkage of the online survey to appropriate people who had been involved in recent ISD projects.

Collecting data from multiple types of respondents helps reduce common-source bias, which could increase measurement errors in a survey study if not addressed carefully (King et al., 2007; Podsakoff et al., 2003). The target respondents came from different backgrounds and had different roles in the projects. Their answers were expected to provide a complete and reliable picture of ISD processes. However, the extra effort required for senior managers to identify appropriate respondents and serve as survey contacts may have reduced the response rate.

## Measures

To reduce possible common-source bias, most instruments were designed to target specific classes of subjects—that is, system developers, user representatives, and/or IS managers. The only exception was system complexity, which was responded to by IS developers because the related system development issues fell primarily into their job responsibilities.

### Team Size and Project Size

Team size was measured by a single item asking for the number of members who worked on an identified ISD team. Project size was measured by a three-item instrument adopted from Barki, Rivard, and Talbot (1993, 2001), asking respondents to rate on a scale of 1 to 5 the extent to which they believed the scheduled number of person-days, the scheduled number of calendar months, and the budget allocated to this project were larger than for other projects in their companies. Target respondents included user representatives, system developers, and IS managers.

### Requirements Uncertainty

The "requirements uncertainty" measure was adapted from Nidumolu's (1995) validated instrument. This instrument used four items centered on the ambiguity about user requirements and needs for a system. Both user representatives and system developers were the target respondents.

### System Complexity

The "system complexity" construct was assessed with nine items based on the instrument developed by McFarlan (1981). McFarlan's instrument has been employed by Tait and Vessey (1988) and McKeen, Guimaraes, and Wetherbe (1994). In this research, McFarlan's instrument was revised by discarding some obsolete components, such as ambiguity of using CPU, hardware, and software, and introducing new components related to design, coding, testing, and installation techniques. The items were responded to by system developers because the related technological issues fell primarily into their job responsibilities.

### Management Support

Management support was measured by two items, asking respondents to rate on a scale of 1 to 5 the extent to which management allocated resources and provided overall support to their project teams. Target respondents included user representatives, system developers, and IS managers.

### Team Performance

Team performance was assessed using the six-item instrument developed in Robey, Smith, and Vijayasarathy (1993). Target respondents included user representatives, system developers, and IS managers.

*System Quality*

System quality was assessed with a fourteen-item instrument adapted from Rivard and colleagues (1997). The instrument asked respondents to indicate, on five-point scales ranging from 1 (strongly disagree) to 5 (strongly agree), the extent to which they believed the system was reliable, adaptable, easy to understand and use, and provided precise, complete, and useful output. Target respondents included user representatives and system developers.

Detailed descriptions of the instruments used in the survey are provided in Appendix 17.1.

## Data Collection

A contact list of IS managers in about 3,400 organizations was purchased from a commercial source. These organizations were mostly business firms, but also included some educational institutions and government agencies. Organization sizes ranged from small (i.e., having less than 250 employees) to large (i.e., having more than 1,000 employees). Contacts were restricted to IS managers defined by their job titles, including chief information officer (CIO), IS manager, IT manager, project managers, and application manager.

Research invitation letters were sent to all of the contacts, with a brief explanation of the research project and requirements for their support and supervision of the survey at their organizations. Of the 3,400 letters, 348 were returned due to invalid addresses. The proportion (about 10.3 percent) is higher than is normal in our experience (about 5 percent), indicating that the quality of the contact list was disappointing. In this research, 110 companies agreed to participate. Survey packages were then mailed to these companies. If return surveys were not received within two weeks of sending out the survey packages, electronic reminders were e-mailed to contact people.

Responding to the surveys were 266 individuals representing 121 ISD project teams from 83 organizations. The respondents included 115 user representatives, 121 system developers, and 30 IS managers. The demographics of the respondents and their organizations, as well as the types of sampled projects, are reported in Tables 17.1 and 17.2.

Twenty-one returned or online-submitted surveys were not complete and had to be deleted from the data set. Thus, 245 complete responses were collected from 108 ISD project teams; each team being represented by at least one developer and one user representative.

## ANALYSES

### Aggregation Analysis

The data analysis of the study was at the team level. Since several measures required responses from multiple subjects within the same team, aggregation analysis was performed to confirm within-team agreement on these survey items prior to the test of the research model. Inter-rater agreement (IRA) was selected to assess the response homogeneity within the sampled project teams. All IRAs of measures involving multiple respondents (reported in Table 17.3, p. 357) were higher than the commonly suggested threshold of 0.70 (Cohen, Doveh, and Eick, 2001), demonstrating satisfactory consistency of the answers collected from subjects in the same teams. Team averages across individual responses were then calculated for these measures to be analyzed in the research model.

Table 17.1

## Demographics of the Respondents

**Individual respondent's gender**

| | |
|---|---|
| Female | 54 |
| Male | 89 |
| Not reported* | 123 |
| Total | 266 |

**Education**

| | |
|---|---|
| High school | 0 |
| Associate degree | 9 |
| Baccalaureate degree | 68 |
| Graduate degree | 66 |
| Not reported* | 123 |
| Total | 266 |

**Age**

| | |
|---|---|
| ≤ 25 | 3 |
| Between 26 and 35 | 22 |
| Between 36 and 45 | 94 |
| Between 46 and 55 | 22 |
| ≥ 55 | 2 |
| Not reported* | 123 |
| Total | 266 |

*Only the online version of the survey questionnaire asked respondents to report their gender, educational level, and age. For space reasons, the paper instrument did not include these questions.

## Construct Validity

The test of construct validity was conducted with partial least squares (PLS)—a structural equation modeling (SEM) technique that has been commonly used in IS research. Similar to other SEM techniques (e.g., LISREL), PLS tests the validity of constructs and the structural model at the same time, and is therefore considered methodologically rigorous when compared with regression-based techniques that separate the test of construct validity (e.g., factor analysis) from the test of research model (Gefen, Straub, and Boudreau, 2000). Two other distinctive features of PLS made the technique a particularly suitable testing tool for our study:

1. PLS has the flexibility of accepting single-item constructs (e.g., team size in this study);
2. The algorithm of PLS is designed to determine explained variance (e.g., the calculation of $R^2$ of dependent variables), making the technique a particularly useful tool for predictive applications and theory building (Gefen, Straub, and Boudreau, 2000).

In this study, we selected PLS-Graph version 3.0 as the primary tool for data analysis. Table 17.3 reports the ICR (internal consistent reliability), AVE (average variance extracted), and

Table 17.2

## Demographics of the Responding Organizations

| Locations of surveyed organizations | Number |
|---|---|
| AZ | 2 |
| CA | 4 |
| FL | 2 |
| IA | 6 |
| IL | 4 |
| KY | 2 |
| MA | 5 |
| MD | 4 |
| MN | 4 |
| MO | 2 |
| NJ | 4 |
| NV | 2 |
| NY | 11 |
| OH | 6 |
| PA | 15 |
| TN | 2 |
| UT | 6 |
| WA | 2 |
| Total | 83 |
| **Industry pattern** | |
| Construction industries | 2 |
| Manufacturing | 21 |
| Transportation, communication, and utilities | 4 |
| Wholesale trade | 2 |
| Retail trade | 2 |
| Finance, insurance, and real estate | 6 |
| Service industries | 38 |
| Public administration | 8 |
| Total | 83 |
| **Organization size** | |
| < 250 | 13 |
| Between 250 and 499 | 9 |
| Between 500 and 999 | 35 |
| ≥ 1,000 | 26 |
| Total | 83 |
| **Project types** | |
| Transaction processing system | 17 |
| Management information system | 13 |
| Decision support system | 7 |
| Expert system | 15 |
| Office automation | 8 |
| Communication system | 13 |
| System integration | 18 |
| Library/knowledge system | 6 |
| Not reported | 24 |
| Total | 121 |

Table 17.3

**Construct Validity and Descriptive Statistics**

| Variables | Mean[1] | Std. deviation[1] | Number of items | ICR[2] | IRA[3] | AVE[4] |
|---|---|---|---|---|---|---|
| 1. Team size | 6.95 | 8.11 | 1 | 1.00 | N/A | 1.00 |
| 2. Project size | 3.01 | 0.61 | 3 | 0.91 | 0.92 | 0.84 |
| 3. User participation | | | 1 | 1.00 | N/A | 1.00 |
| 4. Requirements uncertainty | 3.27 | 0.83 | 4 | 0.89 | 0.79 | 0.67 |
| 5. System complexity | 3.46 | 0.68 | 9 | 0.93 | N/A | 0.61 |
| 6. Management support | 3.20 | 0.59 | 2 | 0.72 | 0.81 | 0.60 |
| 7. Expertise location | 3.95 | 0.62 | 4 | 0.90 | 0.92 | 0.70 |
| 8. Task understanding | 3.87 | 0.72 | 4 | 0.92 | 0.90 | 0.74 |
| 9. Team performance | 3.68 | 0.67 | 6 | 0.92 | 0.87 | 0.66 |
| 10. System quality | 3.97 | 0.62 | 14 | 0.95 | 0.79 | 0.60 |

[1]These statistics were derived by calculating team averages across individual responses for each team and across items of each instrument.
[2]ICR: internal consistency reliability.
[3]IRA: inter-rater agreement.
[4]AVE: average variance extracted.

descriptive statistics (means and standard deviations) of the investigated constructs. Table 17.4 presents the correlations among constructs. All ICRs were greater than 0.7, thus supporting the reliability of the constructs (Thompson, Barclay, and Higgins, 1995). All AVEs were greater than 0.5, suggesting that a large fraction of the variance for each construct was true and not error (Fornell and Larcker, 1981). The square roots of AVEs (reported in Table 17.4 on the diagonal) were greater than any correlation coefficient among constructs, indicating that the measures reflected the values of assigned constructs rather than that of any others (Gefen, Straub, and Boudreau, 2000). Thus, convergent and discriminant validity of the constructs were concluded.

**Model Tests**

The test of the research model and the results are presented in Figure 17.3. Examination of the resulting path significances suggested the rejection of several hypothesized effects of team characteristics on team cognition. More specifically, the effects of project size, management support, and system complexity were not found to be significant on either expertise location or task understanding. Close examination of the correlation matrix in Table 17.4 suggested that these team characteristics might have direct effects on team performance or system quality; effects not mediated by team cognition. The research model was then revised by modeling the effects of the three team characteristics directly onto team performance or system quality. The results of the revised model are presented in Figure 17.4 (p. 360).

The revised model demonstrated overall a good model fit with significant path coefficients (all with $p < 0.05$), acceptable $R^2$, and good construct reliability with high levels of internal consistency

Table 17.4

**Correlations Among Constructs**

| Variables | 1 | 2 | 3 | 4 | 5 | 6 | 7 | 8 | 9 | 10 |
|---|---|---|---|---|---|---|---|---|---|---|
| 1. Team size | **1.00** | | | | | | | | | |
| 2. Project size | –0.07 | **0.92** | | | | | | | | |
| 3. User participation | –0.04 | –0.05 | **1.00** | | | | | | | |
| 4. Requirements uncertainty | 0.26 | 0.34 | 0.01 | **0.82** | | | | | | |
| 5. System complexity | –0.05 | –0.11 | 0.01 | –0.33 | **0.78** | | | | | |
| 6. Management support | –0.11 | 0.15 | –0.13 | –0.06 | 0.08 | **0.77** | | | | |
| 7. Expertise location | –0.32 | –0.09 | –0.28 | –0.28 | –0.05 | 0.12 | **0.84** | | | |
| 8. Task understanding | –0.38 | –0.02 | –0.26 | –0.32 | –0.04 | 0.20 | 0.79 | **0.86** | | |
| 9. Team performance | –0.36 | –0.20 | –0.10 | –0.38 | –0.11 | 0.23 | 0.64 | 0.61 | **0.81** | |
| 10. System quality | –0.21 | –0.06 | –0.13 | –0.25 | 0.19 | 0.20 | 0.39 | 0.36 | 0.60 | **0.77** |

*Note:* The square roots of average variance extracted are presented in boldface in the diagonal.

Figure 17.3    **Initial Test of the Research Model**

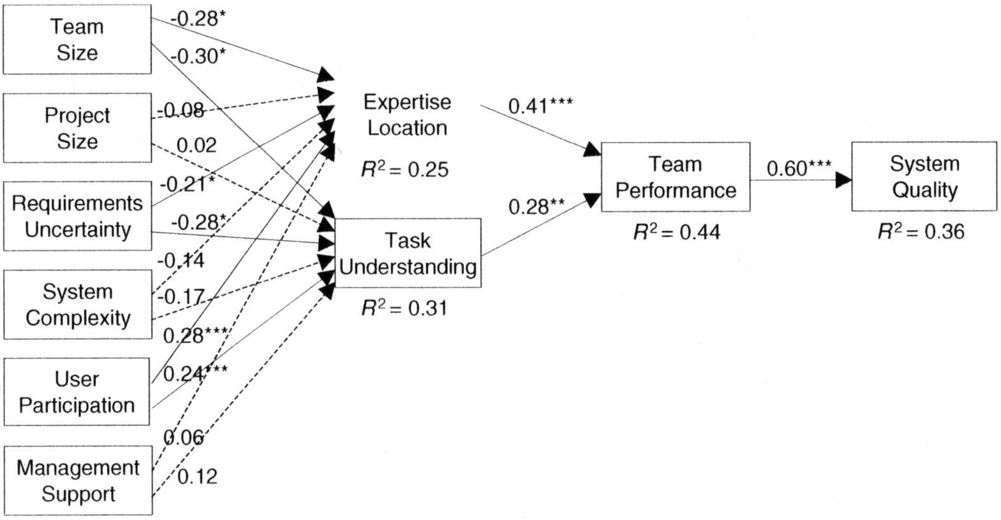

*Notes:* Significance levels of paths: *p < = 0.05; **p < 0.01; ***p < 0.001.
Dashed lines indicate insignificant paths.

(Gefen, Straub, and Boudreau, 2000). In addition, the predictive power on team performance and system quality were satisfactory, with 49 percent of the variance of team performance, and 44 percent of the variance of system quality being explained by the model. Compared with the original research model, the revised model was more parsimonious (total number of paths was reduced from thirteen of the original model to ten of the revised model), while the explained variances of the dependent variables were increased.

## RESULTS, IMPLICATIONS, AND LIMITATIONS

Much of the ISD literature provides guidelines on managing the development process to achieve overall success. However, the effects of environmental characteristics on the productivity of ISD teams have not been extensively investigated. In this study, we identified six environmental characteristics suggested to be important in the literature and tested their effects on team performance and system quality. In addition, team cognition was proposed as the mediating mechanism to explain the way in which these team characteristics may affect the productivity of ISD teams. Results revealed that in our sampled ISD teams:

1. Team size and requirements uncertainty negatively affected the level of team cognition;
2. User participation positively affected the level of team cognition;
3. Team cognition, specified as expertise location and task understanding, had a positive effect on team performance;
4. High levels of team performance led to high quality in resulting systems;
5. Project size had a direct and negative effect on team performance;
6. System complexity had a direct and negative effect on system quality;
7. Management support had a direct and positive effect on team performance.

Figure 17.4  **Revised Research Model**

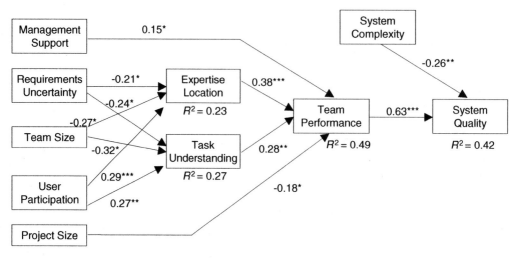

Thus, the effects of team size, requirements uncertainty, and user participation had the expected effect on team cognition, while the effects of project size and management support on team performance were direct and not mediated by team cognition.

Team cognition was shown to have a positive effect on team performance, thus confirming the results of other studies that have involved this mediator (He, Butler, and King, 2007; Ren, Carley, and Argote, 2006). As expected, team performance had a significant positive effect on system quality.

Since the last three results were not hypothesized, but were concluded from the revised model, we shall concentrate on them here.

**Project Size and Team Size Effects on Team Performance**

Project size was found to exert a direct effect on team performance, bypassing the hypothesized mediating mechanism of team cognition. In the literature, project size and team size are both discussed as overall indicators of the scale of ISD projects, and sometimes are used interchangeably. For example, Kraut and Streeter (1995) discussed the implications of project size by the lines of code and the life of the project (pp. 69–70), while measuring the construct using the number of team members in their empirical study (p. 72). The results of this study revealed that the two constructs were distinctive. Not only were the two constructs measured differently (team size was an objective measure of the number of team members, while project size was a perceptual measure and captured the perceived relative scale of investigated projects in comparison to typical projects), their values did not correlate strongly ($r = -0.08$, $p = 0.43$). Also, the two constructs presented different effects on the productivity of ISD teams in the structural model. Team size had negative effects on team cognition, implying that involving more people on an ISD team would increase the difficulty of forming shared mental models within the team, therefore increasing coordination cost and reducing team performance. In contrast, project size had a direct effect on team performance, suggesting that teams working on ambiguously designed projects of large scale will have difficulty in achieving satisfactory performance.

This finding revealed that the existing practice of assuming team size as an aspect of project size might be problematic. Teams with a large number of members may not necessarily be associated with large project scale or the allocation of significant resources. This may be evident in today's Web-based ISD environment, where "project and team size were reported to vary greatly" (Kautz, Madsen, and Norbjerg, 2007, p. 229). Future research is needed to clarify this issue.

## System Complexity Effects on System Quality

Unlike requirements uncertainty, whose hypothesized effects on team cognition were supported by the test results, system complexity was found to have impacts only on system quality. This finding confirmed that technically complicated systems are more difficult to develop; it also suggested that business-related issues may have profound impacts on ISD processes.

Previous studies of ISD complexity have observed that organizational or business-related issues have more significant effects on ISD outcomes than do technical issues (e.g., Xia and Lee, 2004). However, most studies focused on the direct relationship between ISD complexity and ISD outcomes, while the underlying mechanisms through which ISD complexity may affect ISD processes have rarely been investigated. The results of the study suggest that different types of complexity will affect ISD processes in different ways. Business-related issues, or the clarity and stability of user requirements throughout ISD processes as captured by requirements uncertainty, affect the collective understanding of team members of each other's knowledge and expertise as well as of the focal project. In such instances, members' cooperative activities and behavior would inevitably be affected, as would the performance of the team. In contrast, system complexity had little influence either on team cognition or team performance (Table 17.4), but affected the quality of the resulting systems directly. Future research is needed to further explore the mechanisms through which various aspects of ISD complexity affect ISD outcomes.

## Management Support Effects on Team Performance

The results revealed that management support had little effect on team cognition but directly affected team performance. High levels of management support reflect strong commitment from the top management and, presumably, significant allocations of resources. In our sample, support from management did not alter the development of team cognition, suggesting that the involvement of management in an ISD project would hardly change the pattern of interactive activities and behaviors of team members. Rather, management support exerted direct impact on team performance, probably because of the provision of needed resources. The correlation matrix of Table 17.4 reveals a strong correlation between management support and project size ($r = 0.21, p = 0.02$), suggesting the projects that received strong support from management were also perceived to be of large scale, presumably through the allocation of significant resources.

## Managerial Implications

Glass (1999) argued that "the software field needs not better ways of building software . . . but better ways of approaching the building of software" (p. 19). The findings of this study support that argument.

The findings of this research have important implications for ISD practitioners. If environmental characteristics can affect the productivity of ISD project teams in a systematic way, managing these factors may be an efficient solution for managers aiming to enhance their chance of achieving development success. In fact, many of the environmental characteristics that are investigated in this study can be easily manipulated before the allocation and spending of significant time, effort, and resources on a project.

Thus, managers should carefully consider the requirements of a proposed ISD project and provide the ISD team with a favorable environment. More specifically, a smaller team size, a less ambitious scale of project size, the articulation of accurate and stable user requirements, and the use of mature technology to reduce the technical complexity of the development process, as well as high levels of support from users and top management, are expected to help ISD teams to produce quality products and achieve overall development successes.

This means that project plans should be made to include a greater number of smaller modules, and require fewer members on the development team. Moderating the size of the overall development project would also be helpful. The moderation of project complexity should be complemented by the use of more mature technologies. The overall cost of developing new applications with leading-edge technologies appears to be too high, and has thus resulted in less project success. IS managers should curb their enthusiasm for high-tech approaches in favor of more reliable, if less exciting, approaches. These suggestions are in agreement with the pragmatic approach of "smaller is better," which has been proposed in the prescriptive literature based on the observation of numerous ISD practices (Murray, 2000).

The freezing of user requirements is so helpful, according to these results, that it might pay to expend more time and effort on that phase, even at the cost of delaying the project. And, of course, the ever-present "management support" cannot be overlooked. Although it is a cliché to say that greater top management support will result in greater project success because that is true for any activity in an organizational environment, it is nonetheless true.

**Limitations**

Although these results are encouraging, the study has several limitations. One is the relatively small sample size. We collected data from 266 individuals representing 121 ISD teams. Although previous studies that investigated user-participation effects at super-individual levels had similar sample sizes, the sample size of all of these studies raises concern.

We contacted some nonrespondents in order to better understand why they did not cooperate, and found that many organizations restrained their employees from participating in such survey projects due to concerns about distracting them from their work. The research design of matched user–developer responses at the team level further reduced the chance of inducing participation from busy professionals. The following message, which we received from a senior IS manager, may explain many nonresponses:

> One problem I run into personally with your methodology is the number of people within the organization I have to reach out to in order to complete the documentation. Our company is extremely busy during a very difficult economic time. . . . I just can't dedicate so much time to this type of activity.

This explanation identifies a general problem for IS survey researchers, particularly those who require multiple respondents for each unit of analysis (projects, in this case), in an area in which staffs are being reduced and IS survey research is increasing in volume (King and He, 2005).

Tables 17.1 and 17.2 demonstrate great diversity among the respondents as well as their organizations. However, a relatively low response rate increases the risk of nonresponse-induced errors (King and He, 2005). In the field study, it was impossible to perform a systematic comparison between respondents and nonrespondents. Thus, the generalizability of the research results should be treated with some degree of caution.

## SUMMARY

Important ISD environmental factors were studied in terms of their effect on team productivity (defined in terms of team performance and system quality). Team cognition—measured in terms of "expertise location" and "task understanding"—was used as a mediating mechanism. The results demonstrate that in determining team productivity, some environmental factors operate through the mediator and some do not. These results are important to researchers in developing future models of ISD environmental impacts and in developing more comprehensive models of how ISD characteristics impact performance. They are also important to practitioners in providing guidelines for designing successful ISD projects.

## APPENDIX 17.1

**Team Size** (respondent: key user representative, key system developer, and project manager)

1.  For the specified project, how many people were working in the development team?

**Project Size** (respondent: key user representative, key system developer, and project manager)
    For each item the respondent indicated the size of the project in comparison with other IS projects developed in the organization on a 1–5 scale (very low to very high).

1.  the scheduled number of person-days for completing this project was . . .
2.  the scheduled number of months for completing this project was . . .
3.  the dollar budget allocated to this project was . . .

**Requirements Uncertainty** (respondent: key user representative and key system developer)
    For each item the respondent indicated the extent to which he or she agreed with the statement regarding the requirements for the project on a 1–5 scale (strongly disagree to strongly agree).

1.  Requirements fluctuated during the system development process.
2.  Users of this system differed among themselves in the requirements to be met by it.
3.  A lot of effort had to be spent in reconciling the requirements of various users of this system.
4.  It was difficult to customize the system to one set of users without reducing support to other users.

**System Complexity** (respondent: key system developer)
    For each item the respondent indicated the extent to which the project team had problems from using the technology on a 1–5 scale (very easy to very difficult):

1.  The hardware platform
2.  The software platform
3.  The programming language(s)
4.  The telecommunications technology

5. The database technology
6. The design techniques
7. The coding techniques
8. The testing techniques
9. The installation techniques

**Management Support** (respondent: key user representative, key system developer, and project manager)

For each item the respondent indicated the size of the project in comparison with other IS projects developed in the organization on a 1–5 scale (very low to very high).

1. the overall resources that management allocated to this project were . . .
2. the overall "support" from top management was . . .

**Team Performance** (respondent: key user representative, key system developer, and project manager)

For each item the respondent evaluated the performance of the project team on a 1–5 scale (very low to very high).

1. The amount of work the team produced.
2. The efficiency of team operations.
3. The team's adherence to budgets.
4. The team's adherence to the schedule.
5. The quality of work the team produced.
6. The effectiveness of the team's interactions with people outside the team.

**System Quality** (respondent: key user representative, key system developer)

For each item the respondent indicated the extent to which he or she agreed with the statement regarding the quality of the produced system on a 1–5 scale (strongly disagree to strongly agree).

1. The system is reliable (it is always up and running, runs without errors, and does what it is supposed to do).
2. It is easy to tell whether the system is functioning correctly.
3. The system can recover from errors, accidents, and intrusions while maintaining data security and integrity.
4. The system can easily be modified to meet changing user requirements.
5. The system can easily be adapted to a new technical or organizational environment.
6. The system is easy to maintain.
7. The system is easy to understand.
8. The system is easy to use.
9. The output information produced by the system is precise.
10. The output information produced by the system is complete.
11. The output information produced by the system is useful.
12. The output information produced by the system is up to date.
13. The output information produced by the system is reliable.
14. The system performs its functions quickly.

## NOTE

1. Some researchers have used objective or self-report indices to measure project size, such as worker-months (Kim and Lee, 1991), person-hours (Faraj and Spoull 2000), and development hours, months, and cost (McKeen, Guimaraes, and Wetherbe (1994)). These measures are used mainly for demographic analysis of projects.

## REFERENCES

Abdul-Gader, A.H., and Kozar, K.A. 1990. Discourse analysis for knowledge acquisition: the coherence method. *Journal of Management Information Systems*, 6, 4, 61–82.

Ang, S., and Slaughter, S.A. 2001. Work outcomes and job design for contract versus permanent information systems professionals on software development teams. *MIS Quarterly*, 25, 3, 321–350.

Armstrong, D.J., and Hardgrave, B.C. 2007. Understanding mindshift learning: the transition to object-oriented development. *MIS Quarterly*, 31, 3, 453–474.

Barki, H. and Hartwick, J. 1989. Rethinking the concept of user involvement. *MIS Quarterly*, 13, 1, 53–63.

———. 1994. Measuring user participation, user involvement, and user attitude. *MIS Quarterly*, 18, 1, 59–82.

Barki, H.; Rivard, S.; and Talbot, J. 1993. Toward an assessment of software development risk. *Journal of Management Information Systems*, 10, 2, 203–225.

———. 2001. An integrative contingency model of software project risk management. *Journal of Management Information Systems*, 17, 4, 37–69.

Benbya, H., and McKelvey, B. 2006. Toward a complexity theory of information systems development. *Information Technology & People*, 19, 1, 12–34.

Biehl, M. 2007. Success factors for implementing global information systems. *Communications of the ACM*, 50, 1, 53–58.

Brodbeck, F.C. 2001. Communication and performance in software development projects. *European Journal of Work and Organizational Psychology*, 10, 1, 73–94.

Cannon-Bowers, J.A., and Salas, E. 2001. Reflections on shared cognition. *Journal of Organizational Behavior*, 22, 2, 195–202.

Cannon-Bowers, J.A.; Salas, E.; and Converse, S. 1993. Shared mental models in expert team decision making. In N.J. Castellan (ed.), *Individual and Group Decision Making*. Hillsdale, NJ: Erlbaum, pp. 221–246.

Chiang, R., and Mookerjeee, V.S. 2004. Improving software team productivity. *Communications of the ACM*, 47, 5, 89–93.

Cohen, A.; Doveh, E.; and Eick, U. 2001. Statistical properties of the $r_{WG(J)}$ index of agreement. *Psychological Methods*, 6, 3, 297–310.

Cooke, N.J.; Kiekel, P.A.; and Helm, E.E. 2001. Measuring team knowledge during skill acquisition of a complex task. *International Journal of Cognitive Ergonomics*, 5, 3, 297–315.

Cooke, N.J.; Salas, E.; Cannon-Bowers, J.A.; and Stout, R. 2000. Measuring team knowledge. *Human Factors*, 42, 1, 151–173.

Corbin, D.S. 1991. Establishing the software development environment. *Journal of Systems Management*, 42, 9, 28–31.

Curtis, B.; Krasner, H.; and Iscoe, N. 1988. A field study of the software design process for large systems. *Communications of the ACM*, 31, 11, 1268–1287.

DeBrabander, B., and Edstrom, A. 1977. Successful information system development projects. *Management Science*, 24, 2, 191–199.

DeLone, W.H., and McLean, E.R. 1992. Information systems success: the quest for the dependent variable. *Information Systems Research*, 3, 1, 60–95.

———. 2003. The DeLone and McLean model of information systems success: a ten-year update. *Journal of Management Information Systems*, 19, 4, 9–30.

Dillon, R.L.; Pate-Cornell, E.; and Guikema, S.D. 2005. Optimal use of budget reserves to minimize technical and management failure risks during complex project development. *IEEE Transactions on Engineering Management*, 52, 3, 382–395.

Duncan, R.B. 1973. Multiple decision-making structures in adapting to environmental uncertainty: the impact on organizational effectiveness. *Human Relations*, 26, 3, 273–291.

Edstrom, A. 1977. User influence and the success of MIS projects: a contingency approach. *Human Relations*, 30, 7, 589–607.

Eid-Dor, P., and Segev, E. 1978. Organizational context and the success of management information systems. *Management Science*, 24, 10, 1064–1077.

Faraj, S., and Sambamurthy, V. 2006. Leadership of information systems development projects. *IEEE Transactions on Engineering Management*, 53, 2, 238–249.

Faraj, S., and Sproull, L. 2000. Coordinating expertise in software development teams. *Management Science*, 46, 12, 1554–1568.

Fornell, C., and Larcker, D.F. 1981. Evaluating structural equation models with unobservable variables and measurement error. *Journal of Marketing Research*, 18, 1, 39–50.

Garrity, J.T. 1963. Top management and computer profits. *Harvard Business Review*, 41, 4, 6–12.

Gefen, D.; Straub, D.W.; and Boudreau, M. 2000. Structural equation modeling techniques and regression: guidelines for research practice. *Communications of the Association for Information Systems*, 4, 7, 1–78.

Ginzberg, M.J. 1981a. Early diagnosis of MIS implementation failures: promising results and unanswered questions. *Management Science*, 27, 4, 459–478.

———. 1981b. Key recurrent issues in the MIS implementation process. *MIS Quarterly*, 5, 2, 47–59.

Glass, R.L. 1999. Evolving a new theory of project success. *Communications of the ACM*, 42, 11, 17–19.

Guimares, T.; Igbaria, M.; and Lu, M. 1992. The determinants of DSS success: an integrated model. *Decision Sciences*, 23, 2, 409–430.

Hardgrave, B.C.; Wilson, R.L.; and Eastman, K. 1999. Toward a contingency model for selecting an information system prototyping strategy. *Journal of Management Information Systems*, 16, 2, 113–136.

Hartwick, J. and Barki, H. 2001. Communication as a dimension of user participation. *IEEE Transactions on Professional Communication*, 44, 1, 21–36.

He, J.; Butler, B.S.; and King, W.R. 2007. Team cognition: development and evolution in software project teams. *Journal of Management Information Systems*, 24, 2, 267–299.

Hoegl, M., and Gemuenden, H.G. 2001. Teamwork quality and the success of innovative projects: a theoretical concept and empirical evidence. *Management Science*, 12, 4, 435–449.

Hollingshead, A.B. 1998. Group and individual training: the impact of practice on performance. *Small Group Research*, 29, 2, 254–280.

———. 2001. Cognitive interdependence and convergent expectations in transactive memory. *Journal of Personality and Social Psychology*, 81, 6, 1080–1089.

Howcroft, D., and Wilson, M. 2003. Paradoxes of participatory practices: the Janus role of the systems developer. *Information & Organization*, 13, 1, 1–24.

Hwang, M.I., and Thorn, R.G. 1999. The effect of user engagement on system success: a meta-analytical integration of research findings. *Information & Management*, 35, 4, 229–236.

Igbaria, M.; Zinatelli, N.; Cragg, P.; and Cavaye, A.L. 1997. Personal computing acceptance factors in small firms: a structural equation model. *MIS Quarterly*, 21, 3, 279–302.

Ives, B., and Olson, M.H. 1984. User involvement and MIS success: a review of research. *Management Science*, 30, 5, 586–603.

Jackson, S.E.; May, K.E.; and Whitney, K. 1995. Understanding the dynamics of diversity in decision making teams. In R.A. Guzzo and E. Salas (eds.), *Team Effectiveness and Decision Making in Organizations*. San Francisco: Jossey-Bass, pp. 204–261.

Jarvenpaa, S.L., and Ives, B. 1991. Executive involvement and participation in the management of information technology. *MIS Quarterly*, 15, 2, 205–227.

Jiang, J.J.; Klein, G.; and Discenza, R. 2002. Pre-project partnering impact on an information system project, project team and project manager. *European Journal of Information Systems*, 11, 2, 86–97.

Jones, M.C., and Harrison, A.W. 1996. IS project team performance: an empirical assessment. *Information & Management*, 31, 2, 57–65.

Kast, F., and Rosenzweig, J. 1973. *Contingency Views of Organization and Management*. Chicago: Science Research Associates.

Katz, R., and Tushman, M. 1979. Communication patterns, project performance, and task characteristics: an empirical evaluation and integration in an R&D setting. *Organizational Behavior and Human Performance*, 23, 2, 139–162.

Kautz, K.; Madsen, S.; and Norbjerg, J. 2007. Persistent problems and practices in information systems development. *Information Systems Journal*, 17, 3, 217–239.

Kim, S.; and Lee, J. 1991. A contingent analysis of the relationship between IS implementation strategies and IS success. *Information Processing & Management*, 27, 1, 111–128.

King, W.R., and He, J. 2005. External validity in IS survey research. *Communications of the Association for Information Systems*, 16, 880–894.

King, W.R.; Liu, C.; Haney, M.; and He, J. 2007. Method effects in IS survey research: an assessment and recommendations. *Communications of the Association for Information Systems*, 20, 457–482.

Klein, G.; Jiang, J.J.; and Tesch, D.B. 2002. Wanted: project teams with a blend of IS professional orientations. *Communications of the ACM*, 45, 6, 81–87.

Klimoski, R., and Mohammed, S. 1994. Team mental model: construct or metaphor? *Journal of Management*, 20, 2, 403–437.

Kraut, R.E., and Streeter, L.A. 1995. Coordination in software development. *Communications of the ACM*, 38, 3, 69–81.

Kwon, T.H., and Zmud, R.W. 1987. Unifying the fragmented models of information systems implementation. In R.J. Boland and R.A. Hirschheim (eds.), *Critical Issues in Information Systems Research*. Chichester, UK: Wiley, pp. 227–251.

Lawrence, P.R., and Lorsch, J.W. 1967. *Organization and Environment*. Cambridge, MA: Harvard University Press.

Leonard-Barton, D., and Deschamps, I. 1988. Managerial influence in the implementation of new technology. *Management Science*, 34, 10, 1252–1265.

Levesque, L.L.; Wilson, J.M.; and Wholey, D.R. 2001. Cognitive divergence and shared mental models in software development project teams. *Journal of Organizational Behavior*, 22, 2, 135–144.

Lewis, K. 2004. Knowledge and performance in knowledge-worker teams: a longitudinal study of transactive memory systems. *Management Science*, 50, 11, 1519–1533.

Liang, D.W.; Moreland, R.; and Argote, L. 1995. Group versus individual training and group performance: the mediating role of transactive memory. *Personality and Social Psychology Bulletin*, 21, 4, 384–393.

Lucas, H.C. 1982. Alternative structures for the management of information processing. In R. Goldberg and H. Lorin (eds.), *On the Economics of Information Processing*, 2. New York: Wiley-InterScience, pp. 55–61.

Luthans, F., and Stewart, T.I. 1977. A general contingency theory of management. *Academy of Management Review*, 2, 2, 181–195.

MacMillan, J.; Estin, E.E.; and Serfaty, D. 2004. Communication overhead: the hidden cost of team cognition. In E. Salas and S.M. Fiore (eds.), *Team Cognition: Understanding the Factors That Drive Process and Performance*. Washington, DC: American Psychological Association, pp. 61–82.

Mantei, M. 1981. The effect of programming team structures on programming tasks. *Communications of the ACM*, 24, 3, 106–113.

Markus, M.L. 1983. Power, politics, and MIS implementation. *Communications of the ACM*, 26, 6, 430–444.

Markus, M.L., and Mao, J.Y. 2004. Participation in development and implementation: updating an old, tired concept for today's IS contexts. *Journal of the Association for Information Systems*, 5, 11/12, 514–544.

Mason, R.O., and Mitroff, I.I. 1973. A program for research on management information systems. *Management Science*, 19, 5, 475–487.

Mathieu, J.E.; Goodwin, G.F.; Heffner, T.S.; Salas, E.; and Cannon-Bowers, J.A. 2000. The influence of shared mental models on team process and performance. *Journal of Applied Psychology*, 85, 2, 273–283.

McFarlan, F.W. 1971. Problems in planning the information systems. *Harvard Business Review*, 49, 4, 75–89.

———. 1981. Portfolio approach to information systems. *Harvard Business Review*, 59, 5, 142–150.

McKeen, J.D.; Guimaraes, T.; and Wetherbe, J.C. 1994. The relationship between user participation and user satisfaction: an investigation of four contingency factors. *MIS Quarterly*, 18, 4, 427–451.

McKelvey, B. 1999. Avoiding complexity catastrophe in coevolutionary pockets. *Organization Science*, 10, 3, 294–321.

Mohammed, S., and Dumville, B.C. 2001. Team mental models in a team knowledge framework: expanding theory and measurement across disciplinary boundaries. *Journal of Organizational Behavior*, 22, 2, 89–106.

Mohammed, S.; Klimoski, R.; and Rentsch, J. 2000. The measurement of team mental models: we have no shared schema. *Organizational Research Methods*, 3, 2, 123–165.

Moreland, R.L. 1999. Transactive memory: Learning who knows what in work groups and organizations. In L.L. Thompson, J.M. Levine, and D.M. Messick (eds.), *Shared Cognition in Organizations: The Management of Knowledge*. Mahwah, NJ: Erlbaum, pp. 3–31.

Moreland, R.L., and Myaskovsky, L. 2000. Exploring the performance benefits of group training: transactive memory or improved communication? *Organizational Behavior & Human Decision Processes*, 82, 1, 117–133.

Murray, J.P. 2000. Reducing IT project complexity. *Information Strategy*, 16, 3, 30–38.

Nerur, S.; Mahapatra, R.; and Mangalaraj, G. 2005. Challenges of migrating to agile methodologies. *Communications of the ACM*, 48, 5, 73–78.

Nidumolu, S. 1995. The effect of coordination and uncertainty on software project performance: residual performance risk as an intervening variable. *Information Systems Research*, 6, 3, 191–219.

Palanisamy, R. 2005. Strategic information systems planning model for building flexibility and success. *Industrial Management & Data Systems*, 105, 1, 63–81.

Podsakoff, P.M.; MacKenzie, S.B.; Lee, J.Y.; and Podsakoff, N.P. 2003. Common method biases in behavioral research: a critical review of the literature and recommended remedies. *Journal of Applied Psychology*, 88, 5, 879–903.

Purvis, R.L.; Sambamurthy, V.; and Zmud, R.W. 2001. The assimilation of knowledge platforms in organizations: an empirical investigation. *Information Systems Research*, 12, 2, 117–135.

Ravichandran, T., and Rai, A. 1999. Total quality management in information systems development: key constructs and relationships. *Journal of Management Information Systems*, 16, 3, 119–155.

Raymond, L. 1990. Organizational context and information systems success: a contingency approach. *Journal of Management Information Systems*, 6, 4, 5–20.

Ren, Y.; Carley, K.M.; and Argote, L. 2006. The contingent effects of transactive memory: when is it more beneficial to know what others know? *Management Science*, 52, 5, 671–682.

Rivard, S.; Poirier, G.; Raymond, L.; and Bergeron, F. 1997. Development of a measure to assess the quality of user-developed applications. *Data Base*, 28, 3, 44–58.

Robey, D., and Markus, M.L. 1984. Rituals in information system design. *MIS Quarterly*, 8, 1, 5–15.

Robey, D.; Smith, L.A.; and Vijayasarathy, L.R. 1993. Perceptions of conflict and success in information systems development projects. *Journal of Management Information Systems*, 10, 1, 123–139.

Rockart, J.F., and Hofman, J.D. 1992. Systems delivery: evolving new strategies. *Sloan Management Review*, 33, 4, 21–31.

Rowen, R.B. 1990. Software project management under incomplete and ambiguous specifications. *IEEE Transactions on Engineering Management*, 37, 1, 10–21.

Schreyögg, G. 1980. Contingency and choice in organization theory. *Organization Studies*, 1, 4, 305–321.

Sharma, R., and Yetton, P. 2003. The contingent effects of management support and task interdependence on successful information systems implementation. *MIS Quarterly*, 27, 4, 533–555.

Sircar, S.; Nerur, S.P.; and Mahapatra, R. 2001. Revolution or evolution? a comparison of object-oriented and structured system development methods. *MIS Quarterly*, 25, 4, 457–471.

Swanson, B.E. 1974. Management information systems: appreciation and involvement. *Management Science*, 21, 2, 178–188.

Szilagyi, A. Jr., and Wallace, M. 1980. *Organizational Behavior and Performance*. Santa Monica, CA: Goodyear.

Tait, P., and Vessey, I. 1988. The effect of user involvement on system success: a contingency approach. *MIS Quarterly*, 12, 1, 91–108.

Thompson, R.; Barclay, D.W.; and Higgins, C.A. 1995. The partial least squares approach to causal modeling: personal computer adoption and use as an illustration. *Technology Studies: Special Issue on Research Methodology*, 2, 2, 284–324.

Vandenbosch, B., and Higgins, C. 1996. Information acquisition and mental models: an investigation into the relationship between behavior and learning. *Information Systems Research*, 7, 2, 198–214.

Walsh, J.P. 1995. Managerial and organizational cognition: notes from a trip down memory lane. *Organization Science*, 6, 3, 280–321.

Walz, D.B.; Elam, J.J.; and Curtis, B. 1993. Inside a software design team: knowledge acquisition, sharing, and integration. *Communications of the ACM*, 36, 10, 62–77.

Wastell, D., and Sewards, A. 1995. An information system profile of the UK manufacturing sector. *Journal of Information Technology*, 10, 3, 179–189.

Weill, P., and Olson, M.H. 1989. An assessment of the contingency theory of management information systems. *Journal of Management Information Systems*, 6, 1, 59–85.

Wixom, B.H., and Watson, H.J. 2001. An empirical investigation of the factors affecting data warehousing success. *MIS Quarterly*, 25, 1, 17–41.

Xia, W., and Lee, G. 2004. Grasping the complexity of IS development projects. *Communications of the ACM*, 47, 5, 69–74.

Yetton, P.; Martin, A.; Sharma, R.; and Johnston, K. 2000. A model of information systems development project performance. *Information Systems Journal*, 10, 4, 263–289.

Zhang, J., and Faerman, S.R. 2007. Distributed leadership in the development of a knowledge sharing system. *European Journal of Information Systems*, 16, 4, 479–493.

Zmud, R.W. 1980. Management of large software development efforts. *MIS Quarterly*, 4, 2, 45–55.

# CHAPTER 18

# THE MODERATING EFFECTS OF COORDINATED PLANNING ON PROJECT PERFORMANCE

## VICTORIA L. MITCHELL AND ROBERT W. ZMUD

**Abstract:** *Efforts to adapt an organization's information technology (IT) platform to evolving business processes (BP) is a daunting challenge as (1) the nature of an IT platform can facilitate or inhibit process change and (2) overinvestment in the IT platform adds unneeded complexity to process redesign projects and can impair future IT investment initiatives. As a consequence, the process-platform relationship gives rise to considerable project uncertainty, and timely resolution of this uncertainty is a key factor in project performance.*

*It is generally recognized that coordinated planning is an effective means of resolving project uncertainty. The planning literature highlights two distinct coordinated planning approaches—synoptic planning and adaptive planning. Synoptic planning is characterized by the comprehensive integration of planning decisions prior to project implementation, while adaptive planning is characterized by feedback-driven adjustments as a project unfolds. The value of each planning approach has been widely debated, fueled by inconsistent findings among studies examining the relationship between planning and performance.*

*This chapter provides a synthesis of empirical research on coordinated planning and project performance in the context of concurrent development—highlighting the moderating effects of each planning approach for varying conditions of uncertainty. Generally, we find that synoptic planning is more effective in dealing with high levels of uncertainty, while adaptive planning is more effective with low levels of uncertainty. Proper alignment of planning approach with conditions of uncertainty reduces rework, information technologyIT-related problems, and schedule slippage, while enhancing client satisfaction. An agenda for future research is outlined targeting the dynamics of coordination, organizational antecedents, and consequences of each planning approach.*

**Keywords:** *Coordinated Planning, Synoptic Planning, Adaptive Planning, Concurrent Engineering, Project Performance*

It is generally recognized that information technology (IT) has transformed how we do business. Continuing streams of IT investment over the past fifteen years along with the appropriate target of IT initiatives to digitize business processes and fabricate robust, adaptive business platforms have produced significant changes in financial management, operations management, and customer relationship management, among other business practices. However, the interplay between an evolving IT platform and novel work process creates an increasingly challenging problem—how to manage the concurrent development of interdependent operations.

Concurrency in IT platform development and work process development (IT-process development) is difficult to manage because of dynamic or ill-specified requirements, idiosyncratic tacit knowledge, and the complexities that invariably accompany interdependencies. Where knowledge deficits exist, incomplete information and know-how give rise to design uncertainties that obscure the development process. In this context, uncertainty refers to an absence of information or unstable information about the designs (i.e., the IT platform, the business process, and the alignment between these) to be implemented. Excessive design uncertainty, if not managed effectively, tends to require excessive iteration for rework along with excessive communication for coordination, both of which can severely compromise project performance (Krishnan, Eppinger, and Whiteny, 1997; Loch and Terwiesch, 1998).

Prior research indicates planning is an effective means for mitigating design uncertainty (Galbraith, 1973; Segev, 1987; Boynton, Zmud, and Jacobs, 1994). Planning is defined as the effort undertaken to create a pattern in the stream of actions undertaken to develop a program, product, or service (Mintzberg and Waters, 1985). Coordinated planning refers to a pattern of action that facilitates interdependent operations. The pattern of actions that defines coordinated planning is largely unexplored. A few empirical studies in the information systems (IS) literature have substantiated a relationship between project performance and various aspects of coordinated planning; notably cross-functional involvement and strategy coupling (e.g., Lind and Zmud, 1991; Mitchell and Zmud, 1999, 2006; Newkirk and Lederer, 2006; Mitchell and Nault, 2007). These studies suggest that coordinated planning moderates the relationship between uncertainty and performance. Conflicting reports in related research streams both support and refute this view.

One related research stream is strategy formulation. This literature has clearly demonstrated that uncertainty can be mitigated through planning (e.g., Hofer and Schendel, 1978; Porter, 1985Porter, 1985 Mintzberg, 1994). Less clear is the relationship between uncertainty and the manner of planning. Planning is broadly categorized as synoptic or adaptive. Synoptic planning involves a comprehensive assessment to resolve uncertainty prior to implementation. In contrast, adaptive planning attempts to resolve uncertainty through incremental adjustments during implementation. Empirical studies examining the appropriateness of each planning mode under varying conditions of uncertainty have reported conflicting results (e.g., Lindsey and Rue, 1980 Koufteros, Vonderembse, and Jayaram, 2005; Kudla, 1980;).

Another related research stream is concurrency in new product development (NPD). This literature focuses on the relationship between joint planning at the functional level and project performance. Empirical studies have identified predevelopment planning, cross-functional involvement, and task coordination as key performance indicators (Takeuchi and Nonaka, 1986; Ancona and Caldwell, 1992b). Analytical models provide additional insight, revealing the tradeoffs between these indicators and project performance in the context of concurrent development (e.g., Blackburn, Hoedmaker, and van Wassenhove, 1996). For example, Loch and Terwiesch (1998) report that optimal levels of coordination increase with uncertainty and dependence, however, higher levels of uncertainty and dependence make concurrency less attractive. Unfortunately, little empirical work has been done to resolve these contradictions.

The intent of this chapter is to stimulate research on IT-process development in general, and coordinated planning in particular. We begin by drawing an analogy between concurrent design in product development and concurrent design in IT-process development. In this discussion we highlight several aspects of concurrent development (design uncertainty, design change, and coordinated planning) that influence project performance. Then we review related research streams that inform our understanding of coordinated planning. We limit our literature review to normative empirical studies reporting the effects of coordinated planning practices on various aspects of performance. Then, we present empirical work in the IS literature that utilizes these

Figure 18.1   **IT-Process Development in a Concurrent Engineering Context**

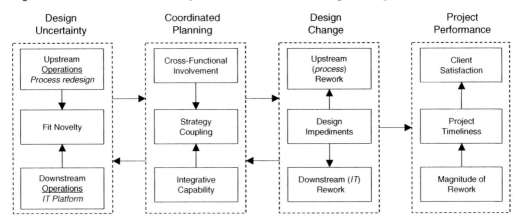

research streams in examining the impact of coordinated planning on IT-process development. A synthesis of these results provides a theoretical framework to explore IT-process development from a concurrency perspective (Figure 18.1).

## CONCURRENT DEVELOPMENT

Concurrent design refers to development activities in projects where two sets of operations are overlapping and interdependent. The product development literature conceptualizes product design as the transformation of a market opportunity and technology possibilities into a design solution (Krishnan and Ulrich, 2001; Gerwin and Barrowman, 2002). The focus of this literature is the design of complex products such as automobiles, aerospace systems, software, and industrial equipment (Mihm, Loch, and Huchzermeier, 2003). Similarly, IT-enabled reengineering initiatives can be conceptualized as IT-process development projects where a business opportunity (or threat) coupled with IT capabilities provide a (re)design solution.

### Design Uncertainty

Concurrent design in product development involves an upstream product definition stage where information about consumer requirements and emerging technology are used to finalize key specifications, and these specifications are used downstream in detailed design and prototyping (Krishnan and Bhattacharya, 2002). Similarly, IT-process development involves the contemporaneous redesign of a firm's IT platform and its business processes, recognizing that IT platforms are assets optimally leveraged in supporting multiple business processes rather than a single business process. Process-platform interdependencies create an upstream environment where concept (product) definition involves the simultaneous consideration of information about new process and platform requirements, along with emerging IT options. These intertwined requirements are used downstream in developing and implementing detailed IT platform and work process designs solutions. Novelty in the assets and activities that comprise a design often results in ambiguous requirement specifications that can obscure the fit between upstream and downstream operations. This "fit novelty" prohibits the early resolution of design uncertainty and is a significant determinant of project performance (Adler, 1995).

Often, these downstream operations cannot be taken "offline" while these new designs are fabricated and implemented. Downstream operations that must continue execution before upstream operations have finalized their requirements rely heavily on the precision and accuracy of upstream specifications for the rapid resolution of design uncertainty (Terwiesch and Loch, 1998). Analytical models indicate that early uncertainty resolution enables these interdependent operations to execute more successfully, while the significant advantage of concurrency is lost with slower uncertainty resolution. Engineering design involves a complex set of relationships among a large number of coupled problems that leads to iterations between upstream and downstream design (Smith and Eppinger, 1997). Fewer iterations and less extensive rework may be experienced when coupled development activities can anticipate each others' results, and the consequence of such coordination can be fewer and shorter project delays. This coordination can be facilitated through communication.

In linking communication and concurrency Blackburn, Hoedemaker, and Van Wassenhove (1996) indicate that if interdependencies cannot be eliminated they must be managed. The involvement of downstream functions in upstream design activities is critical in defining design specifications because of the volatility of functional requirements, which is the chief cause of rework. Thus, a flow forward of preliminary information is needed to begin downstream work. Preliminary information exchange can take place through coordinated planning. In the context of IT-process development, one aspect of coordinated planning is strategy coupling where IT decisions are made in conjunction with a firm's redesign strategy and process design decisions consider IT capabilities, limitations, and future development (Lederer and Mendelow, 1989). The degree of coupling ranges from tight to loose, reflecting the amount of coordinated decision making. Tight strategy coupling attempts to resolve design uncertainty through a high degree of cross-functional involvement and joint planning early in a project's life cycle. In contrast, loose strategy coupling relies on feedback-driven adjustments during implementation and less joint planning up front to promote design flexibility (Horwitch and Thietart, 1987). These ideas suggest that with greater design novelty, coordination through planning requires tight coupling and higher levels of cross-functional involvement to resolve the design uncertainties likely to hinder project performance.

## Project Performance

In the management information systems (MIS) literature, project performance has been conceptualized as both a product and a process (Barki, Rivard, and Talbot, 2001). Product performance refers to the quality of the project outcome—or effectiveness of IT-enabled operations, with the "product" itself being the designs of the operational process and the enabling IT platform. The principle indicator of design quality is *client satisfaction*. Two aspects of product development that influence client satisfaction are project effectiveness and validity. Project effectiveness is concerned with determining whether the newly installed design positively impacts business performance and is typically reflected as measures of goal attainment. Project validity refers to the extent that a new design is "right" for its intended users and is typically reflected as measures of user acceptance (Schultz and Slevin, 1975).

Product performance is affected by process performance. Process performance refers to the quality of the development process—most notably effective planning and efficient implementation. When the development environment is analyzable and stable, it is more likely that process and platform designs can be implemented as intended, delivering expected benefits *on time* and *within budget*. As the process-platform relationship becomes more unpredictable, implementation impediments (e.g., unexpected information and technology requirements) arise for which a further design change or rework becomes more likely. The greater the frequency and *magnitude of rework*, the more difficult it is to deliver the expected benefits within the projected time frame and budget.

## Design Change

The magnitude of rework is contingent on the nature of design change that accumulates over the course of a project. It refers to the extent a process design or a platform design has deviated from its initial blueprint. It does not denote whether this change is beneficial or not, rather its definition is confined to the extent and nature of design deviations that have transpired by the end of a project.

Henderson and Clark (1990) delineate four categories of technological design change in product development—incremental, modular, architectural, and radical—whose progression is related to the magnitude of effort in altering the core design of system components and/or how those components are linked together. Borrowing these categories to define the magnitude of rework in IT and process design, the degree of upstream and downstream rework can be placed on an incremental–radical continuum that captures the level of deviation from the intended process (or platform) design. Here, incremental rework involves *minor* design change; modular, architectural, and radical rework involves *major* design changes. Modular rework is limited to major changes in process or platform components, architectural rework entails major changes to linkages among components, and radical rework involves major changes to both components and linkages (Mitchell and Zmud, 2006; Mitchell and Nault, 2007). Rework involving linkages (architectural and radical change) is more difficult to enact than rework confined to components (modular change) due to the inherent complexities of system interdependence (Henderson and Cockburn, 1994). Thus, performance risk is greater for rework involving architectural and radical design changes than incremental and modular design changes. The later these design changes occur in the project's life cycle, the more difficult it is to deliver the expected benefits within the projected completion period.

Product performance and process performance—captured in the magnitude of rework, client satisfaction, and project timeliness—reflect design uncertainties left unresolved. We know that greater design uncertainty requires greater coordination to define and implement a design (Galbraith, 1974). We also know that planning in the form of cross-functional involvement and strategy coupling can mitigate the uncertainty that impedes project performance (Madnick, 1991; McDonald, 1991). However, significant gaps arise in our understanding of the nature of this relationship.

## COORDINATION IN NEW PRODUCT DEVELOPMENT

Research in new product development suggests project performance can be enhanced through coordination in the form of cross-functional involvement, predevelopment planning, and extensive communication (Krishnan and Loch, 2005). Performance measures in NPD focus on financial indicators (goal attainment), project quality, timeliness, success, and development speed (Brown and Eisenhardt, 1995). Selected studies in this area along with the major research finding of each are listed in Table 18.1. Early studies laid the groundwork for cross-functional involvement in highlighting the role of client (market) issues in generating product revenue (Rothwell et al., 1974). Extending this work, researchers found that stakeholder involvement in cross-functional teams resulted in better performance. Performance improvements were also seen with better product quality, clear product specifications, and extensive preliminary (consumer and technical) assess-

Table 18.1

**Selected Empirical Studies in Product Development**

| Study | Performance measures | Key planning result higher performance related to . . . |
|---|---|---|
| Rothwell (1972) | Product profitability | Identification of user needs |
| | Market share | Senior management involvement |
| Cooper (1979) | Financial indicators | Functional area synergy |
| Zirger and Maidique (1990) | Product profitability | Functional area synergy |
| | | Predevelopment planning |
| Allen (1971, 1977), Katz and Tushman (1981) | Meet technical specifications | Technology gatekeeper |
| | | Frequent external communication |
| Katz and Allen (1985) | Development team performance | Manager involvement |
| Keller (1986) | Project timeliness, budget, product quality | Cohesive internal communication |
| Ancona and Caldwell (1990, 1992) | Project timeliness, efficiency, budget | Task coordination |
| | | External/internal communication of plans, goals, and work breakdown |
| Dougherty (1992) | Project cancellation | Interactive and iterative team communication |
| | Project success | |
| Takeuchi and Nonaka (1986) | Development speed | Use of cross-functional teams |
| Clark and Fujimoto (1991) | Productivity | Overlapping development stages |
| | Product quality | High stakeholder involvement |
| Iansiti (1993) | Development speed | Predevelopment planning |
| Eisenhardt and Tabrizi (1995) | Development speed | Use of cross-functional teams |
| | | Alignment of uncertainty conditions and method of planning |
| Griffin (1997) | Development time | Use of cross-function team |
| | | Use of formal planning processes |

ments (Cooper, 1979; Zirger and Maidique, 1990). According to these studies, higher-performing firms used cross-functional teams, guided by a well-developed predevelopment plan. A related research stream demonstrated the importance of internal communication among team members and manager involvement. This research highlighted the impact of internal information processing activities on uncertainty reduction, which led to better project performance (Allen, 1977; Katz and Allen, 1985).

Shifting the emphasis of performance measures from financial and technical indicators to project timeliness and viability, researchers have empirically tested the impact of specific communication and coordination activities—finding that project performance was enhanced through well-developed internal and external communication channels (Keller, 1986; Ancona and Caldwell, 1992a). Ancona and Caldwell (1992b) also explicated the relationship between boundary-spanning activities and performance. Their work highlighted the importance of accessing internal knowledge and assimilating knowledge external to the firm. Dougherty (1992) showed that information content across teams was increased through cross-functional involvement and that failed projects tended to engage in sequential, rather than concurrent development activities. The culmination of this research provided greater understanding of what types of communication were most beneficial to development projects and the role of cross-functional teams.

Finally, the most recent research has further refined performance to focus on productivity and development speed, reflecting today's dynamic competitive contexts. This empirical work highlighted the importance of cross-functional involvement to coordinate the overlap of development activities. Coordinated overlap of activities coupled with integrated problem solving improved development performance and speeded the development process (Takeuchi and Nonaka, 1986; Clark and Fujimoto, 1991). Iansiti (1993) extended this work, finding that predevelopment planning—particularly planning that integrates new technologies, product expectations, and manufacturing systems—enhanced the performance of development teams under different conditions of uncertainty. Eisenhardt and Tabrizi (1995) empirically examined the effectiveness of different development approaches on project performance. Their results are supported by Griffin's (1997) finding that the use of cross-functional teams in concurrent development reduces development time under conditions of high uncertainty but has no effect under low uncertainty.

## PLANNING PROCESSES IN STRATEGY FORMULATION

The strategy literature highlights two contrasting methods or modes of planning—synoptic and adaptive—that fall on polar ends of a planning continuum (Segars and Grover, 1999). The synoptic planning mode is characterized by the comprehensive integration of planning decisions prior to project implementation. The adaptive planning mode is an incremental approach to planning characterized by feedback–driven adjustments as a project unfolds. Although several other classification schemes have been introduced in the strategy literature, for example, formal/informal (Thune and House, 1970), planned/unplanned (Wood and LaForge, 1979), integrated/nonintegrated (Malik and Karger, 1975), and deliberate/emergent (Mintzberg, 1978), each is largely grounded in this synoptic/adaptive dichotomy.

The synoptic mode is a highly rational, proactive process. Emphasis is placed on establishing goals, monitoring the environment, assessing internal capabilities, evaluating alternatives, and then developing an integrated plan to achieve prespecified goals (Andrews,1971; Hofer and Schendel, 1978). Rooted in the planning school of strategic management, the underlying belief is that systematic planning improves performance (Mintzberg, 1990). This belief is based on two key assumptions: that comprehensive, systematic analysis of the environment and organizational situation reduces uncertainty, and that uncertainty reduction enables the recognition and removal of implementation impediments that would otherwise limit firm performance (Ansoff, 1965; Porter, 1980).

An adaptive mode is an established pattern of activity not explicitly articulated in advance (Mintzberg, 1990, 1994). Derived from the incremental school of strategy formulation, this planning mode is based on the principle of intended rationality. That is, due to cognitive and process limits, comprehensive planning is infeasible under conditions of uncertainty (March and Simon, 1958). Planning is accomplished by breaking large, complex problems into smaller, more manageable pieces. Goals and analysis are intertwined in a repetitive process of feedback-driven adjustments until a successful design emerges (Lindbloom, 1959, Joyce, 1986; Quinn, 1978).

From a decision-making perspective, the major difference between synoptic and adaptive planning is the level of comprehensiveness characterizing each of these planning modes (Fredrickson, 1983). Comprehensiveness is a measure of rationality and is defined as the extent to which organizations attempt to be inclusive in making and integrating strategic decisions (Fredrickson and Mitchell, 1984). Proponents of rationality in strategy formulation argue that strategic decision

Figure 18.2  **Planning Continuum**

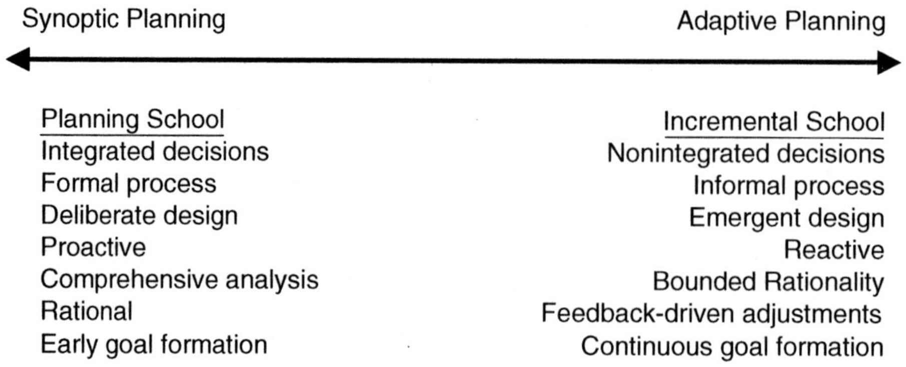

Synoptic Planning                                                          Adaptive Planning

◄──────────────────────────────────────────────────────────────────►

Planning School                                      Incremental School
Integrated decisions                               Nonintegrated decisions
Formal process                                          Informal process
Deliberate design                                        Emergent design
Proactive                                                       Reactive
Comprehensive analysis                               Bounded Rationality
Rational                                      Feedback-driven adjustments
Early goal formation                            Continuous goal formation

making should be exhaustive in analyzing environmental conditions and forecasting the deployment of resources to meet strategic objectives. Here, the term rationality is used in the narrow sense of "functional" rationality (Mannheim, 1950) and refers to the extent to which a series of actions is organized to achieve maximum efficiency. Thus, rationality refers not to the selection of goals but to their implementation (Scott, 1981). If organizations are rational in their decision making, and managers strive to reduce the uncertainty that threatens rationality, then uncertainty is a contingent factor in selecting a planning process to guide implementation (Thompson, 1967). Figure 18.2 depicts the planning continuum and attributes characterizing the polar extremes.

Confronted with different levels of uncertainty, the strategy literature is unclear as to when synoptic planning and adaptive planning respectively prove most effective. Classic studies of planning approach found that organizations that tightly coupled functional strategies outperformed organizations that used loose coupling (Thune and House, 1970; Herold, 1972). Subsequent studies both confirm and refute these findings (Wood and LaFarge, 1979; Malik and Karger, 1975; Grinyer and Norburn, 1975; Rhyne, 1986). In an attempt to explain these inconsistencies, later studies took environmental conditions into consideration. These results are also equivocal (see Table 18.2). For example, under conditions of uncertainty Lindsay and Rue (1980) found synoptic planners outperformed adaptive planners. Contrary to these findings, Kudla (1980) and Frederickson and Mitchell (1984) report that synoptic planning did not improve performance in uncertain environments. In more stable environments, Frederickson (1984) observed that synoptic planning was more effective than adaptive planning. More recently, Brews and Hunt (1999) undertook an empirical study of planning practices among 656 firms to resolve the synoptic–adaptive debate. They report that formal (synoptic) planning practices were associated with higher internal and external performance regardless of conditions of uncertainty. The adaptive (incremental) approach received no support in this study. Their results support other studies demonstrating a strong synoptic planning/performance relationship (Hart and Banbury, 1994; Priem, Rasheed, and Kotulic, 1995).

Although many inconsistencies exist in the NPD and strategy literatures, we consistently find support for specific coordinated planning practices, that is, predevelopment communication, cross-functional teams, managerial involvement, and integrated problem solving. However, inconsistencies do surface regarding the manner of coordination or pattern of decision making most appropriate for a given level of uncertainty. In a NPD study, Eisenhardt and Tabrizi (1995) report that an adaptive approach is most effective under conditions of uncertainty, and that a predictive (synoptic) approach is more effective under more certain circumstances. While consistent results

Table 18.2

**Select Empirical Studies of Coordinated Planning in IT-Process Development**

| Study | Performance measures | Key planning result<br>Higher performance related to . . . |
|---|---|---|
| Mitchell and Zmud (1999) | Client satisfaction<br>Project delay | Tight strategy coupling when uncertainty is high, loose coupling when uncertainty is low |
| Mitchell and Zmud (2006) | Magnitude of rework, IT delay, project delay, budget overrun, and user acceptance | First mover using synoptic planning<br>Late adopter using adaptive planning<br>Early adopter using mixed planning mode |
| Mitchell and Nault (2007) | Magnitude of rework<br>IT delay<br>Project delay | High levels of coordinated planning that mediates the relationship between upstream and downstream rework |

(e.g., Fredrickson, 1984; Fredrickson and Mitchell, 1984) have been reported in the strategy literature, subsequent studies across both literatures provide contradictory findings (e.g., Gerwin and Barrowman, 2002; Brews and Hunt, 1999). These inconsistencies suggest that coordinated planning may in fact serve a moderating role in the relationship between uncertainty and performance.

## COORDINATED PLANNING IN IT-PROCESS DEVELOPMENT

Most work exploring the black box of IT-process development has focused on case studies (e.g., Mitchell and Zmud, 1993, Argyres, 1994; Sherif, et al., 2006) and conceptual frameworks offering guidelines for change (e.g., Hammer, 1990; Davenport and Short, 1990). The insights provided in these studies provide a basis for understanding the interplay between process-platform architectures. Of particular interest is a recent study by Sherif, Zmud, and Browne (2006) that details the importance of coordinated communication in the context of software reuse. They framed software reuse as a coordination problem between upstream operations (software architects) and downstream operations (software developers). The tension between architects and developers was effectively alleviated through two coordination mechanisms—monitoring of upstream and downstream processes and their reciprocal communication—providing information and feedback on design structures and solution effectiveness.

A small set of empirical studies has conceptualized IT-enabled process redesign initiatives as coevolving IT-process development projects. In exploring the effect of joint planning practices on project performance, three studies in particular provide an initial delineation of the coordinated planning construct in a concurrent engineering context (Mitchell and Zmud, 1999, 2006; Mitchell and Nault, 2007). In keeping with the literature on NPD and strategy formulation, these studies operationalize planning as strategy coupling and cross-functional involvement—which individually and collectively influence the relationship between design uncertainty and project performance. The results are provided in Table 18.2.

The first study in this stream explored the interaction between strategy coupling and uncertainty, and its influence on two aspects of project performance—client satisfaction and project timeliness.

In exploring forty-three IT-enabled process-redesign projects in the medical sector, Mitchell and Zmud (1999) developed and validated a six-item measurement scale for strategy coupling. They argue that the pattern of decision making that embodies synoptic and adaptive planning is achieved through tight and loose coupling, respectively. In the context of IT-process development, tight strategy coupling involves the early coordination and integration of design information, akin to March and Simon's (1958) "coordination by plan." Loose strategy coupling relies on "coordination by feedback" where design information is coordinated in response to uncertainty conditions as the project unfolds (Orton and Weick, 1990).

They found that client satisfaction and project timeliness were enhanced when IT and redesign plans were tightly coupled in the presence of high uncertainty, and loosely coupled in the presence of low uncertainty. These results indicate that strategy coupling *moderates* the relationship between design uncertainty and project performance. Tight coupling reduces design uncertainty related to fit novelty by establishing an initial blueprint for design. This blueprint forms the basis for identifying gaps between IT needs and platform capabilities, leaving room for platform improvement early in the project's life cycle. When fit novelty is low, as it is when imitating a process or IT platform, less design uncertainty exists as the vision, goals, and design interdependences have already been revealed. Under these circumstances, loose coupling permits greater flexibility for making incremental adjustments to refine IT-process fit during implementation.

Extending their earlier work, Mitchell and Zmud (2006) examined the relationship between uncertainty and planning mode in predicting the magnitude of rework—a determinant of timely project completion. Set in the context of Miles, Snow and Coleman's adaptive cycle (1978), uncertainty in the form of fit novelty was represented by a firm's technology position. Generally, there are three technology positions—first mover, early adopter, and late adopter—that reflect a pattern of investment in the technologies diffusing through an industry. First movers face greater fit novelty as the nature of process–platform interdependence is not well defined. Early adopters face less fit novelty as they invest in newly introduced process-platform design developed elsewhere. Late adopters primarily invest in proven technologies and operations, where the fit between work process and IT platform is well established. Each technology position embodies a different level of design uncertainty, which leads to rework. To minimize rework, different levels of design uncertainty must be aligned with the appropriate planning mode.

Planning mode was again conceptualized as a synoptic-adaptive continuum with corresponding degrees of strategy coupling and cross-functional involvement (a second dimension of coordinated planning). Synoptic planning was operationalized as tight coupling with cross-functional involvement early in the development process. Adaptive planning was operationalized as loose coupling with less cross-functional involvement up front. Their original coupling instrument was revised—to incorporate timing of IT investments and level of cross-functional involvement in the planning process (Lind and Zmud, 1991). The magnitude of rework was operationalized by a Guttman scale that captured Henderson and Clark's (1990) four types of design change.

Using a sample of 121 IT-process development projects in multi-hospital systems, Mitchell and Zmud validated their planning mode and technology position constructs and conducted a hierarchical log-linear analysis. They report that the magnitude of rework was minimized when first movers used synoptic planning, late adopters used adaptive planning, and early adopters employed aspects of both planning modes—termed a mixed planning mode. A mixed planning mode integrates formal analysis with incremental design (Mintzberg, 1973; Sabherwal and King, 1992). This outcome provides further evidence that coordinated planning moderates the relationship between design uncertainty and both types (IT/process) of rework. Bivariate correlations between magnitude of rework and aspects of project performance indicate the magnitude of rework corresponds with longer IT delays, projects, and budget overruns. An inverse relationship was noted between magnitude of rework and user acceptance of the new operations.

The third study in this stream of work synthesized concepts in the previous two studies. In a partial least squares (PLS) model of concurrent development, Mitchell and Nault (2007) examined the relationships among coordinated planning, design uncertainty, magnitude of rework, and project delays. The coordinated planning instrument was revised to include items regarding business unit and IT alignment (Horner-Reich and Benbasat, 1996), IT consultation, redesign goal clarity, and exploitation of IT capabilities (McDonald, 1991). In addition to synoptic planning, this measure of coordinated planning also reflects Adler's (1995) static coordination (by plan) and Loch and Terwiesch's (1998) pre-communication in concurrent engineering. The instrument does not capture dynamic design adjustments between operations during implementation, which is characteristic of an adaptive planning approach.

Based on a sample of 120 IT-process development projects in health care and telecommunications, this study's results support and confound prior studies. Consistent with the NDP and strategy formulation literature, they report that coordinated planning decreases the magnitude of rework in both upstream (process) and downstream (IT) operations. Interestingly, they report that coordinated planning *mediates* the relationship between process rework and IT rework. In the absence of coordinated planning, process rework has a significant effect on IT rework. In the presence of coordinated planning, that effect is insignificant. Apparently a synoptic approach to coordinated planning is able to raise issues of process-platform fit during strategy formulation that allows for the extensive coordination of process requirements and IT capabilities in formulating a blueprint for design.

They also report that greater uncertainty attributed to fit novelty increases process rework, but has no effect on IT rework and no effect on the amount of coordinated planning. This suggests IT activities can be isolated from some of the uncertainty associated with fit novelty. Finally, they report an indirect effect between process rework and project delay—through IT rework. Thus, tight strategy coupling in the form of synoptic planning and intense cross-functional involvement alleviates design uncertainty early in a project's life cycle, where more precise and stable requirements can be exchanged that make the IT-process relationship more predictable.

## SYNTHESIS

These studies provide a base of understanding for further exploring the management of IT-process development projects from a concurrent engineering perspective. They show that the alignment of design uncertainty and planning mode has a profound effect on project performance. Also uncovered is that this alignment *moderates* the relationship between uncertainty and performance but *mediates* the relationship between IT rework and process rework. In order to minimize rework, the design uncertainty associated with fit novelty can be alleviated with the proper approach to coordinated planning. In effect, project performance is enhanced when high uncertainty is resolved through synoptic planning, when low uncertainty is managed with adaptive planning, and moderate levels of uncertainty are handled with a mixed planning mode. In addition, synoptic planning reduces the need for rework, and reduces the impact of process rework on IT rework.

These results are in keeping with the Planning School advocated in the strategy formulation literature, and coordination studies in new product development. Where dependent operations benefit from bilateral preliminary communication, IT-process development projects require the mutual consideration of IT and work process strategies to effectively reduce design uncertainty. Integrated problem solving through strategy coupling and cross-functional involvement improve at least three aspects of project performance—magnitude of rework, client satisfaction, and timely project completion. Contrary to the findings of Eisenhardt and Tabrizi (1995), Mitchell (1984), and Mitchell and Frederickson (1984), the work of Mitchell and her colleagues lends support to the research findings observed by Gerwin and Barrowman (2002), Brews and Hunt (1999), and Newkirk and Lederer (2006)—that under conditions of uncertainty synoptic planning was more beneficial than adaptive planning, while adaptive planning was a better choice where less uncertainty exists.

Whereas the benefits derived from a new work process are largely attributed to the design of its component tasks and their relationships, its functioning depends on the capabilities of its hosting IT platform. Systematic consideration of IT in the context of process activities allows planners to determine the firm's IT competencies and limitations, and then exploit, or "work-around," these technological realities in designing new processes (McDonald, 1991). Thus, IT-process development depends on management's ability to anticipate, moderate, and eliminate design uncertainties that impede both IT platform and process development and functionality.

## CALL FOR FUTURE WORK

Firms frequently rely on IT-enabled process transformations to turn weak operations into more competitive operations. Ironically, the novel process designs that possess the potential to provide a firm with a competitive edge also promote substantial design uncertainty. The radical enhancing of process activities using IT is dependent on the capabilities embedded within an organization's IT infrastructure, and necessary IT infrastructure investments are contingent on the accurate forecasting of the specific functionalities required by the work processes undergoing change. Thus, the IT infrastructure represents the means for achieving dramatic process change, while the nature of this process change ultimately determines the trajectory of the IT infrastructure. The reciprocal nature of this ends-means relationship, because of increasingly sophisticated IT platforms and business processes, creates an often messy task-technology conundrum: the absence of well-defined fit specifications produces a considerable amount of design uncertainty, which in turn increases the difficulty of deriving—early in a development project—viable fit specifications. As a consequence, IT-process development projects provide a rich context within which to examine the effect of coordinated planning practices on concurrent design, development, and implementation activities.

There are several areas that would benefit from further research activity. These areas correspond with the constructs outlined in Figure 18.1. As a field, the IS literature has borrowed definitions of uncertainty from several reference disciplines. More work is needed to confirm that the nature of uncertainty faced by projects fabricating effective platform-process solutions is the same as that defined in other disciplines. For example, explorations of fit novelty and the nature of inherent design uncertainty across a variety of IT innovations, such as those outlined by Swanson (1994), would improve our understanding of the uncertainty/planning/performance relationship for different types of IT innovations. This enables practitioners to target their planning practices for those uncertainties most likely to arise within specific IT contexts.

While recent research has developed and revised a coordinated planning instrument, further expansion and refinement of the measures is needed. In its current form, the coupling and cross-functional dimensions of the instrument developed by Mitchell and colleagues focus more on synoptic planning than adaptive planning. More attention should be given to the development of adaptive planning items, integrating them with synoptic items, and testing the psychometric properties of this mixed, planning mode scale. Further, the instrumentation developed by Mitchell and colleagues differs markedly from that developed by Newkirk and Lederer (2006), who focus on similar aspects of synoptic and adaptive planning (formal analysis, strategy integration, stakeholder representation, review process, and complexity) and produce similar results. In Figure 18.1, our coordinated planning construct also has an integrative capability dimension. Recently, a scale was developed to measure management's integrative capability in an IT context (Mitchell, 2006) but this instrument is limited to enterprise application integration projects. More work is needed to capture this dimension from a concurrency perspective, and incorporate it with other coordinated planning dimensions in providing a richer formulation of this construct. The fragmentation of planning measures across multiple instruments indicates further instrument development is needed to refine the coordinated planning and uncertainty scales—so they provide a better representation of project planning in an IT context.

The nature of design change (in both the IT platform and in the enhanced business process) is another construct that has received little attention in the IS literature. Borrowing concepts from the NPD literature provides a basis for conceptualizing design change, and exploring its dimensions, role, and impact on project rollout. This aspect of IT-enabled process development and implementation has largely been ignored. In particular, metrics are desired that evaluate a project as it unfolds, facilitating the use of dynamic adjustments beyond trial and error. Performance measures could also be expanded beyond those introduced in the extant research. Finally, more empirical work (quantitative and qualitative as well as positivist and interpretive) is needed to examine the relationships among these constructs so as to increase our collective understanding of how to manage the complexities pervading the joint evolution of IT platforms and the IT-enabled business solutions emerging from these platforms.

## REFERENCES

Argyres, N. 1994. The impact of information technology on coordination: evidence from the B2 stealth bomber. *Organization Science*, 10, 2, 162–180.

Adler, P. 1995. Interdepartmental interdependence and coordination: the case of the design/manufacturing interface. *Organization Science*, 6, 2, 147–167.

Allen, T. 1977. *Managing the Flow of Technology*. Cambridge, MA: MIT Press.

Ancona, D., and Caldwell, D. 1992a. Bridging the boundary. *Administrative Science Quarterly*, 37, 4, 634–666.

———. 1992b. Demography and design: predictors of new product team performance. *Organization Science*, 3, 321–341.

Andrews, K. 1971. *The Concepts of Corporate Strategy*. Homewood, IL: Dow Jones-Irwin.

Ansoff, H. 1965. *Corporate Strategy*. New York: McGraw-Hill.

Barki, H.; Rivard, S.; and Talbot, J. 2001. An integrative contingency model of software project risk management. *Journal of Management Information Systems*, 17, 4, 37–70.

Blackburn, J.; Hoedemaker, G.; and Van Wassenhove, L. 1996. Concurrent software engineering: prospects and pitfalls. *IEEE Transactions on Engineering Management*, 43, 2, 179–188.

Boynton, A.; Zmud, R.; and Jacobs, G. 1994. The influence of IT management practice on IT use in large organizations. *MIS Quarterly*, 18, 3, 299–320.

Brews, P., and Hunt, M. 1999. Learning to plan and planning to learn: resolving the planning school/learning school debate. *Strategic Management Journal*, 20, 10, 889–913.

Brown, S., and Eisenhardt, K. 1995. Product development: Past research, present findings, and future directions. *Academy of Management Review*, 20, 2, 343–378.

Clark, K., and Fujimoto, T. 1991. *Product Development Performance*. Boston: Harvard Business School Press.

Cooper, R. 1979. The dimensions of industrial new product success and failure. *Journal of Marketing*, 43, 93–103.

Davenport, T., and Short, J. 1990. The new industrial engineering: Information technology and business process redesign. *Sloan Management Review* (Summer), 11–26.

Dougherty, D. 1992. Interpretive barriers to successful product innovation in large firms. *Organization Science*, 3, 179–202.

Eisenhardt, K., and Tabrizi, B. 1995. Accelerating adaptive processes: product innovation in the global computer industry. *Administrative Science Quarterly*, 40, 1, 84–111.

Fredrickson, J. 1983. Strategic process research: questions and recommendations. *Academy of Management Review*, 8, 4, 565–575.

———. 1984. The comprehensiveness of strategic decision processes: extension, observations, future directions. *Academy of Management Journal*, 27, 3, 445–466.

Fredrickson, J., and Mitchell, T. 1984. Strategic decision processes: comprehensiveness and performance in an industry with an unstable environment. *Academy of Management Journal*, 27, 2, 399–423.

Galbraith, J. 1973. *Designing Complex Organizations*. Reading, MA: Addison-Wesley.

———. 1974. Organization design: an information processing view. *Interfaces*, 4, 3, 28–36.

Gerwin, D., and Barrowman, N. 2002. An evaluation of research on integrated product development. *Management Science*, 48, 7, 938–953.

Griffin, A. 1997. The effect of project and process characteristics on product development time. *Journal of Marketing Research*, 34, 1, 24–35.

Grinyer, P., and Norburn, D. 1975. Planning for existing markets. *Journal of the Royal Statistical Society*, 138, series A, 70–79.

Hammer, M. 1990. Reengineering work: don't automate, obliterate. *Harvard Business Review* (July–August), 104–111.

Hart, S., and Banbury, C. 1994. How strategy-making processes can make a difference. *Strategic Management Journal*, 15, 4, 251–269.

Henderson, R., and Clark, K. 1990. Architectural innovation: the reconfiguration of existing product technologies and the failure of established firms. *Administrative Science Quarterly*, 35, 9–30.

Henderson, R., and Cockburn, I. 1994. Measuring competence? exploring firm effects in pharmaceutical research. *Strategic Management Journal*, 15, 63–84.

Herold, D. 1972. Long-range planning and organizational performance: a cross-valuation study. *Academy of Management Journal*, March, 91–102.

Hofer, C., and Schendel, D. 1978. *Strategy Formulation: Issues and Concepts*. St. Paul: West Publishing.

Horner-Reich, B., and Benbasat, I. 1996. Measuring the linkage between business and information technology objectives. *MIS Quarterly*, 20, 1, 55–81.

Horwitch, M., and Thietart, R. 1987. The effect of business interdependencies on product R&D: intensive business performance. *Management Science*, 33, 2, 178–197.

Iansiti, M. 1993. Real-world R&D: jumping the product generation gap. *Harvard Business Review*, 71, 3, 138–147.

Joyce, W. 1986. Towards a theory of incrementalism. In R. Lamb and P. Shrivastava (eds.), *Advances in Strategic Management*. Greenwich, CT: JAI Press.

Katz, R., and Allen, T. 1985. Project performance and the locus of influence in the R&D matrix. *Academy of Management Journal*, 28, 67–87.

Keller, R. 1986. Predictors of the performance of project groups in R&D organizations. *Academy of Management Journal*, 29, 715–726.

Koufteros, X.; Vonderembse, M.; and Jayaram, J. 2005. Internal and external integration for product development: the contingency effects of uncertainty, equivocality and platform strategy. *Decision Sciences*, 36, 1, 97–134.

Krishnan, V., and Bhattacharya, S. 2002. Technology selection and commitment in new product development: the role of uncertainty and design flexibility. *Management Science*, 48, 3, 313–327.

Krishnan, V.; Eppinger, S.; and Whitney, D. 1997. A model-based framework to overlap product development activities. *Management Science*, 43, 4, 437–451.

Krishnan, V., and Loch, C. 2005. A retrospective look at production and operations management articles on new product development. *Production and Operations Management*, 14, 4, 433–441.

Krishnan, V., and Ulrich, K. 2001. Product development decisions: a review of the literature. *Management Science*, 47, 1, 1–21.

Kudla, R. 1980. The effects of strategic on common stock returns. *Academy of Management Journal*, 23, 1, 5–20.

Lederer, A., and Mendelow, A. 1989. The coordination of information systems plans with business plans. *Journal of Management Information Systems*, 6, 2, 5–19.

Lind, M., and Zmud, R. 1991. The influence of a convergence in understanding between technology providers and users on information technology innovativeness. *Organization Science*, 2, 2, 195-217.

Lindblom, C. 1959. The science of muddling through. *Public Administration Review*, 19, 120–128.

Lindsay, W., and Rue, L. 1980. Impact of the organization environment on the long-range planning process: a contingency view. *Academy of Management Journal*, 23, 3, 385–404.

Loch, C., and Terwiesch, C. 1998. Communication and uncertainty in concurrent engineering. *Management Science*, 44, 8, 1032–1049.

Madnick, S. 1991. The information technology platform. In M.S. Scott-Morton (ed.), *The Corporation of the 1990s*. New York: Oxford University Press, pp. 27–60.

Malik, Z., and Karger, D. 1975. Long-range planning and organization performance. *Long Range Planning*, 8, 6, 60–64.

McDonald, H. 1991. Business strategy development, alignment, and redesign. In M.S. Scott-Morton (ed.), *The Corporation of the 1990s*. New York: Oxford University Press, pp 159–187.

Mannheim, K. 1950. *Freedom, Power and Democratic Planning*. New York: Oxford University Press.

March, J., and Simon, H. 1958. *Organizations*. New York: Wiley.

Mihm, J.; Loch, C.; and Huchzermeier, A. 2003. Problem-solving oscillations in complex engineering projects. *Management Science*, 46, 6, 733–750.

Miles, R.; Snow, C.; Meyer, A.; and Coleman, H. 1978. Organizational strategy, structure, and process. *Academy of Management Review*, 3, 3, 546–562.

Mintzberg, H. 1973. Strategy-making in three modes. *California Management Review*, 16, 2, 44–53.

———. 1978. Patterns in strategy formation. *Management Science*, 24, 9, 934–948.

———. 1990. Strategy formation: schools of thought. In J. Fredrickson (ed.), *Perspectives on Strategic Management*. New York: Harper and Row.

———. 1994. *The Rise and Fall of Strategic Planning*. New York: Free Press.

Mintzberg, H., and Waters, J. 1985. Of strategies, deliberate and emergent. *Strategic Management Journal*, 6, 3, 257–272.

Mitchell, V. 2006. Knowledge integration and information technology project performance. *MIS Quarterly*, 30, 4, 919–939.

Mitchell, V., and Nault, B. 2007. Cooperative planning, uncertainty and managerial control in concurrent design. *Management Science*, 53, 3, 375–389.

Mitchell, V., and Zmud, R. 1999. The effects of coupling IT and work process strategies in redesign projects. *Organization Science*, 10, 4, 424–438.

———. 2006. Endogenous adaptation: the effects of technology position and planning mode on IT-enabled change. *Decision Sciences*, 37, 3, 325–355.

Newkirk, H., and Lederer, A. 2006. Incremental and comprehensive strategic information systems planning in an uncertainty environment. *IEEE Transactions on Engineering Management*, 53, 3, 380–394.

Orton, D., and Weick, K. 1990. Loosely coupled systems: a reconceptualization. *Academy of Management Review*, 15, 2, 203–223.

Porter, M. 1980. *Competitive Strategy: Techniques for Analyzing Industries and Competitors*. New York: Free Press.

———. 1985. *Competitive Advantage: Creating and Sustaining Superior Performance*. New York: Free Press.

Priem, R.; Rasheed, M.; and Kotulic, A. 1995. Rationality in strategic decision processes, environmental dynamism and firm performance. *Journal of Management*, 21, 5, 913–929.

Quinn, J. 1978. Strategic change: logical incrementalism. *Sloan Management Review*, Fall, 7–21.

Rothwell, R. 1972. *Factors for Success in Industrial Innovations from Project SAPPHO. A Competitive Study of Success and Failure in Industrial Innovation, SPRU*, Brighton.

Rothwell, R.; Freeman, C.; Horsley, A.; Jervis, V.; Robertson, A.; and Townsend, J. 1974. SAPPHO updated: project SAPPHO phase II. *Research Policy*, 3, 258–291.

Rhyne, L. 1986. The relationship of strategic planning to financial performance. *Strategic Management Journal*, 7, 423–436.

Schultz, R., and Slevin, D. 1975. Implementation and organizational validity: an empirical investigation. In R.L. Schultz and D.P. Slevin (eds.), *Implementing Operations Research and Management Science*. New York: Elsevier.

Sabherwal, R., and King, W. 1992. Decision processes for developing strategic applications of information systems: a contingency approach. *Decision Sciences*, 23, 4, 917–944.

Segars, A., and Grover, V. 1999. Profiles of strategic information systems planning. *Information Systems Research*, 10, 3, 199–232.

Segev, E. 1987. Strategy, strategy making, and performance: an empirical investigation. *Management Science*, 33, 2, 258–269.

Scott, R. 1981. *Organizations: Rational, Natural and Open Systems*. Englewood Cliffs, NJ: Prentice Hall.

Sherif, K.; Zmud, R.; and Browne, G. 2006. Managing peer-to-peer conflicts in disruptive information technology innovations: the case of software reuse. *MIS Quarterly*, 30, 2, 339–356.

Smith, R., and Eppinger, S. 1997. Identifying controlling features in engineering design iteration. *Management Science*, 43, 3, 276–293.

Swanson, E. 1994. Information systems innovation among organizations. *Management Science*, 40, 9, 1069–1092.

Takeuchi, H., and Nonaka, I. 1986. The new product development game. *Harvard Business Review*, 64, 1, 137–146.

Thompson, J. 1967. *Organizations in Action*. New York: McGraw-Hill.

Thune, S., and House, R. 1970. Where long-range planning pays off. *Business Horizons*, August, 81–87.

Wood, D., and LaForge, R. 1979. The impact of comprehensive planning on financial performance. *Academy of Management Journal*, 22, 3, 516–526.

Zirger, B., and Maidique, M. 1990. A model of new product development: an empirical test. *Management Science*, 36, 867–883.

# PART IV

# GOALS AND OUTCOMES OF INFORMATION SYSTEMS PLANNING

CHAPTER 19

# INFORMATION STRATEGY

## Confronting Research with Practice

ROLF ALEXANDER TEUBNER, MARTIN MOCKER,
AND ALEXANDER PELLENGAHR

**Abstract:** *Strategic information planning is a top-priority issue in practice, as is obvious from the attention it receives at practitioner conferences and in practitioner publications. As a result, some research efforts have been devoted to related topics. So far, the focus has been on strategic information planning processes as well as on information systems/information technology (IS/IT) and competitive advantage, while its result, the strategic information plan or information strategy has been neglected. Consequently, basic questions regarding the content of information strategy have not been investigated or have only been answered in a normative way until now, leaving the domain of information strategy in obscurity and subject to arbitrariness.*

*In this chapter, we present diverse interpretations of information strategy that can be derived from academic discussion. These range from information strategy as a departmental plan, to information strategy as an application portfolio, to information strategy as enumerated lists, to information strategy as a system of plans. We then discuss the results of fourteen qualitative interviews that we conducted with information strategy professionals in practice.*

*In our interviews, we identify twelve decision areas of practical information strategies and six major rationales behind them. We find that organizational constraints, especially the distinction between corporate- and business-level cases, are major contingencies of the observed differences. Our corporate-level cases homogeneously address issues such as (worldwide) standardization of architectures or applications, and the setting of rights and accountability guidelines that coordinate IS/IT activities across the enterprise. In contrast, business-level cases are widely heterogeneous and idiosyncratic in their information strategic contents. Business information strategies were also much broader in content, including decisions on the application landscape, plans for organizing information functions, and decisions on IS/IT investments.*

*We compare the decision areas identified in our research with those discussed in the academic literature. The academic discussion revolves around topics such as IT and competitive advantage, the IT/IS portfolio and investment decisions. In contrast, practitioners strongly emphasize decisions such as standards, which are almost ignored in the academic discussion on information strategy. This suggests the conclusion that there is a gap between academia and practice with respect to information strategy. This conclusion is also supported by the observation that practitioners almost ignore academic literature, while, on the other hand, practical concerns play no role in the academic discourse. Practitioners regard academic literature as too abstract, time consuming, and irrelevant to their practical needs. Academia will have to focus more on practical needs in order to be better accepted and perceived.*

*Keywords: Strategic Information Planning (SIP), Information Strategy, Information Strategy Research, Information Strategy Content, Strategic Decision Areas, Strategy Rationales, Strategy Contingencies*

## MOTIVATION AND INTRODUCTION

Strategic information planning (SIP) is a top-priority topic in practice. As such it has been among the highest-ranking issues on management agendas for years (Galliers, 1993b; Luftman, Kempaiah, and Nash, 2006; McGee et al., 2005; Watson et al., 1997). It is not surprising that columns in practitioner publications and at conferences are dedicated to the topic as well (e.g., the column "IT Strategien" in *Computerwoche,* a weekly German computer magazine, or the annual practitioner conference "Strategisches IT-Management" hosted by *Handelsblatt,* a daily German business newspaper). Finally, it is not unusual to find managers holding positions such as "head of information technology strategy" in practice, suggesting that this topic deserves special treatment and requires additional resources.

Despite its prominence in practice, SIP is not among the top research issues. This can also be seen from the fact that SIP is less prevalent in academic journals than in practitioner magazines (Lee, Gosain, and Im, 1999). Existing research published on SIP focuses on the process of formation or the strategic impact of information systems/information technology (IS/IT) rather than on information strategy, which is the output of the formation process. For example, Brown (2004) found that only 26 percent of articles are concerned with the content, while 84 percent address the process, of formation. Teo and Ang (2000, p. 275) confirm that "most research seems to focus on the IS planning process itself . . . rather than on the output . . . ," that is, the "strategic plan." Three recently published literature reviews have focused on IT's role alone in gaining and sustaining competitive advantage as only one example of strategic impact (Melville, Kraemer, and Gurbaxani, 2004; Piccoli and Ives, 2005; Wade and Hulland, 2004).

The very focus on the SIP process at the cost of the information strategy is surprising, since, as long as a common understanding of information strategy is lacking—that is, there is no consensus on an information strategy conception (what information strategy is) and its content (which decisions are part of information strategy)—the discussion on process (how to get to the content) necessarily remains vague. As Maritan and Schendel (1997, p. 262) put it: "how can we really understand the process of making strategic decisions without explicitly considering the strategy content of the decisions and how it links to outcome?" In fact, there is still significant vagueness concerning information strategy. For example, various terms are used to describe constructs that differ only slightly: "The problem of terminology is one of the fundamental issues facing those wishing to develop an information strategy. . . . There is a proliferation of terminology and a great deal of ambiguity surrounding its use" (Allen and Wilson, 1996, p. 240). Common terms include "strategic information plan" (Lederer and Salmela, 1996), "IT strategy" (Gottschalk, 1999a) "IS strategy" (Galliers, 1991), "IS/IT strategy" (Chan et al., 1998), and "information strategy" (Smits, et al., 2003). We will discuss later why we use the latter term in this chapter as well.

In addition to the lack of clarity academia already displays within itself, a comparison to practical concerns of information strategy adds another layer of complexity.

An analysis of the topics discussed under the label "information strategy" (the term "IT strategy" seems to be more common in practice) at practitioner conferences and in magazines uncovers that practical information strategies deal with questions that have not frequently been attributed with strategic relevance in research so far. For example, the most frequent "IT strategy" topics in *Com-*

*puterwoche* in 2005 included technology standards (37 articles), IT cost reduction (16 articles), IT security issues (9 articles), and IT provider management (11 articles). This result is confirmed by earlier research on "strategic IT issues" reporting "differences within and between organizations, but particularly in comparison to the academic literature" (Brady et al., 1992, p. 183). More specifically, Doherty and Fulford (2006) complain about the neglect of strategic security issues in research.

On the whole, the indications mentioned above give rise to the assumption that there is a gap between academia and practice in the discussion on information strategy. This assumption is also supported by our experience in teaching master and executive courses on information management. Here, we observe that the academic treatment of information strategy is not part of the agenda and concerns of practitioners. Hence, the need to bring academia and practice more closely together was a strong motivation for the research presented in this chapter. The objective of our research has been to highlight the intersections of academic discussion and practice, and also dissent. A clear idea of these intersections might help us to better align teaching with practical needs. Moreover, it can provide us with a better idea of the practical relevance of the academic discussion. Areas of dissent, in contrast, can highlight training needs in practice or provide a fresh impetus to research that addresses information strategy concerns that have perhaps been ignored in the academic discussion so far.

In this chapter, we contrast academic and practical concerns in SIP. In the following section, we present an overview of existent conceptualizations of information strategy in the academic literature. Then we present the results of an exploratory study on information strategy that we conducted with key professionals in practice. This is followed by a comparative analysis of the findings of both the survey of academic literature and the exploratory study. Finally, we present suggestions for future research.

## STATE OF THE ART OF INFORMATION STRATEGY: A CRITICAL REVIEW

Information strategy is a core responsibility of the top-level IT executive, the chief information officer (CIO). According to a study conducted by Stephens and colleagues (1992), 80 percent of the CIOs surveyed are in charge of planning their company's information strategy. As argued above, the first thing a CIO needs to know when attempting to formulate an information strategy is what must be decided on as part of this strategy. Unfortunately, the academic literature does not give a consistent answer to a CIO interested in knowing what an information strategy is. This inconsistency is already illustrated by the use of different terms for the output of SIP as demonstrated in the previous section.

Besides these different terms, different approaches to substantiating the concept of information strategy can be identified in the literature. We surveyed thirty-five articles covering the output of SIP according to Brown's study (2004). Furthermore, key German (Teubner and Klein, 2002) and English textbooks on information management were taken into account. Based on this work, we identified four approaches: (1) information strategy as a functional departmental plan, (2) information strategy as an application portfolio, (3) information strategy as an enumerated list, and (4) information strategy as a system of plans.

## INFORMATION STRATEGY AS A FUNCTIONAL DEPARTMENTAL PLAN

Interpreting information strategy as a functional strategy builds on the classification of strategies according to the hierarchical levels of a diversified organization (Vancil and Lorange 1975): the

Figure 19.1   **Alignment of Information Strategy with All Other Functional Strategies**

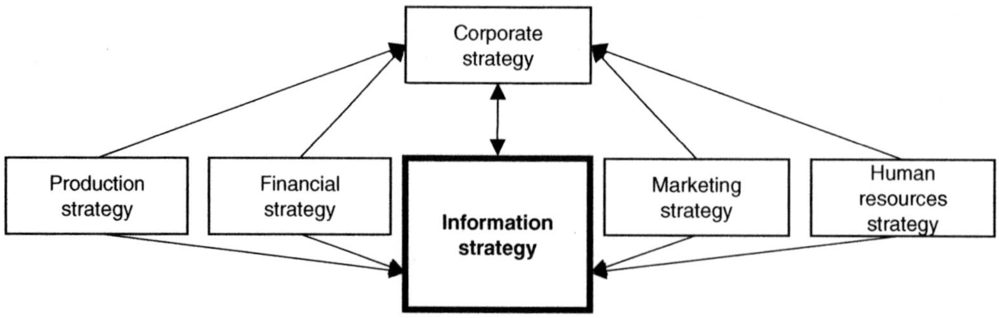

*Source:* Boddy et al. 2005, p. 91.

corporate, business-unit, and functional levels. The functional level comprises departments that are in charge of specific business functions such as marketing, sales, procurement, production, or information processing. Some authors compare information strategy with the strategies of other departments such as marketing or production. Hence, they look upon information strategy simply as a plan for the functional IT department (e.g., Boddy, Boonstra, and Kennedy, 2005, p. 90; Lehner, 1993, p. 16; McLeod, 1998, pp. 40, 48; Smits, Poel, and Ribbers, 2003, p. 65).

Functional strategies are typically derived by breaking down the business strategy and allocating responsibilities for its execution to existing functional departments. This approach assumes that the strategic decisions of the enterprise can be broken down and that strategic actions can be delegated to existing departments. More specifically, it presumes that the respective organizational unit already exists. Following this logic, information strategy is restricted to decisions that lie within the authority of the IS/IT department and excludes decisions at the business and corporate levels.

One problem of viewing information strategy as a departmental strategy lies in the fact that, unlike other functions, the use of information, information systems, and so on permeates the whole enterprise in almost every process (Porter and Millar, 1985). To address this issue, a number of authors propose the alignment of information strategy with all other departmental strategies (see Figure 19.1). However, this alignment introduces a high level of complexity and still does not provide an overall perspective on information strategy.

**Information Strategy as an Application Portfolio**

"It is conventional wisdom and practice" to see the core contents of information strategy as "an application development portfolio" (Earl, 2003, p. 59). Indeed, a significant number of articles suggest this view (e.g., Gottschalk, 1999b; Lederer and Salmela, 1996; Lederer and Sethi, 1992, 1998; Lehner 1993). Here, the primary strategic decision to be made is which information systems should be developed in the future.

The emphasis, especially in the 1980s, was on identifying so-called strategic information systems (SIS)—information systems that help an organization to gain competitive advantage (Senn, 1992, p. 7; Wiseman, 1985, p. 7). Many articles at that time used Porter's five forces model (Porter, 1980) to explain the competitive impact of IS (Eardley and Lewis, 1996). Several research articles addressed the question of how IT/IS can alter any of the five forces (e.g., Bakos and Treacy, 1986; McFarlan, 1984; Porter, 2001; Porter and Millar, 1985). Evidence for this ability of IT was provided mainly in the form of anecdotal case examples. Kettinger and colleagues (1994, Appendix A) list more than sixty SIS case examples.

Later, the scope of the application portfolio widened from its traditional focus on SIS, that is, to "new applications with the potential to create an advantage over competitors," to "embrace the selection of prosaic applications" (Lederer and Sethi, 1992, p. 26). However, the question of which applications to include in the portfolio besides SIS has not yet been answered.

Another criticism is that looking at applications alone is a restricted perspective that misses crucial issues and results in unwanted side effects. For example, the introduction of certain applications can have organizational implications such as new skill requirements that must also be considered. Some authors advocating the application portfolio approach recognize this shortcoming and try to compensate by adding other domains and decisions as components of an information strategy. Galliers (1991, p. 56) demands that "no longer should organisations be looking simply for a prioritised portfolio of information systems applications as the sole outcome of the process." He defines "IT strategy in a broad sense to incorporate the range of issues associated with strategy formation and implementation with respect to information systems" (Galliers, 1993a, p. 283) and makes some suggestions for further issues to be included in information strategy, such as human, organizational, and infrastructural issues. In later work, Galliers (2004) added issues of e-commerce and knowledge management as well. However, due to the lack of any indication as to if and when these extensions will have finally come to a close, proposals to extend the interpretation of information strategy beyond being merely an application portfolio take the form of—somewhat arbitrary—enumerated lists.

## Information Strategy as an Enumerated List

A number of authors present a range of issues that are claimed to have strategic relevance. These issues are typically identified either through literature reviews (e.g., Das, Zahra, and Warkentin, 1991; Flynn and Goleniewska, 1993), surveys among planners (e.g., Conrath, Ang, and Mattay, 1992), or analysis of SIP processes and methods proposed by consultants or tool developers (e.g., Flynn and Goleniewska, 1993; Lederer and Gardiner, 1992; Lederer and Salmela, 1996). Table 19.1 presents examples of the issues derived in each of the three approaches. Furthermore, some authors propose a number of issues as strategic without offering any empirical support (e.g., Heinrich and Lehner, 2005).

Table 19.1 shows that the items to be included in an information strategy differ in number as well as content. The different levels of detail are also striking: some proposals remain vague regarding what has to be planned: for example, should a hardware plan describe the capacities needed or should it go down to the level of actual products? Some proposals even remain on a very abstract level. Bajjaly (1998), for example, lists IS mission, IS objectives, linkage between IS and organizational goals, IS action plans, assignment of tasks to specific people, and mechanisms for management control. Other proposals contain items that can be classified as somewhat operational (i.e., nonstrategic). For example, Lederer and Sethi (1996, p. 37) propose that tools used for system development and maintenance, database specifications, and a sequenced list of projects with cost, risk, and benefit data should be specified in an information strategy. These decisions might also be made on a project management (i.e., implementation) level. Smits, Poel, and Ribbers (2003, p. 73) state that strategies "normally . . . do not include design and project plans." This is because projects are already at the level of operational decision making rather than that of maneuvering action toward the achievement of organizational goals (Steinmann and Schreyögg, 2000, pp. 233, 260 ff). In line with this, the study conducted by Lederer and Sethi (1996, p. 58)

Table 19.1

**Three Examples of Enumerated Lists**

| Das, Zahra, and Warkentin (1991) | Conrath, Ang, and Mattay (1992) | Lederer and Salmela (1996) |
| --- | --- | --- |
| • Distinctive competence emphasized in strategic management information systems (MIS) planning (cost of information, information differentiation for different applications, specialized information for specific market niches)<br>• Dominant information processing technology<br>• Level of computerization of the MIS function<br>• Sources from which the firm obtains its information systems (IS) technology<br>• Contribution of MIS department to systems design and development<br>• Medium by which MIS contributes<br>• Technical processes through which MIS are managed and controlled<br>• Organizational structure of the MIS unit<br>• Administrative policies used to motivate and manage employees in MIS department | • Statement of objectives<br>• Hardware plan<br>• Projection of possible future MIS/EDP (electronic data processing) environment<br>• Recommended implementation plan<br>• Systems development plan<br>• Financial plan<br>• Personnel plan<br>• Facilities plan<br>• Projection of possible future user environment<br>• Organization plan<br>• Education plan<br>• Projection of possible future industry environment<br>• Summary of strengths and weaknesses of staff<br>• Comparison of past IS performance vs. plan<br>• Alternate strategies | • Summary of organization's information technology (IT) strategy<br>• Data and application plan (initial data entities, high-level specification of applications, requirements for data management, security and training, tools for system development and maintenance, cost, benefits, risks, and resource requirements resulting from the plan)<br>• Change management plan: actions that will facilitate adoption of IS plan<br>• Human resources plan: newly required IS skills, new roles/responsibilities<br>• Technical architecture of hardware, supporting databases, and system software<br>• Migration plan: overall approach, key projects, their order of implementation with cost, benefits, risks of each project<br>• Process description: annually updating the plan<br>• Appendix |

concludes that, for example, prescriptions related to database specification are not of importance to strategic information planners. So, the question of how the listed decision areas are strategic is again left open in these proposals.

Another even more fundamental problem of enumerated lists is that it is extremely difficult for a planner to assess whether the proposed lists are exhaustive. One reason for this is that the authors do not explain why the lists can be assumed to be comprehensive. Another reason is that no obvious structure is provided. To address this problem, Das, Zahra, and Warkentin (1991, p. 957) synthesize their nine categories (Table 19.1, column 1) into "four major dimensions . . . by combining related categories." In this indicative way of grouping related issues, they come up with the categories "distinctive competence," "information systems technology," "systems design and development," and "MIS infrastructure." This structure reduces the complexity of the list. Still, the structure remains artificial, since it is applied to a "range of issues" (Galliers, 1993a). Instead of presenting a logic upfront and deriving the proposed items from this concept, the structure is applied to the collection of items ex post. This leaves unclear what the actual components are that have to be decided on (e.g., information technology, information systems, IS/IT organization), how they are related, and why they have to be covered by an information strategy.

### Information Strategy as a System of Plans

In contrast to enumerated lists, systems of plans (e.g., Earl, 1989; Henderson and Venkatraman, 1999; Ward and Peppard, 2004) present domains (potentially in the form of documents or parts of them) of information strategy and their relations in a comprehensible form. Thus, "system of plans" models of information strategy suggest a structure that can be followed in strategy documents.

Earl (1989) presented a very well-received proposition (Allen and Wilson, 1996; Galliers, 1991; Ragu-Nathan et al., 2001; Ward and Peppard, 2004). Meanwhile, it has undergone several extensions (Earl, 1996, 2000) (see Figure 19.2 for the original and extended models). He identifies three domains called "information systems (IS)," "information technology (IT)," and information management (IM)" by asking "What has to be done?" "How does it have to be done?" and "Who should do it where?"

- IS strategy (see Earl, 1989, pp. 67–94) can be seen as an extension of the application portfolio approach. As such, it comprises an "application development portfolio . . . , a 'shopping list' of applications and projects" (ibid., p. 68). It is recognized as business led and demand oriented in that it is about "aligning IS development with business needs."
- IT strategy (ibid., pp. 95–116) is concerned with technology policies and addresses questions related to computer, communication, data, and application architecture. Each of these architecture elements is described by a set of design parameters, schemas (models or blueprints), and policies as well as goals and plans to achieve these goals. According to Earl, the structure of IT strategy is a matrix of elements (computing, communications, data, and applications) and levels (parameters, schemas, policies, and plans). IT strategy is regarded primarily as the supply side of the IS strategy. This becomes evident when Earl equates IT strategy with the "how" in contrast to the "what" of IS strategy. Furthermore, he explicitly recognizes IT strategy as supply oriented and technology focused and sees its main purpose as being "to ensure efficient (especially reliable) and effective delivery of the IS strategy" (Earl 1996, p. 495).
- IM strategy (see Earl, 1989, pp. 117–128) "guides how the organization should run IS/IT activities" (ibid., p. 117). It includes decisions on "the role and structure of IT activities in

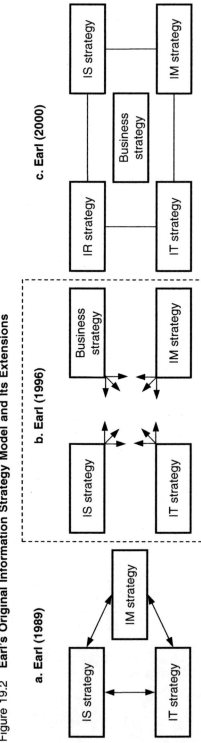

Figure 19.2 Earl's Original Information Strategy Model and Its Extensions

the organization," "relationships between specialists and users and between the centre and divisions or business units," "management controls for IT," "management responsibilities," "performance measurement," and "management processes" (ibid., p. 65 ff). Earl summarizes IM strategy as being "concerned mainly with the relationship between the IS/IT function and the rest of the business" (ibid., p. 118).

The system of plans approach extends enumerated lists with respect to structure and reasoning. Nevertheless, existing strategy models expose some shortcomings as well—because it is one of the best-known models, Earl's is used to demonstrate these shortcomings:

First, the reasoning used is based on common sense posing the three questions "what," "how," and "who" (originally "wherefore"). Whether these questions are intuitively plausible to the reader or not, they do not provide much backing for the distinction of the planning domains or for their relevance. Earl himself is fully aware of the "conjectural" (Earl, 1996, p. 491) nature of his model. He admits that his proposals are "not . . . either complete or fully validated" (ibid., p. 499). Thus, it is not startling that he later adds an entirely new domain to the model labeled "information as a resource" (Earl, 2000), which had not been mentioned in the earlier versions of the model.

A second problem of this common-sense-based approach becomes evident when Earl himself identifies four tasks of information management as elements of IM strategy, namely, planning, organization, control, and technology. He maintains that planning is covered by IS and IT strategy and technology is covered by IT strategy, thus leaving organization and control questions to the IM strategy. However, he gives no reasons for assigning specific management functions to partial (IM, IS, and IT) strategies. It can be argued that something like an "IM strategy" is a misleading strategy concept if it covers only partial management functions. All of this criticism considered, the distinction between IM, IS, and IT strategies is difficult and not well elaborated. Other authors also criticized "the relationship between . . . IT, IS and information management (IM) [as] unclear" (Allen and Wilson, 1996, p. 240).

Third, the interrelationships among the domains (Earl, 1988) and the relations between each domain and business strategy remain ambiguous. For example, Earl (1989) makes sweeping statements on the interrelation of business strategy and "IT," saying, for example, that IT can support business strategy or that IT can create strategic options without shaping them with respect to IT, IS, and IM strategy. Perceiving this as a problem, Earl addresses it in a later publication (Earl, 1996), where he proposes interrelationships between business strategy and the three information strategy domains. But even in this publication the relations are outlined only vaguely: Earl connects each domain with all other domains using four types of relationships for the twelve relations called "clarification," "innovation," "foundation," and "constitution." Each of the four domains is associated with only one type of relationship. Thus, the relationships serve more as an attribute of the domain than an action-oriented description of the relation that would be more helpful for planners in directing their planning logic. Furthermore, one can identify more relationships between the domains using the four types of relationship, which have not been identified by Earl himself. For example, IT strategy—besides acting as a "foundation" for the other domains as proposed by Earl—can also have the role of "innovation."

## INFORMATION STRATEGY IN PRACTICE

The results of the literature review reveal a number of conceptions present in research that also suggest what an information strategy might or should include. In contrast, very little is known about how practitioners conceive information strategy and what they see as its content. What we know from research is that most large organizations claim to have an information strategy (Lehner, 1993; Wilson, 1989). But such surveys do not add to research as long as we do not know what practitioners have in mind when talking about information strategies. The few studies that provide insight into practitioners' concern with information strategy are based on single cases (e.g., Hayward, 1987; Teubner, 2007; Wexelblatt and Srinivasan, 1999) or only a small number of more or less specific companies (Allen and Wilson, 1996; Conrath, Ang, and Mattay, 1992). In order to broaden (and deepen) our understanding of information strategy in practice, we interviewed SIP professionals who, at the same time, were opinion leaders for their views on information strategy.

## Method

In order to learn more about information strategy in practice, we conducted exploratory, qualitative interviews with fourteen practitioners and experts in information strategy making. We chose a qualitative approach for two reasons. First, we were interested in gaining deep insight into practitioners' original understanding. Practitioners can reveal their understanding and use of, and reasoning for, information strategy in open interviews much better than in questionnaires. Second, as the current confusion about the terms already indicates, the state of research described at the beginning of the chapter does not allow the definition of sound constructs and generation of valid hypotheses that can be tested quantitatively. On the contrary, the level of ambiguity in information strategy terminology and concepts suggests a bottom-up, theory-independent, exploratory approach. Qualitative interviews better allow for exploration and real understanding of the "whats" and "whys" of information strategy in practice (Cropley, 2005, p. 49; Miles and Huberman, 1994, p. 5 ff). In using a qualitative approach, we follow other researchers (e.g., Brown, 2004, p. 27), who state—again with an eye toward the current situation in research—that "it may be appropriate for more theory-generating research to be conducted, employing qualitative techniques."

As interviewees, we chose practitioners who present their concepts of information strategy at conferences, have published them elsewhere, or even formally hold the title "head of IT strategy." These practitioners can be assumed to deal with the topic "information strategy" not only marginally in their jobs but as one of their core tasks. They can be seen as experts who have already devoted much thinking to information strategy. Through presenting their understanding at conferences or in publications they are also likely to shape the understanding of other practitioners. Consequently, it is appropriate to start with these experts when turning to practice. To capture a broad picture of information strategy in practice, we selected companies with diverse backgrounds (regarding industry, size, IT organization). Table 19.2 summarizes the research sample in terms of role of the interviewee in the organizations while Table 19.3 displays general characteristics of the firms' organization.

We conducted a total of fourteen interviews, each about two hours long. All interviews, except two phone interviews, were conducted at the respective company's site. All companies are headquartered in a German-speaking country. Four companies are active only in their respective country, and the others are engaged in Europe or even globally. The interviews were conducted in German as this was the native language of the participants. We started each interview by asking the interviewee to give a brief overview of the company's situation and business strategy with a special focus on the IS/IT situation. If the interviewee did not turn to information strategy content himself, we asked which IS/IT decisions were considered strategically relevant within the company. This led to a discussion on the content of information strategy.

We also asked for the effective information strategy, whether its content had changed over time, and, if so, why. We then asked the reasons for viewing this decision as strategic. We also

Table 19.2

**Interviewees**

| No. | Title of participants | Position within information technology (IT)-organization |
|---|---|---|
| 1 | Director IT Strategy | Staff unit to head of department for "IT-infrastructure" |
| 2 | Director IT Development | Head of one department reporting to IT-responsible board member |
| 3 | CIO | Head of IT profit center, represents IT on the corporate level |
| 4 | Director Information Systems | Head of IT department reporting to board member |
| 5 | VP Corporate-IT-Management | Deputy head of corporate IT staff unit |
| 6 | Director IT Department | Head of IT department reporting to board member |
| 7 | Global head of IT Logistics | Head of one department reporting to SBU board member |
| 8 | Deputy head of Corporate IT Strategy | Deputy head of corporate IT staff unit |
| 9 | Head of IT Corporate Strategy | Head of corporate IT staff unit |
| 10 | Head of IT Strategy | Head of IT department (fully outsourced, only two people remaining) |
| 11 | Head of Corporate IT Strategy | Head of corporate IT staff unit |
| 12 | CIO and Chief Process Officer | Head of IT department (also responsible for business processes) reporting to board member |
| 13 | CIO, Director of IT Department | Head of IT department reporting to board member (chief financial officer) |
| 14 | IT Director | Head of main department for IT, reports to CIO |

checked oral descriptions of the content with documents, if there were any, at the site. As far as we were allowed to record the interviews, we transcribed them and conducted a qualitative content analysis (Mayring, 1996). For each interview we coded the decisions and reasons given for why the decision was seen as part of strategy.

**Findings**

In the following section we present the decisions we identified through the interviews as being part of information strategies, grouped together into clusters, that is, decision areas. Then we display the reasons practitioners gave for considering these decisions strategic. In doing so, we present a view of information strategy contents thoroughly grounded in practice. In the last section, we look for contingencies that help to explain why concerns are included in information strategy making in one case, but excluded in other cases.

*Strategy Contents*

Overall, experts were very open in sharing their thinking on information strategy content with us. Many of those who documented their strategies also gave us access to or let us look at their official information strategy documents and presentations, at least at the level of table of contents.

We collected a total of ninety-nine individual decisions, which we grouped into twelve decision areas. We arrived at this grouping by first clustering decisions related to the same object (e.g.,

Table 19.3

## Organizational Characteristics of Research Sample

| No. | Industry | Employees (no.) | Revenue[1] | Organization including IT/IS |
|---|---|---|---|---|
| 1 | Insurance | 2,800 | 2 bn. | Functional organizations, CIO represents IT and organization on the board; IT is main department with three subdepartments including IT-Infrastructure |
| 2 | Insurance | 3,500 | 2 bn. | Two regional headquarters, 500 sales offices, 1,500 partner institutions across northwestern Germany; IT organized in four separate departments reporting to board member |
| 3 | Health care | 60,000 | 4 bn. | Worldwide operating corporation, 3 business units; IT organized as corporate function |
| 4 | Public institution | 1,400 | n/a[2] | Functionally divided public institution, >10 functional departments, operating mainly in Europe; IT organized as functional department |
| 5 | Telecommunication | 240,000 | 50 bn. | Worldwide operating corporation, 3 business units including one for IT services; IT corporate staff unit |
| 6 | Investment Bank | 700 | 24 bn. | Small but worldwide operating bank, legally independent subsidiary of a large corporation; IT organized as a functional department |
| 7 | Logistics | 400,000 | 17 bn. | Worldwide operating corporation with several subsidiaries; 5 business units, one of them including an IT-service provider, IT is corporate staff unit in business units |
| 8 | Universal bank | 20,000 | 320 bn. | Worldwide operating company; 8 business units; IT organized as corporate staff unit plus IT departments in every business unit |
| 9 | Transportation | 250,000 | 30 bn. | Worldwide operating corporation with >5 subsidiaries; 5 business units; IT organized as corporate staff unit plus IT service provider as a subsidiary |
| 10 | Pure online bank | 25 | 48 mn. | Functionally divided company; IT organized as functional department |
| 11 | Transportation | 90,000 | 23 bn. | Worldwide operating corporation, 3 subsidiaries; >5 business units; IT corporate staff unit plus IT service provider as one business unit plus IT departments in every business unit |
| 12 | Financial services | — | 1 bn. | Functionally organized; IT as main department |
| 13 | Ceramics manufacturer | 10,000 | 3 bn. | Worldwide operating company; 3 business units; IT organized as corporate function |
| 14 | Financial services | 900 | 50 bn. | Two regional headquarters, 8 functional departments, CIO represents IT and accounting on the board, IT is main department |

*Notes:* Numbers each at the time of the interview (2002–2005).
[1] 2004 EUR figures: premium income for insurance, assets under management for investment banks, credit volume for banks.
[2] Supranational, public administrative body.

application, set of applications, technical infrastructure, personnel, finance). However, it became apparent that the object alone was insufficient to distinguish the decisions for our purposes. For example, the decision to exchange a number of applications because of unsatisfactory functionality, the general decision on the use of standard vs. custom-built software, and the decision on which applications to include in the application portfolio are certainly all decisions on a set of applications. However, the nature or kind of decision (e.g., a principle, a prioritization, an allocation/ distribution decision, a guideline for action, etc.) differs fundamentally: the first decision is about functionality, the second is about introducing standards in terms of rules, and the last is about an investment decision. Hence, by combining both object and nature of decisions, we identified the twelve homogeneous decision areas:

• *Application landscaping decisions* are related to the functional scope and composition (in contrast to technical design) of the application landscape as a whole. Looking at the application landscape means looking at a blueprint, that is, a holistic view of the applications required to support the business. This aims at answering the question of which applications are needed or need to be changed in order to support the business: "So we developed an IT strategy that was more like a plan for building out IT—with which solutions do we support the business in order to . . . reflect the growth [targeted by the business strategy]" (case 3).

• *Application systems standards* are decisions on the standardization of application systems in functional (process) domains such as accounting or billing. Here the question is not "which functionality is needed" but rather, for example, "for which process domains can we use standard software and where should we use custom-built software" (case 5). Another sample decision is provided by case 7: "we conduct mail business . . . in different countries, in very different facets—you have to make the decision once on whether we want to standardize, do we believe we can standardize that, yes or no."

• *Technical architectural standards* are concerned with the high-level technical structure underlying the application systems and the technical infrastructure. Architectural standards are rules, policies, or guidelines that any application or technical solution has to follow: " . . . no one could bypass that. As in Germany: 'everybody drives in the right lane'" (case 3). Examples include the choice of databases or operating systems to use or the type of architecture (e.g., host-based vs. browser-based, service-oriented architectures vs. monolithic architectures).

• *IT process standards* provide guidelines for developing or operating applications and the technical infrastructure. These may be guidelines on how to manage the life cycle of applications (e.g., evolutionary vs. big-bang changes), which process standard to use for IT operations processes (e.g., the IT Infrastructure Library), project management (e.g., projects in controlled environments methodology), or software engineering (e.g., rational unified process vs. V-model).

• *Investment decisions* focus neither on the functional nor the technical side, but on the prioritization of the allocation of financial resources to concrete initiatives (although functional and technical criteria may serve as a base for this decision). The decision involves a tradeoff between different requests, for example, for projects to build applications or technical infrastructure. The main decision object is the application/project portfolio: "The focus of the documents or the IT strategy work in the business units actually is the portfolio . . . with mid- to long-term projects . . . the decision on which applications, so to speak, get into the portfolio and will then be . . . developed" (case 11).

• *Budgetary decisions* are the decisions on the overall volume of the budget for IT as well as the general apportionment of the budget to business areas or to the budget categories such as personnel, hardware/software investments, external service provision, and so on. The question here is "how much do we want to spend on IT?" and "how do we want to distribute the overall budget to different categories?" (In contrast to "which concrete initiatives should we fund?"): "[this decision includes] we use . . . 70 percent of our resources directly for business areas and we use 30 percent of our resources for the infrastructure. . . . The [resources for business areas] could then be further partitioned by saying: we use 30 percent of the portfolio for the topic 'monetary politics'" (case 4).

• *Decisions on launching IS/IT projects that directly support business strategy* involve engaging in individual projects that are considered relevant for business strategy: "[Whether introducing an application is strategic] depends on what we are talking about. If we talk about an accounting reporting software, then I'd say, that cannot be strategic . . . if it is really [an application for] business scope extension . . . then it gets strategic relevance quickly" (case 6).

• As in any functional department, the IT unit's human resources and their organization must be planned in order to enable efficient conduct of the required activities. The decisions related to these plans are laid down in *human resources and organizational plans of the IS/IT unit*. Decisions include the IT unit's organization into subunits, its personnel and their skills: "how do we develop our [the IT unit's] employees, which core competencies do we see in our employees, how do we ensure employee training?" (case 13).

• *Decisions on the role of the IS/IT unit* determine the self-conception of the IS/IT unit (e.g., as a service provider, technologist, consultant, etc.) that it communicates and enacts toward stakeholders. These decisions affect the positioning of the IS/IT unit toward the business areas and the board of directors, toward its employees and to external stakeholders such as external customers (e.g., should the IS/IT unit serve the external market or not) and potential competitors for providing IS/IT services (e.g., "providing services at competitive price with ongoing benchmarking" [cf. case 13]). The purpose of decisions is marketing the IS/IT unit toward different stakeholders: "the mission expresses the area in which we are [the IT unit is] active. The vision [of the IT unit] . . . is the eventual expression of strategy, which by the way is a very attractive vision for the employees [of the IT unit] here. So really showing a way forward" (case 4).

• *Rights and accountability decisions* regulate the way in which IT decisions are made within the organization. This involves especially the distribution of internal responsibilities for decision rights among different stakeholders within the overall organization and thus goes beyond the IT unit itself. This distribution can be among IT and business stakeholders as well as among corporate- and business-unit-level stakeholders. Rights and accountability decisions also include the introduction of IT control mechanisms such as introducing service-level agreements or charge-out provisions for IT services: "I . . . always see IT strategy in connection with governance. . . . [I]t determines who is allowed to do what, how budgets are determined, how investments [are made]—all these regulations" (case 8).

• *Sourcing decisions* are related to the allocation of IT activities between the company and external parties. Only those activities that are not outsourced are potentially conducted by the IT unit. Hence, this decision area goes beyond decisions on the IT unit. In contrast to rights and accountability decisions, sourcing decisions concern the distribution of responsibilities among internal and external stakeholders and thus cross the boundary of the organization. In case 10, the most prominent example for strategic sourcing decisions, almost all operational, and even some executive, work is outsourced to subcontractors, which is consequently underpinned by the interviewee's statement: "For me, everything relating to questions of outsourcing is strategic" (case 10).

• *Risk mitigation plans and policies* are concerned with avoiding or alleviating technical threats to business continuity, data privacy, or security. In comparison with architectural standards their aim is more specific than just to ensure a technically sound architecture. They address "issues such as disaster recovery work. If something massive happens, how quickly are we able to support the business again?" (case 7).

Figure 19.3 **Information Strategy Content by Case**

| Content of information strategy (decision areas) | Cases | | | | | | | | | | | | | | |
|---|---|---|---|---|---|---|---|---|---|---|---|---|---|---|---|
| | Business unit and/or functional level | | | | | | | | | | Dedicated corporate level | | | | |
| | 1 | 2 | 3 | 4 | 6 | 10 | 11 | 12 | 13 | 14 | 5 | 7 | 8 | 9 | 11 |
| a. Application landscaping | | 2 | 3 | | | | | 2 | 1 | | | | | | |
| b. Application standards | | | 1 | 2 | | | | | | 1 | 2 | 3 | | 2 | |
| c. Architectural standards | 3 | 1 | 3 | 3 | 3 | 3 | 2 | 2 | 3 | | 2 | 2 | 3 | 2 | 2 |
| d. IT process standards | | 2 | | 2 | 3 | | | 2 | | | 1 | | | 3 | 2 |
| e. Portfolio/investment | | | | | | 3 | | 2 | | 2 | | | 1 | | |
| f. Budget | | | 3 | 3 | | 1 | | | | 2 | 1 | | | | |
| g. Strategic IS/IT projects | | | | | 1 | | | | | | | | | | |
| h. HR plan/org. of IT unit | | | | 3 | 1 | | | 2 | 3 | 3 | | | | | |
| i. Role of IS/IT unit | | 1 | 3 | 3 | | | | | 3 | | | | | | |
| j. Rights and accountability | | 3 | 2 | 2 | 3 | | | | | | 3 | 2 | 3 | 3 | 2 |
| k. Sourcing | | | 1 | 3 | | 3 | 2 | 1 | 3 | | 1 | | 1 | | |
| l. Risk mitigation | | | | 2 | | 3 | | 1 | | | | 2 | | | 2 |

While most interviewees looked at information strategy from a business perspective, some had a dedicated corporate perspective (cases 5, 7, 8, 9, and 11). In the corporate-level cases, the information strategy is made across business units. In business-level cases, the scope of the information strategy refers to the whole business in case of a single-entity company, or to one business unit in the case of a divisional organization.[1] We separated these two groups in our analysis.

We differentiated three degrees of coverage. A decision area was rated as low coverage (1) if it was only mentioned as part of the information strategy, but not particularly emphasized, or only covered in making principle decisions (e.g., "Sourcing" was rated "1" if it was covered in the information strategy only by the principle that "we prefer 'buy' over 'make'" (case 12). We rated a decision area as medium coverage (2) if at least some very basic decisions were made or if larger parts of the decision area were covered. In these cases, interviewees typically dwelled on the decision area in more detail. We assigned a rating of high coverage (3) if a decision area was highlighted as one covered extensively in the respective information strategy (e.g., in considering multiple important decisions within the decision area). If the decision was not mentioned or was explicitly stated to be strategically irrelevant, we did not assign any coverage rating. The degrees of coverage of the decision areas for each case are shown in Figure 19.3.

*Strategy Reasoning*

As depicted in Figure 19.3, the importance and multitude of decision areas is very diverse among the companies analyzed. Not only are some of the areas identified more prominently than others (e.g., decision area c), but some of the companies are also concerned with information strategy on a far broader scale than others (compare, e.g., case 4 with case 1). In the following, we display and illustrate reasoning found in practice laying out three decision areas. For the purpose of illustration we chose the decision areas of "architectural standards" (c), "rights and accountability" (j) and "risk mitigation" (l). We chose decision areas c and j because they were frequently addressed in our interviews (cf. Figure 19.3). Thus, they are topics of common interest in practitioners' minds. We added decision area l to them, because this topic, in contrast to its commonness in practice, is not a topic in theory (Doherty and Fulford, 2006).

*Decision Area C—Architectural Standards*

We found architectural standards to be on the information strategy agenda in almost all cases (only cases 2 and 14 have a coverage mark below 2). The companies interviewed look upon standards as an important decision area for two reasons: first and most important, because settling a standard allows cost savings: "if I standardize to one platform across the group, I can save significant money on licenses, I have economies of scale in procurement, I do not need as many specialists, and I do not need as many people on the whole" (case 8). Or as the interviewee in case 5 puts it when he explains why he sets architectural guidelines to reduce the diversity of applications such as DBMS: "simply exploitation of synergies . . . efficiency increases." The second important reason is that choosing a technology standard is a long-term binding decision and a guideline for subsequent decisions: "you cannot change architecture decisions just like that . . . you cannot change that tomorrow or the day after tomorrow all the time. . . . And thus, these are guidelines that simply have relevance, long term durability" (case 13). Thus, architectural rules are often seen as a necessary countermeasure for the "shortsighted view of the business." Without them, infrastructure would soon become a "very costly technology zoo" (case 8). In contrast, an example for a more uncommon rationale is given in one case, where external necessities, namely, SOX 404-imposed constraints, are the drivers of redesign not only of IT-related processes and control structures, but also of the architecture in a standardized way (case 6).

*Decision Area J—Rights and Accountability*

Another important decision area is "rights and accountability." The two main reasons that decisions in this area are regarded strategic are, first, they are fundamental in setting the playing field for other actors or regulating further decisions. In case 9, for example, setting IT governance processes is considered strategic because implementing a rights and accountability framework "is the only chance in a company of this size if you do not want to rule with a drawn pistol." Accordingly, governance is regarded as strategic in case 3 because "it is a very important aspect: I have an application landscape that I would like to introduce. How am I going to do that? What is my authority framework, what are my constraints?" The second salient reason given by the practitioners interviewed is the mid- to long-term perspective of such decisions. They are "tied up for several years" (case 4), have "a mid-term perspective" (case 11), a "long-term character" (case 13), or binding effects "for three to five years" (case 10).

*Decision Area L—Risk Mitigation*

Finally, third, we illustrate the area of risk mitigation and IT security. This topic has become important not only in public awareness (due to phishing, hacking, and the occasional worm) but also in the minds of the IT/IS executives of our cases. Its relevance in practice is also supported by its prominence in IT-related magazines. The most prominent example is case 10, an online-only bank, where risk-related decisions are regarded as strategic in principle. These include decisions about how to control and monitor outsourcing partners, how to work together with international Internet crime experts and virtual crime police departments, or how to minimize the downtime of all technical components deployed. The interviewee explains: "if we had a security breach somewhere, we could [have to] close down the whole business." In another case, running a secure and intruder-proof company-wide network infrastructure is deemed strategic. The reason is that the company has a high turnover of partners and acquisitions and wants to prevent recently sold ex-partner firms from retaining access to the company's database (case 11). In a third case, risk mitigation, pursued by operating a couple of independent data processing centers in a so-called 2½ node concept, is seen as strategic because it determines "whether or not you are able to deliver [and] it secures sustainability." Analogous to this is the argumentation in case 7, where the decision about if and how to operate a decision-control center is considered strategic. It ensures that "things like disaster recovery work, so if something major happens, how quickly are we able to support the business again so that we do not lose any time?" As these examples show, decisions related to risk mitigation touch the very core of the viability of the respective company (or parts of it). This is what makes them strategic in the eyes of the interviewees. Such decisions are essential for survival.

*Consolidating the View*

We have presented three decision areas in order to provide an illustrative picture of practitioners' reasoning for placing issues into the strategy. The examples given above reasonably reflect the impressions we have gotten across all our interviews. We want to consolidate our overall findings by providing two quantitative measures to mirror our impressions appropriately. However, it must be noted that this survey is qualitative in nature and these measures are provided for illustrative purposes only, and hence, by no means claims mathematical precision or statistical relevance.

- The first measure is the ratio of decisions considered strategic because of a specific rationale to all decisions deemed strategic. This measure can be seen as an indicator for the use of a specific rationale, regardless of its commonality across multiple cases.
- The second measure complements the first one. It is the ratio of cases in which a rationale occurs in all cases. This measure can be seen as an indicator of commonality of a rationale across multiple cases, irrespective of the frequency with which it is used (Table 19.4).

The reason by far most often drawn on for calling a decision strategic is its long-term perspective (a). This rationale (possibly among others) is given by the interviewees for nearly half of the decisions named. Nearly a third of all decisions are deemed strategic because they are fundamental or groundbreaking (b), approximately another third due to their contribution to efficiency increases or cost reductions (c). This last reason, on the other hand, occurs in the greatest number of cases, roughly 4/5, and thus leads the "statistic" in this regard. The two other rationales already mentioned, (a) and (b), score a substantial 2/3 each, and together, the three rationales form the top group. They are comparatively common as well as frequently given. The fourth rationale displayed, optimal support of business strategy (d), is a kind of hybrid. It occurs in approximately 2/3 of all cases, but applies to only 1/6 of all decisions. Thus, it justifies only very specific decisions as strategic, especially in light of its commonness across the cases. The two rationales listed last, guarantee of business continuity (e) and having company-wide effects (f), are somewhat "niche-phenomena." Rationale (e) is used in nearly half of all cases, and hence testifies that the entire package of issues revolving around risk and security are familiar and are not taken lightly nowadays—at least among those we surveyed. Rationale (f), on the other hand, is named in only 1/4 of all cases. It is prominent within the corporate-level cases (4 of 14, nearly 1/3)—the "natural" group to relate it to. Nevertheless, the overall ratio of decisions justified by this rationale comes in comparably low as well (around 1/6).

Beyond the rationales displayed in Table 19.4, some rationales were used in only a few cases (Mocker and Teubner, 2007). Perhaps the most striking one was the application of business strategy

Table 19.4

**Reasoning of Information Strategy Content**

| Major rationales | Ratio of decisions | Ratio of cases |
|---|---|---|
| a. Decision is binding, long-term | Approx. 1/2 (> 1/3) | Approx. 2/3 |
| b. Decision is fundamental, serious, ground-breaking | Approx. 1/3 (>1/4) | Approx. 2/3 |
| c. Decision increases efficiency, reduces costs, facilitates synergies | Approx. 1/3 (>1/4) | Approx. 4/5 |
| d. Decision serves optimal support of business strategy | Approx. 1/6 (> 1/10) | Approx. 2/3 |
| e. Decision guarantees business continuity, prevents breakdowns | Approx. 1/6 (> 1/10) | Approx. 1/2 |
| f. Decision has company-wide importance or company-wide impact | Approx. 1/6 (> 1/10) | Approx. 1/4 |

terminology to IT (e.g., scope, vision, mission, market strategy). However, we found that while the same terminology is used, the underlying theory gets lost in a number of cases. Other rationales were extensions to those listed in rows (a) and (b) in Table 19.4. For example, long-term binding is associated with irreversibility, and groundbreaking—with novelty and change.

*Strategy Contingencies*

Our analysis of the interviews shows that rationale (f) is almost exclusively used in identifying decisions as strategic by the participants of the corporate-level cases of our survey. This observation is substantiated by the contents of the respective information strategies. Issues such as standardization and setting rights and accountability are overly prominent in the corporate-level cases compared with the business-level cases. This can be explained by the organizational situation. Common among the corporate-level cases of our survey is that the interviewee typically heads a (very) small central IT department in an international company with dozens or even hundreds of thousands of employees, for example, about 20 vs. 240,000 people (case 5), 30 vs. 250,000 people (case 9), or 15 vs. 20,000 people (case 8). Although we have not calculated the actual numbers for cases 7 and 11, they are very likely equivalent. It is obvious that the viewpoint of information strategy makers in central units of such organizations differs from those of strategy makers within business units or single-entity companies. The interviewee of case 9 puts it this way: "if you go to a company with 10,000 people, much more competencies can be concentrated in a single organizational entity. But here we have 250,000 people and I have got a handful of people—because of time alone we are not able to delve into matters so deeply." The interviewee of case 5 supports this observation: "ultimately, we are a relatively small department under the CIO with 20 people for the whole company. We cannot at all discuss questions like 'Is DB2 better than Oracle'?"

Generally, interviewees at the corporate level stated that they looked at decisions that have "visibility beyond business unit borders" (case 7). In this case, for example, standardizing the global application architecture is considered strategic "because it has an overarching importance" (similarly, case 5). In another case, decisions on seemingly detailed issues (e.g., how many different development architectures the company runs) are regarded as strategic "whenever they have a corporate-wide impact," or "whenever they are of corporate-wide concern" (case 9). Another example is the decision about the intruder-safe network in case 11, which "has strategic relevance

[also] because there is some need for action that has an impact on everybody. It is a corporate issue." In contrast, functionality to be offered by applications (decision area a) or investment prioritization (area e) is not a matter of dedicated corporate information strategies. When these decisions are affected, corporate information strategy is restricted to projects that go beyond business unit borders (e.g., introducing a corporate-wide enterprise resource planning [ERP] system, case 8). These decisions rather happen at the level of functional and domain expertise, that is, the business level. The same holds true for decisions concerning the IT unit (decision areas h and i). These are made in the IT units themselves, not at the corporate level. To sum up, most decisions made on a corporate level involve decisions about standardization or setting guidelines, regardless of their concrete objects (cf. Figure 19.3).

While we observe some homogeneity in the corporate-level cases, the IT-related topics dealt with strategically in the business-level cases display much greater diversity. Paradoxically, as much as the corporate-level cases are unified by their homogeneity, the business-level cases are unified by their heterogeneity. The content of business-level cases' information strategy depends on a wide range of determinants, one of which is the current business strategy. Take, for example, case 6. In this case, the main business strategy of the bank is to grow aggressively while retaining its independence. One way to achieve this is to "opportunistically . . . seize chances wherever they occur"—most of the time, this means setting up new branches or taking over other banks worldwide. Correspondingly, the main goals of the information strategy are twofold. First, it has to support the ongoing independence of the bank by providing a "core platform," which allows freedom of the technological and organizational restrictions of the parent infrastructure. This independence is then fundamental for the second objective, namely, to enable the bank to "answer quickly to changing situations." For example, if a new branch is going to be set up, "we can support that in no time"—mostly due to independence. Subsequent strategic decisions, for example, concerning the technical architecture, are aligned to these maxims. Hence, the main driver for the information strategy content here is the context of business growth and independence.

Another contingency is the organization of the information function. A good example is case 10, a bank that conducts business solely online. Here, the information function is fully outsourced with only two managers remaining. Owing to this and to the status of being an online-only bank, the two managers quite consequently almost exclusively deal with questions regarding (out-)sourcing and risk mitigation. Further examples are cases 3 and 13, where the information function is organized as a corporate function. Its role and position lies somewhere in the middle between the corporate- and business-level cases. On the one hand, in both cases the IT department acts company-wide with international divisions. But unlike the small central staff departments of the corporate-level cases, they do not stop at making fundamental decisions that light the way for other players down the road (e.g., other departments or other companies). The corporate functions are much greater than the small central staff departments of the corporate-level cases. Hence, they not only make abstract decisions but also are in charge of implementing them in practice. In practice this means that questions as to which concrete hardware, OS, ERP or DBMS to deploy are considered as strategic in these cases. As the above examples show, the content of information strategies is highly dependent on the responsibilities and structure of the organizational unit in charge of information strategy development.

While organizational constraints are the most important determinants of the nature of an information strategy, other, perhaps unexpected factors shape it as well. The first factor is the person making the decision. Sometimes, the topics being dealt with strategically depend on a person's educational background and personal preferences. A good example is the participant from case 1. He is a mathematician and highly interested in progress and new developments in the field of information and communication technology. Hence, architectural standards are part and parcel of his information strategy. Questions like .NET vs. CORBA vs. J2EE, Token Ring vs. Ethernet, and so on are prevalent on the strategy agenda. Other topics such as rights and accountability were not mentioned at all. In addition, he was not even fully informed about details of the company's business strategy.

Another example of a constraint that may not come to mind immediately is the historic reputation of the IT department within the company. In case 13, the IT department had the reputation of being highly inefficient and far removed from the real needs of the business. Hence, the current information strategy deals with cost cutting through standardization of architecture and software, on the one hand, and through establishing organizational structures for the immediate support of the business divisions' needs, on the other. The CIO explains that IT was traditionally "almost 50 percent more costly" than it is today, "very little accepted," and "about to be sourced out completely." Only along the path of "tough cost management" and reorganization "closer to the business" through a key-account-structure did IT manage to regain acceptance. Cost efficiency and the role and organization of the IT in a way that allows immediate business support are still dominant topics on the information strategy agenda (Figure 19.3).

We can conclude that an information strategy is a construct that, in practice, is driven not only by objective needs and rationality. The information strategic content and the decisions made are especially affected by factors such as the personality of the decision maker and historical influences.

## DISCUSSION

The objective of our research is to highlight intersections of the academic discussion between information strategy and SIP practice. In the following, we discuss this intersection in three steps. First, we look at the influence of academic literature on practice. Is the literature well perceived so that we can assume a lively transfer of insights from research to practice? Second, we are interested in the concerns that are considered strategic in practice. Which decision areas are regarded as strategic in practice? How do they differ from organization to organization and, eventually, from those discussed in academia? Third, what are the reasons for ascribing strategic importance to specific IT decisions? And, more specifically, does the reasoning of researchers correspond to that of practitioners?

### Perception of the Academic Discussion in Practice

The most striking insight from our interviews may be that common theoretical concepts of information strategy seem to be absent in practice. One explanation is the preliminary state of research, which does not provide practice with convincing strategy concepts or good reasons for when and why specific IT issues are of strategic concern. In order to better understand the influence of academia on practitioners' conceptions of information strategy, we asked the interviewees whether they—as strategy professionals—used any academic literature. We specified that we were interested in the use of any academic textbooks, articles, or other material including online resources. Surprisingly, all fourteen interviewees ignored academic sources in doing their jobs. Indeed, only three practitioners used academic books (Bernhard, Blomer, and Bonn, 2003; Carr, 2004; Weill and Ross, 2004) in constructing information strategy.

An important reason seemed to be a lack of practical use of recommendations from academia. As the interviewee in case 5 (and almost identically, case 7) put it: "of course you can get some suggestions. . . . But at the end of the day you have to make the decisions yourself. . . . And if it goes wrong and you say: well, I'm sorry, but book ABC says that this was exactly the right way, they will say: man, you are mad!" Another respondent stated: "I have to think it through myself anyway" (case 4), indicating that academic literature seems unreliable to him and also cannot be used to gain credibility in the boardroom.

Another reason given by practitioners for not using academic literature is that this literature is not supportive in practice. One complaint is that it is on an overly abstract theoretical level: "In scientific literature, I often miss the concrete guidelines that can immediately be translated into action. If a book on strategy begins with discussing the question 'do I say IS or IT?' over 20 pages, I cannot do anything with it" (case 5). Other interviewees (cases 3, 6, 8) declared that literature was not applicable to the specific situation of their organization. The interviewee in case 3 said: "our situation is too special here," that is, the concepts from academia were regarded as being either too general or—referring to case examples given in literature—too specific to be applicable. A "gedankenexperiment" as elaborate as Earl's might appear too conceptual and hence lack appeal for practitioners to apply it in their individual situation. And structurally more easily approachable constructs, such as enumerated lists, obviously lack acceptance because of their arbitrariness and remoteness to practitioners' practical concerns. Hence, reading books is not considered valuable enough to divert time to: "of course, there is Carr, there are the books of Weill dealing with governance, there are other books from MIT, but naturally, in the day-to-day business there is hardly any time left to wade through big theoretical tomes" (case 5). As a result, the professionals relied on recommendations from management consultants and discussions in practitioner magazines and at conferences rather than on academic sources (e.g., cases 6, 8, 10, 11).

## Strategy Conceptions and Contents

Our interviews do not allow a final conclusion on whether research deficiencies are the reason that academic literature is neglected in practice. It must be said that even more systematic concepts such as Earl's approach are ignored in practice as confirmed by Brady and colleagues (1992, p. 187). However, our research corroborates the belief that the discussion of strategy in academia is detached from practice. For example, while the project portfolio is seen in the literature to be at the heart of an information strategy, it does not play an important role in practice. Only four strategies included this decision to some extent. In all of these cases, the application portfolio was seen as an interface to the business. Other cases did not include setting up a project portfolio in their information strategies. This is not to say that projects were not planned at all, but they were eventually planned project by project. In these cases, the business areas requested cost estimates from the IT department as a basis for initiating a project. As one interviewee (case 3) said: "I am very Adam Smith driven. Let the internal market rule itself." Most of these companies lacked an overall investment plan for the application portfolio as a whole.

Another expectation raised in the literature is that the question of how to gain competitive advantage through the use of IT is a core strategic concern. Yet, identifying SIS or competitive IS/IT resources was hardly on the strategy agenda of the companies we investigated. Looking at the decisions described in the third section of the chapter, most refer to "managing IT" rather than "using IT" to the advantage of the business. The focus is not on how IT can be used to extend the scope of the company or to be more competitive, but on gaining IT synergies, for example, by standardizing IT processes, and so on. Hence, information strategies are directed inward rather than toward competitors. In this respect, the strategies in practice are similar to departmental plans. However, with the exception of case 14, we were unable to confirm that the information strategies were explicitly conceptualized as departmental plans.

Due to a lack of inherent logic and structure, information strategies in practice prima facie are most similar to "enumerated lists." But as far as content is concerned, a closer investigation reveals that they do not correspond very closely to the lists distilled or proposed in the literature. As mentioned above, the portfolio as a key academic concern plays a subordinate role in practice. In contrast, we found standardization to be a major concern, which is hardly addressed by the issue lists in academic literature. Beyond the significant differences in the topics included in the practitioners' strategy agenda as opposed to those discussed in academia, we found that the latter are not used as a reference for setting the strategy agenda in practice. We did not even find evidence that the lists of issues in the literature are noticed or even used as a practical source of ideas. Admittedly, this comes as no surprise, since these lists are highly random and demonstrate an obvious lack of reason.

### Strategy Contingencies

In the absence of theoretically well-reasoned information strategy concepts or models that could serve as a common reference point, our study draws a diverse picture of information strategy contents in practice (Figure 19.3). The breadth of information strategy contents ranges from very narrow and limited (e.g., case 1) to very broad and differentiated (e.g., case 4). Patterns are hard to discern at first sight, with one exception: corporate-level strategies are somewhat coherent in that they concentrate on the organization-wide information infrastructure and the coordination of its management across decentralized IT units, for example, by setting architectural and application systems standards or by issuing rights and decision rules. It is all the more surprising that academic IS literature barely distinguishes between business-level and corporate strategies. There are only few hints in this direction. For example, Andreu, Ricart, and Valor (1992) propose a normative model for integrating strategic business planning with strategic IS/IT planning. This model starts with business planning. Here it distinguishes between a corporate and business unit level as elaborated in the strategic management literature (Vancil and Lorange, 1975). In so doing, the authors also distinguish a corporate and a business unit level of strategic IS/IT planning. However, the consequences for the content of information strategy have not yet been addressed.

Beyond the differentiation of corporate- and business-level strategies, information strategy content seems to be idiosyncratic for each organization. Patterns are weak and nonexclusive (Mocker and Teubner, 2007). In other words, rather than exhibiting dominant designs, the content of information strategies in practice seems to be contingent on characteristics of the organization's external and internal situation. Candidates for contingencies are the industry and the information intensity of the business (online bank vs. financial services vs. production), or the depth of in-house production (case 4), that is, the level of in-/outsourcing (case 10). A further internal organizational characteristic that influences the strategy content is the role of IT, both from the organizational and appreciation points of view. For example, when IT is run as a business on its own, the focus might be more on budget decisions and the role of IT than would be the case for IT as a traditional department without accountability for cost (cf. case 4). When IT plays the role of merely a service function to the organization (cf. case 14), the strategy focus might be the realization of the application project portfolio and the resources available for it (budget, staff). Less objective contingencies such as the personality (e.g., education, interests, prestige) of the decision maker (cases 1, 3), or the historically based reputation of the IT-department (case 13) might also apply.

### Strategy Reasoning

Differences between practitioners and academic discussions were observed not only in the content of information strategies but also in practitioners' reasoning. Rationales such as cost reduction or criticality are prominent in practice but have little foundation in strategy theory.

On the other hand, the most mature academic theories such as the theory on IT and competitive advantage are hardly part of practitioners' thinking. Academics might say that the strategy agenda in practice is too pragmatic, too driven by day-to-day needs, and not reflective of long-term interests. This criticism is also partly supported by the fact that even in cases where rationales from strategy theory are applied, this is done superficially and thus may be misleading. For example, "long-term binding" is often referred to as a criterion for regarding an IT-decision as strategic. Krcmar (1991) demonstrates that many IT decisions result in long-term liabilities. Typical binding periods for hardware decisions are up to five years while for software they are five to seven years. Decisions on data structures may even be binding for up to ten years. Nevertheless, it is questionable whether the choice of a proprietary host computer or the definition of a data structure is strategic in nature (ibid., p. 189).

## CONCLUSIONS AND OUTLOOK

In summary, our research supports the initial hypothesis that there is a gap between information strategy research and practice. Given that the information systems discipline accepts the challenge of offering practical help to managers, researchers have to analyze the reasons for such a disconnect. Has research been unsuccessful in transferring its insights into practice? Has research ignored relevant concerns? Has research even lost touch with practice?

We found some support for affirmative answers to these questions. Only three practitioners in our sample could even quote academic sources on information strategy at all, although they did not say they actually made use of them in their jobs. Instead, practitioners often used the reports of analysts and consultants. In some cases, information strategy formation was perceived more as a game to convince top management than a sophisticated plan for the future of IS/IT. Here, consultants' expertise seems to have much more weight and credibility than academic literature. The following statement (case 11) supports this view: "Typically you get consultants in to develop the IT strategy document. And the next three years you continue it yourself until you realize: okay, now we need a fundamental change and get consultants back in. Thus, systematically you do not need any literature because the crucial point for people dealing with IT strategy . . . is to have an aid for convincing why you want to do it the way you do. And the best aid for convincing is of course you have McKinsey or Cap Gemini or Arthur Andersen or something in the company. Then you do not need to do a lot of convincing anymore. Put in simple terms, this is what's behind it."

Better accessibility to and transfer of the results of academic research might smooth the disconnection between academia and practice to some extent. However, limited transfer is only a minor part of the problem. As our research reveals, it is more important that practical concerns in making information strategy are ignored in the academic discussion. This is not to say that academia should adopt its research agenda for information strategy without reflection. There is a certain risk in directing research toward whatever practitioners demand. Galliers (1995, p. 49) reflectively asks for the "extent to which the research agenda should be dictated by concerns in the world of commerce and industry." One reason he provides for this is that "IT directors too readily follow the latest 'silver bullet' and are taken by the hyperbole surrounding certain of the management fads" (Galliers, 1995, p. 49). And indeed, a comparison of the strategy topics discussed in practitioner magazines with those we found to make up the content of practitioners' information strategies somewhat supports this claim. In other words, current IT trends might influence practitioners' understanding of information strategy that should not be uncritically fed back to research. The recent e-commerce hype may be taken as a prominent example.

Nevertheless, it is necessary for academia to scrutinize information strategies in practice in more detail with a special interest in strategy content and reasoning. Our research suggests that even the construct of information strategy itself must be considerably more differentiated. Corporate-level strategies obviously have concerns and reasoning other than business-level strategies. Moreover, research needs to explore the purposes and contingencies of information strategy in more detail in order to better judge the justification of practitioners' strategy agendas.

## NOTES

This chapter builds on research results that have been presented at the ECIS 2005 and the AMCIS 2007 (cf. Mocker, Teubner 2005 and 2007).

1. The interviewee in case 11 provided both perspectives. For this reason, case 11 appears separately in both groups in Figure 19.3.

## ACKNOWLEDEGEMENTS

The authors acknowledge the support of the BTM Institute.

## REFERENCES

Allen, D.K., and Wilson, T.D. 1996. Information strategies in UK higher education institutions. *International Journal of Information Management,* 16, 4, 239–251.

Andreu, R.; Ricart, J.E.; and Valor, J. 1992. *Information Systems Strategic Planning. A Source of Competitive Advantage.* Blackwell: Oxford.

Bajjaly, S.T. 1998. Strategic information systems planning in the public sector. *American Review of Public Administration,* 28, 1, 75–85.

Bakos, J.Y., and Treacy, M.E. 1986. Information technology and corporate strategy: a research perspective. *MIS Quarterly,* 10, 2, 106–119.

Bernhard, M.G.; Blomer, R.; and Bonn, J. (eds.). 2003. *Strategisches IT-Management 2. Fallbeispiele und praktische Umsetzung.* Düsseldorf: Symposion.

Boddy, D.; Boonstra, A.; and Kennedy, G. 2005. *Managing Information Systems: An Organisational Perspective,* 2d ed. Harlow, UK: Prentice Hall.

Brady, T.; Cameron, R.; Targett, D.; and Beaumont, C. 1992. Strategic IT issues: the views of some major IT investors. *Journal of Strategic Information Systems,* 1, 4, 183–189.

Brown, I.T.J. 2004. Testing and extending theory in strategic information systems planning through literature analysis. *Information Resources Management Journal,* 17, 4, 20–48.

Carr, N.G. 2003. IT doesn't matter. *Harvard Business Review,* 81, 5, 41–49.

———. 2004. *Does IT Matter? Information Technology and the Corrosion of Competitive Advantage.* Boston: Harvard Business School Press.

Chan, Y.E.; Huff, S.L.; Barclay, D.W.; and Copeland, D.G. 1998. Business strategic orientation, information systems strategic orientation, and strategic alignment. *Information Systems Research,* 8, 2, 125–150.

Conrath, D.W.; Ang, J.S.K.; and Mattay, S. 1992. Strategic planning for information systems: a survey of Canadian organizations. *Infor,* 30, 4, 364–378.

Cropley, A.J. 2005. *Qualitative Forschungsmethoden—Eine praxisnahe Einführung,* 2d ed. Eschborn: Verlag Dietmar Klotz.

Das, S.R.; Zahra, S.A.; and Warkentin, M.E. 1991. Integrating the content and process of strategic MIS planning with competitive strategy. *Decision Sciences,* 22, 5, 953–984.

Doherty, N.F., and Fulford, H. 2006. Aligning the information security policy with the strategic information systems plan. *Computers & Security,* 25, 1, 55–63.

Eardley, A., and Lewis, T. 1996. The linkage between IT and business strategy in competitive systems: a reappraisal of some "classic" cases using a competition analysis framework. *International Journal of Technology Management,* 11, 3, 395–411.

Earl, M.J. 1988. Formulation of information systems strategies: emerging lessons and frameworks. In M.J. Earl (ed.), *Information Management: The Strategic Dimension.* Oxford: Oxford University Press, pp. 157–174.

———. 1989. *Management Strategies for Information Technology.* Oxford: Prentice Hall.

————. 1996. Integrating IS and the organization. In M.J. Earl (ed.), *Information Management: The Organizational Dimension.* Oxford: Oxford University Press.

————. 2000. Every business is an information business. In D.A. Marchand, T.H. Davenport, and T. Dickson (eds.), *Mastering Information Management.* London: Prentice Hall, pp. 16–22.

————. 2003. Integrating business and IT strategy. In J.N. Luftman (ed.), *Competing in the Information Age: Align in the Sand.* Oxford: Oxford University Press, 51–61.

Flynn, D.J., and Goleniewska, E. 1993. A survey of the use of strategic information systems planning approaches in UK organizations. *Journal of Strategic Information Systems,* 2, 4, 292–319.

Galliers, R.D. 1991. Strategic information systems planning: myths, reality and guidelines for successful implementation. *European Journal of Information Systems,* 1, 1, 55–64.

————. 1993a. IT strategies: beyond competitive advantage. *Journal of Strategic Information Systems,* 2, 4, 283–291.

————. 1993b. Research issues in information systems. *Journal of Information Technology,* 8, 92–98.

————. 1995. A manifesto for information management research. *British Journal of Management,* 6, 4, 45–52.

————. 2004. Reflections on information systems strategizing. In C. Avgerou, C. Ciborra, and F. Land (eds.), *The Social Study of Information and Communication Technology.* Oxford: Oxford University Press.

Gottschalk, P. 1999a. Implementation of formal plans: the case of information technology strategy. *Long Range Planning,* 32, 3, 362–372.

————. 1999b. Implementation predictors of strategic information systems plans. *Information & Management,* 36, 2, 77–91.

Hayward, R.G. 1987. Developing an information strategy. *Long Range Planning,* 20, 2, 100–113.

Heinrich, L.J., and Lehner, F. 2005. *Informationsmanagement,* 8th ed. Munich and Vienna: Oldenbourg.

Henderson, J.C., and Venkatraman, N. 1999. Strategic alignment: leveraging information technology for transforming organizations. *IBM Systems Journal,* 38, 2, 472–478.

Kettinger, W.J.; Grover, V.; Guha, S.; and Segars, A.H. 1994. Strategic information systems revisited: a study in sustainability and performance. *MIS Quarterly,* 18, 1, 31–58.

Krcmar, H. 1991. Annäherung an Informationsmangement—Managementdisziplin und/oder Technologiedisziplin? In W.H. Staehle and J. Sydow (eds.), *Managementforschung 1.* Berlin: DeGruyter, pp. 63–203.

Lawrence, D.B. 1999. *The Economic Value of Information.* Berlin: Springer.

Lederer, A.L., and Gardiner, V. 1992. The process of strategic information planning. *Journal of Strategic Information Systems,* 1, 2, 76–84.

Lederer, A.L., and Salmela, H. 1996. Toward a theory of strategic information systems planning. *Journal of Strategic Information Systems,* 5, 3, 237–253.

Lederer, A.L., and Sethi, V. 1992. Root causes of strategic information systems planning implementation problems. *Journal of Management Information Systems,* 9, 1, 25–46.

Lederer, A.L., and Sethi, V. 1998. Seven guidelines for strategic information systems planning. *Information Strategy,* 15, 1, 23–28.

Lee, Z.; Gosain, S.; and Im, I. 1999. Topics of interest in IS: evolution of themes and differences between research and practice. *Information and Management,* 36, 5, 233–246.

Lehner, F. 1993. *Informatik-strategien: Entwicklung, Einsatz und Erfahrungen.* Munich and Vienna: Hanser.

Luftman, J.; Kempaiah, R.; and Nash, E. 2006. Key issues for IT executives 2000. *MIS Quarterly Executive,* 5, 2, 27–45.

Maritan, C.A., and Schendel, D.E. 1997. Strategy and decision processes: what is the linkage? In V. Papadakis and P. Barwise (eds.), *Strategic Decisions.* Doredrecht, Boston, London: Kluwer, pp. 259–266.

Mayring, P. 1996. *Einführung in die qualitative Sozialforschung,* 3d ed. Weinheim: Beltz Psychologie Verlags Union.

McFarlan, F.W. 1984. Information technology changes the way you compete. *Harvard Business Review,* 62, 3, 98–103.

McGee, K.; Plummer, D.C.; Comport, J.; Tully, J.; Hafner, B.; Mahoney, J.; Fenn, J.; Morello, D.; McDonald, M.P.; Prentice, S.; and Kutnick, D. 2005. The Gartner scenario 2005: IT leaders' next big decisions. Gartner.

McLeod, R. 1998. *Management Information Systems,* 7th ed. Upper Saddle River, NJ: Prentice Hall.

Melville, N.; Kraemer, K.; and Gurbaxani, V. 2004. Review: information technology and organizational performance: an integrative model of IT business value. *MIS Quarterly,* 28, 2, 283–322.

Miles, M.B., and Huberman, A.M. 1994. *Qualitative Data Analysis,* 2d ed. Thousand Oaks, CA: Sage.

Mocker, M. 2007. Defining the content of information strategy: linking theory and practice. Ph.D. diss. University of Muenster, Muenster.

Mocker, M., and Teubner, R.A. 2005. Towards a comprehensive model of information strategy. *Proceedings of the Thirteenth European Conference on Information Systems*, Regensburg. 26. to 28. of May, 2005.

———. 2006. Information strategy—Research and reality. *Fourteenth European Conference on Information Systems*, Gothenburg. June 12–14, 2006.

Mocker, M., and Teubner, A. 2007. Contents of Information Strategies in Practice. *Proceedings of the Americas Conference on Information Systems*, Keystone. August 9–12, 2007.

Piccoli, G., and Ives, B. 2005. Review: IT-dependent strategic initiatives and sustained competitive advantage: a review and synthesis of the literature. *MIS Quarterly*, 29, 4, 747–776.

Porter, M.E. 1980. *Competitive Strategy*. New York: Free Press.

———. 2001. Strategy and the Internet. *Harvard Business Review*, 79, 3, 62–78.

Porter, M.E., and Millar, V.E. 1985. How information gives you competitive advantage. *Harvard Business Review*, 63, 4, 149–160.

Ragu-Nathan, B.; Ragu-Nathan, T.S.; Tu, Q.; and Shi, Z. 2001. Information management (IM) strategy: the construct and its measurement. *Journal of Strategic Information Systems*, 10, 4, 265–289.

Senn, J.A. 1992. The myths of strategic systems: what defines true competitive advantage? *Information Systems Management*, 9, 3, 7–12.

Smits, M.T.; Poel, K.G.v.d.; and Ribbers, P.M.A. 2003. Assessment of information strategies in insurance companies in the Netherlands. In R.D. Galliers and D.E. Leidner (eds.), *Strategic Information Management*. Oxford: Buttersworth-Heinemann, pp. 64–81.

Steinmann, H., and Schreyögg, G. 2002. *Management—Grundlagen der Unternehmensführung*. Wiesbaden: Gabler.

Stephens, C.S.; Ledbetter, W.N.; Mitra, A.; and Ford, F.N. 1992. Executive or functional manager? the nature of the CIO's job. *MIS Quarterly*, 16, 4, 449–466.

Teo, T.S.H., and Ang, J.S.K. 2000. How useful are strategic plans for information systems? *Behaviour & Information Technology*, 19, 4, 275–282.

Teubner, R.A. 2007. Strategic information systems planning: a case study from the financial services industry. *Journal of Strategic Information Systems*, 16, 1, 105–125.

Teubner, R.A., and Klein, S. 2002. Vergleichende Buchbesprechung Informationsmanagement. *Wirtschaftsinformatik*, 44, 3, 285–294.

Vancil, R.F., and Lorange, P. 1975. Strategic planning in diversified companies. *Harvard Business Review*, 53, 1, 81–90.

Wade, M., and Hulland, J. 2004. Review: the resource-based view and information systems research: review, extension, and suggestions for future research. *MIS Quarterly*, 28, 1, 107–142.

Ward, J., and Peppard, J. 2004. *Strategic Planning for Information Systems*. Chichester, UK: Wiley.

Watson, R.T.; Kelly, G.G.; Galliers, R.D.; and Brancheau, J.C. 1997. Key issues in information systems management: an international perspective. *Journal of Management Information Systems*, 13, 4, 91–116.

Weill, P., and Ross, J.W. 2004. *IT Governance*. Boston: Harvard Business School Press.

Wernerfelt, B. 1995. The resource-based view of the firm: ten years after. *Strategic Management Journal*, 16, 3, 171–174.

Wexelblat, R.L., and Srinivasan, N. 1999. Planning for information technology in a federated organization. *Information & Management*, 35, 265–282.

Wilson, T.D. 1989. The implementation of information system strategies in UK companies: aims and barriers to success. *International Journal of Information Management*, 9, 4, 1989, 245–258.

Wiseman, C. 1985. *Strategy and Computers: Information Systems as Competitive Weapons*. Homewood, IL: Dow Jones-Irwin.

# CHAPTER 20

# HOW INFORMATION TECHNOLOGY INFRASTRUCTURE FLEXIBILITY SHAPES STRATEGIC ALIGNMENT

## A Case Study Investigation with Implications for Strategic IS Planning

### PAUL P. TALLON

**Abstract:** *Strategic alignment or the fit between information technology (IT) and business strategy remains a primary topic of concern among executives worldwide. Over time, the pursuit of alignment has grown more complicated as firms struggle to adapt their business strategy to an increasingly volatile world. Planning for alignment in such situations is fraught with risk as firms seek to understand how much flexibility to add to their IT infrastructure so as to maintain consistently high levels of alignment. In this chapter, we explore six case studies in aerospace, banking, career services, health insurance, printing, and software firms that confirm the complex nature of such decisions. Using data from surveys and detailed interviews of IT and business executives in these six firms, we identify a positive relationship between IT infrastructure flexibility and strategic alignment with strategic information systems planning (SISP) serving as a moderator of this relationship. For example, we reveal that firms with inflexible IT infrastructure exhibit chaotic SISP while those with flexible IT infrastructure have more structured information systems (IS) planning. This result highlights the need for firms to use IS planning processes to consistently monitor the relationship between IT infrastructure flexibility and alignment. Doing so during periods of increased change and uncertainty reduces the risk of being ensnared by rigidity traps that could transform IT into an inhibitor rather than an enabler of change.*

**Keywords:** *Value Disciplines, Strategic Alignment, SISP, IS Planning, Rigidity Traps, IT Business Value, IT Infrastructure Flexibility*

> *Strategy is the act of aligning a company and its environment. That environment, as well as the firm's own capabilities, is subject to change. Thus, the task of strategy is to maintain a dynamic, not a static balance.*
> —Porter (1991, p. 97)

## INTRODUCTION

Despite a plethora of new and emerging technologies such as Web services, utility computing, and radio frequency identification (RFID), executives continue to rank strategic alignment between information technology (IT) and business strategy among the most critical issues facing their firms (CSC, 2001; Luftman, Kempaiah, and Nash, 2006). Whether described in terms of fit (Henderson and Venkatraman, 1993), linkage (Reich and Benbasat, 1996), integration (Broadbent and Weill, 1993; Weill and Broadbent, 1998), or harmony (Luftman, 1996), the intent of alignment remains that of architecting IT to support the business strategy.[1] In recent years, alignment has evolved from cross-referencing of IT and business plans to aligning complex forms of IT to an evolving business strategy (Porter, 1991; Sabherwal and Chan, 2001). Alignment is today considered an exercise in IT resource allocation and control that, on a process-by-process basis, supports the *actual* activities underlying business strategy (Chan et al., 1997; Ravichandran and Lertwongsatien, 2005; Tallon, 2008).

Executives regard change as one of the primary challenges confronting alignment (Luftman, Papp, and Brier, 1999). As a collection of activities—arranged as a value chain, shop, or network (Porter, 1985; Stabell and Fjeldstad, 1998)—strategy can evolve or alter course as firms revise their goals for operating efficiency or market positioning (Porter, 1996). Changes in business strategy are typically motivated by events such as price wars, reduced demand, or the launch of a new product by a competitor (Mendelson and Pillai, 1998). The primary challenge with alignment, however, is whether IT can keep pace with the changes sought by firms, and, beyond this, how firms can better plan for, and architect, IT to respond to change. Not all firms experience change in the same way. For example, in the wood products industry, change is infrequent and incremental. With few disruptive innovations, product life cycles are long and products are commoditized (Christensen, 1997). Meanwhile, in the banking industry, change is both frequent and disruptive. Planning for sudden and unexpected change is a critical element of strategic information systems planning (SISP) if firms are not only to maintain a sense of readiness or agility but also to obtain higher payoffs from IT (Segars and Grover, 1999; Tallon, Kraemer, and Gurbaxani, 2000; Venkatraman and Ramanujam, 1987). If IT is slow to change—as is characteristic of legacy systems that lead to rigidity traps or organizational intransigence (Bharadwaj, 2000)—IT cannot be a source of sustainable advantage. On the other hand, if IT is responsive to change, firms are less likely to experience a decline in firm performance.

Although SISP may be more readily associated with setting overarching or strategic goals for IT (Segars and Grover, 1998), the ever-present threat of change masks a need for firms to reposition SISP to resolve how specific applications and even commoditized IT assets can enhance a firm's preparedness for change. In a world that is competitively *flat* and unpredictable (Friedman, 2006), the task of maintaining alignment has become more complex while the opportunity cost of misalignment has similarly increased (Venkatraman, Henderson, and Oldach, 1993). Firms recognize the benefits of alignment through greater profitability (Chan et al., 1997), better market positioning (Kearns and Lederer, 2003), and superior IT business value (Tallon, Kraemer, and Gurbaxani, 2000), but they do not want to use IT resources that, while beneficial in the short term, could trigger rigidity traps at a later point (Bharadwaj, 2000). If this happens, refocusing IT to support a new or revised strategy could prove difficult for several reasons. Consistent with Porter's (1991) vision of strategy as a dynamic response to environmental change, what firms seek is *dynamic alignment* or a way to maintain tight fit between IT and business strategy even in the face of intense market change (Sabherwal, Hirschheim, and Goles, 2001; Venkatraman, Henderson, and Oldach, 1993). Achieving dynamic alignment is far from certain, however.

Research argues that information systems (IS) planning success is due in part to capabilities such as problem identification, environmental scanning, an ability to react to change, and an ability to use these capabilities for aligning IT with business strategy (Earl, 1993; Segars and Grover, 1998). In the same way that there are differences between intended and actual strategies, in this chapter, we go beyond ex ante predictors of SISP success to investigate what firms are actually doing to achieve and maintain alignment. As Mintzberg and Waters (1985) reveal, the success of any planning process is determined by execution and subsequent performance. Accordingly, we explore what firms have done, vis-à-vis using IT infrastructure flexibility—defined in terms of hardware, software, networks, and technical skills—to generate tighter fit between IT and business strategy while looking behind this relationship for signs of SISP effectiveness.

Using interview and survey data from six case studies, we find that SISP has a profound effect on the link between IT infrastructure flexibility and alignment. We learn, for example, that low IT infrastructure flexibility (or what might be described as IT rigidity) and misalignment can be traced to chaotic or, in some cases, nonexistent IS planning. Meanwhile, high IT infrastructure flexibility and its ability to forge and maintain tight fit during periods of heightened change can be traced to a well-run IS planning process where considerable effort is spent learning and understanding information needs through close interaction with users, exploring IT investment options, alternatives, and risks, and monitoring IT payoffs over time.[2]

We add to the evolving literature on strategic IS planning by providing insights into a range of IT challenges facing firms as they try to achieve alignment in a volatile setting. While the IT artifact is often blamed for firms' inability to react to change (e.g., legacy issues), we find that IT inflexibility is a primary outcome of weak or ineffective IS planning. Trying to curtail rigidity traps through investment in flexible IT will ensure some sense of relief but our analysis shows that in the long term, more effective IS planning, rather than flexible IT, is a necessary first step on the long road toward continuous alignment.

The remainder of this chapter is as follows: in the next section, we provide a summary of what we know from the IS literature concerning the links between IT infrastructure flexibility and alignment. Next, we assess our methodology: we focus first on survey-based measures of IT and business strategy (that we use to quantitatively derive alignment), industry clockspeed (a proxy for environmental volatility), and IT infrastructure flexibility; next we reveal the firms where we collected interview data from business and IT executives. After analyzing our data, we report our results with particular emphasis on the role of SISP in delivering alignment. Finally, we summarize the contribution and limitations of our research and conclude.

## THEORETICAL BACKGROUND

Regardless of definition—fit, integration, linkage, and harmony—the view among IS practitioners and academics is that tighter fit or alignment leads to greater firm performance (Chan et al., 1997; Kearns and Lederer, 2003). Yet, when research has used typologies to evaluate alignment in firms with different strategies, cracks have begun to appear in the general rule that more alignment is always better. Using the Miles and Snow (1978) typology, for example, Sabherwal and Chan (2001) find that *defenders* pursuing a low-cost strategy fail to see any marginal improvement in performance from greater alignment. In a study of specialty retailers, Palmer and Markus (2000) argue that alignment has become a *commodity* as it is no longer able to differentiate between firms on standard retail performance metrics. Last, using the Treacy and Wiersema (1995) typology, Tallon (2008) reveals that customer intimate and product leadership firms realize higher value from IT in processes such as customer relations, marketing, and product enhancement because of higher alignment in these areas, while for operationally excellent firms (similar to defenders in their use of low cost as a primary means of competition), alignment provides little or no marginal benefit.

What is interesting about these findings is that research also shows that low-cost strategies tend to be prevalent in stable environments while niche or differentiation strategies (similar to customer intimate or product leadership under the Treacy and Wiersema [1995] typology) are prevalent in turbulent settings (Porter, 1980; White, 1986). What this means is that firms are unlikely to need a flexible IT infrastructure if they are only competing on low cost; competition in such firms is not based on product or service variety or superior service levels but on productivity and efficiency (Porter, 1996). For instance, Scottrade is a low-cost leader among brokerage firms with $7 commissions. Because each client receives identical treatment, Scottrade has not had to develop IT to reflect different customer segments with varying service expectations or to offer accounts with distinct features and functions for each client. Instead, Scottrade focuses on order handling and transaction speed. In contrast, because U.S. Trust (part of Bank of America) caters to affluent investors with high service expectations, IT has had to satisfy idiosyncratic needs such as providing trading accounts with special money market features or that link to places such as offshore banks, investment trusts, and tax authorities. IT may not be a differentiator in this scenario, but not having a flexible IT platform to offer such services will make it difficult to acquire high net-worth individuals and to operate a successful strategy of customer intimacy. Flexible IT is the price of entry into this high-end market.

Past research by Miller (1993), Miller and Chen (1996), and Miller and colleagues (1996) uses the notion of strategic simplicity to portray a business strategy with a singular focus. *Simplicity,* they note, is often used by firms in a stable setting while *complexity*—denoting a multifocused strategy—is used instead by firms in an unstable setting. In the latter situation, firms face myriad competitive attacks involving product variety, service levels, and low cost. Succeeding in a volatile setting can be a function of organizational slack or an ability to allocate resources to a task as the need arises. Firms may not have the luxury of competing in just one area such as product differentiation if they risk an attack from niche or low-cost competitors.[3] Despite fears of channel conflict, firms may have little choice but to pursue a multifocused strategy. This then leads us to ask whether IT can support a wide range of competitive actions if firms decide to pursue a broad strategy, given that change can now occur in any number of areas whether that is low-cost pricing, the introduction of new and innovative products and services, or a more advanced level of client service.

Prior research argues that an ability to redirect IT resources to counter competitive threats (e.g., to target a low-cost competitor) or to take advantage of new opportunities (e.g., launching a new service), is a key determinant of firm success (Ravichandran and Lertwongsatien, 2005). For IT to boast this level of adaptiveness calls for an awareness of the challenges that IT is likely to face in the medium to long term. This implies that success is based on a formal, comprehensive, and coordinated planning process, and that a key part of this process will entail planning for a flexible IT infrastructure to support the required level of adaptiveness (Bharadwaj, Sambamurthy, and Zmud, 2002; Segars and Grover, 1999; Segars, Grover, and Teng, 1998).

**IT Infrastructure Flexibility: A New Competitive Weapon**

Prior research by Davenport and Linder (1994), Keen (1991), Tallon (2007), Weill and Broadbent (1998), and others identifies the value of using a flexible IT infrastructure to support shared services, best-of-breed applications, and connectivity inside and across firm boundaries, which can scale to accommodate growth in the user base. IT infrastructure consumes over 50 percent of IT budgets (Gurbaxani, Melville, and Kraemer, 1998; Weill and Broadbent, 1998). Much of this spending is said to provide little or largely diminishing value to firms (Carr, 2003), although counterarguments from resource-based theorists would posit that it is not spending but capabilities that generate value (Bharadwaj, 2000; Ray, Muhanna, and Barney, 2005; Sambamurthy, Bharadwaj, and Grover, 2003). In this vein, research emphasizes capabilities that allow IT infrastructure to scale according to different end-user needs or to vary in scope in a way that infrastructure can accommodate an eclectic mix of IT applications, operating systems, and data formats (Duncan, 1995; Keen, 1991). A flexible IT infrastructure is also seen as an essential factor in organizational efforts to improve strategic agility (Weill, Subramani, and Broadbent, 2002).

Exploratory work by Duncan (1995) and Byrd and Turner (2000) conceptualizes IT infrastructure flexibility in terms of four constructs: hardware compatibility, software modularity, network connectivity, and IT skills adaptability—constructs that independently and collectively define IT infrastructure flexibility as the ability of IT infrastructure to easily and quickly scale and evolve according to the needs of the market. In this way, rigidity traps occur when hardware is incompatible, if networks cannot scale, if software cannot be easily customized or altered, or if skills are proprietary or linked to a specific technology platform with little relevance elsewhere. Using these constructs, Tallon (2007) finds that IT infrastructure flexibility is a key predictor of agility or the ease and speed with which firms can revise the configuration or output of key business processes. Equally, Ross, Weill, and Robertson (2006) use architecture maturity as a predictor of process adaptiveness and corporate success. The key point in their results is that as infrastructure matures, it does so by substituting local or process-level flexibility for global or firm-wide flexibility.

## Linking IT Infrastructure Flexibility with Alignment

What then of the link between infrastructure and alignment? In what is now a classic study in the alignment literature, Henderson and Venkatraman (1993) interpret alignment as a sequential link between business strategy and IT strategy, and between IT strategy and IT infrastructure. Business strategy acts as the starting point in this sequence but IT infrastructure is what ultimately decides whether alignment will succeed or not. In later studies, Venkatraman, Henderson, and Oldach (1993) depict human and technological capabilities as necessary for continuous alignment. Human capabilities refer to technical IT skills such as programming, operations, database design, and an ability to represent business knowledge or rules in technical solutions. Technological capabilities, on the other hand, involve the design and application of hardware, software, and networks to meet a range of business needs. Both of these capabilities map to the four elements of IT infrastructure flexibility noted by Byrd and Turner (2000) and Duncan (1995) in their exploratory studies.

Continuous alignment means that whatever strategy a firm would like to pursue, IT will be able to provide the necessary support even if that strategy should evolve or alter direction due to higher volatility. For example, before airlines such as Delta and United added low-cost carriers to their fleet, a key decision was whether the extant IT infrastructure could carry the extra booking load or if an entirely new and separate infrastructure was needed. Other firms such as Abercrombie and Fitch (a fashion retailer) have added separate sports and junior clothing stores to their existing lines with minimal effort. Although these stores attract different demographic segments and use different brand strategies, the underlying IT infrastructure is sufficiently flexible to support the needs of *all* stores at the same time. What this means for alignment is that as firms expand the scale and scope of their strategy by adding new lines of business or by growing the volume of business, IT must be able to match the underlying changes in business strategy so that at no point is the business strategy devoid of IT support.

Besides evaluating the flexible nature of IT infrastructure by asking managers whether IT exhibits certain properties such as allowing the seamless transfer of data between systems, modular system design, or applications interoperability, it is possible to infer certain traits from the physical nature of the IT assets in use within a firm. For example, Oh and Pinsonneault (2006) associate certain

IT systems with different IT strategies: sales force automation, order processing, and customer management systems suggest a sales growth strategy; just in time (JIT), electronic data interchange (EDI), billing, production scheduling, supply chain, and payroll systems reveal a cost reduction or operational efficiency strategy; robotics, computer-aided design (CAD), research and development (R&D), and quality control systems indicate an IT strategy based on quality improvement. The critical issue, as argued by Ray, Barney, and Muhanna, (2004), is that IT resources in isolation are unlikely to have a sustainable impact on firm performance. Rather, it is the combination of IT and non-IT resources such as knowledge or IS–business cohesion that allows IT to deliver superior results. In theory, alignment creates value in a like manner. While it is possible to discover the IT resources that firms use through media reports, the way that IT is embedded or used in business processes is usually difficult to detect. The presence of flexible IT resources is likely to further complicate and frustrate efforts to replicate any advantage a firm may receive from alignment, as seen in past efforts by PC manufacturers to imitate the success of Dell's model by copying their operations and IT systems (Kraemer, Dedrick, and Yamashiro, 2000).

What we can deduce from this discussion is that firms are engaging in certain activities that make it difficult for competitors to replicate their IT-based success. While one could argue that such actions are unplanned (in effect, success is a matter of luck or good fortune), a more likely scenario is that firms plan to align IT with business strategy in a way that makes it difficult for rivals to mimic.[4] If firms expect their business strategy to be buffeted by change and instability, presumably it will take a much more concerted planning effort to sustain alignment over time. Previous studies have not addressed this issue at a detailed level, other than to note that planning is highly complex in a turbulent setting (Lederer and Salmela, 1996; Salmela, Lederer, and Reponen, 2000). In the next section, we examine six different case studies, supplemented with survey data at these firms, in an attempt to provide a more detailed understanding of how strategic IS planning is used to align IT and business strategy, and more important, the role that flexible IT infrastructure plays in maintaining this relationship over time as firms experience a great deal of market volatility.

## Hypothesis Development

Resource-based theories that view valuable, rare, nonsubstitutable, and immobile resources as the ultimate arbiter of superior performance argue that firms with flexible IT infrastructure are more likely to sustain tight fit between IT and business strategy since they are better able to redirect IT around the value chain to support a change in business strategy. IS planning can help to maintain that relationship by creating a platform for firms to monitor environmental or market factors that might precipitate a change in the business strategy. Using these arguments, we propose the following two hypotheses:

H1: IT infrastructure flexibility is positively associated with strategic alignment.
H2: SISP positively moderates the link between IT infrastructure flexibility and strategic alignment.

Prior research on the resource-based view of the firm notes that firms often select particular types of IT resources that match their operating environment (Wade and Hulland, 2004). Firms in a volatile environment have a greater need for flexible IT that can adapt to the ever-changing nature of their business, while in a stable environment, firms are less inclined to pursue flexible IT since the pace of change is less severe. If we extrapolate this argument to the relationship between IT infrastructure flexibility and strategic alignment, it is likely that IT flexibility will prove more important to alignment in a turbulent setting. There may be far fewer opportunities to take advantage of the capabilities of a flexible IT infrastructure in a stable environment. We summarize this argument in our third and final hypothesis:

H3:   Environmental turbulence, denoting the rate of change in the marketplace, positively moderates the link between IT infrastructure flexibility and strategic alignment.

## METHODOLOGY

Case studies are a widely accepted means for developing theories and hypotheses for later testing under large-sample-size methods such as regression or structural modeling (Eisenhardt, 1989; Lee, 1989). Other researchers call for a more balanced approach that combines qualitative and quantitative methods in a way that *traps* the most theoretically astute, parsimonious, and yet the most accurate model behind the data (Kaplan and Duchon, 1988). We adopt such an approach in this study: first using surveys of business and IT executives to examine the relationship between IT infrastructure flexibility and strategic alignment with quantitative measures and sophisticated modeling methods before exposing that relationship to more precise investigation using case studies that offer a qualitative assessment of how and why these variables are related. In order to minimize the risk of respondent bias, we adopt a matched survey protocol. For the first survey, we targeted chief information officers (CIOs) to respond to technical items involving IT infrastructure flexibility; for the second survey, we targeted business executives with responsibility for strategic planning or development. Chief financial officers (CFOs) were used as default respondents in a handful of firms where we were unable to identify executives with overall responsibility for strategic planning.

### Measuring IT Infrastructure Flexibility and Alignment

IT infrastructure flexibility was measured using sixteen items taken from research by Byrd and Turner (2000). These items cover four constructs (four items each): hardware compatibility, software modularity, network connectivity, and IT skills adaptability (all items appear in the appendix). These items have been shown to be valid and reliable in previous research (Byrd and Turner, 2000; Tallon, 2007).

   Measuring alignment presents a more difficult challenge as the literature recognizes that there are several ways to assess fit. Palmer and Markus (2000), for example, conceptualize fit as matching strategic foci where both IT and business strategy are focused on the same set of business goals. Chan and colleagues (1997) and Sabherwal and Chan (2001) see fit in terms of a deviation between an ideal level of IT use and actual IT use, or as interaction terms involving different measures of business strategy. The challenge with using strategy typologies, as the above authors have shown, is that business strategy rarely fits neatly into any of the usual strategy types offered by typologies. Certainly some firms may have a clearly identified strategy but others try to use mixed strategies. Rather than continue with this top-down approach to alignment, we employ a bottom-up approach that identifies business strategy through a variety of business activities and IT strategy according to how IT is used. This bottom-up approach can provide a more realistic assessment of alignment as it emphasizes what activities firms are doing as part of their business strategy and how IT is used to support such activities; these data can then be combined into fit measures.

   Of the six perspectives on how to measure fit—mediation, profile deviation, matching, covariation, moderation, and gestalt (Venkatraman, 1989)—the literature has made widespread use of profile deviation and moderation. Profile deviation uses the difference between actual and ideal IT use (smaller deviations suggest tight fit) while moderation utilizes interaction terms between IT and business strategy. Profile deviation has been used by Sabherwal and Chan (2001) to explore differences in alignment between firms with different strategies using the Miles and Snow typology (1978) while moderation has been used by Chan and colleagues (1997). Tallon (2008) uncovers significant correlations between profile deviation and moderation in reviewing alignment at the process level. In this chapter, we focus on moderation since its range of values is more intuitive (values range from 0 to 1; 0 is worst case misalignment, 1 implies perfect alignment) and its core elements (IT use, business strategy) come from different respondents, thereby limiting respondent bias (Podsakoff et al., 2003). If we used profile deviation, there could be problems of interpretation as has been observed by Sabherwal and Chan (2001).

While business strategy can be measured in a variety of ways, most notably self-typing around an established typology, we use a series of five items to identify the extent to which firms have implemented critical activities within five primary processes: supplier relations, production and operations, product and service enhancement, sales and marketing support, and customer relations. These processes are an abstraction of the generic value chain. Although not exhaustive of all known processes, these areas cover the primary activities in most firms. All items were added to the business executive survey. Respondents were shown a list of activities in each process and asked to assess the extent to which these activities had been implemented on a seven-point Likert scale, anchored on "not implemented" and "fully implemented." In order to evaluate IT use within these same five processes, CIOs were asked to rate the extent of IT use using a seven-point Likert scale, anchored on "low IT use" and "high IT use." In order to derive alignment measures, we could then create five process-level measures as the product of each process-level measure of IT use and its equivalent process-level measure of business strategy. Since IT use and business strategy were measured using seven-point scales, alignment within each process can be assigned a value ranging from 1 ($1 \times 1$: complete misalignment) to 49 ($7 \times 7$: perfect alignment); multiplying each value by 1/49 (a constant) allows for a more intuitive interpretation of these values on a 0 to 1 scale without altering their meaning.

Last, environmental turbulence was assessed using three industry clockspeed measures given by Mendelson and Pillai (1998). Based on earlier research by Fine (1998), industry clockspeed uses objective criteria to determine the rate of change within a firm or its industry. Unlike perceptual measures that often mask the relative changes between industry groups, measures such as product life-cycle duration, customer turnover, or the percentage of sales from products/services launched inside the past two years, offer a more realistic overview of industry change. These three measures were added to the strategic planner's survey.

**Survey-based Data Collection and Analysis**

The population of interest in this study is made up of 2,826 publicly traded firms with revenues in 2001 of $100 million to $3 billion. During 2002, we mailed surveys to a sample of IT and business executives in 1,600 firms. IT respondents were identified in the 2002 directory of Top Computer Executives by ACR while senior business executives with strategic planning oversight were identified on Hoovers.com. Matched surveys were received from 241 firms, yielding a 13 percent response rate; average sales for this group in 2001 amounted to $798 million. Descriptive statistics on our sample are reported in Table 20.1.

To evaluate the validity of our various survey constructs, we first undertook a confirmatory

Table 20.1

**Sample Characteristics** (N = 241)

|  | Frequency | Percent |
|---|---|---|
| Revenues (2001) | | |
| Less than $100 million (M) | 15 | 6.2 |
| $100M–$250M | 75 | 31.1 |
| $250M–$500M | 54 | 22.4 |
| $500M–$1 billion (B) | 44 | 18.3 |
| $1B–$2B | 36 | 14.9 |
| More than $2B | 17 | 7.1 |
| Industry categories | | |
| Electronics and Computing Machinery | 65 | 27.0 |
| Wholesale and Retail | 46 | 19.1 |
| Financial Services | 43 | 17.8 |
| Software Services | 25 | 10.4 |
| Metals and Plastics | 17 | 7.1 |
| Pharmaceuticals and Health Care | 12 | 5.0 |
| Other | 33 | 13.6 |
| Respondents (matched surveys) | | |
| IT Executive Survey | | |
| Chief Information Officer | 116 | 46.2 |
| IT Director | 50 | 20.7 |
| SVP/VP, Information Technology | 49 | 20.3 |
| IT Manager | 26 | 10.8 |
| Business Executive Survey | | |
| SVP/VP Corporate Development | 113 | 46.9 |
| Business Development Officer | 60 | 24.9 |
| VP Strategic Planning | 37 | 15.3 |
| Chief Financial Officer | 31 | 12.9 |

factor analysis. As seen in Table 20.2, the results of our factor analysis confirm that our survey items have factored appropriately. In addition, composite reliability for each factor is in excess of a suggested minimum of 0.8 (Nunnally, 1978), while the average variance extracted (AVE)—a measure of the variance shared among items loading on the same factor—exceeds 0.50 (Fornell and Larcker, 1981). What these results mean for the rest of our analysis is that it is appropriate to collapse or parcel various items together by averaging or weighting by factor loadings, for example, to obtain a single proxy measure for each construct. In effect, this allows us to create a single proxy measure for IT infrastructure flexibility and a single proxy measure for strategic alignment.

We did not add the three measures of industry clockspeed to our factor analysis as they use a very different scale from the seven-point Likert scales used for all other items. Rather, we used cluster analysis to break our sample of firms into two groups: low clockspeed and high clockspeed. Low clockspeed firms have long product life cycles, low customer turnover, and low revenues from new products/services. These firms are reflective of a stable environment where there is

Table 20.2

## Confirmatory Factor Analysis and Descriptive Statistics

| Item | Mean | S.D. | Hardware compatibility | Software modularity | Network connectivity | IT skills adaptability | Strategic alignment |
|------|------|------|------------------------|---------------------|----------------------|------------------------|---------------------|
| HC1 | 5.32 | 1.47 | **0.84** | 0.46 | 0.59 | 0.45 | 0.39 |
| HC2 | 5.00 | 1.60 | **0.82** | 0.47 | 0.61 | 0.35 | 0.39 |
| HC3 | 5.06 | 1.66 | **0.76** | 0.54 | 0.59 | 0.31 | 0.31 |
| HC4 | 3.96 | 1.83 | **0.77** | 0.59 | 0.63 | 0.31 | 0.44 |
| AS1 | 3.74 | 1.69 | 0.48 | **0.85** | 0.56 | 0.35 | 0.38 |
| AS2 | 4.09 | 1.76 | 0.61 | **0.87** | 0.65 | 0.35 | 0.38 |
| AS3 | 4.83 | 1.70 | 0.45 | **0.68** | 0.45 | 0.22 | 0.36 |
| AS4 | 3.95 | 1.60 | 0.44 | **0.68** | 0.48 | 0.35 | 0.34 |
| NC1 | 4.27 | 1.52 | 0.57 | 0.55 | **0.76** | 0.36 | 0.27 |
| NC2 | 4.22 | 1.93 | 0.57 | 0.57 | **0.83** | 0.35 | 0.27 |
| NC3 | 4.41 | 1.54 | 0.69 | 0.58 | **0.91** | 0.43 | 0.36 |
| NC4 | 4.07 | 1.59 | 0.65 | 0.58 | **0.80** | 0.43 | 0.39 |
| ITSA1 | 5.12 | 1.18 | 0.35 | 0.28 | 0.33 | **0.77** | 0.38 |
| ITSA2 | 4.08 | 1.49 | 0.33 | 0.35 | 0.33 | **0.82** | 0.50 |
| ITSA3 | 4.15 | 1.50 | 0.37 | 0.33 | 0.42 | **0.80** | 0.47 |
| ITSA4 | 4.76 | 1.25 | 0.39 | 0.37 | 0.45 | **0.83** | 0.48 |
| SA (SR) | 0.43 | 0.22 | 0.25 | 0.22 | 0.14 | 0.35 | **0.67** |
| SA (PO) | 0.57 | 0.21 | 0.35 | 0.33 | 0.34 | 0.38 | **0.58** |
| SA (PSE) | 0.40 | 0.23 | 0.37 | 0.39 | 0.32 | 0.48 | **0.76** |
| SA (MS) | 0.40 | 0.22 | 0.34 | 0.37 | 0.31 | 0.45 | **0.75** |
| SA (CR) | 0.47 | 0.23 | 0.40 | 0.36 | 0.29 | 0.38 | **0.79** |
| Reliability | | | 0.854 | 0.893 | 0.876 | 0.881 | 0.837 |
| AVE | | | 0.598 | 0.677 | 0.638 | 0.649 | 0.509 |

*Note:* Items in parentheses refer to business processes, SR: supplier relations, PO: production and operations, PSE: product and service enhancement, MS: sales and marketing support, CR: customer relations. Data in boldface represent primary factor loadings.

relatively little or no change. In contrast, high clockspeed firms have short product life cycles, high customer turnover, and rely on new products/services for a large percentage of their sales. Such firms reflect a turbulent environment with a high rate of change. In Table 20.3, we report summary statistics for each group; an analysis of variance (ANOVA) on each measure confirms the presence of significant differences between both groups.

As seen in Figure 20.1, we can then create a scatterplot for both clockspeed groups showing the link between IT infrastructure flexibility and strategic alignment. Adding a regression line to the data reveals a positive association, implying that flexible IT infrastructure facilitates an increase in alignment—this relationship holds for both low and high clockspeed firms. More sophisticated analysis is possible beyond the simple scatterplot and regression results shown here (see Tallon [2006] for a structural model that offers a more detailed assessment of the link between these two variables). At this juncture, our point is to merely indicate the general direction of the relationship

Table 20.3

**Environmental Subgroups** (Low vs. High Clockspeed)

| Clockspeed measures | Low clockspeed ($N = 134$) | High clockspeed ($N = 107$) | $F$ (sig.) |
|---|---|---|---|
| Rate of annual customer turnover (%) | 9.9 | 17.0 | 14.882 |
| Revenues from newly launched products and services (%) | 24.6 | 50.0 | 44.682 |
| Length of product or service lifecycle (months) | 70.7 | 28.2 | 9.733 |

*Note:* All *F*-statistics are significant at $p < 0.001$.

Figure 20.1    **Scatterplot: IT Infrastructure Flexibility and Strategic Alignment**

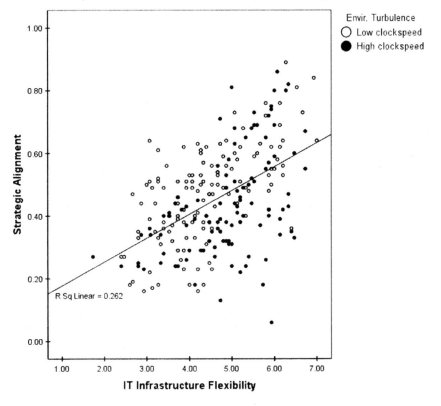

between IT infrastructure flexibility and alignment, using this as a springboard for our subsequent case analysis. From an SISP viewpoint, the question is now: why are some firms able to maintain high IT infrastructure flexibility and high alignment, while others (seen on the lower left corner of Figure 20.1) have much weaker IT infrastructure flexibility (meaning rigidity) and lower alignment? At first glance, environmental turbulence is not an explanatory factor and so we use our case studies to explore whether SISP could help to explain this relationship in more depth.

## Case Studies

During the initial survey phase of the research, a question was added to the end of the CIO survey asking whether the respondent would like to particulate in a case study of IT infrastructure flexibility at a later date. Of the 241 IT executives returning a survey, 74 checked "yes," 121 checked "no." Beginning in late 2003, when a report on the survey results was mailed to each firm, IT executives were again contacted and invited to participate in a case study. Given the time commitment and level of interaction required for case study data collection (multiple interviews, willingness to share minutes of planning meetings, access to IT costs and return on IT investment analyses, etc.), 27 firms eventually agreed to participate. We focus here on just six of those firms—these six were chosen as they roughly follow the outline of the regression line between IT infrastructure flexibility and strategic alignment in Figure 20.1. In Figure 20.2, we identify each of the six case sites as they appear in Figure 20.1. Based on nondisclosure agreements, we use broad industry labels to identify each firm. In Table 20.4, we offer descriptive details on each firm to help readers better understand our case study sites and the general competitive environment in which they operate.

Case study data were collected at each site through a series of semistructured interviews with IT and business executives. Interviews usually lasted for one hour and covered a variety of topics. In the case of IT executives, the discussion centered around their company's interpretation of what it meant to have a flexible IT infrastructure, what IT resources enabled them to be flexible (or not), how they planned for IT, how they monitored developments both inside and outside of IT that might have a bearing on IT planning, and whether chargebacks or similar cost systems were used to recover costs. Interviews typically occurred several months after these IT executives had replied to the earlier survey, the intent being that respondents would be less likely to repeat the data that had been given earlier. While some recall is certainly possible, allowing a period of time to elapse introduces a useful degree of validity into the data collection process. Interviews with business executives were usually arranged with the help of the CIO although in each case the initial request to meet with a named business executive came from the author. In this way, CIOs acted as a conduit to facilitate other interviews but they did not select or censor who could be interviewed.

## Business Strategy: Creating Value for Customers

During many of our interviews, participants (strategic planners or business development officers) struggled to articulate their business strategy when asked to select one of the generic strategies outlined in Porter (1980): low cost, differentiation, niche. The problem was not only that firms tended to have a much broader strategy combining different generic traits but also that the generic labels were confusing; research has found this to be a widespread issue with strategy typologies (White, 1986). Instead, interviewees spoke in terms of how their firms create value for customers. This focus on value creation reflects prior research on value disciplines by Treacy and Wiersema (1995) where firms are said to create value through operational excellence, customer intimacy, or product leadership. Accordingly, we used these terms to assess business strategy in each firm. For example, as noted by a marketing VP at a bank we visited:

> We want to be a low-cost operator for sure but then who isn't these days? We see more opportunity in trying to be responsive to customers' needs. We want to be a one-stop shop for all sorts of different financial needs: car loans, mortgages, retirement planning, education

Table 20.4

**Case Study Site Particulars**

| Firm reference | Company activities | Environmental status | Annual sales |
|---|---|---|---|
| Aerospace | Manufacturer of aircraft parts, very involved in space exploration, large military contracts, highly profitable | Near monopoly position in its current markets<br><br>Low clockspeed | < $1 Billion |
| Banking | Large regional financial services player, has engaged in some recent mergers and acquisitions (M&A) with the goal of broadening its product range | Under a lot of pressure from large national banks<br><br>High clockspeed | < $0.5 Billion |
| Career services | Dominant player in executive search, does not compete with online search sites since most of their positions are highly visible | Few competitors but under growing cost pressure<br><br>Low clockspeed | < $2 Billion |
| Health insurance | National health insurer known for taking a firm line on health costs, active in clinical trials, actively promoting e-health systems | Pressure to redefine future delivery of health care<br><br>Low clockspeed | < $4 Billion |
| Printing | Prints forms, documents of all sorts except newsprint, recent M&A activity has led to a much enlarged firm, very customer focused | Fierce competition based on price and service<br><br>High clockspeed | < $1 Billion |
| Software | Global provider of product life cycle (PLC) software, dominant provider, easy integration with supply chain systems | Competitive industry but less so at this scale<br><br>Low clockspeed | < $1 Billion |

Figure 20.2 **Case Study Sites (Survey Data)**

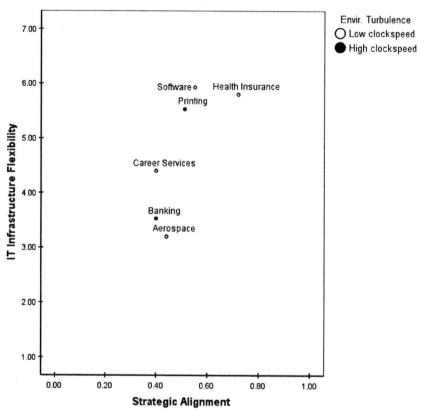

loans, and so on. We want to get to know each customer as if they were our only customer. We see ourselves as moving into relationship-banking where every customer is a market unto themselves. Think about taking a data mining model from grocery retail and apply it to retail banking. That's what we want to be. Every customer has a different experience . . . now if only IT would cooperate!

The only other case study site where we detected a customer-oriented strategy was at a health care insurance provider. While all activities revolved around the customer or patient, the issue was not only to ensure the highest quality of care but to keep control of ever-increasing health care costs. As explained by the director of IT Infrastructure:

We don't need to worry too much about competition. People tend not to change carriers unless they move to another job but we do have to worry about pricing ourselves out of contention with not-for-profits or other nontraditional providers. The problem we see is trying to deal with people [patients] who have unique health needs and that puts a strain on our internal systems . . . someone who needs to see a few specialists for diabetes, heart disease, blindness, mental health, and so on. We don't want to be the provider who always says no, so we need a way to build internal claims and referral systems that bend to the needs of each and every person. It's difficult—it really is difficult. If you want to know why costs are so out of control, you only have to look at what we're trying to do with IT. We want IT to help cut costs but IT also has to be a proxy health care provider. That sort of IT is not cheap. We want to have our cake and eat it too. We want to be cost-focused but also patient-focused.

Two product innovators emerged from among the six firms we studied. A software firm acknowledged the challenges and sometimes the frustration of *eating your own lunch* in order to stay a step ahead of the competition. The other firm (in aerospace) had a different problem with their strategy as the following comment from their CIO illustrates:

We make parts for both the Boeing and Airbus programs. We also make parts for the [NASA] shuttle program. As you can imagine, we don't do a lot of mass production, certainly not for NASA. We innovate around safety—there's a lot more focus on safety post Columbia [the shuttle disaster]. We do a lot of one-off innovation, but the problem with this is that there isn't a huge customer base for what we do! We have to be operationally excellent in order to manage costs. We also have to be constantly plugged into the systems at Boeing and Airbus—all the design and development of aircraft these days is through CATIA [a CAD tool] or something similar. We really don't need to be too flexible just so long as IT doesn't get in the way of being innovative. Sadly, it is right now.

Last, two firms identified themselves as operationally excellent. In the case of a career services firm, they argued that this was not the same as being a low-cost provider. What was remarkable about this firm is its "virtualness"; many operations activities are outsourced but the relationship with human resources (HR) groups in client firms and the initial contact with prospects remains a key strength of the firm and so these activities have been retained in-house. The following comment from the VP of Service Delivery clarifies this idea:

What we do with executive recruitment is not like what Monster.com does; GE will not find its next CEO on an Internet site. Relationships are everything. What we do with temporary jobs is a different story though, we push a lot of that stuff to ASPs [application service providers]. I'd love to be like eBay when it comes to matching up these sorts of jobs, it's about as hands off as you can get. We don't need really flexible systems since the amount of variability that you get on a contract [construction, nursing, secretarial] is limited; they're all much the same. . . . We do need flexibility with executive search but it's not about automation. We want to be a facilitator, bringing together an employer and a future business leader. You can't afford to let IT screw it up so we need humans involved but IT does help.

At the printing firm we visited, the focus was very much on operational excellence but there was a sense that this focus must deliver cost savings for clients. As their CIO commented:

There's a lot of cost pressures these days from print shops in Mexico. The challenge is being able to do small jobs quickly and at a price that dissuades anyone from going someplace else. We've been able to automate a lot of the job setup—customers can submit images online, play around with templates, check on their orders, and so on. We need to be flexible. We have some very large jobs but some very small jobs also. Flexibility is not just a print shop thing. It's about how we interact with clients; it's about billing and being responsive to customers.

From an analysis of the transcripts of our interviews with these executives, it was apparent that in some cases, firms' understanding of their strategy was intertwined with their understanding of the volatile market in which they operated. This is largely consistent with research that sees strategy as a way to align the internal resources of a firm (i.e., capital, labor, IT, knowledge) to the external environment (Miles and Snow, 1978; Porter, 1991; White, 1986). Our reading of the above interview notes suggests that strategy does not automatically decide a firm's position in Figure 20.2, whether on the low-low end of the flexibility-alignment relationship or on the opposite end. However, it can happen that firms espousing product leadership or customer intimacy under the Treacy and Wiersema (1995) typology are more likely to encounter frequent changes within their product portfolio as competitors seek to undermine their market positioning. Research reveals that firms using a low-cost leadership strategy are unlikely to achieve sustainable results (White, 1986), and so they must expand or diversify out into other areas in order to achieve some sense of differentiation. The next and perhaps most critical question that we sought to resolve was how businesses planned for IT infrastructure flexibility if indeed they saw a need for IT to be flexible.

### SISP: Planning a Flexible IT Infrastructure

A significant part of our interviews with business and IT executives was spent discussing SISP or in some cases the reasons why SISP was perceived as weak and ineffective. By focusing the discussion on each side of the IT-business dyad, we could obtain a better sense of the cohesion, partnership, and shared vision for IT in each group. Research shows that closer cooperation between business and IT executives is a key predictor of improved alignment, expanded IT use, and possible competitive advantage (Kearns and Lederer, 2003; Reich and Benbasat, 1996). Our approach to developing this discussion with each group of executives was to leverage some of the existing IS research that describes various elements of SISP and to use this to build talking points or questions. For example, we wanted to know who (business or IT executives) is in charge of environmental scanning. Is the IS function more proactive in suggesting how IT can help the firm to anticipate change or is it more reactive, and if so, how fast is IT in responding to change? We also asked if there was a formal process used to evaluate large IT spending proposals or whether firms did post-implementation audits to identify whether IT was delivering the type of value that was expected of it. In Table 20.5, we provide a descriptive summary of what we learned during this portion of our site visits.

What we discover, for example, is that the IS planning process in our banking and aerospace sites is best characterized as *chaotic*. Part of the challenge in these firms is dealing with disparate systems that somehow fail to communicate with one other. As the bank moves toward a strategy of customer intimacy where checking or savings accounts have customized features that meet the needs of individual customers and where the mix of banking services more accurately reflects customer demographics, the challenge is to combine disparate data pools to provide a single view of each client. As the CIO explains:

> How do you treat a customer who walks in off the street? You've never seen them before and yet they want to open up all sorts of accounts. Is there a way for us to predict whether this customer will be profitable or not? At the moment, we treat everyone the same but going forward, we want to treat each customer differently. We want to be able to mine transactions somehow to predict what products or services a new account holder might want and how we might profit from that . . . building a unified view of a customer

Table 20.5

**SISP Observations**

| Company interviewees | IT planning details | IT metrics |
|---|---|---|
| *Aerospace*<br>• CIO<br>• Director of Customer Accounts | An annual IT plan for the entire firm is divided into four smaller plans for each operating unit. IT planning is complex as the firm is using three ERP systems, the main ERP system is home grown and extremely cumbersome. Integration is a severe challenge. IT is starting to act as a barrier to future expansion yet no upgrade is currently planned.<br>**SISP: Chaotic** | Limited use of chargebacks unless costs are clearly traceable to one or more business units. There is little or no use of ongoing metrics to monitor the return on IT investments. Since the firm is highly profitable, there is no need to curtail or cut IT spending. |
| *Banking*<br>• CIO<br>• VP, Marketing<br>• CFO | With a move toward a customer-centric strategy, IT planning has become very important. IT is now seen as an enabler of business strategy. IT plans are increasingly focused on solving the technical challenges of merging data from myriad systems to form a unified view of each client's accounts.<br>**SISP: Chaotic** | All areas of the bank are intense users of the balanced scorecard, and IT is no different. Key performance metrics are monitored weekly such as transaction accuracy. IT projects do not go through a return on investment analysis. |
| *Career Services*<br>• CIO<br>• VP, Service Delivery | IT is planned around strategic business units. All projects have business owners who are responsible for creating IT business value. IT infrastructure is owned by IT. IT is seen as increasingly strategic.<br>**SISP: In transition from chaotic to structured** | An executive team meets weekly to review client accounts and how IT has been able to support an increase in customer service. |
| *Health Care Insurance*<br>• Head, IT Infrastructure<br>• EVP, Patient Care | A major outsourcing initiative is under way and so a large portion of IT planning revolves around the relationship with the outsourcer and how IT costs will be handled. IT planning is highly structured.<br>**SISP: Structured** | IT performance metrics are linked to a service-level agreement with the outsourcer. All IT costs are carefully monitored and all large budget amounts need approval. |
| *Printing*<br>• CIO<br>• VP, Strategy<br>• VP, Customer Service | The firm maintains a rolling five-year business and IT plan. Each year 200 to 300 IT projects are evaluated. Priorities are set according to what projects best align with the goals of the company and will yield the highest rate of return.<br>**SISP: Structured** | The finance department maintains an IT returns calculator (Excel file) into which data are entered on each new or continuing IT project. Chargebacks are used extensively. The firm does not use post-implementation audits. |
| *Software*<br>• CIO<br>• Infrastructure mgr.<br>• VP, Development | All IT projects in excess of $100k go through a rigorous executive-level approval process. All IT spending is linked to firm strategic objectives. IT is "not core, but context"—an enabler of strategic differentiation but not strategic in and of itself.<br>**SISP: Structured** | 85% of all IT costs are charged back to business units. 80% of IT systems are common to all territories. Post-implementation reviews are required of all large-scale projects. |

is complex. We look across checking accounts, mortgages, credit cards, loans, and so on, and try to find cross-selling opportunities. Getting IT to the point where it can do this is really difficult. We've struggled all along, and what makes it a hundred times worse is when we have a merger . . . we are always putting out fires; data integration is tough and legacy systems do not help one little bit. . . . It would be great to say that our planning is on top of this but it isn't. We get by.

IT planning at the aerospace company is equally challenging because of lingering enterprise resource planning (ERP) problems. A key problem continues to be a home-grown COBOL system that (as of the end of 2005) had over 350 customized modifications added to it. A considerable amount of time (70 percent of the available IT staff hours) is spent maintaining and otherwise integrating the ERP system into computer-aided design (CAD) and other leading-edge systems. A considerable amount of the IT budget is similarly spent on maintaining existing systems although there is general agreement that those resources ought to be spent on more innovative projects. As seen in Table 20.5, we characterize the SISP process at this firm as *chaotic*. Planning does take place but as the CIO argues in the following comment, much of the process is consumed with tactical issues:

A lot of our planning efforts go into dealing with [the ERP system]. We've had a lot of problems with it. We've not been able to earn ISO [International Organization for Standardization] certification because of integration issues . . . swapping it out for something else is not going to be easy. We're not under a lot of pressure yet to rip it out but [the CEO] has told us to start thinking about what to do next. He wants us to be more strategic with IT. We don't have to be strategic; we don't have a lot of competition so as long as we can keep costs under control, we're ok . . . we're flexible where we need to be—in product development—but other than that [the ERP system] has put a damper on our ability to innovate.

We categorize SISP at our career services site as being "In Transition," as IT moves from being a cost center to a source of strategic value. IT infrastructure is a key source of value insofar as it can flex to accommodate the unique needs of each client segment. After the appointment of their first CIO in the late 1990s, IT planning moved from a series of tactical plans to a more integrated or aligned plan. ASPs are a key differentiator for this firm; they use ASPs to generate cost savings, channeling any saved resources to more strategic IT application development, as the following comment from their CIO indicates:

I think we're getting better at planning. We used to spend a lot of time on mundane stuff like billing but to be honest, it never amounted to much. After we outsourced that . . . we focused our planning on how to plug applications into our infrastructure. There are times when we need to scale up in a hurry and infrastructure is what allows us to do that.

Each of the remaining three sites has a well-defined and highly structured SISP process. Although one might argue that firms in low clockspeed environments have no need for flexible IT, we found that IT and business executives were mindful of the need to build a discussion of IT flexibility into their planning process. Incremental change can put pressure on some aspects of a firm's business model and so there is a constant need to keep flexibility in mind, even if change is predictable, as the following comments reveal:

IT planning is one of the most important things we do. IT planning is top down although project proposals can come from anywhere . . . everyone in IT [200-person organization] knows that we plan meticulously . . . we expect those on the business side to work with us. . . . We pay a lot of attention to whether we are getting value from IT or not but it's really the responsibility of the business to drive value from their applications. We have 200–300 IT projects ongoing at any one time and we keep track of them all. (CIO, Printing Company)

We get pushback sometimes from the business side because we chargeback a lot of what we provide, but then we also make them an integral part of our planning process. We're a software company but our IT is not what makes us unique—it helps us get to where we want to be but [our product] is what defines us. There again, if IT is not up to supporting our call centers or if we can't get fixes out, we all suffer. (CIO, Software Company)

There's a huge emphasis today on electronic medical records and we're trying to take the lead on that [in our region]. Then there's a debate about pay for performance. I have to say that planning hasn't been easy. We've had to bring [the outsourcer] into our planning a lot sooner and things don't always work out for us when they have an agenda that doesn't quite gel with ours. I'd like to say though that I'm happy with how we plan. We use internal auditors to cost all aspects of IT and [the outsourcers] know that we expect cost reductions on the basis of whatever they come up with. . . . We've had to pay a lot more attention to how much we spend on IT since [rival health care insurer] has seen their e-health system bomb. . . . We can't afford to mess up when there's such a spot light on health care costs. . . . IT has to deliver value. (Director of IT infrastructure, Healthcare Insurer)

Overall, our interviews highlighted a significant amount of frustration or anxiety with what might be termed inflexible systems. In this context, inflexibility is not only reflective of integration concerns but shows where systems have a difficult time scaling in response to a new advertising campaign or a recent merger. For example, in the bank we studied, there was some concern over a proposal by marketing to offer a high yield Internet savings account—a potential carrot with which to attract new customers:

Our marketing executive was keen to push through a new Internet savings product offering 4 percent [this was 1.5 percent above industry averages at that time] over three months. Great idea but this would blow up our IT systems and create a call center nightmare! There's no way we could sign up a few thousand new accounts a day, not in the timeframe that he's talking about. What happens if customers leave after three months? We still have all this IT capacity lying around. Who's going to pay for that? I know ING [see www.ingdirect.com] has been able to offer a high yield savings account on a large scale but they have deep pockets. We don't. (CIO, Bank)

We did not hear in our interviews that ERP systems are likely to *cause* inflexibility; there was some concern that ERP systems might be slow to react to change (as identified at the aerospace company where their home-grown ERP system was a source of rigidity), but in other instances, we listened as firms said that ERP systems made them more flexible. This was the case, for example, at the health care insurer where their outsourcing deal called for certain core enterprise IT systems to be hosted by the outsourcer. There was a belief (albeit untested) that the outsourcer could provide additional capacity on an as-needed basis, and indeed the insurer's IS planning process assumed that this would be the case when plans called for certain applications to integrate with their core outsourced systems, as their CIO explained:

[The outsourcer] will step up when we need them. When we get to the point where our e-health initiatives or some of our pilots [doctors using PCs to e-mail prescriptions to the pharmacy, for example] begin to roll out in volume, we expect [the ERP system] to be flexible enough to handle the extra load. . . . We went with these guys in part because integration would be easier. . . . We're done fighting integration battles. Let someone else do it.

A critical point to take from this discussion is that IT flexibility is not about being all things to all people. Some firms require flexibility in some parts of the value chain only, rather than in all processes at the same time. For example, the aerospace firm needs flexibility in product design; the bank is also interested in flexibility but only insofar as it involves service innovation as a way to deliver a unique customer experience. The software firm requires flexibility in dealing with requests for patches or where customers are struggling to integrate the software they buy from this firm with other systems. The health care firm, on the other hand, seems interested in flexibility both in terms of operations (claims processing, premium processing, address changes, etc.) and in making it easier for patients and doctors to learn more about alternative sources of medicine, natural remedies, and so on (a value-added service).

## IMPLICATIONS FOR INFORMATION SYSTEMS PLANNING: RESEARCH AND PRACTICE

Research drawn from the resource-based literature notes that sustainable competitive advantage is influenced in part by an ability to leverage IT to respond to external threats and opportunities (Kearns and Lederer, 2003; Kettinger et al., 1994; Ravichandran and Lertwongsatien, 2005). The basic elements of IT infrastructure—servers, PCs, operating systems, networks, and so on—are not a primary driver of performance; rather, performance is driven by the combination of IT and resources such as skills. One skill, in particular, is environmental scanning or an ability to translate market intelligence into executable actions. It can be said that SISP is a process that draws upon skills such as knowing how to use IT to respond to market threats and opportunities. The case of Capital One offers a useful illustration of the power of SISP when an information-based strategy is used to test innovative credit card products (low interest teaser rates, balance transfers, etc.)—products that later redefined the credit card industry (Anand, Rukstad, and Paige, 2001). For firms like Capital One, SISP is a key success factor but it cannot be divorced from the capabilities that the IT artifact provides—capabilities that allow Capital One to run thousands of simultaneous experiments to see what combination of credit card features is likely to be most profitable. Success at Capital One is, therefore, related to the flexibility of their IT infrastructure; if IT was rigid, they would not be able to innovate quickly or to enjoy higher profitability by scaling up their most successful experiments to the mass credit card market. In the same way, it is difficult for us to divorce SISP from the way that some of our six case study firms are using IT infrastructure flexibility, as we explain in more detail below.

As shown previously in Figure 20.2, the six firms presented in this study fall on a continuum extending from low flexibility/low alignment to high flexibility/high alignment. While the positive link between IT infrastructure flexibility and alignment is important, particularly for firms where flexibility or speed to market is an essential competitive attribute, case studies afford a unique opportunity to explore in greater depth the role that SISP plays in nurturing this relationship. In firms where IT inflexibility may be blamed for weak alignment—a logical conclusion implied by the survey results shown in Figure 20.1—there may be a tendency to try to improve alignment by making IT more flexible. Recent innovations in utility computing, Web services, and service-oriented architecture will almost certainly lead to more modular IT systems and greater IT integration both inside and outside firm boundaries, but our case data would suggest that this is not the full story. Rather, inflexible or rigid systems may be symptomatic of a larger problem—namely, a problem with chaotic SISP or in some cases a total lack of planning. Addressing the weak link between IT infrastructure flexibility and alignment through IT alone ignores the fact that ineffective IS planning may still remain. As reported in Table 20.5, chaotic SISP characterizes firms with low IT infrastructure flexibility whereas structured SISP characterizes firms with high IT infrastructure flexibility. Chaotic SISP need not imply that IS planning is disorganized or in total disarray, although it is certainly possible. It also does not coincide with a high clockspeed or volatile environment. It is possible that IS planning could be chaotic in an uncertain environment but our limited case data do not provide evidence of this. Similarly, a stable setting might support a less chaotic IS planning process but our data do not conclusively show this. What we find in our data is that chaotic planning tends to arise because of the difficult challenge of managing inflexible IT. Many times, we heard business and IT executives voice frustration about having to spend inordinate amounts of time planning around core systems that were too important to replace and yet too inflexible to work with other areas of the business. In both the bank and aerospace firms, their CIOs admitted that their IT spending was higher than it should be due to the burden of working with, or fixing, inflexible systems. They also noted, however, that when these systems were first installed, they had been key to enhancing fit with the business strategy. The concern is that when strategy shifts—for example, as the bank moves from operational excellence to customer intimacy—these systems quickly take on the mantle of rigidity. If the bank's managers had more foresight in planning their IT infrastructure needs, data integration issues might have been avoided or at least controlled, as the CIO of the bank describes below:

> The last [IT] guy was too quick to say yes to everything. We have a lot of spaghetti configurations because he didn't have purchasing or configuration standards in place. He didn't stand up to the business and get them to see how little flexibility these systems would provide in future. . . . We're dealing with it now though . . . it really pays to look out a few years and see where the business is going before you invest in IT. He didn't do that!

**Theoretical Implications**

Since case studies are important for theory development, we must ask what our data mean for the literature on SISP and the resource-based view arguing that rare, immobile, and nonsubstitutable IT resources—of which IT infrastructure flexibility is a quintessential form—are a key source of competitive advantage (Barney, 1991; Eisenhardt, 1989). In recent years, the resource-based view has reacted to globalization and an increase in market volatility by embracing the need for capabilities that will allow firms to keep pace with each market change (Eisenhardt and Martin, 2000; Rindova and Kotha, 2001; Teece, Pisano, and Shuen, 1997). IT infrastructure flexibility is one such capability that will allow redirecting or repositioning of resources to whatever activities in the value chain are in most need of support. If IT is to continue to support business strategy—even as that strategy changes (both evolutionary and incremental change)—then it is imperative to have access to a flexible IT infrastructure that is free of rigidities. Our case analysis finds that firms with inflexible IT infrastructure find it more difficult or expensive to undergo strategic change.

While SISP theory argues that alignment and IT flexibility are separate dimensions of SISP effectiveness (Segars and Grover, 1999), our analysis provides a more nuanced interpretation of the theory. We view SISP more as a moderator of the relationship between these variables for the following reasons: in the presence of chaotic IS planning, IT infrastructure flexibility is a weak predictor of alignment, whereas with structured planning, IT infrastructure flexibility is a strong predictor of alignment. This does not conflict with the extant theory of SISP but it does mean that IS planning should be included in future research into continuous alignment or fit between IT and business strategy. Although we have only a small number of case studies, we do not find evidence that environmental change (proxied by clockspeed) moderates the link between IT infrastructure flexibility and alignment, contrary to arguments in the resource-based view (Wade and Hulland, 2004). Taken together, we can argue that IS planning is not necessarily rendered ineffective by a rapidly changing environment—IS planning can be equally effective (or ineffective) in both stable and unstable settings. What makes it difficult to maintain alignment in the face of sudden or abrupt change is how difficult it is for firms to work around IT rigidities—rigidities that, one could argue, are the result of past investment decisions that failed to foresee the consequences of being locked into a particular type of IT. We know from an earlier case study at Dell Computer by Kraemer, Dedrick, and Yamashiro (2000) that Dell was able to foresee a critical downside of committing to SAP, namely, an inability to customize the Dell direct model for each market, and so Dell opted to work with a best-of-breed solution instead, even if this meant living with short-term misalignment due to a potential lack of global systems integration.

**Managerial Implications**

Feeny and Willcocks (1998) describe *architecture planning* as one of nine core IS capabilities for exploiting IT. Architecture planning is not a solitary IS responsibility—it involves close cooperation with business users, a leadership position in crafting a strategic vision for IT, and an understanding of technical issues that might complicate architecture design. Other research explains that these capabilities have a key role to play in the development of an agile enterprise that can easily and quickly respond to the needs of a changing marketplace (Weill, Subramani, and Broadbent, 2002). Our research extends this thinking by showing how key capabilities around IT infrastructure flexibility shape alignment, which, as we know from past studies, will lead to increased firm performance (Chan et al., 1997; Kearns and Lederer, 2003; Sabherwal and Chan, 2001). What we also identify is the frustration felt by some firms that are trying to remove IT rigidities that have stalled or limited their ability to refocus their IT to support a new strategic initiative. In this way, we agree fully with the claims of Prahalad and Krishnan (2002), who, in a study of the dynamic synchronization of IT and business strategy (a term for continuous alignment), conclude that, "a rigid [IT] infrastructure will stymie even the best strategic initiatives, making it difficult to introduce change" (p. 24).

Our analysis also has implications for IT governance, specifically in terms of how IT investments are evaluated. Besides looking at IT payoffs in quantitative terms, a key yardstick by which to evaluate IT is whether it provides firms with options or an ability to move in a strategically different direction. While research on real options is well developed, there is still a dearth of analysis into how firms can apply options thinking to IT projects (Fichman, Keil, and Tiwana, 2006). To the extent that we find examples of chaotic SISP where firms are trying to avoid problems of IT rigidity, real options thinking might help to identify times when IT helps to improve alignment in the short term but at the expense of long-term flexibility. Options thinking would, therefore, highlight the cost of forgoing flexibility, allowing firms to think through how valuable it is for them to remain agile and responsive to future change. Building real options into SISP is still relatively unexplored but it would certainly be a fruitful area for managerial consideration as a way to think about preparing for future alignment between IT and a still-evolving business strategy.

## CONCLUSION

Previous research has repeatedly emphasized the need for cross-referencing between business and IT plans (Kearns and Lederer, 2003). While cross-referencing remains essential for alignment between IT and business strategy, the separation between planned and emergent strategy has compelled researchers to consider alignment in terms of fit between *actual* IT use and *actual* business activities (Chan et al., 1997; Sabherwal and Chan, 2001; Tallon, 2008). While this perspective may be suitable for examining the impact of alignment on *actual* firm performance, it says nothing about whether firms will be able to align IT to changes in their business strategy. If firms are preoccupied with alignment as their end goal, a concern is that their IT choices may inadvertently trigger rigidity traps whereby inflexible IT makes it difficult to respond to change. This may not be an issue for all firms. In low clockspeed sectors such as construction, mining, chemicals, wood products, or metals, firms may experience only incremental or gradual change in strategy over time whereas others in high clockspeed sectors such as fashion retail or electronics are more susceptible to frequent and unannounced changes. For high clockspeed firms, the risk of being caught in a rigidity trap is especially vexing since competitors are likely to seek innovative ways to compete; survival means having the means to counter all such attacks, so there may be a need to refocus IT around new strategic initiatives. For this to happen, firms must invest in a flexible IT infrastructure that can scale according to abrupt capacity needs or that can accommodate a wide range of applications, operating systems, and data formats. Of course, flexibility is not inexpensive, so firms may need to assess the opportunity cost of imposed rigidity before they sanction the additional IT investment needed to deliver flexibility.

A failure to install flexible IT systems can have an adverse economic impact, as JetBlue learned in 2007, when it was unable to reschedule its planes after an ice storm. As described by *CIO Magazine*, "they outgrew the capabilities of systems like their reservation system and the systems that schedule flights and match up pilots and crews with aircraft. Those key systems failed under the stress of what happened. The problem was due to lack of investment; they lost their agility and could not be responsive enough to their customers when an unexpected event occurred and it cost them big time" (Hugos, 2007). The issue here appears to be technical: inflexible IT infrastructure triggers misalignment or a shortfall in IT support due to a change in strategy; change in this case is weather related, something that airlines presumably plan for. If we apply our research results to this event, we might speculate that SISP was lacking or that they failed to fully appreciate the risks from weather outages by adding extra flexibility to their core IT systems.

What our case studies reveal, however, is that IT inflexibility is most likely a symptom of another form of organizational ineffectiveness, namely, bad, incomplete or in some cases nonexistent IS planning. When firms fail to plan for environmental issues that can disrupt their business, it is likely that IT will not have been architected to support a change in their business strategy. As our results show, chaotic planning characterizes firms that are struggling to work through and around IT-based rigidity traps, whose budgets are consumed with fixing rigidities, and that now find themselves struggling to satisfy the needs of a new competitive environment. For example, in the bank we visited, there is a deep-rooted fear that large banks will invade their territory offering free or low-fee checking accounts, mortgage refinancing, and high-yield savings accounts. The only way for the bank to protect itself is to become more customer focused and yet the shared data or systems integration that they need to do this eludes them. In the aerospace firm we visited, a homegrown ERP system continues to pose problems. While their near-monopolistic market status and use of secure government contracts means that their revenues are secure, there is still a fear that all is not well and that at some point, the need to become more agile will force a major systems overhaul. What our data also show is that structured IS planning—a term that signifies use of formal investment appraisal (both before and after an IT investment goes live), equitable use of chargeback procedures, and a portfolio approach to IT project management—is more likely to contribute to the development of flexible IT infrastructure and through this an improved degree of alignment between IT and business strategy.

## Research Contribution

This chapter contributes to the growing literature on alignment in three key respects. First, we use data from matched surveys of business and IS executives at 241 firms to reveal a positive link between IT infrastructure flexibility and strategic alignment.[5] Second, we use case study data from six firms to further evaluate the significance of this relationship. Based on interviews with business and IS executives at these firms—aerospace, banking, career services, health care insurance, printing, and software—we identify that strategic IS planning moderates the link between IT infrastructure flexibility and alignment. Chaotic SISP is prevalent among firms with less flexible IT infrastructure whereas more structured planning procedures accompany firms with flexible IT infrastructure. Rather than classify SISP as a *causal* variable, case study data highlight a complex interplay between SISP processes and the portfolio of IT assets that makes up a firm's IT infrastructure. Often, IS planning is forced to react to earlier IT investments decisions that have resulted in rigidity traps. Third, from our limited case data, we do not find evidence that higher volatility contributes to chaotic planning or that stable environmental conditions contribute to structured planning. However, it is the case that IS planning is more difficult in situations where firms are under constant threat of competitive attack. For example, firms in the fashion retail or electronics sector continue to work with very short life cycles, fickle customers, expectations of higher quality, and often irrational price wars. If firms are to survive and prosper under such conditions, IT infrastructure must be flexible and adaptable. For this to occur, firms must pay careful attention to environmental scanning and SISP, in general.

## Limitations and Future Research

This research has a number of limitations that weaken its contribution. First, we use only six firms for case study purposes. Although these firms are also part of our extended survey effort, there is a possibility that the data gathered in executive interviews is incomplete or biased in any number of ways. We recognize the value of using multiple methods—matched surveys and case studies—to study the same phenomenon. While our interview data reinforce what we found in survey analysis, it is always preferable for theory development and testing to use as large a sample as possible. Second, although we discussed SISP at length during our interviews, we did not collect IS planning data through surveys using any of the measurement constructs developed in earlier IS research. Doing so would have allowed a more systematic measurement of SISP at each of the six sites we visited. Instead, our interpretation reflects an independent content analysis of the transcripts of each interview by the author and a graduate student researcher. Notes were then compared and labels describing SISP were assigned to each firm. Third, although we conducted a number of repeat visits to some firms, our data are not longitudinal. We did observe over the course of several visits, attempts by firms to reposition or change their strategy but this was not systematically done for all firms. Had this happened, we would have been able to give a more precise description of the issues facing IT in each firm, particularly as regards rigidity traps and how firms are trying to overcome them.

Notwithstanding the fact that IS planning has been a fixture in academic IS research for over two decades, much work remains to be done. Despite a great deal of progress in isolating effective IS planning procedures, there is still some question as to whether practitioners are attentive to the prescriptive view of academicians (Teubner, 2007). Our approach has not only been to assess alignment through the lens of what firms are *actually doing* but also to ask pointed questions about SISP. Often, what academics view as obvious requirements for SISP effectiveness are factors that are overlooked or ignored by firms in the rush to get things done. While it might be argued that research needs to be more relevant (besides rigorous), there is also an issue of research transfer to managers. There are, within the realm of SISP, many issues that still frustrate firms and represent fruitful grounds for research. For example, we heard on several occasions (notably from CIOs) a reluctance to commit to long-term IT flexibility projects. This was sometimes an issue of expense (building flexible IT is not always conducive to IT budget-cutting efforts) but rather a question of how CIOs should sell IT flexibility to their business peers. Some firms want to expect the unexpected but the reality is that some events are more expected than others. Future research could benefit enormously from looking at how firms build uncertainty into SISP using real options.

Part of the reality for firms is dealing with crises such as when competitors launch a new product or initiate a sudden price war. Even if firms have not actively planned for these events, there is still some sense of impromptu planning as action plans are quickly put in place. We saw this, for example, at the bank we visited when a regional rival was unexpectedly acquired by a national bank, setting in motion a chain of marketing events at our case site in an attempt to forestall the loss of market share to this now very large rival. For many firms, having a flexible infrastructure helps to eliminate some of the guesswork that firms need to do when reacting to market change; in effect, flexibility provides options that allow firms to respond in a variety of ways. However, when certain unplanned events occur (as this bank learned), SISP proceeds in a different way. Seeing firms respond to crises is an area worthy of future research in that firms often turn to IT to try to restore order to a disrupted business. This form of impromptu IS planning need not produce ineffective results but it is again an area where considerations of flexible IT allow firms to quickly design thoughtful responses to unforeseen and otherwise unplanned events.

**Concluding Remarks**

Despite recent pronouncements that, having acquired the status of a commodity, IT is no longer a source of competitive differentiation (Carr, 2003), executive surveys continue to rank IT effectiveness or the search for higher value from IT among the most critical issues of modern times (Luftman, Kempaiah, and Nash, 2006). Equally, alignment between IT and business strategy remains a perennial managerial concern as firms try to remain competitive in an increasingly flat world (CSC, 2001). Prior research has alluded to the importance of being flexible, adaptable, and responsive to change, yet the technical nature of IT (along with the often significant sunk cost) means that IT is often the least flexible resource available to firms. When IT is unresponsive to change, firms risk stumbling into rigidity traps with the attendant risks of encountering reduced performance (Bharadwaj, 2000). While we do not measure rigidity traps directly, we find that in firms with flexible IT infrastructure, alignment is higher than when IT infrastructure is inflexible. We also discover that chaotic IS planning can prolong rigidity traps. These traps, in turn, complicate subsequent IS planning as firms try to work around the ambiguities of rigid legacy systems. Yet, we also note that structured planning can help firms to anticipate and recognize change much sooner and so architect flexible IT infrastructure to ensure continuous alignment between IT and business strategy, even if that strategy shifts to reflect a new or different market reality. Change does not have to be exogenous to all firms where firms are constantly reacting to change initiated elsewhere. The use of flexible IT enables firms to be more proactive should they decide to set the pace of change within their own industry.

There is universal consensus that firms are now competing in a highly volatile environment where speed, flexibility, and agility are essential to success (Sambamurthy, Bharadwaj, and Grover, 2003). Even the most sophisticated SISP processes are unlikely to capture all adverse events that can occur, so it has fallen to IT to provide a buffer, allowing firms to adapt to any number of situations. Unfortunately, as our data show, IT is not always as flexible as one might wish; rigidity traps are very real and unfortunately very expensive and time consuming to solve. Looking to the future, there is room for improvement in how firms plan for change and how they can plan for IT to continuously align with business strategy, knowing that alignment has been proved to enhance firm performance.

## APPENDIX 20.1. SURVEY INSTRUMENTS
## STRATEGIC PLANNER SURVEY (EXTRACT)

### 1. Business Strategy

Business strategy is reflected in the execution of business activities throughout the firm. For each of the business processes below, please consider the critical business activities on the right, and identify the extent to which these activities have been implemented or enacted by your firm.

| Activities Implemented | | | | | | | | |
|---|---|---|---|---|---|---|---|---|
| Not Implemented | | | | | | Fully Implemented | Business Processes | Critical Business Activities |
| 1 | 2 | 3 | 4 | 5 | 6 | 7 | Supplier Relations | Forge closer links with suppliers; monitor quality; monitor delivery times; gain leverage over suppliers; negotiate pricing. |
| 1 | 2 | 3 | 4 | 5 | 6 | 7 | Production and Operations | Improve throughput, boost labor productivity, improve flexibility and equipment utilization; streamline operations. |
| 1 | 2 | 3 | 4 | 5 | 6 | 7 | Product and Service Enhancement | Embed IT in products; increase pace of development/R&D; monitor design cost; improve quality; support innovation. |
| 1 | 2 | 3 | 4 | 5 | 6 | 7 | Sales and Marketing Support | Spot market trends; anticipate customer needs; build market share; improve forecast accuracy; evaluate pricing options. |
| 1 | 2 | 3 | 4 | 5 | 6 | 7 | Customer Relations | Respond to customer needs; provide after-sales service and support; improve distribution; create customer loyalty. |

## 2. Environmental Change

Please complete the following for a flagship product or service sold by your firm.

N = ____    Average length of the life cycle of the product or service (*in months*).

% = ____    What % of customers is turned over (i.e., lost or replaced) in a year?

% = ____    What % of sales comes from products or services launched in the past 2 years?

## CIO/IT EXECUTIVE SURVEY (EXTRACT)

### 1. Information Technology Use

To what extent is IT used to support critical business activities in each of the following processes? A sampling of critical activities in each process is shown below:

*Supplier Relations*

Forge closer links with suppliers; monitor quality; monitor deliveries; gain leverage over suppliers; negotiate prices

*Production and Operations*

Improve throughput, boost labor productivity, improve flexibility and equipment utilization; streamline operations

*Product and Service Enhancement*

Embed IT in products; expand pace of development/R&D; monitor design cost; improve quality; support innovation

*Marketing and Sales*

Spot market trends; anticipate customer needs; build market share; boost forecast accuracy; evaluate pricing options

*Customer Relations*

Respond to customer needs; provide after-sales service and support; improve distribution; create customer loyalty

|                                 | Low IT Use |   |   |   |   | High IT Use |   |
|---------------------------------|:----------:|:-:|:-:|:-:|:-:|:-----------:|:-:|
| Supplier Relations              | 1 | 2 | 3 | 4 | 5 | 6 | 7 |
| Production and Operations       | 1 | 2 | 3 | 4 | 5 | 6 | 7 |
| Product and Service Enhancement | 1 | 2 | 3 | 4 | 5 | 6 | 7 |
| Marketing and Sales             | 1 | 2 | 3 | 4 | 5 | 6 | 7 |
| Customer Relations              | 1 | 2 | 3 | 4 | 5 | 6 | 7 |

## 2. Information Technology Infrastructure Flexibility

To what extent do you agree with the following statements on IT infrastructure in your firm?

| | Do Not Agree | | | | | Agree Completely | |
|---|---|---|---|---|---|---|---|
| Hardware Compatibility (HC 1—4) | | | | | | | |
| Software applications can be easily transported and used across multiple platforms | 1 | 2 | 3 | 4 | 5 | 6 | 7 |
| Our user interfaces provide transparent access to all platforms and applications | 1 | 2 | 3 | 4 | 5 | 6 | 7 |
| Our firm offers multiple interfaces or entry points (e.g., Web access) to external users | 1 | 2 | 3 | 4 | 5 | 6 | 7 |
| Our firm makes extensive use of middleware to integrate key enterprise applications | 1 | 2 | 3 | 4 | 5 | 6 | 7 |
| Software Modularity (SM 1—4) | | | | | | | |
| Reusable software modules are widely used throughout our systems development unit | 1 | 2 | 3 | 4 | 5 | 6 | 7 |
| Legacy systems within our firm do not hamper the development of new IT applications | 1 | 2 | 3 | 4 | 5 | 6 | 7 |
| Functionality can be quickly added to critical applications based on end-user requests | 1 | 2 | 3 | 4 | 5 | 6 | 7 |
| Our firm can easily handle variations in data formats and standards | 1 | 2 | 3 | 4 | 5 | 6 | 7 |
| Network Connectivity (NC 1—4) | | | | | | | |
| Our company has a high degree of systems interconnectivity | 1 | 2 | 3 | 4 | 5 | 6 | 7 |
| Our systems are sufficiently flexible to incorporate electronic links to external parties | 1 | 2 | 3 | 4 | 5 | 6 | 7 |
| Remote users can seamlessly access centralized data | 1 | 2 | 3 | 4 | 5 | 6 | 7 |
| Data are captured and made available to everyone in the firm in real time | 1 | 2 | 3 | 4 | 5 | 6 | 7 |
| IT Skills Adaptability (ITSA 1—4) | | | | | | | |
| Our IT personnel are encouraged to improve their technical skills | 1 | 2 | 3 | 4 | 5 | 6 | 7 |
| Our IT personnel can quickly develop technical solutions to business problems | 1 | 2 | 3 | 4 | 5 | 6 | 7 |
| Our IT personnel are adept at multitasking | 1 | 2 | 3 | 4 | 5 | 6 | 7 |
| Our IT personnel are trained in a variety of programming methodologies and tools | 1 | 2 | 3 | 4 | 5 | 6 | 7 |

## NOTES

1. In this chapter, we use the terms fit and alignment interchangeably. In each case, the underlying premise is that of using IT to support the business strategy while also evolving the business strategy to take advantage of IT.

2. Just as there are different dimensions of SISP success, there are many activities that fall under the broad rubric of IS planning. As seen in the qualitative portion of this chapter, we chose not to impose limits

on the scope of these activities during our case study interviews. Instead, we invited interviewees to describe their planning activities in general rather than providing them a predetermined activity checklist. This unstructured approach led to many in-depth discussions with interviewees and to important findings that might otherwise have remained hidden.

3. The case of Merrill Lynch (ML) in the late 1990s is illustrative of the risks of failing to adjust one's business strategy to compete in more than one domain. ML did not adopt an online strategy until such time as its market capitalization was less than that of Charles Schwab. ML continued to view brokerage transactions as a value-added service when the industry was moving to a low-cost model. Despite fears of a backlash from commissioned advisers, ML built a low-cost brokerage service—ML Direct—to compete alongside its more expensive broker-assisted services.

4. Some researchers have proposed that firms may align business strategy to IT strategy; in effect, IT strategy is the driving force behind business strategy decisions (Henderson and Venkatraman, 1993. Beyond doing some empirical analysis to determine which comes first, business or IT strategy, logically and practically, it would seem unlikely in modern firms, that executives would delegate strategic decision making for the entire firm to those in charge of IT. Anecdotally, we know that it is difficult for CIOs to be respected by those who see IT as a cost rather than an investment. For this reason, it is more likely that firms will align IT to business strategy—with the latter acting as a fixed anchor.

5. We refer readers to Tallon (2006) for a more intricate analysis of this relationship using structural modeling.

## REFERENCES

Anand, B.N.; Rukstad, M.G.; and Paige, C.H. 2001. *Capital One Financial Corporation (9–700–124)*. Cambridge, MA: Harvard Business School Press.

Barney, J.B. 1991. Firm resources and sustained competitive advantage. *Journal of Management, 17*, 1, 99–120.

Bharadwaj, A. 2000. A resource-based perspective on information technology capability and firm performance: an empirical investigation. *MIS Quarterly, 24*, 1, 169–196.

Bharadwaj, A.; Sambamurthy, V.; and Zmud, R. 2002. Firmwide IT capability: an empirical examination of the construct and its links to performance. Emory University.

Broadbent, M., and Weill, P. 1993. Improving business and information strategy alignment: learning from the banking industry. *IBM Systems Journal, 32*, 1, 162–179.

Byrd, T.A., and Turner, D.E. 2000. Measuring the flexibility of information technology infrastructure: exploratory analysis of a construct. *Journal of Management Information Systems, 17*, 1, 167–208.

Carr, N. 2003. IT doesn't matter. *Harvard Business Review, 81*, 5, 41–49.

Chan, Y.E.; Huff, S.L.; Barclay, D.W.; and Copeland, D.G. 1997. Business strategy orientation, information systems orientation and strategic alignment. *Information Systems Research, 8*, 2, 125–150.

Christensen, C.M. 1997. *The Innovator's Dilemma.* Cambridge, MA: Harvard Business School Press.

Computer Sciences Corporation (CSC). 2001. *Critical Issues in Information Systems Management.* Cambridge, MA.

Davenport, T., and Linder, J. 1994. Information management infrastructure: the new competitive weapon. *Proceedings of the Twenty-seventh Annual Hawaii International Conference on Systems Sciences.* IEEE, pp. 885–899.

Duncan, N. 1995. Capturing flexibility of information technology infrastructure: a study of resource characteristics and their measure. *Journal of Management Information Systems, 12*, 2, 37–57.

Earl, M.J. 1993. Experiences in strategic information systems planning. *MIS Quarterly, 17*, 1, 1–24.

Eisenhardt, K.M. 1989. Building theories from case study research. *Academy of Management Review, 14*, 4, 532–550.

Eisenhardt, K.M., and Martin, J.A. 2000. Dynamic capabilities: what are they? *Strategic Management Journal, 21*, 10–11, 1105–1121.

Feeny, D.F., and Willcocks, L.P. 1998. Core IS capabilities or exploiting information technology. *Sloan Management Review, 39*, 2, 9–21.

Fichman, R.G.; Keil, M.; and Tiwana, A. 2006. Beyond valuation: options thinking in IT project management. *California Management Review, 47*, 2, 74–96.

Fine, C.H. 1998. *Clockspeed: Winning Industry Control in the Age of Temporary Advantage.* Reading, MA: Perseus Books.

Fornell, C., and Larcker, D.F. 1981. Evaluating structural equation models with unobservable variables and measurement error. *Journal of Marketing Research,* 18, 1, 39–50.

Friedman, T.L. 2006. *The World Is Flat.* New York: Farrar, Straus, and Giroux.

Gurbaxani, V.; Melville, N.; and Kraemer, K.L. 1998. Disaggregating the return on investment to IT capital. In J.I. DeGross, R. Hirschheim, and M. Newman (eds.), *Proceedings of the Nineteenth International Conference on Information Systems.* Helsinki, Finland: Association for Information Systems, Atlanta, GA, pp. 376–380.

Henderson, J.C., and Venkatraman, N. 1993. Strategic alignment: leveraging information technology for transforming organizations. *IBM Systems Journal,* 32, 1, 4–16.

Hugos, M. 2007. Doing business in real time: JetBlue and the lessons of business agility. *CIO Magazine Blog.* Available at http://advice.cio.com/node/733?source=nlt_cioinsider (accessed on August 30, 2007).

Kaplan, B., and Duchon, D. 1988. Combining qualitative and quantitative methods in information systems research: a case study. *MIS Quarterly,* 12, 4, 571–586.

Kearns, G.S., and Lederer, A. 2003. A resource-based view of strategic it alignment: how knowledge sharing creates competitive advantage. *Decision Sciences,* 34, 1, 1–29.

Keen, P. 1991. *Shaping the Future: Business Design Through Information Technology.* Boston: Harvard Business School Press.

Kettinger, W.J.; Grover, V.; Guha, S.; and Segars, A. 1994. Strategic information systems revisited: a study in sustainability and performance. *MIS Quarterly,* 18, 1, 31–58.

Kraemer, K.L.; Dedrick, J.; and Yamashiro, S. 2000. Refining and extending the business model with information technology: Dell computer corporation. *Information Society,* 16, 1, 5–21.

Lederer, A., and Salmela, H. 1996. Toward a theory of strategic information systems planning. *Journal of Strategic Information Systems,* 5, 3, 237–253.

Lee, A.S. 1989. A scientific methodology for MIS case studies. *MIS Quarterly,* 13, 1, 33–50.

Luftman, J.N. 1996. Applying the strategic alignment model. In J.N. Luftman (ed.), *Competing in the Information Age: Strategic Alignment in Practice.* New York: Oxford University Press, pp. 43–69.

Luftman, J.N.; Kempaiah, R.; and Nash, E. 2006. Key issues for IT executives 2005. *MIS Quarterly Executive,* 5, 2, 27–45.

Luftman, J.N.; Papp, R.; and Brier, T. 1999. Enablers and inhibitors of business-IT alignment. *Communications of the AIS,* 1, 11, 1–32.

Mendelson, H., and Pillai, R.R. 1998. Clockspeed and informational response: evidence from the information technology industry. *Information Systems Research,* 9, 4, 415–433.

Miles, R.E., and Snow, C.C. 1978. *Organizational Strategy, Structure, and Process.* New York: McGraw-Hill.

Miller, D. 1993. The architecture of simplicity. *Academy of Management Review,* 18, 1, 116–138.

Miller, D., and Chen, M.J. 1996. The simplicity of competitive repertoires: an empirical analysis. *Strategic Management Journal,* 17, 6, 419–439.

Miller, D.; Lant, T.K.; Milliken, F.J.; and Korn, H.J. 1996. The evolution of strategic simplicity: exploring two models of organizational adaptation. *Journal of Management,* 22, 6, 863–887.

Mintzberg, H., and Waters, J.A. 1985. Of strategies, deliberate and emergent. *Strategic Management Journal,* 6, 3, 257–272.

Nunnally, J.C. 1978. *Psychometric Theory,* 2d ed. New York: McGraw-Hill.

Oh, W., and Pinsonneault, A. 2006. On the assessment of the strategic value of information technologies: conceptual and analytical approaches. *MIS Quarterly,* 31, 2, 239–265.

Palmer, J.W., and Markus, M.L. 2000. The performance impacts of quick response and strategic alignment in specialty retailing. *Information Systems Research,* 11, 3, 241–259.

Podsakoff, P.M.; MacKenzie, S.B.; Lee, J.Y.; and Podsakoff, N.P. 2003. Common method bias in behavioral research: a critical review of the literature and recommended remedies. *Journal of Applied Psychology,* 88, 5, 879–903.

Porter, M.E. 1980. *Competitive Strategy: Techniques for Analyzing Industries and Competitors.* New York: Free Press.

———. 1985. *Competitive Advantage.* New York: Free Press.

———. 1991. Towards a dynamic theory of strategy. *Strategic Management Journal,* 12 (Winter), 95–117.

———. 1996. What is strategy? *Harvard Business Review,* 74, 6, 61–77.

Prahalad, C.K., and Krishnan, M.S. 2002. The dynamic synchronization of strategy and information technology. *Sloan Management Review,* 43, 4, 24–33.

Ravichandran, T., and Lertwongsatien, C. 2005. Effect of information systems resources and capabilities on firm performance. *Journal of Management Information Systems*, 21, 4, 237–276.

Ray, G.; Barney, J.; and Muhanna, W.A. 2004. Capabilities, business processes, and competitive advantage: choosing the dependent variable in empirical tests of the resource-based view. *Strategic Management Journal*, 25, 1, 23–37.

Ray, G.; Muhanna, W.A.; and Barney, J. 2005. Information technology and the performance of the customer service process: a resource-based analysis. *MIS Quarterly*, 29, 4, 625–652.

Reich, B.H., and Benbasat, I. 1996. Measuring the linkage between business and information technology objectives. *MIS Quarterly*, 20, 1, 55–81.

Rindova, V.P., and Kotha, S. 2001. Continuous "morphing": competing through dynamic capabilities, form, and function. *Academy of Management Journal*, 44, 6, 1263–1280.

Ross, J.W.; Weill, P.; and Robertson, D.C. 2006. *Enterprise Architecture as Strategy*. Cambridge, MA: Harvard Business School Press.

Sabherwal, R., and Chan, Y.E. 2001. Alignment between business and IS strategies: a study of prospectors, analyzers and defenders. *Information Systems Research*, 12, 1, 11–33.

Sabherwal, R.; Hirschheim, R.; and Goles, T. 2001. The dynamics of alignment: insights from a punctuated equilibrium model. *Organization Science*, 12, 2, 179–197.

Salmela, H.; Lederer, A.; and Reponen, T. 2000. Information systems planning in a turbulent environment. *European Journal of Information Systems*, 9, 1, 3–15.

Sambamurthy, V.; Bharadwaj, A.; and Grover, V. 2003. Shaping agility through digital options: reconceptualizing the role of information technology in contemporary firms. *MIS Quarterly*, 27, 2, 237–263.

Segars, A.H., and Grover, V. 1998. Strategic information systems planning success: an investigation of the construct and its measurement. *MIS Quarterly*, 22, 2, 139–163.

———. 1999. Profiles of strategic information systems planning. *Information Systems Research*, 10, 3, 199–232.

Segars, A.H.; Grover, V.; and Teng, J. 1998. Strategic information systems planning: planning system dimensions, internal co-alignment, and implications for planning effectiveness. *Decision Sciences*, 29, 2, 303–345.

Stabell, C. and Fjeldstad, Ø. 1998. Configuring value for competitive advantage: on chains, shops and networks. *Strategic Management Journal*, 19, 5, 413–437.

Tallon, P.P. 2006. Leveraging IT infrastructure for firm performance: perspectives on IT resource positioning under environmental dynamism. CRITO, University of California, Irvine.

———. 2007. Inside the adaptive enterprise: an information technology capabilities perspective on business process agility. *Information Technology and Management*, 9, 1, 21–36.

———. 2008. A process-oriented perspective on the alignment of information technology and business strategy. *Journal of Management Information Systems*, 24, 3, 231–272.

Tallon, P.P.; Kraemer, K.L.; and Gurbaxani, V. 2000. Executives' perceptions of the business value of information technology: a process-oriented approach. *Journal of Management Information Systems*, 16, 4, 145–173.

Teece, D.; Pisano, G.; and Shuen, A. 1997. Dynamic capabilities and strategic management. *Strategic Management Journal*, 18, 7, 509–533.

Teubner, R.A. 2007. Strategic information systems planning: a case study from the financial services industry. *Journal of Strategic Information Systems*, 16, 1, 105–125.

Treacy, M., and Wiersema, F. 1995. *The Discipline of Market Leaders*. New York: Basic Books.

Venkatraman, N. 1989. The concept of fit in strategy research: toward verbal and statistical correspondence. *Academy of Management Review*, 14, 3, 423–444.

Venkatraman, N., and Ramanujam, V. 1987. Planning system success: a conceptualization and an operational model. *Management Science*, 33, 6, 687–705.

Venkatraman, N.; Henderson, J.C.; and Oldach, S.H. 1993. Continuous strategic alignment: exploiting IT capabilities for competitive success. *European Management Journal*, 11, 2, 139–149.

Wade, W., and Hulland, J. 2004. The resource-based view and information systems research: review, extension, and suggestions for future research. *MIS Quarterly*, 28, 1, 107–142.

Weill, P., and Broadbent, M. 1998. *Leveraging the New Infrastructure: How Market Leaders Capitalize on Information Technology*. Cambridge, MA: Harvard Business School Press.

Weill, P.; Subramani, M.; and Broadbent, M. 2002. Building IT infrastructure for strategic agility. *Sloan Management Review*, 44, 1, 57–65.

White, R.E. 1986. Generic business strategies, organizational context and performance: an empirical investigation. *Strategic Management Journal*, 7, 3, 217–231.

CHAPTER 21

# HOW INFORMATION TECHNOLOGY RESOURCES CAN PROVIDE A COMPETITIVE ADVANTAGE IN CUSTOMER SERVICE

JAY B. BARNEY AND GAUTAM RAY

*Abstract: Information technology (IT) investments, including investments in customer relation-ship management systems, constitute a significant proportion of firms' capital investments. Firms have, however, struggled to measure the payoffs from these investments. In this article, we use the resource-based view of the firm to discuss how different IT resources, individually, and in combi-nation with other IT and non–IT resources, may create value. More specifically, we contend that IT resources create value when IT resources, together with other IT and non-IT resources, allow firms to improve the relative performance of their customer service processes.*

*Keywords: Information Technology, Resource-Based View, IT Resources, Competitive Advantage, Customer Service*

## INTRODUCTION

Firms across the United States and around the globe make significant investments in information technology (IT). The IT sector constitutes about 8 percent of gross domestic product in the U.S. economy (IITA 2007). Currently, IT investments form about 40–45 percent of U.S. capital invest-ment (Montes, 2003). In the past decade, IT investments have been concentrated in enterprise resource planning (ERP), supply chain management (SCM), and customer relationship manage-ment (CRM) systems. However, despite the significant size of these IT investments, chief execu-tive officers (CEOs) and chief information officers (CIO) have struggled to measure the payoffs needed to justify them.

Over the years, various theories have been proposed and numerous studies conducted to measure these payoffs. In the early 1980s, this work focused on how IT could influence industry structure in a way that could give particular firms competitive advantages. Popularized by Porter, the argu-ment was that IT can influence the nature of competition in an industry by influencing competitive forces such as the power of buyers and suppliers, threat of substitution, intra-industry rivalry, and most important, by building barriers against potential new entrants (e.g., Porter and Millar, 1995). Several detailed case studies were written that showed how some firms were able to use IT to attain competitive advantages in this manner (e.g., Vitale, 1985; Vitale and Konsynski, 1988).

However, as IT fell in price and became more widely available, the notion that IT, per se, could act as a barrier to entry began to be questioned. Instead of being a source of competitive advan-tage, IT became a competitive necessity for firms seeking to survive in an industry (Carr, 2003).

444

This commoditization of IT, it was suggested, should lead companies to treat IT like any other commodity—an important part of the production process in a firm, but not a source of competitive advantage. While good IT can help a firm to survive, it cannot help a firm to thrive.

This article develops an alternative point of view. Building on resource-based theory (Barney, 1986, 1991; Grant, 1991; Peteraf, 1993; Stalk, Evans, and Shulman, 1992; Teece, Pisano, and Shuen, 1997; Wernerfelt, 1984), it is suggested that while IT alone is unlikely to be a source of competitive advantage, in combination with other resources controlled by a firm, IT can be such a source. This conclusion is based on the observation that such combinations of IT and IT-related resources not only may enable a firm to increase the satisfaction of its customers but also can do it in ways that competing firms cannot and in ways that competing firms find difficult to imitate. Such valuable, rare, and costly-to-imitate bundles of resources and capabilities are identified by resource-based theory as potential sources of sustained competitive advantage for firms.

For example, Ritz-Carlton has developed a variety of applications that help customer service employees to identify customer preferences so that a room can be customized to a customer's tastes (Berinato, 2002; Sasser, Jones, and Klein, 1994). These applications require the development of a customer preference database direct from customers and customer service personnel, software to gain access to that database, the ability and willingness of customer service personnel to actually use that database to customize rooms and to update the database. In principle, many firms could implement this application. In practice, Ritz-Carlton is one of the few hotel chains to have done so.

Why is this the case? First, Ritz-Carlton customers are more likely to appreciate—and be willing to pay for—this customized service. That is, it is economically valuable for Ritz-Carlton to provide this service. Second, IT professionals and customer service professionals in Ritz-Carlton were apparently able to work closely enough to develop applications that made customization possible and that were easy for customer service personnel to access and update. Third, Ritz-Carlton employees actually use these applications to customize rooms. This may be because of the employees that Ritz-Carlton hires, how they are trained and monitored, and so forth. Firms seeking to imitate Ritz-Carlton's strategy would have to be in the right market segment, have the right kind of relationship between IT and customer service, have to develop the right kinds of applications, and have the right kinds of human resources (HR) systems to ensure that these applications are actually used. Imitating any of these attributes of Ritz-Carlton may be difficult; imitating all of them and having them work together seamlessly is very difficult to accomplish.

In this example, it is not IT per se that gives Ritz-Carlton a competitive advantage, but how IT enables the firm to more fully leverage its resources and capabilities and how IT is linked with these other resources and capabilities. This not only provides a competitive advantage but also makes it difficult for competitors to imitate—at least so far.[1]

In this article we use resource-based theory to examine how distinct IT assets, individually and in combination, affect customer service. The resources examined are: (1) IT–business relationship, (2) technical skills, including application development/implementation methodology, (3) customer service (hardware/software) technologies, (4) IT platform: mainframe and network infrastructure, (5) vendor relationships, (6) customer database, and (7) operating and backend processes. These resources, individually and in combination, may affect customer service and customer satisfaction. This article focuses on IT resources that are identified in the literature (e.g., Bharadwaj, 2000; Powell and Dent-Micallef, 1997; Mata, Fuerst, and Barney, 1995) as being crucial. Many non–IT resources such as organizational culture and human resources practices are complementary to IT and together with IT may lead to competitive advantages. Such non–IT resources are not discussed individually in this article. In the second section we discuss each IT resource individually, and in the third section we discuss the competitive implications of interactions among different resources. Finally, some conclusions are presented.

## INDIVIDUAL INFORMATION TECHNOLOGY RESOURCES[2]

### IT–Business Partnership

IT–business partnership refers to the shared knowledge and understanding between IT managers and customer service managers about customer service processes and how IT can be used to improve customer satisfaction. An organization's IT use is influenced by the absorptive capacity of IT, that is, the presence of IT-related knowledge that binds the firm's IT and line managers (Boynton, Zmud, and Jacobs, 1994). The overlapping pool of *shared knowledge* (i.e., the knowledge that the IT manager possesses about customer service processes, and the knowledge that customer service managers possess about potential opportunities for IT applications to improve customer service) constitutes IT–business partnership. IT–business partnership enables an organization to conceive and implement unique IT applications to improve customer satisfaction (Henderson, 1990; Rockart, 1988).[3]

An IT–business partnership is likely to be a rare resource that is costly to imitate for several reasons (Mata, Fuerst, and Barney, 1995). For example, it is typically developed over long periods of time. The trust, interpersonal relationships, and shared body of firm-specific knowledge between IT and customer service managers, which makes them capable of conceiving novel IT applications, can take years and numerous joint development projects to establish. Thus the development of an IT–business partnership is often a path-dependent and socially complex process. To the extent that an IT–business partnership is valuable and heterogeneously distributed across firms, it can be a source of competitive advantage, since it is not subject to low-cost imitation. Thus, firms that have the firm-specific knowledge and expertise to use IT in unique ways to improve customer service will derive competitive advantage from IT even though all firms may have access to the same information technologies.

### Technical IT Skills/Application Development/Implementation Methodology

Technical IT skills are the skills needed to develop IT applications. Technical IT skills include analysis, design, and programming skills, understanding of operating systems, and experience with databases and networking protocols. While these skills can be very valuable, since they are widely available to firms—through hiring employees or consultants with these skills—they are usually not rare or costly to imitate, and thus, by themselves, they are not likely to be sources of distinctive advantages (Mata, Fuerst, and Barney, 1995). However, if a firm's programmers and analysts develop a specialized understanding of the firm's processes and strategies and are able to conceive unique applications to improve customer service, then such an understanding of a firm's processes and strategies can be a source of competitive advantage.

In contrast to technical skills, application development methodology refers to the higher order (managerial) processes involved in collecting requirements and organizing the development and implementation of IT applications. Carnegie Mellon University's capability maturity model (CMM) is an example of software development methodology. CMM refers to the structured approach to developing and implementing software applications. However, while it is clear that the requirements of each CMM level are well documented, few organizations have achieved the highest level (CMM level 5) of certification. As higher levels of CMM have been associated with more reliable/predictable, higher quality, and lower cost/cycle time of development (Harter, Krishnan, and Slaughter, 2000), firms at higher CMM levels have a competitive advantage in developing and implementing IT applications. Similarly, implementing large IT applications has proved to be a significant challenge (e.g., Worthen, 2002). Since large IT applications are more about managing organizational change than about implementing software applications, this is not surprising. Thus, if a firm has figured out the social aspects of implementing IT projects, that firm can achieve a competitive advantage with application development/implementation methodology.

### Generic Customer Service Information (Hardware/Software) Technologies

Generic customer service technologies refer to the commonly available hardware and software technologies that are used in customer service activities. Generic information technology may include scanning technologies used in the insurance industry, handheld and other point-of-sale (POS) technologies in the retail industry, and the computer telephony integration technologies generally used in call-center applications. Generic information technologies are valuable resources that are used to support customer service processes. However, as seen over the past twenty years, they are usually not difficult to imitate as they can be procured from the market (Mata, Fuerst, and Barney, 1995). Therefore, generic customer service technologies, by themselves, are not likely to be sources of competitive advantage.

In this regard, the level of raw dollar spending on IT is an important resource. Failure to invest in generic information technologies can put a firm at a competitive disadvantage in terms of the performance of its customer service processes. For this reason, firms have a strong incentive to invest in the IT assets necessary to maintain a competitive level of customer service. In this sense investing in IT has almost become a competitive necessity. However, IT spending, per se, is not likely to provide a competitive advantage and explain variance in customer service across firms in an industry. To the extent that IT assets are equally available to all the participants, in a competitive market all the firms will make close-to-optimal IT investments and no firm will gain an advantage from their IT spending per se (Mata, Fuerst, and Barney, 1995; Ray, Muhanna, and Barney, 2005).

### IT Platform

The IT platform is the set of shared capital resources that provides the foundation on which specific IT applications are built. The primary components of the IT platform are: (1) the computing platform (hardware and operating systems), and (2) the communications network. The characteristic of the IT platform makes the speed of implementation, cost, and value of new IT applications different for different firms. This characteristic is described as "flexibility." A flexible IT platform allows for more rapid response to emerging business needs, whereas an inflexible IT platform gets in the way of some important initiatives, limiting the freedom of the company to respond to market forces and innovate. On the other hand, less flexible platforms may allow the efficient execution of a narrow and unchanging set of IT applications in a firm.

The flexibility of the IT platform is manifested in the degree to which a firm's data and applications can be shared and accessed throughout the organization. Such flexibility enables an organization to rapidly build and implement IT applications to respond to emerging market needs. A firm's IT platform is also flexible to the extent that the firm adopts and enforces standards for the components of its IT platform to ensure connectivity and compatibility of its technology platform and shareability of its data and applications.

A flexible IT platform is a complex set of technological resources carefully planned for and developed over time. Because of its path-dependent nature, there can be significant differences across firms in how infrastructure is constituted. Moreover, these differences can be long lasting, since disassembling one platform and erecting a new one can be both costly and time consuming. To the extent that the flexibility of the IT platform varies across firms in an industry, and to the extent that a flexible IT platform enables firms to implement IT applications to support specific processes more efficiently and effectively, the variance in platform flexibility can explain differences in customer service across firms. To the extent that one firm can implement an IT-based strategy that its competitors cannot imitate because of an inflexible IT platform, a flexible IT platform is a strategic resource that can be a source of competitive advantage.

A flexible IT platform is an investment for the future that enables the organization to respond quickly to the market. Therefore, though a flexible IT platform may improve the responsiveness of the IT organization, a flexible IT platform may not have any impact on the current level of performance. By investing in a standard platform that ensures compatibility/connectivity and facilitates the shareability of data across systems and units, an organization sets itself to respond quickly to market demands. Thus, though a flexible IT platform may not improve current performance, it may be necessary for the long-term competitiveness of the organization. Also, the more dynamic a firm's environment, the more valuable a flexible IT platform can be to its long-term survival and growth. The IT platform is thus an enabler (of IT applications), just as highways are enablers of commerce. The IT platform by itself may not provide a competitive advantage, just as highways on their own do not lead to economic growth, but they provide the backbone for commerce that allows economic growth to take place.

A flexible IT platform is more valuable when the firm's environment is dynamic, that is, when the firm actually requires flexibility to respond to changing customer requirements and different and unpredictable competitive moves. In very stable and mature industries where customer needs and competitors' strategies are quite predictable, flexibility may not be very valuable. Investing in a flexible IT platform in such environments may actually hurt economic performance as it will increase the firm's cost of IT operations without any commensurate benefits from the flexibility of its IT platform.

**Vendor Relationships**

IT assets are a complex collection of a large number of hardware and software technologies; and methodologies for developing, implementing, and managing IT applications. An understanding of the firm's competitive environment and business processes and strategies is required to acquire new IT assets and applications. Thus, it is very unlikely that any firm will have the economy of scale and specialization in all of the constituent areas of IT. It is thus not surprising that the IT services market is one of the largest sectors of the U.S. economy. Firms will therefore do well to develop relationships with IT vendors to gain access to services that can lead to a competitive advantage. The literature on strategic alliances and social networks suggests that in more dynamic environments, it is not just the firm's resources that provide a competitive advantage. A firm's ability to identify and gain access to the IT knowledge and expertise that it lacks is a source of competitive advantage. Thus, vendor relationships can be a source of competitive advantage.

**Customer Database**

Customer service applications, over time, allow firms to collect significant transaction histories. These data can be used by firms to develop a profile of each customer so that the firm can offer customized/personalized services to consumers. For example, as discussed earlier, each time a customer visits Ritz-Carlton, any professed preference is recorded by customer service employees. Thus, over time, Ritz-Carlton develops a profile of its customers that allows it to offer each customer a tailor-made room and other services. If the firm is likely to convince the customer to do more business with it, it is likely that the firm will have more information about the customer than any other competitor, in which case, it will be able to offer better service than any of its competitors. Thus, a customer database that is developed over time can be a source of competitive advantage because no competitors will have a comparable database. Mithas, Krishnan, and Fornell (2005) find that CRM systems allow firms to develop customer knowledge that leads to higher customer satisfaction.

## COMPLEMENTARITIES BETWEEN DIFFERENT RESOURCES

The findings regarding individual IT resources have important implications. The technical skills of IT labor and generic customer service technologies alone are not likely to provide a competitive advantage. Investments in generic customer service technologies are a competitive necessity, a cost of being in business. While investments in generic customer service technologies are necessary to provide a competitive level of customer service, they do not provide a competitive advantage. However, this does not mean that these resources are not strategic. In combination with other resources, they can be a source of competitive advantage. This requires that firms develop unique/specific knowledge about how IT can affect the firm's customer service processes and use IT applications to implement improved customer service processes. This is reflected in situations where a firm gains an advantage over its competitors by having superior insight into the use of IT and is manifested in situations where IT allows firms to design and implement customer service processes that are more efficient and effective.

Examples of companies that have gained distinctive advantages through innovative deployment of IT abound (American Airlines–Sabre, Federal Express–Package Tracking system, and Mobil–Speedpass automated payment system). The essential argument here is that a particular IT application may provide only a short-term competitive advantage. However, a firm with unique insight about how to use IT (and access to other IT assets) will be able to innovate continuously to keep ahead of the competition. It is unique insight/knowledge about the innovative use of IT—which we refer to as IT–business partnership—that allows a firm to leverage other IT resources to achieve a competitive advantage (Ray, Muhanna, and Barney, 2005). Thus, the argument is that the complementarity between different IT and non–IT resources is often the source of competitive advantage. In the following paragraphs we discuss the different forms that this complementarity can take.

### IT Resource–IT Resource Complementarity

As discussed in the prior section, IT resources can take many different forms. In this context it is often argued that individual IT resources are easier to imitate. However, a combination of different IT resources is significantly harder to imitate. For example, Bharadwaj (2000) found that firms identified as leaders in the use and application of IT by peers and business leaders have higher profitability (return on assets, return on sales) and lower cost ratio (cost of goods sold to sales) than the control sample. This illustrates causal ambiguity (Barney 1991) about why a firm is successful in using IT strategically. That is, though peers and competitors are able to identify a firm as a leading user of IT, they are not able to neutralize the firm's competitive advantage through imitation. This causal ambiguity increases as the number and interaction among the different IT resources of the firm increase.

Similarly, Tanriverdi (2006) found that the complementarities between IT infrastructure and IT management processes in large multibusiness firms are associated with an increase in performance of diversified firms. This suggests that "IT relatedness" is associated with performance gains. These studies suggest that even if one IT resource alone does not provide a competitive advantage, a combination of IT resources that is rare and inimitable can be a source of competitive advantage.

In the context of e-business environments, Zhu and Kraemer (2002), Zhu (2004) and Zhu and colleagues (2004) find that the integration of front-end functionality (e-commerce capability) and back-end IT infrastructure is associated with e-business value. They also find that the complementarity between front-end e-commerce capability and back-end IT infrastructure led to performance gains in terms of sales per employee, inventory turnover, and cost reduction in the retail industry.

### IT Resource and Non–IT Resource Complementarity

So far, our argument about IT-based competitive advantage has been based on IT resources that lead to innovative IT applications. However, IT can also provide competitive advantage when IT is used to leverage unique/firm-specific non–IT assets. For example, Wal-Mart is able to achieve economies of scale advantage by integrating its distributed stores using IT. The argument is that Wal-Mart is able to realize economy of scale as IT enables it to integrate the purchasing power of all its independent stores. This illustrates that when a firm is able to use IT to leverage some unique non–IT resources—scale effects in this illustration—IT is the lever for gaining a competitive advantage. Wal-Mart is able to achieve a competitive advantage by leveraging its non–IT assets (number of stores–scale) with IT assets (computer hardware/software) that are available to all. Powell and Dent-Micallef (1997), for example, find that IT alone does not provide a sustainable performance advantage, but by using IT to leverage complementary business and human resources, firms have gained sustainable competitive advantages.

### IT-Enabled Business Integration

A third mechanism of IT resource and non–IT resource complementarity is that IT enables integration between firms' customer-side activities with its operations and supplier-side activities. It is clear that to provide superior customer service, firms need to coordinate customer service with operations and supplier-side processes. For example, for Amazon.com to better serve its customers, it must ensure that its warehouses are run efficiently so that books can be delivered to customers expeditiously. This requires that Amazon.com coordinate its activities with suppliers such as logistics providers (e.g., United Parcel Service, the U.S. Postal Service) as well as suppliers such as manufacturers of products and book publishers. Thus, firms need IT to coordinate operations inside the firm as well as IT applications coordinating the firm's activities with their customers and suppliers.

Banker and colleagues (2006) study the impact of plant information systems. They find that just-in-time systems and customer and supplier participation programs mediate the impact of resource planning, operating management, and electronic data interchange systems on plant performance. Similarly, Barua and colleagues (2004) find that firms with higher levels of supplier-side digitization are likely to have higher levels of customer-side digitization and enjoy better financial performance. This indicates that firms that strategize to better serve customers integrate supplier-side activities with customer-side online capabilities to achieve superior performance.

## CONCLUSION

Many studies have been conducted to examine the impact of IT on firm performance. However, an important consideration is that IT influences firm performance through its intermediate impact on the performance of specific business processes (Barua, Kriebel, and Mukhopadhyay, 1995; Davenport, 1993; Hammer and Champy, 1993; Porter, 1991). For example, in a manufacturing company, IT investment may be made to implement a computer-aided design system. In this case, the impact of the investment should be examined on the output of the product design process rather than its impact on firm performance.

There are at least three reasons why the impact of IT resources should be examined on specific business processes rather than on overall firm performance.[4] First, because firms can have competitive advantages in some business processes and competitive disadvantages in others, examining the relationship between the resources/capabilities associated with one process and the firm's overall performance can result in misleading conclusions. In the example described above, IT resources invested in product design affect the outcome of the product design process. The impact of IT on product design may not carry over and affect firm performance if the firm does not perform other activities such as manufacturing and marketing in a competitive manner.

Second, it is possible for a firm's stakeholders to appropriate the profits that can be generated by a firm's resources before those profits are reflected in the firm's overall performance, making firm-level analysis problematic, at least in some cases. In the example above, even if the product design system leads to an improvement in firm performance, no relationship between investments in product design and firm performance would be found if the benefits of the improved performance are appropriated by stakeholders, such as designers, or top management, in the form of higher salaries.

Third, examining the relationship between resources and aggregate firm performance ignores the very mechanism, namely, business processes, through which the firm's resources and capabilities get exposed to the marketplace where their competitive potential can ultimately be realized. Therefore, it is important that the impact of IT be measured at the activity or process level where the prime effects of IT are realized. In this regard, firms can be thought of as entities that perform certain activities whose aggregate impact determines firm performance.

While a firm may implement a CRM system to improve customer service and firm performance, this may not improve customer service and firm performance if the firm is not competitive in other (e.g., supplier management and operations) processes. Though the CRM system may improve customer service activities, this impact may not affect aggregate firm-level performance. Thus, it is important to measure the impact of IT where the first-order effects are realized.

While organizations spend millions on IT to improve business performance, it is often a challenge for CEOs and CIOs to justify investments in IT because of the intangible nature of its benefits. Therefore, a theory explaining how IT investments can affect firm performance would be valuable. In this article, we argued that IT investments per se do not influence performance. Instead, firm-specific IT resources, such as IT–business partnership, drive an organization's use of IT capital and are more likely to be a source of competitive advantage. Similarly, even if an individual IT resource may not provide a competitive advantage, a combination of IT resources can lead to applications that do. From this perspective, the IT resources used in a given process provide a competitive advantage when a firm uses them in combination with other IT and non–IT resources to outperform competitors on the given process.

## NOTES

1. Of course, no competitive advantage lasts forever.
2. This section draws significantly on Mata, Fuerst, and Barney (1995) and Ray, Muhanna, and Barney (2005).
3. Kearns and Sabherwal (2006), for example, found that top managers' knowledge of IT facilitates business managers' participation in strategic IT planning and IT managers' participation in business planning, and that these factors affect strategic IT alignment. Strategic IT alignment leads to quality IT project planning, which affects the business impact of IT.
4. This section draws significantly on Ray, Barney, and Muhanna (2004).

## REFERENCES

Banker, R.D.; Bardhan, I.R.; Chang, H.; and S. Lin. 2006. Plant information systems, manufacturing capabilities, and plant performance. *MIS Quarterly*, 30, 2, 315–337.

Barney, J. 1986. Strategic factor markets: expectation, luck, and business strategy. *Management Science*, 42, 1231–1241.

———. 1991. Firm resources and sustained competitive advantage. *Journal of Management*, 17, 1, 99–120.

Barua, A.; Kriebel, C.H.; and Mukhopadhyay, T. 1995. Information technology and business value: an analytic and empirical investigation. *Information Systems Research*, 6, 1, 3–23.

Barua, A.; Konana, P.; Whinston, A.B.; and Yin, F. 2004. An empirical investigation of net-enabled business value. *MIS Quarterly*, 28, 4, 585–620.

Berinato, S. 2002. Merging business cultures to support common goals. *CIO*, May 15, 202.

Bharadwaj, A.S. 2000. A resource-based perspective on information technology capability and firm performance: An empirical investigation. *MIS Quarterly*, 24, 1, 169–196.

Boynton, A.C.; Zmud, R.W.; and Jacobs, G.C. 1994. The influence of IT management practice on IT use in large organizations. *MIS Quarterly* (September), 299–318.

Carr, N. G. . 2003. IT doesn't matter. *Harvard Business Review*, 81, 5 (May), 41–49.

Davenport, T.H. 1993. *Process Innovation: Reengineering Work Through Information Technology*. Boston: Harvard Business School Press.

Grant, R.M. 1991. The resource-based theory of competitive advantage: implications for strategy formulation. *California Management Review* (Spring), 114–135.

Hammer, M., and Champy, J. 1993. *Reengineering the Corporation: A Manifesto for Business Revolution*. New York: Harper Business.

Harter, D.E.; Krishnan, M.S.; and Slaughter, S.A. 2000. Effects of process maturity on quality, cycle time, and effort in software product development. *Management Science*, 46, 4, 451–466.

Henderson, J.C. 1990. Plugging into strategic partnerships: the critical IS connection. *Sloan Management Review*, 31, 3, 7–18.

Information technology Association of America (IITA). 2007. The U.S. information technology industry: a brief overview. Available at www.itaa.org/news/docs/industryoverview.pdf (accessed August 18, 2008).

Kearns, G., and Sabherwal, R. 2006. Strategic alignment between business and information technology: a knowledge-based view of behaviors, outcome, and consequences. *Journal of Management Information Systems*, 23, 3, 129–162.

Mata, F.J.; Fuerst, W.L.; and Barney, J.B. 1995. Information technology and sustained competitive advantage: a resource-based analysis. *MIS Quarterly* (December), 487–504.

Mithas, S.; Krishnan, M.S.; and Fornell, C. 2005. Why do customer relationship management applications affect customer satisfaction? *Journal of Marketing*, 69 (October), 201–209.

Montes, S.L. 2003. Digital economy 2003 report: information technologies in the US economy. Economics and Statistics Administration, U.S. Department of Commerce.

Peteraf, M.A. 1993. The cornerstones of competitive advantage: a resource-based view. *Strategic Management Journal*, 14, 179–192.

Porter, M.E. 1991. Towards a dynamic theory of strategy. *Strategic Management Journal*, 12, 95–117.

Porter, M.E., and Millar, V.E. 1995. How information gives you competitive advantage. *Harvard Business Review*, 63, 4, 149–160.

Powell, T.C., and Dent-Micallef, A.D. 1997. Information technology as competitive advantage: the role of human, business, and technology resources. *Strategic Management Journal,* 18, 5, 375–405.

Ray, G.; Barney, J.; and Muhanna, W. 2004. Capabilities, business processes, and competitive advantage: choosing the dependent variable in empirical tests of the resource-based view. *Strategic Management Journal,* 25, 1, 2004, 23–37.

Ray, G.; Muhanna, W.; and Barney, J. 2005. Information technology and the performance of the customer service process: a resource-based analysis. *Management Information Systems Quarterly,* 29, 4 (December), 625–652.

Rockart, J.F. 1988. the line takes the leadership—IS management in a wired society. *Sloan Management Review,* 29, 4, 55–64.

Sasser, W.E.; Jones, T.O.; and Klein, N. 1994. Ritz-Carlton: using information systems to better serve the customer. Harvard Business School Case #: 9–395–064.

Stalk, G.; Evans, P.; and Shulman, L.E. 1992. Competing on capabilities: the new rules of corporate strategy. *Harvard Business Review* (March–April), 57–69.

Tanriverdi, H. 2006. Performance effects of information technology synergies in multibusiness firms. *MIS Quarterly,* 30, 1, 57–77.

Teece, D.J.; Pisano, G.; and Shuen, A. 1997. Dynamic capabilities and strategic management. *Strategic Management Journal,* 18, 7, 509–533.

Vitale, M.R. 1985. American Hospital Supply Corp.: the ASAP System (A). Harvard Business School Case #: 9–186–005, 1985.

Vitale, M.R., and Konsynski, B. 1988. Baxter Healthcare Corp.: ASAP Express. Harvard Business School Case #: 9–188–080.

Wernerfelt, B. 1984. A resource-based view of the firm. *Strategic Management Journal,* 5, 171–180.

Worthen, B. 2002. Nestlé's ERP odyssey. *CIO,* May 15.

Zhu, K. 2004. The complementarity of information technology infrastructure and e-commerce capability: a resource-based assessment of their business value. *Journal of Management Information Systems,* 21, 1, 167–202.

Zhu, K., and Kraemer, K. 2002. e-Commerce metrics for net-enhanced organizations: assessing the value of e-commerce to firm performance in the manufacturing sector. *Information Systems Research,* 13, 3, 275–295.

Zhu, K.; Kraemer, K.L.; Xu, S.; and Dedrick, J. 2004. Information technology payoff in e-business environments: an international perspective on value creation of e-business in the financial services industry. *Journal of Management Information Systems,* 21, 1, 17–54.

# CHAPTER 22

# PLANNING FOR SUCCESSFUL ORCHESTRATED E-PROCESS SUPPLY-CHAIN PARTNERSHIPS

OMAR A. EL SAWY, ARVIND MALHOTRA, AND SANJAY GOSAIN

*Abstract: Enterprises in dynamic industries have realized that collaborating with supply-chain partners is even more critical in an e-business environment, and presents new challenges and opportunities. How should enterprises plan for successful orchestrated e-process supply-chain partnerships? This chapter provides guidelines that enable enterprises to orchestrate bridging and bonding without being inflexibly bound to specific supply-chain partners. The wise use of standard electronic business interfaces (SEBIs) enables partners to introduce enriched perspectives into their business environment (bridging) while strengthening their collaborative ties (bonding). The chapter draws from the experience of the formation of the RosettaNet consortium in the information technology industry to provide planning guidelines for process design, information exchange, and knowledge management for more successful supply-chain partnerships.*

*Keywords: Supply Chain, E-Process Model, Partnerships, Collaborative E-Business*

## AN UNLIKELY SCENARIO?

It is July 2007. Tanya Tamaki the vice president and chief process manager for the new product introduction process for BigWig Computers is celebrating with her launch team the successful introduction of a new mobile device—"Zinger"—for field sales employees to access customer information databases. This new product is a high-speed portable device with high-speed "always-on" wireless connection. It allows the sales personnel of large personal and institutional financial services providers to access detailed customer profiles and transactions, videoconference with portfolio managers, and craft personalized portfolio strategies for investors.

Tanya recalled how Bob Chen, the business development manager at Sysint, had approached her just a month earlier and indicated the need for a device that his financial services customers were clamoring for. This required a strategic redirection as BigWig had just released Zinger in computer retail stores as a novelty consumer product. Tanya marveled at how smoothly the transition had gone. A new hardware vendor had been identified that produced a network card with the wireless capabilities needed. Sysint and BigWig had jointly developed the specifications for the product with the financial service customer. The specifications were then zipped off to the customer relationship management (CRM) software publisher (ZeeBell) with specific customization parameters. Software was then delivered to the distributor (Fullfillit) who loaded the software on the devices and added a wireless network card developed by a vendor (NoWireCo) that had been identified specifically for this launch. The completely customized product along with updated technical documentation was delivered to Sysint in the record time of five days.

While this scenario may be ambitious and utopian, it is increasingly likely that we can get closer to it as we become more skilled at planning for more effective information technology (IT)-enabled supply-chain partnerships. It illustrates the opportunities that enterprises have in identifying new market niches and satisfying customers in those niches in collaboration with supply-chain partners. These new opportunities are IT-enabled and allow for different process designs, better information flows, and richer knowledge sharing. But they are also accompanied by a number of challenges.

## THE CHALLENGES OF COLLABORATIVE E-BUSINESS

### Challenge 1: Incompatible Intercompany Process Interfaces

SysInt must learn and maintain different ordering procedures and system interfaces with Fullfillit and BigWig along with other distributors and manufacturers with whom they trade. Consequently, SysInt must spend valuable resources in back-office operations (50 percent by some estimates), which they could otherwise use to make new sales or service their customers.

### Challenge 2: Incompatible Information Formats

BigWig has to provide pre- and post-sale technical support to their resellers, such as SysInt, on tens of thousands of stockkeeping units (SKUs). In turn, SysInt has to grapple with disparate forms of product information collected from hundreds of other manufacturers with no common taxonomy. The lack of product information standards makes the aggregation and dissemination of such content an expensive and inefficient proposition, an effort duplicated by each system integrator/value-added reseller in the supply chain. This problem is further compounded by the content's explosive rate of change due to the burgeoning variety of products.

### Challenge 3: Knowledge Fragmentation

For BigWig to sell Zinger as an integrated solution rather than a novelty product requires integration of knowledge about constituent products from ZeeBell (CRM software) and NoWireCo (wireless card). Even more important, BigWig would never have known that the financial service application market for Zinger existed without mechanisms for knowledge sharing with SysInt. This underlines the fact that the e-business environment requires integration of diverse types of knowledge for design, production, delivery, and servicing of offerings. However, this knowledge is fragmented among the different players in the supply chain.

### Challenge 4: Complex and Changing e-Business Process Interdependencies

The Zinger scenario illustrates that to satisfy an emerging niche market or to satisfy the dynamic needs of existing customers requires adding new partners (ZeeBell and NoWireCo) or reconfiguring processes with existing partners (SysInt). For BigWig to respond to the new business opportunity, it must recognize its existing process dependencies and reconfigured supply-chain processes to reflect the addition of the new network card vendor (NoWireCo).

**Challenge 5: Technology Integration Across Partners and the Enterprise**

To smoothly execute joint transactions, it is required that applications at each of BigWig, SysInt, FullFillit, ZeeBell, and NoWireCo be able to talk to each other and trigger the required sequence of processes from the interface. The SysInt order needs to be understood by BigWig's e-commerce application as well as the applications of ZeeBell, Fullfillit, and NoWireCo in terms of the specific product that is being ordered and the contractual terms that are being solicited. At ZeeBell's (as well as NoWireCo's) end, this has to trigger the appropriate processes that will check on inventory status and allocate product for the order and confirm a delivery schedule to SysInt and Fullfillit. When Fullfillit is assembling the solution, SysInt has to be kept informed of the progress (or any exception). In the end, for accounting purposes, SysInt has to acknowledge to all parties in the supply chain that the solution has been delivered to the customer. This highlights the challenge for the supply chain: the end-to-end processes demand that multiple processes at different players must be simultaneously triggered with very little human intervention. This illustrates the need for industry-wide standards for interfacing processes and information exchange.

## RESPONDING TO THE CHALLENGES: THE STRUCTURAL EVOLUTION OF SUPPLY CHAINS

### The Ghosts of the Silo Structure Past

To begin to understand how supply chains were evolving to respond to the hypercompetitive environment, we conducted interviews with senior-level managers with responsibilities in areas of supply-chain management, purchasing, and distribution from fifteen leading companies in the IT industry. We found that many of the companies in the IT industry supply chain were struggling with the sequential silo-like linking with their partners (Figure 22.1A). In this mode, only the functional entity (such as resellers and system integrators) at the end of the chain was in touch with and possessed knowledge about the customers. The other players derived inferences about customers from information that was passed back along the chain. Thus the farther away the entity was from the customer the harder it was to derive knowledge about the customers, and this was based on information that tended to be incomplete and tardy.

### Toward a More Collaborative Environment

In the IT industry a significant developing trend is "integrated distribution," which makes collaborative use of vendors' and distributors' skills integrating them into one cohesive manufacturing, delivery, and service package. For example, Ingram-Micro, a leading distributor in the IT industry, invested in a 500,000 square foot integration center. This center was designed to assemble products for companies like IBM, HP, Compaq, and so on. To develop this capability, Ingram had to collaborate closely with manufacturers to gain product assembly knowledge. An even more complex relationship was the one formed by Ingram-Micro's competitor Tech Data, called "Factory Direct." Under this initiative Tech Data planned to collaborate closely with manufacturers such as IBM and Compaq, to the extent of having a physical presence at the manufacturer's facility—to form distribution and logistics centers. Using this arrangement, Tech Data would also collaborate with value-added resellers (VARs) to understand and satisfy the VARs' needs. Tech Data would then ship the products directly to the end users on behalf of the VARs, customizing the labels and shipping list with the reseller's logo to maintain the VAR's identity. The arrangements were indicative

**Figure 22.1 A&B    The Structural Evolution of Supply Chains**

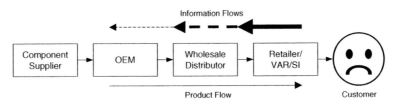

**A. The "Silo-like" Sequential Supply Chain**

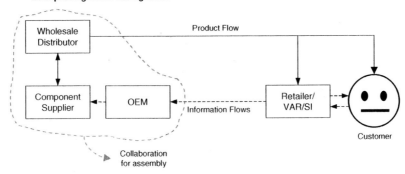

**B. Improving Order Management**

A. The "Silo-like" Sequential Supply-Chain
B. Improving Order Management

of the move toward restructuring supply chains such that partners collaborate on activities around the key processes rather than on specific sequential functional roles such as distribution, sales, and so on (Figure 22.1B).

## A Knowledge-Sharing and -Generating Interorganizational Mode

Similar complex arrangements were starting to be formed between supply-chain partners to improve the new product introduction process. Original equipment manufacturers (OEMs) such as Microsoft and Cisco conducted extensive training for sales employees at large retailers and system integrators (SIs) before introducing new products (Figure 22.1C).

We found that in the most advanced supply-chain relationships each business entity, by virtue of being involved in a customer-touching process, was able to directly derive customer knowledge related to its process. In addition, the customer was actively involved in "co-constructing" the offering and customer competence was co-opted in the value creation. The real competitive advantage came from putting together these process-based knowledge fragments to derive the complete picture (Figure 22.1D).

Executive thinking on the evolution of their supply chains suggested a decoupling of product and information flows. While the physical flows still might invariably be point-to-point and linear in nature, the information flows were increasingly networked. OEMS became information and knowledge hubs in their own supply chain in order to gain control of information flow to and from

Figure 22.1 C & D    **The Structural Evolution of Supply Chains**

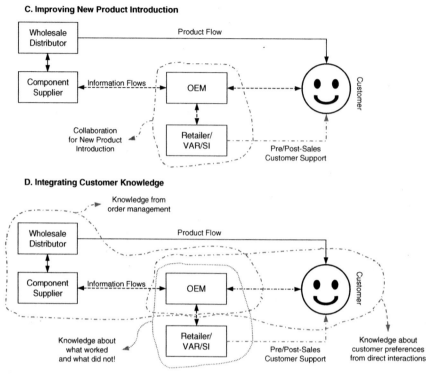

C. Improving New Product Introduction
D. Integrating Customer Knowledge

the customer and to extract more useful knowledge. OEMs then started transforming themselves into original design manufacturers (ODMs) by leveraging the knowledge of their partners and involving them in the design stages of product life cycle.

This began the age of enabling partners to get enriched perspectives into their business environment through rich information exchange with multiple and diverse partners (bridging), while strengthening their collaborative ties with the same partners (bonding). The bridging of information gaps between partners and simultaneously the ability to couple and decouple with partners as needed provide organizations with the ability to sense and respond to hypercompetitive environments.

## RETHINKING SUPPLY-CHAIN CAPABILITIES

At the time of this writing, supply chains in various industries are still not adequately prepared to capitalize on opportunities presented by the e-business environment. Most of them still operate as a series of "smokestacks," with manufacturers, distributors, resellers, and business customers operating efficiently within their own boundaries but deficient when it comes to coordinating activities and sharing information and knowledge with other organizations.

The IT industry in the late 1990s was faced with a highly dynamic market, but was still responding by trying to fine-tune traditional supply-chain organizing models. In our interviews, executives in the IT industry said it was necessary for the industry as a whole to develop new organizing models suited for fast-changing information-intensive business environments. The IT industry is somewhat unique in the challenges it faces. While change is pervasive in most industries, it is particularly intense and high-velocity in the IT industry. It has a high level of technological innovation, which results in high SKU churn due to product rollovers, deflationary pricing, and short product life cycles. IT products also tend to have complex component trees, which creates the need for component sourcing partnerships as well as significant technical support from the customer end. The industry is composed of dynamic players, which leads to the constant emergence of new sources of value, continuous reconfiguration of the market space, and constant erosion of existing sources of value. High growth rates for companies and merger and acquisition activity also lead to process integration challenges. Given these industry characteristics, IT companies are under greater pressure to customize their product and service offerings. The complexity of products also creates higher specialization and the need to coordinate value creation with partners. Therefore, we considered it important to understand the needs of this dynamic industry and how industry executives were beginning to shift their mental frames to gear up for e-business. The new organizing models and practices that emerge from this industry would benefit other industries in competing and prospering in the e-business environment.

In order to reduce misalignments and increase their share of opportunities, the leading companies in the IT industry supply chain came together in early 1998 and formed the RosettaNet Consortium.[1] The mission of RosettaNet was to design, adopt, promote, and facilitate the deployment of quasi-open standard electronic business interfaces (SEBIs) between business partners that would enable them to connect and collaborate with each other without impediments. The SEBIs developed and implemented by RosettaNet Consortium participants focus on both business process standards (called partner interface processes or PIPs) and data dictionary standards for product descriptions and specifications. This allows many-to-many electronic connectivity relationships (bridging) and heralds a much richer and more flexible form of business process connectivity across enterprises (bonding). SEBIs go beyond just standardizing information exchange by also standardizing inter-enterprise process linkages (Gosain et al., 2003).

Initially we focused on understanding the potential impact of SEBIs on IT industry supply chains. To do this, we conducted a number of interviews with high-level IT-industry managers drawn from companies at various tiers in the supply chain. A number of items indicating effectiveness were identified. A survey instrument was prepared and sent to each company on the RosettaNet board. A total of twenty-eight completed responses were received—one from each company.

The survey first asked the respondents to rate twenty-seven metrics, which we identified from the interviews, in terms of their importance in capturing the performance and potential opportunities of the IT-industry supply chain. These included traditional operational measures such as order delivery time, inventory level, and product availability, as well as nontraditional measures such as time to add a new channel partner and percentage of online customer/supplier inquiries. Analysis of our interviews and survey yielded five factors (see Figure 22.2). These factors revealed the underlying thought process of executives in terms of key issues driving IT supply-chain effectiveness in the emergent e-business environment (see Table 22.1).

The factors include some traditional drivers of supply-chain effectiveness such as order management and enterprise integration. But the foremost factor (collaborative process partnering) indicated that a new way of thinking was emerging that goes beyond the traditional transactional view of supply chains. It indicates the emphasis on process alignment across business partners to leverage their collective expertise. Underlying this emphasis is an organizing model suited to the dynamic e-business environment. Our discovery led us to contemplate a new organizing perspective, which we label the "orchestrated e-process" model.

Figure 22.2    **Salient Factors for Supply Chains in the e-Business Environment**

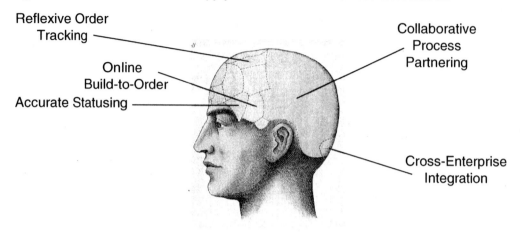

Reflexive Order Tracking

Online Build-to-Order

Accurate Statusing

Collaborative Process Partnering

Cross-Enterprise Integration

Table 22.1

**Key Capabilities Affecting IT Supply Chain Effectiveness in the e-Business Environment**

**Factor 1: Collaborative Process Partnering**
- Flexibility in changing business processes linked to partners
- Understanding of process dependencies on partners
- Understanding how to interface with partners
- Extent to which channel partners provide technical support to each other
- Extent to which channel partners provide marketing support to each other
- Sharing of market knowledge with the channel

**Factor 2: Reflexive Order Tracking**
- Ability of customers to track orders while in transit
- Ability to track shipping status from carriers/shippers
- Ability to react to exceptions caused by channel partners

**Factor 3: Online Build-to-Order**
- Modularity of product/service offerings
- Avoidance of multiple order bookings (phantom orders)
- Sales of product online

**Factor 4: Accurate Status**
- Provision to customers of real-time available-to-promise date
- Appropriate shipping documents

**Factor 5: Cross-Enterprise Integration**
- Extent of integration with partners
- Extent of internal integration in a partner company
- Understanding of how to interface with partners

## The Orchestrated e-Process Model

In order to understand and explicate the orchestrated e-process model of organizing, it is important to establish the key dimensions along which this model may be contrasted with a more traditional IT-enabled supply-chain perspective. Our surveys showed that the two key dimensions were inter-enterprise shared knowledge creation and process management. Further, these dimensions build upon the foundational dimension of inter-enterprise information flows. In order to nurture these capabilities associated with the two dimensions, it is apparent that information flows across organizations need to be affected. Information flows trigger the growth of knowledge, and changes in information flows around processes are key to improving performance. At one leading component manufacturer, the managers we spoke to emphasized the need to achieve process integration and joint creation of capabilities with business partners through sharing product road maps. Similarly, at a computer manufacturer, we found a major effort under way to ensure the coverage, frequency, and quality of information exchange with resellers to better forecast market demand and trends. Thus we identified three core dimensions along which one can understand the intricacies of the underlying model: *knowledge management, process management,* and *information management.*

We label the emerging model of organizing the "orchestrated e-process model." An e-process is a set of business activities executed by a set of enterprises, coordinated through electronic means such as Internet-based applications, with a special emphasis on rich information flows resulting in growth of collective knowledge, while minimizing the role of physical flows and coordination requirements. Orchestration is the dynamic execution and management of the process through collaboration between executing enterprises in order to integrate value creation activities and produce the best value offering for the customers.

Table 22.2 compares and contrasts the orchestrated e-process perspective with the more traditional IT-enabled supply-chain perspective adapted for e-business. The IT-supported supply-chain view marries the functional perspective of sequentially linked enterprises with the automating capabilities of the IT infrastructure. On the other hand, the orchestrated e-process model stresses a collective process-based competence that leverages the IT infrastructure to ensure knowledge-based execution of processes and the extraction of new knowledge from rich information flows.

The orchestrated e-process perspective is based on attention to knowledge management, process management, information management, and infrastructure development from an interorganizational perspective. Groups of enterprises face specific imperatives in each of these dimensions when this perspective is used.

## Knowledge Management: Leveraging Collective Process Competence

The increasing complexity of products and market demands in the e-business environment will require the integration of diverse types of knowledge for design, production, delivery, and servicing of offerings. The orchestrated e-process model emphasizes that competitive advantage will be gained by combining the skills and capabilities of the business partners. The performance of the collective will be determined by the ease with which the partnering enterprises integrate their knowledge resources and bring them to bear on value-creating processes to produce new services and product concepts through communicative and collaborative exchanges. A significant trend developing in the IT industry is "integrated distribution," which makes collaborative use of vendors' and distributors' skills integrating them into one cohesive manufacturing, delivery, and service package. The enterprises in the channel collaborate on activities around the key processes rather than specific sequential

Table 22.2

## Orchestrated e-Process Perspective

| Traditional IT-supported supply-chain perspective | Orchestrated e-process supply-chain perspective |
|---|---|
| *Knowledge management* | *Knowledge management* |
| • Functional perspective of enterprise competence | • Process-based perspective of enterprise competence |
| • Leveraging of individual enterprise competence | • Building and leveraging of collective competence |
| • Dyadic collaboration with adjacent tier partner | • Networked and rich collaboration with a select group of partners |
| • Customer knowledge is derived independently based on information passed across tiers | • Customer knowledge is derived collectively by putting together process-linked information fragments |
| | • New knowledge-based roles appear to facilitate the orchestration (such as knowledge aggregators) |
| *Process management* | *Process management* |
| • Sequential interlinking of siloed enterprise processes | • Rebundling of end-to-end integrated e-processes |
| • Processes optimized for operational efficiency | • Configurational agility and reflexive change derived from flexibility in changing processes linked to partners |
| • Order management process drives the organization of supply chain | • New product introduction process drives the need for orchestration |
| | • New process management roles appear to facilitate the orchestration (such as process brokers) |
| *Information management* | *Information management* |
| • Physical infrastructure and processes are supported by information infrastructure | • Information infrastructure drives the design of physical infrastructure and processes |
| • Information flows are linear and follow the same paths as physical flows | • Information flows are networked and often follow different paths from physical flows |
| • Coordination and statusing information related to transactions ensure operational efficiency | • Rich information flows resulting from collaborative relationships fuel knowledge creation |
| | • New information management roles to facilitate orchestration (such as application service providers) |
| *Infrastructure* | *Infrastructure* |
| • Technology support for transaction information requirements mainly through the use of EDI (electronic data interchange), ERP (enterprise resource planning) systems, supply-chain management systems | • Technology support for collaborative knowledge creation mainly through the use of customer relationship management software, data mining software, collaborative technology |
| • Content exchange standards-enabled infrastructure | • Process and content exchange standards-enabled infrastructure |

functional roles such as distribution, sales, and so on. Thus the key characteristic of the orchestrated e-process model is the process-based perspective of enterprise competence.

In the sequential silo-like linking of functional roles that characterize the IT-enabled supply chains, only the functional entity (such as resellers and system integrators) at the end of the chain was in touch with and possessed knowledge about the customers. The other players derived inferences about customers from information that was passed back along the chain. Thus the farther away the entity was from the customer the harder it was to derive knowledge about the customers, and this was based on information that tended to be incomplete and tardy. But in the orchestrated e-process model of organizing, each business entity, by virtue of being involved in a customer-touching process, can directly derive customer knowledge related to its process. In addition the customer is actively involved in "co-constructing" the offering and customer competence is co-opted in value creation. The real competitive advantage comes from putting together these process-based knowledge fragments to derive the complete picture. This requires the use of new technologies that help partners first store the customer knowledge extracted from their process and then collaboratively combine it with the knowledge of other business enterprises. Once confined to sales reps within a single enterprise, such channel integration technologies extend customer management capabilities across channel partners.

As the orchestrated e-process environment relies on complex information networks to share knowledge and create new knowledge in terms of skills and capabilities, the strategic focus is on channel partnerships (between manufacturers, distributors, retailers, shippers, financiers, and end users) to develop new competencies for a changing business environment. With this comes the need for new knowledge management roles that enable shared knowledge creation through mechanisms such as maintaining repositories of aggregated knowledge, providing a shared context for knowledge exchange, facilitating knowledge growth mechanisms, and so on.

In the next section, we offer some guidelines for companies to use in developing capabilities for participation in orchestrated e-process supply chains.

## SEVEN GUIDELINES FOR DEVELOPING ORCHESTRATED E-PROCESS SUPPLY-CHAIN CAPABILITIES

In this section we provide guidelines for enterprises that recognize the value of participating in orchestrated e-business supply chains. These guidelines range from general implications that follow from this mode of organizing to specific ground issues revealed in our research on the IT industry.

### Market Your Enterprise's e-Process Competencies

In the collaborative process-partnering world, companies in the supply chain specialize in distinctive process competencies, and compete with other companies that possess similar competencies. It is important for managers to recognize and market these competencies to enable them to compete for appropriate roles in as many as possible. In addition to performing roles based on competencies around key orchestrated processes, there is also an opportunity to perform new roles. Such roles emerge with the need to support the orchestrated process partnering mode of organizing, process integration between partners, or the sharing and distribution of knowledge among partners. In the scenario presented at the start of the chapter, BigWig should advertise its competencies in the new product development process to Sysint, while Sysint should advertise its competencies in new product introduction and its complementarities to BigWig. Similarly, it would be advantageous for Zeebell to advertise its customer support process expertise, and for Fulfillit to extol the virtues of its superior fulfillment process.

## Prepare for Rich Information Exchange

Managers must tread a fine line between retaining vital knowledge assets that the organization leverages and sharing enough knowledge with partnering organizations to be able to collaborate effectively. The sharing decision is not an easy one to make particularly when organizations are partnering with different organizations to produce competing offerings. Given the decision on what to share and what not to, it is imperative to exchange information that not only aids coordination but also extends to richer forms in terms of materially impacting core e-processes. For instance, the sharing of product roadmaps between partners is much richer and leads to a better basis for collaboration than the transmission of a "Do you have it?" kind of statusing-information fragment. Managers have to guard against the reaction that their organizations will not share any knowledge if they have not ascertained what they can and cannot share with business partners. This can lead to their organization's not being an integral part of the orchestrated e-process and in the worst case can be the knowledge bottleneck that causes orchestrated e-processes to fail. The Zinger scenario makes it very clear that this would never work unless BigWig and Sysint have a rich information exchange in the new product introduction process for the financial services sector.

## Structure Your Supply-Chain Processes Modularly

In order to maximize the exchange of rich information with partners, enterprises must reduce the amount of coordination information required in this context. Interorganizational modular process design assures that coordination rules are implicit, thus minimizing the need to exchange coordination information. In such a modular design, different enterprises in the supply chain independently (and simultaneously) execute the subprocesses of the overarching supply-chain process with distinct prespecified outputs. The orchestrated e-process model relies on the synthesis of distinctive and complementary modular process capabilities of the partners. Therefore, managers must ascertain the right business partners for their organizations based not on functional and transactional activities but on modular process capabilities.

Modular interorganization process design allows organizations that are conducting the subprocesses to experiment so as to enhance their part of the overall supply-chain process until the time they deliver the prespecified information and physical outputs. Further, the act of engaging in modularly orchestrated supply-chain e-processes allows various enterprises to develop a better understanding of the informational needs of their partners and the core competencies of their partners and how they relate to their own competency. The move toward service-oriented architectures and Web services is enabling enterprises to more easily modularize their e-processes. In our Zinger scenario, Sysint would find it advantageous to keep its customer support process modular, so it can easily redesign it as customer requirements change and it understands what BigWig's information needs are as well.

## Reengineer Outside–In

Traditional process improvement practices target internal organizational processes. In the e-business economy interorganizational processes come to the forefront, and yet these can be a frequent source of problems. Organizations tend to have differences in information systems, process standards, management concerns, interpretations, and so on, which can cause a chasm that is difficult to bridge between partners working together in orchestrated e-processes. Managers must be aware that a key source of competitive advantage in the orchestrated e-process world will be the ability to make it easy for other organizations to do business with you. This requires nurturing a high degree of internal flexibility in order to be able to change interlinked processes and interfaces between partners to respond to ever changing supply-chain conditions. This reflexive adaptation requires that orchestrated e-processes processes be designed for faster learning not just faster execution. It is best for the ecosystem comprised of BigWig, Sysint, Fulfillit, Zeebell, NoWire, and their financial services customers to focus on their interorganizational partnering processes as a first priority.

### Enhance Your Information Absorption Capacity

The orchestrated e-processes depend on intensive information flows. Supply-chain partners must engage in collaborative information exchange (high quality, broad-ranging, and privileged in nature) to gain a complete picture of the hypercompetitive environment. This requires investment in infrastructure to efficiently and effectively procure information from partners (through sharing of broad-ranging and privileged information) and then to blend the information exchanged with internal organizational expertise. Adoption and use of SEBIs is a salient mechanism to engage in collaborative information exchange with supply-chain partners. The shared language of SEBIs allows partners to engage in broad-ranging, high quality information. The network effects created by the use of SEBIs allow enterprises to access a diverse range of information for disparate partners without having to engage in an individual information exchange infrastructure with each partner. SEBIs allow for the exchange of routine transaction information, freeing up key organizational resources for exchanging and leveraging richer information. Further, the act of adopting SEBIs requires partners to understand each others' process and information needs, thereby, placing partners in a better position to provide each other the right information. That is the essence of providing both *bridging* (getting enriched perspectives on the environment) and *bonding* (strengthening their collaborative ties), while not being rigidly bound to partners.

Enterprises engaged in orchestrated e-process supply chains must enhance the information absorption capacity of their enterprises by developing partner-interface–directed information systems. Such systems facilitate the assimilation and transformation of information exchange. Two instances of such systems are interorganizational information interpretation systems and memory systems for interorganizational activities. The former system allows information obtained from partners to be represented in multiple ways (such as data analysis and mining systems). The latter system allows for information related to activities and outcomes with partners to be stored and extracted easily. It is clear from the scenario that Zeebell does this by virtue of its software, but the same should apply to BigWig and Sysint and the entire supply chain as they interact through their e-processes.

### Build Plug-and-Play Infrastructure with Your Industry

Collaboration around the core processes will be the order of the day in the orchestrated e-process world. Many of the activities around the core processes will be coordinated and conducted using the Internet and its future reincarnations as the backbone for communication and execution. It is thus imperative that managers not only ready their organizations internally to easily connect with business partners but also proactively participate in building inter-enterprise infrastructure for process linkages and information exchange interfaces. Several industry-wide initiatives are afoot in this direction as is the case with ANX in the automotive industry and RosettaNet in the IT industry. XML and AJAX technologies have made the implementation of such standards increasingly feasible. Managers are well advised to contribute their organizational resources to shaping these infrastructures that impact their future business activities with current and future business partners. If such an initiative has not been undertaken in their industry, organization managers are well advised to take a leading role in getting them started. This is important in helping to orchestrate e-processes within their industry and could be a source of competitive advantage that allows them to partner with leading suppliers and customers and to seize emerging opportunities that e-business offers. Some industries, such as the IT industry, automotive, financial services, and transportation have been leaders, while others, such as pharmaceuticals and real estate, are currently less well established.

### Collaborate Rather than Coordinate

The gist of the orchestrated e-process supply chain is collaborative intensity focused on information exchange that enhances each enterprise's understanding of its market and allows it to respond to the market in the most expedient manner. While formal mechanisms, such as use of SEBIs, allow for rich information exchange that is explicit and codified, more informal process mechanisms, such as joint decision-making activities with supply-chain partners, are a salient conduit for exchange of tacit and privileged information. Enterprises participating in orchestrated e-process supply chains must develop the competency of engaging with their partners in collaborative activities that go beyond transactional interaction (demand forecasts and manufacturing planning). Joint decisions can be made concerning how to collaboratively create and address new markets, response strategically to imminent threats, and so on.

The act of collaboratively developing, deploying, and using SEBIs also confers upon supply-chain enterprises the adaptive capabilities required to compete in hypermarkets. By deploying and using SEBIs, supply-chain partners signal trust in each other, which is the basis for rich information exchange. Partners engaging in collaborative design and deployment of SEBIs can use the same collaborative platform to learn about each others' process competencies. When the time comes to adapt the supply-chain processes to respond to market shifts, a better understanding of each others' complementarities goes a long way. True collaboration among supply-chain partners occurs around e-processes when bridging and bonding work in concert as the environment shifts. Following the guidelines in this chapter will help to provide an orchestration that blends the discipline of a symphony orchestra with the adaptive improvisation of a jazz ensemble for more successful orchestrated e-process supply-chain partnerships.

### NOTES

This chapter is based on studies and several papers by the three authors (Gosain et al., 2003, 2004; Malhotra, Gosain, and El Sawy, 2005, 2007).

1. RosettaNet (www.rosettanet.org) was then comprised of 28 board members (manufacturing, wholesale distribution, retail, shipping, financing, and end-user companies): Microsoft, Netscape, Oracle, Cisco, SAP, Hewlett-Packard, Intel, Toshiba, ABB, American Express, CHS, Systems, CompUSA, Compaq, Computacenter, Computer 2000, Deutsche Financial Services, EDS, Federal Express, GE Information Services, GSA, Company, IBM, Ingram Micro, Insight, Microage, PC Order, Tech Data, Tech Pacific, and United Parcel Service.

### REFERENCES

Gosain, S.; Malhotra, A.; El Sawy, O.A.; and Chehade, F. 2003. Towards frictionless e-business: the impact of common electronic business interfaces. *Communications of the ACM*, 46, 12, 186–194.
———. 2004. Coordinating for flexibility in e-business supply-chains. *Journal of Management Information Systems*, 21, 3, 39–45.
Malhotra, A.; Gosain, S.; and El Sawy, O.A. 2005. Absorptive capacity configurations in supply chains: gearing for partner-enabled market knowledge creation. *MIS Quarterly*, 29, 1, 145–187.
——— 2007. Leveraging standard electronic business interfaces to enable adaptive supply chain partnerships. *Information Systems Research*, 18, 3, 260–279.

# CHAPTER 23

# PLANNING SUCCESSFUL INTERNET-BASED PROJECTS

## A Risk–Performance Framework

ANANTH SRINIVASAN, R. BRENT GALLUPE, AND ELKE WOLF

*Abstract: Researchers and practitioners of information systems (IS) project management have studied project risk and performance for many years. Most of this work has considered risk and performance as separate aspects of project planning and evaluation. In this research, multiple case studies were conducted to examine the problems decision makers face when separately assessing the risks and the performance of Internet-based projects. From these cases, we develop an integrated framework for planning and managing Internet-based projects. We argue that decisions based on performance assessments can be significantly improved if the performance view is integrated with a risk perspective. For decision makers, the ability to better link project performance to project risk should help mitigate the likelihood of project failure. While we specifically study Internet-based projects in this research, the ideas and results apply more broadly to IT project development and management in general.*

*Keywords: Project Management, Risk Performance Framework, Internet-based Project Performance*

## INTRODUCTION

Among the common outputs of organizational information systems (IS) planning projects in the current environment are Internet-based projects that must be evaluated in detail for their potential efficacy. Projects such as the development of an Internet-based customer relationship management system, the deployment of a remote patient monitoring system, or the implementation of mobile commerce into a multichannel distribution environment require substantial organizational resources and must be evaluated in a detailed and rigorous manner, preferably using a single integrated framework. Any framework for evaluating such projects on a prospective basis should also be applicable to the project as it proceeds. So, a framework would be useful in the planning phase that uses a priori estimates of project characteristics as well as in the execution phase using estimates that are based on actual experience with the project.

Despite the unquestioned enabling and leveraging effect of Internet-based technologies, many projects and initiatives fail, or perform far below expectations. Keil, Rai, and Mann (2000) refer to a study of 8,000 software projects conducted by the Standish Group, which revealed that only 16 percent of these projects were completed on time and on budget. Jiang, Klein, and Ellis (2002) refers to a study of 100 companies that led to slightly more moderate results: only 37 percent of all major information technology (IT) projects were completed on time and 42 percent on budget. Even highly skilled and experienced project managers and other decision makers face serious difficulties trying to achieve acceptable project performance. This is especially true of Internet-based projects that are exposed to high risks. Interest in a systematic approach to managing all aspects of IT projects has heightened in part due to regulatory pressures such as the requirements for Sarbanes-Oxley assessments (Dawson, 2006). Many countries are looking at implementing the equivalent of these assessments to enforce proper organizational governance.

We consider risk and performance as two sides of the same coin and argue that, with a closer link between performance evaluations and the assessment of project risks, more such Internet-based projects might be evaluated positively. The major research question we address in this chapter is: "How can performance assessments be linked with assessments of risks in order to improve project planning and management?"

To answer this question, we conducted a study of selected New Zealand and Canadian firms engaged in Internet-based projects. We analyzed the characteristics of these projects to determine current practices that facilitate and inhibit successful development and deployment of information technologies. From the case descriptions we derived a set of factors that decision makers consider most important in evaluating the performance of their Internet-based projects. We argue that the complexity of such projects, which makes them difficult to evaluate, lies significantly in interdependencies between performance factors and risks. Therefore, we suggest that taking an integrated view of performance and risks could assist the organization in making project-planning decisions.

From this study, we have developed an integrated framework to assess the relationship between risk and performance of Internet-based projects. This framework may improve decisions that must be made in both the planning and execution phases of a project.

We consider our framework to be flexible, so that it can help businesses to further address their risk assessment activities. Therefore, we have aligned our understanding of IS risks with recent regulatory requirements that address IS risks as part of operational risks and guide many businesses in their risk management activities. Regulations such as the Sarbanes-Oxley Act for companies listed on the U.S. Stock Exchange, the New Basel Capital Accord, known as "Basel II" for the banking industry, or Solvency II for the insurance industry are examples of the increased interest of regulators and auditors in ensuring that publicly traded businesses better manage risks and, thus, improve their performance.

The chapter provides a review of the literature related to project performance and risk, and outlines their relevance for this research. After a brief description of the study in the next section, the results revealing six key factors for project performance are presented. Based on these factors and an integrated view of the relationship between performance and risk, a framework for the improvement of decisions concerning Internet-based projects is developed. The chapter concludes with a brief outline of the implications for researchers and practitioners and the limitations of this study, and provides some avenues for further research.

## LITERATURE REVIEW

In this research, we investigate Internet-based projects, as a particular type of IS project. These projects use Internet-related software and hardware, Web-based network technologies, and people such as Web designers and developers. The main characteristics of these projects are complexity and a compressed time for completion (Ramesh, Pries-Heje, and Baskerville, 2002). While many of the ideas that define our work and the outcomes of our research are based on Internet-driven technologies, the implications are wider in that they relate well to any IT-based projects and the associated issues of performance and risk. Clearly, there is a large overlap between the two project types, in that Internet technologies are ubiquitous in IT projects.

Both terms, "performance" and "risk," are widely used in a variety of different contexts. By "performance" we refer to the degree to which a project output (e.g., customer satisfaction) may reach a desired quantity and/or quality. This degree is usually assessed through key criteria or indicators. These criteria most commonly refer to budget and time. IS project performance can be considered an element of overall organizational performance but is to be clearly distinguished from software performance.

"Risk" can generally be defined as a deviation from an expected outcome with an estimated probability. We understand IS risks as part of operational risks, which can be divided into four types: people risks, process risks, system risks, and external risks (BCBS, 2004). With information systems being defined as comprising technology, people using the technology, and processes being supported by the technology, and also as being exposed to influences from outside the organization, IS risks can be of any of the four types. All types can occur throughout the entire life cycle of an IS, that is, in the planning, development, or implementation of projects as well as during the operations stages.

Synthesizing various perspectives on risk management, its common elements are the "identification," "assessment," "mitigation," and "monitoring" of risks (Boehm, 1989; Culp, 2001; Dorofee et al., 1996; Head, 1998; NIST, 2002; OCG, 2001; Schierenbeck and Lister, 2001).

Traditionally, the performance of a project is assessed and monitored through project management techniques. A closer look at common project management approaches, such as PMBOK (Project Management Body of Knowledge) or ISO (International Organization for Standardization) 10006 (see Appendix 23.1), reveals that they cover the assessment and monitoring of performance aspects as well as risks. Although the relationship between performance and risk are well recognized, these approaches do not directly relate them to each other; performance and risk are rather considered as separate factors in common project management approaches. This is also true, for example, regarding the suggestions to apply the balanced scorecard approach (Kaplan and Norton, 1992, 1996) to projects. Only on a holistic organizational level have attempts been made to link organizational performance measurement with enterprise risk management (Beasley et al., 2006). As for projects, while a number of research studies have investigated either performance *or* risks in IS projects, relatively little research has been conducted that addresses both aspects in relation to each other.

## Project Performance Factors

Three major categories of factors affecting project performance can be identified from the research on project performance: people factors, project factors, and technology factors. For example, Yetton and colleagues (2000) investigated the determinants of project performance in form of budget (cost–time) variances and project completion. They identified people factors such as project team dynamics, management support, user participation, and risk management as being the four main determinants of project performance. This indicates a strong relationship between risks and performance but the study does not elaborate on how to address both simultaneously.

Another example is Aladwani (2002) who argued that the focus on task-related outcomes is not sufficient to capture project performance. He added two further dimensions by including organizational and psychological outcomes and developed an integrated performance model of IS projects that relates six categories of variables to performance. These categories are, people characteristics

Table 23.1

**People, Project, Technology Factors for Project Performance**

| Publication | People factors | Project factors | Technology factors |
|---|---|---|---|
| Abdel-Hamid, Sengupta, and Swett (1999) | | Project management goals | |
| Abdel-Hamid (1992) | Managerial turnover | | |
| Aladwani (2002) | Staff expertise | Management advocacy; clear goals; project team size; problem-solving competencies | Support technologies |
| Banker and Kemerer (1992) | Conflicting goals | | |
| Jurison (1999) | Communications, leadership client/user participation | Objectives; problem solving | |
| Yetton et al. (2000) | Project team dynamics, management support, user participation | Risk management | |

and organizational characteristics (people factors), project characteristics, task characteristics, and work processes (project factors), and technology characteristics (technology factors). This study broadened the view of factors affecting performance but again was silent on risk factors.

Banker and Kemerer (1992) investigate different goals between users and project developers on the basis of a principal–agent perspective. Abdel-Hamid, Sengupta, and Swett (1999) studied project factors, such as goals, through a role-playing project-simulation game, and people factors in the form of managerial turnover/succession (Abdel-Hamid, 1992). They found that project managers tend to influence performance by trading quality against cost and vice versa according to their own preferences.

Jurison (1999) performed a comprehensive review of software project management and identified a series of "success factors" involved in managing technology-based projects. The perspective of success factors essentially highlights the facilitators of successful projects. Jurison's list of success factors can also be considered in the people–project–technology framework. For example, "communications," "leadership" and "client/user participation" would be considered people factors while "objectives" and "problem solving" would be considered project factors. Table 23.1 summarizes examples of people, project, and technology performance factors that are covered in the various studies. Our study and the framework we developed are based on these factors.

**Project Risk Factors**

Project risk is a topic receiving increasing attention from IS researchers because of its importance to project outcomes. Considerable interest in a systematic study of risk in the context of IS project implementation has emerged over the past few years. Many researchers have focused on project risk due to the increased interest in distributed software development and associated management issues. Aubert, Patry, and Rivard (2005) discuss the importance of managing risk in the context of outsourcing. Sakthivel (2007) focuses on tradeoffs that must be considered in managing IT project risk with offshore development. Taylor (2006) discussed the importance of clearly defining partner relationships in distributed projects as a mechanism for managing risk.

For example, Applegate, McFarlan, and McKenney (1996) present a framework describing three main dimensions that contribute to project risk; all three dimensions address the broad notion of project complexity. The first dimension considers the size of the project. Typical measures of size include estimated cost, duration, organizational reach, and modularity. The second dimension is related to project structure. This incorporates notions of clarity in requirements specifications, potential impact on organizational process and structural changes, the ability to use prefabricated components, and the ability to impose a structure on the project. The third relates to organizational experience with the technologies involved with the project. This includes resident experience with all aspects of the technology as well as the ability to acquire such experience from sources external to the organization.

Gogan, Fedorowicz, and Rao (1999) elaborate on this framework by suggesting that "time flexibility" and "interdependence" be two additional factors that impact project risk. Time flexibility refers to the ability of an organization to make course corrections during a project, and interdependence refers to the amount of connectivity between various components of the technology. Greater levels of risk are associated with decreased time flexibility and increased interdependence. Both of these factors affect project complexity.

Another example of a project risk framework is the work of Wallace, Keil, and Rai (2004a) who conducted a survey with 507 software project managers and investigated various dimensions of risk. Based on a cluster analysis they identify the six dimensions "team risk," "organizational environment risk," "requirements risk," "planning and control risk," "user risk," and "project complexity risk." They develop a model that assumes these six dimensions are influenced by the "strategic orientation of a project," "sourcing arrangements," and "project scope." While the latter has effects on all six dimensions, the "strategic orientation of the project" influences only "project complexity risk" and "sourcing arrangements" affect only "team risk" and "planning and control risk." The six risk dimensions are assumed to affect "project risk" as a whole, which, in turn, influences "project performance." The study reveals that strategic applications involve higher project complexity risks than informational or transactional applications. Further, it was found that outsourced development projects implied higher team risks as well as higher planning and control risks. This model is developed further by Wallace, Keil, and Rai (2004b).

These frameworks focus on factors that influence project complexity and reflect a general consensus among project risk researchers that assessing project complexity can lead to better project risk assessment. Tsetlin and Winkler (2005) found that project risks are also highly correlated with background risk. These risks have usually been regarded as independent of each other. The results of this study provide further evidence of the problem of complexity in the sense of interdependencies between risks.

## Performance and Risk

Relatively few research studies have considered project performance and risk together. Barki, Rivard, and Talbot (1993) identified a number of risk factors relevant to software development. These factors have partly been confirmed, mapped with risk constructs developed by the Carnegie Mellon Software Engineering Institute (SEI), and further extended in a study of experienced managers by Moynihan (1997). In 2001, Barki, Rivard, and Talbot conducted a longitudinal study of seventy-five software projects and hypothesized that project performance is influenced by the fit between a project's risk exposure and the way in which risk management is performed. They found that performance is lower when the fit is less. Further, they revealed that a different risk management approach is required depending on which performance criteria are used. They found that high risk projects require high levels of "internal integration" (which refers to communication and collaboration), and high levels of formal planning, if the key performance criterion is budget compliance. If the predominant performance criterion is system quality, then high user involvement is called for.

In another study, Lyytinen, Mathiassen, and Ropponen (1998) took a holistic approach to address the notion of risk in software project management. By taking a sociotechnical perspective on the subject, they offer a framework that looks at how risks are managed through "sequential attention shaping" and subsequent process interventions. The contribution of their work is twofold. First, the synthesis of the notion of risk from both managerial theory and software development presents a holistic approach to understanding how projects should be successfully managed. They explicitly consider the interaction of tasks, structures, technologies, and actors in the project management process and argue that looking at any particular framework or methodology (including those referred to earlier in this chapter) might be a limiting exercise.

Fruhauf (2001) argues that risk and project management are so intricately intertwined that the application of any particular methodology must be applied in a pragmatic manner to suit the particular set of circumstances that surround the project. He suggests an explicit integration of risk into all aspects of project planning so that an adequate response can be engineered at any point in the process. The focus is on identifying and being able to manage the risk exposure of a project. This implies an almost continuous process of responding to risk as the primary vehicle for successful project completion.

Our analysis of this project performance and project risk literature provides important guidance for this study. First, overall performance and risk assessment are essential components of complex IS projects, particularly Internet-based projects. It is therefore, crucial to understand these assessments in measurable terms so that they can be explicitly incorporated in project planning, development, and implementation. Second, researchers are beginning to explore the link between project performance, on the one hand, and risk, on the other. Yet, no definitive process has been developed to help project decision makers in this area. Third, the explicit integration of risk exposure with the ongoing process of project evaluation is necessary to ensure that acceptable project performance is achievable.

## RESEARCH METHOD

Our research objective of developing a framework that links performance evaluations with the assessment of risks in order to improve project decisions requires an approach that yields in-depth data of particular projects. The detailed experiences of individuals are critical for our research. We conducted qualitative case study research following the positivist tradition (Darke, Shanks, and Broadbent, 1998) in order to explore "observable" or "measurable" aspects of performance as they are commonly shared between managers of Internet-based projects. We then considered project performance in relationship to specific project risk. Future research may build on this as a first step and continue with, for example, survey research to investigate the value of our framework in practice. In accordance with the definition of case studies provided by Benbasat, Goldstein, and Mead (1987), we investigated performance and risk in their natural setting of Internet projects. The boundaries of the phenomena were not clear at the outset of our study and no systematic variation of variables, that is, no experimental control, was applied. Face-to-face interviews and documentation were chosen as multiple methods for data collection (Benbasat, Goldstein, and Mead, 1987). The interviews were minimally structured in order to generate the richest possible results.

In-depth studies of individual organizations give us rich information about the specifics of how those organizations approach their functions (Yin, 2003). For our research, the predominant benefit of such case studies is that we are able to focus on the complexity of the phenomena (Benbasat, Goldstein, and Mead, 1987), such as the interdependencies between risks and performance, and can obtain detailed data about several aspects of a phenomenon, such as the relationship between performance and risk in Internet-based projects, that otherwise would be difficult to obtain.

We applied the scientific approach for conducting positivist case study research according to Paré (2004) comprising four stages: (1) design of the case study; (2) conduct of the case study; (3) analysis of the case study evidence; and (4) write-up of the case study reports.

## Design of the Case Study

A multiple case study design (Benbasat, Goldstein, and Mead, 1987) allows us to extrapolate patterns about organizations that lay the groundwork for further, generalizable empirical efforts. The use of in-depth case studies enables us to do useful comparisons across organizations at a deeper level of detail. The interviews focus on issues related to the structuring and performance of Internet-based projects in these organizations. With this research design, we attempted to overcome the typical difficulties of single case studies. That is, our design allows for some replicability and, within limits, for some generalizations (Lee, 1999). Our use of multiple case studies is an attempt to balance rigor with depth in our research (Benbasat and Zmud, 1999; Davenport and Markus, 1999; Lyytinen, 1999; Lee, 1999).

Eight organizations, with core competencies significantly related to Internet technologies, that were highly involved in Internet-based projects at the time of the study, were selected for our research. As noted, four of these organizations were located in New Zealand and four were in Canada. We selected eight organizations because we felt this provided enough cases to get in-depth data while at the same time allowing for some degree of generalization. Appendix 23.2 provides more detail about the eight organizations. In order to protect the identity of the organizations that participated in the study, we use generic labels to identify them. Appendix 23.3 shows the documents that were used to solicit participation from those organizations. Organizations were chosen based on the availability of a rich case study that would contribute to this research while satisfying a broad spectrum of industry sectors. We also wanted to do some sort of country-based comparison of our findings and hence looked at case studies in two different countries. We chose one project in each organization that was representative of the Internet projects that each organization had developed. We then conducted interviews with key informants in each of these organizations.

Our research is based on three basic assumptions that informed the structure of the interviews. (Appendix 23.4 provides an overview of the structure of the interviews.) The first assumption is that the key informants in each organization would be able to describe an important Internet-based project with which they were involved and provide detailed information about the performance of that project. The second assumption is that the key informants would be as "objective," that is, balanced, as possible in their descriptions and assessments of the projects. The third assumption is that, through the detailed case descriptions, other factors that affected project performance would emerge from the data.

## Conduct of the Case Study

Table 23.2 summarizes the eight projects selected. The selection covers projects in various types of organizations that take different roles, from technology producers to technology adopters. With

Table 23.2

**Participating Organizations and Their Characteristics**

| Organization | Description | Key projects | Key informant |
|---|---|---|---|
| A | Technology solutions provider (e-commerce focus) | Health sector application | Business Solutions Manager |
| B | Technology infrastructure provider (network infrastructures) | Internal support application | Country Manager |
| C | Financial services; multinational | Role-based portal | Manager Intranet and Knowledge Solutions |
| D | Energy distribution; multinational | Personalization systems | Director of IT Strategic Relationships |
| E | Retail chain | Online business model | Divisional Manager of Online Business |
| F | Consumer products; national | Resource management and governance | Director of IT |
| G | IT services provider | Client interaction projects | Director of Practice |
| H | Insurance services; national | Process automation | VP IS and Technology |

an emphasis on specific ongoing or most recent projects in our interviews, we make sure that the collected data are of high relevance and accuracy.

**Analysis of the Case Study Evidence**

The key informant in each instance was a senior technology officer of the organization and had direct governance over the specific project(s) under consideration. This provided an overview perspective on the Internet-based projects and their relevant performance factors and risks. Each of the semistructured interviews took about two hours. While the informant was asked to focus on a single project and discuss the performance and risk issues of that project, in some cases common threads or some project-specific issues meant that multiple projects were commented on. This enriched the data set as the informants were able to provide multiple dimensions of performance by discussing more than one project. The discussion was minimally structured based on the assumptions that the respondents focused specifically on the issues that they considered to be facilitators and inhibitors of successful project execution. The interviews were audiotaped for subsequent analysis.

The data collected in the interviews were analyzed in three steps. First, all the audiotaped interviews were professionally transcribed. Second, the transcriptions were systematically analyzed for the major performance factors that are associated with the organizations' analysis of their own project performance. The approach that was used focused on identifying emergent high-level *performance factors* as articulated by the key informant. Transcript fragments that made specific reference to performance in the context of the referent project were systematically isolated. The goal was to group related fragments of the transcript under a specific performance factor. Two coders worked in the same fashion; one coded and the other verified. Several iterations of this analysis were required in order to obtain a stable, shared set of performance factors. Third, the transcripts were reanalyzed with the performance factors that had been identified in order to ensure that the identified themes were reflective of a substantial portion of the discourses that were transcribed. A quantitative analysis of the transcript data shows that 89.4 percent of the raw transcript content was coded into these factors.

In order to achieve a high degree of accuracy of results, we attempted to consider the intentions of the interviewees rather than adhering to the literal meaning of words. However, these intentions were captured only from the context of the discussion, so that distortions of statements were avoided and an appropriate level of rigor was assured.

### Write-up of the Case Study Reports

The analysis was performed on the professional transcriptions of the audiotaped interviews. Finally, the results were summarized in case reports.

## RESULTS

From the iterative analysis of the interview transcripts, six main factors were identified within the organizations as criteria used to evaluate project performance: (1) adequate resourcing of projects, (2) building and maintaining of customer relationships, (3) flexibility in project implementation, (4) clarity in outcome specification, (5) leveraging of organizational experience, and (6) understanding of dependencies among organizational processes and technologies. Some of these factors have been identified in other studies (e.g., Barki, Rivard, and Talbot) but no study has identified them as a complete set. What also became clear from the transcripts was the need to directly consider risk when considering performance. This was a common theme for all six factors. This integration of a set of common performance factors with project risk offers new insights for decision making on IS projects. The following briefly describes the six factors and their relationship to project risk. Appendix 23.5 describes the six factors in more detail.

### 1. Resourcing

Providing adequate resources for projects is a key issue in determining project success. What makes this particularly difficult is that the resource requirements in financial terms are not predictable in any precise terms ahead of the commencement of a project and this increases risk. Resourcing is regarded as a combination of financial as well as nonfinancial dimensions, such as the "right signals" from top management about backing the project. The more uncertain the resourcing, the greater the perceived risk.

### 2. Customer Relationships

The nature of the relationships with immediate and extended customers of the project outputs was mentioned repeatedly as an important factor for performance evaluation, minimizing project risk, and consequently, for project success. Managing these relationships in the context of prior experience can reduce risk and be crucial to successfully implementing a particular project.

### 3. Flexibility

The notion of flexibility in project deployment was mentioned as an important factor. This idea refers to the ability of an organization to be able to execute a course correction midway through a project. This is similar to the time flexibility dimension identified by Gogan, Fedorowicz, and Rao (1999). This flexibility is considered to be a risk-minimizing strategy that better enables a project to meet customer expectations.

## 4. Clarity in Outcomes

The importance of being clear as far as project outcomes were concerned was highlighted by all the organizations. While this issue is quite explicitly covered by legal contracts between service providers and external clients (such as those in organizations A and G), it was also critical in the case of internally developed applications (such as those in organizations B and C). Clarity of outcomes appeared to reflect risk in that the fuzzier the outcomes, the greater the perceived risk.

## 5. Experience

The application of prior organizational experience is seen as a key issue in managing projects. This applies to experience in the technology itself as well as processes relating to the application of technology. This is similar to Applegate, McFarlan, and McKenney (1996) "organizational experience" factor. The more relevant prior experience could be applied to a project, the less risky the project was perceived to be.

## 6. Dependencies

The specification of how aspects of the particular projects under discussion were connected with other systems and processes within and outside the organization was identified as a key performance factor. All informants highlighted the importance of identifying and managing these connections between their Internet-based projects. They noted that more connections resulted in greater perceived project risk.

In reanalyzing the interview data in light of the performance factors that were identified, it became clear that underlying much of what the key informants were saying about performance factors was project risk. For example, with the factor "clarity in outcomes," what emerged was a preoccupation with risk, and that clarifying outcomes was a way to mitigate risk in the complex projects that all these organizations had undertaken. Therefore, what evolved was not just the identification of performance factors but the interrelationships of performance factors and project risk. It became clear that a structured process was needed to help these informants understand the risk–performance relationship for Internet-based projects and a way to apply this understanding to future projects. The importance of risk in the context of performance was highlighted from the analysis of the data. While all projects have some inherent risk characteristics, the importance of explicitly incorporating risk within a performance framework appears to be critical. The next section of the chapter develops such a framework.

## DISCUSSION

### Framework Description

Based on the six project performance factors identified in the previous section and the repeated emphasis on project risk on the part of the informants, the risk–performance management framework

Table 23.3

## The Basic Risk–Performance Management Framework (RPMF)

| | | | | Information systems risks | | | | | | | | | | | |
| | | | | Personnel | | | Processes | | | Systems | | | External | | |
| | | | | Risk 1 | Risk 2 | Risk 3 | Risk 1 | Risk 2 | Risk 3 | Risk 1 | Risk 2 | Risk 3 | Risk 1 | Risk 2 | Risk 3 |
|---|---|---|---|---|---|---|---|---|---|---|---|---|---|---|---|
| Performance | Resourcing | Relevance | Means 1 | | | | | | | | | | | | |
| | | | Means 2 | | | | | | | | | | | | |
| | | | Means 3 | | | | | | | | | | | | |
| | Customer relationship | Relevance | Means 1 | | | | | | | | | | | | |
| | | | Means 2 | | | | | | | | | | | | |
| | | | Means 3 | | | | | | | | | | | | |
| | Flexibility | Relevance | Means 1 | | | | | | | | | | | | |
| | | | Means 2 | | | | | | | | | | | | |
| | | | Means 3 | | | | | | | | | | | | |
| | Clarity in outcomes | Relevance | Means 1 | | | | | | | | | | | | |
| | | | Means 2 | | | | | | | | | | | | |
| | | | Means 3 | | | | | | | | | | | | |
| | Experience | Relevance | Means 1 | | | | | | | | | | | | |
| | | | Means 2 | | | | | | | | | | | | |
| | | | Means 3 | | | | | | | | | | | | |
| | Dependencies | Relevance | Means 1 | | | | | | | | | | | | |
| | | | Means 2 | | | | | | | | | | | | |
| | | | Means 3 | | | | | | | | | | | | |

(RPMF) is proposed to aid project decision makers in planning for and managing the complexity of their projects. An example of the use of this framework is found in Appendix 23.6.

The RPMF consists of (1) a *structure,* represented by a two-dimensional grid that describes the elements and their relationships (Table 23.3), and (2) a *process* of how to apply the grid as an instrument to assess performance and risk simultaneously in a project.

### 1. Framework Structure

The framework grid shows the two main dimensions: performance and risk, subdivided into performance factors and risk categories. The performance factors are based on the results of this study. The risk categories are aligned with recent regulatory requirements that guide organizations in their operational risk management activities as described earlier, namely, personnel risks, process risks, systems risks, and external risks. A relevance score is associated with each performance factor, which allows an organization to customize the grid to its particular situation, and the means of achieving high performance for that factor are identified. On the risk dimension, the most crucial risks in each category are identified for an organization in its specific situation.

### 2. Framework Process

The framework process comprises four main steps: (1) defining the relevance of performance factors; (2) identifying the most important possible means; (3) identifying the most crucial IS risks, and (4) identifying and evaluating the impact of IS risks on performance factors. These four steps are explained in detail below.

### Step 1: Defining the Relevance of Performance Factors

Our study has revealed six main performance factors, namely, resourcing, customer relationship, flexibility, clarity in outcomes, experience, and dependencies, which were generally shared across various organizations. However, while these factors may be generally valid across all organizations, their particular relevance and the means by which they can be achieved, are highly organization-specific.

Therefore, the first step of the framework process requires that the organization define the relevance of each performance factor in terms of a degree or weighting regarding the fit with the organizational strategies and goals. This can be done by assigning a particular percentage value to each of the performance factors. These relevance values build, together with the performance factors, the first two columns of the framework grid (Table 23.3).

### Step 2: Identifying the Most Important Possible Means

A high performance for each of the factors identified in Step1 can be achieved by a variety of means (e.g., funding, management time, etc.). The management of performance is assumed to be heavily dependent on the means that are available. However, not all possible means may be available to an organization at a given time in the context of a particular project.

Therefore, the most important available means to achieve each performance factor are identified in the second step of the framework process. This selection can comprise one, two, or more means per performance factor. Again, the selection represents a compromise between accuracy and completeness, on the one hand, and practicability of the framework, on the other. The performance factors and their relevance (Step 1), and these means (Step 2) build the performance dimension on the vertical axis of the framework grid (Table 23.3).

### Step 3: Identifying the Most Crucial IS Risks

Each organization is exposed to an individual set of IS risks, a particular selection of which is most relevant for the project under consideration. Risks are most commonly understood as deviations from an expected outcome to an uncertain extent and with a particular probability of occurrence. As described earlier, we understand IS risks as part of operational risks, four types of which can be distinguished: people, process, systems, and external risks. In this context, people are considered to be employees, and risks emerging from people outside the organization are regarded as external risks. These four categories correspond to the definition of operational risks, as it is used by the Basel Committee on Banking Supervision for the banking industry (BCBS, 2004) and similarly in the Sarbanes-Oxley Act and Solvency II. Since business processes in the banking industry are highly risk sensitive, this field can be regarded as a prototypical example. Similar regulations to Basel II can also be found in the Sarbanes-Oxley Act, for instance, which is not specifically relevant to the banking industry but to all companies listed on the U.S. Stock Exchange, and Solvency II for the insurance industry. Thus, we keep our framework flexible for further integration with operational and overall risk management activities in an organization. In practice, all of these risks may represent inhibitors to the performance of a project. Therefore, we argue that the management of project performance and performance-based decisions can be significantly improved with an approach that takes both performance factors and risks simultaneously into account.

Consequently, in the third step of our framework, the organization identifies those IS risks that are most relevant to the project. In order to make this identification easier, it is performed according to the four categories of personnel risks, process risks, systems risks, and external risks, depending on the area of failure. For instance, if a risk is related mainly to the possible failure of employees in an organization, it is categorized as personnel risk; if the failure lies outside the organization, the risk is categorized as external. Finally, Step 3 of the framework process is scalable in terms of number and categorization of the IS risks. The IS risks differentiated according to the four categories build the risk dimension on the horizontal axis of the framework grid (Table 23.3).

*Step 4: Identifying and Evaluating the Impact of IS Risks on Performance Factors*

In practice, IS risks often represent inhibitors to performance factors. Therefore, as a fourth step in our framework, the organization identifies which IS risks represent inhibitors to which means for performance achievement. Rather than identifying the mere existence of such a relationship, its quality is specified through an evaluation on a rating scale. We suggest values between 1 and 5 as a medium level of granularity. Similar to the previous steps of the framework process, Step 4 is customizable to the specific needs of an organization, for example, in terms of selecting an individual method for the evaluation, that is, scales can be extended to seven or more rating points, or reduced to three traffic light colors/values, dependent on what is needed in the context of the project. The values are then entered into the grid relating IS risks to performance factors.

**The RPMF in Use**

How does this framework enable the project planners to improve their risk-based decisions? First, the RPMF creates transparency and makes project participants more aware of IS risks relevant to the project and their relationship to the project's performance factors. Second, it helps to pro-actively address the problem of IS risks affecting project performance as inhibitors. On the one hand, the weighted sum of the rows reveals which of the performance factors is most affected. On the other hand, the sum of the columns indicates which of the risks exerts the highest impact on the performance of the project, while still considering the interdependencies of the risks. These important circumstances can then be considered in the project plan.

The term "circumstances" indicates that we do not assume a static view, but regard the relationships between IS risks and performance factors as dynamic. Therefore, it is helpful but not sufficient to apply the RPMF only once at the beginning of the project. Instead, the application of the RPMF may be integrated into the project plan, for instance, being applied at several milestones. The evaluations may change over the course of the project and additional IS risks or performance factors may even become important. When the framework is applied iteratively, changes in the results help to illustrate necessary changes for the management of the project. The results further inform the processes of risk management and performance management. The risk management process is considered as comprising the identification, assessment, mitigation, and monitoring of IS risks. Similarly, we regard the performance management process as comprising identification, assessment, facilitation, and monitoring.

However, we emphasize that it is important to apply the framework on the basis of a life cycle perspective. Some IS risks may be predominantly relevant to the development stage, and others to the operation and maintenance stage or to the entire system life cycle. Similarly, the performance factors of the project are relevant to the long-term organizational performance. Therefore, from an organizational perspective, it is necessary to apply the framework in all projects and to incorporate the results into overall risk management as well as organizational performance management.

The RPMF first of all reflects that performance and risk assessment are essential components of complex projects and helps organizations to understand these assessments in measurable terms so that they can be explicitly incorporated in all stages of the system life cycle. Second, it contributes to the exploration of the link between project performance, on the one hand, and IS risks, on the other. In particular, it provides a clear evaluative process that may help decision makers in this area.

Finally, it provides an explicit integration of risk exposure with the ongoing process of project evaluation, which is necessary to ensure that acceptable project performance is achievable. Overall, the risk–performance management framework for Internet-based projects consists of a grid with the two dimensions of performance factors and risk factors. The grid is filled in using a structured process that identifies the relevance of specific performance factors, the means to achieve high performance on those factors, and finally the identification of risks and their strength associated with each of the performance factors. This integration of risk and performance should provide stronger support for project managers beyond the current approaches of considering performance and risk separately.

## CONCLUSIONS

This study began by identifying six project performance factors in Internet-based projects in eight representative organizations. As the data for the projects were being analyzed, it became evident that the project performance factors were tightly linked with project risks. We found that the six main performance factors had strong relationships to risk factors and that a structured process was needed to assist project decision makers to combine performance factors and risk factors into one integrated process so that Internet-based project management could be improved. We have developed a risk–performance management framework (RPMF) that contains a structure and a corresponding process that can meet these needs. We recognize that this framework is based on only eight cases, but we believe this may generate a stream of research that will improve information systems project management by interrelating performance and risk.

The implications of this framework for researchers are that it refocuses project management success factors not on individual factors but on the interrelationship among key project factors. In our view, the integration of relationships between factors holds the potential for developing improved project management approaches. In other words, enhanced project management will develop at the "interfaces" of these factors. A particular strength of the RPMF is its flexibility. It does not assume a generic set of risks that applies to a variety of different organizations or even across industries. Rather, it provides a systematic approach with a wide scope for organization-specific strategic values and priorities. Future research could focus on investigating and refining the RPMF, for example, through other research methods. The use of complexity theory may particularly enhance further development of the framework and its applicability to the uncertain reality of project management. Other work could look at Internet-based projects in other countries. Finally, future research could study the integration of other project elements beyond risk and performance that offer the potential for project management improvement.

For practitioners, we see the implications as twofold. First, the RPMF will provide a new perspective for looking at both project risk and project performance. This new "lens" should help project decision makers focus on aspects of projects that may not have been considered important in the past. Second, the process described in this chapter provides a practical guide to using the framework. The application of the steps should provide confidence to the decision maker that both risk and performance are being considered together, which should result in improved project performance.

## APPENDIX 23.1. PROJECT MANAGEMENT ACCORDING TO PMBOK AND ISO 10006

| PMBOK | ISO 10006 |
|---|---|
| 1. Project integration management | 1. Project initiation and project plan development |
| Project plan development | Interdependency management processes |
| Project plan execution | Interaction management |
| Integrated change control | Change management |
|  | Closure |
| | |
| 2. Project scope management | 2. Scope-related processes |
| Initiation | Concept development |
| Scope planning | Scope development and control |
| Scope definition | Activity definition |
| Scope verification | |
| Scope change control | |
| | |
| 3. Project time management | 3. Activity control |
| Activity definition | Time-related processes |
| Activity sequencing | Activity dependency planning |
| Activity duration estimating | Estimation of duration |
| Schedule development | Schedule development |
| Schedule control | |
| | |
| 4. Project cost management | 4. Schedule control |
| Resource planning | Cost-related processes |
| Cost estimating | Cost estimation |
| Cost budgeting | Budgeting |
| Cost control | Cost control |
| | |
| 5. Project quality management | 5. Resource-related processes |
| Quality planning | Resource planning |
| Quality assurance | Resource control |
| Quality control | |
| | |
| 6. Project human resource management | 6. Personnel-related processes |
| Organizational planning | Definition of project organizational structure |
| Staff acquisition | Staff allocation |
| Team development | Team development |
| | |
| 7. Project communications management | 7. Communication-related processes |
| Communications planning | Communication planning |
| Information distribution | Information |
| Performance reporting | Communication control |
| Administrative closure | |
| | |
| 8. Project risk management | 8. Risk-related processes |
| Risk management planning | Risk identification |
| Risk identification | Risk assessment |

Qualitative risk analysis

Quantitative risk analysis

Risk response planning

Risk monitoring and control

Risk response development

Risk control

9. Project procurement management

Procurement planning

Solicitation planning

Solicitation

Source selection

Contract administration

Contract closeout

9. Purchasing-related processes

Purchasing planning and control

Documentation of requirements

Evaluation of subcontractors

Subcontracting

Contract control

10. Learning from the project

## APPENDIX 23.2. DESCRIPTIONS OF THE EIGHT PARTICIPATING ORGANIZATIONS

### Organization A: Technology Solutions Provider

Organization A is a large multinational provider of technology solutions for users of Internet-based technologies. Its presence in New Zealand is relatively recent going back about ten years and its focus is on networked applications. It supports the development of end-to-end solutions that are built using hardware infrastructures that are manufactured by its infrastructure partner. The focus of A's work is largely e-commerce–related solutions. Its clients are organizations of all sizes and include those from the private and public sectors. The organization has a global presence and therefore its methods adopted in New Zealand are informed by worldwide practices. The project that provided the context for this research was the work done by A in a large government organization. The key informant from A was a high-level manager overseeing the implementation.

### Organization B: Technology Infrastructure Provider

Organization B is a manufacturer and provider of the technology infrastructure used in networked applications. B is a multinational organization with a global presence. Like A, its customer base consists of organizations of all sizes and from different industry sectors. Because of its international presence, practices in New Zealand are informed by worldwide practices. The particular project that provided the data for this study was an internally developed Internet-based solution to support its employees. The system was deployed worldwide so that clients of the system in the New Zealand organization experienced the same system as that seen by its employees in other countries. The key informant who participated in the interview was the country manager based in New Zealand.

### Organization C: Financial Services

Organization C is a multinational financial services firm. It offers a full range of financial products and services mainly across Canada. The focus in this research was on a role-based portal that was under development. A particular emphasis on the design standards that were employed in the development of the project was described. Specifically, the risks associated with developing an important application using an emerging standard was pointed out. The key informant was the manager of Intranet and knowledge solutions

### Organization D: Energy Distributor

Organization *D* is a large multinational energy distribution firm. The discussion in the context of this research was around the issue of providing personalized access to important information to key stakeholders in the firm. In particular, the current attempt at developing a firm-wide application to provide personalized access and the associated organizational and technical issues was the focus. The key informant was the director of IT strategic relationships.

### Organization E: Retailer

Organization *E* is a large retail chain operating several outlets in New Zealand and Australia. The retailer has had a presence in New Zealand for over several decades. It is associated through its parent company with several retail chains in the grocery and department store sectors. The project that served as the context for this study is the development and deployment of an online shopping business model. The model was developed over a period of several years and has been operational for about five years. It is a classic example of a business-to-consumer application of Internet-based technology. The key informant from *E* was the divisional manager, the person in charge of building the online model of the retail business in the organization.

### Organization F: Consumer Products

Organization *F* is a national consumer products firm operating throughout Canada. The key issues that were discussed pertained to resource management and governance of the IT function in the organization. In particular, a current effort dealing with a system to address these issues was the focus of the discussion. The key informant was the director of IT.

### Organization G: IT Services

Organization *G* is an IT services provider that supplies its expertise in business solutions through consultative and system integration services. It has considerable experience in this area and has had a presence in New Zealand for many years. Its client base covers a wide range of industries that includes the public and private sectors and ranges from telecommunications to financial services. In the context of this research, project performance was discussed in terms of how the performance of *G*'s employees is viewed by the organization in the context of client interactions. *G*'s interaction with clients is largely structured on a project basis and therefore it is appropriate to take this focus in addressing the research questions at hand. The key informant from *G* was the director overseeing client interactions.

### Organization H: Insurance Services

Organization *H* is an insurance services firm operating in Canada and offering a wide range of insurance products. The object of the research in this firm dealt with process automation throughout the firm. The traditional nature of the industry and the firm were emphasized and the particular issues surrounding the difficulty of new technology introduction were mentioned as key factors in working through the project. The key informant was the vice president of information systems and technology.

## APPENDIX 23.3. MATERIALS USED IN THE STUDY: INITIAL PARTICIPATION REQUEST

### Research Project

*Performance Assessment in an Internet-based Environment*
*Project Leader:*
*Brief Overview*

The assessment of the performance of organizations engaged in Internet-based projects (the development or deployment of Internet-based technologies in a business context) is an issue of considerable interest to both researchers and practitioners. Performance, as defined in this research project, is considered broadly to encompass the evaluation of a complex organization, a portfolio of projects, or a particular project that the organization embarks on. Short-term financial measures of performance have been used by the markets to decide on the degree of success achieved by such activity. Working under the premise that the adoption of Internet-based technologies in organizations is only going to increase, it is important to study the manner by which these organizations themselves view the issue of their performance. Traditional organizational analysis tells us that performance is a multifaceted phenomenon where short-term financial measures represent one aspect. On the one hand, it is important for organizations to be appreciative of the verdict in the equity markets in order to ensure longevity. However, it is equally important to understand that organizations must be prepared to undergo transformation to leverage new technologies, and these transformations must be subject to appropriate performance assessment. In this research study we wish to investigate how organizations are framing this discourse in order to come to grips with realistically assessing their performance.

### Procedure and Participation

We would like to invite your participation in this project. What this means, in the first instance, is a preliminary indication from you about your willingness to participate. If you indicate that you are (as some of you did at the meeting), we will arrange a meeting with you (or a nominee who has substantial knowledge about performance-related issues in your organization). The meeting will last for about three hours and we will try to schedule it during the early part of December. The meeting will be in the form of an interview with the points to be discussed circulated ahead of the meeting.

We look forward to working with you.

## APPENDIX 23.4. MATERIALS USED IN THE STUDY: INTERVIEW STRUCTURE

### Research Project

*Performance Assessment in an Internet-based Environment*
*Project Leader:*

This note is a follow up to the previously circulated general description of our research project and should be read in conjunction with that description. In preparation for our meeting, this is an outline of the points I would like to cover when we meet. It gives you a rough idea about the sorts of issues that we are interested in. What we want to focus on is the use of Internet-based technologies in your organization. The word "project" in the discussion below is used loosely to refer to a major initiative in your organization. Examples could be:

- New product or process development
- Customer relationship management
- Business process design
- Supply-chain coordination

**Discussion Points**

Consider a particular project that has been recently completed or is in progress in your organization:

- Is the use (development or application) of Internet-based technology an integral part of the project?
- Is the technology Internet based?
- Does the project represent a significant part of the organization's activities?
- What is the (anticipated) duration of the project?
- Approximately how many people are directly involved in the project?
- Approximately what is the level of financial investment in the project?
- What is the extent of reliance on an external organization for the technology that is utilized in this project?

**Performance-Related Issues**

- What are some general evaluation factors that are (or will be) used to evaluate the project (e.g., financial)?
- When were the factors established?
- Who were the people involved in establishing them?
- What is the frequency with which the project's progress is monitored?
- Who is involved in the monitoring?
- What is your assessment of how the project has gone (or is going)?
- What are the major catalysts that are driving the success of the project?
- What are the major detractors that are inhibiting the success of the project?
- What is the role of partner organizations in terms of impact on the progress of the project?

## APPENDIX 23.5. SIX PROJECT PERFORMANCE FACTORS

The following are descriptions of the six project performance factors for Internet-based projects identified from the eight case studies.

### A. Resourcing

All the interview partners talked about the adequate resourcing of projects as a key issue in determining project success. What makes it particularly difficult is that the resource requirements in financial terms are not readily predictable in any precise way in advance of the commencement of a project and this increases risk. Resourcing is regarded as a combination of financial as well as nonfinancial dimensions, such as the "right signals" from top management about backing the project.

Organization A particularly mentioned the notion of resourcing activities as supporting an environment of sharing knowledge throughout an extended community. The organization also pointed out that resourcing is often seen as an "internal matter" involving finances and expertise; however, a broader focus on resources based on influential stakeholders outside the organization (and often from client organizations) can be a useful facilitator of good performance. Organization B mentioned the importance of adequate resourcing, especially from an expertise point of view. Organization C stressed the need for internal resourcing to be well connected with technology standards and providers for harmonizing the design of the applications. Organization D said that resourcing at the overall organizational level has a strong link to specific project resourcing.

## B. Customer Relationships

The nature of the relationships with immediate and extended customers of the project outputs was mentioned repeatedly as an important factor for performance evaluation, minimizing project risk and, consequently, a factor of project success. Immediate customers are those directly involved on the receiving end of the project outputs (online shoppers in Organization E; internal sales force in Organization B). Organization E mentioned that it was important to ensure positive customer experiences as the system continued development. This presented a juggling act where the user experience was managed against a backdrop of system changes. Organization G pointed out that ongoing relationships with clients were so important to the organization that sometimes it even came at a cost to the project. Organization D pointed out that project customers come into a project with prior organizational experience with other implementations. Managing these relationships in the context of prior experience can be crucial to successfully implementing a particular project.

## C. Flexibility

The notion of flexibility in project deployment was mentioned as an important issue. This idea refers to the ability of an organization to be able to execute a course correction midway through a project based on the context of the implementation. This is similar to the time flexibility dimension identified by Gogan and Fedorowicz (1999). There was some divided opinion among the participants as to the importance of flexibility.

Organization A pointed out that being flexible is almost a requirement of their business. When projects last as long as two years in duration, adjustments are bound to be made along the way. Sometimes, this may be infeasible in light of the agreed-upon project outcomes with service providers such as Organization G; in other cases, it might mean the ability to deliver highly successful outcomes such as the system in B that was opportunistically developed during a slow period in the economy. Organization G pointed out that in complex projects it is important to be flexible so that the project can be completed successfully. This is beneficial not only to the customer but also to the organization itself in terms of risk management and long-term customer relationships.

## D. Clarity in Outcomes

The importance of being clear concerning project outcomes was highlighted by all of the organizations. While this issue is explicitly covered by legal contracts between service providers and external clients (such as those in A and G), it was also critical in the case of internally developed applications (such as those in *B* and *C*). Clarity of outcomes appeared to reflect risk in that the fuzzier the outcomes, the greater the perceived risk. Organization *A* also pointed out that a long-term perspective on outcomes must be in place. It is misleading to gauge performance on short-term measures without keeping the long-term implications of the project on the organization and subsequent projects in sight. It was also pointed out by *A* that part of this idea is to position itself strategically through the project deployment in order to gain the visibility required by a solutions provider. It is also important to demonstrate and sometimes deliver outcomes that are unanticipated on the part of the client organization. Organization *G* made the point that with short-term projects, service providers have to be quite clear in stating the outcomes and monitoring them. The monitoring successfully employed standardized and structured ways to gauge performance. These processes were transparent so that all parties were clearly informed about performance issues at all points in time. Longer-term projects presented a higher degree of risk and therefore had to be monitored in a careful way that appropriately took the time frame into account. The development of a good set of metrics was seen as important for service providers. Many of these metrics are financial in nature. However, client satisfaction is considered to be an important indicator of performance. The objectives of the client and the organization can sometimes conflict and this needs to be managed quite carefully.

### E. Experience

The application of prior organizational experience is seen as a key issue in managing projects. This applies to experience in the technology itself as well as processes relating to the application of technology. This is similar to Applegate, McFarlan, and McKenney's (1996) "organizational experience" factor. Organization *A* saw value in applying experience-based templates to all projects in which they were involved. The practice of good documentation of practices was instrumental in leveraging such experience. In a global organization, expertise resides in many parts of the world. The ability of an organization to reach out to its constituencies in appropriate ways is crucial to bringing the right experience to bear on projects. While it is clear that experience in emergent technologies is important, this is only one aspect of overall experience. Experience with process-oriented aspects of workflow was considered to be equally important. Organization *H*'s experience with internal and external design teams presented particular issues of applying broad experience with projects within the specific organizational context.

### F. Dependencies

The specification of how aspects of the particular projects under discussion were connected with other systems and processes within and outside the organization was identified as a key performance factor. Uniformly, all of the participants highlighted the importance of this aspect of managing their Internet-based projects and noted how it affected project risk. Organization *A*'s earlier comments mentioned the effects of a particular project's outcomes on subsequent projects, which is a good example of process dependencies that facilitate good performance. Organization *B* made a strong point about leveraging its experience with technology in all endeavors. The global nature of the company meant that practices had to be more or less in conformance with a worldwide set of norms. Any design in which it engaged used a component-based approach thereby enhancing the possibility of gaining advantage from nonredundant activity. Organization *E* mentioned that it was important to proceed with implementation in small related and dependent steps. Incremental successes were important for the continuity and the longevity of the project. Organization *E* also stated that having good stable systems in place in the organization was an asset that supported the particular project under discussion. The relationship of the organization to its partners in other countries has made it necessary to ensure that the linkages to business practices and processes are kept firmly in focus. Sometimes this had an inhibiting effect but often it served as a benchmark for the particular project at hand. The links between IT processes and management processes presented a particular challenge in Organization C. These links had to be understood clearly and taken into account in the design of the application. Organization C stressed that tight links between internal and external (technology supplier) teams were essential to ensure that any development project worked in synchronized fashion.

## APPENDIX 23.6 AN EXAMPLE OF THE INTEGRATED RISK–PERFORMANCE MANAGEMENT FRAMEWORK FOR INTERNET-BASED PROJECTS

The risk–performance management framework with its grid and its four-step process has been described at a general level in the body of this chapter. The following example explains the application of the framework to an Internet-based project. For this example, we assume the scenario that a bank plans to integrate a mobile banking service as a new channel into its multichannel distribution concept.

### Applying Step 1: Defining the Relevance of Performance Factors

The implementation of a mobile banking service in this example implies significant investments, most of which are assumed to be essential to the project's success—without one of these investments the project would be at risk. Highly qualified personnel are required to staff the project—without them the project cannot succeed.

Offering a mobile distribution channel for banking services mainly aims at retaining existing customers by offering them a channel that is as convenient as possible for any situation and, thus, contributing to customer relationship management.

Moreover, since the development of standards is not yet advanced, information systems for mobile banking with all their components, that is, technical, organizational, and so on, are to be kept as flexible as possible in order to avoid misinvestments and to ensure the potential for later adaptations.

The bank in this scenario is exploring the scope of mobile commerce for banking services. The project is subject to high uncertainty, so that clear outcomes cannot be expected. Further, due to the degree of innovation of the project, prior organizational experience is not available beyond the level that was required for the Internet banking project the bank conducted some years ago.

However, dependencies are regarded as rather high. The mobile channel is to be integrated into the complete set of distribution channels and, if the service is to be of significant value to the customer it must enable transactions. This means that the systems must be integrated with the existing technological infrastructure, particularly the back-end systems of the bank.

All in all, in this example the bank may evaluate the performance factors as follows (see Table 23.4):

- Resourcing: 20 percent
- Customer relationship: 20 percent
- Flexibility: 25 percent
- Clarity in outcomes: 10 percent
- Experience: 10 percent
- Dependencies: 15 percent.

In order to keep the example simple and easy to comprehend, we assume that no customization is needed in terms of additional performance factors.

Table 23.4

**An Example of the Risk–Performance Management Framework for a Mobile Banking Project**

| | | | | | Information systems risks | | | | | | | | | | | | |
| | | | | | Personnel | | | Process | | | Systems | | | External | | | Weighted SUM |
| | | | | | Special know-how required | Degree of outsourcing | Lack of acceptance | Time-to-market | Strategic relevance | Unauthorized use | Path dependency | Low usability | Clarity of requirements | Standards | Volatility of customer needs | Legal/regulatory changes | |
| Performance | Resourcing | 20% | Top management involvement | 5 | 5 | 2 | | | | | | | | | | | 2 |
| | | | Early acquisition of skills | | | | | | | | | | | | | | |
| | | | Increase stakeholder's value | | | | | | | | | | | | | | |
| | Customer relationship | 20% | Market research | | | | | | | | | | | | | | 0 |
| | | | Positive experiences | | | | | | | | | | | | | | |
| | | | Trust | | | | | | | | | | | | | | |
| | Flexibility | 25% | Agile methodologies | | | | | | | | | | | | | | 0 |
| | | | Redundant knowledge and skills | | | | | | | | | | | | | | |
| | | | Early warning mechanisms | | | | | | | | | | | | | | |
| | Clarity in outcomes | 10% | Precise definitions | | | | | | | | | | | | | | 0 |
| | | | Long-term specification | | | | | | | | | | | | | | |
| | | | QS of SLAs | | | | | | | | | | | | | | |
| | Experience | 10% | Hiring qualified personnel | | | | | | | | | | | | | | 0 |
| | | | Training existing personnel | | | | | | | | | | | | | | |
| | | | High quality documentation | | | | | | | | | | | | | | |
| | Dependencies | 15% | Relating activities to business processes | | | | | | | | | | | | | | 0 |
| | | | Identifying relationships with other projects | | | | | | | | | | | | | | |
| | | | Identifying relationships with external developments | | | | | | | | | | | | | | |
| | | | SUM | 5 | 5 | 2 | 0 | 0 | 0 | 0 | 0 | 0 | 0 | 0 | 0 | 0 | |

## Applying Step 2: Identifying the Most Important Possible Means

The aspects that have been gathered from the case studies for each of the factors suggest some initial ideas about the means that would be relevant for the participating organizations. These means are considered for this example of a bank (Table 23.4). However, each organization has to identify its own means that are available to achieve the performance factors, according to its strategies and goals.

So, for the bank, the means to achieve the performance criterion of resourcing could be to involve top management as early as possible, in order to create a supportive environment. Further, the early acquisition of knowledge and skills for this cutting-edge technology, for instance, through hiring new and/or training existing staff, can significantly contribute to adequate resourcing. A third means could be to address the bank's assets from a stakeholder's perspective, for example, to increase long-term values and the viability of the organization. (Calculating a generous budget is a theoretical means to address this performance criterion, but is not considered feasible in times of serious cost pressure and economic downturns.)

Customer relationships can be addressed through conducting market research, in order to investigate the actual demand related to the willingness to pay for a mobile banking service. Close collaboration with the marketing and investor relations department can help to base the project on firsthand, high quality information on customers. Another means to support the performance criterion of customer relationships is to create early positive customer experiences, for example, to start the mobile banking service with a pilot group of "power customers" and to make sure not to launch the service too early while serious bugs remain. A climate of trust can be supported by addressing the most serious security issues and communicating the solution to customers, as well as by reassuring them about the confidential treatment of their personal data.

The best possible flexibility of the project could be achieved, for instance, through the use of agile development methodologies, such as DSDM (Stapleton, 1997), Adaptive Software Development (Highsmith, 2000), SCRUM (Sutherland, 2004), Crystal Methodologies (developed by Cockburn and Highsmith, 2008), and the like. Additional enhancements could involve making sure that the most important knowledge and skills in the project team are redundant and to install early warning mechanisms to identify when milestones of the project cannot be met on time or on budget. Again, interdependencies between the activities and related risks need to be considered, as opposed to looking at each early warning indicator separately.

Legal contracts can help the bank to clarify outcomes, although this does not cover changes that become necessary during the development process. A long-term specification can address this issue right from the beginning, although there are a number of changes that cannot be anticipated at that stage. A continuous quantification of financial impacts of all changes can at least help to keep outcomes clear within financial constraints. In addition, measuring or monitoring outcomes, for example, the information provided, usefulness, customer satisfaction, and retention, helps to keep track of the desired outcomes of the project. In order to measure and monitor outcomes, precise project success indicators need to be identified at the beginning of the project. However, these indicators can also be subject to change, which renders monitoring outcomes particularly difficult in Internet-based projects.

As has been mentioned earlier, experience prior to the start of the project is not expected to be available. So, technology-related experience can be acquired either through training existing or hiring new staff. Process-related experience usually needs to be trained within the organization. Beyond directly acquiring experience, good documentation is essential for the bank to facilitate knowledge transfer. This is essential, if parts of the project have been outsourced. In practice, projects often fail in the end when external personnel leave without having transferred their knowledge to internal staff.

### Applying Step 3: Identifying the Most Crucial IS Risks

As outlined earlier, IS risks for this research are defined as the deviation from an expected outcome to an uncertain extent and a probability of occurrence due to the failure of

   a.   technical systems, and/or
   b.   processes that are supported through information systems, and/or
   c.   people who use information systems, and/ or
   d.   external events that affect or cause failure of information systems.

The bank in this example may perceive the following IS risks as most crucial for their mobile banking project (Table 23.4). They may, for instance, determine that the project is most exposed to personnel risks in the sense of special know-how that is required, a high degree of outsourcing, and a serious lack of user acceptance if the system cannot be properly integrated into the back-end systems and no transaction services can be offered to customers.

One of the most crucial process risks may be an extremely short time to market. Further, "mobile banking" service and market entry are of significant strategic relevance, since the bank expects to lose a large number of existing premium customers if it is not among the first movers. In addition, the service is subject to unauthorized use, in particular, as long as no specific processes have been implemented and established in practice.

The greatest system risks may be the dependency on new technology and the implied path dependency and risk of low usability on the devices available to customers. Since the bank tries to be among the first movers, there are few comparable systems.

With a highly innovative technology, there are usually no standards available, so that the bank has to face the external risk that standards will be developed that are incompatible with the technology it has chosen. Since "mobile banking" service is fairly new to customers, their needs are presumably highly volatile compared with a service that has already reached the level of a commodity. Finally, an important external risk that can always affect business processes and thereby have an impact on systems supporting them, lies in legal and regulatory changes. This is particularly crucial for the banking industry.

### Applying Step 4: Identifying and Evaluating the Impact of IS Risks on Performance Factors

In this fourth step the bank first identifies those IS risks that have an impact on the performance factors and evaluates the relationship between these IS risks and performance factors. For each of the IS risks identified in Step 3, the strength of its impact on each of the performance factors is assessed. In this example, the assessment is done in the form of a five-point rating.

### REFERENCES

Abdel-Hamid, T.K. 1992. Investigating the impact of managerial turnover/succession on project performance. *Journal of Management Information Systems,* 9, 2, 127–144.

Abdel-Hamid, T.K.; Sengupta, K.; and Swett, C. 1999. The impact of goals on software project management: an experimental investigation. *MIS Quarterly,* 23, 4, 531–555.

Aladwani, A.M. 2002. An integrated performance model of information systems projects. *Journal of Management Information Systems,* 19, 1, 185–210.

Applegate, L.; McFarlan, F.W.; and McKenney, J.L. 1996. *Corporate Information Systems Management: Text and Cases.* Boston: Irwin.

Aubert, B.A.; Patry, M.; and Rivard, S. 2005. A framework for information technology outsourcing risk management. *DATA BASE for Advances in Information Systems,* 36, 4, 9–28.

Banker, R.D., and Kemerer, C.F. 1992. Performance evaluation metrics for information systems development: a principal–agent model. *Information Systems Research,* 3, 4, 379–400.

Barki, H.; Rivard, S.; and Talbot, J. 1993. Toward an assessment of software development risk. *Journal of Management Information Systems,* 10, 2, 203–225.

———. 2001. An integrative contingency model of software project risk management. *Journal of Management Information Systems,* 17, 4, 37–69.

Basel Committee on Banking Supervision (BCBS). 2004. *International Convergence of Capital Measurement and Capital Standards.* Available at www.bis.org/publ/bcbs107.pdf (accessed on October 5, 2006).

Beasley, M.; Chen, A.; Nunez, K.; and Wright, L. 1992. Working hand in hand: balanced scorecard and enterprise risk management. *Strategic Finance,* 87, 9, 49–55.

Benbasat, I., and Zmud, R.W. 1999. Empirical research in information systems: the practice of relevance. *MIS Quarterly,* 23, 1, 3–16.

Benbasat, I.; Goldstein, D.K.; and Mead, M. 1987. The case research strategy in studies of information systems. *MIS Quarterly,* 11, 3, 369–386.

Boehm, B.W. 1989. *Software Risk Management.* Washington, DC: IEEE Computer Society.

Cockburn, A. and and J. Highsmith. 2008. About Methodologies. Available at http://alistair.cockburn.us/cAbout-methodologies (accessed August 7, 2008).

Culp, C.L. 2001. *The Risk Management Process: Business Strategy and Tactics.* New York: Wiley.

Darke, P.; Shanks, G.; and Broadbent, M. 1998. Successfully completing case study research: combining rigour, relevance and pragmatism. *Information Systems Journal,* 8, 4, 273–289.

Davenport, T.H., and Markus, M.L. 1999. Rigor vs. relevance revisited: response to Benbasat and Zmud. *MIS Quarterly,* 23, 1, 19–23.

Dawson, J. 2006. The role of information technology management in managing the preparation for Sarbanes-Oxley assessments. *Proceedings of SIGMIS-CPR06,* Claremont, CA, 147–149.

Dorofee, A.J.; Walker, J.A.; Alberts, C.J.; Higuera, R.P.; Murphy, R.L.; and Williams, R.C. 1996. Continuous risk management guidebook. Carnegie Mellon Software Engineering Institute (SEI), Pittsburgh, PA.

Fruhauf, K. 2001. The intertwining between risk and project management. Tutorial presentation. *Twenty-Third International Conference on Software Engineering,* Toronto.

Gogan, J.L.; Fedorowicz, J.; and Rao, A. 1999. Assessing risks in two projects: a strategic opportunity and a necessary evil. *Communications of the AIS,* 1, 4, 2–33.

Head, G.L. 1998. *The Risk Management Process.* New York: Risk Management Society.

Highsmith, J.A. 2000. *Adaptive Software Development: A Collaborative Approach to Managing Complex Systems.* New York: Dorset House.

Jiang, J.J.; Klein, G.; and Selwyn Ellis, T. 2002. A measure of software development risk. *Project Management Journal,* 33, 3, 30–41.

Jurison, J. 1999. Software project management: a manager's view. *Communications of the AIS,* 2, 3, 2–56.

Kaplan, R.S., and Norton, D.P. 1992. The balanced scorecard: measures that drive performance. *Harvard Business Review,* 83, 7/8, 172–180.

———. 1996. *The Balanced Scorecard: Translating Strategy into Action.* Boston: Harvard Business School Press.

Lee, A.S. 1999. Rigor and relevance in MIS research: beyond the approach of positivism alone. *MIS Quarterly,* 23, 1, 29–33.

Lyytinen, K. 1999. Empirical research in information systems: on the relevance of practice in thinking of MIS research. *MIS Quarterly,* 23, 1, 25–27.

Lyytinen, K.; Mathiassen, L.; and Ropponen, J. 1998. Attention shaping and software risk: a categorical analysis of four classical risk management approaches. *Information Systems Research,* 9, 3, 233–255.

Moynihan, T. 1997. How experienced project managers assess risk. *IEEE Software,* 14, 3, 35–41.

National Institute of Standards and Technology (NIST). 2002. *Risk Management Guide for Information Technology Systems—Recommendations of the National Institute of Standards and Technology.* NIST Special Publications SP 800-30.

Office of Government Commerce (OGC). 2001. *OGC Guidelines on Managing Risk.* London.

Paré, G. 2004. Investigating information systems with positivist case study research. *Communications of the AIS,* 13, 1, 233–264.

Ramesh, B.; Pries-Heje, J.; and Baskerville, R. 2002. Internet software engineering: a different class of processes. *Annals of Software Engineering,* 14, 4, 169–195.

Sakthivel, S. 2007. Managing risk in offshore systems development. *Communications of the ACM,* 50, 4, 69–75.

Schierenbeck, H., and Lister, M. 2001. *Value Controlling.* Munich: Oldenbourg.

Stapleton, J. 1997. *DSDM—Dynamic Systems Development Method: The Method in Practice.* Reading, MA: Addison-Wesley.

Sutherland, J. 2004. Jeff Sutherland's SCRUM. Available at www.jeffsutherland.org/scrum/index.html (accessed November 9, 2004).

Taylor, H. 2006. Critical risks in outsourced IT projects: the intractable and the unforeseen. *Communications of the ACM,* 49, 11, 75–79.

Tsetlin, I., and Winkler, R. 2005. Risky choices and correlated background risk. *Management Science,* 51, 9, 1336–1345.

Wallace, L.; Keil, M.; and Rai, A. 2004a. Understanding software project risk: a cluster analysis. *Information & Management,* 42, 1, 115–125.

———. 2004b. How software project risk affects project performance: an investigation of the dimensions of risk and an exploratory model. *Decision Sciences,* 35, 2, 289–321.

Yetton, P.; Martin, A.; Sharma, R.; and Johnston, K. 2000. A model of information systems development project performance. *Information Systems Journal,* 10, 4, 263–289.

Yin, R.K. 2003. *Case Study Research: Design and Methods.* Beverly Hills, CA: Sage.

# EDITORS AND CONTRIBUTORS

**Yoris A. Au** is an Assistant Professor in the Department of Information Systems and Technology Management of the College of Business at the University of Texas at San Antonio. He received a Ph.D. in Business Administration with a concentration in Information and Decision Sciences from the Carlson School of Management, University of Minnesota. His research has been published in the *Journal of Management Information Systems, Information Systems and E-Business Management, Electronic Commerce Research and Applications,* and *Communications of the AIS.* He currently serves as an Associate Editor for *Electronic Commerce Research and Applications.* His early industry experience is in the areas of databases, software development, and computer and network operations. His more recent positions have been in technology management consulting with Andersen Consulting/Accenture, and as general manager of an Internet startup, which later became the first publicly listed Internet company in Indonesia.

**Jay B. Barney** is Chase Chair for Excellence in Corporate Strategy at the Fisher College of Business at the Ohio State University. His research focuses on the relationship between costly-to-copy firm skills and capabilities and sustained competitive advantage. He has published more than eighty-five articles in leading journals such as the *Academy of Management Review, Management Science,* the *Sloan Management Review,* and the *Journal of Management.* He serves on the editorial board of the *Strategic Management Journal,* has been Associate Editor for the *Journal of Management,* Senior Editor for *Organization Science,* and currently is Associate Editor of the *Strategic Entrepreneurship Journal.* He has presented scholarly papers at more than sixty universities worldwide; has published five books; and has been honored for his research and teaching, including election as a Fellow of the Academy of Management.

**Michel Benaroch** is a Whitman Research Fellow and Professor of Information Systems in the Martin J. Whitman School of Management, Syracuse University. His current research interests focus on the economic valuation and management of IT investments and their risk, as well as on designing declarative ontology-centered modeling formalisms. He has published in a variety of outlets, including *Information Systems Research, Journal of Management Information Systems, MIS Quarterly, International Journal of Economic Dynamics and Control, Decision Sciences, IEEE Transactions on Engineering Management, IEEE Transactions on Knowledge and Data Engineering, International Journal of Human–Computer Studies, Information Retrieval,* and *Decision Support Systems.*

**Ganesh D. Bhatt** is an Associate Professor in the Department of Information Science and Systems at Morgan State University. His research interests are in the area of IS strategy; knowledge management; and IT and organizations. His research has been accepted by journals such as *JMIS, CACM, OMEGA, Decision Support Systems, International Journal of Human Computer Studies,* and *International Journal of Operations and Production Management.*

**Christine V. Bullen** joined the Howe School of Management at Stevens Institute of Technology as a Senior Lecturer in August 2002, where she is the coordinator for the Strategic Issues course and Director of the IT Outsourcing Concentration. Her current research focuses on IT workforce trends. Prior to Stevens, she was a Distinguished Lecturer at Fordham University. From 1976 to 1993, she was Assistant Director of the MIT Sloan School Center for Information Systems Research. Her body of research has focused on strategic planning for the IT function and the organizational impact of IT. Her research at MIT included the launching of the concepts of critical success factors and IT strategic alignment. She received her MS in Management from the MIT Sloan School and will shortly be awarded the Ph.D. degree from Stevens Institute of Technology. She is an active member of SIM, AIS and INFORMS, and a founding member of the Global Sourcing Council.

**Michael J. Davern** is Associate Professor of Accounting and Business Information Systems and Director of the Master of Business and Information Technology at the University of Melbourne. He obtained his Ph.D. in Information and Decision Sciences from the Carlson School of Management at the University of Minnesota, and was previously on the faculty of the Stern School of Business, New York University. A major theme in Dr. Davern's research is the business impact of information technology from behavioral, business process, and economic perspectives, particularly in the context of decision technologies. His work appears in a diverse range of outlets including *Journal of Management Information Systems, Decision Support Systems, Communications of the ACM, International Journal of Accounting Information Systems,* and *Australian Accounting Review,* among others. Some of his current work is supported by an Australian Research Council Linkage Grant (LP#0774949).

**Kim Huat Goh** is currently an Assistant Professor in the Information Technology and Operations Management Division at the Nanyang Business School, Nanyang Technological University, Singapore. He completed his doctorate in Business Administration with an emphasis on Information and Decision Sciences at the Carlson School of Management, University of Minnesota in 2007. His research interests include examining the strategic value of IT at the firm and industry levels, latency issues pertaining to IT payoffs, and the strategic analysis of B2B electronic markets. His articles have been published in *MIS Quarterly,* and in the proceedings of the International Conference on Information Systems, the Hawaii International Conference on Systems Science, and the Academy of Management. He was also runner-up for the "best doctoral research" award at the 2006 INFORMS Conference on Information Systems and Technology.

**R. Brent Gallupe** is a Professor of Information Systems at the business school of Queens University in Kingston, Canada. He is also Associate Dean of the faculty.

**Sanjay Gosain** is a Web strategy analyst with Capital Group Companies, Inc. Prior to his current role, he was an Assistant Professor of Information Systems in the Decision and Information Technologies Department at the Robert H. Smith School of Business, University of Maryland. He completed his Ph.D. in Business Administration at the Marshall School of Business, University of Southern California. Dr. Gosain's research broadly addresses the drivers of effective information technology (IT) design, use, and value leverage in corporate settings. Sanjay is interested in examining consumer behavior and information search on the Web and implications for firm strategy. He is also interested in examining strategic issues related to organizational transformations that leverage IT. His research articles have been presented at international conferences and published in leading academic journals.

**Varun Grover** is the William S. Lee (Duke Energy) Distinguished Professor of IS at Clemson University. Prior to this, he was Business Partnership Foundation Fellow, Distinguished Researcher, and Professor of IS at the University of South Carolina. Dr. Grover has published extensively in the information systems field, with over 160 publications in refereed journals. Five recent articles have ranked him in the top three researchers (from over 4,000) based on publications in the top IS journals over the past decade. His work has appeared in journals such as *ISR, JMIS, MISQ, CACM, Decision Sciences, IEEE Transactions, California Management Review,* and others. He has received numerous awards for his research and teaching from USC, Clemson, the Decision Sciences Institute, the Association for Information Systems, Anbar, and PriceWaterhouseCoopers. Currently, Varun is serving as Senior Editor of the *MISQ, JAIS,* and *Database: Advances in IS;* Associate or Advisory Editor of nine other journals including the *JMIS, International Journal of Electronic Commerce,* and *Journal of Business Process Management.*

**Jun He** is an Assistant Professor of MIS at the University of Michigan-Dearborn. He has an MBA from Tsinghua University and a PhD degree from the University of Pittsburgh. His research interests include systems design and development, knowledge management, and methodological issues. He has presented a number of papers at meetings of the Association for Computing Machinery (ACM) and the Americas' Conference on Information Systems (AMCIS), published in journals such as *Communications of the Association for Information Systems, Information & Management, Journal of Management Information Systems,* and in the book *Current Topics in Management.*

**Rudy Hirschheim** (B.A., M.Sc., Ph.D.) is Ourso Family Distinguished Professor of Information Systems in the E.J. Ourso College of Business, Louisiana State University. He has previously been on the faculties of the University of Houston, Templeton College-Oxford, the London School of Economics, and McMaster University. He has also worked as a Senior Consultant with the National Computing Centre in Manchester, England. He has held visiting appointments at: University of New South Wales (Australia), University of Bayreuth (Germany), University of Paris-Dauphine (France), and Monash University (Australia). He is Co-Consulting Editor of the John Wiley Series in Information Systems. He is Senior Editor for *JAIS* and on the editorial boards of the journals: *JMIS, ISJ, JSIS, JIT,* and *Information & Organization;* and has previously been on the boards of *EJIS* and *MISQ.* In 2006, he was awarded an honorary doctorate by the Faculty of Science, University of Oulu (Finland).

**Wei-Lin Hsu** is an Associate Professor, head of the Department of Information Engineering and Informatics, and head of the Computer Center, Tzu Chi College of Technology, Taiwan. He received his Ph.D. in Computing and Informatics from the University of Leeds, UK. He has more than ten years of working experience relevant to IS/IT planning in the higher education and non-profit organization sectors. His research interests include strategic IS/IT planning, organizational transformation through IS/IT, and methodological approaches for studying the impact of IS/IT on organization.

**Anand Jeyaraj** holds a Ph.D. from the University of Missouri–St. Louis. He is an Assistant Professor of Information Systems in the Raj Soin College of Business at Wright State University, Dayton, Ohio. His research interests are primarily in information systems with overlaps in organizational behavior and social networks, and include the adoption, diffusion, and assimilation of information systems innovations, information systems success, information systems development methodologies, and impacts of information systems. His research has appeared in *Management Science, Communications of the ACM,* and *Journal of Information Technology.* He has also presented his research at the Americas Conference on Information Systems, Diffusion Interest Group in Information Technology, and the Annual Conference of the Academy of Management.

**Robert J. Kauffman** is the W.P. Carey Chair in IS, W.P. Carey School of Business, Arizona State University. He was Director of the MISRC, Professor and Chair of Information and Decision Sciences at the Carlson School of Management, University of Minnesota. He has taught at NYU and the University of Rochester. His graduate degrees are from Cornell and Carnegie Mellon. His research focuses on IT strategy, investment valuation, adoption, economic development, and e-commerce. His articles have appeared in *Organization Science, JMIS, CACM, Management Science, MISQ,* and *ISR,* and elsewhere. He won a 2006 Outstanding Research Award from IEEE's International Society for Engineering Management for research on standards drift in technology adoption in *IEEE Transactions on Engineering Management.* He also received a 2006 Best Research Award from the *Journal of the Association for IS.* He was recognized at ICIS 2007 for contributing a "top five" research paper in the IS discipline.

**William R. King** holds the title University Professor at the University of Pittsburgh. He is the author of 15 books and more than 300 papers that have appeared in the leading journals in management science, strategic planning, and information systems. He has served as Founding President of the Association for Information Systems (AIS), President of TIMS (a predecessor to INFORMS) and as Editor-in-Chief of the *MIS Quarterly.* In 2004, he was given the Leo Lifetime Exceptional Achievement Award by AIS.

**Albert L. Lederer** is a Professor of Management Information Systems in the College of Business and Economics at the University of Kentucky (UK). He earned his MS in Computer and Information Sciences and his Ph.D. in Industrial and Systems Engineering from the Ohio State University. He received his B.A. in Psychology from the University of Cincinnati. He has over ten years of full-time industry experience in information systems. Before joining UK, he served on the faculties of Oakland University and the University of Pittsburgh. The focus of his research for two decades continues to be information systems planning. His work has appeared in *MIS Quarterly, Information Systems Research, Journal of Management Information Systems, Communications of the ACM,* and other outlets.

**Gwo-Guang Lee** is a Professor and Head of the Department of Information Management, National Taiwan University of Science and Technology, Taiwan. He received his Ph.D. in Information Management from the University of Leeds, UK, in 1993. His research has been published in numerous international journals such as *Journal of Information Technology* (SCI), *Behaviour and Information Technology* (SSCI), *Journal of Information Science* (SSCI), *Business Process Management Journal,* and *International Journal of Retail and Distribution Management.* His recent research emphasizes e-commerce, knowledge management, strategic information systems planning, organizational learning, and business reengineering.

**Jerry N. Luftman** is Associate Dean of Graduate Information Systems Programs and Distinguished Professor at Stevens Institute of Technology, Hoboken New Jersey. His career includes strategic positions in management (Information Technology, including CIO and consultant), management consulting, Information Systems, and executive education. After a notable twenty-two-year career with IBM, and over fifteen years at Stevens, Dr. Luftman's experience combines the strengths of practitioner, consultant, and academic. His framework for assessing IT–business alignment maturity is considered key in helping companies around the world understand, define, and scope an appropriate strategic planning direction that leverages Information Technology. Dr. Luftman is the founder and leader of Stevens graduate IS Programs, one of the largest in the world. He is the author of twelve books, of which the most recent is *Competing in the Information Age: Align in the Sand* (Oxford University Press). His active membership in the Society for Information Management (SIM) includes being the VP of Academic Affairs for the SIM Executive Board.

**Arvind Malhotra** is an Associate Professor of Entrepreneurship and Innovation at the Kenan-Flagler Business School, University of North Carolina at Chapel Hill. His research and teaching focus on innovation, successful innovative organizational and interorganizational structures; adoption of innovative technologies, such as wireless, by consumers and organizations; and knowledge management. He has consulted, conducted applied research projects, or led executive development workshops with major U.S. corporations. Dr. Malhotra has received research grants from the Society for Information Management Advanced Practices Council, Dell, Carnegie-Bosche Institute, National Science Foundation, RosettaNet consortium, UNC-Small Grants Program, and the Marketing Sciences Institute. His papers have been published in leading academic journals such as *Harvard Business Review, Journal of Management Information Systems, MIS Quarterly, Manufacturing and Service Operations Management, Journal of Knowledge Management,* and *Communications of the ACM.* He received the best paper award from *MIS Quarterly,* the top information science journal, in 2001. Two of his papers have earned the prestigious Society for Information Management's Best Paper Award. He has also written practice-focused articles for the *Financial Times* and the *Times of India.* He received his Ph.D. in Business Administration and his M.S. in Industrial and Systems Engineering from the University of Southern California.

**James D. McKeen** is a Professor of MIS at the School of Business, Queen's University at Kingston, Canada, and is the founding Director of the Monieson Centre, which conducts multiuniversity, collaborative research focused on generating value through knowledge in organizations. Jim received his Ph.D. in Business Administration from the University of Minnesota. He has been working in the field of MIS for many years as a practitioner, researcher, and consultant and is a frequent speaker at business and academic conferences. His research has been widely published in various journals including the *MIS Quarterly, Knowledge Management Research and Practice, Journal of Information Technology Management,* the *Communications of the Association of Information Systems, MIS Quarterly Executive,* the *Journal of Systems and Software,* the *International Journal of Management Reviews, Information and Management, Communications of the ACM, Computers and Education, OMEGA, Canadian Journal of Administrative Sciences, Journal of MIS, KM Review, Journal of Information Science and Technology,* and *Database.* Dr. McKeen is the coauthor of three books on IT management with Heather Smith. Their latest book is *IT Strategy in Action* (Pearson Prentice Hall, 2008). He currently serves on a number of editorial boards.

**Victoria L. Mitchell** is an Associate Professor in the Haskayne School of Business at the University of Calgary in Alberta, Canada. She has a Ph.D. in Information Systems, an M.B.A. and a B.Sc. in Nursing from Florida State University, and a B.A. from Oakland University. Most recently her research focuses on IT-enabled change, information and organization design, and IT in health care. Her research has appeared in *Organization Science, Management Science, Decision Sciences,* and *MIS Quarterly,* among others. She has been on the faculty at the Ohio State University, the University of California at Los Angeles, the University of Washington, and North Carolina State University.

**Martin Mocker** was a Fellow of the ERCIS Research Group on Strategic Information Management until 2007. He is currently a Senior Consultant with McKinsey & Company's Business Technology Office. He received a Ph.D. in Information Systems from the University of Muenster in 2007 for a dissertation on information strategy. He received a Masters Degree in computer science from the University of Dortmund in 2002.

**Henry E. Newkirk** is an Associate Professor of Management Information Systems in the College of Business at East Carolina University. He holds a Ph.D. from the University of Kentucky, an M.B.A. from East Carolina University, and a B.S. in Chemistry from North Carolina State University. He worked for over seventeen years in the telecommunications industry with Sprint. His research interests include strategic information systems planning and electronic commerce. His publications have appeared in the *IEEE Transactions on Engineering Management, Information and Management, International Journal of Electronic Commerce, Journal of Strategic Information Systems, Journal of Computer Information Systems,* and *International Journal of Information Management.* He is a member of the Association for Information Systems, Decision Sciences Institute, and INFORMS, and has presented his research at their conferences.

**Samuel Otim** is a Ph.D. candidate in Information Systems at Clemson University. He also holds a Ph.D. in economics from Monash University (Australia), and an M.S. in Information Technology from Rochester Institute of Technology (New York). His research interests include the economics of information systems, electronic commerce, knowledge management, information systems strategy, interorganizational systems, and organizational impact of information technology. His work has been published in the *European Journal of Information Systems* and he has articles under review in major IS journals, such as *MIS Quarterly* and *Journal of Management Information Systems.* He has previously taught courses in the IS area at State University of New York at Brockport and University of Maryland University College.

**Alexander Pellengahr** is Fellow of the ERCIS Research Group on Strategic Information Management. He did his masters thesis on the contents of information strategies in practice. He received a Masters Degree in Information Systems from the University of Muenster in 2007. During and prior to his studies, he worked for several companies in the field of IT. He also spent seven months in Australia, working for a worldwide operating producer of polymer-based products.

**George Philip** is a Professor of Management and Information Systems in the Queen's University Management School, Belfast BT7 1NN, United Kingdom. His research interests are: strategic planning and IS strategy, IS management, IT and business transformation, management of technological change including risk management and e-commerce/e-government. He has published over ninety papers in international journals and conference proceedings. He has been a Visiting Professor in IS at the Australian National University (Canberra) in 2003 and Erskine Visiting Fellow at the University of Canterbury (NZ) in 2001. He has also served as an expert assessor (on research proposals) to the European Commission (Luxembourg) for the e-Content research initiative under the Framework 6 Programme. He has conducted invited seminars at a number of universities in NZ, Australia, and at the Japan Advanced Institute for Science and Technology (JAIST). Combining a multidisciplinary background, he has been teaching Information Systems at postgraduate and undergraduate levels in the UK for several years and in Canada and NZ.

**T.S. Ragu-Nathan** is Professor of Information Systems and Operations Management in the College of Business Administration at the University of Toledo. He holds a Ph.D. in Management Information Systems from the University of Pittsburgh. He has published in several journals including *Information Systems Research, Decision Sciences, OMEGA: International Journal of Management Science, Journal of Management Information Systems, Journal of Information Systems,* and *Journal of Strategic Information Systems.* His current research interests are in information systems strategy, quality issues in information systems, and use of information technology in manufacturing, supply-chain management, and e-commerce.

**Gautam Ray** is an Assistant Professor of Information Systems at the Carlson School of Management at the University of Minnesota. He received his Ph.D. from the Ohio State University. His research interests are in the area of the impact of information technology on firms and markets, specifically about how firms make choices to take advantage of opportunities provided by information technology. His research has been published in journals such as *Communications of the ACM, Journal of Management Information Systems, Management Science, Marketing Science, MIS Quarterly,* and the *Strategic Management Journal.* He is an Associate Editor for *Information Systems Research.*

**Frederick J. Riggins** is an Assistant Professor in the Department of Information and Decision Sciences of the Carlson School of Management, University of Minnesota. His research focuses on new business models for Internet-based commerce, strategies for implementing interorganizational systems, measuring the value of information systems, and policies affecting the diffusion of information technology. He has spoken at many conferences and published in leading academic journals including *Management Science, Communications of the ACM, Journal of Management Information Systems, Journal for the Association for Information Systems, International Journal of Electronic Commerce,* and *Journal of Organizational Computing and Electronic Commerce.* He received his Ph.D. from the Graduate School of Industrial Administration at Carnegie Mellon University, where he was winner of the 1994 William W. Cooper Doctoral Dissertation Award in Management Science. Before joining the Carlson School, he was a professor at Georgia Tech.

**John F. Rockart** is currently Senior Lecturer Emeritus at the MIT Sloan School of Management. Before retiring, he held the George and Sandra Schussel Distinguished Senior Lecturer of Information Technology Chair at the Sloan School. Following his doctoral work at MIT, Dr. Rockart joined the MIT faculty in 1968. For twenty-five years (1975 to 2000), he was Director of the Center for Information Systems Research at the Sloan School. During this time, the Center produced more than 300 research papers in the field of information technology. In 2004, the Association for Information Systems named Dr. Rockart as recipient of its LEO award for Lifetime Exceptional Achievement in Information Systems. He received his undergraduate degree from Princeton and his M.B.A. from Harvard.

**Sherry D. Ryan** is an Associate Professor of Information Technology and Decision Sciences at the University of North Texas. She received her Ph.D. in IS from the University of Texas at Arlington and an M.B.A. from the University of Southern California. Prior to returning to academia she worked for IBM, teaching courses and speaking at national conferences. Her research interests include IT investment decisions, knowledge management and IT training, and human resource issues. Her work has appeared in journals including *Journal of Management Information Systems, Decision Support Systems, Information and Management, DATA BASE, Journal of Information Resources Management, Journal of Organizational and End User Computing,* and others.

**Rajiv Sabherwal** received a Ph.D. from the University of Pittsburgh in 1989. He is University of Missouri System Curators' Professor, Emery C. Turner Professor of Information Systems, and Director of the Ph.D. Program in Business Administration at the University of Missouri, St. Louis. He is a Departmental Editor for *IEEE Transactions on Engineering Management*, recently completed a three-year term as Senior Editor at *MIS Quarterly*, and serves on the editorial boards of *Management Science, Information Systems Research, Journal of MIS*, and *Journal of AIS*. He has served as Program Co-Chair and Consortium Co-Chair for the Americas Conference on Information Systems, and Track Co-Chair for ICIS. He will be Conference Co-Chair for ICIS, 2010. His research focuses on information systems planning, knowledge management and business intelligence, and social aspects of systems development. His work appears in numerous journals, including *Management Science, California Management Review, Organization Science, Information Systems Research, MIS Quarterly*, and *European Journal of Information Systems*.

**Omar A. El Sawy** is Professor of Information Systems at the Marshall School of Business at the University of Southern California. From 2001 through 2007, he was Director of Research, Center for Telecom Management at USC. His interests include redesigning and managing IT-based value chains and capabilities for dynamic environments, business models for digital platforms, business process transformation, and designing vigilant information systems for fast-response environments. El Sawy holds a Ph.D. from Stanford Business School, an M.B.A. from the American University in Cairo, and a BSEE in Telecommunications from Cairo University. Prior to joining USC in 1983, he worked as an engineer and manager for twelve years, first at NCR Corporation, and then as a manager of computer services at Stanford University. Dr. El Sawy is the author of over eighty papers and his writings have appeared in both information systems and management journals. He serves on several journal editorial boards, and is a six-time winner of the Society for Information Management's Paper Awards Competition, as well the Association of Information Systems' Publication of the Year Award in 2007.

**Albert Segars** is the RBC Centura Distinguished Professor and Chair of the Entrepreneurship area at the University of North Carolina's Kenan-Flagler Business School. His areas of expertise include innovation, technology management, and product commercialization. He also examines how firms create effective innovation, invention, and proof-of-concept processes for the design of products and services. His recent articles on these topics appear in *California Management Review, Communications of the ACM*, and *IEEE Transactions on Engineering Management*. Dr. Segars is an active consultant with such organizations as Apple Computer, Siemens, Xerox, Red Hat, IBM, Sprint, Merrill Lynch, Ford, Bank of America, GlaxoSmithKline, U.S. EPA, and the Department of the Navy. He serves state and federal governments as a speaker and expert on technology transfer and implementation for economic development.

**Heather A. Smith** is Senior Research Associate with Queen's University School of Business, specializing in IT management issues. A former senior IT manager, she is a founder and co-director (with James McKeen) of the IT Management Forum, the CIO Brief, and the KM Forum, which facilitate interorganizational learning among senior executives, and coauthor (with James McKeen) of *Management Challenges in IS: Successful Strategies and Appropriate Action* (1996). She is also a Research Associate with the Lac Carling Congress on E-Government, the Society for Information Management, and Chair of the IT Excellence Awards University Advisory Council, and a member of the editorial board of *MISQ-Executive*. Her research is published in *CAIS, MIT Sloan Management Review, KMRP, JIST, JITM, Information and Management, Database, CIO Canada*, and the

*CIO Governments Review.* Her book with James McKeen, *Making IT Happen: Critical Issues in IT Management,* was published by Wiley in January 2003 and she is the coauthor of two new books—*Information Technology and Organizational Transformation: Solving the Management Puzzle* (Butterworth-Heinemann) and *IT Strategy in Action* (Pearson Prentice Hall).

**Ananth Srinivasan** is a Professor of Information Systems and Digital Commerce at the University of Auckland Business School. He is also a co-director of the Centre of Digital Enterprise, a research center focused on digital technology implementation in organizations.

**Cidambi Srinivasan** is a Professor of Statistics in the College of Arts and Sciences at the University of Kentucky. He earned his M.STAT and Ph.D. in Statistics from the Indian Statistical Institute, Calcutta, India. Before joining the University of Kentucky, he served on the faculty of Indiana University, Bloomington. His research activities focus on statistical decision theory, Bayesian inference, artificial neural networks, and social networks with applications to business and engineering. His work has appeared in *Annals of Statistics, Journal of the American Statistical Association, International Journal of Electric Commerce, IEEE Transactions On Systems and Cybernetics, Journal of Neurocomputing, Journal of Strategic Information Systems,* and *Journal of Organizational Computing and Electronic Commerce.*

**Monideepa Tarafdar** is Associate Professor of Information Systems at the University of Toledo. She has an undergraduate degree in Physics and a graduate degree in Telecommunications and Electronics Engineering from the University of Calcutta, India. Her doctoral degree is in Management Information Systems from the Indian Institute of Management Calcutta. Her research has appeared in *Information Systems Research, Journal of Management Information Systems, Journal of Strategic Information Systems, Journal of Computer Information Systems, Information Resources Management Journal,* and *Journal of Cases on Information Technology.* Her current research interests are in the areas of information systems and business innovation, IT–business alignment, managing individual and organizational adjustments required for effective IT use, and information systems planning for Net-enabled organizations.

**Paul P. Tallon** is Assistant Professor of Information Systems at the Wallace E. Carroll School of Management, Boston College and a Research Associate at the Center for Research on Information Technology and Organizations (CRITO) at the University of California, Irvine. He previously worked as an IT auditor and chartered accountant with PricewaterhouseCoopers in Dublin, Ireland, and New York, New York. His research has appeared in the *Journal of Management Information Systems, Communications of the ACM,* the *Journal of Global IT Management,* the *Journal of Strategic Information Systems, Information Technology and Management,* and *Communications of the AIS.* He previously co-edited a volume in the *Advances in MIS* series published by M.E. Sharpe on the topic of advanced empirical methods in IS and e-commerce research. His research interests include the economic, social, and organizational impacts of IT, strategic alignment, real options, IT portfolio analysis, and the economics of information management.

**Thompson S.H. Teo** is an Associate Professor in the Department of Decision Sciences at the School of Business, National University of Singapore. His research interests include strategic use of IT, e-commerce, e-government, adoption and diffusion of IT, strategic IT management and planning, and offshoring. He has published more than eighty papers in international refereed journals such as *Communications of the ACM, Communications of the AIS, Database for Advances* *in Information Systems, Decision Support Systems, European Journal of Information Systems, IEEE Transactions on Engineering Management, Information and Management, Journal of the AIS, Journal of Information Technology, Journal of Management Information Systems, MISQ Executive,* and *Omega.* He has co-edited four books on IT and e-commerce, and is on the editorial board of several international refereed journals. He is a two-time winner of the Society for Information Management (SIM) Paper Competition Award.

**Rolf Alexander Teubner** is Reader in Information Management at the University of Muenster in Germany and Director of the Research Group on Strategic Information Management at the European Research Center for Information Systems (ERCIS). He teaches Information Management in several Master and Executive Programs and is an Associate Professor at Educatis University, Graduate School of Management, Switzerland. Alexander served for several years as manager and member of the board of a digital image processing company. He received a Ph.D. in Information Systems from the University of Muenster in 1997 and a Masters degree in business administration from the University of Dortmund/Germany in 1991.

**Elke Wolf** is an independent consultant and adjunct faculty member of the University of Auckland Business School. She has considerable experience working with financial institutions in Europe in technological risk assessment.

**Robert W. Zmud** is Professor, Michael F. Price Chair in MIS, and George Lynn Cross Research Professor at the Michael F. Price College of Business at the University of Oklahoma. His research interests focus on the organizational impacts of information technology and on the management, implementation, and diffusion of information technology. He is currently a Senior Editor for *Information Systems Research* and *MISQ Executive,* and sits on the editorial boards of *Academy of Management Review* and *Information and Organization.* He is a fellow of both AIS and DSI. He holds a Ph.D. from the University of Arizona and an M.S. from MIT.

# SERIES EDITOR

**Vladimir Zwass** is Gregory Olsen Endowed Chair and Distinguished Professor of Computer Science and Management Information Systems at Fairleigh Dickinson University. He holds a PhD in Computer Science from Columbia University. Professor Zwass is the Founding Editor-in-Chief of the *Journal of Management Information Systems*, one of the three top-ranked journals in the field of Information Systems; the Journal has celebrated 25 years of its publication. He is also the Founding Editor-in-Chief of the *International Journal of Electronic Commerce*, ranked as the top journal in its field. More recently, Dr. Zwass has been the Founding Editor-in-Chief of the monograph series *Advances in Management Information Systems*, whose objective is to codify the knowledge and research methods in the field. Dr. Zwass is the author of six books and several book chapters, including entries in the *Encyclopaedia Britannica*, as well as of a number of papers in various journals and conference proceedings. Vladimir Zwass has received several grants, consulted for a number of major corporations, and is a frequent speaker to national and international audiences. He is a former member of the Professional Staff of the International Atomic Energy Agency in Vienna, Austria.

# INDEX

*Italicized* locators indicate a chart outside of the page range of the topic.